A DICTIONARY
OF
BASIC
JAPANESE
GRAMMAR

A DICTIONARY OF BASIC JAPANESE GRAMMAR

日本語基本文法辞典

Seiichi Makino
and
Michio Tsutsui

The Japan Times

First cloth-bound edition: March 1986
First paperback edition: March 1989
18th printing: January 1994

ISBN 4-7890-0454-6

Cover: CADEC Inc.

Published by The Japan Times, Ltd.
5-4, Shibaura 4-chome, Minato-ku, Tokyo 108, Japan

Printed in Japan

Preface

This is a dictionary of basic Japanese grammar designed primarily for first and second year Japanese students and for teachers of Japanese. After having examined major textbooks being used in Japan and the United States we have chosen what we believe to be basic grammatical items. Our descriptions and explanations have incorporated the recent findings in Japanese linguistics which we felt were of practical significance.

We have spent three years and a half preparing this dictionary. Each of us initially prepared half of the original draft: approximately 200 entries. Upon completion of the first draft of the dictionary (i.e., Entries, Appendixes, Characteristics of Japanese Grammar, and Grammatical Terms), we closely examined, discussed and improved our individual drafts. Therefore, every part of this dictionary has virtually been written by both of us.

Naturally we owe a great deal to our predecessors whose works are listed in the references. Our heart-felt thanks go to them, although we could not acknowledge them individually in each entry where we used their insightful explanations. We would also like to acknowledge many profitable discussions with our colleagues at the University of Illinois, Urbana-Champaign and at the Summer Japanese School of Middlebury College, Middlebury, Vermont. For fear of omission, we would rather not attempt a comprehensive listing of names. Even so we would like to mention four individuals whose technical assistance has made it possible to publish this dictionary: First, Mr. Burr Nelson of the University of Illinois and Mrs. Sharon Tsutsui, who have edited our English and provided us with valuable comments and suggestions from the user's viewpoint; also, Mr. Mamoru Yoshizawa, who has patiently and conscientiously assisted with the proofreading; and, last but not least Mr. Masayuki Ishida of The Japan Times, who has done such conscientious editing: he has been a perfect midwife for the birth of our progeny and our special thanks go to him.

Spring 1986

Seiichi Makino
Michio Tsutsui

TABLE OF CONTENTS

To the Reader

This dictionary consists of the following parts:

A. *Grammatical Terms* contains brief explanations or informal definitions of the grammatical terms frequently used in this book. If the reader finds that he is not familiar with these terms, we suggest he read this section carefully.

B. *Characteristics of Japanese Grammar* introduces the reader to the major characteristics of Japanese grammar and the important concepts involved. The reader should read through this section before he starts to consult the dictionary. Some entries from the *Main Entries* section refer the reader to topics in this section which provide broader perspectives on those entries.

C. *Main Entries* constitutes the core of this book. Each entry is organized as follows:

---

① [entry name]　　② [part of speech]

　　③ [meaning / function]　　④ [English counterpart(s)]
　　　　　　　　　　　　　　　　　　[antonym]
　　　　　　　　　　　　　　　　⑤ [related expression(s)]

⑥ ♦ **Key Sentence(s)**

⑦ **Formation**

⑧ **Examples**

⑨ **Note(s)**

⑩ **[Related Expression(s)]**

---

① [entry name]: Each entry is given in romanized spelling followed by its *hiragana* version. Entries are alphabetically ordered based on their romanized spellings.

② [part of speech]: Each entry is followed by its part of speech.

③ [meaning / function]: The general meaning or function of the entry is given in the box below the entry name.

④ [English counterpart(s)]: English expressions equivalent to the entry are given to the right of the box. When the entry has an antonym, it is provided, as in (ANT. xxx).

⑤ [related expression(s)]: Items which are related semantically to the entry are listed as [REL. aaa; bbb; **ccc** (ddd)]. Expressions in non-bold type like aaa are explained in the entry under 【Related Expression(s)】 (⑩). Expressions in bold type like **ccc** contain comparisons to the entry under 【Related Expression(s)】 for **ccc**. Parenthesized expressions like (ddd) are explained in the **ccc** entry.

⑥ ◆**Key Sentence**(s): Key sentences present basic sentence patterns in frames according to sentence structure. The parts in red color are recurrent elements. The same is true of *Formation*.

⑦ **Formation**: The word formation rules / connection forms for each item are provided with examples.

⑧ **Examples**: Example sentences are provided for each entry.

⑨ **Note**(s): Notes contain important points concerning the use of the item.

⑩ 【**Related Expression(s)**】: Expressions which are semantically close to the entry are compared and their differences are explained.

D. *Appendixes* contains information such as tables of verb / adjective conjugations, a list of connection rules for important expressions and a list of counters.

E. *Indexes* contains three indexes: the grammar index, the English index and the Japanese index. The reader, therefore, has three means of access to the word he is looking up.

List of Abbreviations

Adj(*i*) = *i*-type adjective (e.g. *takai* 'high, expensive', *yasui* 'inexpensive')
Adj(*na*) = *na*-type adjective (e.g. *genkida* 'healthy', *shizukada* 'quiet')
Adv. = adverb
Aff. = affirmative
ANT. = antonym
Aux. = auxiliary
Conj. = conjunction
Cop. ≐ copula (= *da* / *desu*, *datta* / *deshita*)
Fml. = formal (= -*des*-, -*mas*-)
Gr. = Group
Inf. = informal
Irr. = Irregular (e.g. *kuru* 'come', *suru* 'do')
KS = Key Sentence
LSV = Location + Subject + Verb
N = Noun
Neg. = negative
Nom. = nominalizer (= *no* and *koto*)
NP = Noun Phrase
Phr. = phrase
Pl. = plural
Pot. = potential
Pref. = prefix (e.g. *o*-, *go*- 'politeness markers')
Pro. = pronoun
Prt. = particle
REL. = Related Expression
S = Sentence
Sinf = Sentence that ends with an informal predicate (e.g. *Nihon ni iku* of *Nihon ni iku n desu* 'It is that I am going to Japan.')
SLV = Subject + Location + Verb
S.o. = someone
S.t. = something
SOV = Subject + Object + Verb
SV = Subject + Verb
Str. = structure

Suf. = suffix (e.g. *-sa* ' -ness ', *-ya* ' store ')

V = Verb

Vcond = conditional stem of Gr. 1 Verb (e.g. *hanase* of *hanaseba* ' if s.o. talks ')

Vinf = informal form of verbs (e.g. *hanasu* ' talk ', *hanashita* ' talked ')

V*masu* = *masu*-stem of Verb (e.g. *hanashi* of *hanashimasu* ' talk ')

Vneg = informal negative form of Gr. 1 verb (e.g. *hanasa* of *hanasanai* ' s.o. doesn't talk ')

Vstem = stem of Gr. 2 Verb (e.g. *tabe* of *taberu* ' eat ')

V*te* = *te*-form of Verb (e.g. *hanashite* ' talk and ~ ', *tabete* ' eat and ~ ', *kite* ' come and ~ ', *shite* ' do and ~ ')

Vvol = volitional form of Verb (e.g. *hanasō* ' let's talk ', *tabeyō* ' let's eat ', *koyō* ' let's come ', *shiyō* ' let's do it ')

WH-word = an interrogative word (e.g. *nani* ' what ', *doko* ' where ', *dare* ' who ', *itsu* ' when ', *dō* ' how ', *naze* ' why ')

List of Symbols

⇨ = See or refer to.

? = The degree of unacceptability is indicated by the number of question marks, three being the highest.

* = ungrammatical or unacceptable (in other words, no native speaker would accept the asterisked sentence.)

{A / B}C = AC or BC (e.g. {V/Adj(*i*)}inf = Vinf or Adj(*i*)inf)

ø = zero (in other words, nothing should be used at a place where ø occurs. Thus, Adj(*na*) {ø / *datta*} *kamoshirenai* is either Adj(*na*) *kamoshirenai* or Adj(*na*) *datta kamoshirenai*.)

Grammatical Terms

The following are brief explanations of some grammatical terms most frequently used in this dictionary.

Active Sentence　A sentence which describes an action from the agent's point of view. (Cp. Passive Sentence)　In active sentences, the subject is the agent. Sentences (a) and (b) below are an active and a passive sentence, respectively.

(a) 先生はジョンをしかった。
　　Sensei wa Jon o shikatta.
　　(The teacher scolded John.)

(b) ジョンは先生にしかられた。
　　Jon wa sensei ni shikarareta.
　　(John was scolded by the teacher.)

Agent　One who initiates and / or completes an action or an event.　The agent is not always in the subject position.　Compare the positions of the agent *Bill* in (a) and (b).

(a) ビルはマーサをぶった。
　　Biru *wa Māsa o butta.*
　　(Bill hit Martha.)

(b) マーサはビルにぶたれた。
　　*Māsa wa **Biru** ni butareta.*
　　(Martha was hit by Bill.)

Appositive Clause (**Construction**)　A clause which modifies a noun (or noun phrase) and explains *what* the modified noun is.　In (a), *Meari ga Tomu ni atta* 'Mary met Tom' is an appositive clause, and is what *jijitsu* 'the fact' refers to.

(a) 私はメアリーがトムに会った事実を知っている。
　　*Watashi wa Meari ga Tomu ni atta **jijitsu** o shitte iru.*
　　(I know the fact that Mary met Tom.)

Auxiliary Adjective　A dependent adjective that is preceded by and attached to a verb or another adjective. The bold-printed parts of the following sentences are typical auxiliary adjectives.

(a) 私はジョンに行って欲しい。
Watashi wa Jon ni itte **hoshii**.
(I want John to go there.)

(b) この辞書は使いやすい。
Kono jisho wa tsukai**yasui**.
(This dictionary is easy to use.)

(c) 私はすしが食べたい。
Watashi wa sushi ga tabe**tai**.
(I want to eat *sushi*.)

(d) ベスは大学を出たらしい。
Besu wa daigaku o deta **rashii**.
(Beth seems to have graduated from college.)

(e) 花子は淋しいようだ。
Hanako wa sabishii **yōda**.
(Hanako looks lonely.)

(f) このお菓子はおいしそうだ。
Kono o-kashi wa oishi**sōda**.
(This cake looks delicious.)

Auxiliary Verb A verb which is used in conjunction with a preceding verb or adjective. The bold-faced words of the following sentences are typical auxiliary verbs.

(a) ビルは今手紙を書いている。
Biru wa ima tegami o kaite **iru**.
(Bill is writing a letter now.)

(b) 窓が開けてある。
Mado ga akete **aru**.
(The window has been opened. (= The window is open.))

(c) 僕は宿題をしてしまった。
Boku wa shukudai o shite **shimatta**.
(I have done my homework.)

(d) 私は友達にお金を貸してあげた。
Watashi wa tomodachi ni o-kane o kashite **ageta**.

(I loaned money to my friend.)

(e) このコンピューターは高すぎる。
*Kono konpyūtā wa taka**sugiru***.
(This computer is too expensive.)

(f) ジョージはスポーツカーを欲しがっている。
*Jōji wa supōtsukā o hoshi**gatte iru***.
(Lit. George is showing signs of wanting a sports car. (=George wants a sports car.))

(g) あっ！雨が降って来た！
*A! Ame ga futte **kita**!*
(Gee! It's started to rain!)

Compound Particle   A particle which consists of more than one word but functions like a single particle.   For example, the compound particle *to shite wa* consists of the particle *to*, the *te*-form of *suru* and the particle *wa*, but it is used like a single particle to mean ' for '.   (Cp. Double Particle)

Compound Sentence   A sentence which consists of clauses combined by coordinate conjunctions such as *ga* meaning ' but ' or by the *te*-forms of verbs, adjectives or the copula meaning ' ~ and '.

(a) 僕は泳いだがスミスさんは泳がなかった。
*Boku wa oyoida **ga** Sumisu-san wa oyoganakatta.*
(I swam but Mr. Smith didn't.)

(b) 吉田さんは東京に行って鈴木さんに会った。
*Yoshida-san wa Tōkyō ni it**te** Suzuki-san ni atta.*
(Mr. Yoshida went to Tokyo and met Mr. Suzuki.)

Contrastive Marker   A particle which marks contrast. For example, when X is contrasted with Y, it is typically marked by the particle *wa*. X and Y usually appear in S_1 and S_2, respectively in S_1 *ga* S_2, as shown in (a).

(a) ジョンは来たが，ビルは来なかった。
*Jon **wa** kita ga, Biru **wa** konakatta.*
(John came here. But Bill didn't.)

Coordinate Conjunction   A conjunction that combines two sentences without subordinating one to the other. A typical coordinate conjunction is *ga* 'but'. Example:

(a) 走っていますが，ちっともやせません。

*Hashitte imasu **ga**, chitto mo yasemasen.*

(I'm running, but I haven't lost any weight at all.)

Direct Object　The direct object of a verb is the direct recipient of an action represented by the verb. It can be animate or inanimate. An animate direct object is the direct experiencer of some action (as in (a) and (b) below). An inanimate direct object is typically something which is created, exchanged or worked on, in short, the recipient of the action of the verb (as in (c), (d) and (e) below).

(a) 山口先生は学生をよくほめる。

*Yamaguchi-sensei wa **gakusei** o yoku homeru.*

(Prof. Yamaguchi often praises his students.)

(b) かおりは一郎をだました。

*Kaori wa **Ichirō** o damashita.*

(Kaori deceived Ichiro.)

(c) 僕は本を書いた。

*Boku wa **hon** o kaita.*

(I wrote a book.)

(d) 一郎はみどりにスカーフをやった。

*Ichirō wa Midori ni **sukāfu** o yatta.*

(Ichiro gave a scarf to Midori.)

(e) 私はドアを開けておいた。

*Watashi wa **doa** o akete oita.*

(I kept the door open.)

Although direct objects are marked by the particle *o*, nouns or noun phrases marked by *o* are not always direct objects, as shown in (f) and (g).　(⇨ *o*^{2}; *o*^{4})

(f) 花子は一郎の大学入学を喜んだ。

*Hanako wa Ichirō no daigakunyūgaku **o** yorokonda.*

(Hanako was glad that Ichiro entered college.)

(g) トムはその時公園を歩いていた。

*Tomu wa sono toki kōen **o** aruite ita.*

(At that time Tom was walking in the park.)

Double Particle   A sequence of two particles. The first particle is usually a case particle and the second is an adverbial particle such as *wa* 'topic / contrast marker', *mo* 'also, even', and *shika* 'only'.

(a) 東京からは田中さんが来た。
    *Tōkyō **kara wa** Tanaka-san ga kita.*
    (Lit. From Tokyo Mr. Tanaka came.)

(b) 私はミラーさんとも話した。
    *Watashi wa Mirā-san **to mo** hanashita.*
    (I talked with Mr. Miller, too.)

Embedded Sentence   A sentence within another sentence is an embedded sentence. The bold-faced part of each sentence below is the embedded sentence. An embedded sentence is marked by a subordinate conjunction such as *kara* 'because', *keredomo* 'although', *node* 'because', *noni* 'although', *to* 'if', the quote marker *to* 'that', a nominalizer (*no* or *koto*) or the head noun of a relative clause.

(a) 山田は頭が痛いと言った。
    *Yamada wa **atama ga itai** to itta.*
    (Yamada said that he had a headache.)

(b) 山田は頭が痛いので学校を休んだ。
    *Yamada wa **atama ga itai** node gakkō o yasunda.*
    (Yamada didn't go to school, because he had a headache.)

(c) 山田は外国に行くのが大好きだ。
    *Yamada wa **gaikoku ni iku** no ga dai-sukida.*
    (Yamada loves to go to a foreign country.)

(d) 山田は空手を習ったことがある。
    *Yamada wa **karate o naratta** koto ga aru.*
    (Yamada has learned *karate* before.)

Hearer   The person who receives a spoken or written message. In this dictionary the term "hearer" is used in a broader sense to mean the person to whom the speaker or the writer communicates.

Imperative Form   A conjugated verb form that indicates a command, as in *Hanase!* 'Talk!', *Tabero!* 'Eat it!', *Shiro!* 'Do it!' or *Koi!* 'Come!'.

Indefinite Pronoun   A pronoun which does not refer to something specifically. *No* in B's sentence in (a) is an indefinite pronoun. Here, *no* is used for *jisho* 'dictionary', but does not refer to a specific dictionary.

(a) A : どんな辞書が欲しいんですか。
       Donna jisho ga hoshii n desu ka.
       (What kind of dictionary do you want?)

     B : 小さいのが欲しいんです。
       *Chisai **no** ga hoshii n desu.*
       (I want a small one.)

Intransitive Verb   A verb which does not require a direct object. The action or state identified by the intransitive verb is related only to the subject of the sentence. For example, the verb *hashitta* 'ran' in (a) is an intransitive verb because the action of running is related only to the subject.

(Cp. Transitive Verb)

(a) 鈴木さんは走った。
     *Suzuki-san wa **hashitta**.*
     (Mr. Suzuki ran.)

Intransitive verbs typically indicate *movement* (such as *iku* 'go', *kuru* 'come', *aruku* 'walk', *tobu* 'fly', *noru* 'get onto'), *spontaneous change* (such as *naru* 'become', *kawaru* 'change', *tokeru* 'melt', *fukuramu* 'swell', *hajimaru* 'begin'), *human emotion* (such as *yorokobu* 'rejoice', *kanashimu* 'feel sad', *omou* 'feel'), and *birth / death* (such as *umareru* 'be born', *shinu* 'die').

(⇒ Appendix 3)

I-type Adjective   An adjective whose nonpast prenominal form ends with *i*. Examples of *i*-type adjectives are *takai* 'high, expensive' and *tsuyoi* 'strong', as seen in (a).

(Cp. *Na*-type Adjective)

(a) 高い本
     *tak**ai** hon*
     (an expensive book)

     強い人
     *tsuyo**i** hito*
     (a strong person)

I-type adjectives are further subdivided into two types : *i*-type adjectives which end with *shi-i* and those with non-*shi-i* endings. Most adjectives with *Shi-i* endings express human emotion (such as *ureshii* 'happy', *kanashii* 'sad', *sabishii* 'lonely', *kurushii* 'painful'); the non-*shi-i* adjectives are used for objective descriptions (such as *kuroi* 'black', *shiroi* 'white', *hiroi* 'spacious', *takai* 'high, expensive').

Na-type Adjective An adjective whose nonpast prenominal form ends with *na*. For example, *shizukada* 'quiet' and *genkida* 'healthy' are *na*-type adjectives, as in (a). (Cp. *I*-type Adjective)

(a) 静かな家
shizukana ie
(a quiet house)

元気な人
genkina hito
(a healthy person)

Na-type adjectives are very similar to nouns. Some *na*-type adjectives can be used as real nouns as shown in (b). All *na*-type adjectives behave as nouns when they are used before the copula *da*, as shown in (c).

(b) 健康は大事ですよ。
Kenkō *wa daijidesu yo.*
(Health is important, you know.)

Cp. 健康な人
kenkōna hito
(a healthy person)

ご親切は忘れません。
*Go-**shinsetsu** wa wasuremasen.*
(I'll never forget your kindness.)

Cp. 親切な人
shinsetsuna hito
(a kind person)

(c) この人は元気 / 学生 {だ / です / だった / でした / じゃない / じゃありません / じゃなかった / じゃありませんでした。}
*Kono hito wa **genki** / **gakusei** {da / desu / datta / deshita / janai / jaarimasen / janakatta / jaarimasendeshita.}*
(This person {is / was / isn't / wasn't} healthy / a student.)

Nominalizer A nominalizer is a particle that makes a sentence into a noun phrase or clause. There are two nominalizers *no* and *koto*: the former represents the speaker's empathetic feeling towards an event / state expressed in the nominalized noun phrase / clause; the latter represents the speaker's relatively anti-empathetic feeling towards an event / state.　　　　　　　($\Rightarrow$ *no*[3]; *koto*[2])

Noun Phrase / Clause		Particle	Predicate
Sentence	Nominalizer		
日本語を読む *Nihongo o yomu*	の / こと *no / koto*	は *wa*	難しい。 *muzukashii.*
(Reading Japanese is difficult.)			

The nominalized sentence can be used in any position where an ordinary noun or a noun phrase / clause can be used.

Passive Sentence　　A sentence which describes an action by someone from the viewpoint of someone else who is affected by that action. (Cf. Active Sentence) (a) and (b) are passive sentences.

(a)　私はビルにぶたれた。
　　Watashi wa Biru ni butareta.
　　(I was beaten by Bill.)

(b)　太郎は秋子に泣かれた。
　　Tarō wa Akiko ni nakareta.
　　(Lit. Taro was annoyed by the fact that Akiko cried. (=Taro was annoyed by Akiko's crying.))

Potential Form　　A verb form that expresses competence in the sense of 'can do s.t.' The formation is as follows:

Gr. 1 Verbs	Vcond＋る *ru*	e.g.	話せる 'can talk' *hanase-ru*

Gr. 2 Verbs　Vstem＋られる　e.g.　食べられる 'can eat'
　　　　　　　　　　　rareru　　　　*tabe-rareru*

　　　　　　　Vstem＋れる　e.g.　食べれる 'can eat'
　　　　　　　　　　　reru　　　　*tabe-reru*

Irr. Verbs　　来る　　　　　　　来られる 'can come'
　　　　　　　kuru　　　　　　*korareru*
　　　　　　　　　　　　　　　　来れる
　　　　　　　　　　　　　　　　koreru

する	出来る 'can do'
suru	*dekiru*

Predicate   The part of a sentence which makes a statement about the subject. The core of the predicate consists either of a verb, an adjective, or a noun followed by a form of the copula *da*.   Optionally, objects and other adjectival and / or adverbial modifiers may be present.   In (a), (b) and (c) the predicates are printed in bold type.

(a) 松本さんは**よく映画を見る**。
    Matsumoto-san wa **yoku eiga o miru**.
    (Mr. Matsumoto sees movies often.)

(b) 私の家は**スミスさんのより新しい**。
    Watashi no ie wa **Sumisu-san no yori atarashii**.
    (My house is newer than Mr. Smith's.)

(c) ジョンは**日本語の学生です**。
    Jon wa **nihongo no gakusei desu**.
    (John is a student of Japanese language.)

Prenominal Form   The verb / adjective form which immediately precedes a noun and modifies it.   The bold-faced verb and adjectives in (a), (b), (c) and (d) are prenominal forms.

(a) 私が**読む** / **読んだ**新聞
    watashi ga **yomu** / **yonda** shinbun
    (the newspaper I read)

(b) **大きい** / **大きかった**家
    ōkii / **ōkikatta** ie
    (a big house / a house which used to be big)

(c) **立派な** / **立派だった**建物
    rippana / **rippadatta** tatemono
    (a magnificent building / a building which used to be magnificent)

(d) **おいしそうな** / **おいしそうだった**ケーキ
    oishisōna / **oishisōdatta** kēki
    (a delicious-looking cake / a cake which looked delicious)

Punctual Verb　　A verb that represents a momentary action which either occurs once, as in (a), or can be repeated continuously, as in (b).

(a)　知る　　'get to know'
　　shiru
　　死ぬ　　'die'
　　shinu
　　始まる　　'begin'
　　hajimaru
　　結婚する　　'get married'
　　kekkonsuru
　　やめる　　'stop s.t.'
　　yameru
　　似る　　'resemble'
　　niru

(b)　落とす　　'drop'
　　otosu
　　もぎる　　'pluck off'
　　mogiru
　　ける　　'kick'
　　keru
　　跳ぶ　　'jump'
　　tobu
　　打つ　　'hit'
　　utsu

With the auxiliary verb *iru* (i.e., *iru*[2]), the punctual verbs in (a) express a state after an action was taken, and those as in (b) express either a repeated action or a state after an action was taken.　　　　　　　　　　(⇒ Appendix 2)

Stative Verb　　A verb which represents a state of something or someone at some point in time, as in (a).　　　　　　　　　　(⇒ Appendix 2)

(a)　ある
　　aru
　　(exist (of inanimate things))
　　いる
　　iru
　　(exist (of animate things))

いる
iru
(need)
出来る
dekiru
(can do)

Subject   The subject is an element of a sentence which indicates an agent of an action in active sentences (as in (a)) or an experiencer of an action (as in (b)) or someone or something that is in a state or a situation (as in (c), (d), (e) and (f)). The subject is normally marked by the particle *ga* in Japanese unless it is the sentence topic.

(a) ジョンがりんごを食べた。
     Jon *ga ringo o tabeta.*
     (John ate an apple.)

(b) メアリーが先生にほめられた。
     Meari *ga sensei ni homerareta.*
     (Mary was praised by her teacher.)

(c) ナンシーはきれいだ。
     Nanshi *wa kireida.*
     (Nancy is pretty.)

(d) ドアが開いた。
     Doa *ga aita.*
     (The door opened.)

(e) 机が一つある。
     Tsukue *ga hitotsu aru.*
     (Lit. One table exists. (＝There is a table.))

(f) 空が青い。
     Sora *ga aoi.*
     (The sky is blue.)

Subordinate Clause   A clause which is embedded into a main clause with a subordinate conjunction. Typical subordinate conjunctions are *ba* 'if', *kara* 'because', *node* 'because', *keredo* 'although' and *noni* 'although'. Thus, in (a) below, the bold-faced clause with the subordinate conjunction *node* is embedded into the main clause *Nakayama-san wa gakkō o yasunda*, 'Mr. Nakayama was absent from school.'

(a) 中山さんは**頭が痛かったので**学校を休んだ。

*Nakayama-san wa **atama ga itakatta node** gakkō o yasunda.*

(Mr. Nakayama was absent from school because he had a headache.)

The informal form of a verb / adjective is usually used in a subordinate clause.

Transitive Verb   A verb that requires a direct object. It usually expresses an action that acts upon s.o. or s.t. indicated by the direct object. Actions indicated by transitive verbs include *real causatives* (such as *ikaseru* 'make / let s.o. go', *korosu* 'kill', *miseru* 'show', *nakasu* 'make s.o. cry', *noseru* 'put, place'), *exchange* (such as *ageru* 'give', *morau* 'receive', *kureru* 'give'), *creation* (such as *tsukuru* 'make', *kaku* 'write', *kangaeru* 'think'), *communication* (such as *hanasu* 'speak', *oshieru* 'teach', *tsutaeru* 'convey a message') and others. Note that some English transitive verbs are intransitive in Japanese.

(a) 私は車が**ある**。

*Watashi wa kuruma ga **aru**.*

(Lit. With me a car exists. (＝I have a car.))

(b) 僕はお金が**いる**。

*Boku wa o-kane ga **iru**.*

(Lit. To me money is necessary. (＝I need money.))

(c) スミスさんは中国語が**分かる**。

*Sumisu-san wa chūgokugo ga **wakaru**.*

(Lit. To Mr. Smith Chinese is understandable. (＝Mr. Smith understands Chinese.))

(d) 私はフランス語が少し**出来る**。

*Watashi wa furansugo ga sukoshi **dekiru**.*

(Lit. To me French is a bit possible. (＝I can speak French a little.))

(e) 木下さんは東京でお父さんに**会った**。

*Kinoshita-san wa Tōkyō de o-tō-san ni **atta**.*

(Mr. Kinoshita met his father in Tokyo.)

(f) 私にはベルが**聞こえなかった**。

*Watashi ni wa beru ga **kikoenakatta**.*

(Lit. To me the bell wasn't audible. (＝I wasn't able to hear the bell.))

(g) ここからは富士山が**見えます**よ。

*Koko kara wa Fujisan ga **miemasu** yo.*

(Lit. From here Mt. Fuji is visible. (＝We can see Mt. Fuji from here.))

(h) 私達は新幹線に乗りました。
*Watashitachi wa shinkansen ni **norimashita**.*
(We rode a bullet train.)

(i) 私は母に似ているらしい。
*Watashi wa haha ni **niteiru** rashii.*
(It seems that I resemble my mother.)

Volitional Sentence　A sentence in which a person expresses his will.　The main verb in such sentences is in the volitional form, as in (a).

(a) 僕が行こう / 行きましょう。
*Boku ga **ikō** | **ikimashō**.*
(I will go.)

WH-question　A question that asks for information about *who, what, where, which, when, why* and *how*, as exemplified by (a) through (f) below.

(Cp. Yes-No Question)

(a) 誰が来ましたか。
***Dare** ga kimashita ka.*
(Who came here?)

(b) 何を食べますか。
***Nani** o tabemasu ka.*
(What will you eat?)

(c) どこに行きますか。
***Doko** ni ikimasu ka.*
(Where are you going?)

(d) いつ大阪へ帰りますか。
***Itsu** Ōsaka e kaerimasu ka.*
(When are you going back to Osaka?)

(e) どうして買わないんですか。
***Dōshite** kawanai n desu ka.*
(How come you don't buy it?)

(f) 東京駅へはどう行きますか。
*Tōkyō eki e wa **dō** ikimasu ka.*
(How can I get to Tokyo Station?)

WH-word An interrogative word which corresponds to English words such as *who, what, where, which, when, why* and *how*. The following are some examples.

(a) 誰 'who'
 dare
 何 'what'
 nani | nan
 どこ 'where'
 doko
 いつ 'when'
 itsu
 どうして / なぜ 'how come / why'
 dōshite | naze
 どう 'how'
 dō

Note that Japanese WH-words are not always found in sentence-initial position; they are frequently found after a topic noun phrase, as shown in (b) and (c) below.

(b) きのうのパーティーには誰が来ましたか。
 *Kinō no pāti ni wa **dare** ga kimashita ka.*
 (Lit. To yesterday's party, who came there? (=Who came to yesterday's party?))
 Cp. 誰がきのうのパーティーに来ましたか。
 ***Dare** ga kinō no pāti ni kimashita ka.*
 (Who came to yesterday's party?)

(c) 日本では何をしましたか。
 *Nihon de wa **nani** o shimashita ka.*
 (Lit. In Japan what did you do? (=What did you do in Japan?))
 Cp. 何を日本でしましたか。
 ***Nani** o nihon de shimashita ka.*
 (What did you do in Japan?)

Yes-No Question A question that can be answered by *hai | ē* 'yes' or *ie* 'no'. (Cp. WH-question) Examples follow:

(a) A : 上田さんは来ましたか。
 Ueda-san wa kimashita ka.
 (Did Mr. Ueda come?)

B : はい，来ました。
Hai, kimashita.
(Yes, he did.)

(b) A : 鈴木さんは学生ですか。
Suzuki-san wa gakusei desu ka.
(Is Mr. Suzuki a student?)

B : いいえ，そうじゃありません。
Ie, sō ja arimasen.
(No, he isn't.)

Characteristics of Japanese Grammar

1. Word Order

Japanese is typologically classified as an *SOV* (Subject + Object + Verb) language, whereas English is classified as *SVO*. An important fact about Japanese word order is that each sentence ends in a verb, an adjective or a form of the copula, and that the order of the other sentence elements is relatively free, except for the topic noun or noun phrase, which normally comes at sentence-initial position. A sample sentence follows.

(1)

Subject (topic)		Location		Direct Object		Verb (transitive)
スミスさん	は	日本	で	日本語	を	勉強している。
Sumisu-san	*wa*	*Nihon*	*de*	*nihongo*	*o*	*benkyōshite iru.*
(Mr. Smith is studying Japanese in Japan.)						

The Location and the Direct Object can be switched, but the Subject (topic) and the Verb must normally be in sentence-initial and sentence-final positions, respectively.

The word order principle for Japanese is *the modifier precedes what is modified*. This principle holds whether the modified word is dependent or fully independent. The function of the modifier is to specify the meaning of the modified word. Thus, in (1), the verb *benkyōshite iru* 'is studying' is modified by the preceding elements Subject, Location and Direct Object. Observe the following phrases and clauses.

(2)

Adjective	Noun
赤い	車
akai	*kuruma*
(a red car)	

(3)

Noun Phrase	
Relative Clause	Noun
父　が　きのう　読んだ	本
chichi ga kinō yonda	*hon*
(a book which my father read yesterday)	

(4)

Noun	Particle
スミスさん *Sumisu-san*	は *wa*
(Mr. Smith (topic))	
スミスさん *Sumisu-san*	が *ga*
(Mr. Smith (subject))	
スミスさん *Sumisu-san*	を *o*
(Mr. Smith (object))	
スミスさん *Sumisu-san*	も *mo*
(Mr. Smith also)	
スミスさん *Sumisu-san*	に *ni*
(to / by / from Mr. Smith)	
スミスさん *Sumisu-san*	から *kara*
(from Mr. Smith)	
スミスさん *Sumisu-san*	より *yori*
((more ~) than Mr. Smith)	

(5)

Subordinate Clause	
Sentence	Conjunction
日本　へ　行く *Nihon　e　iku*	から *kara*
(Because I go to Japan)	
日本　へ　行く *Nihon　e　iku*	けれど *keredo*
(Although I go to Japan)	
日本　へ　行く *Nihon　e　iku*	と *to*
(When I go to Japan)	
日本　へ　行く *Nihon　e　iku*	なら *nara*
(If you go to Japan)	

Note: A subordinate clause precedes a main clause.

(6)

Nominalized Noun Phrase	
Sentence	Nominalizer
音楽　を　聞く *ongaku o kiku*	の / こと *no / koto*
(to listen / listening to music)	

In (2) and (3) where the modified word is an independent noun the basic principle holds; in (4) (5) and (6) where the second element is a dependent word, such as a particle, conjunction, or nominalizer, the basic modificational principle also holds, because the meaning of the modified word is fully specified by the modifier. Unlike independent words, however, dependent words require modifiers.

It is important for students of Japanese to recognize and understand some of the most basic Japanese sentence types and their word order. Examples of these basic sentence types are given below:

(7) a. X *wa* Y *da* / X *ga* Y *da* 'Speaking of X, X is Y / It is X that is Y'

X (subject / topic)	Prt	Y	Copula
田中さん *Tanaka-san*	は *wa*	学生 *gakusei*	だ / です。 *da / desu.*
(Mr. Tanaka is a student.)			

(In answer to the question: Who is a student?)

X (subject)	Prt	Y	Copula
田中さん *Tanaka-san*	が *ga*	学生 *gakusei*	だ / です。 *da / desu.*
(Lit. It is Mr. Tanaka who is a student. (=Mr. Tanaka is a student.))			

b. =(1) *SOV*

c. *S Adj*

Subject (topic)	Prt	Adj (*i*)
山川さん *Yamakawa-san*	は *wa*	若い / 若いです。 *wakai / wakaidesu.*
(Mr. Yamakawa is young.)		

Subject (topic)	Prt	Adj (*na*)
山川さん *Yamakawa-san*	は *wa*	元気だ / 元気です。 *genkida / genkidesu.*
(Mr. Yamakawa is healthy.)		

d. X *wa* Y *ga* ~ 'Speaking of X, Y ~'

X (topic, experiencer)	Prt	Y	Prt	Predicate
本田さん *Honda-san*	は *wa*	テニス *tenisu*	が *ga*	上手だ / 上手です。 *jōzuda / jōzudesu.*
(Mr. Honda is good at tennis.)				

X (topic, possessor)	Prt	Y	Prt	Predicate
象 Zō	は wa	鼻 hana	が ga	長い / 長いです。 nagai / nagaidesu.
(An elephant has a long trunk.)				

e. *SV* (=Subject+Verb)

Subject (topic)	Prt			Verb (intransitive)
スミスさん Sumisu-san	は wa	学校 gakkō	に ni	行く / 行きます。 iku / ikimasu.
(Mr. Smith goes to school.)				

f. *LSV* (=Location+Subject+Verb)

Location (topic)	Prt	Prt	Subject	Prt	Quantity	Verb (existence)
この町 Kono machi	(に) (ni)	は wa	大学 daigaku	が ga	二つ futatsu	ある / あります。 aru / arimasu.
(In this town there are two universities.)						

g. *SLV* (=Subject+Location+Verb)

Subject (topic)	Prt	Location	Prt	Quantity	Verb (existence)
大学 Daigaku	は wa	この町 kono machi	に ni	二つ futatsu	ある / あります。 aru / arimasu.
(Speaking of universities, there are two of them in this town.)					

Finally, as shown in the following diagram, any major element listed vertically in (1) through (8) can be a topic marked by *wa*. The element with a lower number tends to be used towards the beginning of a sentence. The order of elements within the predicate is usually much more complex than that shown below. An adverb, which is omitted in the chart, can be positioned at any place before the Core Predicate, as long as it is positioned before or after NP+Prt. The normal position for an adverb, however, is right before the word it modifies.

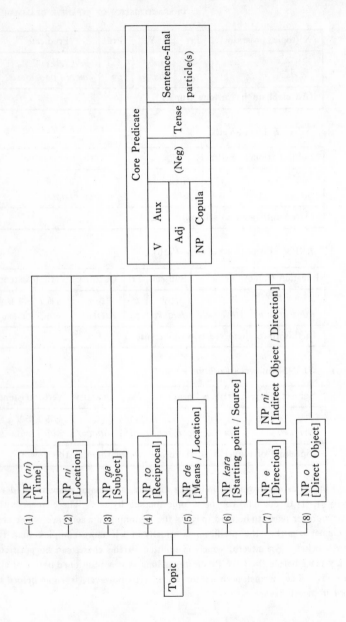

2. Topic

Topic is a key concept in understanding Japanese. Roughly speaking, the topic of a sentence is what the sentence is about. For example, in (1), the topic is *Hanako* and the rest of the sentence provides information about *Hanako*.

(1) 花子は学生です。
     Hanako wa gakusei desu.
     (Hanako is a student.)
     [(Speaking of Hanako,) Hanako is a student.]

Topics are presented using various topic-marking devices. Among these, *wa* is the most frequent marker. (For other topic-markers, see *wa*[1] (は).)

When a topic is presented it must be something both the speaker and the hearer can identify from their knowledge. Usually a topic is something that has been mentioned in a previous discourse, something the speaker and the hearer perceive through their five senses, a proper noun or a generic noun, as seen in (2).

(2) a. 昔々，一人のおじいさんが住んでいました。**おじいさんは**とても貧乏で
         でした。(*O-ji-san* was mentioned previously.)
         Mukashimukashi, hitori no o-ji-san ga sunde imashita. **O-ji-san**
         wa *totemo binbōdeshita.*
         (Once upon a time, there lived an old man. The old man was very
         poor.)

     b. これは私のペンです。(*Kore* is what the speaker and the hearer see.)
         Kore wa *watashi no pen desu.*
         (This is my pen.)

     c. 鈴木さんは日本人です。(*Suzuki-san* is a proper noun.)
         Suzuki-san wa *nihonjin desu.*
         (Mr. Suzuki is Japanese.)

     d. くじらはほ乳動物です。(*Kujira* is a generic noun.)
         Kujira wa *honyūdōbutsu desu.*
         (Whales are mammals.)

In general, any noun phrase (NP) can be topicalized, although subject NPs are the ones most frequently topicalized. (3) presents additional examples. As seen below, when an NP is topicalized, the particle which follows may or may not be retained depending on the particle.

(3) a. スミスさんは日本へ行きました。
        *Sumisu-san **wa** Nihon e ikimashita.*
        (Mr. Smith went to Japan.)

    b. その映画はもう見ました。
        *Sono eiga **wa** mō mimashita.*
        (I already saw the movie.)

    c. 日本(へ / に)はまだ行ったことがない。
        *Nihon (**e** / **ni**) **wa** mada itta koto ga nai.*
        (I haven't been to Japan yet.)

    d. まり子には本をあげた。
        *Mariko **ni wa** hon o ageta.*
        (To Mariko, I gave a book.)

    e. アメリカからはスミスさんが来た。
        *Amerika **kara wa** Smisu-san ga kita.*
        (As for ((lit.) from) America, Mr. Smith came (from there).)

Finally, in discourse, once a topic is established, it does not need to be repeated unless another topic is presented. Consider the following passage, consisting of four sentences (a) – (d) in (4).

(4) a. 太郎はまだアメリカに行ったことがない。
        ***Tarō wa** mada Amerika ni itta koto ga nai.*
        (Taro has not been to America yet.)

    b. いつも行きたいと思っているがお金がないから行けない。
        Itsumo ikitai to omotte iru ga o-kane ga nai kara ikenai.
        (He always thinks he wants to go, but since he has no money, he cannot go.)

    c. お父さんは働いてお金をためなさいと言う。
        ***O-tō-san wa** hataraite o-kane o tamenasai to iu.*
        (His father tells him to work and save money.)

    d. でも太郎はお父さんにお金を出してほしいのだ。
        *Demo **Tarō wa** o-tō-san ni o-kane o dashite hoshii no da.*
        (But Taro wants his father to give him money.)

Here, (4a) introduces a topic, *Tarō*. Since (4b) is a statement about *Tarō* and *Tarō* is an established topic at this point, *Tarō wa* does not have to be repeated here. (4c), however, presents a new topic, *o-tō-san*. Since this topic is still in effect when the topic returns to *Tarō* in (4d), *Tarō wa* has to be reintroduced. A topic must also be presented if a sentence is the first sentence of a new paragraph, even if the last sentence of the preceding paragraph has the same topic.

3. Ellipsis

In language it is universally observed that strategies exist to minimize the effort of conveying messages. The most common strategies are ellipsis, contraction, abbreviation and the use of pronouns. Of these, ellipsis (i.e., the omission of words) is the most efficient and occurs frequently in Japanese.

Generally speaking, elements which can be understood from the context and / or from the situation can be omitted in Japanese unless ellipsis makes the sentence ungrammatical. For example, in (1), B does not repeat *Tarō wa* and *sono mise de* because they can be understood.

(1) A : 太郎はその店で何を買いましたか。
       Tarō wa sono mise de nani o kaimashita ka.
       (What did Taro buy at the store?)

    B : ペンを買いました。
       Pen o kaimashita.
       (He bought a pen.)

Kaimashita, however, cannot be omitted in normal conversation even though it can be understood here, because Japanese sentences (or clauses) must end with a *core predicate* (that is, either a verb, an adjective or a noun phrase which is followed by a form of the copula). Therefore, without the core predicate *kaimashita*, this sentence is ungrammatical. (In informal conversation, B might reply "pen" in answer to A's question, but an answer of this sort is considered abrupt.)

The following are some general rules of ellipsis in Japanese.

(A) If X is the topic of a sentence (often marked by *wa*) and it is also the topic of the sentence which follows it, X can be omitted in the second sentence.
                              (See (4) in 2. *Topic*.)

(B) In question-and-answer discourse, if an element X is shared in the question and the answer, X can be omitted in the answer unless X is the core predicate. Example:

(2) A : 田中さんはむかえに来てくれましたか。
       Tanaka-san wa mukae ni kite kuremashita ka.
       (Did Mr. Tanaka come to pick you up?)

    B : はい、来てくれました。
       Hai, kite kuremashita.
       (Yes, he did.)

(3) A : あなたはアメリカにいた時，学生でしたか。
          Anata wa Amerika ni ita toki gakusei deshita ka.
          (Were you a student when you were in America?)

     B : はい，そう / 学生 でした。   (*Sō* is more commonly used.)
          Hai, sō / gakusei deshita.
          (Yes, I was.)

(Refer again to (1). In yes-no question situations, even predicates can be omitted in very informal conversation.)

(C) If the referent of X is something very close to the speaker and the hearer, and X can be understood from the context and / or the situation, X can be omitted as in (4) – (6). (The parenthesized words can be omitted.)

(4) A : (あなたは)行きますか。
          (*Anata wa*) *ikimasu ka.*
          (Are you going?)

     B : はい，(私は)行きます。
          Hai, (*watashi wa*) *ikimasu.*
          (Yes, I am.)

(5) A : (私達は)行きましょうか。
          (*Watashitachi wa*) *ikimashō ka?*
          (Shall we go?)

     B : いや，(私達は)よしましょう。
          Iya, (*watashitachi wa*) *yoshimashō.*
          (No, let's not.)

(6) A : (これは / それは)何ですか。
          (*Kore wa / Sore wa*) *nan desu ka.*
          (What is this / that?)

     B : (それは / これは)花子からのプレゼントです。
          (*Sore wa / Kore wa*) *Hanako kara no purezento desu.*
          (That / This is a present from Hanako.)

(A) – (C) concern the ellipsis of content words such as nouns and verbs. However, ellipsis in Japanese is not limited to content words. The following are some general rules regarding the ellipsis of particles in conversation.

(D) If the referent of X in X *wa* is psychologically close to the speaker and the hearer, *wa* tends to drop unless X is under focus. Examples:

(7) a. わたくし（は）山田ともうします。

       Watakushi (wa) Yamada to mōshimasu.

       (Lit. I call myself Yamada. (=I am Yamada.))

    b. 君（は）今，何年生ですか。

       Kimi (wa) ima nan-nensei desu ka.

       (What year (in school) are you in now?)

    c. この本（は）おもしろいよ。

       Kono hon (wa) omoshiroi yo.

       (This book is interesting.)

    d. あの人（は）誰ですか。

       Ano hito (wa) dare desu ka.

       (Who is that person?)

(E) The subject marker *ga* can be omitted if the sentence conveys information which is expected by the hearer or which is very closely related to the hearer. Examples:

(8) a. あ，電車（が）来た。

       A, densha (ga) kita.

       (Oh, here comes the train.)

    b. みなさん，お食事（が）出来ました。

       Minasan, o-shokuji (ga) dekimashita.

       (Folks, the meal is ready now.)

    c. 今日田中さんから君に電話（が）あったよ。

       Kyō Tanaka-san kara kimi ni denwa (ga) atta yo.

       (There was a phone call for you today from Mr. Tanaka.)

    d. もしもし，くつのひも（が）ほどけてますよ。

       Moshimoshi, kutsu no himo (ga) hodokete masu yo.

       (Excuse me, your shoelace is untied.)

(F) The direct object marker *o* can be omitted unless the NP *o* is under focus. (*O* drops more frequently in questions.) Examples:

(9) a. コーヒー（を）飲みませんか。

       Kōhi (o) nomimasen ka.

       (Wouldn't you like coffee?)

    b. じゃ，それ（を）もらいます。

       Ja, sore (o) moraimasu.

       (Then, I'll take it.)

c.　今晩電話 (を) ください。

　　Konban denwa (o) kudasai.

　　(Please give me a call tonight.)

Rules (A) – (F) concern the ellipsis of parts of simple sentences or clauses. There are, however, cases in which entire clauses are omitted. (G) is a general rule regarding this sentential ellipsis.

(G)　If the message conveyed by a main clause can be understood from the context and / or the situation, the main clause can be deleted.　Examples:

(10)　A :　きのうパーティーに来なかったね。

　　　　Kinō pāti ni konakatta ne.

　　　　(You didn't come to the party yesterday.)

　　　B :　うん，ちょっと忙しかったから (行けなかった)。

　　　　Un, chotto isogashikatta kara (ikenakatta).

　　　　(Yeah, (I couldn't come) because I was busy.)

(11)　田中先生に聞いたら (どうですか)？

　　　Tanaka-sensei ni kiitara (dō desu ka)?

　　　(Lit. (How will it be) if you ask Prof. Tanaka?　(= Why don't you ask Prof. Tanaka?))

(12)　お茶がはいりましたけど (いかがですか)。

　　　O-cha ga hairimashita kedo (ikaga desu ka).

　　　(Lit. Tea is ready now, but (how would you like it?))

Additionally, ellipsis can take place for psychological reasons.　That is, the speaker may omit a part of a sentence either because he considers it rude, because he feels uncomfortable saying it or because he doesn't know how to say it, etc. For example, if he is offered food he cannot eat, he may say, *Sore wa chotto*, ' (lit.) That is, a little,' implying *Sore wa chotto taberaremasen*, ' I can hardly eat it.'　Or, if the speaker hears someone's unhappy news, he may say, *Sore wa dōmo*, ' (lit.) That is, very,' meaning *Sore wa kanashii koto desu ne*, ' That is a sad thing.'

Finally, it is noted that since ellipsis is common in Japanese, Japanese sentences are often ambiguous in isolation.　They are interpreted correctly only if they are in proper contexts and / or situations.　Examples:

(13)　a.　ぼくは雪子はあまり好きじゃない。　　しかし (ぼくは)

　　　Boku wa Yukiko wa amari sukijanai.　Shikashi (boku wa)

　　　春子は好きだ。

　　　***Haruko wa sukida*.**

　　　(I don't like Yukiko very much.　But, I like Haruko.)

b. ぼくは雪子はあまり好きじゃない。　　しかし**春子は**

*Boku wa Yukiko wa amari sukijanai.　Shikashi **Haruko wa***

(雪子が)**好きだ。**

(*Yukiko ga*) **sukida**.

(I don't like Yukiko very much.　But, Haruko likes her.)

(14)　a. 私はいい人を見つけたので，さっそく**田中さんに**

*Watashi wa ii hito o mitsuketa node, sassoku **Tanaka-san ni***

(その人に)**会ってもらった。**

(*sono hito ni*) **atte moratta**.

(I found a good man, so I asked Mr. Tanaka to see him right away.)

b. 私はいい人を見つけたので，さっそく(その人に)

Watashi wa ii hito o mitsuketa node, sassoku (sono hito ni)

田中さんに会ってもらった。

***Tanaka-san ni atte moratta**.*

(I found a good man, so I asked him to see Mr. Tanaka right away.)

4. Personal Pronouns

One of the peculiarities of Japanese personal pronouns is that there is more than one pronoun for the first and second person and that traditionally there have been no third person pronouns. The most frequently used first and second person pronouns are listed below:

Personal Pronouns / Levels of Formality	Singular	
	First Person 'I'	Second Person 'You'
Very Formal	わたくし *watakushi*	none
Formal	わたし あたくし *watashi* *atakushi* (female)	あなた *anata*
Informal	ぼく あたし *boku* *atashi* (male) (female)	きみ *kimi* (male)
Very Informal	おれ *ore* (male)	おまえ あんた *omae* *anta* (male)

Personal Pronouns / Levels of Formality	Plural	
	First Person 'We'	Second Person 'You'
Very Formal	わたくしども *watakushi**domo***	none
Formal	わたくしたち *watakushi**tachi*** わたしたち *watashi**tachi***	あなたがた *anata**gata***
Informal	ぼくたち あたしたち *boku**tachi*** *atashi**tachi*** (male) (female) ぼくら あたしら *boku**ra*** *atashi**ra*** (male) (female)	きみたち あなたたち *kimi**tachi*** *anata**tachi*** (male) きみら *kimi**ra*** (male)
Very Informal	おれたち *ore**tachi*** (male)	おまえたち あんたたち *omae**tachi*** *anta**tachi*** (male) おまえら あんたら *omae**ra*** *anta**ra*** (male)

Note: (Male) / (female) means that the particular pronoun is used by a male / female speaker, respectively.

The first person singular pronoun *watakushi* has at least six contracted forms. The way the contraction (i.e., omission of sounds) takes place is as follows:

wataku̸shi → watashi (formal)
w̸atakushi → atakushi (formal, female)
w̸átaku̸shi → atashi (informal, female)
w̸ataku̸s̸h̸i → atai (very informal / vulgar, female)
wat̸ak̸u̸shi → washi (informal, older male)
wat̸ak̸u̸shi → as̸shi (very informal, adult male of the Bay area of Tokyo)

The fact that there is more than one pronoun for the first and second person leads us to suspect that Japanese first and second person pronouns are not pure pronouns but are a kind of noun. In fact, these 'pronouns' can be freely modified by adjectives or by relative clauses as in (1) and cannot be repeated in a single sentence as in (2), which supports the idea that they are similar to regular nouns.

⑴ a. 忙しい私はテレビも見られない。
*Isogashii **watashi** wa terebi mo mirarenai.*
(Lit. Busy me cannot see even TV. (=I cannot even watch TV because I'm so busy.))

b. 音楽が好きな私は一日中音楽を聞いている。
*Ongaku ga sukina **watashi** wa ichinichijū ongaku o kiite iru.*
(Lit. I who like music is listening to music all day long. (=Because I like music, I listen to it all day long.))

c. 若いあなたにはまだ分からないでしょう。
*Wakai **anata** ni wa mada wakaranai deshō.*
(Lit. Young you probably won't understand it. (=Since you are young, you probably won't understand it.))

⑵ a. *私は私の部屋で私の友達と話していた。
****Watashi** wa **watashi** no heya de **watashi** no tomodachi to hanashite ita.*
(I was talking with my friend in my room.)
→ 私は ø 部屋で ø 友達と話していた。
*   **Watashi** wa ø heya de ø tomodachi to hanashite ita.*

b. *あなたはきのうあなたの部屋であなたの友達と何をしていましたか。
****Anata** wa kinō **anata** no heya de **anata** no tomodachi to nani o shite imashita ka.*

(What were you doing yesterday with your friend in your room?)
→ **あなた**はきのう ø 部屋で ø 友達と何をしていましたか。

Anata wa kinō ø heya de ø tomodachi to nani o shite imashita ka.

It is also important to note that Japanese first and second person pronouns are deleted unless it is necessary to emphasize *me*-ness or *you*-ness. Under normal communicative situations, who is speaking to whom is obvious, so Japanese speakers simply omit these pronouns. Students of Japanese, therefore, should avoid using first and second person pronouns whenever possible.

In addition to first and second person pronouns, there are other ways to refer to the speaker or the addressee, as summarized in the following chart.

Kinds & Conditions	Self-address Forms	Alter-address Forms
Kinship terms	お父さん (your father) o-tō-san お母さん (your mother) o-kā-san おじいさん (your grandpa) o-ji-san おばあさん (your grandma) o-bā-san おじさん (your uncle) oji-san おばさん (your aunt) oba-san	お父さん o-tō-san お母さん o-kā-san おじいさん o-ji-san おばあさん o-bā-san おじさん oji-san おばさん oba-san
Social role terms	先生 (your teacher) sensei	先生 sensei 社長 (president of a company) shachō 課長 (section chief) kachō
Occupational terms	none	魚屋さん (fish monger) sakana-ya-san 肉屋さん (butcher) niku-ya-san
First / Last names	花子 Hanako	花子さん Hanako-san 田中さん Tanaka-san

Within a family, if the speaker is considered superior (primarily in terms of age) to the addressee (Speaker>Addressee), he may use a kinship term as a form of self-address, but if not, he can use only a first person pronoun in self-address. If the addressee is considered superior to the speaker (Addressee> Speaker), the speaker has to employ the kinship term of the addressee when addressing him, or he must use a second person pronoun or the addressee's name (optionally with -san or -chan). Outside the family, in an Addressee> Speaker situation, the speaker has to employ the addressee's social role term when addressing him. If the situation is Speaker>Addressee, the speaker cannot use his own social role term as a form of self-address, except for the term *sensei* when it refers to elementary and junior high school teachers.

Occupational terms such as *sakana-ya* ' fish monger ', *niku-ya* ' butcher ' and *hana-ya* ' florist ' are used as address forms by attaching -san to them. (⇨ **-ya**) Also, a female first name is employed by a young girl as a self-address form in very informal speech as in (3).

(3) あのね，京子きのう一郎さんとデートしたのよ。
*Ano ne, **Kyōko** kinō Ichirō-san to dēto shita no yo.*
(You know what? I (=Kyoko) had a date with Ichiro yesterday!)

There is no real third person pronoun in Japanese. As shown in (4), all English third person pronouns have no corresponding forms in Japanese.

(4) a. 山田さんは去年アメリカに行った。英語が勉強したかったのだ。
Yamada-san wa kyonen Amerika ni itta. Eigo ga benkyōshitakatta no da.
(Mr. Yamada went to America last year. *He* wanted to study English.)

b. 上田さんは十年前に買った車にまだ乗っている。
Ueda-san wa jūnen mae ni katta kuruma ni mada notte iru.
(Mr. Ueda is still driving the car which *he* bought ten years ago.)

c. A : ボブはきのう来ましたか。
Bobu wa kinō kimashita ka.
(Did Bob come see you yesterday?)

B : ええ，来ましたよ。
Ē, kimashita yo.
(Yes, *he* did.)

d. A : 田中さん達，遅いわねえ。
Tanaka-san-tachi, osoi wa nē.
(Miss Tanaka and the people with her are late, aren't they?)

B: 忘れているんじゃないかしら。

Wasurete iru n ja nai ka shira.

(I wonder if *they* have forgotten about this.)

e. ここから大阪まで車で一時間かかる。

Koko kara Ōsaka made kuruma de ichijikan kakaru.

(*It* takes one hour from here to Osaka.)

f. 今七時です。

Ima shichiji desu.

(*It* is seven now.)

During the past century or so, however, the third person pronouns *kare* 'he', *kanojo* 'she', *karera* 'they (male)' and *kanojora* 'they (female)' have begun to be employed primarily in novels translated into Japanese and in Japanese novels. These pronouns are also fairly widely used in current spoken Japanese. Like first and second person pronouns, they are treated very much like nouns, as seen in (5).

(5) a. 僕の**彼女**, とてもきれいなんだ。

*Boku no **kanojo**, totemo kireina n da.*

(My girl friend is very pretty, you know.)

b. 大学を出た**彼**はすぐ結婚した。

*Daigaku o deta **kare** wa sugu kekkonshita.*

(Lit. He who finished college got married right away. (=He got married right after graduation from college.))

There is one condition governing the use of third person pronouns:

The speaker / writer is psychologically somewhat distant from the referent of the pronoun.

5. Passive

The concept of passive in Japanese, which is called *ukemi* (受身) (lit. body which receives something), is considerably different from its English counterpart. The Japanese passive contains two elements: an event (i.e., an action by someone / something) and a person or thing which is affected by that event. For example, if someone runs away and it affects someone else, that action can be expressed by the passive construction. Or, if someone smokes and it affects someone else, that can be a passive situation. In other words, the common characteristic of the Japanese passive is that the event is not under the control of those affected by it. Note that the person in the first situation above has no control over someone's running away and the one in the second has no control over someone's smoking.

Passive situations are expressed in various ways according to the situation. The most common way is to use the passive forms of verbs. (⇨ **rareru**[1]) For instance, the above situations can be expressed as in (1), using passive verb forms.

(1) a. 山田さんは奥さんに逃げ**られた**。
    *Yamada-san wa okusan ni nige**rareta**.*
    (Lit. Mr. Yamada's wife ran away on him.)

  b. 太郎は春子にたばこをすわ**れた**。
    *Tarō wa Haruko ni tabako o suwa**reta**.*
    (Lit. Taro had a cigarette smoked by Haruko on him.)

Notice here that in (1a) the verb *nigeru* 'run away' is intransitive and in (1b) there is a direct object *tabako* 'cigarette'. Neither (1a) nor (1b) can be expressed using the English passive construction "*be*+past participle". This type of construction, however, is frequently found in Japanese and is called 'the indirect passive'. In indirect passive sentences the thing affected by the event is usually human and how the person is affected is interpretable only from the context. The sentences in (1) show situations where someone is negatively affected. The following is an example where the person is positively affected.

(2) 木村さんは美人に横に座ら**れて**うれしそうだ。
   *Kimura-san wa bijin ni yoko ni suwara**rete** ureshi sōda.*
   (Lit. Mr. Kimura, having a pretty woman sit beside him, looks happy.)

In indirect passive sentences the agent of the event is usually animate and the action is volitional. Therefore, the following examples are all unacceptable.

(3) a. *私は石に頭に落ちられた。

   *Watashi wa ishi ni atama ni ochira**reta**.

   (*My head was fallen on by a rock.)

   b. *トムは交差点のまん中で車に止まられた。

   *Tomu wa kōsaten no mannaka de kuruma ni tomara**reta**.

   (*Tom was stopped in the middle of the intersection by his car.)

There are, however, a very few exceptions, as seen in (4).

(4) 僕は雨に降られた。

   Boku wa ame ni fura**reta**.

   (Lit. It rained on me.)

The passive forms of verbs can also express what is called direct passive. (5) presents some examples.

(5) a. ジョンはビルにぶたれた。

   Jon wa Biru ni buta**reta**.

   (John was hit by Bill.)

   b. この絵は十九世紀に描かれた。

   Kono e wa jūkyū-seiki ni kaka**reta**.

   (This picture was painted in the nineteenth century.)

   c. 酒は米から作られる。

   Sake wa kome kara tsukura**reru**.

   (*Sake* is made from rice.)

As seen in (5), direct passive sentences have passive equivalents in English. It is noted that in direct passive sentences, too, the conditions mentioned above are satisfied. That is, in (5a) there is a person, John, who was affected by an event, Bill's hitting, and the event was not under John's control. The difference between direct passive and indirect passive is that in direct passive sentences a person / thing is *directly* affected by an event (i.e., a person / thing is the direct receiver of someone's / something's action) as in (5), while in indirect passive sentences the effect of an event on a person is indirect (i.e., a person is not the direct receiver of someone's / something's action), as seen in (1) – (4).

In general, when a passive sentence is used, it is about the person / thing which is affected by the event, and when what is affected is human, the sentence takes the viewpoint of the person rather than the agent of the event.

(See 9. Viewpoint.)

Some passive situations are also expressed by the verb *morau* ' get ', as in (6).

(6) a. マーガレットはポールにイヤリングをもらった。

　　　*Māgaretto wa Pōru ni iyaringu o **moratta**.*

　　　(Margaret got a pair of earrings from Paul.)

　　b. メアリーはスティーブにアパートに来てもらった。

　　　*Meari wa Sutību ni apāto ni kite **moratta**.*

　　　(Mary had Steve come to her apartment. (=Steve came to Mary's apartment for her.))

　　c. 私は父にカメラを買ってもらった。

　　　*Watashi wa chichi ni kamera o katte **moratta**.*

　　　(I had my father buy me a camera. (=My father bought a camera for me.))

When *morau* is used, the event always affects the person *positively*. (This is not the case with sentences with *rareru*.) In this case, also, the speaker's viewpoint is that of the person affected by the event.　　　　　　　(⇨ ***morau***[1,2])

　　Naru ' become ' can also express some passive situations. Compare the following pairs of sentences with *suru* ' do ' and *naru*.

(7) a. 山口さんはアメリカに行くことにした。

　　　*Yamaguchi-san wa Amerika ni iku koto ni **shita**.*

　　　(Mr. Yamaguchi has decided to go to America.)

　　b. 山口さんはアメリカに行くことになった。

　　　*Yamaguchi-san wa Amerika ni iku koto ni **natta**.*

　　　(It's been decided that Mr. Yamaguchi is going to America.)

(8) a. 先生はフレッドを停学にした。

　　　*Sensei wa Fureddo o teigaku ni **shita**.*

　　　(The teacher suspended Fred from school.)

　　b. フレッドは停学になった。

　　　*Fureddo wa teigaku ni **natta**.*

　　　(Fred was suspended from school.)

Here, again, the viewpoint in the (b) sentences is that of the person affected by the event, and the agent of the event is not the speaker's main concern.

　　　　　　　　　　　　　　　　　　　(⇨ ***koto ni naru***; ***naru***)

6. Politeness and Formality

All languages are equipped with polite expressions and Japanese is no exception. What makes Japanese polite expressions distinctly different from those of other languages is that the Japanese system involves grammar as well as lexical items. Basically, there are two ways to be polite in Japanese; one is to elevate the speaker's superior, i.e., a person who is older and higher in social status than the speaker. Expressions of this type are called *Honorific Polite Expressions*. The other method is to lower the speaker or his in-group members, and thus elevate his superior indirectly. Expressions of this type are called *Humble Polite Expressions*.

With *Honorific Polite Expressions*, the subject of the sentence is the speaker's superior and the form of the main predicate is an honorific form, as shown below:

(A) *Honorific Polite Verbs*
   Regular Formation

Nonpolite (Dictionary Form)	Honorific Polite	
	o- V*masu* *ni naru*	Passive Form
話す (talk) *hanasu*	お話し に なる *o-hanashi* *ni naru*	話される *hanasareru*
教える (teach) *oshieru*	お教え に なる *o-oshie ni naru*	教えられる *oshiereru*

   Irregular Forms

Nonpolite (Dictionary Form)	Honorific Polite
見る (see) *miru*	ご覧 に なる *goran ni naru* (Gr. 1)
知って いる (know) *shitte iru*	ご存知 だ *gozonji da*
居る / 来る / 行く (be / come / go) *iru / kuru / iku*	いらっしゃる *irassharu* (Gr. 1)
くれる (give (to me)) *kureru*	くださる *kudasaru* (Gr. 1)
食べる (eat) *taberu*	召し上がる *meshiagaru* (Gr. 1)
する (do) *suru*	なさる *nasaru* (Gr. 1)
来る / 行く / 居る (come / go / be) *kuru / iku / iru*	おいで に なる (Gr. 1) *oide ni naru*

着る (wear) *kiru*	お召し に なる (Gr. 1) *omeshi ni naru*
死ぬ (die) *shinu*	おなくなり に なる (Gr. 1) *o-nakunari ni naru*
言う (say) *iu*	おっしゃる (Gr. 1) *ossharu*

The following are typical examples of sentences using honorific polite verbs:

(1) a. 先生はアメリカの大学で日本語を**お教えになります**。
     *Sensei wa Amerika no daigaku de nihongo o **o-oshie ni narimasu**.*
     (The professor will teach Japanese at an American college.)

    b. 先生はアメリカの大学で日本語を**教えられます**。
     *Sensei wa Amerika no daigaku de nihongo o **oshieraremasu**.*
     (The professor will teach Japanese at an American college.)

    c. 先生はゴルフを**なさる**と**おっしゃいました**。
     *Sensei wa gorufu o **nasaru** to **osshaimashita**.*
     (The professor told me that he's going to play golf.)

Sentence (1a) with its longer honorific expression, is more polite than (1b), which has a shorter honorific expression. Notice also that the honorific form in (1b) is the same as the passive form. An important characteristic of the honorific and passive form is *indirectness*, the origin of honorific politeness. Sentence (1c) includes the irregular verbs *nasaru* ' do ' and *ossharu* ' say '. Such verbs as *nasaru* and *ossharu* which are irregular must be memorized one by one. Note that the following honorific polite verbs are Gr. 1 verbs, but are irregular in their conjugations of formal nonpast and imperative forms.

Inf Neg	Fml Nonpast	Inf Nonpast	Conditional	Imperative
いらっしゃらない *irassharanai*	いらっしゃいます *irasshaimasu*	いらっしゃる *irassharu*	いらっしゃれば *irasshareba*	いらっしゃい *irasshai*
くださらない *kudasaranai*	くださいます *kudasaimasu*	くださる *kudasaru*	くだされば *kudasareba*	ください *kudasai*
なさらない *nasaranai*	なさいます *nasaimasu*	なさる *nasaru*	なされば *nasareba*	なさい *nasai*
おっしゃらない *ossharanai*	おっしゃいます *osshaimasu*	おっしゃる *ossharu*	おっしゃれば *osshareba*	おっしゃい *osshai*

The honorific polite form of V*te iru* is formed as shown in the following chart.

Honorific Polite Forms of V te iru.

Nonpolite	Honorific Polite	
	V*te* **irassharu**	**o**- V*masu* **da** / **de irassharu**
読んでいる (be reading) *yonde iru*	読んでいらっしゃる *yonde* **irassharu**	お読みだ / でいらっしゃる **o**-*yomi* **da** / **de irassharu**
教えている (be teaching) *oshiete iru*	教えていらっしゃる *oshiete* **irassharu**	お教えだ / でいらっしゃる **o**-*oshie* **da** / **de irassharu**

The use of the honorific polite V*te iru* is exemplified by (2) below. Here again the longer version is more polite than the shorter one. Thus, the hierarchy of politeness is: *o*- V*masu de irassharu* > V*te irassharu* > *o*- V*masu da*.

(2) a. 先生は今ご本をお読みでいらっしゃいます。
　　　　Sensei wa ima go-hon o **o-yomi de irasshaimasu**.
　　　　(The professor is reading a book.)

　　　b. 先生は今ご本を読んでいらっしゃいます。
　　　　Sensei wa ima go-hon o **yonde irasshaimasu**.

　　　c. 先生は今ご本をお読みだ。
　　　　Sensei wa ima go-hon o **o-yomi da**.

(B) *Honorific Polite Adjectives*
　　 Regular Formation (Adj(*i*))

Nonpolite (Dictionary Form)	Honorific Polite **o**- Adj(*i*) inf
若い　(young) *wakai*	お若い **o**-*wakai*
強い　(strong) *tsuyoi*	お強い **o**-*tsuyoi*

Irregular Forms

Nonpolite	Honorific Polite
いい / よい　(good) *ii / yoi*	およろしい **o**-*yoroshii*

Regular Formation (Adj(*na*))

Nonpolite	Honorific Polite
	o- Adj(*na*)stem {*da* / *de irassharu*}
元気だ (healthy) *genkida*	お元気{だ / でいらっしゃる} *o-genki* {*da* / *de irassharu*}
きれいだ (pretty) *kireida*	おきれい{だ / でいらっしゃる} *o-kirei* {*da* / *de irassharu*}

There are additional polite adjectival forms (such as *o-wakō gozaimasu* (from *wakai* 'young'), *o-tsuyō gozaimasu* (from *tsuyoi* 'strong')), but such hyperpolite forms are now seldom used by younger native speakers, except in greetings such as *o-hayō gozaimasu* (from *hayai* 'early'), *o-medetō gozaimasu* 'Congratulations!' (from *medetai* 'auspicious') and *arigatō gozaimasu* 'Thank you very much' (from *arigatai* 'grateful'). Adjectives which can be used in honorific polite sentences are limited to those which refer to personal characteristics. Examples follow:

(3) a. お若いですね。
    O-wakaidesu *ne.*
    (You are young, aren't you?)

  b. お父さんはお元気でいらっしゃいますか。
    O-tō-san wa ***o-genkide irasshaimasu*** *ka.*
    (Lit. Is your father healthy? (=How is your father's health?))

In terms of humble polite expressions, the subject of the sentence is the speaker or someone in his in-group rather than the speaker's superior. The humble polite predicates are listed below:

(C) *Humble Polite Verbs*
    Regular Formation

Nonpolite (Dictionary Form)	Humble Polite *o-* V*masu* **suru** / **itasu**
話す (talk) *hanasu*	お話する / いたす *o-hanashi* **suru** / **itasu**
教える (teach) *oshieru*	お教えする / いたす *o-oshie* **suru** / **itasu**

Irregular Formation

Nonpolite (Dictionary Form)	Humble Polite
見る (see) *miru*	拝見する / いたす *haiken suru / itasu* (Gr. 1)
借りる (borrow) *kariru*	拝借する / いたす *haishaku suru / itasu*
飲む / 食べる / もらう (drink / eat / receive) *nomu / taberu / morau*	いただく *itadaku* (Gr. 1)
する (do) *suru*	いたす *itasu* (Gr. 1)
来る / 行く (go) *kuru / iku*	まいる *mairu* (Gr. 1)
言う (say) *iu*	申す *mōsu* (Gr. 1)
会う (meet) *au*	お目にかかる *o-me ni kakaru* (Gr. 1) (お会いする / いたす) (*o-ai suru / itasu*)
いる (be) *iru*	おる *oru* (Gr. 1)
やる / あげる (give) *yaru / ageru*	さしあげる *sashiageru* (Gr. 2)
知っている (know) *shitte iru*	存じている *zonjite iru* (Gr. 2)

Typical sentences containing humble polite expressions follow:

(4) a. 私がそのお荷物を**お持ち**します。
   *Watashi ga sono o-nimotsu **o o-mochi shimasu**.*
   (I will carry your luggage.)

   b. 母が**お連れ**いたします。
   *Haha ga **o-tsure itashimasu**.*
   (My mother will take you there.)

Sentence (4b) with its longer humble expression is more humble than (4a) with a shorter humble expression.

In addition to the two major polite expressions (i.e., Honorific Polite and Humble Polite Expressions), there is what might be called *Neutral Polite Expression*. It is called 'neutral' because its predicate *de gozaimasu* can be honorific-, humble- or neutral-polite, as shown in the following chart.

(D) *Neutral Polite Form of Copula ' da '*

Nonpolite	Neutral Polite
(a) 先生は病気だ。 *Sensei wa byōki da.* (The professor is ill.)	Speaker's superior *wa* / *ga* **o-** / **go-** ~ **de go-zaimasu**. (Honorific)
	先生はご病気でございます。 *Sensei wa **go-**byōki **de gozaimasu**.*
(b) 私は学生だ。 *Watashi wa gakusei da.* (I am a student.)	Speaker *wa* / *ga* ~ **de gozaimasu**. (Humble)
	私は学生でございます。 *Watakushi wa gakusei **de gozaimasu**.*
(c) あれは議事堂です。 *Are wa gijidō desu.* (That's the Diet building.)	Inanimate object *wa* / *ga* ~ **de gozaimasu**. (Neutral)
	あれは議事堂でございます。 *Are wa gijidō **de gozaimasu**.*

In (Da) the speaker is being polite to the person referred to by the subject. In (Db) the speaker is being humble towards the addressee and in (Dc) the speaker is just using polite speech; it is not directed towards the inanimate object referred to by the subject.

In the case of honorific polite expressions in general, the polite prefix *o-* or *go-* is attached to someone or something belonging to the human subject of a sentence. Although the prefixes *o-* and *go-* are normally attached to Japanese and Sino-Japanese nouns, respectively, the prefix *o-* can be attached to highly Japanized nouns such as *benkyō* (勉強) 'study', *cha* (茶) 'tea' and *denwa* (電話) 'telephone'. *Go-*, however, is never attached to traditional Japanese nouns. Example sentences in which *o-* or *go-* are used are given below:

(5) a. 先生はお車をお持ちですか。

*Sensei wa **o**-kuruma o o-mochi desu ka.*

(Do you have a car, Professor?)

b. 田中先生はご本をお書きになった。

*Tanaka-sensei wa **go**-hon o o-kaki ni natta.*

(Prof. Tanaka has written a book.)

The prefixes *o-* and *go-* can also be attached to things which are not related to the speaker's superior, especially to basic items related to clothing, food and housing. The purpose of such usage is to make a sentence sound more elegant. Female speakers tend to use *o-* and *go-* in this way more frequently than males. Example sentences follow:

(6) a. 今晩はお刺身とお吸い物にしましょうか。

*Konban wa **o**-sashimi to **o**-suimono ni shimashō ka.*

(Shall we make it *sashimi* and clear soup tonight?)

b. お手洗いはどこですか.

***O**-tearai wa doko desu ka.*

(Where is the washroom?)

It is also important to note that there is a stylistic distinction between the *informal* and *formal* styles, independent of the honorific-, humble-, and neutral-polite distinctions. The formal style is normally used when one is NOT speaking intimately or personally with someone who belongs to his in-group. The informal style is used when one is speaking with one's own in-group or when a verb, an adjective or the copula is used in specific grammatical positions, such as right before *hazu da* 'be expected to' or *tsumori da* 'intend to', as shown in (7). (⇨ Appendix 4 (C), (D), (E), (I), (J) and (K))

(7) a. 先生は今日研究室にいらっしゃる /* いらっしゃいますはずです。

*Sensei wa kyō kenkyūshitsu ni **irassharu** / *__irasshaimasu__ hazu desu.*

(The professor is expected to be at his office today.)

b. 私が先生にご連絡する /*ご連絡しますつもりです。

*Watashi ga sensei ni **go-renrakusuru** / *__go-renrakushimasu__ tsumori desu.*

(I intend to contact you, Professor.)

The formal style is marked by *-mas-* or *-des-* as shown in the following chart.

Styles / Predicates		Informal		Formal	
		Nonpast	Past	Nonpast	Past
Verbals	Verb	食べる *taberu* (eat)	食べた *tabeta* (ate)	食べます *tabemasu* (eat)	食べました *tabemashita* (ate)
	Adj (*i*)	広い *hiroi* (is wide)	広かった *hirokatta* (was wide)	広いです *hiroidesu* (is wide)	広かったです *hirokattadesu* (was wide)
Nominals	Adj (*na*)	きれいだ *kireida* (is pretty)	きれいだった *kireidatta* (was pretty)	きれいです *kireidesu* (is pretty)	きれいでした *kireideshita* (was pretty)
	Noun	本だ *hon da* (is a book)	本だった *hon datta* (was a book)	本です *hon desu* (is a book)	本でした *hon deshita* (was a book)

Students of Japanese will usually be exposed to the formal style in their beginning textbook, because it is the proper stylistic register for adults. They should be aware, however, that the informal style is more basic than the formal style, as evidenced by the fact that native children master the informal style first.

It is interesting to note that whenever the speaker takes a *speaker-oriented position* he switches his style from formal to informal, even in a formal situation. For example, a student speaking with his professor would use the formal style during conversation. But, if he were stung by a bee while talking, he would use the informal *itai* ' ouch ', rather than the formal form *itaidesu*, because getting stung is purely a speaker-oriented matter. This is an extreme case, but there are many situations where the informal style must be used due to speaker-orientation. This results in a formal discourse interspersed with informal verbals and nominals.

Finally, in practical terms, what are the appropriate situations for polite sentences? Generally speaking, an inferior uses polite speech to an addressee or to the person presented as the topic of a sentence. Typical situations are the following:

You are:	Your addressee is:
student	teacher, professor
subordinate	boss
salesperson	customer
junior	senior

Sometimes, an older person uses polite expressions when he is asking a favor of a younger person. Under such circumstances, the older person feels psychologically inferior to the person he is addressing.

Another appropriate situation for polite speech involves discourse among adults of equal status who do not know each other well. Formal Japanese is also used at such occasions as ceremonies, public speeches and public announcements. The informal style, then, is normally reserved for communication among equals who are on intimate terms.

7. Sentence-final Particles

In Japanese there is a group of particles called sentence-final particles. In non-inverted sentences, sentence-final particles are placed at the end of a main clause and indicate the function of the sentence or express the speaker's emotion or attitude toward the hearer in a conversational situation. (Personal letters, which are a sort of conversation between the sender and the receiver, may also contain sentence-final particles.) Some of these particles are used exclusively by male or exclusively by female speakers, so they also function to mark the speaker's sex. In what follows, we will take some common sentence-final particles and see how they are used.

(1) is a declarative sentence. If the sentence-final particles *ka* and *ne* are affixed to (1), as in (2) and (3), the sentence becomes a question ((2)) and a sentence of confirmation ((3)).

(1) 山田さんは先生です。
   Yamada-san wa sensei desu.
   (Mr. Yamada is a teacher.)

(2) 山田さんは先生ですか。
   *Yamada-san wa sensei desu **ka**.*
   (Is Mr. Yamada a teacher?)

(3) 山田さんは先生ですね。
   *Yamada-san wa sensei desu **ne**.*
   (Mr. Yamada is a teacher, isn't he?)

Ne is also used to soften requests and invitations, and it often expresses the speaker's friendliness.

(4) 来て（ください）ね。
   *Kite (kudasai) **ne**.*
   (Please come.)

(5) 一緒に行きましょうね。
   *Isshoni ikimashō **ne**.*
   (Let's go together, shall we?)

Ne can be used with polite imperatives but not with plain imperatives.

(6) 学校へ行きなさいね。
   *Gakkō e ikinasai **ne**.*
   (Go to school, okay?)

(7) *学校へ行けね。
   *Gakkō e ike **ne**.

Na functions as the negative imperative marker when it is used with informal nonpast verbs.

(8) a. こっちへ来るな。
   Kotchi e kuru **na**.
   (Don't come this way.)

   b. 動くな。
   Ugoku **na**.
   (Don't move.)

When *na* is affixed to informal declarative or invitational sentences, it sometimes functions like *ne*, with the limitation that it is used only by men.

(9) a. 一郎は一年生だな。
   Ichirō wa ichi-nensei da **na**.
   (Ichiro is a freshman, isn't he?)

   b. 一緒に行こうな。
   Isshoni ikō **na**.
   (Let's go together, shall we?)

Na is also used by men in monologue situations.

(10) a. おかしいな。誰もいない。どうしたんだろう。
   Okashii **na**. Dare mo inai. Dō shita n darō.
   (It's strange. There's nobody. What's wrong, I wonder?)

Sometimes *na* is used with formal sentences in older men's speech. This *na* conveys the feeling of weak assertion.

(11) a. それはちょっと難しいですな。
   Sore wa chotto muzukashii desu **na**.
   (That's a bit difficult.)

Yo, *zo* and *ze* are used for assertion. Some English equivalents are " I tell you ", " you know ", " believe me ", and " I'd say ". *Zo* and *ze* are exclusively used in informal male speech.

(12) a. 私は知りませんよ。
   Watashi wa shirimasen **yo**.
   (I don't know. Believe me.)

    b. おれは負けないぞ。
       *Ore wa makenai **zo**.*
       (I won't lose!)

    c. これは金だぜ。
       *Kore wa kin da **ze**.*
       (Hey, this is gold!)

Yo and *ze* are also used with invitational sentences.

(13) 今晩は飲もうよ / ぜ。
    *Konban wa nomō **yo** / **ze**.*
    (Let's drink tonight!)

Wa is affixed only to declarative sentences by female speakers. It gives sentences a feminine flavor and sometimes expresses a light assertion. It is used in both formal and informal speech.

(14) a. 私はまだ十八ですわ。
       *Watashi wa mada jūhachi desu **wa**.*
       (I am still eighteen.)

    b. あたし、うれしいわ。
       *Atashi, ureshii **wa**.*
       (I'm happy.)

Wa can be used with *ne* and *yo* but not with *ka*, as in (15).

(15) a. これ、高いわね。
       *Kore, takai **wa ne**.*
       (This is expensive, isn't it?)

    b. 私も行くわよ。
       *Watashi mo iku **wa yo**.*
       (I'm going, too.)

    c. *田中さんも来るわか.
       Tanaka-san mo kuru **wa ka.*
       (Is Mr. Tanaka coming, too?)

Nē, *nā* and *wā* are used in exclamatory sentences. *Nē* can also convey the idea of confirmation. *Nā* is usually used by men, but can be heard in conversations by younger women. *Wā* is used only by women.

(16) a. きれいだねえ。　(Male)
       *Kireida **nē**.*
       (Isn't it pretty!)

b. きれいだわねえ。　(Female)

*Kireida wa **nē**.*

(Isn't it pretty!)

c. 鈴木君はよく働くなあ。　(Male)

*Suzuki-kun wa yoku hataraku **nā**.*

(Boy, Mr. Suzuki works hard!)

d. すてきだわあ。　(Female)

*Sutekida **wā**.*

(It's wonderful!)

Some sentence-final particles appear in questions in informal speech. For example, in informal male speech *kai* and *dai* mark yes / no questions and WH-questions, respectively. 　　　　　　　　　　　　　　(⇨ ***dai***; ***kai***)

(17)　a. これは君の本かい。　(Male)

*Kore wa kimi no hon **kai**.*

(Is this your book?)

b. これはだれの本だい。　(Male)

*Kore wa dare no hon **dai**.*

(Whose book is this?)

In informal female speech the sentence-final *n(o) desu ka* becomes *no* spoken with rising intonation. In this use *no* is almost a female question marker. Examples follow:

(18)　a. 友子さん，パーティーに行かないの?　(Female)

*Tomoko-san, pāti ni ikanai **no**?*

(Aren't you going to the party, Tomoko?)

b. 何を買うの?　(Female)

*Nani o kau **no**?*

(What are you going to buy?)

Kashira and *kanā* also appear in sentence-final position and express the speaker's uncertainty about a proposition. The former is usually used by female speakers and the latter by male speakers.

(19)　a. 私にも出来るかしら。　(Female)

*Watashi ni mo dekiru **kashira**.*

(Can I do it, too, I wonder?)

b. あしたは雨かなあ。　(Male)

*Ashita wa ame **kanā**.*

(Will it rain tomorrow, I wonder?)

As we have seen in the various examples above, sentence-final particles play an important role in determining the function of a sentence. Also, by using these particles in conversation, a speaker expresses his / her emotion or attitude toward the hearer as well as his / her masculinity / femininity.

8. Sound Symbolisms—*giseigo* and *gitaigo*

Japanese is abundant in sound symbolisms in the form of *phonomimes* (= *onomatopoeia*, **giseigo**), *phenomimes* (= **gitaigo**) and *psychomimes* (= **gitaigo**). All languages have phonomimes or direct phonetic representations of actual sounds in every day life, such as the English *bang*, *bowwow*, *cock-a-doodle-do* and *meow*. English phonomimes are normally considered children's language and are not fully integrated into adult language. In Japanese, however, not only *phonomimes* but also *phenomimes* (phonetic representations of phenomena perceptible by non-auditory senses) and *psychomimes* (phonetic representations of human psychological states) are an integral part of adult spoken and written Japanese. Therefore, it is of vital importance that students of Japanese learn these sound symbolisms as part of their ordinary vocabulary.

A summary of sound symbolisms is given below. Each sound symbolism is an adverb associated with a specific verb. The adverb is normally followed by the quote marker *to*, because the sound symbolism is perceived as a quotation. The examples contain the verb that typically co-occurs with the given sound symbolism.

(A) *Voiceless* and *Voiced Consonants*

Voiced consonants tend to represent something big, heavy, dull or dirty; whereas voiceless consonants represent something small, light, sharp or pretty.

a. きらきら((と)光る)　　((shine) sparklingly)
   kirakira ((to) hikaru)

b. ころころ((と)転がる)　((small object) rolls)
   korokoro ((to) korogaru)

c. ぽたぽた((と)落ちる)　((small amount of liquid) drips)
   potapota ((to) ochiru)

d. さくさく((と)切る)　　((cut) a thin, light object)
   sakusaku ((to) kiru)

a′. ぎらぎら((と)光る)　　((shine) dazzlingly)
    giragira ((to) hikaru)

b′. ごろごろ((と)転がる)　((heavy object) rolls)
    gorogoro ((to) korogaru)

c′. ぼたぼた((と)落ちる)　((large amount of liquid) drips)
    botabota ((to) ochiru)

d'. ざくざく((と)切る)　　　((cut) a thick, heavy object)
　　zakuzaku ((to) kiru)

(B) *Velar Consonants—k and g*

The velar consonants [k] and [g] tend to represent hardness, sharpness, clear-cutness, separation, detachment or sudden change.

a. かちかち(に凍る)　　　((freeze) hard)
　　kachikachi (ni kōru)

b. くっきり((と)見える)　　((be visible) clearly)
　　kukkiri ((to) mieru)

c. きっぱり((と)別れる)　　((separate from people) once and for all)
　　kippari ((to) wakareru)

d. がらっ(と変わる)　　　((completely) change)
　　garat (to kawaru)

e. ぐっ(と引く)　　　　　((pull) with a jerk)
　　gut (to hiku)

f. ぽっくり((と)死ぬ)　　　((die) suddenly)
　　pokkuri ((to) shinu)

(C) *Dental Fricative Consonant—s*

The dental fricative consonant [s] tends to represent a quiet state or a quiet and quick motion. [sh] in particular seems to represent some quiet human emotion.

a. さっ(と立ち上がる)　　((stand up) quickly)
　　sat (to tachiagaru)

b. するする((と)滑る)　　　((slide) smoothly)
　　surusuru ((to) suberu)

c. しとしと((と)降る)　　　((it rains) quietly)
　　shitoshito (to furu)

d. しんみり((と)話す)　　　((talk) quietly and intimately)
　　shinmiri ((to) hanasu)

e. しん(とする)　　　　　((be) quiet)
　　shin (to suru)

f. しょんぼり((と)する)　　((be) despondent)
　　shonbori ((to) suru)

g.　こそこそ((と)逃げる)　　((escape) secretly)
　　kosokoso ((to) nigeru)

h.　しゅん(とする)　　　　((be) dispirited)
　　shun (to suru)

i.　ひっそり((と))する)　　((be) quiet)
　　hissori ((to) suru)

(D)　*Liquid Consonant—r*

The liquid consonant [r] tends to represent fluidity, smoothness or slipperiness.

a.　すらっ(としている)　　((figure) is slim)
　　surat (to shite iru)

b.　すらすら((と)答える)　　((answer) with great ease)
　　surasura ((to) kotaeru)

c.　くるくる((と)まわる)　　((turn) round and round)
　　kurukuru ((to) mawaru)

d.　つるつる(している)　　((be) slippery)
　　tsurutsuru (shite iru)

e.　ぬるぬる(している)　　((be) slimy)
　　nurunuru (shite iru)

f.　さらさら((と)流れる)　　((flow) smoothly)
　　sarasara ((to) nagareru)

g.　たらたら((と)流れる)　　((sweat or blood) drip continuously)
　　taratara ((to) nagareru)

(E)　*Nasal Consonants—m and n*

The nasal sounds tend to represent tactuality, warmth and softness.

a.　むくむく(している)　　((of a dog or a cat) is plump)
　　mukumuku (shite iru)

b.　むちむち(している)　　((be) plump)
　　muchimuchi (shite iru)

c.　なよなよ((と)している)　　((be) slender and delicate)
　　nayonayo ((to) shite iru)

d.　にちゃにちゃ(する)　　((be) sticky)
　　nichanicha (suru)

e. にゅるにゅる(している)　　　((be) slimy)
　　nyurunyuru (shite iru)

f. ぬるぬる(している)　　　　((be) slimy)
　　nurunuru (shite iru)

g. ねちねち(している)　　　　((be) sticky)
　　nechinechi (shite iru)

(F) *Voiceless Bilabial Plosive——p*

The voiceless bilabial plosive (=stop) [p] tends to represent explosiveness, crispiness, strength and suddenness.

a. ぱっ(と明るくなる)　　　　((become bright) suddenly)
　　pat (to akaruku naru)

b. ぴしゃり(と叩く)　　　　　(whack)
　　pishari (to tataku)

c. ぴん(とくる)　　　　　　　(come to (me) in a flash)
　　pin (to kuru)

d. ぺらぺら((と)しゃべる)　　(gibber, speak fluently)
　　perapera ((to) shaberu)

e. ぴんぴん(している)　　　　((be) peppy)
　　pinpin (shite iru)

f. ぷい(と出て行く)　　　　　((leave) suddenly)
　　pui (to dete iku)

g. ぷつっ(と切れる)　　　　　((break) suddenly)
　　putsut (to kireru)

h. ぽっかり((と)浮かぶ)　　　((float) suddenly)
　　pokkari ((to) ukabu)

(G) *Semi-vowel—y*

The semi-vowel [y] tends to represent weakness, slowness and softness.

a. よいよい(になる)　　　　　(have locomotor ataxia, loss of reflexes)
　　yoiyoi (ni naru)

b. よぼよぼ(になる)　　　　　((become) senile)
　　yoboyobo (ni naru)

c. よれよれ(になる)　　　　　((become) worn-out)
　　yoreyore (ni naru)

d. ゆらゆら((と)ゆれる)　　((sway) like waves)
   yurayura ((to) yureru)

e. ゆっくり(話す)　　　　((speak) slowly)
   yukkuri (hanasu)

f. やんわり(と言う)　　　((tell) softly)
   yanwari (to iu)

g. よちよち((と)歩く)　　((walk) totteringly)
   yochiyochi ((to) aruku)

(H) *Back High Vowel—u*

The back high vowel [u] tends to represent something that has to do with human physiology or psychology.

a. うとうと(する)　　　　(doze)
   utouto (suru)

b. うきうき(する)　　　　((be) buoyant)
   ukiuki (suru)

c. うすうす(感づく)　　　((perceive) dimly)
   usuusu (kanzuku)

d. うずうず(する)　　　　(itch for action)
   uzuuzu (suru)

e. うつらうつら(する)　　(doze)
   utsurautsura (suru)

f. うっかり(する)　　　　((be) off guard)
   ukkari (suru)

g. うっとり(する)　　　　((be) enchanted)
   uttori (suru)

h. うら(さびしい)　　　　(somewhat (lonely))
   ura (sabishii)

i. うんざり(する)　　　　((be) fed up with)
   unzari (suru)

(I) *Back Vowel—o*

The back vowel [o] tends to represent something basically negative with regard to human psychology.

a. おずおず(している)　　　((be) nervous and timid)
   ozuozu (shite iru)

b. おどおど(している)　　((be) very nervous)
   odoodo (*shite iru*)

c. おろおろ(する)　　((be) in a dither)
   orooro (*suru*)

d. おたおた(する)　　(don't know what to do)
   otaota (*suru*)

e. おめおめ(とだまされる)　　((be deceived) in a shameless manner)
   omeome (*to damasareru*)

(J) *Front Vowel—e*

The front vowel [e] tends to represent something vulgar.

a. へべれけ(になる)　　((become) dead drunk)
   hebereke (*ni naru*)

b. へらへら((と)笑う)　　((laugh) meaninglessly when embarrassed)
   herahera ((*to*) *warau*)

c. てらてら(光る)　　(be glossy)
   teratera (*hikaru*)

d. めそめそ((と)泣く)　　(sob)
   mesomeso ((*to*) *naku*)

In addition to the regular sound symbolisms there are some basic words that can be explained in terms of (B) and (E) above. Consider the following semantically similar words that are indispensable in Japanese grammar.

Velars	Nasals
が *ga* (subject marker)	の *no* (subject marker in relative and nominalized clauses)
から *kara* (because)	ので / もの *node* / *mono* (because)
から(貰う) *kara* (*morau*) ((receive) from)	に(貰う) *ni* (*morau*) ((receive) from)

か **ka** (or)	の **no** (a particle for combining nouns)
けれど / が **keredo / ga** (although / but)	のに **noni** (although)
こと **koto** (nominalizer)	の **no** (nominalizer)
こと **koto** (an intangible thing)	もの **mono** (a tangible thing)

The words with the nasal [n] sound more personal, subjective and speaker-oriented than their counterparts with the velar [k] or [g].

It is also to be noted that (C) above would tend to explain why *i*-type adjectives that end in *-shi* as in *kanashii* 'sad', *sabishii* 'lonely', *tanoshii* 'enjoyable', *ureshii* 'happy' represent human emotive psychological states.

Also note that the glottal stop is often used to create more emphatic and / or more emotive versions of a given sound, as in *pitari* vs. *pittari* 'tightly', *yahari* vs. *yappari* 'as expected', *bakari* vs. *bakkari* 'only', *yohodo* vs. *yoppodo* 'to a great extent', *to* vs. *tte* 'that', *i*-type adj. stem+*kute* (e.g., sabishi*kute* 'be lonely and ～') vs. *i*-type adj. stem+*kutte* (e.g., sabishi*kutte*), etc.

It is important for students of Japanese to learn basic sound symbolisms, (especially, phenomimes and psychomimes) relatively early in their Japanese language study. These words are an indispensable part of the basic vocabulary of any adult speaker. More importantly, the acquisition, use and understanding of Japanese sound symbolisms allow the student to appreciate the keen sensibility of Japanese language and culture toward directly perceptible objects.

9. Viewpoint

There is more than one way to describe a state or an event, and the choice of expressions depends, in part, on the viewpoint from which the state or event is described. To illustrate this, let us suppose that a person A hit a person B. This event can be expressed by either (1a) or (1b).

(1)　a.　A hit B.
　　　b.　B was hit by A.

Both (1a) and (1b) state the same fact, but the speaker's (or writer's) viewpoint is different. That is, when (1a) is chosen, the speaker is describing the event from A's point of view or a neutral viewpoint, and when (1b) is used, the speaker's description is from B's point of view.

There are several principles and rules concerning viewpoint; some are universal and others are specific to Japanese. The following are rather universal principles:

(A) Within a single sentence (excluding coordinate sentences) the viewpoint should be consistent.

(B) When a sentence includes the structure A's B, (e.g., John's wife) the speaker is taking A's viewpoint rather than B's.

(C) When the speaker (or writer) empathizes with someone, the speaker tends to take that person's viewpoint.

(D) The speaker usually describes a situation or an event from his own viewpoint rather than from others' when he is involved in the situation or the event.

(E) It is easier for the speaker to take the viewpoint of the person in a sentence subject position than to take the viewpoint of a person in other positions.

(F) It is easier for the speaker to take the viewpoint of the person who has been established as a discourse topic than to take the viewpoint of someone who has just been introduced in the discourse.

(G) Under normal circumstances the speaker cannot take the viewpoint of a dead person.

Although many of the grammatical principles concerning viewpoint are rather universal, as seen above, there are a number of viewpoint-related expressions which are important and specific to Japanese. Some rules concerning these expressions are listed below:

(H) The following giving / receiving verbs require the viewpoints shown in (2).

(2) a. やる，あげる，さしあげる (give): the giver's or a neutral viewpoint
yaru　ageru　sashiageru (when they are used as auxiliary verbs,
only the giver's viewpoint)

b. くれる，くださる (give): the receiver's viewpoint
kureru　kudasaru

c. もらう，いただく (get; receive): the receiver's viewpoint
morau　itadaku

(H), together with (A) and (D), explains the unacceptability of the following sentences. (⇨ *ageru*[1,2]; *kureru*[1,2]; *morau*[1,2])

(3) a. *一郎は私にパンをあげた。
*Ichirō wa **watashi ni** pan o **ageta**.
(Ichiro gave me some bread.)

b. *私は和男にペンをくれた。
*Watashi wa Kazuo ni pen o **kureta**.
(I gave Kazuo a pen.)

c. *花子は私にえんぴつをもらった。
*Hanako wa **watashi ni** enpitsu o **moratta**.
(Hanako received a pencil from me.)

(I) The passive construction, whether direct or indirect, requires the viewpoint of the referent of the subject. (Cp. (E))

Together with (A), (B) and (D), this explains the unnaturalness of sentences like (4). (⇨ *rareru*[1])

(4) a. *私のむすこは私にしかられた。
*Watashi no musuko wa watashi ni **shikarareta**.
(My son was scolded by me.)

b. *私の家内は私に秘密の手紙を読まれた。
*Watashi no kanai wa watashi ni himitsu no tegami o **yomareta**.
(My wife had her secret letter read by me.)

(J) When the verb *kuru* 'come' is used, the speaker's viewpoint is somewhere close to the arrival point. When *kuru* is used as an auxiliary verb, the viewpoint is the point *to* which an action is directed or a change proceeds.

(K) When the verb *iku* ' go ' is used, the speaker's viewpoint is somewhere close to the departure point.   When *iku* is used as an auxiliary verb, the viewpoint is the point *from* which an action is directed or a change proceeds.

(J) and (K) explain the unacceptability of the sentences in (5) and (6) under the given conditions.   (⇨ *iku*[1,2]; *kuru*[1,2])

(5) a. [The speaker is in Japan.]
         *私は来年アメリカへ来ます。
         *Watashi wa rainen Amerika e **kimasu**.
         (I will come to America next year.)

     b. [The speaker is in America.]
         *私は去年アメリカへ行きました。
         *Watashi wa kyonen Amerika e **ikimashita**.
         (I went to America last year.)

(6) a. *私はどろぼうにおそいかかって来た。
         *Watashi wa dorobō ni osoikakatte **kita**.
         (Lit. I came to attack the robber.)

     b. *どろぼうは私におそいかかって行った。
         *Dorobō wa watashi ni osoikakatte **itta**.
         (Lit. The robber went to attack me.)

(L) When adjectives like *hoshii* ' want ' (lit. desirable), *ureshii* ' happy ' and *kanashii* ' sad ' which describe one's personal feelings are used with the third person subject, the speaker empathizes with that person, which usually implies that the speaker is taking the viewpoint of that person.
                                                                   (Cp. (C))

Thus, if the subject is someone the speaker is unable to empathize with, the adjectives mentioned in (L) cannot be used, as in (7).   (⇨ *garu*; *hoshii*; *tai*)

(7) a. *見知らぬ人がたばこが欲しい。
         *Mishiranu hito ga tabako ga **hoshii**.
         (A stranger wants a cigarette.)

     b. *通りがかりの人がうれしい。
         *Tōrigakari no hito ga **ureshii**.
         (A passerby is happy.)

(M) Kinship terms can be used for the first person and (less commonly) the second person.   In this case the proper kinship term for the first person (or the second person) is selected from the viewpoint of someone X with whom the speaker empathizes. The person X is usually lower in status than the person for whom a kinship term is used. (e.g., one's little brother) (Cp. 4. Personal Pronouns)

(8) a. [From an elder brother to his younger brother]

兄さんに見せてごらん。

Ni-san *ni misete goran.*

(Let me see it.)

b. [From an uncle to his niece]

おじさんがしてあげよう。

Oji-san *ga shite ageyō.*

(I'll do it for you.)

c. [Spoken by a mother to her daughter Yoshiko from the viewpoint of the daughter's little brother Hiroshi]

お姉ちゃん，ひろしに貸してあげなさい。

O-nē-chan, *Hiroshi ni kashite agenasai.*

(*Yoshiko*, let Hiroshi have it.)

(N) When a reflexive pronoun *jibun* 'self' is used, the speaker tends to empathize with the referent of *jibun*, which implies that the speaker's viewpoint is that of the referent. (⇨ ***jibun***[1])

In (9) the referent of *jibun* is Hanako and the speaker is taking Hanako's viewpoint.

(9) 花子は太郎が自分を愛していると信じていた。

*Hanako wa Tarō ga **jibun** o aishite iru to shinjite ita.*

(Hanako believed that Taro loved her.)

(10) is unnatural because the viewpoint is inconsistent.

(10) *妻は私が自分を今でも愛していると信じている。

Tsuma wa watashi ga **jibun o ima demo aishite iru to shinjite iru.*

(My wife believes that I still love her.)

A DICTIONARY
OF
BASIC
JAPANESE
GRAMMAR

(Main Entries)

Seiichi Makino and Michio Tsutsui

日本語基本文法辞典

ageru¹ あげる   *v. (Gr. 2)*

> S.o. gives s.t. to a person who is not a member of the giver's in-group but whose status is about equal to that of the giver.

give
【REL. **kureru**¹ (*morau*¹)】

◆**Key Sentence**

Topic (subject)		Indirect Object		Direct Object		
私	は	良子	に	花	を	あげた / あげました。
Watashi	*wa*	*Yoshiko*	*ni*	*hana*	*o*	*ageta / agemashita.*
(I gave Yoshiko flowers.)						

Examples

(a) 大野さんは山本さんに本をあげた。
 Ōno-san wa Yamamoto-san ni hon o ageta.
 (Ms. Ono gave Mr. Yamamoto a book.)

(b) 君はアンに何をあげましたか。
 Kimi wa An ni nani o agemashita ka.
 (What did you give to Ann?)

Notes

1. *Ageru* is one of a set of giving and receiving verbs; the meaning is 'give'. However, *ageru* cannot be used when the indirect object is the first person (i.e., *I* or *we*) or a person with whom the speaker empathizes (usually a member of the speaker's in-group). Thus, (1a) and (1b) are ungrammatical.

 (1) a. *花子は私に本をあげた。
  Hanako wa **watashi ni hon o **ageta**.*
  (Hanako gave me a book.)

 b. *花子は私のむすこに本をあげた。
  Hanako wa **watashi no musuko ni hon o **ageta**.*
  (Hanako gave my son a book.)

The reason for this is as follows: *Ageru* requires the giver's point of view or a neutral point of view when describing an event. When an event involves the first person or a person the speaker empathizes with, however, the event is normally described from that person's point of view. (See Characteristics of Japanese Grammar, 9. Viewpoint.) Therefore, if the first person or a person the speaker empathizes with is a recipient in *ageru*-sentences, a viewpoint conflict arises, making the sentences ungrammatical. The grammatical sentences for (1a) and (1b) are (2a) and (2b), respectively.   (⇨ *kureru*[1])

(2) a. 花子は私に本をくれた。
    *Hanako wa watashi ni hon o **kureta**.*
    (Hanako gave me a book.)

   b. 花子は私のむすこに本をくれた。
    *Hanako wa watashi no musuko ni hon o **kureta**.*
    (Hanako gave my son a book.)

2. The humble polite version of *ageru* is *sashiageru*. Example:

(3) 私は先生に本をさしあげました。
    *Watashi wa sensei ni hon o **sashiagemashita**.*
    (I gave my teacher a book.)

The degree of politeness expressed in *sashiageru* is higher than that of *kudasaru* and *itadaku*, which are the polite versions of *kureru* and *morau*, respectively.   (⇨ *kureru*[1], REL. II)

3. When the giver is in a higher position than the recipient or the recipient is a person very close to the speaker, *yaru* is used instead of *ageru*. Examples:

(4) a. 私は弟に本をやった。
    *Watashi wa otōto ni hon o **yatta**.*
    (I gave my little brother a book.)

   b. ひろしは猫にミルクをやった。
    *Hiroshi wa neko ni miruku o **yatta**.*
    (Hiroshi gave milk to the cat.)

   c. [Tom is the speaker's intimate friend.]
    私はトムにケーキをやりました。
    *Watashi wa Tomu ni kēki o **yarimashita**.*
    (I gave a cake to Tom.)

A

ageru² あげる *aux. v.* (*Gr.* 2)

> S.o. gives some action as a favor to a person who is not a member of the giver's in-group but whose status is about equal to that of the giver.

do s.t. for s.o.; do s.o. a favor by doing s.t.
【REL. ***kureru***² (*morau*²)】

♦ **Key Sentences**

(A)

Topic (subject)		Indirect Object		Direct Object		V*te*	
私	は	信男さん	に	ネクタイ	を	買って	あげた / あげました。
Watashi	*wa*	*Nobuo-san*	*ni*	*nekutai*	*o*	***katte***	*ageta / agemashita.*
(I bought a tie for Nobuo.)							

(B)

Topic (subject)		Direct Object		V*te*	
僕	は	春子さん	を	なぐさめて	あげた / あげました。
Boku	*wa*	*Haruko-san*	*o*	***nagusamete***	*ageta / agemashita.*
(I consoled Haruko.)					

Formation

V*te*　あげる
　　　ageru

話して　　あげる　　(talk for s.o.'s sake)
hanashite ageru

食べて　あげる　(eat for s.o.'s sake)
tabete ageru

Examples

(a) 君はお母さんに何をしてあげましたか。
　　Kimi wa o-kā-san ni nani o shite agemashita ka.
　　(What did you do for your mother?)

(b) 田中さんはスミスさんに本を貸してあげた。
　　Tanaka-san wa Sumisu-san ni hon o kashite ageta.
　　(Mr. Tanaka lent a book to Mr. Smith.)

Notes

1. *Ageru* is used as an auxiliary verb with the *te*-form of verbs. The meaning of V*te ageru* is ' do s.t. for s.o.' or ' do s.o. a favor by doing s.t.' The restriction which applies to *ageru¹* also applies to *ageru²*. Namely, sentences with V*te ageru* are descriptions from the viewpoint of the benefactor (i.e., the person in subject position); therefore, the indirect object must not be the first person or a person the speaker empathizes with. (⇨ *ageru¹*, Note 1) Thus, (1a) and (1b) are ungrammatical.

   (1) a. *花子は私に日本語を教えてあげた。
             *Hanako wa **watashi ni** *nihongo o oshiete* **ageta**.
             (Hanako taught me Japanese.)

        b. *メアリーは私のむすめにペンを買ってあげた。
             *Meari wa **watashi no musume ni** *pen o katte* **ageta**.
             (Mary bought a pen for my daughter.)

The grammatical sentences for (1a) and (1b) are (2a) and (2b), respectively.
                                         (⇨ *kureru²*)

   (2) a. 花子は私に日本語を教えてくれた。
             Hanako wa watashi ni nihongo o oshiete **kureta**.

        b. メアリーは私のむすめにペンを買ってくれた。
             Meari wa watashi no musume ni pen o katte **kureta**.

2. As in KS (B), if the person receiving the benefit is the direct object of the sentence, the indirect object is omitted. Therefore, (3a) and (3b) are ungrammatical.

   (3) a. *僕は春子さんに春子さんをなぐさめてあげた。
             *Boku wa **Haruko-san ni** *Haruko-san o nagusamete ageta*.

        b. *僕は春子さんになぐさめてあげた。
             *Boku wa **Haruko-san ni** *nagusamete ageta*.

3. When the main verb is intransitive, *ageru* is not used along with *ni*. The following sentence is ungrammatical.

   (4) *私達はジョンに働いてあげた。
             Watashitachi wa Jon* **ni *hataraite* **ageta**.
             (We worked for John.)

In this case, *no tame ni* ' for the sake of ' is used, as in (5). (⇨ *tame* (*ni*))

(5) 私達はジョンのために働いた。
　　*Watashitachi wa Jon **no tame ni** hataraita.*
　　(We worked for John's sake.)

4. The humble polite version of V*te ageru* is V*te sashiageru*. Example:

(6) 私は先生にピアノをひいてさしあげました。
　　*Watashi wa sensei ni piano o hiite **sashiagemashita**.*
　　(I played the piano for my teacher.)

The degree of politeness expressed in V*te sashiageru* is higher than that of V*te kudasaru* and V*te itadaku*, which are the polite versions of V*te kureru* and V*te morau*, respectively.　　　　(⇨ **kureru**[1], REL. II)

5. When the benefactor is in a higher position than the recipient or is of equal status and his relationship to the recipient is close, V*te yaru* is used instead of V*te ageru*. Examples:

(7) a. 私は妹にレコードを買ってやった。
　　　 *Watashi wa imōto ni rekōdo o katte **yatta**.*
　　　 (I bought my little sister a record.)

　　b. じゅんは猫に魚を焼いてやった。
　　　 *Jun wa neko ni sakana o yaite **yatta**.*
　　　 (Jun roasted fish for his cat.)

　　c. [John is the speaker's close friend.]
　　　 私はジョンにラジオを貸してやりました。
　　　 *Watashi wa Jon ni rajio o kashite **yarimashita**.*
　　　 (I lent John my radio.)

---

aida ⟨**ni**⟩ 間 ⟨に⟩　　*phr.*

| the space between two temporal or physical points | during (the time when); while 【REL. *nagara*; ***uchi ni***】 |

A

♦**Key Sentences**

(A)

Subordinate Clause				Main Clause
	V*te*			
私　　が　ご飯　を *Watashi ga gohan o*	**食べて** **tabete**	いる *iru*	間 *aida*	山田さん　　は　テレビ　を *Yamada-san wa terebi o* 見て　いた / いました。 *mite ita / imashita.*
(While I was eating my meal, Mr. Yamada was watching TV.)				

(B)

Subordinate Clause					Main Clause
	V*te*				
私　　が　ご飯　を *Watashi ga gohan o*	**食べて** **tabete**	いる *iru*	間 *aida*	に *ni*	山田さん　　が　来た / *Yamada-san ga kita /* 来ました。 *kimashita.*
(While I was eating my meal, Mr. Yamada came in.)					

Formation

(i) V*te* いる 間 （に）
　　　 iru aida (ni)

　　話して　いる 間 （に）　　(while s.o. is talking)
　　hanashite iru aida (ni)

　　食べて いる 間 （に）　　(while s.o. is eating)
　　tabete iru aida (ni)

(ii) Adj (*i*) 間 （に）
　　　　　 aida (ni)

　　高い　間 （に）　　(while s.t. is expensive)
　　takai aida (ni)

(iii) Adj (*na*) stem な 間 （に）
　　　　　　　 na aida (ni)

静かな　　間　(に)　　(while s.t. is quiet)
shizukana aida (ni)

(iv)　N　の　間　(に)
no aida (ni)

夏休み　　　の　間　(に)　　(during the summer vacation)
natsuyasumi no aida (ni)

Examples

(a) スミスさんは日本にいる間英語を教えていました。
Sumisu-san wa Nihon ni iru aida eigo o oshiete imashita.
(Mr. Smith was teaching English (all during the time) while he was in Japan.)

(b) 子供達がテレビを見ている間私は本を読んでいました。
Kodomotachi ga terebi o mite iru aida watashi wa hon o yonde imashita.
(I was reading a book (all during the time) while my children were watching TV.)

(c) 高橋さんはアメリカにいる間にゴルフを覚えました。
Takahashi-san wa Amerika ni iru aida ni gorufu o oboemashita.
(Mr. Takahashi learned golf while he was in America.)

(d) 中川さんのお母さんは中川さんがパリに留学している間に病気になりました。
Nakagawa-san no o-kā-san wa Nakagawa-san ga Pari ni ryūgakushite iru aida ni byōki ni narimashita.
(Mr. Nakagawa's mother became ill while he was studying in Paris.)

(e) 秋子は子供がいない間に本を読む。
Akiko wa kodomo ga inai aida ni hon o yomu.
(Akiko reads books while her children are not at home.)

Notes

1. The subjects for the *aida*-clause (=subordinate clause) and the main clause can be different as in Exs. (b), (d) and (e) or can be the same as in Exs. (a) and (c). When the subjects are different, the subject in the *aida*-clause is marked not by *wa* but by *ga*.

2. The verb before *aida* is normally nonpast V*te iru* or *iru*, regardless of the tense of the main clause.

3. *Aida*, if followed by *ni*, a particle of specific time point, means that the time span of an event identified by the main clause falls within the time span of an event identified by the *aida*-clause, as in Exs. (c), (d) and (e). *Aida* without *ni*, as in Exs. (a) and (b), indicates that the two events are assumed to cover the same span of time. Thus, if the main verb is a punctual verb, *aida* should be used with *ni*. The following sentence, therefore, is ungrammatical.

(1) *山田さんがパリに留学している間お母さんが病気になった。

Yamada-san ga Pari ni ryūgakushite iru **aida o-kā-san ga byōki ni natta.*

(*Mr. Yamada's mother became ill (all during the time) while he was studying in Paris.)

The difference between *aida ni* and *aida* can be diagrammed as follows:

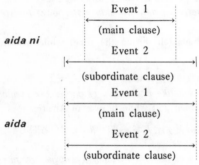

4. A noun or an adjective can be used before *aida*.

(2) 夏休みの間レストランでアルバイトをしました。

*Natsuyasumi **no aida** resutoran de arubaito o shimashita.*

(During the summer vacation I worked part time at a restaurant.)

(3) 夏休みの間にガールフレンドが出来ました。

*Natsuyasumi **no aida ni** gārufurendo ga dekimashita.*

(During the summer vacation I found a girl friend.)

(4) 長い間母に手紙を書いていません。

*Nagai **aida** haha ni tegami o kaite imasen.*

(I haven't written to my mother for a long time.)

(5) 若い間に本を出来るだけたくさん読みなさい。

*Wakai **aida ni** hon o dekiru dake takusan yominasai.*

(Read as many books as you can while you are young.)

5. The non-temporal *aida* which means 'space between' or 'relationship' is used in the structure *A to B* (*to*) *no aida* 'between A and B' as in:

(6) 日本とアメリカ（と）の間には海しかない。
    Nihon to Amerika (to) no aida ni wa umi shika nai.
    (There is only ocean between Japan and America.)

(7) 山口と僕（と）の間は決して悪くない。
    Yamaguchi to boku (to) no aida wa kesshite warukunai.
    (The relationship between Yamaguchi and me is not bad at all.)

The usage of *aida* meaning 'relationship' in (7) is a metaphorical extension of physical space between two persons.

6. The verb *iru* '(an animate object) exists' can be used by itself, as in Ex. (c), due to its stative nature. Some adjectives such as *takai* 'expensive', *yasui* 'cheap', *atatakai* 'warm', *suzushii* 'cool', *wakai* 'young' can also be used in this way, as follows:

(8) 若い間にスポーツをいろいろした方がいいです。
    Wakai aida ni supōtsu o iroiro shita hō ga iidesu.
    (It's better to do various sports while you are young.)

These adjectives, however, sound a little more natural with *uchi ni* 'while'.   (⇨ **uchi ni**)

[Related Expression]

If the subjects of the main and subordinate clauses are identical and if the verbs are action verbs, *aida* can be replaced by *nagara*, but with different meaning.

[1] 雪子はご飯を食べている間テレビを見ていた。
    Yukiko wa gohan o tabete iru aida terebi o mite ita.
    (Yukiko was watching TV while she was eating her meal.)

[2] 雪子はご飯を食べながらテレビを見ていた。
    Yukiko wa gohan o tabenagara terebi o mite ita.
    (Lit. Yukiko was primarily watching TV, although simultaneously she was eating her meal. (=Yukiko was eating her meal while watching TV.))

[1] and [2] focus on 'duration of some action/state' and 'accompanying minor action', respectively.   (⇨ **nagara**)

A

amari あまり   *adv.*

> The degree of s.t. is not great.   (not) very much; (not) very

♦ **Key Sentence**

Topic (subject)			Predicate (negative)
この　本 *Kono hon*	は *wa*	あまり *amari*	よくない / よくありません。 *yokunai / yokuarimasen.*
(This book is not very good.)			

Examples

(a) 鈴木さんはあまり食べない。
    Suzuki-san wa amari tabenai.
    (Miss Suzuki does not eat much.)

(b) 私はあまり速く走れません。
    Watashi wa amari hayaku hashiremasen.
    (I cannot run very fast.)

Notes

1. The adverb *amari* usually occurs in negative sentences, meaning 'not very (much)'. *Amari* is one of a group of adverbs which co-occur with negative predicates. They include:

  (1) *zenzen* '(not) at all'; *mettani* 'rarely, seldom'; *kesshite* 'never, by no means'; *sappari* '(not) at all'; *sukoshimo* '(not) a bit'; *chittomo* '(not) a bit'

2. *Anmari* is a phonological variant of *amari* and usually used in conversation.

3. In limited situations, *amari* can be used in affirmative sentences, too. In this case, it means 'very; too' with a negative implication. Examples:

  (2) a. スコットが**あまり**失礼なことを言うのでサリーは怒って帰ってしまった。
      *Sukotto ga **amari** shitsureina koto o iu node Sari wa okotte kaette shimatta.*
      (Since Scott was very rude (lit. said very rude things), Sally got mad and went home.)

     b. 井上さんは**あまり**酒を飲んだので病気になった。
      *Inoue-san wa **amari** sake o nonda node byōki ni natta.*

(Mr. Inoue drank too much and became ill.)

c. それは**あんまり**です。
   *Sore wa **anmari** desu.*
   (You're (lit. That's) too cruel.)

---

aru¹ ある   *v. (Gr. 1)*

| An inanimate thing exists. | be; exist; have |
| | 【REL. *iru¹*; *motte iru*】 |

◆ **Key Sentences**

(A)

Topic (location)		Subject		Quantifier	
この　町 *Kono machi*	(に) は (*ni*) *wa*	大学 *daigaku*	が *ga*	三つ *mittsu*	ある / あります。 *aru / arimasu.*

(Lit. In this town are three universities. (=There are three universities in this town.))

(B)

Topic (subject)		Noun (location)			
エッフェル塔 *Efferutō*	は *wa*	パリ *Pari*	に *ni*		ある / あります。 *aru / arimasu.*

(The Eiffel Tower is in Paris.)

Examples

(a) 私のアパート(に)はテレビが二台ある。
   Watashi no apāto (ni) wa terebi ga nidai aru.
   (There are two TV sets in my apartment.)

(b) デトロイトはミシガン州にあります。
   Detoroito wa Mishigan-shū ni arimasu.
   (Detroit is in the State of Michigan.)

(c) 和田さんのうち(に)はクーラーがない。

　　Wada-san no uchi (ni) wa kūrā ga nai.

　　(There is no air-conditioner at Mr. Wada's.)

Notes

1. *Aru* expresses the existence of or the possession of *inanimate things* including abstract things such as events and problems. Thus, (1) is ungrammatical.

　　(1)　*この町には日本人がある。

　　　　　**Kono machi ni wa nihonjin ga aru.*

　　　　　(There are Japanese in this town.)

　　For animate things, *iru*[1] is used. 　　　　　　　　　(⇨ *iru*[1])

2. The negative informal form of *aru* is not *aranai* but *nai*.

3. Two sentence patterns can be used with *aru*. The KS (A) pattern is used when a location is presented as a topic. In this case, what exists is under focus. In this pattern, the location marker *ni* can optionally drop. The KS (B) pattern is used when something which exists is presented as a topic. In this case, where it exists is under focus. Compare the two patterns in (2).

　　(2)　A：早稲田大学はどこにありますか。

　　　　　Waseda Daigaku wa doko ni arimasu ka.

　　　　　(Where is Waseda University?)

　　　　B：早稲田大学は東京にあります。

　　　　　Waseda Daigaku wa Tōkyō ni arimasu.

　　　　　(Waseda University is in Tokyo.)

　　　　A：東京には早稲田大学しかありませんか。

　　　　　Tōkyō ni wa Waseda Daigaku shika arimasen ka.

　　　　　(Lit. Are there no universities in Tokyo but Waseda University? (＝Is Waseda University the only university in Tokyo?))

　　　　B：いいえ、東京には大学がたくさんあります。

　　　　　Īe, Tōkyō ni wa daigaku ga takusan arimasu.

　　　　　(No, there are many universities in Tokyo.)

4. A thing (whether animate or inanimate) can also occur in the location position of KS (A). In this case, the sentence expresses possession rather than existence. Examples:

(3) a. この車(に)はカー・ステレオがある。

   ***Kono kuruma* (*ni*) *wa* kā sutereo ga *aru*.**

   (Lit. There is a car stereo in this car. (=This car has a car stereo.))

b. 私(に)は車がある。

   ***Watashi* (*ni*) *wa* kuruma ga *aru*.**

   (Lit. There is a car with me. (=I have a car.))

Note that even if *aru* expresses the idea of possession, possessed things are marked not by *o* but by *ga*. This is because *aru* essentially indicates existence.

5. When *aru* is used to express the idea of having and the object is animate, that object must be someone who maintains a very close relationship with the possessor, such as a family member, a relative or a friend. Thus, (4) is acceptable, but (5) is odd.

(4) 私(に)は子供が三人ある。

   Watashi (*ni*) *wa* kodomo ga sannin aru.

   (I have three children.)

(5) ??私(に)は運転手がある。

   ??*Watashi* (*ni*) *wa* untenshu ga aru.

   (I have a chauffeur.)

Since *aru* in this usage is a possessive expression, it cannot be used in situations where the idea indicates existence. Thus, (6) is unacceptable.

(6) *私(に)は母がもうありません。

   **Watashi* (*ni*) *wa* haha ga mō arimasen.

   (I don't have my mother now.)

In this case, *iru* must be used.

6. When *aru* is used for events such as parties and concerts, the particle marking locations must be *de* as in (7).　　　　　　　　(⇨ ***de*¹; *ni*⁶**)

(7) 今日サムのうちで / *にパーティーがある。

   *Kyō Samu no uchi **de** / ***ni** pātī ga aru.

   (There is a party at Sam's today.)

〔Related Expressions〕

I. There is another possessive expression, *motte iru*, which is the *te*-form of *motsu* 'hold' followed by the auxiliary verb *iru*. However, *motte iru* is used only when the possessor is animate and the possessed thing is inanimate. Thus, [1] is acceptable, but [2] and [3] are not.

[1] ジョンはいい車を持っている。
*Jon wa ii kuruma o **motte iru**.*
(John has a good car.)

[2] *ジョンは妹を持っている。
Jon wa imōto o **motte iru.*
(John has a younger sister.)

[3] *この車はクーラーを持っている。
Kono kuruma wa kūrā o **motte iru.*
(This car has an air-conditioner.)

Groups and organizations of people such as political parties, countries, institutions and companies can also be possessors in sentences with *motte iru*, as in [4].

[4] この大学はいい図書館を持っている。
*Kono daigaku wa ii toshokan o **motte iru**.*
(This university has a good library.)

II. *Iru*¹ is also used to express existence. However, *iru*¹ is used only for animate objects.   (See Note 1.)

---

aru² ある   *aux. v. (Gr. 1)*

| S.t. has been done to s.t. and the resultant state of that action remains. | have been done; be done 【REL. *iru*²; *oku*】 |

◆ **Key Sentence**

Topic (subject)			V*te*	
それ *Sore*	は *wa*	もう ジョン に *mō Jon ni*	**話して** **hanashite**	ある / あります。 *aru / arimasu.*
(It's been told to John already.)				

V*te* ある
    aru

話して ある   (has been told)
hanashite aru

食べて ある   (has been eaten)
tabete aru

Examples

(a) 飲み物はもう買ってあります。
   Nomimono wa mō katte arimasu.
   (Drinks have already been bought.)

(b) 窓が開けてある。
   Mado ga akete aru.
   (The window has been open / is open.)

Notes

1. *Aru* is used with V*te* as an auxiliary verb. Two points are indicated by the V*te aru* expression:

  (A) Someone did something to X. (Thus, V*te* is usually a transitive verb.)

  (B) X is still in that state.

  X is most frequently marked by the topic marker *wa* or the subject marker *ga*; occasionally it is marked by the direct object marker *o*.

2. The agent is usually omitted because he is unimportant, unknown or obvious.

[Related Expressions]

There are expressions similar to V*te aru*, namely, V*te iru* and V*te oku*. Let us compare [1] and [2] with Ex. (b).

[1] 窓が開いている。
   *Mado ga aite **iru**.*
   (The window is open.)

[2] 私は窓を開けておく。
   *Watashi wa mado o akete **oku**.*
   (I open / will open the window (in advance).)

[1] simply means that the window is open. It doesn't imply that someone opened it. *Aite*, the *te*-form of *aku* ' open ', is an intransitive verb. As seen in [2], V*te oku* means ' do s.t. in advance for future convenience '. An important difference between V*te aru* and V*te oku* is that the former expresses a state, while the latter expresses an action. Note that in V*te oku* sentences, the agent is not omitted unless it is known.

ato de あとで   *conj.*

Some state or action takes place at a time (not always immediately) after another state or action has taken place.	after 【REL. *tara*; *te kara*】 (ANT. *mae ni*)

♦**Key Sentences**

(A)

Topic (subject)		Subordinate Clause			Predicate
			Vinf·past		
メイソンさん *Meison-san*	は *wa*	日本 へ *Nihon e*	行った ***itta***	あと で *ato de*	病気 に なった / *byōki ni natta* / なりました。 *narimashita.*
(Mr. Mason became ill after he went to Japan.)					

(B)

Topic (subject)		Noun (event)			
私 *Watashi*	は *wa*	授業 ***jugyō***	の *no*	あと で *ato de*	図書館 に 行った / *toshokan ni itta* / 行きました。 *ikimashita.*
(After the class I went to the library.)					

Formation

KS(A):

Vinf·past　あと　で
　　　　　　ato de

話した　　あと　で　　(after s.o. has talked/had talked)
hanashita ato de

食べた　あと　で　　(after s.o. has eaten/had eaten)
tabeta ato de

KS(B):

N　の　あと　で
　　no ato de

勉強　の　あと　で　　(after study)
benkyō no ato de

Examples

(a) ご飯を食べたあと(で)すぐ勉強しました。
　　Gohan o tabeta ato (de) sugu benkyōshimashita.
　　(I studied right after I had eaten my meal.)

(b) 山田さんはビールを飲んだあと(で)寝てしまった。
　　Yamada-san wa biru o nonda ato (de) nete shimatta.
　　(Mr. Yamada fell asleep after he drank beer.)

(c) 戦争が終わったあと(で)東京にもどりました。
　　Sensō ga owatta ato (de) Tōkyō ni modorimashita.
　　(I went back to Tokyo after the war ended.)

(d) 食事のあとでテニスをした。
　　Shokuji no ato de tenisu o shita.
　　(I played tennis after my meal.)

Note

The particle *de* may be omitted in informal speech.

[Related Expressions]

　I. Vinf·past *ato de* is crucially different from V*te kara* in two respects: V*te kara* is very awkward if the main clause expresses something beyond the control of the subject or the speaker of the sentence. Vinf·past *ato de* is free from such restriction.

[1] 私がうちへ帰ったあとで / ??? 帰ってから雨が降った。

Watashi ga uchi e kaetta ato de / ??? *kaette kara ame ga futta.*

(It rained after I came home.)

Secondly, V*te kara* indicates 'the space of time following after', but Vinf·past *ato de* indicates 'any space of time after'. Thus,

[2] 日本へ来てから / *来たあとで何年になりますか。

Nihon e kite kara / *kita ato de nannen ni narimasu ka?*

(How many years have passed since you came to Japan?)

(⇨ *kara*²)

II. Vinf·past *ato de* can be replaced by Vinf·past *ra* when the latter is used with a purely temporal meaning (i.e., 'after', 'when'). Thus, Exs. (a), (b) and (c) can be rephrased as [3a], [3b] and [3c], respectively.

[3] a. ご飯を食べたらすぐ勉強しました。

   Gohan o tabetara sugu benkyōshimashita.

   b. 山田さんはビールを飲んだら寝てしまった。

   Yamada-san wa bīru o nondara nete shimatta.

   c. 戦争が終わったら東京にもどりました。

   Sensō ga owattara Tōkyō ni modorimashita.

However, if Vinf·past *ra* has a non-temporal meaning (i.e., 'if'), it cannot be replaced by Vinf·past *ato de*, as illustrated by [4].

[4] a. 日本へ行ったら / *行ったあとでいいでしょう。

   Nihon e ittara / *itta ato de ii deshō.*

   (Lit. It would be nice if you go to Japan. (=You should go to Japan.))

   b. これを読んだら / *読んだあとでどうですか。

   Kore o yondara / *yonda ato de dō desuka.*

   (Lit. How would it be if you read this. (=Why don't you read this?))

(⇨ *tara*)

ba ば   *conj.*

a conjunction which indicates that the preceding clause expresses a condition	if 【REL. ***tara*** (*nara*, *to⁴*)】

♦ **Key Sentence**

Subordinate Clause (condition)		Main Clause
この　薬　を　**飲め** *Kono kusuri o **nome***	ば *ba*	よく　なる / なります。 *yoku naru / narimasu.*
(If you take this medicine, you'll get well.)		

Formation

(i) Gr. 1 verbs:　Vcond ば
　　　　　　　　　　　　 ba

　　　　　　　　話せば　　(if s.o. talks)
　　　　　　　　hanaseba

(ii) Gr. 2 verbs:　Vstem れば
　　　　　　　　　　　　　 reba

　　　　　　　　食べれば　　(if s.o. eats)
　　　　　　　　tabereba

(iii) Irr. verbs:　来る → 来れば　　(if s.o. comes)
　　　　　　　　kuru　 *kureba*

　　　　　　　　する → すれば　　(if s.o. does)
　　　　　　　　suru　 *sureba*

(iv) Adjs (*i*):　　Adj (*i*) stem ければ
　　　　　　　　　　　　　　 kereba

　　　　　　　　高ければ　　(if s.t. is expensive)
　　　　　　　　takakereba

(v) Adjs (*na*):　Adj (*na*) stem {なら（ば）/ で　あれば}
　　　　　　　　　　　　　　 {*nara(ba)* / *de areba*}

　　　　　　　　{静かなら（ば）　/ 静かで　あれば}　　(if s.t. is quiet)
　　　　　　　　{*shizukanara(ba)* / *shizukade areba*}

(vi) N+cop.:　　N {なら（ば）/ で　あれば}
　　　　　　　　　　 {*nara(ba)* / *de areba*}

B

{先生　なら(ば) / 先生　で あれば}　(if s.o. is a teacher)
{*sensei nara(ba)* / *sensei de areba*}

Examples

(a) これは松本先生に聞けば分かります。
Kore wa Matsumoto-sensei ni kikeba wakarimasu.
(You'll understand it if you ask Prof. Matsumoto.)

(b) その町は車で行けば三十分で行ける。
Sono machi wa kuruma de ikeba sanjuppun de ikeru.
(You can get to that town in thirty minutes if you go by car.)

(c) 安ければ買います。
Yasukereba kaimasu.
(I'll buy it if it's cheap. / I would buy it if it were cheap.)

(d) 時間があれば京都へも行きたい。
Jikan ga areba Kyōto e mo ikitai.
(If I have time, I want to go to Kyoto, too. / If I had time, I would want to go to Kyoto, too.)

(e) 見たければ見なさい。
Mitakereba minasai.
(If you want to see it, see it.)

(f) 出来ればこれもやってください。
Dekireba kore mo yatte kudasai.
(Please do this, too, if you can.)

Notes

1. " S₁ *ba* S₂ " basically expresses a general conditional relationship between the two propositions represented by S_1 and S_2. S_1 represents a condition and S_2 a proposition which holds or will hold true under the condition. (*Ba* is, in fact, the origin of the topic marker *wa*.)

2. S_2 can be a statement of the speaker's volition or hope, as in Exs. (c) and (d). (⇨ ***to***⁴)

3. S_2 can be a command, a request or a suggestion, as in Exs. (e) and (f). In this case, however, S_1 cannot be an action. Thus, in (1) and (2) *ba* is ungrammatical. (⇨ ***nara***; ***tara***)

(1) 山本さんが来たら / *来れば知らせてください。
*Yamamoto-san ga **kitara** / *kureba shirasete kudasai.*
(If Mr. Yamamoto comes in, please let me know.)

⑵ シカゴへ行く(の)なら / *行けばバスで行ったらどうですか。

*Shikago e **iku** (**no**) **nara** | *ikeba basu de ittara dō desu ka.*

(If you go to Chicago, why don't you go by bus?)

B

4. S_1 can express both factual and counterfactual conditions. Thus, Exs. (c) and (d) can be either factual or counterfactual statements.

(⇨ ***ba yokatta***)

5. S_1 can be a state or an event in the past if it is counterfactual or habitual. Examples:

⑶ もっと安ければ買いました。

Motto yasukereba kaimashita.

(I would have bought it if it had been much cheaper.)

⑷ 雨が降ればよく家で本を読んだものだ。

Ame ga fureba yoku ie de hon o yonda mono da.

(When it rained, I often read at home.)

However, S_1 cannot be a single factual event in the past even if it represents a condition, as seen in (5). (⇨ ***tara***)

⑸ 日本へ行ったら / *行けば日本語が上手になった。

*Nihon e **ittara** | *ikeba nihongo ga jōzuni natta.*

(I became good at Japanese when I went to Japan.)

6. "S_1 *ba* S_2" does not mean more than a conditional relationship; therefore, this construction cannot be used when the speaker wants to suggest something by a conditional sentence. For example, (6) does not suggest that one should not approach the cage. It is acceptable only when it means, as a mere conditional statement, that one is in danger under the condition that one gets close to the cage.

⑹ そのおりに近づけばあぶないですよ。

Sono ori ni chikazukeba abunaidesu yo.

(It is dangerous if you get close to the cage.)

(In order to suggest that one should not approach the cage, *chikazuku to* or *chikazuitara* is used instead of *chikazukeba*.)

7. There are some idiomatic expressions which utilize the "S_1 *ba* S_2" construction. (⇨ ***ba yokatta***; ***nakereba naranai***; ***to ieba***)

bakari ばかり　　*prt.*

B

a particle which indicates that s.t. is the only thing or state which exists, or the only action s.o. will take, takes, is taking or took

only; just; be ready to do s.t.; have just done s.t.; just did s.t.; be just doing s.t.; about 〖REL. *hodo* (*kurai*); *shika* (*dake*); *tokoro da*[2]〗

♦ **Key Sentences**

(A)

Topic (subject)		Vinf·nonpast		
デザート	は	**食べる**	ばかり	に　なって　いる　います。
Dezāto	*wa*	***taberu***	*bakari*	*ni natte iru imasu.*

(Lit. The only thing left to do with the dessert is to eat it. (＝The dessert is ready to eat.))

(B)

Topic (subject)		V*te*		
友子	は	**遊んで**	ばかり	いる / います。
Tomoko	*wa*	***asonde***	*bakari*	*iru / imasu.*

(Lit. The only thing Tomoko is doing is playing. (＝Tomoko is doing nothing but playing.))

(C)

Topic (subject)			Vinf·past		
私	は	昼ご飯　を	**食べた**	ばかり	だ / です。
Watashi	*wa*	*hirugohan o*	***tabeta***	*bakari*	*da / desu.*

(Lit. I had my lunch and haven't done anything else since then. (＝I have eaten my lunch.))

(D)

Topic (subject)		Adj		
この　レストラン	は	**安い**	ばかり	だ / です。
Kono resutoran	*wa*	***yasui***	*bakari*	*da / desu.*

(Lit. The only merit of this restaurant is that the food is inexpensive. (＝This restaurant is just cheap.))

(E)

Topic (subject)		Noun		
デニス *Denisu*	は *wa*	**ビール** **biru**	ばかり *bakari*	飲んで いる / います。 *nonde iru / imasu.*
(Dennis is drinking only beer.)				

(F)

Topic (subject)		Quantifier		
私 *Watashi*	は *wa*	**ひと月** **hitotsuki**	ばかり *bakari*	パリ に いた / いました。 *Pari ni ita / imashita.*
(I was in Paris for about a month.)				

Formation

(i) Vinf·nonpast ばかり
　　　　　　　　　bakari

　　話す　ばかり　　(be ready to talk)
　　hanasu bakari

　　食べる ばかり　　(be ready to eat)
　　taberu bakari

(ii) V*te* ばかり
　　　　　bakari

　　話して　ばかり　　(be just talking)
　　hanashite bakari

　　食べて ばかり　(be just eating)
　　tabete bakari

(iii) Vinf·past ばかり
　　　　　　　　bakari

　　話した　ばかり　　(have just talked)
　　hanashita bakari

　　食べた ばかり　(have just eaten)
　　tabeta bakari

(iv) {Adj (*i*) inf·nonpast / Adj (*na*) stem な} ばかり
　　　　　　　　　　　　　　　　　　na 　*bakari*

高い　ばかり　(just expensive)
takai bakari

静かな　ばかり　(just quiet)
shizukana bakari

(v) N　ばかり
　　　bakari

先生　ばかり　(only teachers)
sensei bakari

(vi) N　Prt　ばかり
　　　　　　bakari

学生　に　ばかり　(only to students)
gakusei ni bakari

(vii) Quantifier　ばかり
　　　　　　　　bakari

一時間　ばかり　(about an hour)
ichijikan bakari

Examples

(a) このレポートはあと結論を書くばかりだ。
   Kono repōto wa ato ketsuron o kaku bakari da.
   (The only thing left to do with this report is to write a conclusion.)

(b) 春江は泣いてばかりいて何も話そうとしない。
   Harue wa naite bakari ite nanimo hanasō to shinai.
   (Harue is just crying and won't talk about anything.)

(c) 松山さんは今シカゴに着いたばかりです。
   Matsuyama-san wa ima Shikago ni tsuita bakari desu.
   (Mr. Matsuyama has just arrived in Chicago now.)

(d) この仕事はめんどうなばかりであまりもうかりません。
   Kono shigoto wa mendōna bakari de amari mōkarimasen.
   (This job is just troublesome and doesn't bring us big profits.)

(e) この寮に住んでいるのは男子学生ばかりだ。
   Kono ryō ni sunde iru no wa danshi gakusei bakari da.
   (The students who are living in this dorm are all boys.)

(f) フィッシャー先生はリサとばかり話している。
   Fisshā-sensei wa Risa to bakari hanashite iru.
   (Prof. Fisher is talking only with Lisa.)

(g) 十人ばかりの友達が手伝ってくれました。
Jūnin bakari no tomodachi ga tetsudatte kuremashita.
(About ten friends helped me.)

Notes

1. The basic idea which *bakari* expresses is that there is nothing except what is stated. When Vinf·nonpast precedes *bakari*, the whole expression means there is nothing left to do (to complete something) but what is stated by the verb. In some contexts, Vinf·nonpast *bakari* means that someone does nothing but what is stated. Example:

   ⑴ 彼は笑うばかりで何も説明してくれない。
   *Kare wa **warau bakari** de nanimo setsumeishite kurenai.*
   (He just laughs and doesn't explain anything to me.)

2. When Vinf·past precedes *bakari*, the whole expression means that there has been almost no time for anything to happen since what is stated took place. That is, something has just happened, or someone has just done something.

3. When *bakari* follows " N *ga* " or " N *o*", *ga* or *o* drops. The directional *e* and *ni* may be either deleted or retained. Other case particles do not drop when they are followed by *bakari*.

4. *Bakari* in classical Japanese expressed the speaker's conjecture and this usage is still seen in the " Quantifier *bakari*" pattern, where *bakari* means 'about'.

ba yokatta ばよかった   *phr.*

a phrase which expresses the speaker's regret	I wish ~ had done s.t. **[**REL. *te yokatta*]

♦ **Key Sentence**

Subordinate Clause (condition)		Main Clause
先生 に *Sensei ni*	聞け ば **kike** ba	よかった / よかったです。 *yokatta / yokattadesu.*
(I wish I had asked my teacher.)		

Formation

(i) Gr. 1 verbs:　Vcond　ば よかった
　　　　　　　　　　　　　　ba yokatta

　　　　　　　　　　話せ　ば よかった　　(I wish s.o. had talked)
　　　　　　　　　hanase ba yokatta

(ii) Gr. 2 verbs:　Vstem　れば よかった
　　　　　　　　　　　　　　reba yokatta

　　　　　　　　　食べれば よかった　　(I wish s.o. had eaten)
　　　　　　　　　tabereba yokatta

(iii) Irr. verbs:　来る → 来れば よかった　　(I wish s.o. had come)
　　　　　　　　　kuru　kureba yokatta

　　　　　　　　　する → すれば よかった　　(I wish s.o. had done)
　　　　　　　　　suru　sureba yokatta

Examples

(a)　あの本を読めばよかった。
　　　Ano hon o yomeba yokatta.
　　　(I wish I had read that book.)

(b)　ウェルズさんは日本へ行けばよかったね。
　　　Ueruzu-san wa Nihon e ikeba yokatta ne.
　　　(I wish Mr. Wells had gone to Japan, don't you?)

(c)　ああ，もっと英語を勉強しておけばよかったなあ。
　　　Ā, motto eigo o benkyōshite okeba yokatta nā.
　　　(Oh, I wish I had studied English harder!)

Notes

1. Vcond *ba yokatta* is an idiomatic expression which means 'I wish ~ had done s.t.' It consists of a conditional clause with *ba* and *yokatta* 'was good' and literally means 'It would have been good if ~ had done s.t.'

2. When there is no subject in a *ba*-clause sentence, the first person is the implicit subject.

3. This expression is often used with exclamatory words such as *ā* 'oh' and the sentence-final particle of exclamation *nā*, as in Ex. (c).

4. "S.o. (other than the first person) wishes ~ had done s.t." is expressed using this phrase and the verb *omou* 'think', as in (1).

(⇒ *iru*², Note 4; *to*³)

⑴ ビルは日本へ行けばよかったと思っている。

Biru wa Nihon e ikeba yokatta to omotte iru.

(Lit. Bill thinks that it would have been good if he had gone to Japan. (=Bill wishes he had gone to Japan.))

[Related Expression]

In " Vcond *ba yakatta* ", Vcond *ba* expresses a counterfactual action or state in the past. In a similar expression " V*te yokatta* ", V*te* expresses a factual action or state in the past. Compare [1] with Ex. (a).

[1] あの本を読んでよかった。

Ano hon o yonde yokatta.

(Lit. It was good that I read that book. (=I'm glad I read that book.))

dai だい　　*prt.*

---

a sentence-final particle which indi-　　【REL. *ka*²; *kai*】
cates a WH-question in informal male
speech

♦ **Key Sentences**

(A)

Subject		Adj (*na*) stem / N	
どこ	が	**静か**	だい。
Doko	*ga*	***shizuka***	*dai*.
(What place is quiet?)			

(B)

Sentence (informal)†			
だれ が 行く	ん	だい。	
*Dare ga **iku***	*n*	*dai*.	
(Who is going?)			

†*Da* after Adj (*na*) stem and N changes to *na*.

Formation

(i) {Adj (*na*) stem / N} だい
　　　　　　　　　　　　dai

　　静か　だい　　(s.t. is quiet?)
　　shizuka dai

　　先生　だい　　(s.o. is a teacher?)
　　sensei dai

(ii) {V / Adj (*i*)} inf ん だい
　　　　　　　　　　n dai

　　{話す　/話した}　ん だい　　(s.o. talks / talked?)
　　{*hanasu* / *hanashita*} *n dai*

　　{高い / 高かった} ん だい　　(s.t. is / was expensive?)
　　{*takai* / *takakatta*} *n dai*

(iii) {Adj (*na*) stem / N} {な / だった} ん だい
　　　　　　　　　　　　　{*na* / *datta*} *n dai*

{静かな　／静かだった} ん だい　　(s.t. is / was quiet?)
{*shizukana* / *shizukadatta*} *n dai*

{先生　な／先生　だった} ん だい　　(s.o. is / was a teacher?)
{*sensei na* / *sensei datta*} *n dai*

D

Examples

(a) 新しい仕事はどうだい。
Atarashii shigoto wa dō dai.
(How's your new job?)

(b) あの人はだれだい。
Ano hito wa dare dai.
(Who is that person?)

(c) 何がおかしいんだい。
Nani ga okashii n dai.
(What's funny?)

(d) どの人が佐藤先生なんだい。
Dono hito ga Satō-sensei na n dai.
(Which person is Prof. Sato?)

Notes

1. *Dai* can also be used with declarative sentences for emphasis in boys' speech, as in (1)

    (1) a. これは僕のだい。
        Kore wa boku no dai.
        (This is mine.)

        b. 僕も行くんだい。
        Boku mo iku n dai.
        (I will go, too.)

2. When *dai* is used with interrogative sentences, the sentences must be WH-questions. Thus, the following sentences are ungrammatical.

    (2) a. *あの人は先生だい。
        *Ano hito wa sensei dai.
        (Is that person a teacher?)

        b. *村田さんも行くんだい。
        *Murata-san mo iku n dai.
        (Is Mr. Murata going, too?)

For yes-no questions, *kai* is used.　　　　　　　　　(⇨ *kai*)

3. Questions with *dai*, as in KS (A), and those with *n dai*, as in KS (B), correspond to questions without *no desu* and those with *no desu* in formal speech, respectively. (⇨ **no da**)

4. *Dai* actually consists of the copula *da* and the particle *i*. Thus, it can follow only *na*-type adjective stems, nouns and noun equivalents. The following sentences are ungrammatical because *dai* follows a verb or an *i*-type adjective.

  (3) a. *だれが行くだい。
      **Dare ga iku dai.*
      (Who is going?)

   b. *どれがおもしろいだい。
      **Dore ga omoshiroi dai.*
      (Which one is interesting?)

N dai can follow verbs and *i*-type adjectives, as in KS (B) and Ex. (c), because *n* is a nominalizer (the colloquial form of *no*[3]) and it changes the preceding sentence into a noun equivalent.

5. In informal male speech, questions as in (3) are expressed as in (4), with rising intonation.

  (4) a. だれが行く？
      Dare ga iku?
      (Who is going?)

   b. どれがおもしろい？
      Dore ga omoshiroi?
      (Which one is interesting?)

6. The past form of *dai* is *dattai*, but it is not frequently used. The more frequently used past form of *dai* is *datta* with rising intonation, as seen in (5).

  (5) a. 新しい仕事はどうだった？
      Atarashii shigoto wa dō datta?
      (How was your new job?)

   b. どこが静かだった？
      Doko ga shizukadatta?
      (What place was quiet?)

[Related Expression]

In informal speech, the question marker *ka* (i.e., *ka*[2]) is not usually used.

The following chart summarizes the endings for informal questions.

Formal	Male, informal	Female, informal	Note
yes-no question	Sinf かい; Sinf *kai*	Sinf	*Da* after Adj (*na*) stem and N drops.
yes-no question with *no desu*	Sinf の かい; Sinf の *no kai* *no*	Sinf の *no*	*Da* after Adj (*na*) stem and N changes to *na*.
WH-question	Sinf; {Adj (*na*) stem / N} だい *dai*	Sinf	*Da* after Adj (*na*) stem and N drops.
WH-question with *no desu*	Sinf ん だい; Sinf の *n dai* *no*	Sinf の *no*	*Da* after Adj (*na*) stem and N changes to *na*.

Sinf *ka* is used in very informal speech or in vulgar speech. Female informal endings can also be used by male speakers.

dake だけ   *prt.*

a particle which expresses a limit imposed upon something that is growing and expanding	only; just; alone; merely; that's all 【REL. *shika* (*bakari*)】

◆**Key Sentences**

(A)

Subject		Predicate
スミスさん **Sumisu-san**	だけ（が） *dake* (*ga*)	来た / 来ました。 *kita* / *kimashita*.
(Only Mr. Smith came.)		

(B)

		Number-Counter		
私　は　日本　へ *Watashi wa Nihon e*		一度 ***ichido***	だけ *dake*	行った / 行きました。 *itta / ikimashita.*
(I went to Japan only once.)				

(C)

Sentence	Vinf	
雪子さん　とは *Yukiko-san to wa*	デート　した ***dēto shita***	だけ　だ / です。 *dake da / desu.*
(I just dated Yukiko, that's all.)		

(D)

Sentence	Adj (*i*) inf	
この　家　は *Kono ie wa*	大きい ***ōkii***	だけ　だ / です。 *dake da / desu.*
(This house is big, that's all.)		

(E)

Sentence	Adj (*na*) stem		
この　お菓子　は　色　が *Kono o-kashi wa iro ga*	きれい ***kirei***	な **na**	だけ　だ / です。 *dake da / desu.*
(This cake has pretty colors, that's all.)			

Formation

(i) N だけ (が) / (を)
　　　dake (ga) / (o)

　　先生　だけ　(が) / (を)　　(the teacher alone (subject) / (direct object))
　　sensei dake (ga) / (o)

(ii) N {だけ Prt / Prt だけ}　　(where Prt=particles other than *ga*, *o*, and
　　　{*dake* Prt / Prt *dake*}　*wa*)

　　先生　{だけ　に / に　だけ}　　(only to the teacher / to the teacher alone)
　　sensei {dake ni / ni dake}

(iii) {V / Adj (*i*)} inf だけ {だ / です}
                    dake {*da* / *desu*}

  {話す / 話した} だけ {だ / です}   (s.o. talks / talked, that's all)
  {*hanasu* / *hanshita*} *dake* {*da* / *desu*}

  {高い / 高かった} だけ {だ / です}   (s.t. is / was expensive, that's all)
  {*takai* / *takakatta*} *dake* {*da* / *desu*}

(iv) Adj (*na*) stem {な / だった} だけ {だ / です}
                  {*na* / *datta*} *dake* {*da* / *desu*}

  {静かな / 静かだった} だけ {だ / です}   (s.t. is / was quiet, that's
  {*shizukana* / *shizukadatta*} *dake* {*da* / *desu*} all)

Examples

(a) 佐藤さんだけ(が)会議に出ました。
    Satō-san dake (ga) kaigi ni demashita.
    (Only Mr. Sato attended the conference.)

(b) 小さい和英辞典だけ(を)買いました。
    Chisai waeijiten dake (o) kaimashita.
    (I bought only a small Japanese-English dictionary.)

(c) 僕にだけ / だけに話して下さい。
    Boku ni dake / dake ni hanashite kudasai.
    (Please tell it only to me / to me alone.)

(d) この車はアルコールでだけ / だけで動きます。
    Kono kuruma wa arukōru de dake / dake de ugokimasu.
    (This car runs only on alcohol (and on nothing else) / on alcohol alone
    (so it needs nothing else).)

(e) あの先生には一度だけ会いました。
    Ano sensei ni wa ichido dake aimashita.
    (I met that professor only once.)

(f) 朝はコーヒーを一杯飲むだけです。
    Asa wa kōhi o ippai nomu dake desu.
    (In the morning I just drink a cup of coffee, that's all.)

(g) この本は高いだけでおもしろくない。
    Kono hon wa takai dake de omoshirokunai.
    (This book is just expensive and is not interesting.)

(h) テニスは好きなだけで上手じゃない。
    Tenisu wa sukina dake de jōzuja nai.
    (I just like tennis, and I'm not good at it.)

(i) それは学生だけのパーティーだった。
Sore wa gakusei dake no pāti datta.
(It was a party for students only.)

(j) 出来るだけゆっくり話して下さい。
Dekiru dake yukkuri hanashite kudasai.
(Please speak as slowly as possible.)

Notes

1. When *dake* modifies a preceding noun, as in Exs. (a), (b), (c), and (d), the particle that is used with the noun can be positioned before or after *dake*, except for the particles *ga*, *o* and *wa*, which can be optionally used only after *dake*.

2. The optional positionings of the particles other than *ga*, *o* and *wa* create a subtle semantic difference. Distinctive emphasis is placed on the particle, yielding a meaning of exclusiveness in the case of N+Prt+ *dake*. No meaning of exclusiveness is implied in the case of N+*dake* +Prt.

3. If *dake* is used in:

$$\sim \begin{Bmatrix} \{V\ /\ Adj\ (i)\}\ inf \\ \{Adj\ (na)\ stem\ \{na\ /\ datta\}\} \end{Bmatrix} + dake\ \{da\ /\ desu\}$$

as illustrated by KSs (C), (D) and (E), *dake* modifies the entire preceding part and means ' ~, that's all.'
Compare (1a) and (1b) below:

(1) a. 魚だけ（を）食べた。
*Sakana **dake** (o) tabeta.*
(I ate only fish.)

　　b. 魚を食べただけだ。
*Sakana o tabeta **dake** da.*
(I ate fish, that's all.)

In (1a) *dake* modifies only the preceding noun *sakana* ' fish ', while in (1b) *dake* modifies the entire preceding part of the sentence *sakana o tabeta* ' I ate fish.'

4. V(Potential)+*dake* as in Ex. (j) means ' as much as one can ~ '.

(2) a. 食べられるだけ食べたい。
*Taberareru **dake** tabetai.*
(I'd like to eat as much as I can (eat).)

b. 踊れるだけ踊ろう。
   *Odoreru **dake** odorō.*
   (Let's dance as much as we can (dance).)

D

dake de (**wa**) **naku** ~ (**mo**) だけで(は)なく～(も)   *phr.*

not only X but also Y, where X and Y can be either a noun, a verb, an adjective

not only ~ but also ~
【REL. *bakari de* (*wa*) *naku* ~ (*mo*)】

♦ **Key Sentences**

(A)

Topic (subject)			Vinf	
あの 人 *Ano hito*	は *wa*	よく *yoku*	**勉強する** **benkyōsuru**	だけ で (は) なく よく *dake de* (*wa*) *naku yoku* 遊ぶ / 遊びます。 *asobu / asobimasu.*
(He not only studies hard, but also plays a lot.)				

(B)

Topic (subject)			Adj (*i*) inf	
あの 人 *Ano hito*	は *wa*	頭 が *atama ga*	いい **ii**	だけ で (は) なく よく 勉強 *dake de* (*wa*) *naku yoku benkyō* (も) する / します。 (*mo*) *suru / shimasu.*
(He is not only smart; he studies hard, too.)				

(C)

Topic (subject)		Adj (*na*) stem		
この うち *Kono uchi*	は *wa*	きれい *kirei*	な *na*	だけ で (は) なく とても *dake de (wa) naku totemo* 安い (です)。 *yasui (desu).*
(This house is not only beautiful but it is also inexpensive.)				

(D)

Subject				Predicate
Noun		Noun		
ジョン *Jon*	だけ で (は) なく *dake de (wa) naku*	メアリー *Meari*	も *mo*	来た / 来ました。 *kita / kimashita.*
(Not only John but also Mary came here.)				

<u>Formation</u>

(i) {V / Adj (*i*)} inf だけ で (は) なく   (not only ~)
　　　　　　　　　dake de (wa) naku

　　{話す　/ 話した}　だけ で (は) なく   (s.o. not only speaks /
　　{*hanasu* / *hanashita*} *dake de (wa) naku*   spoke ~)

　　{高い / 高かった} だけ で (は) なく   (s.t. is / was not only
　　{*takai* / *takakatta*} *dake de (wa) naku*   expensive ~)

(ii) Adj (*na*) stem {な / だった} だけ で (は) なく   (not only ~)
　　　　　　　　　　{*na* / *datta*}　*dake de (wa) naku*

　　{静かな　/ 静かだった}　だけ で (は) なく   (s.t. is / was not only
　　{*shizukana* / *shizukadatta*} *dake de (wa) naku*   quiet ~)

(iii) N {ø / だった} だけ で (は) なく   (not only ~)
　　　　{ø / *datta*}　*dake de (wa) naku*

　　{先生　/ 先生　だった} だけ で (は) なく   (not only teachers / not
　　{*sensei* / *sensei datta*} *dake de (wa) naku*   only s.o. was a teacher)

Examples

(a) あの人は小説を読むだけではなく書きます。
Ano hito wa shōsetsu o yomu dake de wa naku kakimasu.
(He not only reads novels but also writes them.)

(b) ブラウンさんは日本へ行っただけではなく住んだこともあります。
Buraun-san wa Nihon e itta dake de wa naku sunda koto mo arimasu.
(Mr. Brown has not only been to Japan, but has also lived there.)

(c) このアパートは高いだけでなく大変狭いです。
Kono apāto wa takai dake de naku taihen semaidesu.
(This apartment is not only expensive but it is also very small.)

(d) 幸子は頭がよかっただけではなく、とても親切でした。
Sachiko wa atama ga yokatta dake de wa naku, totemo shinsetsu-deshita.
(Sachiko was not only bright but was also very kind.)

(e) この車はきれいなだけではなく，よく走ります。
Kono kuruma wa kireina dake de wa naku, yoku hashirimasu.
(This car is not only pretty but also runs well.)

(f) 日本人だけでなくアメリカ人もよく働きます。
Nihonjin dake de naku amerikajin mo yoku hatarakimasu.
(Not only Japanese but also Americans work hard.)

(g) 中村さんはアメリカやヨーロッパだけではなく東南アジアにもよく出張します。
Nakamura-san wa Amerika ya Yōroppa dake de wa naku Tōnan Ajia ni mo yoku shutchōshimasu.
(Mr. Nakamura makes a business trip not only to America and Europe but also to Southeast Asia.)

(h) ジョンソンさんは日本語だけではなく中国語も話せます。
Jonson-san wa nihongo dake de wa naku chūgokugo mo hanasemasu.
(Mr. Johnson can speak not only Japanese but also Chinese.)

Note

In " Noun ~ *dake de (wa) naku* Noun ~ *mo* ", the two nouns can be followed by various particles.

(1) 手紙は友達（から）だけではなく先生からも来ました。
*Tegami wa tomodachi (**kara**) dake de wa naku sensei **kara** mo kimashita.*
(Letters came not only from my friends but also from my teachers.)

(2) 手紙は友達(に)だけではなく先生にも書きました。

*Tegami wa tomodachi (**ni**) dake de wa naku sensei **ni** mo kakimashita.*

(I wrote letters not only to my friends, but also to my teachers.)

【Related Expression】

In the majority of cases *dake* can be replaced by *bakari*. When one needs to define limitation in a rigid way, however, *dake* is preferable. For example:

[1] [Teacher to his student.]

あしたまでに十課だけ /?? ばかりでなく十一課も勉強しておきなさい。

*Ashita made ni jukka **dake** | ?? **bakari** de naku jūikka mo benkyō-shite okinasai.*

(Study not only Lesson 10 but also Lesson 11 by tomorrow.)

(⇨ *dake*)

---

darō だろう   *aux.*

an auxiliary indicating the speaker's conjecture which is not based on any particular information or evidence	probably 【REL. ***kamoshirenai*** (*ni chigainai*); ***yōda*** (*rashii, sōda*[2])】

◆**Key Sentence**

Sentence (informal)†	
アンダーソンさん は 日本 へ 行く *Andāson-san wa Nihon e **iku***	だろう / でしょう。 *darō	deshō.*
(Ms. Anderson will probably go to Japan.)	

†*Da* after Adj (*na*) stem and N drops.

Formation

(i) {V / Adj (*i*)} inf だろう
　　　　　　　　　　darō

{話す　/ 話した}　　だろう　　(s.o. will probably talk / probably talked)
{*hanasu* / *hanashita*}　*darō*

{高い　/ 高かった}　　だろう　　(s.t. is / was probably expensive)
{*takai* / *takakatta*}　*darō*

(ii) {Adj (*na*) stem / N}　{ø / だった}　だろう
　　　　　　　　　　　　　　{ø / *datta*}　*darō*

{静か　/ 静かだった}　　だろう　　(s.t. is / was probably quiet)
{*shizuka* / *shizuka datta*}　*darō*

{先生　/ 先生　　だった}　だろう　　(s.o. is / was probably a teacher)
{*sensei* / *sensei datta*}　　*darō*

Examples

(a) あのアパートは高いでしょう。
　　Ano apāto wa takai deshō.
　　(That apartment is probably expensive.)

(b) ロジャーはスキーが上手だろう。
　　Rojā wa ski ga jōzu darō.
　　(Roger is probably good at skiing.)

(c) あの人は中国人だろう。
　　Ano hito wa chūgokujin darō.
　　(That man is probably Chinese.)

Notes

1. *Darō* is originally the informal conjecture form of the copula *da*, but it is used as an auxiliary of conjecture. The formal version is *deshō*.

2. Probability adverbs such as *tabun*, *osoraku* and *kitto* are sometimes used with *darō* or *deshō*. The speaker's conjecture sounds more certain with *tabun* or *osoraku*, and even more certain with *kitto*. Examples:

　(1) アンダーソンさんは**たぶん**日本へ行くだろう。
　　　*Andāson-san wa **tabun** Nihon e iku darō.*
　　　(Ms. Anderson will most probably go to Japan.)

　(2) アンダーソンさんは**きっと**日本へ行くだろう。
　　　*Andāson-san wa **kitto** Nihon e iku darō.*
　　　(I'm almost certain that Ms. Anderson will go to Japan.)

3. *Darō* / *deshō* with the question marker *ka* makes questions softer or less direct. Compare (3) and (4).

(3) 大じょうぶですか。
　　 *Daijōbu **desu ka**.*
　　 (Is it all right?)

(4) 大じょうぶでしょうか。
　　 *Daijōbu **deshō ka**.*
　　 (I wonder if it's all right.)

4. S *darō* / *deshō* with rising intonation asks for the hearer's agreement.

(5) a. 君も行くだろう？
　　　 *Kimi mo iku **darō**?*
　　　 (You will go too, (am I) right?)

　　 b. これ、きれいでしょう？
　　　 *Kore, kirei **deshō**?*
　　　 (Isn't this pretty?)

The sentence-final particle *ne* also asks for the hearer's agreement, but S *darō* / *deshō* with rising intonation is softer or less direct. (⇨ **ne**) Compare (5a) with (6).

(6) 君も行くね。
　　 *Kimi mo iku **ne**.*
　　 (You will go too, won't you?)

~dasu ~出す　*aux. v.* (*Gr. 1*)

S.t. that has been latent is realized.

out; begin to; start to
【REL. ~*hajimeru*】
(ANT. ~*owaru*)

♦ **Key Sentence**

Subject		V*masu*	
車	が	**動き**	出した / 出しました。
Kuruma	*ga*	***ugoki***	*dashita* / *dashimashita*.
(The car started to move.)			

Formation

V*masu* 出す
　　　 dasu

話し出す　　(s.o. starts to talk)
hanashidasu

食べ出す　　(s.o. starts to eat)
tabedasu

Examples

(a) 急に雨が降り出した。
　　Kyūni ame ga furidashita.
　　(Suddenly it began to rain.)

(b) 一歳になって初めて歩き出した。
　　Issai ni natte hajimete arukidashita.
　　(Lit. He started to walk only after he became a year old. (= He didn't start to walk until he was a year old.))

(c) そのアイディアはだれが考え出したんですか。
　　Sono aidia wa dare ga kangaedashita n desu ka.
　　(Who thought out that idea?)

(d) 一時間ぐらいかけてとうとうその本屋を探し出した。
　　Ichijikan gurai kakete tōtō sono hon-ya o sagashidashita.
　　(After spending about an hour, I finally located that bookstore.)

Notes

1. *Dasu* in V*masu*+*dasu* is used as an auxiliary verb. When it is used as a full verb, it means 'cause something to become visible'.

2. V*masu*+*dasu* is normally ambiguous; one meaning is '~ out' and the other is 'begin to ~'. Thus, *tsukuridasu* means 'turn out' or 'begin to make'.

3. V*masu*+*dasu* conjugates as a Gr. 1 Verb.

	さない *sanai*	(inf, neg, nonpast)
	します *shimasu*	(fml, nonpast)
話し出- *hanashida-* 食べ出- *tabeda-*	す *su*	(inf, nonpast)
	せば *seba*	(conditional)
	そう *sō*	(volitional)
	して *shite*	(*te*-form)
	した *shita*	(inf, past)

4. V*masu*+*owaru* ' finish ~ing ' is an antonym of V*masu*+*dasu* / *hajimeru*.

[Related Expression]

~*dasu* in the sense of ' begin to ~' is different from ~*hajimeru* in that the former indicates a non-volitional and abrupt beginning while the latter is more broadly used. Thus,

[1] そろそろ歩き始めましょう / *歩き出しましょうか。
*Sorosoro **arukihajimemashō** / *arukidashimashō ka.*
(It's getting late. Shall we begin to walk?)

[2] 私達が歩き始めた / 歩き出した時山田達が来た。
*Watashitachi ga **arukihajimeta** / **arukidashita** toki Yamada-tachi ga kita.*
(When we started to walk, Yamada and his company came.)

[3] どうしてか分からなかったが，男は急におこり出した /?? おこり始めた。
*Dōshite ka wakaranakatta ga, otoko wa kyūni **okoridashita** / ??okori-hajimeta.*
(I don't know why, but the man suddenly started to get angry.)

de¹ で   *prt.*

| a particle which indicates location, except for location of existence | at; in; on **【REL.** *ni*⁴; *ni*⁶; *o*²**】** |

♦**Key Sentence**

Topic (subject)		Noun (location)		Predicate (non-existential)
私達 *Watashitachi*	は *wa*	きっ茶店 *kissaten*	で *de*	コーヒー を 飲んだ / 飲みました。 *kōhī o nonda / nomimashita.*

(We drank coffee at a coffee shop.)

Examples

(a) ゆり子はデパートで働いています。
   Yuriko wa depāto de hataraite imasu.
   (Yuriko is working at a department store.)

(b) オーストラリアでは十二月は夏だ。
   Ōsutoraria de wa jūnigatsu wa natsu da.
   (In Australia it is summer in December.)

(c) 島崎さんは日本では元気でした。
   Shimazaki-san wa Nihon de wa genkideshita.
   (Mr. Shimazaki was healthy in Japan.)

(d) ヘレンは初めて舞台で歌った。
   Heren wa hajimete butai de utatta.
   (Helen sang on the stage for the first time.)

Note

*De*¹ cannot be used to indicate location of existence. (⇨ *ni*⁶) However, if the existential verb *aru* '(inanimate things) exist' occurs with an event, *de* is used, as in (1).

(1) a. 今晩ジムの家で / *にパーティーがあります。
    *Konban Jimu no ie de / *ni pāti ga arimasu.*
    (There's a party at Jim's tonight.)

   b. きのうこの部屋で / *にプライス先生の講演があった。
    *Kinō kono heya de / *ni Puraisu-sensei no kōen ga atta.*
    (We had Prof. Price's lecture in this room yesterday.)

de² で   *prt.*

| a particle which indicates the use of s.t. for doing s.t. | by; for; from; in; on; using; with |

【REL. *o tsukatte*】

♦ **Key Sentence**

Topic (subject)			Noun (means)		
宮本さん	は	毎日	バス	で	会社 へ 行く / 行きます。
Miyamoto-san	*wa*	*mainichi*	***basu***	*de*	*kaisha e iku / ikimasu.*

(Mr. Miyamoto goes to his company by bus everyday.)

Examples

(a) 日本人ははしでご飯を食べる。
    Nihonjin wa hashi de gohan o taberu.
    (Japanese people eat rice with chopsticks.)

(b) 私達は日本語で話した。
    Watashitachi wa nihongo de hanashita.
    (We talked in Japanese.)

(c) 私はその映画をテレビで見ました。
    Watashi wa sono eiga o terebi de mimashita.
    (I saw the movie on TV.)

(d) とうふは大豆で作ります。
    Tōfu wa daizu de tsukurimasu.
    (We make *tofu* from soybeans.)

(e) ラリーはこのいすを十ドルで買った。
    Rari wa kono isu o jūdoru de katta.
    (Larry bought this chair for ten dollars.)

(f) ベッツィーはそのレポートを一日で書いたそうだ。
    Bettsi wa sono repōto o ichinichi de kaita sōda.
    (I heard that Betsy wrote the report in one day.)

Notes

1. In general, *de*² indicates something which is used when someone or something does something.   Typically, it indicates means and instruments as in KS and Exs. (a) – (c).

2. Since *de* also indicates reason and cause, the phrase *nan de*, which consists of *nan* 'what' and *de*, is ambiguous: One meaning is 'by means of what (=how)' and the other is 'for what reason (=why)'. Thus, (1) can be interpreted in two ways.

⑴ 本田さんは何で大阪へ行くんですか。
   Honda-san wa nan de Ōsaka e iku n desu ka.
   (How / Why is Mr. Honda going to Osaka?)

[Related Expression]

De² can be used instead of the phrase ~ *o tsukatte* 'by using ~', except when the preceding noun refers to a human being. Examples:

[1] 私達はタクシーを使って / で来ました。
   *Watashitachi wa takushī **o tsukatte** / **de** kimashita.*
   (We came by taxi.)

[2] 私は子供を使って / *で家具を動かした。
   *Watashi wa kodomo **o tsukatte** / ***de** kagu o ugokashita.*
   (Lit. I moved the furniture using my children.)

---

de³ で *prt.*

a particle (apparently derived from the *te*-form of *desu*) that indicates a weak causal relationship	and; because of; due to; because 【REL. *kara³*; **node**】

◆**Key Sentence**

	Noun (cause)		
山口さん　　は *Yamaguchi-san wa*	病気 **byōki**	で *de*	学校　を　休んだ / 休みました。 *gakkō o yasunda / yasumimashita.*
(Lit. Mr. Yamaguchi was ill and absented himself from school. (=Because Mr. Yamaguchi was ill, he didn't come to school.))			

Examples

(a) あしたは期末試験で大変です。
   Ashita wa kimatsushiken de taihen desu.
   (I'm having an awful time because of tomorrow's final exam.)

(b) 大雨で橋がこわれた。

Ōame de hashi ga kowareta.

(Lit. Because of heavy rain the bridge broke down. (=Heavy rain destroyed the bridge.))

(c) きのうは夜，仕事でとても疲れた。

Kinō wa yoru, shigoto de totemo tsukareta.

(Lit. Because of my work I got very tired last night. (=I worked so hard last night that I got very tired.))

(d) 父は交通事故で入院しました。

Chichi wa kōtsūjiko de nyūinshimashita.

(My father was hospitalized due to a traffic accident.)

Notes

1. Some of the uses of *de*³ (such as KS and Ex. (a)) are very close to the *te*-form of *desu*. For example, KS can be paraphrased into two sentences (1a) and (1b):

   (1) a. 山口さんは病気でした。

   　　　Yamaguchi-san wa byōki deshita.

   　　　(Mr. Yamaguchi was ill.)

   　　b. 山口さんは学校を休みました。

   　　　Yamaguchi-san wa gakkō o yasumimashita.

   　　　(Mr. Yamaguchi was absent from school.)

   And KS can be considered to be the result of combining the two sentences using the *te*-form of *desu* which basically means ' be ~ and '.

2. A noun that precedes *de*³ expresses something that is beyond human control (such as illness, flood, accident, rain, and fire). It is also to be noted that *de*³ co-occurs with any noun, if a predicate expresses something that is beyond human control. If the co-occurring predicate expresses something that is controllable, the particle *de* is no longer *de*³; it is *de*² of means. (⇨ **de²**) Compare (2a) and (2b) below:

   (2) a. 卵でアレルギーになる。

   　　　*Tamago **de** arerugī ni naru.*

   　　　(Lit. Eggs cause me allergy. (=I'm allergic to eggs.))

   　　b. 卵でオムレツを作る。

   　　　*Tamago **de** omuretsu o tsukuru.*

   　　　(I make an omelette with eggs.)

(2a) and (2b) contain a noncontrollable predicate *arerugi ni naru* 'become allergic' and a controllable predicate *omuretsu o tsukuru* 'make an omelette', respectively. Therefore, *de* in (2a) and (2b) are *de³* and *de²*, respectively.

[Related Expression]

The particle *de³* is a very loose marker of cause due to its origin; in contrast, *kara³* and *node* are clear subordinate conjunctions of cause / reason.

(⇨ ***kara³***; ***node***)

de⁴ で   *prt.*

a particle which indicates the time when s.t. terminates or the amount of time a period of activity has taken	at; on; in 【REL. *ni¹*】

♦ **Key Sentence**

Topic (subject)		Noun (time)		
春学期 *Harugakki*	は *wa*	五月　十日 ***gogatsu tōka***	で *de*	終わる / 終わります。 *owaru / owarimasu.*
(The spring term ends on May 10.)				

Examples

(a) このコンサートは十時で終わります。
   Kono konsāto wa jūji de owarimasu.
   (This concert will be over at ten o'clock.)

(b) 私のパスポートは六月できれる。
   Watashi no pasupōto wa rokugatsu de kireru.
   (My passport expires in June.)

(c) アメリカに来てから今日で三年になる。
   Amerika ni kite kara kyō de sannen ni naru.
   (It's been three years since I came to America.)

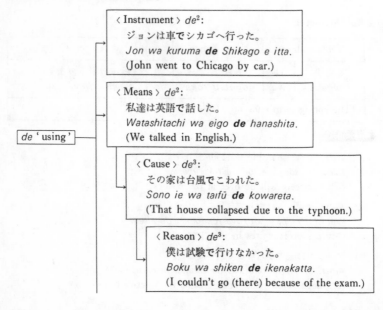

Notes

1. In general, X *de*[4] indicates that something lasts for a period of time up to X.

2. When X in X *de* refers to a duration of time, as in (1), it is the *de* of means rather than the *de* of termination time.   (⇨ ***de***[2])

   (1) 山田さんは一週間でそのレポートを書いた。

      Yamada-san wa isshūkan de sono repōto o kaita.

      (Mr. Yamada wrote the report in a week (lit. using a week).)

[Related Expression]

Ni[1] can be used in place of *de*[4] in KS and Exs. (a) and (b), as in [1].

   [1] 春学期は五月十日で / に終わる。

      *Harugakki wa gogatsu tōka **de** / **ni** owaru.*

      (The spring term ends on May 10.)

When *de* is used, the nuance is that the spring term lasts up to May 10. When *ni* is used, however, the sentence simply indicates the time when the spring term ends.

★Semantic Derivations of *De*

〈 Instrument 〉 *de*[2]:

ジョンは車でシカゴへ行った。

*Jon wa kuruma **de** Shikago e itta.*

(John went to Chicago by car.)

〈 Means 〉 *de*[2]:

私達は英語で話した。

*Watashitachi wa eigo **de** hanashita.*

(We talked in English.)

de ' using '

〈 Cause 〉 *de*[3]:

その家は台風でこわれた。

*Sono ie wa taifū **de** kowareta.*

(That house collapsed due to the typhoon.)

〈 Reason 〉 *de*[3]:

僕は試験で行けなかった。

*Boku wa shiken **de** ikenakatta.*

(I couldn't go (there) because of the exam.)

〈 Material 〉 *de²*:

私は毛糸でくつ下をあんだ。

*Watashi wa keito **de** kutsushita o anda.*

(I knit socks with wool.)

〈 Place 〉 *de¹*:

道子はいつも図書館で勉強する。

*Michiko wa itsumo toshokan **de** benkyōsuru.*

(Michiko usually studies at the library.)

〈 Required time 〉 *de²*:

木村さんは三日でこのレポートを書いた。

*Kimura-san wa mikka **de** kono repōto o kaita.*

(Mr. Kimura wrote this report in three days.)

〈 Time 〉 *de⁴*:

仕事は五時で終わります。

*Shigoto wa goji **de** owarimasu.*

(My work ends at five o'clock.)

〈 Required cost 〉 *de²*:

私はこの本を十ドルで買った。

*Watashi wa kono hon o jūdoru **de** katta.*

(I bought this book for ten dollars.)

demo でも   *prt.*

the *te*-form of *desu* plus *mo* 'even'   even

♦ Key Sentences

(A)

Subject		Predicate
先生 ***Sensei***	でも *demo*	まちがう / まちがいます。 *machigau / machigaimasu.*
(Even a teacher makes mistakes.)		

(B)

Topic (subject)		Direct Object		Verb
私 *Watashi*	は *wa*	難しい　　仕事 ***muzukashii shigoto***	でも *demo*	する / します。 *suru / shimasu.*
(I will even do a difficult job.)				

(C)

Noun	Prt		
ここ ***Koko***	から ***kara***	でも *demo*	富士山　が　見える / 見えます。 *Fujisan ga mieru / miemasu.*
(Even from here you can see Mt. Fuji.)			

Formation

(i) N でも
　　　　demo

　先生　が　(subject) →　先生　でも　(even a teacher)
　sensei ga　　　　　　*sensei demo*

　先生　を　(object) →　先生　でも　(even a teacher)
　sensei o　　　　　　*sensei demo*

(ii) N+Prt でも
　　　　　demo

　先生　と　でも　(even with a teacher)
　sensei to demo

　東京　から　でも　(even from Tokyo)
　Tōkyō kara demo

D

(a) 子供でもそんなことは分かりますよ。

Kodomo demo sonna koto wa wakarimasu yo.

(Even a child can understand that sort of thing.)

(b) お会いしたいんですが，日曜日でもかまいませんか。

O-ai shitai n desu ga, nichiyōbi demo kamaimasen ka.

(I'd like to see you, but is it all right to see you even on Sunday?)

(c) あの人は魚でも肉でも食べます。

Ano hito wa sakana demo niku demo tabemasu.

(Lit. He eats anything, whether it be fish or meat. (=He eats both fish and meat.))

1. WH-word+*demo* yields the following meaning depending on which WH-word is used.

だれでも	*dare **demo***	(no matter who it is; anyone)
何でも	*nan **demo***	(no matter what it is; anything)
いつでも	*itsu **demo***	(no matter when; any time)
どこでも	*doko **demo***	(no matter where it is; any place)
どれでも	*dore **demo***	(no matter which it is)

   (1) あの図書館はだれでも入れます。

   Ano toshokan wa dare demo hairemasu.

   (Anyone can enter that library.)

   (2) いつでもかまいませんよ。

   Itsu demo kamaimasen yo.

   (Any time will be fine.)

2. The particle *demo* should not be confused with the particle combination *de+mo*, as in (1) below where *de* is a particle of location (=*de*[1]), and in (2) where *de* is a particle of means (=*de*[2]).

   (1) 日本でもインフレが大きな問題になっている。

   *Nihon **de mo** infure ga ōkina mondai ni natte iru.*

   (In Japan, too, inflation is a big problem.)

   (2) そこはバスでも行けますか。

   *Soko wa basu **de mo** ikemasu ka.*

   (Can you also get there by bus?)

   (⇒ ***de***[1]; ***de***[2])

dō どう　　*adv.*

> an interrogative adverb which asks about the state of s.o. / s.t. or the way of doing s.t.　　　　how; in what way

♦ **Key Sentence**

Topic (subject)		
お母さん	は	どう（です　か）。
O-kā-san	*wa*	*dō (desu ka)*.
(How's your mother?)		

Examples

(a) 新しいアパートはどうですか。
　　Atarashii apāto wa dō desu ka.
　　(How's your new apartment?)

(b) コーヒーはどうですか。
　　Kōhi wa dō desu ka.
　　(How is the coffee? / Would you like coffee? / How about coffee?)

(c) 土曜日はどう？
　　Doyōbi wa dō?
　　(How about Saturday?)

Notes

1. The polite version of *dō* is *ikaga*. In very informal speech *desu ka* is omitted after *dō* or *ikaga*.

2. *Dō* and *ikaga* are also used to offer or suggest something, as in Exs. (b) and (c). In this case, *dō* or *ikaga* are asking about the state of the hearer's mind regarding the offer or suggestion rather than about the state of what is being offered or suggested.

3. *Dō* is also used to ask the way of doing something. In this case, *ikaga* is usually not used. Example:

　(1) この言葉はどう読みますか。
　　　Kono kotoba wa dō yomimasu ka.
　　　(How do you read this word?)

4. The idiomatic expression *dō shite* 'lit. doing what' is used to ask manners, reasons or causes. Examples:

(2)　どうして日本語を勉強しているんですか。
　　Dō shite nihongo o benkyōshite iru n desuka.
　　(How (= In what way) are you studying Japanese? / Why are you studying Japanese?)

(3)　この木はどうして枯れたんですか。
　　Kono ki wa dō shite kareta n desu ka.
　　(Why did this tree die?)

As seen in (2), unless the context is clear, *dō shite* is sometimes ambiguous. (The interrogative adverb *naze* 'why' is unambiguous but less colloquial than *dō shite*.)

e へ　*prt.*

> a particle that indicates the direction toward which some directional movement or action proceeds

to; towards
[REL. *made*; *ni*[4]; *ni*[7]]

E

◆**Key Sentence**

	Noun (location)		
私　は　先週 *Watashi wa senshū*	京都 ***Kyōto***	へ *e*	旅行　に　行った / 行きました。 *ryokō ni　itta / ikimashita.*
(I went on a trip to Kyoto last week.)			

Examples

(a) 私は札幌のうちへ飛行機で帰った。
　　Watashi wa Sapporo no uchi e hikōki de kaetta.
　　(I went back home to Sapporo by plane.)

(b) 地震だったのでいそいで外へ出た。
　　Jishin datta node isoide soto e deta.
　　(It was an earthquake, so I went outside quickly.)

(c) 父へ手紙を出したが，まだ返事が来ない。
　　Chichi e tegami o dashita ga, mada henji ga konai.
　　(I sent a letter to my father, but his reply has not come yet.)

[Related Expressions]

I. The particles *e*, *made*, and *ni*[7] focus on direction, course (up to ~), and point of contact, respectively. Thus,

　　[1] はるばる東京まで / ?に / ?へ来た。
　　　　*Harubaru Tōkyō **made** / ?**ni** / ?**e** kita.*
　　　　(I came all the way to Tokyo.)

　　[2] 東京に / へ / *まで十二時に着いた。
　　　　*Tōkyō **ni** / **e** / *__made__ jūniji ni tsuita.*
　　　　(I arrived in Tokyo at 12:00 o'clock.)

　　[3] ニューヨークへ / まで / *にの便はもうありません。
　　　　*Nyūyōku **e** / **made** / *__ni__ no bin wa mō arimasen.*
　　　　(There isn't any flight to / as far as New York any more.)

[4] ここまで / *へ / *にの道は悪かったでしょう。
*Koko **made** / *e / *ni no michi wa warukatta deshō.*
(Your way here must have been rough.)

In actuality, native speakers use *e* and *ni*[7] (of point of contact) almost interchangeably except in the case of [3] (i.e., *ni* cannot be followed by *no*).

II. Even the *ni*[4] of direct contact meaning 'into; onto' can be replaced by *e* as in:

[5] お風呂に / へ入った。
*O-furo **ni** / **e** haitta.*
(Lit. I entered into a bath. (=I took a bath.))

[6] 机の上に / へ乗った。
*Tsukue no ue **ni** / **e** notta.*
(I got onto the table.)

[7] 黒板に / へ漢字を書いた。
*Kokuban **ni** / **e** kanji o kaita.*
(I wrote *kanji* on the blackboard.)

ga[1] が　*prt.*

⎰ a particle which indicates the subject ⎱　　　【REL. *wa*[1] (は)】

◆**Key Sentence**

Subject		Predicate
雨	が	降って いる / います。
Ame	*ga*	*futte　iru / imasu.*
(Lit. Rain is falling (＝It's raining.))		

Examples

(a) 私の部屋にはステレオがあります。
　　Watashi no heya ni wa sutereo ga arimasu.
　　(There is a stereo in my room.)

(b) あ，のり子が走っている。
　　A, Noriko ga hashitte iru.
　　(Oh, Noriko is running.)

(c) A : このレストランは何がおいしいですか。
　　　　Kono resutoran wa nani ga oishiidesu ka.
　　　　(What is good in this restaurant?)

　　B : ステーキがおいしいです。
　　　　Sutēki ga oishiidesu.
　　　　(Steak is good.)

Notes

1. *Ga* marks the subject of a sentence when the information expressed by the subject is first introduced in a discourse. When the subject is presented as the topic (that is, the information has already been introduced into the discourse), however, the topic marker *wa* replaces *ga*. (⇨ **wa**[1] (は)) Consider the following discourse, a typical opening in folktales, which illustrates the different uses of *ga* and *wa*.

　　(1) 昔々一人のおじいさんが住んでいました。おじいさん**は**とても貧乏でした。
　　　　*Mukashimukashi hitori no o-ji-san **ga** sunde imashita. O-ji-san **wa** totemo binbōdeshita.*
　　　　(Once upon a time there lived *an* old man. He (lit. *the* old man) was very poor.)

In the first sentence, *o-ji-san* 'old man' appears for the first time in the discourse; *o-ji-san* is the subject but not the topic in this sentence. Therefore, it is marked by *ga*. The second sentence tells something about the old man introduced in the first sentence. *O-ji-san* is now the topic; therefore, it is marked by *wa* rather than *ga*. Note the parallelism here between *ga* and *wa* in Japanese and *a* and *the* in English.

2. *Ga* is also replaced by *wa* if the subject is in contrast with another element. For example, in Ex. (c), B could also say:

(2) ステーキはおいしいです。
   *Sutēki **wa** oishiidesu.*
   (Stéak is good (but other food is not). / (I don't know about other food but at least) Stéak is good.)

Here, *sutēki* 'steak' is newly introduced in the discourse and is not the topic; yet it is marked by *wa*. This is because *sutēki*, in this case, is being contrasted with other food.

3. Since WH-words like *nani* 'what', *dare* 'who' and *doko* 'what place' can never be topics, they are never marked by *wa*, as in (3).

(3) 今晩だれが / *は来ますか。
   *Konban dare **ga** / ***wa** kimasu ka.*
   (Who is coming tonight?)

4. The subject in subordinate clauses is marked by *ga* unless it is a contrasted element, as seen in (4).

(4) a. 私はデビーが / *はフランスへ行くことを知らなかった。
   *Watashi wa Debi **ga** / ***wa** Furansu e iku koto o shiranakatta.*
   (I didn't know that Debbie was going to France.)

   b. ジーンは僕が / *はアパートを出た時まだ寝ていた。
   *Jin wa boku **ga** / ***wa** apāto o deta toki mada nete ita.*
   (Gene was still in bed when I left my apartment.)

   c. 私が / *はきのう見た映画はドイツの映画だった。
   *Watashi **ga** / ***wa** kinō mita eiga wa Doitsu no eiga datta.*
   (The movie I saw yesterday was a German film.)

Note that topics are not presented in subordinate clauses.

5. In relative clauses, the subject may be marked by *no*, as in (5).

(⇒ Relative Clause, Note 3)

(5)　私のきのう見た映画はドイツの映画だった。

　　　*Watashi **no** kinō mita eiga wa Doitsu no eiga datta.*

　　　(The movie I saw yesterday was a German film.)

6. In some expressions, elements which are considered to be direct objects are presented as subjects and are marked by *ga*.　　(⇨ *~ **wa** ~ **ga***)

(6)　a.　僕はスポーツカーが欲しい。

　　　　　*Boku wa supōtsukā **ga** hoshii.*

　　　　　(I want a sports car.　(Lit. To me, a sports car is desirable.))

　　　b.　春子はスペイン語が分かる。

　　　　　*Haruko wa supeingo **ga** wakaru.*

　　　　　(Haruko understands Spanish.　(Lit. To Haruko, Spanish is understandable.))

7. To sum up the important rules concerning *ga*,

(A)　*Ga* marks the subject when it is newly introduced in a discourse.

(B)　*Wa* replaces *ga* when the subject is a topic or a contrasted element.

(C)　WH-words are always marked by *ga* when they are the subject of a sentence.

(D)　The subject in subordinate clauses is marked by *ga* unless it is a contrasted element.

(E)　When predicates are transitive adjectives or stative transitive verbs, the elements which correspond to the direct object in English are marked by *ga*.

〔Related Expression〕

The topic marker *wa* is often mistaken for a subject marker. It appears to be a subject marker because it often replaces *ga*. (See Notes 1 and 2, and Characteristics of Japanese Grammar, 2. Topic.)　　　　　(⇨ ***wa***¹ (は))

ga² が　　*conj.*

a disjunctive coordinate conjunction that combines two sentences	but 〔REL. *daga*; *dakedo*; *demo*; *keredomo*; *shikashi*〕

◆ **Key Sentence**

Sentence₁		Sentence₂
ジョン は 来た / 来ました *Jon wa kita / kimashita*	が *ga*	メアリー は 来なかった / 来ませんでした。 *Meari wa konakatta / kimasendeshita.*
(John came but Mary didn't (come).)		

Formation

S₁ が S₂
  ga

太郎 は 泳いだ が 次郎 は 泳がなかった。   (Taro swam but Jiro didn't
Tarō wa oyoida ga Jirō wa oyoganakatta.   swim.)

Examples

(a) 私はビールは飲むが酒は飲まない。
    Watashi wa bīru wa nomu ga sake wa nomanai.
    (I drink beer but don't drink *sake*.)

(b) 旅行をしたいがお金がない。
    Ryokō o shitai ga o-kane ga nai.
    (I want to travel but I don't have money.)

Notes

1. *Ga²*, like *but* in English, combines two sentences which express contrastive ideas. However, *ga* is much weaker than *but* in that it is sometimes used simply to combine two sentences for stylistic reasons even if those two sentences do not represent contrastive ideas. For example, the *ga* in (1) is used simply as a transition word to connect two sentences.

   (1) a. パーティーをします**が**来ませんか。
           *Pāti o shimasu **ga** kimasen ka.*
           (We'll have a party. Wouldn't you like to come?)

       b. 田中さんは私のうちにも時々来ます**が**おもしろい人ですね。
           *Tanaka-san wa watashi no uchi ni mo tokidoki kimasu **ga***
           omoshiroi hito desu ne.
           (Mr. Tanaka sometimes comes to my place, too. He is an
           interesting person, isn't he?)

2. *Ga²* makes a sentence unit with the preceding sentence, not with the following sentence. Thus, it is wrong to place a comma before *ga* or to start a sentence with *ga*, as in (2) and (3).

(2) *ジョンは来た，がメアリーは来なかった。
　　Jon wa kita, ga Meari wa konakatta.
　　(John came, but Mary didn't come.)

(3) *ジョンは来た。がメアリーは来なかった。
　　Jon wa kita. Ga Meari wa konakatta.
　　(John came. But Mary didn't come.)

3. S_1 and S_2 in " S_1 *ga* S_2 " must be in the same form whether formal or informal, because they are both independent clauses. (4) and (5) are stylistically awkward.　　　　　　　　　　　　　　　　(⇨ *keredomo*)

(4) ??太郎は泳ぎましたが次郎は泳がなかった。
　　??*Tarō wa **oyogimashita** ga Jirō wa **oyoganakatta**.*
　　(Taro swam but Jiro didn't (swim).)

(5) ?太郎は泳いだが次郎は泳ぎませんでした。
　　?*Tarō wa **oyoida** ga Jirō wa **oyogimasendeshita**.*
　　(Taro swam but Jiro didn't (swim).)

4. S_2 in " S_1 *ga* S_2 " is often omitted when it is understandable from the context and / or the situation, or when the speaker doesn't want to continue for some reason (e.g., the sentence is too direct, impolite, embarrassing, etc.). Examples:

(6) 大じょうぶだと思いますが。
　　Daijōbuda to omoimasu ga.
　　(I think it's all right but . . .)

(7) トムはよく勉強するんですが。
　　Tomu wa yoku benkyōsuru n desu ga.
　　(Tom studies hard but . . .)

5. When " S_1 *ga* S_2 " expresses contrastive ideas, the contrastive *wa* typically appears in S_1 and S_2, as in KS and Ex. (a).　　　　(⇨ *wa¹* (は))

[Related Expressions]

Daga, dakedo, demo, shikashi and *keredomo* express the same idea as *ga*. However, the first four cannot make compound sentences like *ga* does; they must occur at the beginning of a sentence, as in [1].　　　(See Note 2.)

[1] a. S_1 *ga* S_2.
　　b. *S_1 *daga / dakedo / demo / shikashi* S_2.
　　c. S_1. *Daga / Dakedo / Demo / Shikashi* S_2.

Keredomo differs from *ga* in that *keredomo* is a subordinate conjunction meaning 'although'. That is, in "S₁ *keredomo* S₂", S₁ *keredomo* is a subordinate clause and S₂ is a main clause. In "S₁ *ga* S₂", on the other hand, both S₁ and S₂ are independent clauses.

~**garu** ~がる   *aux. v. (Gr. 1)*

| an auxiliary verb attached to a psy-chological / physiological adjective meaning a person other than the speaker shows signs of ~ | show signs of ~ |

G

♦ **Key Sentences**

(A)

Topic (subject)		Direct Object		Adj (*i*) stem	
一男 *Kazuo*	は *wa*	スポーツカー *supōtsukā*	を *o*	欲し ***hoshi***	がった / がりました。 *gatta / garimashita.*

(Lit. Kazuo showed signs of wanting a sports car. (=Kazuo wanted a sports car.))

(B)

Topic (subject)		Direct Object		Adj (*i*) stem V*masu*		
上田さん *Ueda-san*	は *wa*	アイスクリーム *aisukurimu*	を *o*	食べ ***tabe***	た ***ta***	がった / がりました。 *gatta / garimashita.*

(Lit. Mr. Ueda showed signs of wanting to eat ice cream. (=Mr. Ueda wanted to eat ice cream.))

Formation

Adj (*i* / *na*) stem がる
　　　　　　　　　　garu

うれしがる　　(s.o. shows signs of being glad)
ureshigaru

めんどうがる　　(s.o. shows signs of being bothered)
mendōgaru

Examples

(a) スーザンは一人で淋しがっています。

Sūzan wa hitori de sabishigatte imasu.

(Susan feels lonely by herself.)

(b) 子供が眠たがっている。

Kodomo ga nemutagatte iru.

(My child wants to go to sleep.)

Notes

1. There is a group of adjectives which, in the present tense, usually requires the first person (or a person with whom the speaker can empathize) as subject. If the subject of a sentence in which these adjectives occur is not the first person (or one with whom the speaker can empathize), then *garu* is attached to the adjective. Observe the accompanying change of particles from *ga* into *o*.

(1) a. 僕は犬がこわい。

Boku wa inu **ga** kowai.

(Lit. To me dogs are scary. (=I am scared of dogs.))

b. 深田さんは犬をこわがっている。

Fukada-san wa inu **o** kowagatte iru.

(Mr. Fukada fears dogs.)

(2) a. 僕はスポーツカーが欲しい。

Boku wa supōtsukā **ga** hoshii.

(I want a sports car.)

b. 一男はスポーツカーを欲しがっている。

Kazuo wa supōtsukā **o** hoshigatte iru.

(Kazuo wants a sports car.)

If an adjective appears in an embedded clause (except a nominalized clause), the *garu* attachment is unnecessary even if the tense is nonpast and the subject is a person with whom the speaker cannot empathize. Thus,

(3) a. 深田さんは犬がこわいと言った。

Fukada-san wa inu ga **kowai** to itta.

(Mr. Fukada said that he is scared of dogs.)

b. 一男はスポーツカーが欲しいそうだ。

Kazuo wa supōtsukā ga **hoshii** sōda.

(I heard that Kazuo wants a sports car.)

(⇨ **hoshii**[1], Note 3)

2. *Garu* conjugates as a Gr. 1 verb. Thus,

欲しが-
hoshiga-

らない	(inf, neg, nonpast)
ranai	
ります	(fml, nonpast)
rimasu	
る	(inf, nonpast)
ru	
れば	(conditional)
reba	
ろう	(volitional)
rō	
って	(*te*-form)
tte	
った	(inf, past)
tta	

3. The following psychological and physiological adjectives are commonly used with *garu*.

Psychology		Physiology	
(Adj (*i*))		(Adj (*i*))	
欲しい *hoshii*	(want)→欲しがる *hoshi**garu***	痛い *itai*	(painful)→痛がる *ita**garu***
うれしい *ureshii*	(happy)→うれしがる *ureshi**garu***	苦しい *kurushii*	(painful)→苦しがる *kurushi**garu***
淋しい *sabishii*	(lonely)→淋しがる *sabishi**garu***	かゆい *kayui*	(itchy)→かゆがる *kayu**garu***
～たい *~tai*	(want to)→～たがる *~ta**garu***	寒い *samui*	(cold)→寒がる *samu**garu***
こわい *kowai*	(scary)→こわがる *kowa**garu***	暑い *atsui*	(hot)→暑がる *atsu**garu***
羨しい *urayamashii*	(envious)→羨しがる *urayamashi**garu***	だるい *darui*	(languid)→だるがる *daru**garu***
おもしろい *omoshiroi*	(amusing)→おもしろがる *omoshiro**garu***	くすぐったい *kusuguttai*	(ticklish)→くすぐったがる *kusugutta**garu***

(Adj (*na*))
迷惑だ (troublesome)→迷惑がる *meiwakuda*　　　　*meiwaku**garu***
いやだ　　(dislike)→いやがる *iyada*　　　　　*iya**garu***

4. A limited number of ~*garu* forms have derived noun forms. The form is ~*gari* (*ya*), meaning 'a person who shows signs of being ~'.

（⇨ **-ya**）

淋しがり (屋)
sabishigari (*ya*)
(a person who always feels lonely)

こわがり (屋)
kowagari (*ya*)
(a person who is easily frightened)

寒がり (屋)
samugari (*ya*)
(a person who is sensitive to cold)

暑がり (屋)
atsugari (*ya*)
(a person who is sensitive to heat)

goro ごろ　　*suf.*

approximately (with a specific point of time)	about; around 【REL. *kurai* / *gurai*】

◆ **Key Sentence**

Topic (subject)		Noun (time)		Predicate
鈴木さん *Suzuki-san*	は *wa*	朝　七時 *asa*　**shichiji**	ごろ *goro*	うち を 出る / 出ます。 *uchi o deru / demasu.*
(Mr. Suzuki leaves home at about 7:00 o'clock in the morning.)				

Formation

N (time) ごろ（に）
　　　　　goro (*ni*)

三時 ごろ（に）　（at about 3 o'clock）
sanji *goro* (*ni*)

Examples

(a)　A：いつごろ北京に行きますか。
　　　Itsu goro Pekin ni ikimasu ka.
　　　(About when are you going to Beijing?)

　　B：来年の六月ごろ行きます。
　　　Rainen no rokugatsu goro ikimasu.
　　　(I'm going there around June of next year.)

(b)　A：今朝は何時ごろまで寝ていましたか。
　　　Kesa wa nanji goro made nete imashita ka.
　　　(Until about what time were you asleep this morning?)

　　B：十時ごろまで寝ていました。
　　　Jūji goro made nete imashita.
　　　(I was asleep until about 10 o'clock.)

(c)　去年の今ごろは大雪でしたね。
　　Kyonen no ima goro wa ōyuki deshita ne.
　　(About this time last year it snowed heavily, didn't it?)

Notes

1. *Goro* is used with a specific point of time. Thus, the following sentence is unacceptable.

　(1)　*夜ごろテレビを見ていました。
　　　*Yoru **goro** terebi o mite imashita.
　　　(*I was watching TV about at night.)

2. Depending on the speaker's perspective, time expressions other than exact time expressions can be perceived as points in time. Thus, in Ex. (a), the month of June is a point in time from the speaker's viewpoint. In these cases, *goro* seems easier to use grammatically if there is some distance between the time of the event and the time of speech, as seen in the following examples.

(2) ??来年の夏ごろ山中さんに会います。

   ??*Rainen no natsu **goro** Yamanaka-san ni aimasu.*

   (*I will see Mr. Yamanaka around next summer.)

(3) 再来年の夏ごろ山中さんに会います。

   *Sarainen no natsu **goro** Yamanaka-san ni aimasu.*

   (I will see Mr. Yamanaka in the summer in a couple of years.)

(4) ?? 去年の夏ごろ山中さんに会いました。

   ??*Kyonen no natsu **goro** Yamanaka-san ni aimashita.*

   (*I met Mr. Yamanaka around the summer of last year.)

(5) おととしの夏ごろ山中さんに会いました。

   *Ototoshi no natsu **goro** Yamanaka-san ni aimashita.*

   (I met Mr. Yamanaka sometime during the summer of the year before last.)

[Related Expression]

Goro is different from *kurai | gurai* ' about' in that the latter is used with specific quantity expressions. Thus,

[1] 僕は三時ごろに寝ました。

   *Boku wa sanji **goro** ni nemashita.*

   (I went to sleep at about 3 o'clock.)

[2] 僕は三時間ぐらい寝ました。

   *Boku wa sanjikan **gurai** nemashita.*

   (I slept about three hours.)

goto ni ごとに   *prt.*

S.t. takes place regularly in succession after a certain temporal or spatial interval.	every **[REL.** *mai*; *oki ni*]

◆Key Sentences

(A)

Topic (subject)		Number-Counter		
私 *Watashi*	は *wa*	三時間 **san-jikan**	ごと に *goto ni*	薬 を 飲んだ / 飲みました。 *kusuri o nonda / nomimashita.*

(I took medicine every three hours.)

(B)

Topic (subject)		Noun		
正月 *Shōgatsu*	は *wa*	家 **ie**	ごと に *goto ni*	門松 を 立てる / 立てます。 *kadomatsu o tateru / tatemasu.*

(They put up pine tree decorations at every house on New Year's Day.)

Examples

(a) 一課ごとに試験がある。
Ikka goto ni shiken ga aru.
(There is a test after every lesson.)

(b) 学期ごとに先生がかわる。
Gakki goto ni sensei ga kawaru.
(Every semester teachers change.)

(c) 木村さんは会う人ごとに挨拶している。
Kimura-san wa au hito goto ni aisatsushite iru.
(Mr. Kimura greets every one he meets.)

(d) 三日ごとにテニスをしています。
Mikka goto ni tenisu o shite imasu.
(I'm playing tennis every third day.)

[Related Expression]

Qki ni indicates that something is repeated at certain intervals. Although its usage is comparable to *goto ni*, note the distinct difference in meanings in examples [1a] and [1b].

[1] a. この電車は二駅おきに止まる。
*Kono densha wa futa eki **oki ni** tomaru.*
(This train stops at every third station.)

b. この電車は二駅ごとに止まる。

*Kono densha wa futa eki **goto ni** tomaru.*

(This train stops at every other station.)

When a time expression precedes *oki ni* or *goto ni*, there is no difference in meaning, if an event takes place at one point in time as in [2a]. But there is difference in meaning, if an event takes place within a certain period of time as in [2b].

[2] a. 電車は五分おきに / ごとに出る。

*Densha wa gofun **oki ni** / **goto ni** deru.*

(The train leaves every five minutes.)

b. 私は二日おきに / ごとに花子と会っている。

*Watashi wa futsuka **oki ni** / **goto ni** Hanako to atte iru.*

(I'm seeing Hanako every third day / every other day.)

~hajimeru ~はじめる   *aux. v. (Gr. 2)*

S.o. / s.t. begins to do s.t. or begins
to be in some state.

begin to
【REL. *~dasu*; *kuru*[2]】
(ANT. *~owaru*)

◆ **Key Sentence**

	V*masu*	
あした から レポート を *Ashita kara repōto o*	**書き** ***kaki***	はじめる / はじめます。 *hajimeru / hajimemasu.*
(I'll begin to write my paper tomorrow.)		

Formation

V*masu*   はじめる
          hajimeru

話しはじめる   (s.o. begins to talk)
hanashihajimeru

食べはじめる   (s.o. begins to eat)
tabehajimeru

Examples

(a) 私は八月から源氏物語を読みはじめました。
    Watashi wa hachigatsu kara Genjimonogatari o yomihajimemashita.
    (I began to read *The Tale of Genji* in August.)

(b) 日本の経済は1964年の東京オリンピックのころから強くなりはじめた。
    *Nihon no keizai wa sen-kyūhyaku-rokujūyo(n)nen no Tōkyō Orinpikku no
    koro kara tsuyoku narihajimeta.*
    (The Japanese economy began to strengthen about the time of the 1964
    Tokyo Olympics.)

(c) A: いつから切手を集めはじめたんですか。
       Itsu kara kitte o atsumehajimeta n desu ka.
       (When did you start to collect stamps?)

    B: 子供の時から集めはじめました。
       Kodomo no toki kara atsume hajimemashita.
       (I started to collect them when (lit. since) I was a child.)

Notes

1. V*masu*+*hajimeru* conjugates exactly like the Gr. 2 Verb *hajimeru*.

話しはじめ- *hanashihajime-* 食べはじめ- *tabehajime-*	ない *nai*	(inf, neg, nonpast)
	ます *masu*	(fml, nonpast)
	る *ru*	(inf, nonpast)
	れば *reba*	(conditional)
	よう *yō*	(volitional)
	て *te*	(*te*-form)
	た *ta*	(inf, past)

2. For the sentence (1) below, there are two honorific versions, depending on which part of V*masu*+*hajimeru* is changed into an honorific form; if the V*masu* is changed into an honorific form, it will become (2a) and if the entire V*masu*+*hajimeru* is changed into an honorific form, it will become (2b).

  (1) 先生は本を書きはじめた。
      *Sensei wa hon o **kakihajimeta**.*
      (The teacher began to write a book.)

  (2) a. 先生はご本をお書きになりはじめた。
         *Sensei wa go-hon o **o-kaki ni narihajimeta**.*

     b. 先生はご本をお書きはじめになった。
        *Sensei wa go-hon o **o-kakihajime ni natta**.*

        (⇨ *o ~ ni naru*)

3. *~hajimeru* is normally attached to a non-punctual verb (such as *yomu* 'read', *kaku* 'write' and *miru* 'see'). If the subject is plural, however, the verb can be a punctual verb (such as *tsuku* 'arrive', *kuru* 'come' and *shinu* 'die'). (⇨ Appendix 2D) Thus,

(3) 上田さんは新聞を読みはじめました。
Ueda-san wa shinbun o yomihajimemashita.
(Mr. Ueda began to read a newspaper.)

(4) 人々 / *花子が会場に着きはじめました。
*Hitobito | *Hanako ga kaijō ni tsukihajimemashita.*
(People / *Hanako began to arrive at the meeting room.)

hazu はず   *n.*

```
a dependent noun which expresses
the speaker's expectation that s.t. will
take place or took place or that s.o. /
s.t. is or was in some state
```

I expect that ~ ; It is expected
that ~ ; ~ is expected to; I am
fairly certain that ~ ; should;
ought to; It is natural that ~ ;
No wonder ~

◆Key Sentence

Sentence (informal)†	
クラークさん は パーティー に **行く** *Kurāku-san wa pātī ni **iku***	はず だ / です。 *hazu da / desu.*
(I expect that Mr. Clark will go to the party.)	

†*Da* after Adj (*na*) and N changes to *na* and *no*, respectively.

Formation

(i) {V / Adj (*i*)} inf はず だ
　　　　　　　　　hazu da

　　{話す　 / 話した}　はず だ　　(It is expected that s.o. will talk / talked.)
　　{*hanasu | hanashita*} *hazu da*

　　{高い / 高かった}　はず だ　　(It is expected that s.t. is / was expensive.)
　　{*takai | takakatta*} *hazu da*

(ii) Adj (*na*) stem　{な / だった} はず だ
　　　　　　　　　{*na | datta*}　*hazu da*

　　{静かな　 /静かだった}　はず だ　　(It is expected that s.t. is / was
　　{*shizukana | shizukadatta*} *hazu da*　　quiet.)

(iii) N {の / だった} はず だ
　　　　{no / datta}　hazu da

　　{先生 の / 先生 だった} はず だ　　(It is expected that s.o. is / was a
　　{sensei no / sensei datta}　hazu da　teacher.)

(a) 大野先生はサンドラを知っているはずです。
　　Ōno-sensei wa Sandora o shitte iru hazu desu.
　　(I expect that Prof. Ono knows Sandra.)

(b) あの本は高かったはずだ。
　　Ano hon wa takakatta hazu da.
　　(I expect that book was expensive.)

(c) そのアパートはきれいなはずです。
　　Sono apāto wa kireina hazu desu.
　　(I expect that apartment is clean.)

(d) カールソンさんは昔先生だったはずだ。
　　Kāruson-san wa mukashi sensei datta hazu da.
　　(I'm fairly sure that Ms. Carlson was a teacher before.)

1. "S *hazu*" expresses the speaker's expectation, not in the sense of hoping or looking forward to something, but in the sense that the proposition expressed by S should be true or come true. Thus, when the speaker uses *hazu*, he is not merely guessing, but stating a proposition based on reliable information or knowledge. (⇒ ***darō***; ***rashii***; ***sōda*²**; ***yōda***)

2. *Hazu* is a dependent noun and cannot be used alone. It is always modified by a sentence or a demonstrative such as *sono* 'that' and *konna* 'like this'. "Demonstrative *hazu*" is used when a proposition is known to the hearer from the context, as in (1).

　(1) A : マーサも来ますか。
　　　　　Māsa mo kimasu ka.
　　　　　(Is Martha coming, too?)

　　　　B : はい，**そのはず**です。
　　　　　Hai, **sono hazu** *desu.*
　　　　　(Yes, I expect so.)

3. Negative expectations can be expressed in two ways:
(A) S (negative) *hazu da*

(2) クラークさんはパーティーに行かないはずだ。

*Kurāku-san wa pātī ni ika**nai hazu** da.*

(Lit. I expect that Mr. Clark is not going to the party.

(= I don't expect that Mr. Clark is going to the party.))

(B) S *hazu wa / ga nai*

(3) クラークさんはパーティーに行くはずは / がない。

*Kurāku-san wa pātī ni iku **hazu wa / ga** nai.*

(Lit. I have no expectation that Mr. Clark is going to the party.

(= It is improbable that Mr. Clark will go to the party.))

The assertion in (3) is stronger than that in (2).

4. "S *hazu*" can also be used when the speaker has discovered the reason for an event or a state. In this case, *hazu* means "It is natural that ~." or "No wonder ~." and can be paraphrased as "S *wake da.*" (⇨ **wake da**) Example:

(4) 高いはずだ。これは金だ。

*Takai **hazu** da. Kore wa kin da.*

(No wonder this is expensive. It's gold.)

5. When "S *hazu*" modifies a noun, that is, when "S *hazu*" is a relative clause, *no* follows, as in (5).　　　　　　　(⇨ Relative Clause)

(5) 山口さんに出したはずの手紙が床に落ちていた。

*Yamaguchi-san ni dashita **hazu no** tegami ga yuka ni ochite ita.*

(I found the letter I thought I had sent to Mr. Yamaguchi on the floor.)

---

hodo ほど　　*prt.*

a particle which indicates an extent or a degree to which s.o. / s.t. does s.t. or is in some state	to the extent of; to the extent that ~; (not as) ~ as ~; about 〖REL. *bakari*; *kurai*〗

♦**Key Sentences**

(A)

Topic (subject)		Noun		Predicate (negative)
私 *Watashi*	は *wa*	**ケン** ***Ken***	ほど *hodo*	強くない / 強くありません。 *tsuyokunai* / *tsuyokuarimasen*.
(Lit. I'm not strong to Ken's extent. (=I'm not as strong as Ken.))				

(B)

Topic (subject)		Sentence (informal)†		Predicate
この　仕事 *Kono shigoto*	は *wa*	子供　でも　**出来る** *kodomo demo **dekiru***	ほど *hodo*	やさしい / やさしいです。 *yasashii* / *yasashiidesu*.
(Lit. This job is easy to the extent that even a child can do it. (=This job is so easy that even a child can do it.))				

†*Da* after Adj(*na*) and N changes to *na* and *de aru*, respectively.

Formation

(i) N ほど
　　　　hodo

　　君　ほど　　(as you)
　　kimi hodo

(ii) Demonstrative ほど
　　　　　　　　　hodo

　　それ　ほど　　(to that extent)
　　sore hodo

(iii) Sinf ほど
　　　　hodo

　　家　が　倒れる　ほど　　(to the extent that houses would fall down)
　　ie ga taoreru hodo

Examples

(a) 僕は君ほど速く歩けません。
　　Boku wa kimi hodo hayaku arukemasen.
　　(I can't walk as fast as you can.)

(b) ジェニファーほどよく勉強する学生はいない。

　　Jenifā hodo yoku benkyōsuru gakusei wa inai.

　　(There is no student who studies as hard as Jennifer.)

(c) 私は西田さんがあれほどピアノがひけるとは思わなかった。

　　Watashi wa Nishida-san ga are hodo piano ga hikeru to wa omowana-katta.

　　(I didn't think that Mr. Nishida could play the piano that well (lit. to that extent).)

(d) ルイスさんの日本語は太田先生も外国人だと気づかなかったほど上手です。

　　Ruisu-san no nihongo wa Ōta-sensei mo gaikokujin da to kizukanakatta hodo jōzudesu.

　　(Mr. Lewis's Japanese is so good that even Prof. Ota didn't notice he was a foreigner.)

H

Notes

1. When *hodo* is preceded by a noun, the predicate must be negative, as in KS(A), Exs. (a) and (b). The following sentences are ungrammatical.

　　(1)　*私は太郎ほど強い。

　　　　Watashi wa Tarō **hodo tsuyoi.*

　　　　(I am as strong as Taro.)

　　(2)　*フットボールほどおもしろいスポーツはたくさんある。

　　　　Futtobōru **hodo omoshiroi supōtsu wa takusan aru.*

　　　　(There are many sports which are as interesting as football.)

If a sentence or a demonstrative modifies *hodo*, however, the predicate of the main clause can be either affirmative or negative, as in KS(B), Ex. (d) and (3).

　　(3)　その仕事はそれほどやさしいんですか。

　　　　*Sono shigoto wa sore **hodo** yasashii n desu ka.*

　　　　(Is that job that easy (lit. easy to that extent)?)

2. When *hodo* is used with a quantifier, it means 'about'. Example:

　　(4)　ビールを三本ほど飲みました。

　　　　*Biru o sanbon **hodo** nomimashita.*

　　　　(I drank about three bottles of beer.)

[Related Expressions]

Bakari and *kurai* also mean 'about' when they are used with a number and a counter. The difference among the three is that *bakari* and *hodo* can be used with an exact number or amount of something, whereas *kurai* cannot, as seen in [1].

[1] そのりんごを二つばかり / ほど / *くらいください。
    *Sono ringo o futatsu **bakari** | **hodo** | *kurai kudasai.*
    (Please give me two of those apples.)

In the situation in [1] the speaker does not want *about* two apples but *exactly* two apples, and, in this case, *kurai* cannot be used. It is a very common practice in Japanese to avoid asking for exact numbers or amounts, and the practice comes from the idea that being straightforward or direct is impolite. This can be observed in many verbal and nonverbal expressions in Japanese and also in the manners of the Japanese people.

---

hō ga ii ほうがいい   *phr.*

<table>
<tr><td>It is strongly suggested that s.o. do s.t.</td><td>had better do s.t.
【REL. *tara dō desu ka*】</td></tr>
</table>

◆**Key Sentence**

	Vinf·past	
日本語 の 本 を *Nihongo no hon o*	読んだ **yonda**	ほう が いい / いいです。 *hō ga ii / iidesu.*
(You'd better read Japanese books.)		

Formation

Vinf·past ほう が いい
　　　　　hō ga ii

話した ほう が いい   (had better talk)
hanashita hō ga ii

食べた ほう が いい   (had better eat)
tabeta hō ga ii

Examples

(a) 野菜も食べたほうがいいよ。

Yasai mo tabeta hō ga ii yo.

(You'd better eat vegetables, too.)

(b) もう帰ったほうがいいですか。

Mō kaetta hō ga iidesu ka.

(Had I better go home now?)

(c) 和子はもっと英語を勉強したほうがいいね。

Kazuko wa motto eigo o benkyōshita hō ga ii ne.

(Kazuko had better study English harder.)

Notes

1. Vinf·past *hō ga ii* is an idiomatic expression of the comparative structure and expresses a strong suggestion.   (⇨ ~ **hō ga** ~ **yori**)

2. The second person subject in declarative sentences and the first person subject in interrogative sentences are usually omitted. (KS and Exs. (a) and (b)) When the subject is the third person, it is not omitted unless it can be clearly understood from the context. In this case, the speaker is telling the hearer what the speaker suggests for the third person. (Ex. (c))

3. Vinf·nonpast can be substituted for Vinf·past, as in (1).

　　(1) 日本語の本を読むほうがいい。

　　　　*Nihongo no hon o **yomu** hō ga ii.*

　　　　(You'd better read Japanese books.)

The meaning of Vinf·nonpast *hō ga ii* is almost the same as that of Vinf·past *hō ga ii* if it is used in situations of suggestion. However, Vinf·past *hō ga ii* may express a stronger suggestion than Vinf·nonpast *hō ga ii*. For instance, in the following example, Vinf·past *hō ga ii* is more appropriate.

　　(2) お前, このごろ麻薬をやってるそうだな。そんなもの**止めた** / ??止めるほうがいいぜ。

　　　　*Omae, konogoro mayaku o yatteru sō da na. Sonna mono **ya-meta** / ??**yameru** hō ga ii ze.*

　　　　(I heard you are taking drugs these days. You'd better stop such things, I tell you.)

4. "Had better not do s.t." is expressed by Vneg *nai hō ga ii*. Example:

(3) コーヒーを飲まないほうがいい。

*Kōhi o **nomanai** hō ga ii.*

(You'd better not drink coffee.)

Note that the verb must be in the nonpast negative form in this expression. The following is ungrammatical.

(4) *コーヒーを飲まなかったほうがいい。

Kōhi o **nomanakatta hō ga ii.*

(You'd better not drink coffee.)

H

~hō ga ~yori ~ほうが~より   *phr.*

| In comparing two entities, one is in some state or does s.t. more than the other. | ~ be more (Adj.) than ~ ; ~ do s.t. more (Adv.) than ~ do 【REL. *yori*】 |

◆**Key Sentences**

(A)

Noun₁			Noun₂		Predicate
石田さん ***Ishida-san***	の *no*	ほう　が *hō ga*	私 ***watashi***	より *yori*	若い / 若いです。 *wakai / wakaidesu.*
(Mr. Ishida is younger than I am.)					
私 ***Watashi***	の *no*	ほう　が *hō ga*	上田さん ***Ueda-san***	より *yori*	よく 食べる / 食べます。 *yoku taberu / tabemasu.*
(I eat more than Ms. Ueda does.)					

(B)

Sentence₁ (informal)†		Sentence₂ (informal)†		Predicate
車　で 行く ***Kuruma de iku***	ほう　が *hō ga*	バス で 行く ***basu de iku***	より *yori*	安い / 安いです。 *yasui / yasuidesu.*
(Going by car is cheaper than going by bus.)				

†*Da* after Adj(*na*) and N changes to *na* and *de aru*, respectively.

Formation

KS(A):

N の ほう が N より
no hō ga yori

先生 の ほう が 学生 より (Teachers are more ~ than students.)
sensei no hō ga gakusei yori

KS(B):

(i) {V / Adj (*i*)} inf ほう が; {V / Adj (*i*)} inf・nonpast より
  hō ga *yori*

{話す / 話した} ほう が (Talking / Having talked is more ~);
{*hanasu* / *hanashita*} *hō ga*

聞く より (than hearing)
kiku yori

{食べる / 食べた} ほう が (Eating / Having eaten is more ~);
{*taberu* / *tabeta*} *hō ga*

寝る より (than sleeping)
neru yori

{高い / 高かった} ほう が (Being / Having been expensive is more ~);
{*takai* / *takakatta*} *hō ga*

安い より (than being cheap)
yasui yori

(ii) Adj (*na*) stem {な / だった} ほう が; Adj (*na*) stem な より
  {*na* / *datta*} *hō ga* *na yori*

{静かな / 静かだった} ほう が (Being / Having been quiet is more
{*shizukana* / *shizukadatta*} *hō ga* ~);

きれい な より (than being pretty)
kirei na yori

(iii) N {で ある / だった} ほう が; N で ある より
  {*de aru* / *datta*} *hō ga* *de aru yori*

{先生 で ある / 先生 だった} ほう が (Being / Having been a
{*sensei de aru* / *sensei datta*} *hō ga* teacher is more ~);

学生 で ある より (than being a student)
gakusei de aru yori

Examples

(a) このカメラのほうがあのカメラより好きです。
Kono kamera no hō ga ano kamera yori sukidesu.
(I like this camera better than that camera.)

(b) ジェフのほうが私より速く走れる。
Jefu no hō ga watashi yori hayaku hashireru.
(Jeff can run faster than I can.)

(c) 私が話すほうが君が話すよりいいでしょう。
Watashi ga hanasu hō ga kimi ga hanasu yori ii deshō.
(It's probably better for me to talk than for you to talk.)

(d) もちろん，安いほうが高いよりうれしいです。
Mochiron, yasui hō ga takai yori ureshiidesu.
(Of course, I'm happier when it is cheap than when it is expensive.)

(e) 子供は元気なほうが静かなより安心だ。
Kodomo wa genkina hō ga shizukana yori anshinda.
(Talking about children, you feel more at ease when they are lively than when they are quiet.)

(f) 私は女であるほうが男であるより楽しいと思う。
Watashi wa onna de aru hō ga otoko de aru yori tanoshii to omou.
(I think it's more enjoyable to be a woman than to be a man.)

Notes

1. In Japanese there are no comparative forms of adjectives and adverbs. The idea of comparison is expressed by the " X *no hō ga* Y *yori* " pattern. Y *yori* may be omitted if it is clear from the context or the situation. Example:

   (1) A : トムとジョンとどちらが強いですか。
   Tomu to Jon to dochira ga tsuyoidesu ka.
   (Who is stronger, Tom or John?)

   B : トムのほうが(ジョンより)強いです。
   Tomu no hō ga (Jon yori) tsuyoidesu.
   (Tom is stronger (than John).)

2. In the " S₁ *hō ga* S₂ *yori* " pattern (KS(B)), S₁ can be either nonpast or past. S₂, however, is always nonpast regardless of the tense of S₁ and the main clause. There are two cases in which S₁ is past. First, S₁ can be past when the whole sentence is about a present or future action or state. In this case, the sentence sounds rather hypothetical. Example:

(2) 私が話したほうが君が話すよりいいでしょう。

*Watashi ga **hanashita** hō ga kimi ga hanasu yori ii deshō.*

(It would probably be better if I talk rather than if you talk.)

S_1 can also be past if the whole sentence is about a past action or state. In this case the sentence is counterfactual. Example:

(3) 私が話したほうが君が話すよりよかった。

*Watashi ga **hanashita** hō ga kimi ga hanasu yori yokatta.*

(It would have been better if I had talked rather than you.)

3. Y *yori* can precede X (*no*) *hō ga*, as in (4).

(4) あのカメラよりこのカメラのほうが好きです。

Ano kamera yori kono kamera no hō ga sukidesu.

(I like this camera better than that camera.)

4. X *no hō* is a noun phrase; therefore, it can also be a direct object, an indirect object, etc. However, when it is used for something other than the subject, the " Y *yori* X *no hō* (*o, ni*, etc.)" order is preferable. Examples:

(5) a. 私はビールより酒のほうをよく飲む。

Watashi wa biru yori sake no hō o yoku nomu.

(I drink *sake* more than beer.)

b. 学生は川田先生より木村先生のほうによく質問に行く。

Gakusei wa Kawada-sensei yori Kimura-sensei no hō ni yoku shitsumon ni iku.

(Students go to Prof. Kimura to ask questions more often than to Prof. Kawada.)

【Related Expression】

The idea of comparison can be expressed by the " X *wa* Y *yori* " pattern, too. (⇒ **yori**) However, when this pattern is used, X must have already been established as a topic. Thus, in a context like [1], the " X *wa* Y *yori* " pattern cannot be used.

[1] A : トムとジョンとどちらが強いですか。

Tomu to Jon to dochira ga tsuyoidesu ka.

(Who is stronger, Tom or John?)

B : トムのほうが / *トムは（ジョンより）強いです。

*Tomu **no hō ga** / *Tomu wa (Jon yori) tsuyoidesu.*

(Tom is stronger (than John).)

On the other hand, in a context like [2], the "X *wa* Y *yori*" pattern is preferable, because X has already been established in the previous sentence.

[2] トムはとても強いです。彼は / ??彼のほうがジョンより強いです。
*Tomu wa totemo tsuyoidesu. Kare **wa** / ??Kare **no hō ga** Jon yori tsuyoidesu.*
(Tom is very strong. He is stronger than John.)

H

hoshii[1] ほしい

S.t. is desired by the speaker.   want (s.t.)
                                                    【REL. *tai*】

♦ **Key Sentences**

(A)

Topic (experiencer)		Desired Object		
私	は	車	が	ほしい / ほしいです。
Watashi	*wa*	*kuruma*	*ga*	*hoshii / hoshiidesu.*
(I want a car.)				

(B)

Topic (experiencer)		Desired Object		
弟	は	僕 の 自転車	を	ほしがって いる / います。
Otōto	*wa*	*boku no jitensha*	*o*	*hoshigatte iru / imasu.*
(My little brother wants my bike.)				

Examples

(a) 私は日本人の友達がほしい。
Watashi wa nihonjin no tomodachi ga hoshii.
(I want a Japanese friend.)

(b) あなたは今何がほしいですか。
Anata wa ima nani ga hoshiidesu ka.
(What do you want now?)

(c) パムはステレオをほしがっている。

Pamu wa sutereo o hoshigatte iru.

(Pam wants a stereo.)

Notes

1. The *i*-type adjective *hoshii* expresses a person's desire for some object. Like other stative transitive adjectives, *hoshii* takes the *wa-ga* construction, where the experiencer is marked by *wa* and the desired object by *ga*. (In subordinate clauses the experiencer is also marked by *ga*.)　　　　　　　　　　　　　　　　　　　　(⇨ *~ wa ~ ga*)

2. Since *hoshii* expresses a very personal feeling, the experiencer is usually the first person in declarative sentences and the second person in interrogative sentences, as in KS(A), Exs. (a) and (b). The third person's desire is usually expressed by *hoshigatte iru* 'Lit. be showing the sign of wanting (s.t.)', as in KS(B) and Ex. (c). (⇨ *garu*) It is noted that when *hoshigatte iru* is used, the desired object is marked by *o*.

3. It is, however, acceptable to use *hoshii* in connection with the third person experiencer in the following situations:

   (1) *In the past tense*

   モーリスはいいステレオがほしかった。

   *Mōrisu wa ii sutereo ga hoshi**katta**.*

   (Maurice wanted a good stereo set.)

   (2) *In indirect / semi-direct speech*

   a. ジョイもほしいと言っている。

   *Joi mo hoshii **to itte iru**.*

   (Joy says she wants it, too.)

   b. オスカーもほしいそうだ。

   *Osukā mo hoshii **sōda**.*

   (I heard that Oscar wants it, too.)

   (3) *In explanatory situations*

   パメラはイヤリングがほしいんです。

   *Pamera wa iyaringu ga hoshii **n desu**.*

   ((The explanation is that) Pamela wants a pair of earrings.)

   　　　　　　　　　　　　　　　　　　　　　　　　　(⇨ *no da*)

(4) *In conjecture expressions*

a. フランシスはうで時計がほしいらしい。
*Furanshisu wa udedokei ga hoshii **rashii**.*
(It seems that Francis wants a wrist watch.)

b. コニーは人形がほしいようだ。
*Koni wa ningyō ga hoshii **yōda**.*
(It appears that Connie wants a doll.)

hoshii² ほしい   *aux. adj. (i)*

| want s.o. (who is not higher in status than the speaker) to do s.t. | want (s.o.) to do (s.t.) 【REL. *moraitai*; **tai**】 |

◆ **Key Sentence**

Topic (experiencer)		Indirect Object			Vte	
私	は	あなた	に	英語 を	教えて	ほしい / ほしいです。
Watashi	*wa*	*anata*	*ni*	*eigo o*	***oshiete***	*hoshii / hoshiidesu.*
(I want you to teach me English.)						

Formation

Vte ほしい
    hoshii

話して ほしい   (want (s.o.) to talk)
hanashite hoshii

食べて ほしい   (want (s.o.) to eat)
tabete hoshii

Examples

(a) 私は子供達に私と一緒に住んでほしい。
Watashi wa kodomotachi ni watashi to isshoni sunde hoshii.
(I want my children to live together with me.)

(b) あなたはだれに来てほしいですか。

Anata wa dare ni kite hoshiidesu ka.

(Who do you want to come?)

Notes

1. *Hoshii* is used as an auxiliary with V*te* to mean ' want (s.o.) to do (s.t.) '. When the experiencer wants a person X to do something, X is marked by *ni*. *Hoshii* is not used if X has a higher status than the experiencer. Thus, the following sentence is not appropriate when the speaker is a student of Prof. Yoshida's. (See Related Expression, [2] for the correct sentence in that situation.)

   (1) 私は吉田先生に来てほしい。

   Watashi wa Yoshida-sensei ni kite hoshii.

   (I want Prof. Yoshida to come.)

2. When V*te hoshii* is used, the experiencer is usually the first person in declarative sentences (KS, Ex. (a)) and the second person in interrogative sentences (Ex. (b)). If the experiencer is the third person, V*te moraita-gatte iru* ' (lit.) be showing the sign of wanting to receive the favor of doing s.t. from s.o.' is used, as in (2). (⇨ *morau*²; *tai*; *garu*)

   (2) アダムスさんはフランシスにこの仕事をしてもらいたがっている。

   Adamusu-san wa Furanshisu ni kono shigoto o shite moraita-gatte iru.

   (Mr. Adams wants Francis to do this job.)

[Related Expression]

The same idea can also be expressed by V*te moraitai.* (⇨ *morau*²; *tai*) Example:

   [1] 私はあなたに英語を教えてもらいたい。

   Watashi wa anata ni eigo o oshiete moraitai.

   (I want you to teach me English.)

This pattern can be used when the experiencer wants someone who has higher status to do something. In this case, *itadaku*, the humble version of *morau*, is used instead of *morau*. Example:

   [2] 私は吉田先生に来ていただきたい。

   Watashi wa Yoshida-sensei ni kite itadakitai.

   (I would like Prof. Yoshida to come.)

ichiban 一番 *adv.*

| a superlative marker | most |

♦ **Key Sentence**

Noun			Subject			Adjective
クラス	(の中) で	大川さん	が	一番	頭 が いい。	
Kurasu	*(no naka) de*	*Ōkawa-san*	*ga*	*ichiban*	*atama ga ii.*	
(Mr. Okawa is the brightest in the class.)						

Formation

(i) 一番　　Adj (*i* / *na*)
　　ichiban

　　一番　　{高い / 高かった}　　(s.t. is / was the highest)
　　ichiban {*takai* / *takakatta*}

　　一番　　{静かだ　 / 静かだった}　　(s.t. is / was the most quiet)
　　ichiban {*shizukada* / *shizukadatta*}

(ii) 一番　　{Adj (*i*) stem く / Adj (*na*) stem に}
　　Ichiban　　　　　　*ku*　　　　　　*ni*

　　一番　　高く　　(most highly)
　　ichiban *takaku*

　　一番　　静かに　　(most quietly)
　　ichiban *shizukani*

Examples

(a) A : この中でどの映画が一番おもしろいですか。
　　　　Kono naka de dono eiga ga ichiban omoshiroidesu ka.
　　　　(Among these, which movie is the most interesting?)

　　B : この日本の映画でしょう。
　　　　Kono Nihon no eiga deshō.
　　　　(This Japanese movie, I guess.)

(b) A : 松本さんと池田さんと清水さんの中で、だれが一番(よく)出来ますか。
　　　　Matsumoto-san to Ikeda-san to Shimizu-san no naka de, dare ga ichiban (yoku) dekimasu ka.
　　　　(Among Mr. Matsumoto, Mr. Ikeda and Mr. Shimizu, who is the best student (lit. can do best)?)

B：池田さんです。

Ikeda-san desu.

(Mr. Ikeda is.)

(c) 日本で一番きれいな所はどこですか。

Nihon de ichiban kireina tokoro wa doko desu ka.

(Lit. Where is the most scenic place in Japan? (＝Which place is the most scenic in Japan?))

Note

Ichiban cannot be affixed directly to a noun as in **ichiban sensei*, meaning 'the best teacher'. It should precede an adjective, as in *ichiban ii sensei*. If the meaning is predictable, however, the adverbial form of adjectives, esp. *yoku* 'well, frequently', may be omitted, as in Ex. (b).

I

iku¹ 行く   *v. (Gr. 1)*

> S.o. or s.t. moves in a direction away from the speaker or the speaker's viewpoint.

go; come

【REL. *kuru*¹】

◆**Key Sentences**

(A)

Topic (subject)			Noun (direction)		
田中さん *Tanaka-san*	は *wa*	来週 *raishū*	アメリカ ***Amerika***	へ / に *e / ni*	行く / 行きます。 *iku / ikimasu.*
(Mr. Tanaka is going to America next week.)					

(B)

Topic (subject)		N (location)		N (location)		N (means)		
私 *Watashi*	は *wa*	東京 *Tōkyō*	から *kara*	大阪 *Ōsaka*	まで *made*	バス *basu*	で *de*	行った / *itta* / 行きました。 *ikimashita.*
(I went from Tokyo to Osaka by bus.)								

Examples

(a) 私は毎朝八時に会社に行く。
　　Watashi wa maiasa hachiji ni kaisha ni iku.
　　(I go to work (lit. my company) at eight every morning.)

(b) A：今晩私のうちでパーティーをしますが来ませんか。
　　　Konban watashi no uchi de pātī o shimasu ga kimasen ka.
　　　(We are going to have a party at my place tonight. Wouldn't you like to come?)

　　B：はい，行きます。
　　　Hai, ikimasu.
　　　(Yes, I'll come (lit. go).)

(c) あなたにもその知らせは行きましたか。
　　Anata ni mo sono shirase wa ikimashita ka.
　　(Lit. Did the notice go to you, too? (=Did you get the notice, too?))

(d) その村にもバスは行っている。
　　Sono mura ni mo basu wa itte iru.
　　(The bus goes to the village, too.)

Notes

1. *Iku*[1] is used when someone or something moves in a direction away from the speaker or in a direction away from the speaker's viewpoint, which is not necessarily the speaker's position. (⇨ *kuru*[1]) For example, in the following situation, *iku* is used when the speaker (point C) places his viewpoint near point A.

　　(1) X さんは B に行った。
　　　　X-san wa B ni itta.
　　　　(Mr. X went to B.)　　Mr. X

2. When someone goes to his own "home base" (e.g., *uchi* 'home'), *uchi ni iku* is ungrammatical. In this case, *kaeru* 'return' is used as in *uchi ni kaeru* 'go home'.

3. There are cases where both *kuru* and *iku* can be used with different shades of meaning. Examples:

(2) 君のうちに息子が**来ませんでした** / **行きませんでした**か。

Kimi no uchi ni musuko ga **kimasendeshita** / **ikimasendeshita** ka.

(Didn't my son go to your house?)

(3) [The speaker lives in San Francisco and is calling his friend in New York who is coming to Los Angeles.]

スミスさんは来月ロスアンジェルスに**来る** / **行く**そうですね。

Sumisu-san wa raigetsu Rosuanjerusu ni **kuru** / **iku** sōdesu ne.

(Mr. Smith, I was told that you're coming to Los Angeles next month.)

In (2), when the speaker uses *kuru*, he is putting himself psychologically in the addressee's location; when he uses *iku*, he is not. In (3), *kuru* is more appropriate than *iku* because, in general, a speaker is more empathetic with a location close to his own. The choice of *iku* here definitely implies that the speaker is unusually unempathetic with his neighboring location.

---

iku² 行く   *aux. v. (Gr. 1)*

Some action or state keeps changing from the point in time at which the speaker first describes the action.

go on ~ing; continue; grow; become

【REL. *kuru*²】

◆**Key Sentence**

		V*te*	
これ から は *Kore kara wa*	寒く *samuku*	**なって** ***natte***	行く / 行きます　よ。 *iku	ikimasu　yo.*
(It will get colder (and continue to be that way) from now on.)				

Formation

V*te* 行く
　　iku

話して　行く　　(s.o. continues to talk)
hanashite iku

食べて 行く　　(s.o. continues to eat)
tabete iku

Examples

(a) これからは毎日本を一冊読んで行くつもりです。
　　Kore kara wa mainichi hon o issatsu yonde iku tsumori desu.
　　(I intend to keep reading one book a day from now on.)

(b) これからは暖かくなって行きますよ。
　　Kore kara wa atatakaku natte ikimasu yo.
　　(It will grow warmer (and continue in that way) from now on.)

(c) その頃から日本の経済は強くなって行った。
　　Sono koro kara Nihon no keizai wa tsuyoku natte itta.
　　(The Japanese economy grew stronger (and continued to grow that way) from that time on.)

(d) 分からないことをノートに書いて行った。
　　Wakaranai koto o nōto ni kaite itta.
　　(I went on taking notes on things I didn't understand.)

Notes

1. The point in time at which the action starts is the present time in Exs. (a) and (b) and the past in Exs. (c) and (d), respectively.

2. The following examples use *iku* as a full verb meaning 'to go', and are not the usage of *iku²*.

　　(1) 毎日会社にバスに乗って行く。
　　　　Mainichi kaisha ni basu ni notte iku.

(Lit. I ride a bus every day and go to my company. (=I go to work every day by bus.))

⑵ あのレストランでコーヒーを飲んで行きましょう。

Ano resutoran de kōhi o nonde ikimashō.

(Lit. Let's drink coffee at that restaurant and go. (=Let's drink coffee at that restaurant and then continue on our way.))

【Related Expression】

When a change of state is expressed by *iku²*, as in Exs. (b) and (c), *iku²* can be replaced by *kuru²*, as in [1a] and [1b] below.

[1] a. これからは暖かくなって来ますよ。

Kore kara wa atatakaku natte kimasu yo.

(It will grow warmer from now on.)

b. その頃から日本の経済は強くなって来た。

Sono koro kara Nihon no keizai wa tsuyoku natte kita.

(The Japanese economy grew stronger from that time on.)

The *iku²* versions here are more impersonal and objective than the *kuru²* versions. The latter versions stress that some change is going to involve or has involved the speaker himself, while the former versions are impersonal statements.

---

iru¹ いる *v. (Gr. 2)*

An animate thing exists.	be; exist; stay
	【REL. *aru¹*】

♦ Key Sentences

(A)

Topic (location)			Subject		Quantifier	
この　町	(に)	は	日本人	が	たくさん	いる / います。
Kono machi	(ni)	wa	nihonjin	ga	takusan	iru / imasu.
(Lit. In this town are many Japanese. (=There are many Japanese in this town.))						

(B)

Topic (subject)		Noun (location)		
リー	は	この 寮	に	いる / います。
Ri	*wa*	*kono ryō*	*ni*	*iru / imasu.*
(Lee is in this dorm.)				

Examples

(a) この動物園にはパンダがいます。
　　Kono dōbutsuen ni wa panda ga imasu.
　　(There are pandas in this zoo.)

(b) スチーブはいまロビンのアパートにいる。
　　Suchibu wa ima Robin no apāto ni iru.
　　(Steve is in Robin's apartment now.)

Notes

1. *Iru*¹ expresses existence in terms of animal life. It cannot be used for plant life or inanimate things. Thus, the following sentence is ungrammatical.

　　(1)　*このキャンパスには木がたくさんいる。
　　　　Kono kyanpasu ni wa ki ga takusan **iru.*
　　　　(There are many trees on this campus.)

　　For plants and inanimate things, *aru* is used.　　　　　　　　(⇨ **aru**¹)

2. Two sentence patterns can be used with *iru*¹. In the KS(A) pattern, a location is presented as the topic and what exists there is under focus. In this pattern the location marker *ni* can optionally drop. In the KS(B) pattern, on the other hand, what exists is presented as the topic and where it exists is under focus.　　　　　　　　(⇨ **aru**¹, Note 3)

3. An animate thing or a group or organization of animate things such as a football team can also be in the location position, as seen in (2).

　　(2)　a.　私(に)は子供が三人いる。
　　　　　　Watashi (ni) wa kodomo ga sannin iru.
　　　　　　(Lit. There are three children with me. (=I have three children.))

　　　　b.　このチーム(に)はいいクオーターバックがいる。
　　　　　　Kono chimu (ni) wa ii kuōtābakku ga iru.

(Lit. There is a good quarterback in this team. (= This team has a good quarterback.))

iru² いる *aux. v.* (*Gr.* 2)

> S.o. or s.t. is doing s.t. he or it started some time ago, or is in a state created by an action he or it took some time ago.

be ~ing; have done (s.t.)
【REL. *aru*²】

◆ **Key Sentence**

Topic (subject)			V*te*	
佐々木さん *Sasaki-san*	は *wa*	酒 を *sake o*	飲んで ***nonde***	いる / います。 *iru / imasu.*
(Mr. Sasaki is drinking *sake*.)				

Formation

V*te* いる
　　　iru

話して　いる　　(be talking)
hanashite iru

食べて　いる　　(be eating)
tabete iru

Examples

(a) 和江は新聞を読んでいる。
　　Kazue wa shinbun o yonde iru.
　　(Kazue is reading a newspaper.)

(b) このりんごはくさっている。
　　Kono ringo wa kusatte iru.
　　(This apple is rotten.)

(c) 木が倒れている。

Ki ga taorete iru.

(A tree has fallen down (and is lying there).)

(d) 私は鈴木さんを知っています。

Watashi wa Suzuki-san o shitte imasu.

(I know Miss Suzuki.)

Notes

1. *Iru* is used as an auxiliary verb with V*te* and expresses the continuation of an action or state. In general, if V*te* expresses an action which can continue or be repeated, V*te iru* expresses the continuation of the action. If V*te* is a verb indicating a momentary action which cannot be repeated, V*te iru* expresses the idea that something happened to X and X maintains the state which was created by that event. KS and Ex. (a) are examples of the first usage and Exs. (b), (c) and (d) are examples of the second usage. Note in Ex. (d) that *shiru*, the dictionary form of *shitte*, means 'to get to know' and *shitte iru* expresses the continuation of the state after the speaker got to know Miss Suzuki, which is expressed by *know* in English. It is also noted, however, that 'not to know' is not *shitte inai*, but *shiranai*. (⇒ **shiru**)

2. V*te iru* also expresses a habitual action, which is a special sort of repeated action. Example:

(1) 私は毎日四マイル走っている。

*Watashi wa mainichi yonmairu **hashitte iru**.*

(I run four miles every day.)

3. When V*te* is a motion verb such as *iku* 'go', *kuru* 'come' and *kaeru* 'return', the meaning of V*te iru* is not 'be ~ing'. For example, *itte iru* means 'to have gone to some place and to still be there'. The sentences in (2) provide examples.

(2) a. 次郎はアメリカに行っている。

*Jirō wa Amerika ni **itte iru**.*

(Jiro has gone to America and is there.)

b. ベックさんはもう家に帰っています。

*Bekku-san wa mō ie ni **kaette imasu**.*

(Mr. Beck has already returned home and is there.)

4. The verb *sumu* 'live' requires the "V*te iru*" pattern if the sentence ex-

presses a present state. Also, verbs like *iu* 'say' and *omou* 'think' with a third person subject require the "V *te iru*" pattern if the sentence expresses a present state. Examples:

(3) a.　私は東京に**住んでいる** / *住む。
　　 *Watashi-wa Tōkyō ni **sunde iru** / *sumu.*
　　 (I live in Tokyo.)

　　 b.　ウェストさんは日本語はやさしいと**思っている** / *思う。
　　 *Uesuto-san wa nihongo wa yasashii to **omotte iru** / *omou.*
　　 (Mr. West thinks that Japanese is easy.)

I

*iru*³ いる　　*v. (Gr. 1)*

> S.o. or s.t. needs s.t.　　　　　　　　need

◆**Key Sentence**

Topic (experiencer)		Necessary Object		
君たち *Kimitachi*	は *wa*	英和辞典 *eiwa-jiten*	が *ga*	いる / いります。 *iru / irimasu.*
(You need an English-Japanese dictionary.)				

Examples

(a)　私は今お金がいる。
　　 Watashi wa ima o-kane ga iru.
　　 (I need money now.)

(b)　何か道具がいりますか。
　　 Nanika dōgu ga irimasu ka.
　　 (Do you need some tools?)

(c)　この車はガソリンがたくさんいる。
　　 Kono kuruma wa gasorin ga takusan iru.
　　 (This car needs a lot of gas.)

Notes

1. *Iru* 'need' takes the *wa-ga* construction, where the experiencer (that

is, the person or thing that needs something) is followed by *wa* and the necessary object by *ga*.   (⇨ **~ wa ~ ga**)

2. *Iru* 'need' is a Gr. 1 verb; thus, the negative form is *iranai*, the polite form is *irimasu* and the *te*-form is *itte*.   (Cp. **iru**[1]; **iru**[2])

3. The experiencer can also take the particle *ni*, as in (1).

   (1) a. この子にはいい家庭教師がいる。

           *Kono ko **ni** wa ii kateikyōshi ga iru.*

           (This child needs a good tutor. (Lit. For this child, a good tutor is necessary.))

       b. このプロジェクトには人と金がいる。

           *Kono purojekuto **ni** wa hito to kane ga iru.*

           (This project needs people and money. (Lit. For this project people and money are necessary.))

4. In subordinate clauses, the experiencer is followed by either *ga* or *ni*, as in (2), unless the sentence is contrastive. (In that case, *wa* follows.)

                                      (⇨ **wa**[1] (は))

   (2) この車が / にガソリンがたくさんいることを知っていましたか。

        *Kono kuruma **ga** / **ni** gasorin ga takusan iru koto o shitte ima-shita ka.*

        (Did you know that this car needs a lot of gas?)

jibun¹ 自分   *pro.*

a reflexive pronoun that refers (back)   ~self; own
to a human subject with whom the   **[REL. *jibun*²]**
speaker is empathizing

♦**Key Sentences**

(A)

Topic (subject)				
土田 *Tsuchida*	は *wa*	幸子 が *Sachiko ga*	自分 *jibun*	を 愛して いる こと を 知らなかった / *o aishite iru koto o shiranakatta* / 知りませんでした。 *shirimasendeshita.*
(Tsuchida didn't know that Sachiko loved him (lit. himself).)				

(B)

Sentence₁
ゆかり は 歩きながら 考えて いた。 *Yukari wa arukinagara kangaete ita.*
(Yukari was walking while thinking.

	Sentence₂			
健一 は *Ken'ichi wa*	自分 *jibun*	が 本当 に 好きなん だろう か。 *ga hontō ni sukina n darō ka.*		
Does Kenichi really love me (lit. myself)?)				

Examples

(a) 中川は自分が京大に入れると思っていなかった。
Nakagawa wa jibun ga Kyōdai ni haireru to omotte inakatta.
(Nakagawa didn't think that he (lit. himself) could enter Kyoto University.)

(b) 一郎は冬子が自分に会いに来た時うちにいなかった。
Ichirō wa Fuyuko ga jibun ni ai ni kita toki uchi ni inakatta.
(Ichiro wasn't at home when Fuyuko came to see him (lit. himself).)

J

(c) 道子は一男に自分の車で行かせた。

Michiko wa Kazuo ni jibun no kuruma de ikaseta.

(Michiko made Kazuo go there in his / her own car.)

(d) ジョンはメアリーのことを思っていた。彼女は自分と結婚してくれるんだろうか。自分を捨てて，ボブと結婚するんだろうか。

Jon wa Meari no koto o omotte ita. Kanojo wa jibun to kekkonshite kureru n darō ka. Jibun o sutete, Bobu to kekkonsuru n darō ka.

(John was thinking of Mary. Is she going to marry me (lit. myself)? Is she going to leave me (lit. myself) and marry Bob?)

Notes

1. *Jibun*¹ is an empathy marker that normally refers back to the subject of the main clause as in KS(A), Exs. (a), (b) and (c), or to the discourse topic as in KS(B) and Ex. (d).

2. When *jibun* is an empathy marker, its referent (i.e., the subject of the sentence) is normally a passive experiencer. In other words, the referent is not an agent (i.e., someone who initiates and / or completes an action).

$(\Rightarrow \boldsymbol{jibun}^2)$

3. Ex. (c) is an ambiguous sentence, because *jibun* can refer to either the main subject *Michiko* or to *Kazuo*. *Jibun*'s reference to *Kazuo* is not a counterexample of *jibun*'s strong tendency to refer to the subject, however, because *Kazuo* is semantically the subject of the verb *iku* ' go '. Also to be noted is that *Michiko* is an agent of the causative action, but *Kazuo* is a passive experiencer of the causative action. Indeed, it is easier to look at *Kazuo* as the object of the speaker's empathy, because he is a passive experiencer. It is very likely that *jibun* is not an empathy marker but a contrastive marker when it refers to an agent *Michiko*. Other similar ambiguous sentences follow:

(1) a. 道子は一男に**自分**の車で行ってもらった。

*Michiko wa Kazuo ni **jibun** no kuruma de itte moratta.*

(Lit. Michiko received from Kazuo a favor of going there in her / his own car. (=Michiko had Kazuo go there in her / his own car.))

b. 道子は一男に**自分**の車で行かれた。

*Michiko wa Kazuo ni **jibun** no kuruma de ikareta.*

(Lit. Michiko is annoyed by the fact that Kazuo went there by her / his own car. (=Michiko had Kazuo go there in her / his own car.))

Note that *jibun* in (1a, b) is an empathy marker when it refers to *Michiko* and is a contrastive marker when it refers to *Kazuo*.   (⇨ ***jibun***²)

4. The referent of *jibun* in a complex sentence has to be conscious of the situation expressed in the main clause. Compare (2a) and (2b):

   (2) a. 友子は**自分**が死ぬ前に子供が大学に入った。

          *Tomoko wa **jibun** ga shinu mae ni kodomo ga daigaku ni haitta.*

          (Lit. Speaking of Tomoko, before she (lit. herself) died, her child entered college. (= Before Tomoko died, her child entered college.))

      b. *友子は**自分**が死んだあとで子供が大学に入った。

          Tomoko wa **jibun ga shinda ato de kodomo ga daigaku ni haitta.*

          (Lit. Speaking of Tomoko, after she (lit. herself) had died, her child entered college. (= After Tomoko died, her child entered college.))

The sentence (2b) is ungrammatical because one can hardly empathize with a dead person.

J

---

jibun² 自分   *pro.*

a reflexive pronoun that refers (back) to a human subject, the referent of which is contrasted with s.o. else	~self; own 【REL. *jibun*¹】

◆Key Sentences

(A)

Topic (subject)			
日本人 *Nihonjin*	は *wa*	自分 *jibun*	の 国 の 文化 を ユニーク だ と 思って *no kuni no bunka o yuniku da to omotte* いる / います。 *iru / imasu.*
(The Japanese think that their country's culture is unique.)			

(B)

Topic (subject, agent)			
メアリー *Meari*	は *wa*	自分 *jibun*	で 何 でも する / します。 *de nan demo suru / shimasu.*
(Mary does everything by herself.)			

(C)

Topic (subject)			
一男 *Kazuo*	は *wa*	自分 *jibun*	を 励ました / 励ましました。 *o hagemashita / hagemashimashita.*
(Kazuo braced himself.)			

Examples

(a) 自分を知ることが一番難しい。
Jibun o shiru koto ga ichiban muzukashii.
(To know yourself is the hardest.)

(b) マイクはいつも自分の寮の部屋で勉強している。
Maiku wa itsumo jibun no ryō no heya de benkyōshite iru.
(Mike is always studying in his own dorm room.)

(c) 小林は自分からしたいと言った。
Kobayashi wa jibun kara shitai to itta.
(Kobayashi voluntarily (lit. from himself) said that he wanted to do it.)

(d) 先生はご自分の家で私に会って下さった。
Sensei wa go-jibun no ie de watashi ni atte kudasatta.
(The professor kindly met me at his own house.)

Note

Jibun is a contrastive marker if at least one of the following three conditions is met: (1) *its referent is an agent* (as in KSs (B), (C), Exs. (b), (c) and (d)). (2) *the subject is generic* (as in KS(A) and Ex. (a)). (3) *jibun cannot be replaced by an implicit third person pronoun (ø) or by an explicit third person pronoun* (such as *kare* 'he' and *kanojo* 'she'). KS(C) satisfies the condition (3), because if *jibun* is replaced by ø or *kare* 'he', the meaning of the sentence changes into 'Kazuo encouraged him.'

[Related Expression]

Jibun is *jibun¹* if the referent does not satisfy any of the three conditions given in Note; if it satisfies at least one of them it is *jibun²*.

J

ka[1] か   *prt.*

a particle which marks an alternative	(either) ~ or ~
	【REL. *soretomo*】

♦**Key Sentences**

(A)

Topic (subject)		Noun₁		Noun₂			Predicate
私	は	電車	か	バス	(か)	で	行く / 行きます。
Watashi	*wa*	*densha*	*ka*	*basu*	*(ka)*	*de*	*iku / ikimasu.*
(I will go either by train or by bus.)							

(B)

Sentence₁ (informal)†		Sentence₂ (informal)†		
トム が 行く	か	メアリー が 行く	か	どちらか だ / です。
Tomu ga iku	*ka*	*Meari ga iku*	*ka*	*dochiraka da / desu.*
(Either Tom will go or Mary will go.)				

†*Da* after Adj(*na*) stem and N drops.

Formation

KS(A):

N₁ か N₂ (か)
  ka   *(ka)*

先生 か 学生 (か)   (either a teacher or a student)
sensei ka gakusei (ka)

KS(B):

(i) {V / Adj (*i*)} inf か
                    ka

{話す / 話した} か   (either s.o. talks / talked or)
{*hanasu* / *hanashita*} *ka*

{高い / 高かった} か   (either s.t. is / was expensive or)
{*takai* / *takakatta*} *ka*

(ii) {Adj (*na*) stem / N}   {ø / だった} か
                          {ø / *datta*} *ka*

{静か / 静かだった} か   (either s.t. is / was quiet or)
{*shizuka* / *shizukadatta*} *ka*

{先生 / 先生 だった} か   (either s.o. is / was a teacher or)
{*sensei* / *sensei datta*} *ka*

(a) 私は毎朝ジュースかミルクを飲む。
   Watashi wa maiasa jūsu ka miruku o nomu.
   (I drink either juice or milk every morning.)

(b) それはボブかマークがします。
   Sore wa Bobu ka Māku ga shimasu.
   (As for that, either Bob or Mark will do it.)

(c) 肉が高かったか一郎が肉がきらいだったかどちらかだ。
   Niku ga takakatta ka Ichirō ga niku ga kiraidatta ka dochiraka da.
   (Either meat was expensive or Ichiro didn't like meat.)

(d) 手紙を書くか電話をかけるかどちらかしてください。
   Tegami o kaku ka denwa o kakeru ka dochiraka shite kudasai.
   (Either write a letter or make a call, please.)

(e) 食べるか話すかどちらかにしなさい。
   Taberu ka hanasu ka dochiraka ni shinasai.
   (Lit. Decide on either eating or talking. (=Just do one thing, eat or talk.))

Notes

1. The basic function of *ka* is to mark an alternative. It can mark either nouns or sentences. When it marks nouns, the final *ka* is usually omitted. When it marks sentences, the sentences are subordinate clauses; that is, they must be in the informal form. The topic marker *wa* must not be used.

2. *Ka* cannot be used to connect two questions. Thus, the following sentences are ungrammatical.

   (1) a. *これはあなたのですか。か私のですか。
       Kore wa anata no desuka. **Ka watashi no desu ka.*
       (Is this yours or mine?)

      b. *私と一緒に来ますか。かここにいますか。
       Watashi to isshoni kimasu ka. **Ka koko ni imasu ka.*
       (Will you come with me? Or will you stay here?)

   In this case, *soretomo* is used instead of *ka*.   (⇨ ***soretomo***)

【Related Expression】

Soretomo is also used with alternatives. However, the function of *soretomo* is to *connect* two alternatives, not to *mark* an alternative. Thus, *soretomo* appears with *ka*, not in place of *ka*. Examples:

[1] 肉が高かったか，**それとも**一郎が肉がきらいだったかどちらかだ。
Niku ga takakatta ka, **soretomo** *Ichirō ga niku ga kiraidatta ka dochiraka da.*
(Either meat was expensive or Ichiro didn't like meat.)

[2] 私と一緒に来ますか。**それとも**ここにいますか。
Watashi to isshoni kimasu ka. **Soretomo** *koko ni imasuka.*
(Will you come with me? Or will you stay here?)

Soretomo is optional in [1], but not in [2].

K

ka² か *prt.*

a sentence-final particle which indicates that the preceding sentence is interrogative	whether; if **【REL.** *dai* (*kai*)**】**

♦Key Sentences

(A)

Sentence†	
よし子 は　大学　へ 行く / 行きます *Yoshiko wa daigaku e　iku / ikimasu*	か。 *ka.*
(Is Yoshiko going to college?)	

†In informal speech, *da* after Adj (*na*) stem and N drops.

(B)

	Sentence (informal)†			
私　は テリー に *Watashi wa Teri ni*	ナンシー が 日本 へ **行く** *Nanshi ga Nihon e **iku***	か *ka*	と *to*	聞いた / *kiita /* 聞きました。 *kikimashita.*
(I asked Terry whether Nancy was going to Japan.)				

†*Da* after Adj (*na*) stem and N drops.

Formation

(i) {V / Adj (*i*)}　か
　　　　　　　　　ka

　{話す　 / 話します}　　か　(Will (or Does) s.o. talk? (informal / formal))
　{*hanasu* / *hanashimasu*}　*ka*

　{高い / 高いです}　か　　(Is s.t. expensive? (informal / formal))
　{*takai* / *takaidesu*}　*ka*

(ii) {Adj (*na*) stem / N}　{ø / です} か
　　　　　　　　　　　　　　{ø / *desu*} *ka*

　{静か　 / 静かです}　　か　(Is s.t. quiet? (informal / formal))
　{*shizuka* / *shizukadesu*}　*ka*

　{先生 / 先生　です} か　(Is s.o. a teacher? (informal / formal))
　{*sensei* / *sensei desu*}　*ka*

Examples

(a) あなたは学生ですか。
　Anata wa gakusei desu ka.
　(Are you a student?)

(b) これは何ですか。
　Kore wa nan desu ka.
　(What is this?)

(c) 友達は漢字が難しいかと聞いた。
　Tomodachi wa kanji ga muzukashii ka to kiita.
　(My friend asked if *kanji* is difficult.)

(d) 私はジャンにだれが来たかとたずねた。
　Watashi wa Jan ni dare ga kita ka to tazuneta.
　(I asked Jan who had come.)

(e) 僕は山崎先生がきのう何を言ったか忘れてしまった。
Boku wa Yamazaki-sensei ga kinō nani o itta ka wasurete shimatta.
(I've forgotten (completely) what Prof. Yamazaki said yesterday.)

(f) 私は健二にお金を貸したかどうか思い出せない。
Watashi wa Kenji ni o-kane o kashita ka dō ka omoidasenai.
(I cannot remember if I lent Kenji some money.)

Notes

1. The question marker *ka* is a special use of the *ka* which marks an alternative (i.e., *ka¹*). For example, KS(A) came from (1), with the parenthesized part omitted. (⇒ **ka¹**)

   (1) よし子は大学へ行きますか。(それとも行きませんか。)
   Yoshiko wa daigaku e ikimasu ka. (Soretomo ikimasen ka.)
   (Is Yoshiko going to college? (Or is she not?))

2. Unless it is very informal, an interrogative sentence is marked by *ka* whether it is a yes-no question or a WH-question. (⇒ *dai*; *kai*) Note that in Japanese interrogative sentences, the word order is the same as that of the corresponding declarative sentence. Also, an interrogative sentence is pronounced with rising intonation whether it is a yes-no question or a WH-question.

3. *Ka* remains in indirect questions as in KS(B), Exs. (c) and (d).

4. When the informal forms of *na*-type adjectives and the copula precede the question marker *ka*, *da* drops. A possible reason is that *da*, the informal form of *desu*, expresses a strong assertion and it conflicts with the question marker *ka*, which expresses the speaker's uncertainty about something. (⇒ *kai*; *kamoshirenai*; *kashira*)

ka ⟨dō ka⟩ か(どうか)   *prt.*

a marker for an embedded yes-no question	whether or not; if (~ or not)

◆**Key Sentence**

Embedded Yes-No Question (informal)†		Verb (cognition)
鈴木さん が 大学 に 入った か *Suzuki-san ga daigaku ni haitta ka*	(どう か) (は) (*dō ka*) (*wa*)	知らない / 知りません。 *shiranai / shirimasen.*
(I don't know whether or not Mr. Suzuki entered college.)		

†*Da* after Adj (*na*) stem and N drops.

Formation

(i) {V / Adj (*i*)} inf か（どう か）
　　　　　　　　　ka (dō　ka)

　　{話す　/ 話した}　か（どう か）　　(whether or not s.o. talks / talked)
　　{*hanasu / hanashita*} *ka (dō　ka)*

　　{高い / 高かった}　か（どう か）　　(whether or not s.t. is / was expensive)
　　{*takai / takakatta*} *ka (dō ka)*

(ii) {Adj (*na*) stem / N}　{ø / だった} か（どう か）
　　　　　　　　　　　　　{ø / *datta*} *ka (dō　ka)*

　　{静か　/ 静かだった}　か（どう か）　　(whether or not s.t. is / was
　　{*shizuka / shizukadatta*} *ka (dō　ka)*　　quiet)

　　{先生　/ 先生　だった} か（どう か）　　(whether or not s.o. is / was a
　　{*sensei / sensei datta*} *ka (dō　ka)*　　teacher)

Examples

(a) 小川さんが結婚しているかどうか知っていますか。
　　Ogawa-san ga kekkonshite iru ka dō ka shitte imasu ka.
　　(Do you know if Mr. Ogawa is married or not?)

(b) フォークナーの小説がおもしろいかどうか知らない。
　　Fōkunā no shōsetsu ga omoshiroi ka dō ka shiranai.
　　(I don't know if Faulkner's novels are interesting.)

(c) 山口先生がお元気かどうか存じません。
　　Yamaguchi-sensei ga o-genki ka dō ka zonjimasen.
　　(I don't know if Prof. Yamaguchi is healthy.)

Notes

1. When the optional *dō ka* is used, the embedded question has to be a yes-no question. If it is not used, then the question can be either a yes-no question or a WH-question.

(1) レストランで何を食べた**か** / ***かどうか**覚えていますか。
*Resutoran de **nani** o tabeta **ka** | ***ka dō ka** oboete imasu ka.*
(Do you remember what you ate at the restaurant?)

(2) その時だれと一緒にいた**か** / ***かどうか**覚えていますか。
*Sono toki **dare** to isshoni ita **ka** | ***ka dō ka** oboete imasu ka.*
(Do you remember who you were with at that time?)

2. Typical final verbs include, among others, verbs of knowing, examining, understanding, asking, remembering, and deciding.

3. Sinf *ka* (*dō ka*) can be used as a noun phrase that takes particles such as *ga* and *o*.

(3) 仕事をやめるかどうかが問題だった。
Shigoto o yameru ka dō ka ga mondai datta.
(Whether or not to quit the job was the question.)

(4) 大学院に行くかどうかを今考えています。
Daigakuin ni iku ka dō ka o ima kangaete imasu.
(I'm now thinking about whether or not I will go to graduate school.)

K

---

kai かい   *prt.*

a sentence-final particle which marks yes-no questions in informal male speech	【REL. *dai* (*ka*[2])】

♦**Key Sentences**

(A)

Sentence (informal)†	
日本語　は　**おもしろい** *Nihongo wa **omoshiroi***	かい。 *kai.*
(Is Japanese interesting?)	

†*Da* after Adj (*na*) stem and N drops.

(B)

Sentence (informal)†		
上野さん は アメリカ へ 行く *Ueno-san wa Amerika e **iku***	の *no*	かい。 *kai.*
(Is Mr. Ueno going to America?)		

†*Da* after Adj (*na*) stem and N changes to *na*.

Formation

KS(A):

(i) {V / Adj (*i*)} inf かい
　　　　　　　　　　kai

　　{話す　／話した}　かい　　(Does (or Will) / Did s.o. talk?)
　　{*hanasu* / *hanashita*} *kai*

　　{高い／高かった} かい　(Is / Was s.t. expensive?)
　　{*takai* / *takakatta*} *kai*

(ii) {Adj (*na*) stem / N}　{ø / だった} かい
　　　　　　　　　　　　　{ø / *datta*}　*kai*

　　{静か　／静かだった}　かい　(Is / Was s.t. quiet?)
　　{*shizuka* / *shizuka*datta} *kai*

　　{先生　／先生　だった} かい　(Is / Was s.o. a teacher?)
　　{*sensei* / *sensei datta*}　*kai*

KS(B):

(i) {V / Adj (*i*)} inf の かい
　　　　　　　　　　no kai

　　{話す　／話した}　の かい　　(Does (or Will) / Did s.o. talk?)
　　{*hanasu* / *hanashita*} *no kai*

　　{高い／高かった} の かい　(Is / Was s.t. expensive?)
　　{*takai* / *takakatta*} *no kai*

(ii) {Adj (*na*) stem / N}　{な / だった} の かい
　　　　　　　　　　　　　{*na* / *datta*}　*no kai*

　　{静かな　／静かだった}　の かい　(Is / Was s.t. quiet?)
　　{*shizuka*na / *shizuka*datta} *no kai*

　　{先生　な／先生　だった} の かい　(Is / Was s.o. a teacher?)
　　{*sensei* na / *sensei datta*}　*no kai*

Examples

(a) 日本語を勉強するかい。
Nihongo o benkyōsuru kai.
(Will you study Japanese?)

(b) このアパートは静かかい。
Kono apāto wa shizuka kai.
(Is this apartment quiet?)

(c) 君達は学生かい。
Kimitachi wa gakusei kai.
(Are you students?)

(d) その本は難しいのかい。
Sono hon wa muzukashii no kai.
(Is the book difficult?)

(e) あの人は先生なのかい。
Ano hito wa sensei na no kai.
(Is that person a teacher?)

Notes

1. Since *kai* is used in informal speech, preceding sentences must be in the informal form. The following sentences are unacceptable.

   (1) a. *日本語はおもしろいです(の)かい。
          *Nihongo wa **omoshiroidesu** (no) kai.*
          (Is Japanese interesting?)

        b. *上野さんはアメリカへ行きます(の)かい。
          *Ueno-san wa Amerika e **ikimasu** (no) kai.*
          (Is Mr. Ueno going to America?)

2. *Kai* is used only for yes-no questions. Thus, the following sentences are ungrammatical.

   (2) a. *どこへ行く(の)かい。
          Doko e iku (no) kai.
          (Where are you going?)

        b. *あの人はだれ(なの)かい。
          Ano hito wa dare (na no) kai.
          (Who is that person?)

(In these sentences, *dai* is used. (⇨ ***dai***))

3. Questions in the KS(A) pattern and those in the KS(B) pattern correspond to questions without *no desu* and those with *no desu* in formal speech, respectively. (⇨ **no da**)

4. Questions in female informal speech can be formed by dropping *kai* in male informal questions and using rising intonation. Examples:

   (3) a. 日本語はおもしろい (の)?
            Nihongo wa omoshiroi (no)?
            (Is Japanese interesting?)

        b. 上野さんはアメリカへ行く (の)?
            Ueno-san wa Amerika e iku (no)?
            (Is Mr. Ueno going to America?)

        c. あの人は先生 (なの)?
            Ano hito wa sensei (na no)?
            (Is that person a teacher?)

For a summary of the endings for informal questions, see *dai*, Related Expression.

K

---

kamoshirenai かもしれない   *aux. adj (i)*

can't tell if ~   might
                            【REL. *darō*; *ni chigainai*; *sōda*[2]】

♦ **Key Sentences**

(A)

	Vinf	
午後 雨 が *Gogo ame ga*	降る ***furu***	かもしれない / かもしれません。 *kamoshirenai / kamoshiremasen.*
(It might rain in the afternoon.)		

(B)

	Adj (*i*) inf	
あの 先生 の 授業 は *Ano sensei no jugyō wa*	**つまらない** ***tsumaranai***	かもしれない / かもしれません。 *kamoshirenai / kamoshiremasen.*
(That teacher's class might be dull.)		

(C)

	Adj (*na*) stem	
京都 の 桜 は まだ *Kyōto no sakura wa mada*	**きれい** ***kirei***	かもしれない / かもしれません。 *kamoshirenai / kamoshiremasen.*
(The cherry blossoms in Kyoto might still be beautiful.)		

Formation

(i) {V / Adj (*i*)} inf かもしれない
                kamoshirenai

    {話す / 話した} かもしれない (s.o. might talk / might have talked)
    {*hanasu / hanashita*} *kamoshirenai*

    {高い / 高かった} かもしれない (s.t. might be high / might have been
    {*takai / takakatta*} *kamoshirenai* high)

(ii) {Adj (*na*) stem / N} {ø / だった} かもしれない
                     {ø / *datta*}   *kamoshirenai*

    {静か / 静かだった} かもしれない (s.t. might be quiet / might have
    {*shizuka / shizuka datta*} *kamoshirenai* been quiet)

    {先生 / 先生 だった} かもしれない (s.o. might be a teacher / might
    {*sensei / sensei datta*} *kamoshirenai* have been a teacher)

Examples

(a) 今年の冬は大変寒くなるかもしれません。
    Kotoshi no fuyu wa taihen samuku naru kamoshiremasen.
    (It might be very cold this winter.)

(b) あの人は今日のパーティーのことを忘れたかもしれません。
    Ano hito wa kyō no pāti no koto o wasureta kamoshiremasen.
    (He might have forgotten about today's party.)

(c) この映画はあなたにはつまらないかもしれません。
    Kono eiga wa anata ni wa tsumaranai kamoshiremasen.
    (This movie might be uninteresting for you.)

(d) 中国語の文法は日本語の文法より簡単かもしれない。

Chūgokugo no bunpō wa nihongo no bunpō yori kantan kamoshirenai.

(Chinese grammar might be simpler than Japanese grammar.)

(e) あれは鈴木先生かもしれないよ。

Are wa Suzuki-sensei kamoshirenai yo.

(That might be Prof. Suzuki.)

[Related Expressions]

I. The probability of accuracy predicted by a *kamoshirenai* sentence is lower than that of a *darō* sentence and much lower than that of a *ni chigainai* sentence as diagrammed below:

low probability ←————————————————→ high probability
kamoshirenai < *darō* < *ni chigainai*

The Japanese weatherman on radio or TV, for example, employs *deshō* (the formal version of *darō*) in his forecasts as in the following:

[1] 関東地方，あすは小雨が一日中降るでしょう。

*Kantō-chihō, asu wa kosame ga ichinichijū furu **deshō**.*

(Tomorrow, in the Kanto area it will probably be drizzling all day long.)

II. V*masu* / Adj (*i* / *na*) stem *sōda* is used when the speaker's conjecture is based primarily on visual or other perceptual evidence, but *kamoshirenai* is not; rather the latter is used when that conjecture is based on logical reasoning. Thus,

[2] あっ！ このケーキ（は）おいしそうですね。

A! Kono kēki (wa) oishisōdesu ne.

(Look, this cake looks good, doesn't it?)

[3] *あっ！ このケーキ（は）おいしいかもしれませんね。

A! Kono kēki (wa) oishii **kamoshiremasen ne.*

(*Look, this cake might be good, might it not?)

(⇨ **yōda**)

kara[1] から   *prt.*

| a particle which indicates a starting point or a source | from; since; out of 【REL. *ni*[3]; *o*[3]】 |

♦ **Key Sentence**

Topic (subject)	Noun		
パーティー は *Pāti* *wa*	八時 ***hachiji***	から *kara*	始まる / 始まります。 *hajimaru / hajimarimasu.*
(The party starts at (lit. from) eight o'clock.)			

Examples

(a) 今日の授業は一時から三時までです。
    Kyō no jugyō wa ichiji kara sanji made desu.
    (Today's class is from one o'clock till three o'clock.)

(b) このバスはニューヨークから来た。
    Kono basu wa Nyūyōku kara kita.
    (This bus came from New York.)

(c) ここから富士山が見えるよ。
    Koko kara Fujisan ga mieru yo.
    (You can see Mt. Fuji from here.)

(d) そのタイプライターはだれから借りたんですか。
    Sono taipuraitā wa dare kara karita n desu ka.
    (Who did you borrow the typewriter from?)

(e) 酒は米から作る。
    Sake wa kome kara tsukuru.
    (*Sake* is made out of rice.)

(f) つまらないことからけんかになった。
    Tsumaranai koto kara kenka ni natta.
    (Lit. It became a quarrel from a trifle. (=We started to quarrel over a trifle.))

Note

Kara basically indicates a temporal or spatial starting point (Exs. (a), (b) and (c)) or a source (Exs. (d), (e) and (f)). As seen in Exs. (d), (e) and (f), a source can be a person, material, a cause or a reason.

kara² から　　*conj.*

| after / since a point in time at which s.t. takes place | after; having done s.t.; since (time) |

【REL. ***ato de***; *te*-form of verb**】**

♦ **Key Sentence**

	V*te*		
雪子　は　晩ご飯　を *Yukiko wa bangohan o*	**食べて** ***tabete***	から *kara*	映画　に　行った / 行きました。 *eiga ni　itta / ikimashita.*
(After eating her supper, Yukiko went to a movie.)

Formation

V*te* から
　　　kara

話して　　から　　(after talking)
hanashite kara

食べて　から　　(after eating)
tabete kara

Examples

(a) 私は友達に電話してからうちを出た。
Watashi wa tomodachi ni denwashite kara uchi o deta.
(I left home after making a call to my friend.)

(b) ジョーンズさんはいつもシャワーを浴びてから寝ます。
Jōnzu-san wa itsumo shawā o abite kara nemasu.
(Mr. Jones always goes to bed after taking a shower.)

(c) 私達がこの家を買ってからもう十年になる。
Watashitachi ga kono ie o katte kara mō jūnen ni naru.
(It's already been ten years since we bought this house.)

(d) 二年前に交通事故を起こしてから，ミラーさんは車に乗らないようにしています。
Ninen mae ni kōtsūjiko o okoshite kara, Mirā-san wa kuruma ni noranai yōni shite imasu.
(Since he caused a traffic accident two years ago, Mr. Miller has been trying not to drive a car.)

Notes

1. V*te kara* S means 'S after doing s.t.' or 'S since ~ did s.t.' The usage of *kara²* is an extended use of *kara¹*.

2. *Te kara* is not to be confused with *ta kara* in which *kara* is used as a conjunction of cause / reason.　　　　　　　　　　　(⇨ *kara³*)

   (1) a. ジョギングをしてからシャワーを浴びた。
           Jogingu o shite kara shawā o abita.
           (After jogging, I took a shower.)

        b. ジョギングをしたからシャワーを浴びた。
           Jogingu o shita kara shawā o abita.
           (Because I jogged, I took a shower.)

[Related Expression]

Kara in V*te kara* can be omitted if the main verb does not indicate a high degree of volitional control on the part of the speaker as in the cases of a strong suggestion, determination or a command. Thus, in KS and Exs. (a), (b) and (c) *kara* can drop, but in Ex. (d), [1a] and [2a] it cannot.

  [1] a. 勉強が終わってからテニスをしましょう。
         Benkyō ga owatte kara tenisu o shimashō.
         (Let's play tennis after we've finished studying.)

       b. *勉強が終わって，テニスをしましょう。
         **Benkyō ga owatte, tenisu o shimashō.*
         (*We've finished studying, and let's play tennis.)

  [2] a. 勉強が終わってから遊びなさい。
         Benkyō ga owatte kara asobinasai.
         (Play after you've finished studying.)

       b. *勉強が終わって遊びなさい。
         **Benkyō ga owatte asobinasai.*
         (*You've finished studying, and play.)

The difference between *te kara* and *te* is that the former focuses more on chronological order and volitional planning than the latter does.

kara³ から   *conj.*

┌─────────────────────────────┐
a subordinate conjunction which ex-   so; since; because
presses a reason or a cause   【REL. *node*】
└─────────────────────────────┘

◆Key Sentences

(A)

Subordinate Clause (reason / cause)		Main Clause
来年 日本 へ 行く *Rainen Nihon e iku*	から *kara*	日本語 を 勉強して いる / います。 *nihongo o benkyōshite iru / imasu.*
(I'm studying Japanese because I'm going to Japan next year.)		

(B)

A:
どう して 日本語 を 勉強して いる ん {だ / です か}。 *Dō shite nihongo o benkyōshite iru n {da / desu ka}.*
(Why are you studying Japanese?)

B: Sentence (informal)		
来年 日本 へ **行く** *Rainen Nihon e **iku***	から *kara*	だ / です。 *da / desu.*
(It's because I'm going to Japan next year.)		

Formation

KS(B):

Sinf から
　　　kara

{話す / 話した}   から   (because s.o. (will) talk / talked)
{*hanasu* / *hanashita*} *kara*

{高い / 高かった}   から   (because s.t. is / was expensive)
{*takai* / *takakatta*} *kara*

{静かだ / 静かだった}   から   (because s.t. is / was quiet)
{*shizukada* / *shizukadatta*} *kara*

{先生　だ / 先生　だった} から　　(because s.o. is / was a teacher)
{*sensei da* / *sensei datta*} *kara*

Examples

(a) 春子は十七だからまだお酒を飲めない。
Haruko wa jūshichi da kara mada o-sake o nomenai.
(Haruko is seventeen, so she can't drink *sake* yet.)

(b) 今日は忙しいですからあした来てください。
Kyō wa isogashii desu kara ashita kite kudasai.
(Please come tomorrow because I'm busy today.)

(c) A : どうしてきのう学校を休んだんですか。
Dō shite kinō gakkō o yasunda n desu ka.
(Why were you absent from school yesterday?)

B : 頭が痛かったからです。
Atama ga itakatta kara desu.
(It was because I had a headache.)

Notes

1. S *kara* represents a reason or a cause. Thus, S₁ *kara* S₂ corresponds to 'S₂ because / since S₁', 'Because / since S₁, S₂', or 'S₁, so S₂'. Note that the order of S₁ and S₂ is not always the same in English, while in Japanese *kara* clauses (i.e., S₁) always precede main clauses (i.e., S₂).

2. In subordinate clauses predicates are usually in the informal form. However, since the degree of subordination or dependency of S₁ in "S₁ *kara* S₂" is rather low, S₁ may be in the formal form in very formal speech, as in Ex. (b).

3. When a main clause is known to the hearer from the context, the KS(B) pattern is used. In this case, the *kara* clause must be in the informal form. The following sentence is unacceptable.

　(1) *来年日本へ行きますからだ / です。
　Rainen Nihon e ikimasu kara da / desu.
　(It's because I'm going to Japan next year.)

4. In question-and-answer situations as in KS(B) and Ex. (c), abbreviated forms are occasionally used. For example, speaker B may say (2) in the KS(B) situation.

　(2) 来年日本へ行きますから。
　Rainen Nihon e ikimasu kara.
　(Because I'm going to Japan next year.)

In this sentence, the main clause *nihongo o benkyō shite imasu* 'I'm studying Japanese' has been omitted.

kashira かしら   *prt.*

> a sentence-final particle which ex-   I wonder
> presses the idea that the female
> speaker wonders about s.t.

♦**Key Sentence**

Sentence (informal)†	
松本さん　は **来る** *Matsumoto-san wa **kuru***	かしら。 *kashira.*
(I wonder if Mr. Matsumoto will come.)	

†*Da* after Adj (*na*) stem and N drops.

Formation

(i) {V / Adj (*i*)} inf かしら
　　　　　　　　　kashira

　{話す　 / 話した}　 かしら　 (I wonder s.o. (will) talk / talked)
　{*hanasu* / *hanashita*} *kashira*

　{高い / 高かった} かしら　 (I wonder s.t. is / was expensive)
　{*takai* / *takakatta*} *kashira*

(ii) {Adj (*na*) stem / N} {ø / だった} かしら
　　　　　　　　　　　　{ø / *datta*}　*kashira*

　{静か　 / 静かだった}　 かしら　 (I wonder s.t. is / was quiet)
　{*shizuka* / *shizuka*datta} *kashira*

　{先生　 / 先生　 だった} かしら　 (I wonder s.o. is / was a teacher)
　{*sensei* / *sensei* datta}　*kashira*

K

Examples

(a) あの先生の授業はおもしろいかしら。
   Ano sensei no jugyō wa omoshiroi kashira.
   (I wonder if that teacher's class is interesting.)

(b) 幸子さんは何が好きかしら。
   Sachiko-san wa nani ga suki kashira.
   (I wonder what Sachiko likes.)

(c) あの人はだれかしら。
   Ano hito wa dare kashira.
   (I wonder who that person is.)

Notes

1. Etymologically, *kashira* comes from *ka shiranai* 'I don't know (if) ~', but now expresses the idea "I wonder".

2. *Kashira* is usually used by female speakers in rather informal speech. The male version is *kanā*, which is used only in fairly informal situations. The formation rules of *kanā* are exactly the same as those for *kashira*.

3. Sfml *kashira* is acceptable if the situation is very formal. Example:

   (1) そこは**静かですか**しら。
      *Soko wa **shizukadesu** kashira.*
      (I wonder if that place is quiet.)

4. Since *kashira* and *kanā* mean 'I wonder' (present tense), they cannot be used for expressions like "I wondered" and "Mr. Smith wondered". For such expressions, "A *wa* Sinf *kashira* / *kanā to omou*" is used. Here, A is the person who wonders; *to omou* literally means 'think that'. Examples:

   (2) a. 私は松本さんは来るかしらと思った。
        *Watashi wa Matsumoto-san wa kuru **kashira to omotta**.*
        (I wondered if Mr. Matsumoto would come.)

      b. 山本さんは小川さんは先生かしらと思った。
        *Yamamoto-san wa Ogawa-san wa sensei **kashira to omotta**.*
        (Ms. Yamamoto wondered if Mr. Ogawa was a teacher.)

-kata 方　*suf.*

> a noun-forming suffix that indicates a way or a manner in which one does s.t.

a way of; a manner of; how to 【REL. *hōhō*】

◆**Key Sentence**

	V*masu*	
ケーキ の Kēki　no	作り方 ***tsukuri****kata*	を 教えて ください。 o oshiete kudasai.
(Please show me how to make a cake.)		

Formation

V*masu*　方
　　　　kata

話し　方　　(way / manner of speaking)
hanashikata

食べ 方　　(way / manner of eating)
tabekata

Examples

(a) この漢字の書き方が分かりません。
　　Kono kanji no kakikata ga wakarimasen.
　　(I don't know how to write this *kanji*.)

(b) あの人の歩き方はおもしろいですね。
　　Ano hito no arukikata wa omoshiroidesu ne.
　　(His manner of walking is amusing, isn't it?)

(c) 日本語の勉強の仕方を教えてください。
　　Nihongo no benkyō no shikata o oshiete kudasai.
　　(Please teach me how to study Japanese language.)

Notes

1. V*masu*＋*kata* is in itself ambiguous, meaning either 'way' or 'manner'. Thus,

    (1) 飲み方が大事です。
    　　Nomikata ga daijidesu.

is ambiguous: it means either 'The way of drinking is important' or 'The manner in which one drinks is important.' The separate meanings become clearer in an extended context:

(2) この薬は飲み方が大事です。必ず食前に飲んでください。
Kono kusuri wa nomikata ga daijidesu. Kanarazu shokuzen ni nonde kudasai.
(It's important to know how to take this medicine. Be sure to take it before every meal.)

(3) スープは飲み方が大事です。
Sūpu wa nomikata ga daijidesu.
(In eating soup the manner (in which one eats it) is important.)

2. Sino-Japanese *suru*-verbs such as *benkyō-suru* 'study', *denwa-suru* 'telephone', *ryōri-suru* 'cook', *setsumei-suru* 'explain' and *sōdan-suru* 'consult' need the particle *no* before *shikata* as in:

(4) 勉強 / 電話 / 料理 / 説明の仕方
*benkyō / denwa / ryōri / setsumei **no** shikata*
(a way / manner of studying / telephoning / cooking / explanation)

[Related Expression]

Kata can be replaced by *hōhō* but only when *kata* means 'a way of doing s.t.' *Hōhō* roughly corresponds to the English word 'method'; it means a relatively complicated way of doing s.t. Ex. (c) can be rewritten as [1].

[1] 日本語の勉強の方法を教えてください。
*Nihongo no benkyō no **hōhō** o oshiete kudasai.*
(Please teach me a method for studying Japanese.)

kawari ni かわりに   *phr.*

S.t. (including an action) replaces s.t. else.	in place of ~ ; instead of; to make up for ~ ; although; but **[REL.** *keredo(mo)*; *shikashi***]**

♦ **Key Sentences**

(A)

Noun		Noun	Predicate
先生 **Sensei**	の かわり に *no kawari ni*	私 *watashi*	が 教えた / 教えました。 *ga oshieta / oshiemashita.*
(I taught in place of my teacher.)			

(B)

Sentence (informal)†		
土曜日 に 仕事 を **する** *Doyōbi ni shigoto o **suru***	かわり に *kawari ni*	月曜日 は 休む / *getsuyōbi wa yasumu /* 休みます。 *yasumimasu.*
(To make up for working on Saturdays, I take Mondays off.)		

†*Da* after Adj (*na*) stem and N changes to *na* and *no*, respectively.

K

Formation

(i) N の かわり に
   no kawari ni

   先生 の かわり に   (in place of the teacher)
   sensei no kawari ni

(ii) {V / Adj (*i*)} inf かわり に
                    kawari ni

   {話す / 話した}   かわり に   (instead of talking / talked but)
   {hanasu / hanashita} kawari ni

   {食べる / 食べた} かわり に   (instead of eating / ate but)
   {taberu / tabeta} kawari ni

   {高い / 高かった} かわり に   (s.t. is / was expensive but ~)
   {takai / takakatta} kawari ni

(iii) Adj (*na*) stem {な / だった} かわり に
                   {na / datta} kawari ni

   {静かな / 静かだった} かわり に   (s.t. is / was quiet but ~)
   {shizukana / shizukadatta} kawari ni

Examples

(a) ビールのかわりに酒を買いました。
Biru no kawari ni sake o kaimashita.
(I bought *sake* instead of beer.)

(b) わたしのかわりに父が行ってもいいですか。
Watashi no kawari ni chichi ga itte mo iidesu ka.
(Can my father go there in place of me?)

(c) 今日は夜おそくまで踊るかわりにあしたは一日中勉強します。
Kyō wa yoru osoku made odoru kawari ni ashita wa ichinichijū benkyō-shimasu.
(I'll study all day tomorrow to make up for dancing until late tonight.)

(d) 手伝ってあげるかわりに飲ませてくださいよ。
Tetsudatte ageru kawari ni nomasete kudasai yo.
(I'll help you, so (to make up for it) please (lit. let me drink) buy me a drink, OK?)

(e) 僕のアパートは不便なかわりに家賃が安い。
Boku no apāto wa fubenna kawari ni yachin ga yasui.
(My apartment is inconvenient, but the rent is cheap.)

(f) 英語を教えてあげたかわりに日本語を教えてもらった。
Eigo o oshiete ageta kawari ni nihongo o oshiete moratta.
(I taught him Japanese, so (to make up for it) he taught me English.)

(g) その車は安かったかわりによく故障した。
Sono kuruma wa yasukatta kawari ni yoku koshōshita.
(That car was inexpensive, but it often broke down.)

Note

In N_1 *no kawari ni* N_2, N_2 is regarded as the substitute for N_1, which is the originally intended item. In S_1inf *kawari ni* S_2, an action or a state identified by S_2 takes place to make up for a counter-action or counter-state represented in S_1.

[Related Expressions]

In S_1 *kawari ni* S_2, *kawari ni* can be replaced by *keredo(mo)* 'although' or *shikashi* 'but'. Note, however, that the converse is not always acceptable. Thus, *keredo(mo)* and *shikashi* in [1] below cannot be replaced by *kawari ni*, because the meaning of 'making up for ~' is missing, but the same conjunctions in [2] can be replaced by *kawari ni*, because the compensative meaning is present there.

[1] 私は甘いものをたくさん食べる**けれど（も）**／。しかし／*かわりに歯は強い。
*Watashi wa amai mono o takusan taberu **keredo(mo)** / . Shikashi /
***kawari ni** ha wa tsuyoi.*
(Although I eat a lot of sweets, I have strong teeth.)

[2] 私は甘いものをたくさん食べる**けれど（も）**／。しかし／かわりに歯をよく
磨く。
*Watashi wa amai mono o takusan taberu **keredo(mo)** / . Shikashi /
kawari ni ha o yoku migaku.*
(Although I eat a lot of sweets, I brush my teeth well.)

keredomo けれども   *conj.*

a disjunctive subordinate conjunction that combines two sentences	although; though 【REL. ***ga*²** (*daga, dakedo, demo, shikashi*)】

♦ **Key Sentence**

Subordinate Clause (informal)		Main Clause
私　は　**言わなかった** *Watashi wa **iwanakatta***	けれども *keredomo*	トム　は　知って　いた／いました。 *Tomu wa shitte ita / imashita.*
(Although I didn't tell him, Tom knew (about it).)		

Formation

Sinf けれども
　　　keredomo

{話す／話した}　けれども　　(Although s.o. (will) talk / talked)
{*hanasu / hanashita*} *keredomo*

{高い／高かった}　けれども　　(Although s.t. is / was expensive)
{*takai / takakatta*} *keredomo*

{静かだ／静かだった}　けれども　　(Although s.t. is / was quiet)
{*shizukada / shizukadatta*} *keredomo*

{先生　だ／先生　だった}　けれども　　(Although s.o. is / was a teacher)
{*sensei da / sensei datta*} *keredomo*

Examples

(a) この本は高いけれどもいい本ですよ。

Kono hon wa takai keredomo ii hon desu yo.

(Although it is expensive, this book is a good book.)

(b) 僕はドイツ語があまり好きじゃないけれども勉強しなければならない。

Boku wa doitsugo ga amari sukijanai keredomo benkyōshinakereba na-ranai.

(Although I don't like German very much, I have to study it.)

(c) 大野さんは九十歳だけれどもとても元気だ。

Ōno-san wa kyūjussai da keredomo totemo genkida.

(Although Mr. Ono is ninety years old, he is very healthy.)

Notes

1. S₁ *keredomo* S₂ means 'Although S₁, S₂'. Here, S₁ *keredomo* is a subordinate clause, therefore it is usually in the informal form. However, in very polite speech, S₁ can be in the formal form, as in (1).

   (1) この本は高いですけれどもいい本ですよ。

     *Kono hon wa **takaidesu** keredomo ii hon desu yo.*

     (Although it is expensive, this book is a good book.)

2. The informal forms of *keredomo* (listed from least formal to most formal) are *kedo* < *kedomo* < *keredo*.

kikoeru 聞こえる   *v. (Gr. 2)*

> S.t. is passively and spontaneously audible.

audible; (can) hear; it sounds 【REL. *kikeru*】

♦ **Key Sentence**

Topic (experiencer)		Audible Object			
私	(に) は	うぐいす の 声	が	よく	聞こえる / 聞こえます。
Watashi	*(ni) wa*	*uguisu no koe*	*ga*	*yoku*	*kikoeru / kikoemasu.*

(Lit. To me the cries of a nightingale are clearly audible. (=I can clearly hear the cries of a nightingale.))

Examples

(a) その音は小さすぎて聞こえない。

Sono oto wa chisasugite kikoenai.

(That sound is too weak and is not audible.)

(b) 大山さんの声は大きいので隣の部屋の人にもよく聞こえる。

Ōyama-san no koe wa ōkii node tonari no heya no hito ni mo yoku kikoeru.

(Mr. Oyama's voice is so loud that people in the neighboring rooms can hear him.)

(c) 私にはお寺のかねの音が聞こえたが，弟には聞こえなかった。

Watashi ni wa o-tera no kane no ne ga kikoeta ga, otōto ni wa kikoe-nakatta.

(I could hear the sound of the temple bell, but my younger brother couldn't.)

(d) テーラーさんの作った文は変に聞こえる。

Tērā-san no tsukutta bun wa hen ni kikoeru.

(The sentences which Mr. Taylor made sound strange.)

K

〔Related Expression〕

Kikoeru is different from the regular potential form of *kiku* 'hear' (i.e., *kikeru*), in that the former indicates a passive, auditory potentiality, whereas the latter indicates that the speaker (or the subject of sentence) can hear sound not passively but actively. Thus,

[1] 僕は耳が聞こえない / *聞けない。

*Boku wa mimi ga **kikoenai** / *kikenai*.

(I am deaf.)

[2] こんなに後ろに座るとよく聞こえない / *聞けないよ。

*Konna ni ushiro ni suwaru to yoku **kikoenai** / *kikenai yo.*

(If we sit this far back, we won't be able to hear well.)

[3] いいステレオを買ったからレコードが聞ける / *聞こえる。

*Ii sutereo o katta kara rekōdo ga **kikeru** / *kikoeru*.

(I bought a good stereo set, so I can listen to records.)

[4] 音楽がうるさくて話が聞こえない / 聞けない。

*Ongaku ga urusakute hanashi ga **kikoenai** / **kikenai**.*

(The music is so loud that the conversation is inaudible / we cannot hear the conversation.)

Note that in [4] both *kikeru* and *kikoeru* are possible, depending on the speaker's perception of the situation; if he perceives the situation to be inalterable, he uses *kikoeru*; if not, he uses *kikeru*.

kiraida きらいだ   *adj.* (*na*)

S.t. or s.o. is what s.o. does not like.

don't like; dislike
(ANT. *sukida*)

◆ **Key Sentence**

Topic (experiencer)		Disliked Object		
私	は	チーズ	が	きらいだ / きらいです。
Watashi	*wa*	*chīzu*	*ga*	*kiraida / kiraidesu*.
(I don't like cheese.)				

Examples

(a) 僕は冬がきらいだ。
   Boku wa fuyu ga kiraida.
   (I dislike winter.)

(b) ホワイトさんはフットボールが大きらいです。
   Howaito-san wa futtobōru ga dai-kiraidesu.
   (Mr. White hates football.)

Notes

1. *Kiraida* is a *na*-type adjective which requires the "*wa-ga* construction". (⇨ **~ wa ~ ga**) The experiencer (i.e., the person who dislikes some thing) is marked by *wa* and the disliked object by *ga*. Note that the disliked object is marked by *ga*, not by *o*.

2. In subordinate clauses, *wa* marking the experiencer changes into *ga*, as seen in (1).

(1) a. 私がチーズがきらいなことはみんな知っている。
   *Watashi **ga** chizu ga kiraina koto wa minna shitte iru.*
   (Everybody knows that I don't like cheese.)

   b. 僕がきらいな季節は冬です。
   *Boku **ga** kiraina kisetsu wa fuyu desu.*
   (The season I don't like is winter.)

3. "Dislike a lot" is expressed by *dai-kiraida*, as in Ex. (b).

K

koto[1] こと   *n.*

| a thing which is intangible | thing; what
【REL. *mono*】 |

♦ **Key Sentences**

(A)

Adj		
いい	こと	を 教えて あげよう / あげましょう。
Ii	*koto*	*o oshiete ageyō / agemashō.*
(Lit. I'll tell you a good thing. (=I have a good suggestion for you.))		

(B)

Relative Clause		
論文 に 書いた	こと	を 話して ください。
Ronbun ni kaita	*koto*	*o hanashite kudasai.*
(Please tell me what you wrote in your thesis.)		

(C)

	Noun			
ブラウンさん は *Buraun-san wa*	**日本 の 大学** **Nihon no daigaku**	の *no*	こと *koto*	を よく 知って いる / *o yoku shitte iru /* います。 *imasu.*

(Mr. Brown knows a lot (of things) about Japanese universities.)

Formation

(i) {V / Adj (*i*)} inf こと
　　　　　　　　　　koto

　　{話す　/ 話した} こと　　(what s.o. (will) says / said)
　　{*hanasu* / *hanashita*} *koto*

　　{おもしろい / おもしろかった} こと　　(what is / was interesting)
　　{*omoshiroi*　/ *omoshirokatta*} *koto*

(ii) Adj (*na*) stem　{な / だった} こと
　　　　　　　　　　{*na* / *datta*} *koto*

　　{大事な / 大事だった} こと　　(what is / was important)
　　{*daijina* / *daijidatta*} *koto*

(iii) N　の こと
　　　　no koto

　　先生　の こと　　(things about the teacher)
　　sensei no koto

Examples

(a) 大事なことはもう全部話しました。
　　Daijina koto wa mō zenbu hanashimashita.
　　(I already told you everything that's important.)

(b) 先生が言ったことを覚えていますか。
　　Sensei ga itta koto o oboete imasu ka.
　　(Do you remember what (=the thing which) the teacher said?)

(c) 試験のことは忘れなさい。
　　Shiken no koto wa wasurenasai.
　　(Forget about the exam.)

1. *Koto* means a thing which is intangible. Thus, (1) is ungrammatical.

   (1) *おいしいことはありませんか。

   　　Oishii **koto wa arimasen ka.*

   　　(Lit. Isn't there a delicious thing?)

2. N *no koto*, whose literal meaning is 'thing of N', is often used with such verbs as *shitte iru* 'know', *hanasu* 'talk' and *wasureru* 'forget', and means 'know about N', 'talk about N', etc.

3. *Koto* is used as a nominalizer, too. (⇨ *koto*²) Ex. (b), for instance, is ambiguous without proper context. That is, it means either 'Do you remember the thing which the teacher said?' or 'Do you remember (the fact) that the teacher said (it)?'

[Related Expression]

Mono also means 'thing', but it means 'a tangible thing'. Compare *koto* and *mono* in the following sentences:

[1] 黒いもの / *ことが見えましたか。

　　*Kuroi **mono** / ***koto** ga miemashita ka.*

　　(Lit. Did you see a black thing?)

[2] おもしろいこと / *ものを話してください。

　　*Omoshiroi **koto** / ***mono** o hanashite kudasai.*

　　(Please tell us interesting things.)

K

---

koto² こと　　*nom.*

| a nominalizer used to indicate the speaker's relative lack of empathy with the content of the sentence he is nominalizing | to ~ ; ~ing; that [REL. *no*³] |

♦ **Key Sentence**

Sentence (informal)†		
小説　を　**書く** *Shōsetsu o **kaku***	こと *koto*	は　難しい　（です）。 *wa muzukashii (desu).*
(Writing a novel is hard.)		

†*Da* after Adj (*na*) stem and N changes to *na* and *de aru*, respectively.

Formation

(i) {V / Adj (*i*)} inf こと
　　　　　　　　　koto

　　{話す / 話した}　　　こと　　((the fact) that s.o. talks / talked)
　　{*hanasu* / *hanashita*} *koto*

　　{高い / 高かった} こと　　((the fact) that s.t. is / was expensive)
　　{*takai* / *takakatta*} *koto*

(ii) Adj (*na*) stem {な / だった} こと
　　　　　　　　　　{*na* / *datta*}　*koto*

　　{静かな　 /静かだった}　こと　　((the fact) that s.t. is / was quiet)
　　{*shizukana* / *shizukadatta*} *koto*

(iii) N {で ある / で あった / だった} こと
　　　{*de aru* / *de atta* / *datta*}　　*koto*

　　{先生　である / 先生　であった / 先生　だった} こと　　((the fact) that
　　{*sensei de aru* / *sensei de atta*　/ *sensei datta*}　*koto*　s.o. is / was a
　　　　　　　　　　　　　　　　　　　　　　　　　　　　　teacher)

Examples

(a) 若い時にいい友達を作ることはとても大事だ。
　　Wakai toki ni ii tomodachi o tsukuru koto wa totemo daijida.
　　(It is very important to make good friends when one is young.)

(b) 大学四年の時フランスに留学することを考えています。
　　Daigaku yonen no toki Furansu ni ryūgakusuru koto o kangaete imasu.
　　(I am thinking of studying in France during my senior year.)

(c) 日本の文化がおもしろいことは分かるが，ユニークだとは思わない。
　　Nihon no bunka ga omoshiroi koto wa wakaru ga, yuniku da to wa omowanai.
　　(I know that Japanese culture is interesting, but I don't think that it is unique.)

(d) スイスがきれいなことは写真で知っています。

Suisu ga kireina koto wa shashin de shitte imasu.

(From pictures I know that Switzerland is beautiful.)

(e) あの人がいい人であることはたしかです。

Ano hito ga ii hito de aru koto wa tashikadesu.

(Lit. It is certain that he is a good person. (=He is without doubt a good person.))

Note

The nominalizer *koto* turns not just a verb or adjective but an entire sentence into a noun phrase. For example, in KS the sentence *shōsetsu o kaku* 'one writes a novel' becomes a complex noun phrase. Once a sentence has become a noun phrase, it can be used anywhere a regular noun phrase can be used. Thus, it can function as the subject, as in KS or Exs. (a) and (e), or as the direct object, as in Exs. (b) and (d), and so on.

[Related Expression]

In contrast to another nominalizer *no*, *koto* tends to indicate something the speaker does not feel close to. Thus, in KS, the nominalizer *koto* indicates that the speaker of the sentence is not personally involved in writing a novel; in other words, he is stating the sentence in general or objective terms. The nominalizer *no*, however, indicates something which the speaker can directly perceive or empathize with. (⇨ ***no***³) Therefore, if *koto* in KS is replaced by *no*, the nominalizer now indicates that the speaker of the sentence is somehow personally involved with writing a novel; in short, he is empathetic with an act of writing a novel. A few typical examples in which *no* or *koto* are unacceptable are given.

[1] a. 僕は静江が泳ぐの / *ことを見ていた。

*Boku wa Shizue ga oyogu **no** / *****koto** o mite ita.*

(I was watching Shizue swim.)

b. お母さんがこんなに心配しているの / ??ことが分からないの？

*O-kā-san ga konna ni shinpaishite iru **no** / ??**koto** ga wakaranai no?*

(Don't you understand that I am (lit. your mom is) really worried?)

c. ジェーンはビルが洗濯するの / *ことを手伝った。

*Jēn wa Biru ga sentakusuru **no** / ***koto** o tetsudatta.*

(Jane helped Bill do laundry.)

d.　この町ではいい音楽を聞くこと / *のが出来る。

　　*Kono machi de wa ii ongaku o kiku **koto** / ***no** ga dekiru.*

　　(I can listen to good music in this town.)

e.　見ること / *のは信じること / *のだ。

　　*Miru **koto** / ***no** wa shinjiru **koto** / ***no** da.*

　　(To see is to believe.)

Incidentally, the difference between *koto* and *no* is apparently due to the difference in the initial sounds *k* and *n*; the velar sound *k* is used to symbolize a harsh, metallic, impersonal sound and the nasal sound *n* is used to symbolize a soft, warm, personal sound.

(⇨ Characteristics of Japanese Grammar, 8. Sound Symbolisms)

K

koto ga aru¹ ことがある　　*phr.*

There was a time when ~.	S.o. has done s.t.; S.o. has had an experience doing s.t.; There was a time when ~.

◆**Key Sentences**

Sentence (informal, past)	
私　は ヨーロッパ へ 行った *Watashi wa Yōroppa e **itta***	こと が ある / あります。 *koto ga aru / arimasu.*
(I have been to Europe.)	
レタス が とても 高かった *Retasu ga totemo **takakatta***	こと が ある / あります。 *koto ga aru / arimasu.*
(There was a time when lettuce was very expensive.)	

Formation

Sinf·past　こと が ある
　　　　　　koto ga aru

話した　　こと が ある　　(have talked)
hanashita koto ga aru

高かった こと が ある   (There was a time when s.t. was expensive.)
takakatta koto ga aru

静かだった こと が ある   (There was a time when s.t. was quiet.)
shizukadatta koto ga aru

先生 だった こと が ある   (There was a time when s.o. was a teacher.)
sensei datta koto ga aru

Examples

(a) 私は中学校で英語を教えたことがあります。
Watashi wa chūgakkō de eigo o oshieta koto ga arimasu.
(I have taught English at a junior high school.)

(b) 小川さんはまだゴルフをしたことがない。
Ogawa-san wa mada gorufu o shita koto ga nai.
(Mr. Ogawa hasn't played golf yet.)

(c) 私は日本の小説をよく読んだことがある。
Watashi wa Nihon no shōsetsu o yoku yonda koto ga aru.
(There was a time when I read a lot of Japanese novels.)

(d) スーザンは一時ジャズがとても好きだったことがある。
Sūzan wa ichiji jazu ga totemo sukidatta koto ga aru.
(There was a time when Susan liked jazz a lot.)

(e) 私はプロ野球選手だったことがあります。
Watashi wa puro-yakyū senshu datta koto ga arimasu.
(There was a time when I was a professional baseball player.)

Notes

1. In general, Sinf·past *koto ga aru* expresses the idea that there was a time when someone or something was in some state or did something.

2. More specifically, Sinf·past *koto ga aru* expresses one's experience. In this case, Sinf·past *koto ga aru* is an extended use of the possession expression "A *wa* B *ga aru*", where B is a past action rather than a possessed thing. (⇨ ***aru***[1], Note 4) This extended use of the expression of possession for the expression of experience in Japanese is parallel to that in English. Compare (1) and (2).

   (1) [Possession]
   私は車がある。
   Watashi wa *kuruma* ***ga aru***.
   (*I have* a car.)

K

(2) [Experience]

私は [ロシア語を勉強したこと]past action **がある**。

Watashi wa [*roshiago o benkyōshita koto*]past action **ga aru**.

(*I have* [studied Russian.]past action)

3. In the Sinf·past *koto ga aru* structure, a past time adverb can be used
in S.

(3) 私は五年前に日本へ行ったことがある。

*Watashi wa gonen mae ni Nihon e it**ta koto** ga aru.*

(I went to Japan five years ago. (Lit. I have been to Japan five
years ago.))

(3) expresses the ideas "I have been to Japan" and "It was five years
ago" at the same time. However, in this usage, the time expressed
cannot be too close to the present. (4) is unacceptable.

(4) *私はきのうさしみを食べたことがある。

Watashi wa **kinō sashimi o tabe**ta koto** ga aru.*

(Lit. I have eaten *sashimi* yesterday.)

K

koto ga aru² ことがある   *phr.*

There are times when ~.   There are times when ~.

◆**Key Sentence**

Sentence (informal, nonpast)†	
私　は　朝　ふろ　に　入る *Watashi wa asa furo ni* **hairu**	こと　が　ある／あります。 *koto ga aru / arimasu.*
(There are times when I take a bath in the morning.)	

†*Da* after Adj(*na*) stem and N changes to *na* and *no* / *de aru*, respectively.

Formation

(i) V / Adj (*i*) inf·nonpast　こと　が　ある

　　　　　　　　　　　　　koto ga aru

話す こと が ある　　(There are times when s.o. talks.)
hanasu koto ga aru

高い こと が ある　　(There are times when s.t. is expensive.)
takai koto ga aru

(ii) **Adj (na) stem** な こと が ある
　　　　　　　　na koto ga aru

静かな こと が ある　　(There are times when s.t. is quiet.)
shizukana koto ga aru

(iii) **N** {の / である} こと が ある
　　　{*no / de aru*} *koto ga aru*

{先生 の / 先生 である} こと が ある　　(There are times when s.o.
{*sensei no / sensei de aru*} *koto ga aru*　　is a teacher.)

Examples

(a) たかしは朝ご飯を食べずに学校へ行くことがある。
Takashi wa asagohan o tabezu ni gakkō e iku koto ga aru.
(There are times when Takashi goes to school without eating breakfast.)

(b) この店のミルクはたまに古いことがある。
Kono mise no miruku wa tamani furui koto ga aru.
(Occasionally there are times when the milk in this store is old.)

(c) アメリカで日本へのみやげを買うとそれが日本製であることがよくある。
Amerika de Nihon e no miyage o kau to sore ga Nihon-sei de aru koto ga yoku aru.
(Often there are times when we find out that a souvenir we've bought in America for someone in Japan is made in Japan.)

(d) 最近のいわゆる自然食品は本当の自然食品じゃないことがある。
Saikin no iwayuru shizenshokuhin wa hontō no shizenshokuhin ja nai koto ga aru.
(There are times these days when so-called natural foods are not genuine natural foods.)

Notes

1. Sinf·nonpast *koto ga aru* expresses the idea that something happens from time to time.

2. Adverbs of frequency such as *yoku* 'often', *tokidoki* 'sometimes' and *tamani* 'occasionally' are sometimes used with this expression, as in Exs. (b) and (c).

koto ga dekiru ことが出来る　*phr.*

> Doing s.t. is possible.

can; be able to
【REL. *rareru*[2]】

◆**Key Sentence**

Topic (experiencer)		Subject		
		Vinf·nonpast	Nom	
田口さん *Taguchi-san*	は *wa*	中国語　を *chūgokugo o*	**話す** ***hanasu***	こと *koto* が *ga*	出来る / *dekiru* / 出来ます。 *dekimasu*.

(Lit. For Mr. Taguchi speaking in Chinese is possible. (= Mr. Taguchi can speak Chinese.))

Formation

Vinf·nonpast こと が 出来る
　　　　　koto ga dekiru

話す　　こと が 出来る　　(s.o. can talk)
hanasu koto ga dekiru

食べる こと が 出来る　　(s.o. can eat)
taberu koto ga dekiru

Examples

(a) 新幹線に乗れば大阪まで三時間で行くことが出来る。
　　Shinkansen ni noreba Ōsaka made sanjikan de iku koto ga dekiru.
　　(If you take a bullet train, you can get to Osaka in three hours.)

(b) 小田は六つの時バッハをひくことが出来た。
　　Oda wa muttsu no toki Bahha o hiku koto ga dekita.
　　(Oda was able to play Bach at the age of six.)

(c) ジョンソンさんは日本語で手紙を書くことが出来る。
　　Jonson-san wa nihongo de tegami o kaku koto ga dekiru.
　　(Mr. Johnson can write letters in Japanese.)

Notes

1. Vinf·nonpast *koto ga dekiru* is a potential form meaning 'can', or 'be able to ~'. This potential form is used in the "*wa-ga* construction":

N (animate) **wa** (∼ Vinf·nonpast) *koto* **ga** *dekiru*.

where N is an animate experiencer and the noun phrase ∼ Vinf·nonpast *koto* is a subject noun phrase nominalized by *koto*. The meaning of the structure is 'N can V' (lit. 'For N Ving ∼ is possible.').

(⇨ ∼ **wa** ∼ **ga**)

2. If a verb is closely associated with its direct object, as in (1) and (2) below, *o* V *koto* can be deleted.

(1) ナンシーはピアノ(を弾くこと)が出来る。
Nanshi wa piano (**o hiku koto**) ga dekiru.
(Nancy can play the piano.)

(2) 岡本さんはロシア語(を話すこと)が出来る。
Okamoto-san wa roshiago (**o hanasu koto**) ga dekiru.
(Mr. Okamoto can speak Russian.)

The *o* V *koto* deletion is unacceptable in the following sentence, however, because there is no close association between the verb and its direct object.

(3) スミスさんは日本語の新聞{を読むこと / *ø}が出来る。
Sumisu-san wa nihongo no shinbun {**o yomu koto** / *ø} ga dekiru.
(Mr. Smith can read Japanese newspapers.)

[Related Expression]

A shorter potential form of verb, i.e., *rareru*[2] can replace the longer potential form *koto ga dekiru* without a change in basic meaning. Thus, Exs. (a), (b) and (c) can be rewritten as [1], [2] and [3], respectively.

[1] 新幹線に乗れば大阪まで三時間で行ける。
Shinkansen ni noreba Ōsaka made sanjikan de **ikeru**.

[2] 小田は六つの時バッハが / をひけた。
Oda wa muttsu no toki Bahha ga / o **hiketa**.

[3] ジョンソンさんは日本語で手紙が書ける。
Jonson-san wa nihongo de tegami ga **kakeru**.

Basically, the difference between the shorter and the longer potential form is one of style; namely, the shorter version is more colloquial and less formal than the longer one.

koto ni naru ことになる *phr.*

> An event takes place as if spontaneously, irrespective of the speaker's volition.

it will be decided that ~ ; come about ~ ; be arranged that ~ ; turn out that ~

【REL. *koto ni suru*】

♦ **Key Sentences**

(A)

Topic (experiencer)			Vinf·nonpast	Nom	
私 *Watashi*	は *wa*	来年 大阪 に *rainen Ōsaka ni*	**転勤する** **tenkinsuru**	こと *koto*	に なった / *ni natta /* なりました。 *narimashita.*

(Lit. It has been decided that I will transfer to Osaka next year. (=I'm going to be transferred to Osaka next year.))

(B)

Topic (place)			Vinf·nonpast
日本 で *Nihon de*	は *wa*	車 は 道 の 左側 を *kuruma wa michi no hidarigawa o*	**走る** **hashiru**

Nom	
こと *koto*	に なっている / います。 *ni natte iru / imasu.*

(In Japan cars are supposed to be driven on the left side of the street.)

Formation

Vinf·nonpast こと に {なる / なった}
　　　　　 koto ni {naru / natta}

話す こと に {なる / なった}
hanasu koto ni {naru / natta}
(it will be decided / it has been decided that s.o. will talk)

食べる こと に {なる / なった}
taberu koto ni {naru / natta}
(it will be decided / it has been decided that s.o. will eat)

Examples

(a) 私は来月から会社に勤めることになりました。
Watashi wa raigetsu kara kaisha ni tsutomeru koto ni narimashita.
(It has been decided that I will be employed at a company beginning next month.)

(b) 多分ジャンセンさんは日本で英語を教えることになるでしょう。
Tabun Jansen-san wa Nihon de eigo o oshieru koto ni naru deshō.
(Perhaps it will turn out that Mr. Jansen will teach English in Japan.)

(c) 来年六月に結婚することになりました。
Rainen rokugatsu ni kekkonsuru koto ni narimashita.
(It's been arranged that I will get married next June.)

(d) スミスさんは日本で英語を教えることになっている。
Sumisu-san wa Nihon de eigo o oshieru koto ni natte iru.
(Mr. Smith is supposed to teach English in Japan.)

(e) 今日山田先生に会うことになっています。
Kyō Yamada-sensei ni au koto ni natte imasu.
(Today (it's been arranged that) I'm seeing Prof. Yamada.)

K

Notes

1. This construction is used when some decision or arrangement is made by some unspecified agent. Semantically this construction is close to the passive, because the experiencer has no control over the event.

2. Even when the experiencer himself decides to do s.t., it sounds more indirect, and therefore, more humble for him to use this construction rather than to use *koto ni suru* 'decide to do'. (⇨ ***koto ni suru***)

3. *Koto ni natte iru*, as in KS(B) and Exs. (d) and (e), indicates that some decision took place at some point in the past and that the result of that decision is still in effect, sometimes to the extent that it has become a rule or a custom.

koto ni suru ことにする *phr.*

| A volitional decision to do s.t. is made. | decide to 【REL. *koto ni kimeru*; *koto ni naru*】 |

◆ **Key Sentences**

(A)

Topic (agent)			Vinf·nonpast	Nom	
私 *Watashi*	は *wa*	会社 を *kaisha o*	**やめる** *yameru*	こと *koto*	に した / しました。 *ni shita / shimashita.*
(I decided to quit my company.)					

(B)

Topic (agent)			Vinf·nonpast	Nom	
私 *Watashi*	は *wa*	毎日　三十分　ぐらい 運動を *mainichi sanjuppun gurai undō o*	**する** *suru*	こと *koto*	に している / *ni shite iru /* します。 *imasu.*
(I make it a rule to exercise for about 30 minutes every day.)					

Formation

(i) Vinf·nonpast こと に {する / した}
　　　　　　　koto ni {suru / shita}

話す　こと に {する / した}　　(s.o. decides / has decided to talk)
hanasu koto ni {suru / shita}

食べる こと に {する / した}　　(s.o. decides / has decided to eat)
taberu koto ni {suru / shita}

Examples

(a) 今年の夏は北海道を旅行することにしました。
Kotoshi no natsu wa Hokkaidō o ryokōsuru koto ni shimashita.
(I've decided to make a trip in Hokkaido this summer.)

(b) 京都までバスで行くことにしましょう。

 Kyōto made basu de iku koto ni shimashō.

 (Let's (lit. decide to) go as far as Kyoto by bus.)

(c) 毎日漢字を十覚えることにしました。

 Mainichi kanji o tō oboeru koto ni shimashita.

 (I've decided to memorize ten *kanji* every day.)

(d) 私は肉をあまり食べないことにしている。

 Watashi wa niku o amari tabenai koto ni shite iru.

 (I make it a rule not to eat very much meat.)

Notes

1. If one decides not to do something, the verb before *koto ni suru* should be negated as in:

 (1) ピクニックに行こうと思ったんですが，行か**ない**ことにしました。

 *Pikunikku ni ikō to omotta n desu ga, ika**nai** koto ni shimashita.*

 (I thought I would go to the picnic, but I've decided not to.)

2. *Koto ni suru* is a more complex version of N *ni suru* 'decide on N', 'make it N'. (⇨ **~ *ni suru***) The complexity is due to a noun phrase nominalized by *koto*. (⇨ ***koto***²) An example of N *ni suru* is given below:

 (2) A : 何にしますか。

  Nan ni shimasu ka.

  (What are you going to have (lit. decide on)?)

 B : ハンバーガーにします。

  Hanbāgā ni shimasu.

  (I'll have (lit. decide on) a hamburger.)

[Related Expressions]

I. *Koto ni suru* indicates someone's volitional decision, whereas *koto ni naru* indicates a non-volitional decision. Therefore, if you perceive a given decision to be your own decision, you should use *koto ni suru*; on the other hand, if you don't perceive a given decision to be your own, you should use *koto ni naru* instead. That is why *koto ni suru* and *koto ni naru* are very awkward in [1a] and [1b], respectively.

 [1] a. 私は大阪に転勤することになりました / ???しました。

  *Watashi wa Ōsaka ni tenkinsuru koto ni **narimashita** / ??? **shimashita**.*

  (Lit. It has been decided that I will transfer to Osaka. (= I'm going to be transferred to Osaka.))

K

b. 僕はたばこをやめることにしました / ???なりました。
   *Boku wa tabako o yameru koto ni **shimashita** / ???**narima-
   shita***.
   (I've decided to quit smoking.)

II. *Koto ni suru* and *koto ni kimeru* 'determine to do s.t.' are virtually
identical in meaning. The difference is that the former is an idiom and,
therefore, frequently used in colloquial speech, while the latter is appropriate when the speaker is talking about a relatively important decision
in a rather decisive manner. Also, *koto ni suru* can be used to mean
' I hereby decide to ∼ ' but *koto ni kimeru* cannot. Thus, [1] below
cannot be rephrased by *koto ni kimeru*.

[1] 私は会社をやめることにします / ???きめます。
    *Watashi wa kaisha o yameru koto ni **shimasu** / ???**kimemasu***.
    (I've decided to quit my company.)

K

koto wa こと は   *phr.*

| Speaking of proposition X, X is cer-tainly true. | indeed one does s.t. alright, (but ∼); indeed ∼ (but ∼); do ∼ (but ∼) |

◆ **Key Sentence**

Topic (subject)		Predicate₁					Predicate₂
		V₁ inf		V₂			
私 *Watashi*	は *wa*	テニスを *tenisu o* **する** *suru*	ことは *koto wa*	**する / します** *suru / shimasu*	が *ga*	上手じゃない / 上 *jōzujanai / jō-* 手じゃありません。 *zujaarimasen.*

(I do play tennis, but I am not good at it.)

Formation

(i) {V₁ / Adj (*i*)₁} inf こと は {V₂ / Adj (*i*)₂}
      koto wa   (where {V₁ / Adj (*i*)₁} = {V₂ / Adj(*i*)₂})

話す こと は {話す ／話します} (s.o. does talk)
hanasu koto wa {hanasu / hanashimasu}

話した こと は {話した ／話しました} (s.o. did talk)
hanashita koto wa {hanashita / hanashimashita}

高い こと は 高い(です) (s.t. *is* expensive)
takai koto wa takai(desu)

高かった こと は 高かった(です) (s.t. *was* expensive)
takakatta koto wa takakatta(desu)

(ii) {Adj (*na*) stem₁ な こと / N₁} は {Adj (*na*) stem₂ / N₂} {だ / です}
      na koto   *wa*   *{da / desu}*
    (where {Adj (*na*) stem₁ / N₁} = {Adj (*na*) stem₂ / N₂})

静かな こと は 静か {だ / です} (s.t. *is* quiet)
shizukana koto wa shizuka {da / desu}

いい 人 は いい 人 {だ / です} (s.o. *is* a good person)
ii hito wa ii hito {da / desu}

(iii) {Adj (*na*) stem₁ / N₁} だった こと は {Adj (*na*) stem₂ / N₂} {だった / でした}
       datta koto wa   *{datta / deshita}*
    (where {Adj (*na*) stem₁ / N₁} = {Adj (*na*) stem₂ / N₂})

静かだった こと は 静か {だった / でした} (s.t. *was* quiet)
shizukadatta koto wa shizuka {datta / deshita}

いい 人 だった こと は いい 人 {だった / でした} (s.o. *was* a good
ii hito datta koto wa ii hito {datta / deshita} person)

Examples

(a) ジョーンズさんは日本語を話すことは話しますが，簡単なことしか言えません。
Jōnzu-san wa nihongo o hanasu koto wa hanashimasu ga, kantanna koto shika iemasen.
(Mr. Jones does speak Japanese, but he can say only simple things.)

(b) ボストン シンフォニーの切符は買えたことは買えましたが，大変悪い席でした。
Bosuton Shinfoni no kippu wa kaeta koto wa kaemashita ga, taihen warui seki deshita.
(I could buy a ticket for the Boston Symphony alright, but it was a very bad seat.)

(c) この店は安いことは安いですが，ものがよくありません。
   Kono mise wa yasui koto wa yasui desu ga, mono ga yokuarimasen.
   (This store is inexpensive alright, but its goods are of poor quality.)

(d) 今日の試験は難しかったことは難しかったがよく出来た。
   Kyō no shiken wa muzukashikatta koto wa muzukashikatta ga yoku dekita.
   (Today's exam was indeed difficult, but I did well on it.)

(e) 私のアパートは駅に近くて便利なことは便利ですが，家賃がとても高いです。
   Watashi no apāto wa eki ni chikakute benrina koto wa benridesu ga, yachin ga totemo takaidesu.
   (My apartment is close to the station and convenient alright, but the rent is very high.)

(f) その女の子が好きだったことは好きでしたが，結婚はしなかったんです。
   Sono onna no ko ga sukidatta koto wa sukideshita ga, kekkon wa shinakatta n desu.
   (I did like the girl, but I didn't marry her.)

(g) あの人はいい人はいい人だったけれど頑固だったね。
   Ano hito wa ii hito wa ii hito datta keredo gankodatta ne.
   (He was indeed a good person, but he was stubborn, wasn't he?)

Notes

1. In this construction, when the main verb is in the past tense the tense of the first verb / adjective can be changed into the nonpast tense. Thus, Exs. (b) and (d) could be (1) and (2), respectively. The switched versions are more common in conversation.

   (1) ボストン シンフォニーの切符は**買える**ことは買えましたが大変悪い席でした。
      *Bosuton Shinfoni no kippu wa **kaeru** koto wa kaemashita ga taihen warui seki **deshita**.*

   (2) 今日の試験は**難しい**ことは難しかったがよく**出来た**。
      *Kyō no shiken wa **muzukashii** koto wa muzukashikatta ga yoku **dekita**.*

2. The verb / adjective / noun before *koto wa* is normally marked in the informal form even if the final predicate is marked in the formal form.

3. Normally this construction is followed by a disjunctive conjunction such as *ga* 'but', *keredo* 'but, although' and *shikashi* 'but'.

~kudasai ～ください *aux. v.* (imperative form)

> an auxiliary verb which indicates a polite request

please do s.t.

◆ **Key Sentences**

(A)

	V*te*	
日本語 で *Nihongo de*	**書いて** ***kaite***	ください。 *kudasai.*
(Please write in Japanese.)		

(B)

	Vneg		
英語 を *Eigo o*	**使わ** ***tsukawa***	ないで *nai de*	ください。 *kudasai.*
(Please don't use English.)			

K

Formation

(i) V*te* ください
　　　　kudasai

　話して　ください　　(Please talk.)
　hanashite kudasai

　食べて ください　　(Please eat.)
　tabete kudasai

(ii) Vneg ないで ください
　　　　nai de kudasai

　話さない で ください　　(Please don't talk.)
　hanasanai de kudasai

　食べない で ください　　(Please don't eat.)
　tabenai de kudasai

Examples

(a) この言葉の意味を教えてください。
　Kono kotoba no imi o oshiete kudasai.
　(Please tell me the meaning of this word.)

(b) 夜おそく電話しないでください。

　　Yoru osoku denwashinai de kudasai.

　　(Please don't call me late at night.)

Notes

1. *Kudasai* is the polite imperative form of *kudasaru*, the honorific version of *kureru* 'give (me)' and is used as an auxiliary verb with the *te*-form of verbs.　　　　　　　　　　　　　　　　　　　　　(⇨ *kureru*[2])

2. *Dōzo* emphasizes the speaker's request and makes it more polite.

　　⑴　どうぞ教えてください。

　　　　Dōzo *oshiete kudasai.*

　　　　(Please tell me.)

3. In very informal speech, *kudasai* may drop. (This form of request is often used by female speakers.)

　　⑵　a.　早く来て。

　　　　　　Hayaku kite.

　　　　　　(Please come quickly.)

　　　　b.　まだ帰らないで。

　　　　　　Mada kaeranai de.

　　　　　　(Please don't go home yet.)

4. The negative question form, seen in (3), makes a request more polite.

　　⑶　あした八時に来てくださいませんか。

　　　　Ashita hachiji ni kite ***kudasaimasen ka****.*

　　　　(Would you please come at eight o'clock tomorrow?)

5. *Kure*, the imperative form of *kureru*, can also be used in place of *kudasai* in informal male speech. {V*te* / V*neg nai de*} *kure* is the least polite request form.

　　⑷　a.　僕と一緒に来てくれ。

　　　　　　Boku to isshoni kite ***kure****.*

　　　　　　(Come with me (please).)

　　　　b.　アパートには来ないでくれ。

　　　　　　*Apāto ni wa ko****nai de kure****.*

　　　　　　(Don't come to my apartment (please).)

-kun 君 *suf.*

a suffix attached to the first or last name of a male equal or to the first or last name of a person whose status or rank is lower than the speaker's

【REL. *-sama* (-chan; -san)】

Formation

(i) Last Name 君
              kun

山田　君　(Mr. Yamada)
Yamada-kun

(ii) First Name 君
                kun

太郎 君　(Taro)
Tarō-kun

(iii) Last Name First Name 君
                         kun

山田　太郎 君　(Mr. Taro Yamada)
Yamada Tarō-kun

Examples

(a) もし，もし，一郎君いますか。
Moshi, moshi, Ichirō-kun imasu ka.
(Hello, is Ichiro in?)

(b) 田口君が来年結婚するそうだ。
Taguchi-kun ga rainen kekkonsuru sōda.
(I heard that Mr. Taguchi will get married next year.)

(c) 田口一郎君，昇進おめでとう。
Taguchi Ichirō-kun, shōshin omedetō.
(Mr. Ichiro Taguchi, congratulations on your promotion.)

Note

A male may address females of lower rank by *-kun*. A female student may address males of equal or lower rank by *-kun*. Such addresses are commonly used in situations such as schools and companies.

kurai くらい *prt.*

┌─────────────────────────────────┐
approximate quantity or extent
└─────────────────────────────────┘

approximately; about
【REL. *goro*; *hodo* (*bakari*)】

♦ **Key Sentence**

	Number-Counter		
東京 から サンフランシスコ まで 飛行機 で *Tōkyō kara Sanfuranshisuko made hikōki de*	**九時間** **kujikan**	くらい *kurai*	かかる / か *kakaru* / *ka-* かります。 *karimasu.*
(It's about nine hours by plane from Tokyo to San Francisco.)			

Formation

(i) Number-Counter くらい
　　　　　　　　　　　　 kurai

　　四冊 　くらい　　(about four volumes)
　　yonsatsu kurai

　　百人 　　くらい　　(about a hundred people)
　　hyakunin kurai

(ii) Demonstrative {Pronoun / Adjective} くらい
　　　　　　　　　　　　　　　　　　　　　 kurai

　　{これ / この} くらい　　(about this much / to about this extent)
　　{*kore* / *kono*} *kurai*

　　{それ / その} くらい　　(about that much / to about that extent)
　　{*sore* / *sono*} *kurai*

　　{あれ / あの} くらい　　((referring to an object that is removed from both
　　{*are* / *ano*} *kurai*　　the speaker and the hearer) about that much /
　　　　　　　　　　　　　　　 to about that extent)

　　{どれ / どの} くらい　　(about how much? / to about what extent?)
　　{*dore* / *dono*} *kurai*

(iii) Interrogative Pronoun くらい
　　　　　　　　　　　　　　　 kurai

　　いくら くらい　　(about how much?)
　　ikura kurai

Examples

(a) A : その車はいくらぐらいでしたか。
　　　Sono kuruma wa ikura gurai deshita ka.
　　　(About how much was that car?)

　　B : 百五十万円くらいでした。
　　　Hyakugojūman'en kurai deshita.
　　　(It was about 1,500,000 yen.)

(b) スミスさんは京都に四か月くらい行っていました。
　　Sumisu-san wa Kyōto ni yonkagetsu kurai itte imashita.
　　(Mr. Smith was in Kyoto for about four months.)

(c) 山田さんぐらい英語が出来れば楽しいでしょうね。
　　Yamada-san gurai eigo ga dekireba tanoshii desyō ne.
　　(It must be fun to be able to speak English as well as Mr. Yamada
　　(lit. to the extent of Mr.Yamada).)

(d) 私だってそれぐらいのことは分かりますよ。
　　Watashi datte sore gurai no koto wa wakarimasu yo.
　　(Even I can understand that sort of thing (lit. things of that extent).)

Note

Kurai may be freely replaced by *gurai* without a change in meaning.

K

kureru[1] くれる　　*v. (Gr. 2)*

> S.o. whose status is not higher than
> the speaker's gives s.t. to the first
> person or to s.o. with whom the
> speaker empathizes.

give
【REL. *ageru*[1]; *morau*[1]】

♦**Key Sentence**

Topic (subject)		Indirect Object		Direct Object		
大川さん	は	(私	に)	本	を	くれた / くれました。
Ōkawa-san	*wa*	(*watashi*	*ni*)	*hon*	*o*	*kureta / kuremashita.*
(Mr. Okawa gave me a book.)						

Examples

(a) ビルは(君に)何をくれましたか。
　　Biru wa (kimi ni) nani o kuremashita ka.
　　(What did Bill give to you?)

(b) 川村さんは私のむすめにレコードをくれた。
　　Kawamura-san wa watashi no musume ni rekōdo o kureta.
　　(Mr. Kawamura gave my daughter a record.)

Notes

1. *Kureru*, which is one of a set of giving and receiving verbs, means 'give'. Unlike the English *give*, however, *kureru* is used only when the receiver is the first person or someone with whom the speaker empathizes (usually a member of the speaker's in-group). Thus, (1) is unacceptable. (If the speaker empathizes with Mr. Ito, (1) is considered acceptable. Addressing someone as "Mr. Ito", however, is too formal in such a situation.)

   (1) *川口さんはいつも伊藤さんにたばこをくれる。
   　　*Kawaguchi-san wa itsumo Itō-san ni tabako o kureru.
   　　(Mr. Kawaguchi always gives Mr. Ito cigarettes.)

2. When the giver is the first person, *kureru* cannot be used.

   (2) *私は中島さんに酒をくれた。
   　　*Watashi wa Nakajima-san ni sake o kureta.
   　　(I gave Mr. Nakajima *sake*.)

   In this case, *ageru* must be used.

   (3) 私は中島さんに酒をあげた。
   　　Watashi wa Nakajima-san ni sake o ageta.
   　　(I gave Mr. Nakajima *sake*.)

   Note that when the subject is the first person, *kureru*-sentences are not grammatical even if the receiver is someone the speaker empathizes with, as in (4).

   (4) *私は兄さんにチョコレートをくれた。
   　　*Watashi wa ni-san ni chokorēto o kureta.
   　　(I gave my elder brother chocolates.)

   The reason for this is as follows: *Kureru* requires the receiver's point of view when describing an event, and when an event involves the first person, the event is normally described from the first person's point of view. Therefore, if the first person is the giver in *kureru*-sentences, a viewpoint conflict arises, making the sentences ungrammatical. (In this case, *ageru* must be used.)

3. The polite (honorific) version of *kureru* is *kudasaru* (Gr. 1 verb; The *masu*-form is *kudasaimasu*). Example:

(5) 先生は（私に）本をくださいました。
    *Sensei wa (watashi ni) hon o **kudasaimashita**.*
    (My teacher gave me a book.)

4. The indirect object is often omitted if it refers to the speaker in declarative sentences or to the hearer in interrogative sentences.

(See KS and Ex. (a).)

[Related Expressions]

I. [1] compares the differences among the three giving and receiving verbs *ageru*, *kureru* and *morau* in terms of viewpoint when A gives X to B. The eye sign " ∀ " indicates which viewpoint the sentence requires.

[1] a. **A** は B に X をあげた。
         A *wa B ni X o ageta.*
         ∀ (or neutral)
         (A gave X to B.)

     b. A は **B** に X をくれた。
         *A wa **B** ni X o kureta.*
              ∀
         (A gave X to B.)

     c. **B** は A に X をもらった。
         B *wa A ni X o moratta.*
         ∀
         (B got X from A.)

If the first person or a person the speaker empathizes with is involved in a giving-receiving situation, the NP which refers to him must occur in the positions with " ∀ ". The reason for this is as follows: When the first person or someone the speaker empathizes with is involved in a giving-receiving situation, the situation is normally described from his viewpoint, and if the NP which refers to him occurs in the positions without " ∀ ", a viewpoint conflict arises.

II. [2] summarizes the plain forms and polite forms of giving and receiving verbs:

[2]

	(I) give (s.o.)	(s.o.) gives (me)	(I) get / receive (from s.o.)
Plain form	① やる *yaru* (to s.o. of lower status) ② あげる *ageru*	② くれる *kureru*	① もらう *morau*
Polite form	② さしあげる *sashiageru* (very humble)	① くださる *kudasaru* (honorific) (*masu*-form : *kudasaimasu*)	① いただく *itadaku* (humble)

((①: Gr. 1 verb; ②: Gr. 2 verb)

Note the different degree of politeness in each verb (particularly, *yaru*, *ageru* and *sashiageru*).

kureru[2] くれる　　*aux. v. (Gr. 2)*

S.o. does s.t. as a favor to the first person or to s.o. with whom the speaker empathizes.

do s.t. (for me or s.o.); do me or s.o. a favor by doing s.t. 【REL. *ageru*[2]; **kureru**[1]; *morau*[2]】

◆ **Key Sentences**

(A)

Topic (subject)	Indirect Object	Direct Object	V*te*	
父　　は *Chichi*　*wa*	(私　　に) (*watashi*　*ni*)	カメラ　を *kamera*　*o*	買って **katte**	くれた / くれました。 *kureta* / *kuremashita*.
(My father bought a camera for me.)				

(B)

Topic (subject)		Direct Object		V*te*	
道男 *Michio*	は *wa*	私 *watashi*	を *o*	**なぐさめて** **nagusamete**	くれた / くれました。 *kureta / kuremashita.*
(Michio consoled me.)					

Formation

V*te* くれる
　　kureru

話して　くれる　　(s.o. (will) talks for my sake)
hanashite kureru

食べて　くれる　　(s.o. (will) eats for my sake)
tabete kureru

Examples

(a) 母は(私に)ケーキを焼いてくれた。
　　Haha wa (watashi ni) kēki o yaite kureta.
　　(My mother baked a cake for me.)

(b) ウォーカーさんは私のむすこに英語を教えてくれている。
　　Wōkā-san wa watashi no musuko ni eigo o oshiete kurete iru.
　　(Ms. Walker is kindly teaching my son English.)

(c) 子供達は(あなたに)何をしてくれましたか。
　　Kodomotachi wa (anata ni) nani o shite kuremashita ka.
　　(What did your children do for you?)

Notes

1. *Kureru* is used as an auxiliary verb with V*te*. The meaning of V*te kureru* is "someone does the first person (or someone with whom the speaker empathizes) a favor by doing something". Like sentences with *kureru* as a main verb, sentences with V*te kureru* are stated from the viewpoint of the person who receives the favor and the receiver must be the first person or someone the speaker empathizes with (usually a member of the speaker's in-group). Thus, (1a) is grammatical, but (1b) is not. (⇒ *kureru*¹)

　　(1) a. 知らない人が私にコーラを買ってくれた。
　　　　　 Shiranai hito ga watashi ni kōra o katte kureta.
　　　　　 (A stranger bought cola for me.)

b. *私は知らない人にコーラを買ってくれた。

*Watashi wa shiranai hito ni kōra o katte kureta.

(I bought cola for a stranger.)

(In the case in (1b), *ageru* 'give' must be used. (⇨ **ageru**²)) Note that if the subject is the first person, sentences with V*te kureru* are ungrammatical even if the person who receives the favor is someone the speaker empathizes with, as in (2). (See **kureru**¹, Note 2.)

(2) *私は**母に**ケーキを焼いて**くれた**。

*Watashi wa **haha ni** kēki o yaite **kureta**.

(I baked a cake for my mother.)

In this case, *ageru* must be used. (⇨ **ageru**²)

2. As in KS(B), if the person receiving the benefit of the action is the direct object, the indirect object is omitted. Therefore, (3a) and (3b) are ungrammatical.

(3) a. *道男は私に私をなぐさめてくれた。

*Michio wa **watashi ni** watashi o nagusamete kureta.

b. *道男は私になぐさめてくれた。

*Michio wa **watashi ni** nagusamete kureta.

3. If the main verb of the sentence is intransitive, the person receiving the benefit of the action is not marked by *ni*. Therefore, (4) is ungrammatical.

(4) *みんなは私に働いてくれた。

*Minna wa watashi **ni** hataraite kureta.

(Everybody worked for me.)

In this case, *no tame ni* 'for the sake of' is used, as in (5). (⇨ **tame**)

(5) みんなは私のために働いてくれた。

Minna wa watashi **no tame ni** hataraite kureta.

(Everybody worked for my sake.)

4. The polite (honorific) version of V*te kureru* is V*te kudasaru*. Example:

(6) 先生は私に本を貸してくださった。

Sensei wa watashi ni hon o kashite **kudasatta**.

(My teacher kindly lent me a book.)

5. Note that in sentences like " Mr. A taught me ∼ ", " Mr. A bought me ∼ " and " Mr. A lent me ∼ ", which usually imply that the speaker received some sort of favor, V*te kureru* (or *kudasaru*) should be used,

though in English this is not usually explicitly expressed. In Japanese, without the auxiliary verbs *kureru* or *kudasaru*, such sentences don't convey the idea that the speaker received a favor.

6. The indirect object is often omitted if it refers to the speaker in declarative sentences or to the hearer in interrogative sentences.

(See KS(A), Exs. (a) and (c).)

〔Related Expressions〕

Ageru, *kureru* and *morau* and all their polite and non-polite versions are used as auxiliary verbs with V*te*. (Auxiliary verbs *ageru*, *kureru* and *morau* are explained under *ageru²*, *kureru²* and *morau²*, respectively.) When these verbs are used as auxiliary verbs, the same viewpoint rules stated in *kureru¹* Related Expression I apply, except that there is no neutral viewpoint.

K

kuru¹ 来る *v. (Irr.)*

~~~
S.o. or s.t. moves in a direction towards the speaker or the speaker's
viewpoint or area of empathy.
~~~

come; visit; show up
〔REL. *iku¹*〕

◆**Key Sentence**

	Noun (place)		
田中さん が あした *Tanaka-san ga ashita*	**うち** **uchi**	へ / に *e / ni*	来る / 来ます。 *kuru / kimasu.*
(Mr. Tanaka will come to my home tomorrow.)				

Examples

(a) ナンシーはきのうパーティーに来ましたか。
Nanshī wa kinō pāti ni kimashita ka.
(Did Nancy come to the party yesterday?)

(b) 来週木口さんが名古屋に来るそうだ。
Raishū Kiguchi-san ga Nagoya ni kuru sōda.
(I was told that Mr. Kiguchi is coming to Nagoya next week.)

(c) もし，もし，家内が来たらすぐ帰るように言ってください。

Moshi, moshi, kanai ga kitara sugu kaeru yō ni itte kudasai.

(Hello, please tell my wife to come home right away if she (lit. comes to see you) drops by.)

(d) 今日はまだ新聞が来ない。

Kyō wa mada shinbun ga konai.

(Today's newspaper hasn't come yet.)

(e) 僕の研究室にあした来てください。

Boku no kenkyūshitsu ni ashita kite kudasai.

(Please come to my office tomorrow.)

Note

Kuru commonly describes a movement towards a place where the speaker physically exists, as in KS and Ex. (d). However, it can also describe a movement in a direction where the speaker has placed his viewpoint or where he feels strong empathy. For example, in Ex. (a) the speaker, who apparently did not attend the party, is taking the viewpoint of the hearer, who did attend. In Ex. (c) the speaker is phoning and is not at the hearer's house, yet he is taking the hearer's viewpoint, a typical example of the psychological fusion between speaker and hearer. In Ex. (b), it is possible that the speaker lives nearer Nagoya than Mr. Kiguchi does and feels that Mr. Kiguchi is entering his (the speaker's) territory or area of strong empathy. And again, in Ex. (e), the use of *kuru* indicates that the speaker's office as well as his house can be considered his territory or area of empathy.

[Related Expression]

If a movement is towards a place where the speaker can place his viewpoint, *kuru* is used, but if a movement is towards a place where the speaker cannot place his viewpoint, *iku* is used. (⇨ *iku¹*)

In Exs. (a) and (c) both *kuru* and *iku* are acceptable. The difference is that the use of *kuru* shifts the focus of the sentence to the hearer's viewpoint while *iku* shifts it to the speaker's viewpoint.

kuru² 来る *aux. v. (Irr.)*

<table>
<tr><td>An auxiliary verb which indicates the beginning of some process or continuation of some action up to a current point of time.</td><td>come about; grow; come to; begin to
【REL. ~*hajimeru*】</td></tr>
</table>

♦ Key Sentences

(A)

	V*te* (process)	
私　　は コンピューター が　少し *Watashi wa　conpyūtā　ga sukoshi*	**分かって** **wakatte**	来た / 来ました。 *kita / kimashita.*
(Now I have begun to understand computers.)		

(B)

	V*te*	
私　　は いろいろ 日本　の　歴史書 を *Watashi wa　iroiro Nihon no rekishisho o*	**読んで** **yonde**	来た / 来ました。 *kita / kimashita.*
(Up to now I've been reading various Japanese histories.)		

Formation

(i) V*te* 来る
　　　　 kuru

　　ふくらん で 来る / 来た　　(s.t. begins / has begun to swell)
　　fukuran de kuru / kita

　　大きく なって 来る / 来た　　(s.t. begins / has begun to grow big)
　　ōkiku　natte　kuru / kita

Examples

(a) テニスをしていたら急に雨が降って来た。
　　Tenisu o shite itara kyūni ame ga futte kita.
　　(Suddenly, while we were playing tennis, it began to rain.)

(b) 午後から頭が痛くなって来ました。
　　Gogo kara atama ga itaku natte kimashita.
　　(Lit. My head began to ache in the afternoon.　(=My headache started in the afternoon.))

(c) 私はこのごろ太って来ました。

Watashi wa konogoro futotte kimashita.

(I've started to gain weight these days.)

(d) あの子はこのごろずいぶんきれいになって来たね。

Ano ko wa konogoro zuibun kireini natte kita ne.

(That girl has become very pretty lately, hasn't she?)

(e) 今までたくさん本を読んで来ましたが，これからも読んで行くつもりです。

Ima made takusan hon o yonde kimashita ga, kore kara mo yonde iku tsumori desu.

(Up to now I have read quite a few books and I intend to read from now on, too.)

(f) 今まで遊んで来ましたが，これからは一生懸命勉強するつもりです。

Ima made asonde kimashita ga, kore kara wa isshōkenmei benkyōsuru tsumori desu.

(Up to now I haven't been working hard (lit. have been playing), but from now on I intend to work very hard.)

Notes

1. V*te kuru* expresses *inception* as in Exs. (a) through (d), or *continuation* of s.t. up to a current point of time, as in Exs. (e) and (f). In the former case the V is a verb that indicates a process that takes some time to complete, such as *naru* 'become', *wakaru* 'understand', *futoru* 'gain weight', *yaseru* 'lose weight', *fukuramu* 'swell' and *chijimu* 'shrink'. In the latter case the V is any non-punctual verb.

2. In the following sentences *kuru* is used more as a full verb than as an auxiliary verb. The meaning of V*te kuru* is the same as that of V*te* (i.e., ' V and ') and of *kuru*.　　　　　　　　　　　　　(⇨ *kuru*¹)

   (1) 私は会社にバスに乗って来ます。

   Watashi wa kaisha ni basu ni notte kimasu.

   (Lit. I ride a bus and come to my company. (＝I come to work by bus.))

   (2) 四時までには帰って来てください。

   Yoji made ni wa kaette kite kudasai.

   (Lit. Please return and come here by 4:00. (＝Please come back by 4:00.))

(3) おいしいケーキを買って来ました。
   Oishii kēki o katte kimashita.
   (Lit. I bought a delicious cake and came here. (＝I bought you a delicious cake.))

(4) 友達をうちに連れて来た。
   Tomodachi o uchi ni tsurete kita.
   (I brought my friends to my house.)

(5) あの本持って来た？
   Ano hon motte kita?
   (Did you bring that book (lit. carry that book and come)?)

(6) ちょっと見て来るよ。
   Chotto mite kuru yo.
   (Lit. I'll just look and come back here. (＝I'll just go and take a look at it.))

(7) 傘を取って来ます。
   Kasa o totte kimasu.
   (Lit. I'll get my umbrella and come back here. (＝I'll go and get my umbrella.))

3. Note that the experiencer of the *inception* process or the *continuation* of the action must be the speaker himself or someone with whom the speaker empathizes. In other words, in this usage, what is expressed by V*te kuru*² involves the speaker in a very intimate way.

[Related Expression]

When *kuru*² means *inception* (the beginning of a process, that is), it is very close to V*masu hajimeru* 'begin to ～' Exs. (a) through (d) can all be paraphrased using V*masu hajimeru*. However, *kuru* implies that s.t. happens to the speaker or whomever he can empathize with, whereas V*masu hajimeru* lacks the speaker's involvement with a process of inception. (⇨ **～hajimeru**)

mada まだ　*adv.*

~~~
S.o. or s.t. is in some state he or it
was in some time ago.
~~~
still; (not) yet
【REL. *mō*】

♦**Key Sentences**

(A)

Topic (subject)			Predicate (affirmative)
木村君 *Kimura-kun*	は *wa*	まだ *mada*	昼ご飯 を **食べて いる** / **います**。 *hirugohan o **tabete iru** / **imasu**.*
(Mr. Kimura is still eating his lunch.)			

(B)

Topic (subject)			Predicate (negative)
太田さん *Ōta-san*	は *wa*	まだ *mada*	その こと を **知らない** / **知りません**。 *sono koto o **shiranai** / **shirimasen**.*
(Mr. Ota still doesn't know about it.)			

Examples

(a) お酒はまだありますか。
　　O-sake wa mada arimasu ka.
　　(Do you still have *sake*?)

(b) 私はまだ日本へ行ったことがない。
　　Watashi wa mada Nihon e itta koto ga nai.
　　(I have not been to Japan yet.)

(c) A: もう昼ご飯を食べましたか。
　　　　Mō hirugohan o tabemashita ka.
　　　　(Have you eaten your lunch yet?)

　　B₁: いいえ，まだ食べていません。
　　　　Īe, mada tabete imasen.
　　　　(No, I haven't eaten it yet.)

　　B₂: いいえ，まだです。
　　　　Īe, mada desu.
　　　　(No, not yet.)

Notes

1. *Mada* expresses the idea that someone or something is in the same state that he or it was in some time ago. In affirmative sentences, *mada* always corresponds to 'still'. In negative sentences, however, it corresponds to 'yet' when an action has not yet been taken, and 'still' in other situations, as in Ex. (c) and KS(B), respectively.

2. The abbreviated sentence seen in B₂ of Ex. (c) is used only when the response to a question is a negative one.

[Related Expression]

The concept which *mada* expresses is opposite to that of *mō*. [1] illustrates the difference between the idea conveyed by *mada* and the one conveyed by *mō*.

[1] a. *mada* <u>X is in the state A</u>⎯⎯⎯⎯⎯→ time

                              ↑

                  point of reference

                  (X is still in the state A)

    b. *mō* <u>X is in the state A</u>| ⎯⎯⎯→ time

                            ↑

                  point of reference

                  (X is not in the state A any more.)

M

---

made まで   *prt.*

a particle to indicate a spatial, temporal or quantitative limit or an unexpected animate / inanimate object	as far as; till; up to; until; through; even **[REL. *made ni*]**

♦Key Sentences

(A)

	Noun (time)		Noun (time)		
きのうは *Kinō wa*	三時 ***sanji***	から *kara*	五時 ***goji***	まで *made*	友達　と テニス をした / *tomodachi to tenisu o shita /* しました。 *shimashita.*
(Yesterday I played tennis from three to five with my friend.)					

(B)

Noun (location)		Noun (location)		
東京 ***Tōkyō***	から *kara*	京都 ***Kyōto***	まで *made*	新幹線　で 三時間　かかる / *shinkansen de sanjikan kakaru /* かかります。 *kakarimasu.*
(It takes three hours by bullet train from Tokyo to Kyoto.)				

(C)

Subordinate Clause			Main Clause
	Vinf·nonpast		
私　が *Watashi ga*	行く ***iku***	まで *made*	うち で 待って いて ください。 *uchi de matte ite kudasai.*
(Please wait at home until I get there.)			

(D)

	Number-Counter		
この ホール は *Kono hōru wa*	二千人 ***nisennin***	まで *made*	入れる / 入れます。 *haireru / hairemasu.*
(This hall can hold up to 2,000 people.)			

(E)

	Noun (unex-pected object)	
あの 人 は ねずみ や スカンク は もちろん *Ano hito wa nezumi ya sukanku wa mochiron*	**蛇** **hebi**	まで *made*
	好きだ / 好きです。 *sukida / sukidesu.*	
(He even likes snakes, not to mention rats and skunks.)		

Formation

(i) Noun (time / location) まで
                   made

  五時 / 学校 まで   (until five / as far as school)
  goji / gakkō made

(ii) Vinf·nonpast まで
             made

  話す まで   (until s.o. talks / talked)
  hanasu made

  食べる まで   (until s.o. eats / ate)
  taberu made

(iii) Number-Counter まで
               made

  四十人   まで   (up to forty people)
  yonjūnin made

  五枚   まで   (up to five sheets of paper)
  gomai made

Examples

(a) アメリカ人は毎週月曜日から金曜日まで働く。
    Amerikajin wa maishū getsuyōbi kara kin'yōbi made hataraku.
    (Americans work every week from Monday through Friday.)

(b) 駅から大学までは歩いて十分ぐらいです。
    Eki kara daigaku made wa aruite juppun gurai desu.
    (Lit. It's about 10 minutes from the station to the university on foot.
    (= It's about a ten-minute walk from the station to the university.))

(c) スミスさんは刺身はもちろん，なっとうまで食べるんですよ。

Sumisu-san wa sashimi wa mochiron, nattō made taberu n desu yo.

(Mr. Smith even eats fermented soybeans, not to mention raw fish.)

(d) 飛行機が出るまでロビーで友達と話していた。

Hikōki ga deru made robi de tomodachi to hanashite ita.

(Until the plane left I was talking with my friend in the lobby.)

Note

' *X made* ' and ' until X ' do not have the same meaning when X represents a duration of time. For example, in (1) *raishū no getsuyōbi made* means that the speaker will be absent next Monday; therefore, the corresponding English is ' until next *Tuesday* '.

(1) 私は来週の月曜日まで休みます。

Watashi wa raishū no getsuyōbi made yasumimasu.

(I'll be absent until next Tuesday.)

made ni　までに　　*prt.*

a particle that indicates a time limit on / for an action	by; by the time (when) 【REL. *made*; *made de*; *mae ni*】

♦Key Sentences

(A)

	Noun (time)		
私　は *Watashi wa*	十時 *jūji*	まで に *made ni*	帰る / 帰ります。 *kaeru / kaerimasu.*
(I'll come home by 10 o'clock.)			

(B)

Subordinate Clause			Main Clause
	Vinf·nonpast		
学校 が *Gakkō ga*	**始まる** **hajimaru**	までに *made ni*	この 本 を 読んで おいて ください。 *kono hon o yonde oite kudasai.*
(Please read this book (in advance) by the time school starts.)			

Formation

KS(A):

N (time) まで に
      made ni

五時 まで に   (by five o'clock)
goji made ni

あした まで に   (by tomorrow)
ashita made ni

KS(B):

Vinf·nonpast まで に
      made ni

話す   まで に   (by the time s.o. talks / talked)
hanasu made ni

食べる まで に   (by the time s.o. eats / ate)
taberu made ni

Examples

(a) A：何時までに空港に行けばいいでしょうか。
    Nanji made ni kūkō ni ikeba ii deshō ka.
    (By what time should I go to the airport?)

    B：出発の一時間前までに来てください。
    Shuppatsu no ichijikan mae made ni kite kudasai.
    (Please come one hour before departure.)

(b) 僕はこのレポートを一月二十日までに書きあげなければならないんだ。
    Boku wa kono repōto o ichigatsu hatsuka made ni kakiagenakereba naranai n da.
    (I have to finish writing this paper by January 20.)

(c) ジェット機がパリに着くまでに本を三冊読んでしまいました。

Jettoki ga Pari ni tsuku made ni hon o sansatsu yonde shimaimashita.

(By the time the jet got to Paris, I had finished reading three books.)

【Related Expressions】

I. *Made ni* cannot be used with a verb that indicates a continuous action. Instead, *made* 'continuously until / to X' is used.

[1] 山田は来月まで / *までにいる。

*Yamada wa raigetsu **made** / ***made ni** iru.*

(Yamada will stay here *until* / *by* next month.)

[2] 私は五時まで / *までに待っている。

*Watashi wa goji **made** / ***made ni** matte iru.*

(I'll be waiting *until* / *by* five o'clock.)

II. When *made ni* 'by' is preceded by an informal nonpast verb, it may be replaced by *mae ni* 'before'. The difference between the two is the same as the English 'by' vs. 'before'. Thus, if *made ni* in Ex. (c) is replaced by *mae ni*, the sentence means 'Before the jet got to Paris I had finished reading three books.' More examples of the different uses follow:

[3] a. 来月までに / *前にこの仕事をします。

*Raigetsu **made ni** / ***mae ni** kono shigoto o shimasu.*

(I will finish this work *by* / *before* next month.)

b. 授業前に / *までに郵便局に行く。

*Jugyō **mae ni** / ***made ni** yūbinkyoku ni iku.*

(I will go to the post office *before* / *by* class.)

III. *Made de*, a particle which means 's.t. continues until / up to X (and stops at X, although it can continue beyond X)' is similar to *made ni*. The differences in meaning can be seen in the examples below. In [4] *made ni* is unacceptable because Lesson 10 is not the limit of domain (which is Lesson 20). In [5] *made de* is unacceptable because no important items appear after Lesson 10.

[4] この教科書は二十課までありますが今学期は十課までで / *までに終わります。

*Kono kyōkasho wa nijukka made arimasu ga kongakki wa jukka **made de** / ***made ni** owarimasu.*

(There are up to twenty lessons in this textbook, but this semester we will stop at Lesson 10.)

[5] この教科書は二十課までありますが，大事なことは十課までに / ???
までで全部出て来ます。

*Kono kyōkasho wa nijukka made arimasu ga, daijina koto wa
jukka **made ni** / ???**made de** zenbu dete kimasu.*

(There are (lit. up to) twenty lessons in this textbook, but the
important items are introduced (lit. appear) by Lesson 10.)

---

mae ni 前に   *conj.*

in front of or before some situation comes about	before; in front of
	【REL. ***made ni***; *uchi ni*】
	(ANT. *ato de*; *ushiro ni*)

M

◆**Key Sentences**

(A)

Subordinate Clause			Main Clause
	Vinf·nonpast		
ジャクソンさん は 日本 へ *Jakuson-san wa Nihon e*	行く *iku*	前 に *mae ni*	日本語 を　勉強した / *nihongo o benkyōshita /* しました。 *shimashita.*
(Mr. Jackson studied Japanese before he went to Japan.)			

(B)

Noun (event)			
旅行 *Ryokō*	の *no*	前 に *mae ni*	風邪 を 引いた / 引きました。 *kaze o hiita / hikimashita.*
(Before the trip I caught cold.)			

(C)

Noun (place)			
駅 **Eki**	の *no*	前 に *mae ni*	たばこ屋 が ある / あります。 *tabako-ya ga aru / arimasu.*
(There is a tobacco shop in front of the station.)			

Formation

(i) Vinf·nonpast 前 に
         mae ni

話す　前　に　　(before s.o. talks / talked)
hanasu mae ni

食べる　前　に　　(before s.o. eats / ate)
taberu mae ni

(ii) N の 前 に
     no mae ni

朝ご飯　の 前 に　　(before breakfast)
asagohan no mae ni

Examples

(a) 日本人はご飯を食べる前に「いただきます。」と言う。
Nihonjin wa gohan o taberu mae ni " Itadakimasu." to iu.
(The Japanese say " *Itadakimasu* " (lit. I humbly receive (this food))
before eating their meals.)

(b) テイラーさんは日本へ行く前にハワイに寄りました。
Teirā-san wa Nihon e iku mae ni Hawai ni yorimashita.
(Mr. Taylor stopped in Hawaii before he went to Japan.)

(c) 私は試験の前に映画を見に行った。
Watashi wa shiken no mae ni eiga o mi ni itta.
(Before the exam I went to see a movie.)

Notes

1. *Mae ni* is used when the speaker knows when something is going to take
place. Thus, the following uses of *mae ni* are marginal.

    (1) ?雨が降る前に帰りましょう。
        ?*Ame ga furu **mae ni** kaerimashō.*
        (Let's go home before it rains.)

(2) ??忘れる前に言っておこう。

　　??*Wasureru **mae ni** itte okō.*

　　(I'll say it (in advance) before I forget.)

(See Related Expression for proper expressions.)

2. The verb before *mae ni* is always nonpast, even if the tense of the main verb is past, as in Ex. (b).

【Related Expression】

When the speaker knows that something is about to happen but does not know exactly when it is to happen, *uchi ni* 'before' is used instead of *mae ni*. Thus, *mae ni* in (1) and (2) of Note 1 should be replaced by *nai uchi ni*, as in [1] and [2].　　　　　　　　　　　　　　　　　　　　　(⇨ **uchi ni**)

[1] 雨が降ら**ないうちに**帰りましょう。

　　*Ame ga fura**nai uchi ni** kaerimashō.*

　　(Let's go home before it rains.)

[2] 忘れ**ないうちに**言っておこう。

　　*Wasure**nai uchi ni** itte okō.*

　　(I'll say it (in advance) before I forget.)

M

---

mai- まい　　*pref.*

a prefix which means 'every (unit of time)'	every; per 〖REL. *goto ni*〗

♦ **Key Sentence**

	Noun of time	
私　は *Watashi wa*	毎 *mai* 日 **nichi**	一マイル　泳ぐ / 泳ぎます。 *ichimairu oyogu / oyogimasu.*
(I swim one mile every day.)		

毎　N of time
mai

毎　朝　　(every morning)
mai **asa**

毎　月　　(every month)
mai **tsuki**

(a) 弘は毎晩道子に電話しているそうだ。
Hiroshi wa maiban Michiko ni denwashite iru sōda.
(I heard that Hiroshi calls Michiko every evening.)

(b) 台風は毎時二十キロの速さで北に進んでいる。
Taifū wa maiji nijukkiro no hayasa de kita ni susunde iru.
(The typhoon is moving north at a speed of twenty kilometers per hour.)

(c) 私は毎年一度は日本へ行く。
Watashi wa maitoshi ichido wa Nihon e iku.
(I go to Japan at least once every year.)

(d) ジーンは毎食サラダを食べる。
Jin wa maishoku sarada o taberu.
(Jean eats salad at every meal.)

1. *Mai* is prefixed to nouns which express a unit of time. Nouns like *shoku* 'meal' can also be used, as seen in Ex. (d). In this case, *shoku* implies the time at which one eats. However, the following phrases are all unacceptable because the nouns following *mai* do not indicate a time or period of time. (The correct expressions are given in parentheses.)

　　(1)　a.　*毎人　　　　　'every person'　(すべての人 / 人はみんな)
　　　　　　mai-hito / nin　　　　　　　(*subete no hito / hito wa minna*)

　　　　b.　*毎先生　　　　'every teacher'　(すべての先生 /
　　　　　　mai-sensei　　　　　　　　(*subete no sensei /*
　　　　　　　　　　　　　　　　　　　先生はみんな)
　　　　　　　　　　　　　　　　　　　sensei wa minna)

　　　　c.　*毎家　　　　　'every house'　(すべての家 / 家はみんな)
　　　　　　mai-ie / ka / ya　　　　　　(*subete no ie / ie wa minna*)

Mai cannot be used when nouns of time are preceded by numbers; thus, the following phrases are unacceptable. (⇨ **goto ni**)

(2) a. *毎三日 'every three days'
   *mai-mikka

   b. *毎二年 'every other year'
   *mai-ninen

   c. *毎一週 'every one week'
   *mai-isshū

(See Related Expresssion [1a] for correct expressions.)

2. *Mai* is usually used with Japanese-origin words of one or two syllables or shorter Chinese-origin words. Thus, compounds like those in (3) are awkward.

(3) a. ???毎休み 'every holiday'
   ???*mai-yasumi*

   b. ???毎クリスマス 'every Christmas'
   ???*mai-kurisumasu*

   c. *毎子供の日 'every Children's Day'
   *mai-kodomo-no-hi

(See Related Expression [1b] for correct expressions.)

[Related Expression]

Goto ni also means 'every', but its usage differs from that of *mai*. First, *goto ni* is not a prefix but a suffix. Second, it is used with nouns of time preceded by numbers or specific dates, as seen in [1]. (⇨ **goto ni**)

[1] a. *Period of time*
   三日ごとに 'every three days'
   mikka goto ni

   一時間ごとに 'every hour'
   ichijikan goto ni

   b. *Specific date*
   クリスマスごとに 'every Christmas'
   Kurisumasu goto ni

   子供の日ごとに 'every Children's Day'
   Kodomo-no-hi goto ni

(Cf. 日ごとに 'day after day'; 年ごとに 'year after year')
 hi-goto ni   *toshi-goto ni*

Third, unlike *mai*, *goto ni* can also be used with other noun phrases, as seen in [2].

[2] ジョンは会う人ごとに日本語であいさつをした。
 Jon wa au hito goto ni nihongo de aisatsu o shita.
 (John greeted every person he met in Japanese.)

mama まま   *n.*

An already given situation or condition remains unaltered.	as it is; unchanged; undisturbed; leave as is, remain 【REL. *nai de*; *zu ni*】

♦Key Sentences

(A)

Topic (subject)		Direct Object		Vinf·past			
弟 *Otōto*	は *wa*	テレビ *terebi*	を *o*	つけた ***tsuketa***	まま *mama*		寝て しまった / しまいました。 *nete shimatta / shimaimashita.*
(My younger brother went to sleep leaving the TV on.)							

(B)

Topic (subject)		Direct Object		Vinf·past			
弟 *Otōto*	は *wa*	テレビ *terebi*	を *o*	つけた ***tsuketa***	まま *mama*	に *ni*	して おいた / おきました。 *shite oita / okimashita.*
(My younger brother left the TV on.)							

(C)

Topic (subject)		Direct Object		Vinf·past		
弟	は	テレビ	を	つけた	まま	だ / です。
Otōto	*wa*	*terebi*	*o*	***tsuketa***	*mama*	*da* / *desu*.

(My younger brother has left the TV on.)

(D)

Topic (subject)		Noun			
この 部屋	は	**きのう**	の	まま	だ / です。
Kono heya	*wa*	***kinō***	*no*	*mama*	*da* / *desu*.

(This room is as it was yesterday.)

(E)

Topic (Direct Object)		Demonstrative Pronoun			
ここ	は	**この**	まま	に	して おく / おきます。
Koko	*wa*	***kono***	*mama*	*ni*	*shite oku* / *okimasu*.

(I'll leave this place as it is.)

(F)

Subject		Vinf·past			
テレビ	が	**ついた**	まま	に	なって いる / います。
Terebi	*ga*	***tsuita***	*mama*	*ni*	*natte iru* / *imasu*.

(The TV was turned on and is still on).

(G)

	Vinf·past			Noun		
帽子 を	**かぶった**	まま	の	学生	が 教室 に いた / いました。
Bōshi o	***kabutta***	*mama*	*no*	*gakusei*	*ga kyōshitsu ni ita* / *imashita*.

(A student who kept his hat on was in the classroom.)

Formation

(i) Vinf·past まま
       mama

(電気を)つけた　まま　　(leaving (the light) on)
(denki o) tsuketa mama

(ii) Adj (*i*) まま
        mama

大きい まま　　(as s.t. is big)
ōkii　mama

(iii) {Adj (*na*) stem な / N の} まま
                na　*no mama*

不便な　まま　　(leaving s.t. inconvenient)
*fuben*na *mama*

昔　　　の まま　　(leaving s.t. as it was)
mukashi no mama

Examples

(a) 電気をつけたまま寝てしまいました。
   Denki o tsuketa mama nete shimaimashita.
   (I fell asleep leaving the light on.)

(b) ビールを買ったまま飲まなかった。
   Bīru o katta mama nomanakatta.
   (I bought beer, but I didn't drink it.)

(c) 聞いたままを友達に話しました。
   Kiita mama o tomodachi ni hanashimashita.
   (I told my friend exactly what I heard.)

(d) あの人はあれからずっと寝たままだ。
   Ano hito wa are kara zutto neta mama da.
   (He's been in bed (lit. all along) since then.)

(e) 高山さんはアメリカへ行ったまま帰らなかった。
   Takayama-san wa Amerika e itta mama kaeranakatta.
   (Mr. Takayama went to America never to return.)

(f) 車のエンジンをかけたままにしておいた。
   Kuruma no enjin o kaketa mama ni shite oita.
   (I left the car engine on.)

(g) 今のままにしておいてください。

Ima no mama ni shite oite kudasai.

(Please leave it as it is now.)

Notes

1. The verb before *mama* has to be nonpast if the verb is negative as in (1).

    (1) a. ドアを閉め**ないまま**出かけてしまった。

          *Doa o shime**nai mama** dekakete shimatta.*

          (I left my house with the door open.)

       b. さようならの挨拶も**しないまま**行ってしまった。

          *Sayōnara no aisatsu mo shi**nai mama** itte shimatta.*

          (She went away without even saying goodbye.)

If a verb that precedes *mama o* is non-volitional, the verb can be nonpast even if the main transitive verb is past, as shown in (2):

    (2) a. 言われる / 言われたままを払った。

          ***Iwareru* / *Iwareta* mama o haratta.**

          (I paid money as I was told to.)

       b. 思っている / いたままを書いて見た。

          *Omotte **iru** / **ita** mama o kaite mita.*

          (I wrote exactly as I felt.)

2. When *mama* is followed directly by a verb (other than *suru*) as in KS(A) and Exs. (a), (b) and (e), *de* can be inserted between *mama* and the verb. Thus, KS(A) can be rephrased as follows:

    (3) 弟はテレビをつけたままで寝てしまった。

        *Otōto wa terebi o tsuketa mama **de** nete shimatta.*

        (Lit. My younger brother left the TV on, and went to sleep. (= My younger brother went to sleep leaving the TV on.))

The difference between the *mama* version and the *mama de* version is minimal; the latter sounds more like a coordinate construction as illustrated by the literary translation of (3).

[Related Expressions]

Vinf·nonpast·neg *mama* can be paraphrased using *nai de* or *zu ni*, as in:

    [1] ドアを閉め**ないまま** / **ないで** / **ずに**出かけてしまった。

        *Doa o shime**nai mama** / **nai de** / **zu ni** dekakete shimatta.*

        (He left his house with the door open.)

The *mama* version focuses on the unaltered situation, but the *nai de* / *zu ni* versions focus primarily on the negative aspect of the verb. The translation of the former and the latter are ' He left with the door open.' and ' He left without closing the door.', respectively.   (⇨ ***nai de***)

~**mashō** ~ましょう   *aux.*

a verb ending which indicates the first person's volition or invitation in formal speech	I / We will do s.t.; Let's do s.t. 【REL. ~*masen ka*】

◆**Key Sentences**

(A)

Subject (first person)				V*masu*	
私 *Watashi*	が *ga*	彼 に *kare ni*		話し ***hanashi***	ましょう。 *mashō.*
(Í will talk to him.)					

(B)

		V*masu*	
映画 に *Eiga ni*		行き ***iki***	ましょう。 *mashō.*
(Let's go to a movie.)			

Formation

V*masu* ましょう
        mashō

話しましょう   (I / We will talk; Let's talk.)
hanashimashō

食べましょう   (I / We will eat; Let's eat.)
tabemashō

Examples

(a) 私達が手伝いましょう。
Watashitachi ga tetsudaimashō.
(Wé will help you.)

(b) 私が行きましょうか。
Watashi ga ikimashō ka.
(Shall Í go there?)

(c) ビールを飲みましょう。
Biru o nomimashō.
(Let's drink beer.)

(d) 車で行きましょうか。
Kuruma de ikimashō ka.
(Shall we go by car?)

Notes

1. *Mashō* is a formal verb ending which is used to express the first person's volition (KS(A), Exs. (a) and (b)) or invitation (KS(B), Exs. (c) and (d)).

2. The sentence in the KS(A) pattern, which includes the subject X *ga*, implies that 'not others but X will do something'. If the sentence doesn't carry such an implication but simply states the first person's volition, the subject is usually omitted. Compare the following sentences:

   (1) a. そのかばんを持ちましょう。
   Sono kaban o mochimashō.
   (I'll carry that bag.)

   b. 私がそのかばんを持ちましょう。
   Watashi ga sono kaban o mochimashō.
   (I will carry that bag.)

3. In invitation situations like KS(B), the subject is usually omitted. (Exs. (c) and (d))

4. *Mashō* with the question marker *ka* asks whether the hearer will accept the speaker's volitional action or invitation. (Exs. (b) and (d))

5. Negative volition is usually expressed by simple nonpast negatives, as seen in (2).

   (2) 私はパーティーに行きません。
   Watashi wa pāti ni ikimasen.
   (I won't go to the party.)

(The negative volitional ending *mai*, as in *ikumai* 'won't go', is not commonly used in modern colloquial Japanese.)

6. " Let's not do s.t." is expressed by different constructions.

   (A) Vinf *no wa yamemashō / yoshimashō.* (Lit. Let's stop doing s.t.)
      Example:

      ⑶ パーティーに行くのはやめましょう / よしましょう。
         Pāti ni iku no wa yamemashō / yoshimashō.
         (Let's not go to the party.)

   (B) Vneg *naide okimashō* (Lit. Let's leave ~ undone.)   (⇨ **oku**)
      Example:

      ⑷ フレッドには言わないでおきましょう。
         Fureddo ni wa iwanaide okimashō.
         (Let's not tell Fred.)

7. In indirect speech or in sentences with verbs like *omou* 'think' and *kesshinsuru* 'make up one's mind', the informal volitional form is used. (For the informal volitional forms of verbs, see Appendix 1.)

   ⑸ 村田さんはコーヒーを飲もうと言った。
      Murata-san wa kōhī o nomō to itta.
      (Mr. Murata suggested we drink coffee.)

   ⑹ 私は来年日本へ行こうと思います。
      Watashi wa rainen Nihon e ikō to omoimasu.
      (I think I will go to Japan next year.)

8. Unlike English, in Japanese the volitional future and the simple future are expressed by different forms. Thus, " I think I will see a movie." is expressed by either (7) or (8).

   ⑺ 私は映画を見ようと思う。
      Watashi wa eiga o miyō to omou.

   ⑻ 私は映画を見ると思う。
      Watashi wa eiga o miru to omou.

(7) is an example of the volitional future, in which the speaker's volition is expressed, while (8) is an example of the simple future.

[Related Expression]

An invitation by the speaker can also be expressed through negative questions, as in [1].

[1] パーティーに行きませんか。

*Pāti ni **ikimasen ka**.*

(Wouldn't you (like to) go to the party?)

In invitation situations, negative questions are more polite than *mashō*-sentences because the former are asking whether or not the hearer will do something and, therefore, are hearer-oriented, while the latter do not consider the hearer's volition and are more speaker-oriented.

---

mieru 見える   *v. (Gr. 2)*

S.o. or s.t. is passively / spontaneously visible.

be visible; (can) see; look ~

【REL. *mirareru*】

M

♦**Key Sentences**

(A)

Topic (experiencer)		Visible Object		
私 *Watashi*	(に)は (*ni*) *wa*	遠く の もの *tōku no mono*	が *ga*	よく 見える / 見えます。 *yoku mieru / miemasu.*

(Lit. To me distant objects are very visible. (=I can see distant objects very well.))

(B)

Topic (location)		Visible Object		
窓 から *Mado kara*	(は) (*wa*)	海 *umi*	が *ga*	見える / 見えます。 *mieru / miemasu.*

(Lit. From the window the ocean is visible. (=We can see the ocean from the window.))

(C)

	Visible Object		Adj (adverbial form) / N+*ni*	
今日 は *Kyō wa*	山 *yama*	が *ga*	近く *chikaku*	見える / 見えます。 *mieru* / *miemasu*.
(Today the mountains look near.)				

Examples

(a) 私には木の上の小さな鳥が見えた。
   Watashi ni wa ki no ue no chisana tori ga mieta.
   (I could see small birds on the tree.)

(b) 東京タワーからは東京の町がよく見える。
   Tōkyō Tawā kara wa Tōkyō no machi ga yoku mieru.
   (From Tokyo Tower you can get a good view of the towns of Tokyo.)

(c) あの人は年よりずっと若く見える。
   Ano hito wa toshi yori zutto wakaku mieru.
   (He looks much younger than his age.)

(d) 女の人は夜きれいに見える。
   Onna no hito wa yoru kireini mieru.
   (Women look beautiful at night.)

(e) 中島さんは学生に見える。
   Nakajima-san wa gakusei ni mieru.
   (Mr. Nakajima looks like a student.)

Notes

1. *Mieru* can mean 'look ~' if it is preceded by the adverbial form of an Adj (*i*) as in Ex. (c) or of an Adj (*na*) as in Ex. (d) or by a N *ni* as in Ex. (e).

2. *Mieru* can be used as a polite version of *kuru* 'come' as in:

   (1) お母さん，お客さんが**見えた**よ。
      *O-kā-san, o-kyaku-san ga **mieta** yo.*
      (Mom, we have company!)

   (2) 学会には上田先生も**見えた**。
      *Gakkai ni wa Ueda-sensei mo **mieta**.*
      (Lit. To the academic meeting appeared Prof. Ueda, too. (=Prof. Ueda also attended the academic conference.))

Mieru can be used as an honorific polite verb because it is a more indirect reference to a superior's act of 'coming'. In other words, the speaker is referring to a superior's appearance as if it were a spontaneous, natural phenomenon of 'visibility'.

3. A visible object is marked by *ga*, not by *o*.

[Related Expression]

Mieru is different from the regular potential form of *miru*, i.e., *mirareru*, in that *mieru* indicates that s.t. or s.o. is passively visible regardless of the volition of the speaker; *mirareru*, on the other hand, indicates that the speaker or the subject of the sentence can see s.t. or s.o. actively rather than passively. Thus,

[1] 僕は目が**見えない** / *見られない。
   *Boku wa me ga **mienai** / *mirarenai.*
   (I'm blind.)

[2] テレビを買ったからテレビが**見られる** / *見える。
   *Terebi o katta kara terebi ga **mirareru** / *mieru.*
   (Because I bought a TV I can now watch TV.)

[3] あの映画はどこで**見られます** / *見えますか。
   *Ano eiga wa doko de **miraremasu** / *miemasu ka.*
   (Where can we see the movie?)

[4] よく**見えない** / *見られないからステージの近くに行こう。
   *Yoku **mienai** / *mirarenai kara sutēji no chikaku ni ikō.*
   (We can't see it well, so let's go closer to the stage.)

[5] 隣に高いビルが立ったので山が**見え** / **見られ**なくなった。
   *Tonari ni takai biru ga tatta node yama ga **mie** / **mirare** naku natta.*
   (Because a tall building was built next door, the mountains are not visible any more / we can't see the mountains any more.)

Note that in [5] both *mieru* and *mirareru* are possible, depending on how the speaker perceives the visible object; if he thinks that the situation is beyond his control and has to give up looking at the mountains, he uses *mieru*; if not, he uses *mirareru*.

miru みる　　*aux. v. (Gr. 2)*

> do s.t. to see what it's like or what
> will happen

do s.t. and see; try to do s.t.
【REL. *yō to suru*】

♦ **Key Sentence**

Topic (subject)			V*te*	
私	は	日本 の 小説 を	読んで	みる / みます。
Watashi	*wa*	*Nihon no shōsetsu o*	*yonde*	*miru / mimasu.*

(I will read Japanese novels (to see what they are like).)

Formation

V*te*　みる
　　　miru

話して　　みる　　(try to talk)
hanashite miru

食べて　みる　　(try to eat)
tabete miru

Examples

(a) おもしろそうなコンサートだったので行ってみました。
　　Omoshiro sōna konsāto datta node itte mimashita.
　　(Since it seemed interesting, I went to the concert (to see what it was like).)

(b) ここの刺身はおいしいですよ。食べてみますか。
　　Koko no sashimi wa oishiidesu yo. Tabete mimasu ka.
　　(*Sashimi* here is good.　Will you try it?)

Note

Miru is used as an auxiliary verb with V*te* meaning 'make an attempt at
doing s.t. to see what it is like or what will happen'.

【**Related Expression**】

A similar expression, ~ *yō to suru*, means simply 'try to do s.t.' When
these two expressions are used in the past tense, however, their meanings are
not the same.　For example, [1a] means that Mr. Brown did put on Tom's
undershirt, whereas [1b] means that Mr. Brown tried to put it on, with the
implication that he couldn't or didn't actually do it.

[1] a. ブラウンさんはトムのシャツを**着てみた**。
       *Buraun-san wa Tomu no shatsu o **kite mita**.*
       (Mr. Brown tried Tom's undershirt on.)

    b. ブラウンさんはトムのシャツを**着ようとした**。
       *Buraun-san wa Tomu no shatsu o **kiyō to shita**.*
       (Mr. Brown tried to put Tom's undershirt on.)

mo[1] も   *prt.*

a particle which indicates that a proposition about the preceding element X is also true when another similar proposition is true	too; also; (not) ~ either

M

♦ **Key Sentences**

(A)

Subject		
私	も	学生 だ / です。
Watashi	*mo*	*gakusei da / desu.*
(Lit. I, too, am a student. (= I'm a student, too.))		

(B)

Topic (subject)		Direct Object		
私	は	スペイン語	も	話す / 話します。
Watashi	*wa*	*supeingo*	*mo*	*hanasu / hanashimasu.*
(I speak Spanish, too.)				

(C)

Topic (subject)		Indirect Object			
私 *Watashi*	は *wa*	村山さん *Murayama-san*	に *ni*	も *mo*	プレゼント を あげる / *purezento o ageru* / あげます。 *agemasu.*

(I will give a present to Mr. Murayama, too.)

Formation

(i) N も
　　　 mo

　　私　　　 も　　 (I, too / me (as direct object), too)
　　watashi mo

(ii) N (Prt) も
　　　　　 mo

　　日本　(に) も　　 (in / to Japan, too)
　　Nihon (ni) mo

　　アメリカ (へ) も　　 (to America, too)
　　Amerika (e) mo

(iii) N Prt も
　　　　　 mo

　　先生　 に も　　 (to / for the teacher, too (indirect object))
　　sensei ni mo

　　フランス から も　　 (from France, too)
　　Furansu kara mo

　　イギリス で も　　 (in England, too)
　　Igirisu de mo

　　友達　　 と も　　 (with my friend, too)
　　tomodachi to mo

Examples

(a) ハートさんは日本へ行った。ルイスさんも（日本へ）行った。
　　Hāto-san wa Nihon e itta. Ruisu-san mo (Nihon e) itta.
　　(Mr. Hart went to Japan. Mr. Lewis also went to Japan.)

(b) 林さんはテニスをします。(彼は)ゴルフもします。

Hayashi-san wa tenisu o shimasu. (Kare wa) gorufu mo shimasu.

(Mr. Hayashi plays tennis. He plays golf, too.)

(c) この町では新しい魚が買えません。隣の町でも(新しい魚が)買えません。

Kono machi de wa atarashii sakana ga kaemasen. Tonari no machi de mo (atarashii sakana ga) kaemasen.

(You can't buy fresh fish in this town. You can't buy it in the next town, either.)

Notes

1. In general, when the element X *mo* appears in a sentence, a related sentence with the element Y (plus particle if necessary) in place of X *mo* is presupposed. For example, when a speaker states (1), a sentence like (2) is presupposed.

  (1) 私はニューヨークへも行った。
  *Watashi wa Nyūyōku e **mo** itta.*
  (I went to New York, too.)

  (2) 私はボストンへ行った。
  Watashi wa Bosuton e itta.
  (I went to Boston.)

Thus, when X *mo* appears in a sentence, X *mo* is always the element under focus in that sentence.

2. There are cases in which X *mo* is used, although it does not exactly replace the element Y in the presupposed sentence. For example, (3b) can be spoken after (3a).

  (3) a. 私の家は居間がせまい。
   Watashi no ie wa ima ga semai.
   (The living room of my house is small.)

  b. それに台所も不便だ。
   *Sore ni daidokoro **mo** fubenda.*
   (On top of that, the kitchen is inconvenient, too.)

In this case, the speaker implies that his house is inconvenient when he says (3a), and this implication is the presupposition of (3b), where the speaker elaborates on the inconvenience.

3. " X *mo* A *da* " cannot be used to mean 'X is also A' in the sense that

X is A as well as something else. " X *mo* A *da* " can be used only when
" Y *wa* / *ga* A *da* " is presupposed. Thus, (4) does not mean (5). (In
fact, (4) is nonsensical if it is stated by the same person.)

⑷ 私は医者だ。　　　　*私も先生だ。
　*Watashi wa isha da. *Watashi **mo** sensei da.*

⑸ I am a (medical) doctor. I am also a teacher.

The idea that someone is a doctor as well as a teacher is expressed as
in (6).

⑹ 私は医者だ。　　　　そして先生でもある。
　*Watashi wa isha da. Soshite sensei **de mo aru**.*

(I am a (medical) doctor and also a teacher.)

*mo*² も　*prt.*

| a marker which indicates emphasis | even; as many / much / long / ...as; (not) even (one); (not) any |

♦**Key Sentences**

(A)

Topic (subject)		Noun			
グレーさん *Gurē-san*	は *wa*	こんな　難しい　漢字 ***konna muzukashii kanji***	も *mo*	読める / 読めます。 *yomeru / yomemasu.*	
*(Mr. Gray can read even difficult *kanji* like this.)*					
ハリスさん *Harisu-san*	は *wa*	こんな　やさしい　漢字 ***konna yasashii kanji***	も *mo*	読めない / 読めません。 *yomenai / yomemasen.*	
*(Mr. Harris cannot read even easy *kanji* like this.)*					

(B)

Topic (subject)			Quantifier		Predicate (affirmative)
私	は	漢字 を	八千	も	知って いる / います。
Watashi	*wa*	*kanji o*	***hassen***	*mo*	*shitte iru / imasu.*
(I know as many as eight thousand *kanji*.)					

(C)

Topic (subject)			*One*	Counter		Predicate (negative)
私	は	漢字 を	一	つ	も	知らない / 知りません。
Watashi	*wa*	*kanji o*	***hito***	***tsu***	*mo*	*shiranai / shirimasen.*
(I don't know even one *kanji*.)						

(D)

Topic (subject)		WH-word		Predicate (negative)
私	は	何	も	食べなかった / 食べませんでした。
Watashi	*wa*	***nani***	*mo*	*tabenakatta / tabemasendeshita.*
(I didn't eat anything.)				

(E)

Topic (subject)			V*masu*		
ナンシー	は	私 の 話 を	聞き	も	しない / しません。
Nanshī	*wa*	*watashi no hanashi o*	***kiki***	*mo*	*shinai / shimasen.*
(Nancy doesn't even listen to me.)					

M

Formation

KS(A): See *mo*[1] Formation.

KS(B):

Quantifier も
          mo

五十 も   (as many as fifty)
gojū mo

百人   も   (as many as a hundred people)
hyakunin mo

KS(C):

One Counter も
          mo

一人　も　　((not) even one person)
hitori mo

一つ　も　　((not) even one ~)
hitotsu mo

KS(D):

WH-word も
          mo

何も　　((not) anything)
nanimo

だれも　　((not) anybody)
daremo

KS(E):

V*masu* も しない
       mo shinai

話し　も しない　　(don't even talk)
hanashi mo shinai

食べ　も しない　　(don't even eat)
tabe mo shinai

Examples

(a) 春男は一年生のたし算もまともに出来ない。
    Haruo wa ichinensei no tashizan mo matomoni dekinai.
    (Haruo cannot do even the first-year addition correctly.)

(b) 今日は車が十台も売れた。
    Kyō wa kuruma ga jūdai mo ureta.
    (As many as ten cars sold today.)

(c) そのパーティーには女の子は一人も来なかった。
    Sono pāti ni wa onna no ko wa hitori mo konakatta.
    (No (lit. Not even one) girl came to the party.)

(d) だれもそのことを知りません。
    Daremo sono koto o shirimasen.
    (Nobody knows about it.)

(e) 私は木村さんがくれた本をまだ見もしていない。

Watashi wa Kimura-san ga kureta hon o mada mi mo shite inai.

(I haven't even seen the book Mr. Kimura gave me yet.)

Notes

1. *Mo* as an emphatic marker is an extended use of *mo¹*. (⇨ **mo¹**) The following examples show the transition of meaning from the original idea 'also' to the emphatic use 'even'.

   (1) a. グレーさんは非常に難しい漢字も読める。

   *Gurē-san wa hijōni muzukashii kanji **mo** yomeru.*

   (Lit. Mr. Gray can read very difficult *kanji*, too. (=Mr. Gray can read even very difficult *kanji*.))

   b. ハリスさんは非常にやさしい漢字も読めない。

   *Harisu-san wa hijōni yasashii kanji **mo** yomenai.*

   (Lit. Mr. Harris cannot read very easy *kanji*, either. (=Mr. Harris cannot read even very easy *kanji*.))

2. *Nanimo* and *daremo* are used only in negative sentences. Other WH-words with *mo* can be used in both affirmative sentences and negative sentences.

   (2) いつも　　(always; anytime)
   itsumo

   どこも　　(everywhere; anywhere)
   dokomo

   どちらも　　(both; neither of the two ~)
   dochiramo

   どうも　　(somehow)
   dōmo

Note the following examples:

   (3) a. 大木君はいつも人に親切だ。

   *Ōki-kun wa **itsumo** hito ni shinsetsuda.*

   (Mr. Oki is always kind to people.)

   b. 小山はいつも約束を守らない。

   *Koyama wa **itsumo** yakusoku o mamoranai.*

   (Koyama never keeps his promise.)

3. V*masu mo* is always followed by a negative form of *suru* 'do' as in KS(E) and Ex. (e).

mō もう　　*adv.*

> S.o. or s.t. is no longer in the same
> state that he or it was in some time
> ago.

(not) any more; (not) any longer;
already; yet; now
【REL. *mada*】

♦**Key Sentences**

(A)

Topic (subject)			Predicate (affirmative)
私	は	もう	昼ご飯　を　**食べた** / **食べました**。
Watashi	*wa*	*mō*	*hirugohan o* **tabeta** / **tabemashita**.
(I have already eaten my lunch.)			

(B)

Topic (subject)			Predicate (negative)
ヒルさん	は	もう	日本語　を　**勉強して　いない** / **いません**。
Hiru-san	*wa*	*mō*	*nihongo o* **benkyōshite inai** / **imasen**.
(Mr. Hill is not studying Japanese any longer.)			

Examples

(a)　A：もう宿題をしましたか。
　　　　Mō shukudai o shimashita ka.
　　　　(Have you done your homework yet (or already)?)

　　　B：はい，もうしました。
　　　　Hai, mō shimashita.
　　　　(Yes, I've already done it.)

(b)　私はもう酒を飲みません。
　　　Watashi wa mō sake o nomimasen.
　　　(I won't drink *sake* any more.)

(c)　春男君はもう大じょうぶです。
　　　Haruo-kun wa mō daijōbudesu.
　　　(Haruo is all right now.)

Notes

1. *Mō* expresses the idea that someone or something is not in the same state he or it was in some time ago.   Thus, *mō* corresponds to 'already' or 'now' in affirmative declarative sentences, 'yet' or 'already' in affirmative interrogative sentences, and '(not) any more' or '(not) any longer' in negative sentences.

2. The opposite concept of *mō* is expressed by *mada*.   (⇨ **mada**)

~**mo** ~**mo** ～も～も   *str.*

the repeated use of a particle meaning 'also' to list elements belonging to the same part of speech

both ~ and ~ ; neither ~ nor

M

♦**Key Sentences**

(A)

Noun		Noun		
田中さん *Tanaka-san*	も *mo*	中山さん *Nakayama-san*	も *mo*	デパート に 勤めて いる / います。 *depāto ni tsutomete iru / imasu.*
(Both Mr. Tanaka and Mr. Nakayama are working for a department store.)				

(B)

	Noun	Prt		Noun	Prt		
京都 へ は *Kyōto e wa*	バス *basu*	で *de*	も *mo*	電車 *densha*	で *de*	も *mo*	行ける / 行けます。 *ikeru / ikemasu.*
(We can go to Kyoto either by bus or by electric train (lit. by both bus and electric train).)							

(C)

	Adj (*i*) stem			Adj (*i*) stem			
この うち は *Kono uchi wa*	広く *hiroku*	も *mo*		狭く *semaku*	も *mo*		ない / *nai* / ありません。 *arimasen.*
(This house is neither big nor small.)							

Formation

(i) N(Prt) も N(Prt) も (N(Prt) も)
       mo   *mo*   *mo*

先生 も 学生 も   (both teachers and students)
sensei mo gakusei mo

(ii) Adj (*i*) stem く も Adj (*i*) stem く も Neg
          ku mo   *ku mo*

大きく も 小さく も ない   (s.t. is neither big nor small)
ōkiku mo chisaku mo nai

(iii) {Adj (*na*) stem / N} で も {Adj (*na*) stem / N} で も Neg
              de mo   *de mo*

便利で も 不便で も ない   (s.t. is neither convenient nor incon-
benride mo fubende mo nai   venient)

先生 で も 学生 で も ない   (s.o. is neither a teacher nor a
sensei de mo gakusei de mo nai   student)

Examples

(a) 日本人もアメリカ人もよく働く。
Nihonjin mo amerikajin mo yoku hataraku.
(Both Japanese and Americans work hard.)

(b) 山川さんは酒もたばこもやりません。
Yamakawa-san wa sake mo tabako mo yarimasen.
(Mr. Yamakawa neither drinks nor smokes.)

(c) 弟にも妹にも本を買ってやりました。
Otōto ni mo imōto ni mo hon o katte yarimashita.
(I bought books for both my younger brother and younger sister.)

(d) 和枝は美人でも不美人でもない。
Kazue wa bijin demo fubijin demo nai.
(Kazue is neither beautiful nor ugly.)

(e) この建物はきれいでも立派でもありません。
Kono tatemono wa kireide mo rippade mo arimasen.
(This building is neither pretty nor magnificent.)

Notes

1. Noun *mo* Noun *mo* can be used as the subject as in Ex. (a), as the direct object as in Ex. (b), as the indirect object as in Ex. (c) or in any other way in which a regular noun phrase is used.   (⇨ ***mo***[1])

2. Although Noun *mo* Noun *mo* can be an indefinitely long noun phrase, normally Noun *mo* is not repeated more than three or four times.

3. The predicate that corresponds to the Noun *mo* Noun *mo* phrase can be affirmative as in Exs. (a) and (c) or negative as in Exs. (b), (d) and (e).

mono (da) もの(だ)   *n.*

| The speaker presents some situation as if it were a tangible object. | because; how could ~!; used to; should like to; should 【REL. *kara*; *no da*】 |

M

◆ **Key Sentences**

(A)

A:	B:
どうして 行かない の? *Dōshite ikanai no?*	だって, 忙しい もの。 *Datte, isogashii mono.*
(How come you don't go there?)	('Cause I'm busy.)

(B)

	Vinf		
よく あんな 男 と デート *Yoku anna otoko to dēto*	**出来る** ***dekiru***	もの *mono*	だ / です! *da / desu!*
(How could you date that kind of guy!)			

(C)

	Vinf·past		
昔　は　よく　映画　を *Mukashi wa yoku eiga o*	見た ***mita***	もの *mono*	だ／です。 *da / desu.*
(I used to see movies a lot.)

(D)

	V*masu*			
こんな　いい　うち　に　一度　住んで *Konna　ii　uchi ni ichido sunde*	見 ***mi****tai*	たい	もの *mono*	だ／です。 *da / desu.*
(I'd like to live in such a nice house.)

(E)

	Vinf·nonpast		
朝　人　に　会ったら「おはよう」と *Asa hito ni　attara　"Ohayō" to*	言う ***iu***	もの *mono*	だ／です。 *da / desu.*
(You should say "Good morning" when you see people in the morning.)

(F)

	V*masu*			
年　を　取ると　昔　のこと を *Toshi o　toru to mukashi no koto o*	話し ***hanashi****tagaru*	たがる	もの *mono*	だ／です。 *da / desu.*
(When one gets old, he wants to talk about his past.)

Formation

(i) {Vinf / V*masu tai*} もの　だ
　　　　　　　　　mono da

　　話す　　もの　だ　　(s.o. should talk)
　　hanasu mono da

　　話した　　もの　だ　　(s.o. used to talk)
　　hanashita mono da

　　話したい　もの　だ　　(s.o. would like to talk)
　　hanashitai mono da

(ii) {Adj (*i*) / Adj (*na*)} inf もの （だ）
                                    mono (da)

高い　もの　　　　（'Cause s.t. is expensive)
takai mono

高かった　もの　　　（'Cause s.t. was expensive)
takakatta mono

高かった　もの　だ　　(s.t. used to be expensive)
takakatta mono da

静かだ　　もの　　　（'Cause s.t. is quiet)
shizukada mono

静かだった　　もの　　（'Cause s.t. was quiet)
shizukadatta mono

静かだった　もの　だ　(s.t. used to be quiet)
shizukadatta mono da

Examples

(a) A : どうして食べないの？
        Dōshite tabenai no?
        (Why don't you eat it?)

    B : だって，まずいもの。
        Datte, mazui mono.
        ('Cause it doesn't taste good.)

(b) A : どうしてその本，読まないんだい？
        Dōshite sono hon, yomanai n dai?
        (Why don't you read that book?)

    B : だって，よく分からないんだもの。
        Datte, yoku wakaranai n da mono.
        ('Cause I don't understand it well.)

(c) よくそんなばかなことをしたものだ！
    Yoku sonna bakana koto o shita mono da!
    (How could you do such a foolish thing!)

(d) 月日の立つのは早いものだ。
    Tsukihi no tatsu no wa hayai mono da.
    (Lit. The passing of days and months is so quick! (=How fast time flies!))

(e) 昔はこの川にも魚がいたものだ。

Mukashi wa kono kawa ni mo sakana ga ita mono da.

(There used to be fish in this river, too.)

(f) 一度是非一緒にテニスをしたいものですね。

Ichido zehi isshoni tenisu o shitai mono desu ne.

(I'd like to play tennis with you once.)

(g) 人の家に行く時はおみやげを持って行くものです。

Hito no ie ni iku toki wa o-miyage o motte iku mono desu.

(When you visit someone, you should take a gift with you.)

(h) 好きな仕事をしていると病気にならないものだ。

Sukina shigoto o shite iru to byōki ni naranai mono da.

(When you are doing work you love, you don't become ill.)

Notes

1. Because the speaker presents a situation before *mono* (*da*) as if it were a tangible object, this structure tends to convey differing degrees of emotion. KSs (A) through (F) represent emotive excuse, exclamation, nostalgic reminiscence, desire, indirect command and conviction, respectively. Note, however, that the emotion expressed here is not an instantaneously appearing emotion instigated by a current event but an emotion nurtured in one's mind for a relatively long period time.

2. When *mono* indicates a reason or an excuse it is used only in very informal speech.

3. *Mono* is contracted into *mon* in very colloquial speech.

4. The usage of *mono* in KS(A) does not take *da* / *desu*, unless it appears in a subordinate clause, as in (1).

   (1) 金がない**もんで**映画も見られないんだ。

   *Kane ga nai **mon de** eiga mo mirarenai n da.*

   (Because I don't have money, I can't see even a movie, you know.)

[Related Expression]

In KSs(A), (C), (D), (E) and (F) *mono* can be replaced by *no*, but with a slightly different meaning. *Mono* sounds more emotive than *no*, probably due to the semantic difference between *mono* 'a tangible object' and *no* 'a nominalizer of a directly perceptible state or action'. Thus, the *mono* (*da*) version is more indirectly emotive, and is not necessarily geared to the current moment, whereas the *no* (*da*) version is more directly emotive and is geared to the current moment. Observe the following:

[1]　今ビールが飲みたいん / *ものです。
　　*Ima biru ga nomitai **n** / *__mono__ desu.*
　　(I'd like to drink beer now.)

[2]　今すぐ会いに行くん / *ものです。
　　*Ima sugu ai ni iku **n** / *__mono__ desu.*
　　(You should go see him at once.)

Note that *mono* in KS(A) can be replaced by *kara*, but the latter is free from the emotive overtones which are attached to *mono*.

morau[1] もらう　　*v. (Gr. 1)*

The first person or s.o. the speaker empathizes with receives s.t. from s.o. whose status is not as high as the receiver's.

get; receive; be given
【REL. *kureru*[1] (*ageru*[1])】

M

◆Key Sentence

Topic (subject) (Receiver)		Giver		Direct Object		
(私	は)	山本さん	に	本	を	もらった / もらいました。
(*Watashi*	*wa*)	*Yamamoto-san*	*ni*	*hon*	*o*	*moratta / moraimashita.*
(I got a book from Mr. Yamamoto.)						

Examples

(a)　山川さんは橋本さんにウイスキーをもらった。
　　Yamakawa-san wa Hashimoto-san ni uisuki o moratta.
　　(Mr. Yamakawa got whiskey from Mr. Hashimoto.)

(b)　(あなたは)モリスさんに何をもらったの？
　　(Anata wa) Morisu-san ni nani o moratta no?
　　(What did you get from Mr. Morris?)

Notes

1. *Morau*, which is one of a set of giving and receiving verbs, means 'get'. Unlike the English *get*, however, *morau* is used only when the receiver is the first person or someone with whom the speaker empathizes (usually a member of the speaker's in-group). Thus, (1) is unacceptable.

　(1) *山本さんは私に酒をもらった。
　　　*Yamamoto-san wa watashi ni sake o moratta.
　　　(Mr. Yamamoto got *sake* from me.)

The reason for this is as follows: *morau* requires the receiver's point of view when describing an event, and when an event involves the first person, the event is normally described from the first person's point of view. Therefore, if the first person is the giver in *morau*-sentences, a viewpoint conflict arises, making the sentences ungrammatical. (The situation seen in (1) is usually described using *ageru*.)　　(⇨ **ageru**¹)

2. The humble polite version of *morau* is *itadaku*. Example:

　(2) 私は先生に本をいただいた。
　　　Watashi wa sensei ni hon o **itadaita**.
　　　(I was given a book by my teacher.)

3. The giver can also be marked by the source *kara* 'from' (i.e., *kara*¹).
　　　　　　　　　　　　　　　　　　　　　　　　　　　　　(⇨ **ni**³)

　(3) 私は山本さんに / から本をもらった。
　　　Watashi wa Yamamoto-san **ni** | **kara** hon o moratta.
　　　(I got a book from Mr. Yamamoto.)

However, if the giver is not human, *kara* is more appropriate than *ni*, as seen in (4).

　(4) 私は日本政府から / ??にお金をもらった。
　　　Watashi wa Nihonseifu **kara** | ??**ni** o-kane o moratta.
　　　(I received some money from the Japanese government.)

This seems to be due to the fact that *kara*¹ carries the idea of source, while *ni* conveys the idea of direct contact. That is, unlike the situation in (3), the speaker in (4) does not have direct contact with the giver, the Japanese government, when receiving money. Rather, the Japanese government in (4) is merely the source of the money received.

4. In declarative sentences, if the subject is the speaker, it is often

omitted. Similarly, in interrogative sentences, if the subject is the hearer, it is often omitted.   (See KS and Ex. (b).)

morau[2] もらう   *aux. v. (Gr. 1)*

The first person or s.o. the speaker empathizes with receives some benefit from an action by someone whose status is not as high as the receiver's.

receive benefit from an action by s.o.; have s.t. done by s.o.; have s.o. do s.t.
【REL. *kureru*[2] (*ageru*[2])】

♦ **Key Sentences**

(A)

Topic (subject) (Receiver)		Giver		Direct Object		V*te*	
(私 *(Watashi*	は) *wa)*	父 *chichi*	に *ni*	カメラ *kamera*	を *o*	買って *katte*	もらった / *moratta /* もらいました。 *moraimashita.*
(My father bought a camera for me.)							

(B)

Topic (subject) (Receiver)		Giver		V*te*	
(私 *(Watashi*	は) *wa)*	友達 *tomodachi*	に *ni*	来て *kite*	もらった / もらいました。 *moratta / moraimashita.*
(I had my friend come (for my benefit).)					

Formation

V*te* もらう
　　　 morau

話して　もらう　　(have s.o. talk for my sake)
hanashite morau

食べて もらう　　(have s.o. eat for my sake)
tabete morau

(a) 木村さんは大野さんに車を貸してもらった。
Kimura-san wa Ōno-san ni kuruma o kashite moratta.
(Mr. Kimura had Mr. Ono lend him his car.)

(b) (君は)ベックさんに何をしてもらいましたか。
(Kimi wa) Bekku-san ni nani o shite moraimashita ka.
(Lit. What did you have Mr. Beck do for you?　(＝What did Mr. Beck do for you?))

(c) ジョンソンさんは鈴木さんに日本語を教えてもらっている。
Jonson-san wa Suzuki-san ni nihongo o oshiete moratte iru.
(Mr. Johnson has Mr. Suzuki teaching him Japanese.)

Notes

1. *Morau* is used as an auxiliary verb with V*te*. The meaning of V*te morau* is 'receive some benefit from someone's action' or 'have someone do something for s.o.'s sake'. Like sentences with *morau* as a main verb, when the auxiliary verb *morau* is used, the recipient of the favor (i.e., the person in the subject position) must be the first person or someone with whom the speaker empathizes (usually a member of the speaker's in-group). Thus, (1a) is grammatical, but (1b) is not.

(1) a. 私は隣の人にペンを貸してもらった。
Watashi wa *tonari no hito ni pen o kashite moratta.*
(Lit. I had the man next to me lend me a pen.　(＝I borrowed a pen from the man next to me.))

b. *隣の人は私にペンを貸してもらった。
Tonari no hito wa watashi ni *pen o kashite moratta.*
(Lit. The man next to me had me lend him a pen.　(＝The man next to me borrowed a pen from me.))

Note that if the giver of the favor is the first person, sentences with V*te morau* are ungrammatical even if the recipient of the favor is someone the speaker empathizes with, as in (2).　(⇨ **morau¹**, Note 1)

(2) *弟は私にラジオを貸してもらった。
Otōto wa watashi ni *rajio o kashite moratta.*
(My younger brother had me lend him a radio.)

3. The humble polite version of *morau* as an auxiliary verb is *itadaku*. Example:

> ⑶ 私は先生に本を貸していただいた。
>
> *Watashi wa sensei ni hon o kashite **itadaita**.*
>
> (Lit. I had my teacher lend me a book. (＝I borrowed a book from my teacher.))

4. Unlike sentences with *morau¹*, the giver cannot be marked by *kara* in sentences with *morau²*.

5. In declarative sentences, if the subject is the speaker, it is often omitted. Similarly, in interrogative sentences, if the subject is the hearer, it is often omitted.　　　　　　　　　　　　　　(KS(A)(B) and Ex. (b).)

na な　　*prt.*

> a negative imperative marker used
> by a male speaker in very informal
> speech

Don't do ~

♦**Key Sentence**

	Vinf・nonpast	
たばこ を *Tabako o*	吸う ***suu***	な！ *na!*
(Don't smoke!)

Formation

Vinf・nonpast　な
　　　　　　　na

話す　な　(Don't talk!)
hanasu na

食べる　な　(Don't eat!)
taberu na

Examples

(a) 酒をあまり飲むな！
　　Sake o amari nomu na!
　　(Don't drink too much *sake*!)

(b) そんな所にもう行くな！
　　Sonna tokoro ni mō iku na!
　　(Don't go to such a place any more!)

(c) あんな男とは結婚するな！
　　Anna otoko to wa kekkonsuru na!)
　　(Don't marry that kind of man!)

(d) もう帰って来るな！
　　Mō kaette kuru na!
　　(Don't come home any more!)

Notes

1. ~ *na* is a strong negative imperative and is seldom used except in highly

emotional situations. However, the addition of *yo* after *na* serves to soften the force of the statement.

(1) 酒をあまり飲むなよ。
    *Sake o amari nomu **na yo**.*
    (Don't drink too much *sake*, OK?)

2. A female speaker normally does not use the *na* imperative. She uses Vneg *nai de*, as in *hanasanai de* ' Don't talk.' or *tabenai de* ' Don't eat.'
    (⇨ **~ kudasai**, Note 3)

---

nado など   *prt.*

> a marker that indicates exemplification

and so on; and the like; for example; things like ~
【REL. *nanka*】

◆**Key Sentence**

	Noun		Noun	
日本 の 食べ物 の 中 で は *Nihon no tabemono no naka de wa*	**すし** **sushi**	や *ya*	**てんぷら** **tenpura**	など が 好き *nado ga suki-* だ / 好きです。 *da / sukidesu.*
(Among Japanese foods I like things like *sushi* and *tenpura*.)

Examples

(a) A: 冬休みはどこに行きましょうか。
    Fuyuyasumi wa doko ni ikimashō ka.
    (Where shall we go during the winter vacation?)

    B: ハワイなどどうですか。
    Hawai nado dō desu ka.
    (How about Hawaii, for example?)

(b) 大学ではフランス語やドイツ語などを勉強した。
    Daigaku de wa furansugo ya doitsugo nado o benkyōshita.
    (In college I studied French and German and the like.)

(c) この大学には中国や韓国などから学生が大勢来ます。

　　Kono daigaku ni wa Chūgoku ya Kankoku nado kara gakusei ga ōzei kimasu.

　　(A lot of students from China, Korea and so on come to this college.)

(d) A : 経済学を専攻するつもりですか。

　　Keizaigaku o senkōsuru tsumori desu ka.

　　(Are you going to major in economics?)

　　B : いいえ，経済学など専攻するつもりはありません。

　　Īe, keizaigaku nado senkōsuru tsumori wa arimasen.

　　(No, I have no intention of majoring in things like economics.)

(e) A : この翻訳をしてくださいませんか。

　　Kono hon'yaku o shite kudasaimasen ka.

　　(Could you kindly translate this for me?)

　　B : こんな難しいもの，私などには出来ません。

　　Konna muzukashii mono, watashi nado ni wa dekimasen.

　　(A person like me cannot translate such a difficult thing.)

Notes

1. A particle normally follows *nado*, as in:

   nado {*wa* / *ga* / (*o*) / (*ni*) / *kara* / *de* / *e* / *yori* / etc.}

   Particles other than *ga*, *o*, and *wa* can precede *nado*, but, depending on the context, this order gives the sentence a more derogatory meaning. Examples:

   (1) 箸でなど食べられない。

   　　*Hashi **de nado** taberarenai.*

   　　(We can't eat with damned chopsticks.)

   (2) 箸などで食べる人もいる。

   　　*Hashi **nado de** taberu hito mo iru.*

   　　(Some people eat it with chopsticks (and the like).)

2. If the main predicate is negated, as in Exs. (d) and (e), *nado* often conveys a sense of humbleness especially when the subject is the speaker or a member of his in-group. In other cases, it is generally derogatory.

[Related Expression]

Nanka is the informal, colloquial version of *nado*. It is used as *nado* is used except that in a context conveying undesirability or contempt there is more emphasis on the derogatory meaning.

nagara ながら *conj.*

a conjunction which indicates that
the action expressed by the preceding
verb takes place concurrently or simultaneously with the action expressed in the main clause

while; over; with
【REL. *aida*】

♦ **Key Sentence**

Topic (subject)			Secondary Action	V*masu*	
田口さん *Taguchi-san*	は *wa*	いつも *itsumo*	新聞 を *shinbun o*	読み ***yomi***	ながら *nagara*
Primary Action					
朝ご飯　を　食べる / 食べます。 *asagohan o taberu / tabemasu.*					
(Mr. Taguchi always reads a newspaper while eating his breakfast.)					

Formation

V*masu* ながら
　　　nagara

話し　ながら　　(while talking / talk while doing s.t.)
hanashi nagara

食べ ながら　　(while eating / eat while doing s.t.)
tabe nagara

Examples

(a) 歩きながら本を読むのはあぶないですよ。
Aruki nagara hon o yomu no wa abunaidesu yo.
(It is dangerous to read while walking.)

(b) 山口さんは笑いながら私の話を聞いていた。
Yamaguchi-san wa warai nagara watashi no hanashi o kiite ita.
(Mr. Yamaguchi was listening to me with a smile. (Lit. While smiling,
Mr. Yamaguchi was listening to my story.))

N

(c) 私は寝ながら小説を読むのが好きだ。

Watashi wa ne nagara shōsetsu o yomu no ga sukida.

(I like to read novels in bed. (Lit. While in bed, I like to read novels.))

(d) ものを食べながら話してはいけません。

Mono o tabe nagara hanashite wa ikemasen.

(Don't talk with food in your mouth. (Lit. You must not talk while eating things.))

(e) 木村君は会社で働きながら学校に行っている。

Kimura-kun wa kaisha de hataraki nagara gakkō ni itte iru.

(Mr. Kimura works for a company while going to school.)

Notes

1. V*masu nagara* expresses an action that occurs concurrently or simultaneously with another action. The action expressed by V*masu nagara* is always secondary to the action expressed in the main clause. Thus, in (1), B is acceptable as a response to A, but C is not.

   (1) A: ちょっと話がしたいんですが。

   Chotto hanashi ga shitai n desu ga.

   (I'd like to have a little talk with you.)

   B: じゃ，コーヒーを飲み**ながら**話しましょう。

   *Ja, kōhī o nomi **nagara** hanashimashō.*

   (Then, let's talk over a cup of coffee.)

   C: *じゃ，話し**ながら**コーヒーを飲みましょう。

   Ja, hanashi **nagara kōhī o nomimashō.*

   (Then, let's drink a cup of coffee while talking.)

   Note that in English, "while ~ing" is not always the secondary action.

2. V*masu nagara* cannot be used when the subjects of the two actions are different, as in (2).

   (2) *ルームメートがステレオを聞きながら私は勉強した。

   **Rūmumēto ga sutereo o kiki nagara watashi wa benkyōshita.*

   (I studied while my roommate was listening to the stereo set.)

   (In this case, *aida* is used. (⇨ **aida**))

~nai de ～ないで *phr.*

a negative *te*-form of a verb	do not do s.t. and; without doing ~

【REL. *nakute*; *zu ni*】

◆**Key Sentence**

Topic (subject)		Adverbial Clause		
			Vneg	
ナンシー *Nanshi*	は *wa*	きのう　朝ご飯を *kinō asagohan o*	食べ **tabe** ない で *nai de*	学校 へ 行った / *gakkō e　itta /* 行きました。 *ikimashita.*

(Nancy went to school yesterday without eating her breakfast.)

Formation

Vneg　ない で
　　　nai de

話さない　で　　(without talking)
hanasanai de

食べない　で　　(without eating)
tabenai de

Examples

(a) 中田さんは大阪に行かないで京都に行った。
　　Nakada-san wa Ōsaka ni ikanai de Kyōto ni itta.
　　(Mr. Nakada didn't go to Osaka; he went to Kyoto.)

(b) 辞書を使わないで読んでください。
　　Jisho o tsukawanai de yonde kudasai.
　　(Please read it without using a dictionary.)

(c) まだ帰らないでください。
　　Mada kaeranai de kudasai.
　　(Please don't go home yet.)

(d) 電話しないで欲しい。
　　Denwashinai de hoshii.
　　(Lit. I want you not to call me. (=Don't call me.))

(e) やかましくしないでもらいたい。
　　Yakamashiku shinai de moraitai.
　　(Lit. I want you not to make noises. (=Don't make any noise.))

(f) まだあるから買わないでおきました。
　　Mada aru kara kawanai de okimashita.
　　(Because I still have it, I didn't buy it (in advance).)

Notes

1. If a *nai de* clause expresses something one is expected to do, as in KS where there is the expectation that Nancy should eat breakfast, the translation is 'without ~ing', but if not, it is 'do not do ~ and ~', as in Ex. (a).

2. ~*nai de* is often used to combine two sentences as in KS and Exs. (a) and (b) but can also be used with *kudasai* 'please do s.t.', as in Ex. (c), *hoshii* 'want', as in Ex. (d), *morau* 'receive a favor', as in Ex. (e), and *te oku* 'do s.t. in advance', as in Ex. (f).

3. ~*nai de* is used only with verbs. It cannot be used with adjectives.

4. In cases where no auxiliaries such as *kudasai*, *hoshii*, *morau* and *te oku* are used, *nai de* implies that the speaker is emphasizing negation, because somehow the proposition expressed in the *nai de* clause is contrary to his expectation.

[Related Expressions]

I. ~*nai de* can be replaced by ~ *zu ni*, if *de* of *nai de* somehow retains the original meaning of 'and', as in KS, Exs. (a), (b) and (f). Thus, the sentences in [1] are all grammatical, but those in [2] are all ungrammatical:

　　[1] a. ナンシーはきのう朝ご飯を食べずに学校へ行った。
　　　　　 *Nanshī wa kinō asagohan o tabe**zu ni** gakkō e itta.*　(Cp. KS)

　　　　b. 中田さんは大阪に行かずに京都に行った。
　　　　　 *Nakada-san wa Ōsaka ni ika**zu ni** Kyōto ni itta.*　(Cp. Ex. (a))

　　　　c. 辞書を使わずに読んでください。
　　　　　 *Jisho o tsukawa**zu ni** yonde kudasai.*　(Cp. Ex. (b))

　　　　d. まだあるから買わずにおきました。
　　　　　 *Mada aru kara kawa**zu ni** okimashita.*　(Cp. Ex. (f))

　　[2] a. ＊まだ帰らずにください。
　　　　　 *＊Mada kaera**zu ni** kudasai.*　(Cp. Ex. (c))

b. *電話せずに欲しい。
  *Denwase**zu ni** hoshii. (Cp. Ex. (d))

The only difference between *nai de* and *zu ni* is that of style: *zu ni* is used in formal speech or written Japanese. The formation is exactly the same as *nai de*, namely, Vinf·neg *zu ni*. However, the *zu ni* form for *suru*-verbs is not *shi zu ni*, but *se zu ni*, as in *benkyōsezu ni* ' without studying '.

II. ~*nai de* can be replaced by *nakute* only when the *nai de* clause indicates some cause for human emotion which is expressed in the main clause. Otherwise, the *nakute* version is unacceptable, as in [5].

[3] 僕は英語が話せないで / ???ずに / なくて恥ずかしかった。
  *Boku wa eigo ga hanase**nai de** / ???**zu ni** / **nakute** hazukashi-katta.*
  (I felt ashamed because I couldn't speak English.)

[4] スージーが遊びに来ないで / ???ずに / なくて助かった。
  *Sūji ga asobi ni ko**nai de** / ???**zu ni** / **nakute** tasukatta.*
  (I felt relieved, because Susie didn't come see me.)

[5] a. 一郎は帽子を脱がないで / ずに / *なくて部屋に入った。
  *Ichirō wa bōshi o nuga**nai de** / **zu ni** / *__nakute__ heya ni haitta.*
  (Ichiro entered the room without taking off his hat.)

  b. 見ないで / *ずに / *なくてください。
  *Mi**nai de** / *__zu ni__ / *__nakute__ kudasai.*
  (Please don't look at it.)

  c. 食べないで / ずに / *なくておいた。
  *Tabe**nai de** / **zu ni** / *__nakute__ oita.*
  (I left it uneaten.)

It is also noted that the idea of ' X is not Y but Z ' is expressed by *nakute* rather than *nai de*, as in [6].

[6] 私は学生ではなくて / *ないで先生です。
  *Watashi wa gakusei de wa **nakute** / *__nai de__ sensei desu.*
  (I am not a student but a teacher.)

~nakereba naranai ～なければならない *phr.*

> It won't do if s.o. does not take some action or if s.o. or s.t. is not in some state.

have to; must; need

【REL. ~nai to ikenai; ~nakereba ikenai; ~nakute wa ikenai; ~nakute wa naranai; ~neba naranai】

(ANT. ~nai de mo ii; ~nakute mo ii; ~te wa ikenai; ~te wa naranai)

◆Key Sentences

(A)

A:
今日 は　働かなくて　も いい ん です か。
Kyō wa hatarakanakute mo ii n desu ka.
(Don't you have to work today?)

B:	Vinf·neg	
いいえ,	働か	なければ なりません。
Īe,	**hataraka**	nakereba narimasen.
(Yes, I have to work.)		

(B)

Topic (subject)		Adj (*i*) stem		
バスケットボール の　選手	は	大き	く	なければ ならない /
Basukettobōru no senshu	wa	**ōki**	ku	nakereba naranai /
				なりません。
				narimasen.
(Basketball players have to be big.)				

(C)

Topic (subject)		Adj (*na*) stem		
図書館 *Toshokan*	は *wa*	**静か** ***shizuka***	で *de*	なければ ならない / なりません。 *nakereba naranai / narimasen.*
(Libraries have to be quiet.)				

(D)

	Topic		Noun		
この 仕事 *Kono shigoto*	は *wa*		**学生** ***gakusei***	で *de*	なければ ならない / なりません。 *nakereba naranai / narimasen.*
(Lit. Speaking of this job, it has to be students. (=Only students can apply for this job.))					

Formation

(i) Vneg なければ ならない
　　　 nakereba naranai

　　話さなければ　ならない　(s.o. has to talk)
　　hanasanakereba naranai

　　食べなければ ならない　(s.o. has to eat)
　　tabenakereba naranai

(ii) Adj (*i*) stem く なければ ならない
　　　　　　　　 ku nakereba naranai

　　安くなければ　ならない　(s.t. has to be inexpensive)
　　yasukunakereba naranai

(iii) {Adj (*na*) stem / N} で なければ ならない
　　　　　　　　　　 de nakereba naranai

　　静かでなければ　ならない　(s.t. has to be quiet)
　　shizukadenakereba naranai

　　先生　で なければ ならない　(s.o. has to be a teacher)
　　sensei de nakereba naranai

Examples

(a) 私はあした朝五時に起きなければなりません。
　　Watashi wa ashita asa goji ni okinakereba narimasen.
　　(I have to get up at five tomorrow morning.)

(b)　あの部屋はもう少し広くなければなりません。
　　　Ano heya wa mō sukoshi hirokunakereba narimasen.
　　　(That room has to be a bit larger.)

(c)　この仕事をするためには英語が上手でなければならない。
　　　Kono shigoto o suru tame ni wa eigo ga jōzu de nakereba naranai.
　　　(To do this job, your English has to be good.)

(d)　このゴルフ場を使うためにはメンバーでなければならない。
　　　Kono gorufujō o tsukau tame ni wa menbā de nakereba naranai.
　　　(To use this golf course, you have to be a member.)

Notes

1. Vneg *nakereba naranai* expresses the idea of obligation. The contracted forms Vneg *nakerya naranai* and Vneg *nakya(a) naranai* are also used in conversation. Sometimes, *naranai* is omitted if the context is clear. Example:

　(1)　もう帰らなければ / 帰らなけりゃ / 帰らなきゃ(あ)。
　　　Mō kaeranakereba | kaeranakerya | kearanakya(a).
　　　(I have to go home now.)

2. Negative obligation, i.e., " do not have to " cannot be expressed by the negative form of this pattern. It is expressed by ~*nakutemo ii* ' It is all right if ~ doesn't do s.t.'　　　　　　　　　　(⇨ ~ *te mo ii*)

[Related Expression]

In addition to ~*nakereba naranai | ikenai* there are at least four other expressions of obligation. They are as follows:

　[1]　a.　話さなくてはならない / いけない。
　　　　　Hanasanakute wa naranai | ikenai.

　　　b.　話さないといけない / *ならない。
　　　　　*Hanasanai to ikenai | *naranai.*

　　　c.　話さねばならない / *いけない。
　　　　　*Hanasaneba naranai | *ikenai.*

[1c] is the written version of ~*nakereba naranai*. [1a], [1b] and *hanasa nakereba naranai | ikenai* carry essentially the same meaning. *Nakute wa* is often contracted into ~*nakucha*, ~*nakuchā*, ~*nakutcha*, and ~*nakutchā*.

~**naku naru** ～なくなる　　*phr.*

> It has reached the point where some state or action does not take place any more.

not ~ any more
【REL. *yōni naru*; *mō ~ nai*】

◆**Key Sentence**

	Vinf·neg	
やさしい 漢字 も *Yasashii kanji mo*	**書け** ***kake***	なく なった / なりました。 *naku natta / narimashita.*
(I cannot even write easy *kanji* any more.)		

Formation

(i) Vinf·neg　なく　なる　　where V is often a potential verb
　　　　　　naku naru

　　{話さ　/話せ}　なく　なる　　(s.o. doesn't / can't talk any more)
　　{*hanasa* / *hanase*} *naku naru*

　　{食べ / 食べられ} なく　なる　　(s.o. doesn't / can't eat any more)
　　{*tabe* / *taberare*} *naku naru*

(ii) Adj (*i*) stem　く　なく　なる
　　　　　　　　　ku naku naru

　　高く　　なく　なる　　(s.t. isn't expensive any more)
　　takaku naku naru

(iii) {Adj (*na*) stem / N} {で　は / じゃ} なく　なる
　　　　　　　　　　　　　{*de wa* / *ja*}　　*naku naru*

　　{静かで　　は / 静かじゃ} なく　なる　　(s.t. isn't quiet any more)
　　{*shizukade wa* / *shizukaja*} *naku naru*

　　{先生　で　は / 先生　じゃ} なく　なる　　(s.o. isn't a teacher any more)
　　{*sensei de wa* / *sensei ja*}　　*naku naru*

Examples

(a) 前は酒をよく飲んでいたが，この頃は飲まなくなりました。
　　Mae wa sake o yoku nonde ita ga, konogoro wa nomanaku narimashita.
　　(I used to drink *sake* a lot, but now I don't drink any more.)

(b) 彼は前よく電話をかけて来ましたが，もうかけて来なくなりました。

   Kare wa mae yoku denwa o kakete kimashita ga, mō kakete konaku nari-mashita.

   (He used to call me frequently, but he doesn't call me any more.)

(c) 日本語はもう難しくなくなりました。

   Nihongo wa mō muzukashikunaku narimashita.

   (Japanese isn't difficult for me any more.)

(d) この郊外も地下鉄が来て不便ではなくなった。

   Kono kōgai mo chikatetsu ga kite fubende wa naku natta.

   (This suburban area is no longer inconvenient because there is a subway now (lit. the subway has reached here).)

(e) やっと大学を出て学生ではなくなりました。

   Yatto daigaku o dete gakusei de wa naku narimashita.

   (I finally graduated from college and am not a student any longer.)

[Related Expressions]

Compare *naku naru*, Vinf·neg *yōni naru* and *mō ~nai* in the following sentences:

[1] 日本語が話せなくなった。

   *Nihongo ga hanase**naku natta**.*

   (I cannot speak Japanese any more.)

[2] 日本語が話せないようになった。

   *Nihongo ga hanase**nai yōni natta**.*

   (I've reached the point where I can't speak Japanese.)

[3] 日本語がもう話せない。

   *Nihongo ga **mō** hanase**nai**.*

   (I cannot speak Japanese any more.)

[1] and [2] focus on both process and result, but [3] focuses only on result. Thus, [1] and [2] can take time expressions indicating the period of change, such as *ichinen no uchi ni* 'within a year', *kyūni* 'suddenly', *tōtō* 'finally', but [3] cannot. [1] is different from [2] in that the latter focuses on an indirect, circumstantial cause for the change, whereas the former focuses on a more direct one. Thus, [1] implies that the speaker cannot speak Japanese any more because he has simply forgotten Japanese but [2] implies that he cannot speak Japanese because the situation is such that there are no native speakers around to speak with.   (⇒ *yōni naru*)

~nakute ~なくて　*phr.*

a *te*-form of the negative *nai*, which indicates a cause / reason for a state or action	do not do s.t. and ~ ; is not ~ and ~ ; because ~ do not do s.t. 【REL. *nai de*; *nai kara*; *nai node*; *nakute mo*】

◆ **Key Sentence**

Sentence (cause)			Sentence (effect)
	Vinf·neg		
朝　七時　に *Asa shichiji ni*	起きられ ***okirare***	なくて *nakute*	会社　に　遅れた / 遅れました。 *kaisha ni okureta / okuremashita.*
(I couldn't get up at seven and was late for work (at my company).)			

Formation

(i) Vinf·neg　なくて　　where V is often a potential verb
　　　　　　nakute

　　{話さ　/ 話せ}　なくて　　(s.o. doesn't / can't talk and ~)
　　{*hanasa / hanase*} *nakute*

　　{食べ / 食べられ}　なくて　　(s.o. doesn't / can't eat and ~)
　　{*tabe / taberare*} *nakute*

(ii) Adj (*i*) stem　く　なくて
　　　　　　　　　ku nakute

　　高く　　なくて　　(s.t. isn't expensive and ~)
　　takaku nakute

(iii) {Adj (*na*) stem / N} {で　は / じゃ} なくて
　　　　　　　　　　　　{*de wa / ja*}　*nakute*

　　{静かで　は / 静かじゃ}　なくて　　(s.t. isn't quiet and ~)
　　{*shizukade wa / shizukaja*} *nakute*

　　{先生　で　は / 先生　じゃ}　なくて　　(s.o. isn't a teacher and ~)
　　{*sensei de wa / sensei ja*}　*nakute*

Examples

(a) 先生の説明が分からなくて困りました。
　　Sensei no setsumei ga wakaranakute komarimashita.
　　(I didn't understand the teacher's explanation and had a difficult time.)

(b) 日本では日本語が話せなくて残念でした。

Nihon de wa nihongo ga hanasenakute zannendeshita.

(It's regrettable that I couldn't speak Japanese in Japan.)

(c) 試験は難しくなくてよかったですね。

Shiken wa muzukashiku nakute yokattadesu ne.

(Lit. The exam wasn't difficult and it was good, wasn't it? (=Aren't you glad that the exam wasn't difficult?))

(d) 字が上手じゃなくて恥ずかしいんです。

Ji ga jōzuja nakute hazukashii n desu.

(My handwriting is so poor that I feel ashamed.)

(e) きびしい先生じゃなくてよかった。

Kibishii sensei ja nakute yokatta.

(Lit. He wasn't a strict teacher and it was good. (=I'm glad that he wasn't a strict teacher.))

[Related Expressions]

I. *Nakute mo* means '(even) if ~ not ~'.

  [1] 小川は頭がいいから勉強しなくても東大に入れるよ。

  *Ogawa wa atama ga ii kara benkyōshi**nakute mo** Tōdai ni haireru yo.*

  (Ogawa is bright, so he can enter Tokyo University even if he doesn't study.)

  [2] この難しい漢字は覚えなくてもいいですか？

  *Kono muzukashii kanji wa oboe**nakute mo** iidesu ka?*

  (Is it all right if I don't memorize this difficult *kanji*?)

II. The cause and effect relation indicated by *nakute* is much weaker and more indirectly presented than that of *nai kara* or *nai node*. Thus, KS can be rewritten in four versions, including *nai de*, as shown in [3].

  [3] 朝七時に起きられなくて / ないで / なかったから / なかったので会社に遅れました。

  *Asa shichiji ni okirare**nakute** / **nai de** / **nakatta kara** / **nakatta node** kaisha ni okuremashita.*

The most direct presentation of the cause-effect relation is *nakatta kara*, and the presentation becomes more indirect in the following order: *nakatta node*, *nai de*, and *nakute*. For an excuse for one's lateness the least direct one is of course preferred, because the more indirect, the politer the expression.   (⇨ **kara** ; **node** ; **-te**)

nara なら   *conj.*

> a conjunction which indicates that the preceding sentence is the speaker's supposition about the truth of a present or past fact or the actualization of something in the future

if it is true that; if it is the case that; if; would; could 【REL. *tara* (*ba*, *to*[4])】

♦ **Key Sentence**

Sentence₁			Sentence₂
松田　が　来る *Matsuda ga kuru*	(の) (*no*)	なら *nara*	僕　は　行かない／行きません。 *boku wa　ikanai / ikimasen.*

(If it is true that Matsuda will come, I won't go.)

Formation

(i) {V / Adj (*i*)} inf (の) なら
                  (*no*) *nara*

  {話す　／話した}　(の) なら   (if it is true that s.o. talks / talked)
  {*hanasu* / *hanashita*} (*no*) *nara*

  {高い／高かった} (の) なら   (if it is true that s.t. is / was expensive)
  {*takai* / *takakatta*} (*no*) *nara*

(ii) {Adj (*na*) stem / N}   {ø / だった (の)} なら
                      {ø / *datta* (*no*)} *nara*

  {静か　／静かだった　(の)} なら   (if it is true that s.t. is / was quiet)
  {*shizuka* / *shizukadatta* (*no*)} *nara*

  {先生／先生　だった (の)} なら   (if it is true that s.o. is / was a
  {*sensei* / *sensei datta* (*no*)} *nara*   teacher)

Examples

(a) シカゴへ行くのならバスで行きなさい。
   Shikago e iku no nara basu de ikinasai.
   (If you go to Chicago, go by bus.)

(b) 杉田が来たのなら僕は帰る。
   Sugita ga kita no nara boku wa kaeru.
   (If Sugita has come, I'll go home.)

(c) そんなに高いのなら買えません。

Sonna ni takai no nara kaemasen.

(If it is that expensive, I can't buy it.)

(d) 山田さんが好きなら手紙を書いたらどうですか。

Yamada-san ga suki nara tegami o kaitara dō desu ka.

(If you like Mr. Yamada, why don't you write a letter to him?)

(e) 高橋先生ならそのことを知っているでしょう。

Takahashi-sensei nara sono koto o shitte iru deshō.

(Lit. If it is Prof. Takahashi, he probably knows about it. (=Prof. Takahashi would probably know about it.))

Notes

1. Basically, S *nara* expresses the speaker's supposition concerning the truth of a present or past fact or the actualization of something in the future.

2. *Nara* is the simplified form of *naraba*, the conditional form of the copula *da*. (⇨ *ba*) In modern Japanese, however, *ba* is usually omitted.

3. Since *nara* is the simplified conditional form of the copula, it requires a noun or a noun equivalent. Thus, if the preceding element is not a noun, it is nominalized by *no* (⇨ *no*[3]), although this *no* is optional in modern Japanese. (The stems of *na*-type adjectives behave like nouns; therefore, they can precede *nara* without being nominalized. See Formation (ii).)

4. When S₁ is nonpast, S₁ *nara* S₂ cannot be used if it is nonsensical to suppose the truth of S₁. Thus, the sentences in (1) – (3) are all unacceptable. (1) is unacceptable because it never fails to become ten o'clock; (2) is unacceptable because one can never tell whether it is true or not that it will rain tomorrow; (3) is unacceptable because the speaker already knows it is true that he wants to go.

 (1) *十時になるならバスが来るはずです。

   *Jūji ni naru **nara** basu ga kuru hazu desu.*

   (Lit. The bus is expected to come if it is true that it becomes ten o'clock.)

 (2) *あした雨が降るなら試合はないでしょう。

   *Ashita ame ga furu **nara** shiai wa nai deshō.*

   (If it is true that it will rain tomorrow, there will probably be no game.)

(3) *僕が行きたい**なら**，和子も行きたがっているはずです。

　Boku ga ikitai **nara, Kazuko mo ikita gatte iru hazu desu.*

　(If it is true that I want to go, I expect that Kazuko also wants to go.)

As seen above, S_1 *nara* S_2 cannot be used (A) if S_1 never fails to happen, (B) if one can never tell if it is true or not that S_1 will happen, or (C) if the speaker already knows S_1 is the fact.

If S_1 is counterfactual, S_1 *nara* S_2 can be used. For example, (4) is acceptable because S_1 expresses the speaker's counterfactual feeling. Note that in this case the nominalizer *no* is preferred.

(4) 僕が行きたい**のなら**だれにも言わずに一人で行くよ。

　*Boku ga ikitai **no nara** dare ni mo iwazu ni hitori de iku yo.*

　(If it were the case that I wanted to go, I would go by myself without telling anybody.)

5. S_1 *nara* S_2 cannot be used if the completion or actualization of S_1 brings about S_2.

(5) *春子のアパートへ行く / 行った**なら**一郎がいた。

　Haruko no apāto e iku / itta **nara Ichirō ga ita.*

　(When I went to Haruko's apartment, Ichiro was there.)

(6) *テープレコーダーを買う / 買った**なら**テープをくれた。

　Tēpurekōdā o kau / katta **nara tēpu o kureta.*

　(When I bought a tape-recorder, they gave me a tape.)

If S_2 does not express a past event or a present habitual event, but expresses a present state, the speaker's opinion, volition, judgment, command, request or suggestion, S_1 *nara* can be used as in (7).

(7) a. ニューヨークへ行く（**の**）**なら**リンカーン・センターがおもしろいですよ。(Opinion)

　　　*Nyūyōku e iku (**no**) **nara** Rinkān Sentā ga omoshiroidesu yo.*

　　　(If you go to New York, Lincoln Center is interesting.)

　　b. ニューヨークへ行く（**の**）**なら**リンカーン・センターへ行きます。(Volition)

　　　*Nyūyōku e iku (**no**) **nara** Rinkān Sentā e ikimasu.*

　　　(If I go to New York, I will go to Lincoln Center.)

　　c. テープレコーダーを買う / 買った**なら**テープをくれるはずです。(Judgment)

　　　*Tēpurekōdā o kau / katta **nara** tēpu o kureru hazu desu.*

(If you buy / have bought a tape-recorder, they should give you a tape.)

6. When S₂ in S₁ *nara* S₂ is past, S₁ must be a past event or state. For example, in (8), S₁ represents a past event, and S₁ *nara* indicates that the speaker supposes the truth of S₁.

(8) 雨が降った(の)なら試合はなかったはずです。
   *Ame ga futta (**no**) **nara** shiai wa nakatta hazu desu.*
   (If it is true that it rained, there should have been no game.)

(8) can also be used in a counterfactual situation where it means 'If it were true that it rained, there should have been no game.' In this case the nominalizer *no* is preferred.

7. *No nara* often becomes *n nara* in conversation.

~nasai ~なさい   *aux. v.*

> a polite imperative used by superiors such as parents or teachers to their inferiors (=people of younger age and of lower rank)

Do s.t.
【REL. ~*kudasai*】

♦ **Key Sentence**

	V*masu*	
もっと たくさん *Motto takusan*	食べ **tabe**	なさい。 *nasai.*
(Eat more.)		

Formation

V*masu* なさい
    nasai

話しなさい   (Talk.)
hanashinasai

食べなさい   (Eat.)
tabe*nasai*

Examples

(a) 遊ばないで勉強しなさい。
Asobanaide benkyōshinasai.
(Don't play. Study.)

(b) 早くうちに帰って来なさいよ。
Hayaku uchi ni kaette kinasai yo.
(Come home early, OK?)

(c) もうおそいから歯を磨いて寝なさい。
Mō osoi kara ha o migaite nenasai.
(It's late now, so brush your teeth and go to bed.)

Notes

1. ~*nasai* is the imperative form of the verb *nasaru* 'do' (polite honorific).

2. ~*nasai* is the polite version of nonpolite imperatives.

(⇨ Appendix 1, Basic Conjugations)

(1) a. 読みなさい。(a polite imperative)
Yominasai.
(Read it.)

b. 読め！(a nonpolite imperative)
Yome!
(Read it!)

(2) a. 食べなさい。(a polite imperative)
Tabenasai.
(Eat it.)

b. 食べろ！(a nonpolite imperative)
Tabero!
(Eat it!)

[Related Expression]

In contrast to *nasai*, *kudasai* is used by an inferior towards his superior when he asks a favor of the latter.

[1] 先生，文法を**教えてください** / ***教えなさい**。
Sensei, bunpō o **oshiete kudasai** / ***oshienasai**.
(Professor, please teach me grammar.)

ne ね　*prt.*

| a sentence-final particle that indicates the speaker's request for confirmation or agreement from the hearer about some shared knowledge | English tag question (such as isn't it?; is it?; don't you?; do you?); you know |

♦ **Key Sentence**

Sentence	
坂本さん　　は　たばこ　を　吸わない / 吸いません *Sakamoto-san wa tabako　o　suwanai / suimasen*	ね。 *ne.*
(Mr. Sakamoto doesn't smoke, does he? / Mr. Sakamoto, you don't smoke, do you?)	

Examples

(a)　A：今日はいい天気ですね。

　　　Kyō wa ii tenki desu ne.

　　　(Today is a fine day, isn't it?)

　　B：本当にそうですね。

　　　Hontō ni sō desu ne.

　　　(Isn't it!)

(b)　あなたは学生ですね。

　　Anata wa gakusei desu ne.

　　(You are a student, aren't you?)

(c)　パーティーにいらっしゃいますね？

　　Pāti ni irasshaimasu ne?

　　(You are going to the party, aren't you?)

Notes

1. In this construction the sentence preceding *ne* can be any informal or formal sentence except nonpolite imperative. Thus,

　　(1)　a.　*読めね。

　　　　　Yome **ne.*

　　　　　(Read it, will you?)

　　　　b.　読みなさいね。

　　　　　*Yominasai **ne**.*

　　　　　(Read it, will you?)

c. 読んでくださいね。

   *Yonde kudasai **ne**.*

   (Please read it, will you?)

2. *Ne* can be used as a request for either confirmation or agreement from the addressee. When a sentence expresses the speaker's strong impression of something, *ne* indicates the speaker's request for agreement from the hearer, as in Ex. (a). When a sentence expresses something emotively neutral, *ne* indicates the speaker's request for confirmation from the hearer, as in KS and Exs. (b) and (c). Here, however, KS can also be a request for agreement, if the speaker is surprised that Mr. Sakamoto doesn't smoke. These two uses of *ne* have different intonations: the *ne* of agreement uses falling intonation and the *ne* of confirmation uses rising intonation. The *ne* of agreement becomes *nē* if the speaker is excited about the content of his statement. In other words, S *nē* is an exclamatory sentence, as in (2).

   (2) A: おもしろい映画でしたねえ！

      *Omoshiroi eiga deshita **nē**!*

      (It was such an interesting film, wasn't it!)

      B: そうでしたねえ！

      *Sō deshita **nē**!*

      (Wasn't it!)

On the other hand, the *ne* of confirmation has no exclamatory overtones; it implies something like 'I am assuming X but can you confirm it?' Thus, in KS the speaker doesn't like people who smoke, and for some reason or other, he wants to confirm that Mr. Sakamoto is not one of those people.

3. *Ne* is sometimes used in a non-sentence-final position to draw the hearer's attention to something or to confirm that the hearer has understood what has been said up to that point. *Ne* is typically used in this manner in telephone conversations.

   (3) もしもし，今晩ね，銀座で飲んでから帰るからね，十一時半頃になるよ。

      *Moshi moshi, konban **ne**, Ginza de nonde kara kaeru kara **ne**, jūichijihan goro ni naru yo.*

      (Lit. Hello, tonight, OK? I go home after drinking in Ginza, you understand?, so I'll be home around 11:30. (=Hello, tonight I'll go to the Ginza to drink, so I'll be home around 11:30.))

N

4. {~*te* / *kara*} *ne* is specifically used to give a reason or a cause for the speaker's state of mind or feelings in a very indirect and vague fashion. Examples follow:

(4) a. あの先生はとてもきびしくて / きびしいからね。

   Ano sensei wa totemo kibishikute / *kibishii* **kara ne**.

   ((It's because) that teacher is very strict, you know?)

   b. ゆうべは飲みすぎて / 飲みすぎたからね。

   Yūbe wa nomisugite / *nomisugita* **kara ne**.

   ((It's because) I drank too much last night, you know?)

Ne here indicates the speaker's request for agreement from the hearer based on shared knowledge.

5. The *ne* of confirmation or agreement is used after another sentence-final particle *yo* of assertion. *Yo ne* means ' I assert that ~ but don't you agree? / am I right? '. This *ne* is pronounced with rising intonation

(5) a. 英語が分かるよね。

   Eigo ga wakaru **yo ne**.

   (Lit. I assert that you understand English but am I right? (=You understand English, don't you?))

   b. あの先生はいい先生ですよね。

   Ano sensei wa ii sensei desu **yo ne**.

   (That teacher is a good teacher. Don't you think so?)

6. The *ne* of confirmation or agreement is used after another sentence-final particle, the question marker *ka*. *Ka ne* means ' I am not sure if ~, am I right? '. The *ne* of *ka ne* is pronounced with falling intonation.

(6) a. 山下君は京大に入れますかね。

   *Yamashita-kun wa Kyōdai ni hairemasu***ka ne**.

   (Lit. I'm not sure whether Mr. Yamashita can get into Kyoto University, but am I right? (=I'm not sure whether Mr. Yamashita can get into Kyoto University. What do you say?))

   b. あの先生はいい先生ですかね。

   Ano sensei wa ii sensei desu **ka ne**.

   (I doubt that he is a good teacher.)

ni¹ に   *prt.*

> a particle that indicates a point of time at which s.t. takes place

at; in; on
【REL. *de*⁴】

♦Key Sentence

Topic (subject)			Noun (time)		
私 *Watashi*	は *wa*	毎朝 *maiasa*	六時半 ***rokujihan***	に *ni*	起きる / 起きます。 *okiru* / *okimasu.*
(I get up at six thirty every morning.)					

Examples

(a) 私は四月一日に生まれました。
    Watashi wa shigatsu tsuitachi ni umaremashita.
    (I was born on April 1st.)

(b) 今朝は五時半にうちを出ました。
    Kesa wa gojihan ni uchi o demashita.
    (This morning I left home at five thirty.)

(c) 来年の夏(に)外国旅行をするつもりです。
    Rainen no natsu (ni) gaikokuryokō o suru tsumori desu.
    (I intend to make a trip abroad next summer.)

(d) 子供が学校に行っている間に手紙を書いた。
    Kodomo ga gakkō ni itte iru aida ni tegami o kaita.
    (I wrote a letter while my children were away at school.)

(e) 田中は大学にいる時(に)今の奥さんと出会った。
    Tanaka wa daigaku ni iru toki (ni) ima no okusan to deatta.
    (Tanaka met his present wife when he was in college.)

Notes

1. There are a number of time expressions that cannot take *ni*; the typical ones are *asa* 'morning', *ashita* 'tomorrow', *kinō* 'yesterday', *kyō* 'today', *ototoi* 'the day before yesterday', *rainen* 'next year', *saikin* 'lately', etc. Generally speaking, if a time expression can be specified uniquely in terms of digits, the adverb can take *ni*; otherwise, it cannot. *Getsuyōbi* 'Monday' is the 'first' day of the week, so it can take *ni*. So can

kurisumasu 'Christmas', because it is December 25. But *kyō* 'today' cannot take *ni*, because 'today' cannot be uniquely specified by date.

2. *Ni* is optional with certain time nouns, such as *natsu* 'summer' (as in Ex. (c)) and *toki* 'time' (as in Ex. (e)). The version with *ni* stresses the point of time more than the version without *ni* does.

3. The time noun *aida* also takes *ni* if the event in the main clause does not continue for the entire duration of the event in the *aida* clause, as seen in Ex. (d). If the event in the main clause covers the same duration as the event in the *aida* clause, *ni* cannot be used.   (⇒ **aida** (**ni**))

  (1) 子供が学校に行っている間手紙を書いていた。

      *Kodomo ga gakkō ni itte iru **aida** tegami o kaite ita.*

      (I was writing letters while my children were away at school.)

4. When a specific time expression takes *goro* 'about' as in (2), *ni* may drop.

      (2) 今朝五時半頃(に)起きました。

          *Kesa gojihan **goro** (ni) okimashita.*

          (I got up at about five thirty.)

5. *Ni* as a particle for a point of time can be used freely with various time expressions, as long as it occurs with a time expression that can be uniquely specified in terms of digits.   (⇒ Note 1)

      (3) a. 一時五分に

              *ichiji gofun **ni***

              (at 1:05)

          b. 三月四日に

              *sangatsu yokka **ni***

              (on March 4)

          c. 月曜日に

              *getsuyōbi **ni***

              (on Monday)

          d. 千九百八十四年に

              *sen-kyūhyaku-hachijūyo(n)nen **ni***

              (in 1984)

          e. 二十一世紀に

              *nijūisseiki **ni***

              (in the 21st century)

6. *Ni* is optional with the names of the four seasons. Thus,

(4) 春(に)結婚します。
*Haru (**ni**) kekkonshimasu.*
(I'm getting married in the Spring.)

*ni*² に *prt.*

＿＿＿＿＿＿＿＿＿＿＿＿＿＿＿＿＿＿＿
an indirect object marker   to; for
＿＿＿＿＿＿＿＿＿＿＿＿＿＿＿＿＿＿＿

◆**Key Sentence**

Topic (subject)		Indirect Object		Direct Object		
私	は	母	に	手紙	を	よく 書く / 書きます。
Watashi	*wa*	***haha***	*ni*	*tegami*	*o*	*yoku kaku / kakimasu.*
(I often write letters to my mother.)						

Examples

(a) 父は僕に時計をくれた。
Chichi wa boku ni tokei o kureta.
(My father gave me a watch.)

(b) 加藤先生はアメリカ人の学生に日本文学を教えている。
Katō-sensei wa amerikajin no gakusei ni nihonbungaku o oshiete iru.
(Prof. Kato is teaching Japanese literature to American students.)

(c) 私は妹にお金を少しやりました。
Watashi wa imōto ni o-kane o sukoshi yarimashita.
(I gave a little money to my younger sister.)

(d) 今井さんに電話しましたがいませんでした。
Imai-san ni denwashimashita ga imasendeshita.
(I called Mr. Imai, but he wasn't there.)

(e) 大川先生は学生に色々な辞書を見せた。
Ōkawa-sensei wa gakusei ni iroirona jisho o miseta.
(Prof. Okawa showed various dictionaries to his students.)

N

Notes

1. In this construction, as seen in KS, the verb is typically transitive and is related to an action that involves something that can be transferred from one person to another, such as *ageru* 'give', *hanasu* 'talk', *kureru* 'give', *miseru* 'show', *nageru* 'throw', *oshieru* 'teach' and *yaru* 'give'.

2. Any transitive verb used in the V*te ageru* or V*te kureru* construction can take *ni*, if the verb does not take a human direct object. For example, *yomu* 'read', which does not take a human object, can take *ni²*, if used in the V*te ageru* or V*te kureru* construction, as shown in (1), but *homeru* 'praise', which takes a human object, cannot take *ni*, as shown in (2).

   (1) 小さい時お母さんは私によく本を読んでくれた。
       *Chisai toki o-kā-san wa watashi **ni** yoku hon o yonde kureta.*
       (When I was small, my mother often read me books.)

   (2) 先生は私を / *にほめてくださいました。
       *Sensei wa watashi **o** / *ni homete kudasaimashita.*
       (My teacher praised me.)

An intransitive verb can never take *ni* even if it is used in the V*te ageru* or V*te kureru* construction. Thus,

   (3) ジョンはメアリーの / *にパーティーに来てあげた。
       *Jon wa Meari **no** / *ni pāti ni kite ageta.*
       (John came to Mary's party (for her sake).)

                                        (⇨ ***ageru²***; ***kureru²***)

---

ni³ に   *prt.*

a particle that indicates an agent or a source in passive, causative, *morau* / *te morau* and other receiving constructions	by; from 【REL. *kara¹*】

♦ **Key Sentences**

(A)

Sentence (passive)			
Topic (subject)	Agent	Direct Object	Verb (passive)
一男　は *Kazuo*　*wa*	友達　に ***tomodachi***　*ni*	手紙　を *tegami*　*o*	読まれた / 読まれました。 ***yoma***reta / ***yoma***remashita.
(Kazuo's friend read his (=Kazuo's) letter (and Kazuo was unhappy).)			

(B)

Sentence (causative)			
Topic (subject)	Agent	Direct Object	Verb (causative)
秋子　は *Akiko*　*wa*	浩　に ***Hiroshi***　*ni*	ご飯　を *gohan*　*o*	作らせた / 作らせました。 ***tsukura***seta / ***tsukura***semashita.
(Akiko made Hiroshi fix a meal.)			

(C)

Topic (subject)	Agent	Direct Object	V*te*	
私　は *Watashi*　*wa*	父　に ***chichi***　*ni*	車　を *kuruma*　*o*	買って ***katte***	もらった / もらいました。 *moratta / moraimashita.*
(Lit. I had my car bought by my father.　(=My father bought me a car.))				

(D)

Topic (subject)	Source		
ジェーン　は *Jēn*　*wa*	山野　先生　に ***Yamano-sensei***　*ni*	生け花　を *ikebana*　*o*	習った / 習いました。 *naratta / naraimashita.*
(Jane took lessons in flower arranging from Mrs. Yamano.)			

Examples

(a) その子はお母さんに叱られました。

　　Sono ko wa o-kā-san ni shikararemashita.

　　(The child was scolded by its mother.)

(b) A：そのネクタイはだれにもらったんですか。

　　Sono nekutai wa dare ni moratta n desu ka.

　　(Lit. From whom did you receive that tie? (＝Who gave you that tie?))

　B：父にもらいました。

　　Chichi ni moraimashita.

　　(Lit. I received it from my father. (＝My father did.))

(c) 僕はアメリカ人に英語を教えてもらった。

　　Boku wa amerikajin ni eigo o oshiete moratta.

　　(I had an American teach me English.)

(d) 兄は私に五時間も運転させました。

　　Ani wa watashi ni gojikan mo untensasemashita.

　　(My older brother made me drive for as long as five hours.)

(e) A：吉田さんが結婚したそうですよ。

　　Yoshida-san ga kekkonshita sōdesu yo.

　　(I heard that Mr. Yoshida got married.)

　B：そうですか。だれに聞きましたか。

　　Sō desu ka. Dare ni kikimashita ka.

　　(Is that right? Who told you so?)

N

Notes

1. *Ni*³ is typically used in passive, causative, *morau / te morau* constructions and with verbs such as *kariru* 'borrow', *kiku* 'hear', *morau* 'receive', *narau* 'learn', *osowaru* 'learn' which require a noun phrase representing the source of the direct object.

　　　　　　　　　　　　　　　(⇨ **rareru**; **saseru**; **morau**¹; **morau**²)

2. Nouns that take *ni*³ as in KSs (A), (B) and (C) all represent agents of the main verb's action. Thus, KSs (A), (B) and (C) include (1), (2) and (3), respectively as part of their meaning.

　(1) 友達が手紙を読んだ。

　　　Tomodachi ga tegami o yonda.

　　　(His friend read a letter.)

　(2) 浩がご飯を作った。

　　　Hiroshi ga gohan o tsukutta.

　　　(Hiroshi fixed a meal.)

(3) 父が車を買った。

　　Chichi ga kuruma o katta.

　　(My father bought a car.)

3. *Ni³* of source as in KS (D), Exs. (b) and (e) can be replaced by *kara¹*, but *ni³* of agent, as in KSs (A), (B), (C), Exs. (a), (c) and (d), cannot.

[Related Expression]

The difference between *ni³* (of source) and *kara¹* is that the former indicates the speaker's psychological closeness to a human source, whereas the latter doesn't. This difference explains why *ni³* is ungrammatical if the source is an impersonal institution to which the speaker can hardly feel close, as shown in [1].

[1] ヒルさんは文部省から / *に奨学金をもらいました。

　　*Hiru-san wa monbushō **kara** / ***ni** shōgakukin o moraimashita.*

　　(Mr. Hill has received a scholarship from the Ministry of Education.)

---

ni⁴ に　*prt.*

N

| a particle that indicates the surface of s.t. upon which some action directly takes place | on; onto
【REL. *de¹*; *e* (*made*, *ni⁷*); *ni⁶*】 |

♦Key Sentence

Subject				Direct Object		Verb (action)
子供	が	紙	に	絵	を	描いた / 描きました。
Kodomo	*ga*	**kami**	*ni*	*e*	*o*	*kaita / kakimashita.*
(A child has drawn a picture on the paper.)						

Examples

(a) ここにあなたの名前と住所を書いてください。

　　Koko ni anata no namae to jūsho o kaite kudasai.

　　(Please write your name and address here.)

(b) ヘリコプターが山の上におりました。

   Herikoputā ga yama no ue ni orimashita.

   (A helicoptor landed on the top of the mountain.)

(c) オーバーはハンガーにかけてください。

   Ōbā wa hangā ni kakete kudasai.

   (Please hang your overcoat on the hanger.)

(d) そんな所に立っていると危ないですよ。

   Sonna tokoro ni tatte iru to abunaidesu yo.

   (It's dangerous to keep standing in such a place.)

[Related Expressions]

   I. *Ni*⁴ should not be confused with *de*¹, a particle that indicates a location
   in which some action takes place. (⇨ **de**¹) Consider the difference in
   meaning between [1a] and [1b]:

   [1] a. 道に絵を描いた。

      *Michi **ni** e o kaita.*

      (I drew a picture *on* the street.)

      b. 道で絵を描いた。

      *Michi **de** e o kaita.*

      (I drew a picture *in* the street.)

   II. *Ni*⁴ should not be confused with *ni*⁶, a particle that indicates the location
   where someone or something exists. (⇨ **ni**⁶) Examples:

   [2] a. その寺は京都にある。

      *Sono tera wa Kyōto **ni** aru.*

      (That temple is in Kyoto.)

      b. 私は部屋にいた。

      *Watashi wa heya **ni** ita.*

      (I was in the room.)

ni[5] に *prt.*

> a particle which indicates purpose when s.o. moves from one place to another

> to do s.t.; in order to do s.t. 【REL. *tame ni*】

♦ **Key Sentence**

Topic (subject)			V*masu*		Verb (motion)
私 Watashi	は wa	デパートへ 贈り物 を depāto e okurimono o	買い **kai**	に ni	行った / 行きました。 itta / ikimashita.
(I went to a department store to buy a gift.)					

Formation

V*masu* に
　　　 ni

話し に　　(to talk)
hanashi ni

食べ に　　(to eat)
tabe ni

Examples

(a) 学生が質問をしに来た。
　 Gakusei ga shitsumon o shi ni kita.
　 (A student came to ask questions.)

(b) そこへ何をしに行くんですか。
　 Soko e nani o shi ni iku n desu ka.
　 (Lit. To do what are you going there?　(=For what are you going there?))

(c) 村井さんは昼ご飯を食べにうちへ帰った。
　 Murai-san wa hirugohan o tabe ni uchi e kaetta.
　 (Mr. Murai went home to eat his lunch.)

Notes

1. V*masu ni*, meaning 'to do s.t.', can be used only with verbs of motion, (i.e., verbs which express a movement from one place to another), such

as *iku* ' go ', *kuru* ' come ', *kaeru* ' return ', *hairu* ' enter ' and *deru* ' leave '. Verbs like *aruku* ' walk ', *hashiru* ' run ' and *oyogu* ' swim ' are not considered motion verbs because they express a manner of movement rather than a movement from one place to another. Therefore, the following sentence is ungrammatical.

(1) *私は桜の花を見に公園を歩いた。
    **Watashi wa sakura no hana o mi ni kōen o aruita.*
    (I walked through the park to see cherry blossoms.)

2. If the verb in V*masu ni* is a compound verb of the structure N *suru*, such as *shigotosuru* ' work ', *benkyōsuru* ' study ' and *shitsumonsuru* ' ask a question ', *suru* is sometimes omitted.

(2) a. 大山さんは仕事(し)に行った。
       Ōyama-san wa shigoto(shi) ni itta.
       (Mr. Oyama went to work.)

    b. 学生が質問(し)に来た。
       Gakusei ga shitsumon(shi) ni kita.
       (A student came to ask questions.)

【Related Expression】

N

Vinf·nonpast *tame ni* is also used to express purpose in an action. However, the uses of Vinf·nonpast *tame ni* and V*masu ni* differ in some ways. First, unlike V*masu ni*, Vinf·nonpast *tame ni* can be used with any verb. Examples:

[1] 私は子供の写真を撮るためにカメラを買った。
    *Watashi wa kodomo no shashin o toru **tame ni** kamera o katta.*
    (I bought a camera to take pictures of my child.)

[2] 私はアメリカ人の友達と話すために英語を勉強している。
    *Watashi wa amerikajin no tomodachi to hanasu **tame ni** eigo o benkyōshite iru.*
    (I'm studying English in order to speak with my American friend.)

Second, when V*masu ni* and Vinf·nonpast *tame ni* are used with verbs of motion, V*masu ni* can be used without a directional phrase, but Vinf·nonpast *tame ni* cannot, unless that information is clear from the context. Examples:

[3] 僕は酒を飲みに行った。
    *Boku wa sake o nomi **ni** itta.*
    (I went (somewhere) to drink.)

[4] a. 僕は酒を飲むために友達の家に行った。

*Boku wa sake o nomu **tame ni** tomodachi no ie ni itta.*

(I went to his friend's house to drink.)

b. *僕は酒を飲むために行った。

Boku wa sake o nomu **tame ni itta.*

(I went to drink.)

Third, when Vinf·nonpast *tame ni* and V*masu ni* are used with verbs of motion, Vinf·nonpast *tame ni* usually expresses a rather important purpose, while V*masu ni* can be used even to express something insignificant. Examples:

[5] a. 喫茶店へコーヒーを飲みに行った。

*Kissaten e kōhi o nomi **ni** itta.*

(I went to a coffee shop to drink coffee.)

b. ??喫茶店へコーヒーを飲むために行った。

*??Kissaten e kōhi o nomu **tame ni** itta.*

(I went to a coffee shop to drink coffee.)

N

ni⁶ に *prt.*

~~~~~~~~~~~~~~~~~~~~~~~~~~~~~~
a particle which indicates the location where s.o. or s.t. exists
~~~~~~~~~~~~~~~~~~~~~~~~~~~~~~

in; at; on

【REL. *de¹*; *ni⁴*】

◆Key Sentences

(A)

Topic (subject)			Noun (location)		Verb (existence)
ヒルさん *Hiru-san*	は *wa*	今 *ima*	ジョンソンさん の アパート *Jonson-san no apāto*	に *ni*	いる / います。 *iru / imasu.*
(Mr. Hill is at Mr. Johnson's apartment now.)					

(B)

Topic (location)			Subject		Verb (existence)
私　の　クラス ***Watashi no kurasu***	に *ni*	は *wa*	中国人　の　学生 *chūgokujin no gakusei*	が *ga*	いる / います。 *iru / imasu.*
(There is a Chinese student in my class.)					

Examples

(a) その本はこの学校の図書館にあります。
Sono hon wa kono gakkō no toshokan ni arimasu.
(That book is in this school's library.)

(b) この学校にはプールがない。
Kono gakkō ni wa pūru ga nai.
(There is no swimming pool at this school.)

(c) 加藤さんは大阪に住んでいます。
Katō-san wa Ōsaka ni sunde imasu.
(Mr. Kato lives in Osaka.)

(d) 庭に桜の木が立っている。
Niwa ni sakura no ki ga tatte iru.
(There is a cherry tree standing in the yard.)

(e) この作文には文法のまちがいがたくさん見られる。
Kono sakubun ni wa bunpō no machigai ga takusan mirareru.
(Lit. A lot of grammatical mistakes can be seen in this composition.
(=There are a lot of grammatical mistakes in this composition.))

(f) 花子がみのるの隣に座っている。
Hanako ga Minoru no tonari ni suwatte iru.
(Hanako is sitting next to Minoru.)

Notes

1. *Ni*[6] indicates the location where someone or something exists. Verbs such as *iru* '(animate things) exist', *aru* '(inanimate things) exist' and *sumu* 'live' typically occur with the locational *ni*.　　　(⇨ ***aru***[1]; ***iru***[1])

2. The verb *aru* often takes the particle *ni*, but when *aru* is used for an event, *ni* cannot be used. In this case, *de* is used.　　(⇨ ***aru***[1]; ***de***[1])

3. Noun phrases with *ni* often occur as topics, as in KS(B) and Ex. (b).

4. If a location phrase which indicates the existence of someone or something modifies a noun phrase, as in ' an apartment *in New York*', *ni* cannot be used. In this case, *no* is used.   (⇨ *no*¹)

   (1) ニューヨーク**の** / ***に**アパート

       *Nyūyōku **no** / *ni apāto*

       (an apartment in New York)

[Related Expressions]

  I. *De*¹ also indicates location, but not a location where someone / something exists. Thus, in the following sentences *de* is ungrammatical.

    [1] a. 私のうちに / *ではテレビがない。

          *Watashi no uchi **ni** / *de wa terebi ga nai.*

          (There is no TV set in my house.)

        b. スミスさんは今会議室に / *でいる。

          *Sumisu-san wa ima kaigishitsu **ni** / *de iru.*

          (Mr. Smith is in the conference room now.)

On the other hand, *ni* is used only to indicate the location where someone / something exists, but not an event; therefore, in the following sentences, *ni* is ungrammatical.

    [2] a. 私はいつも図書館で / *に勉強する。

          *Watashi wa itsumo toshokan **de** / *ni benkyōsuru.*

          (I always study at the library.)

        b. このラケットは日本で / *には五万円ぐらいだ。

          *Kono raketto wa Nihon **de** /*ni wa goman'en gurai da.*

          (This racket costs about 50,000 yen in Japan.)

        c. そのパーティーはトムの家で / *にあった。

          *Sono pātī wa Tomu no ie **de** / *ni atta.*

          (The party was held at Tom's.)

  II. In some sentences, both the locational *ni* and the locational *de* can be used. For example, in [3] both *ni* and *de* are appropriate.

    [3] 私は京都に / でいい家を見つけた。

       *Watashi wa Kyōto **ni** / **de** ii ie o mitsuketa.*

       (I found a good house in Kyoto.)

However, the nuances of a sentence with *ni* and that with *de* are different. Namely, the sentence with *ni* implies that " I found a good house which is in Kyoto", while the one with *de* means " In Kyoto I found a good house". Therefore, in [4] the *ni* version and the *de* version mean different things.

[4]　私は東京に / で仕事を見つけた。
　　Watashi wa Tōkyō ni / de shigoto o mitsuketa.
　　(I found a job in Tokyo.)

Namely, in the sentence with *ni*, the job is in Tokyo and the place the speaker found it might not have been Tokyo. On the other hand, the sentence with *de* means that the place the speaker found the job was Tokyo and the place where he is going to work is not necessarily Tokyo.

---

ni⁷ に　*prt.*

| a particle which indicates a place toward which s.o. or s.t. moves | to; toward 【REL. *e*】 |

◆**Key Sentence**

Topic (subject)			Noun (place)		
私 *Watashi*	は *wa*	きのう *kinō*	サンフランシスコ ***Sanfuranshisuko***	に *ni*	行った / 行きました。 *itta / ikimashita.*
(I went to San Francisco yesterday.)					

Examples

(a) ジムは来年アメリカに帰る。
　　Jimu wa rainen Amerika ni kaeru.
　　(Jim is going back to America next year.)

(b) いつか私のうちに来ませんか。
　　Itsuka watashi no uchi ni kimasen ka.
　　(Wouldn't you like to come to my house sometime?)

(c) 彼らは角のレストランに入った。
　　Karera wa kado no resutoran ni haitta.
　　(They entered the restaurant around the corner.)

★Semantic Derivations of *Ni*

⟨ Direct Contact ⟩ *ni*⁴
黒板に絵を描いた。
Kokuban ni e o kaita.
(I drew a picture on the blackboard.)

⟨ Locational existence ⟩ *ni*⁶
ここに電話がある。
Koko ni denwa ga aru.
(Here is a telephone.)

ni ⟨ contact ⟩

⟨ Direction ⟩ *ni*⁷
私はロンドンに行った。
Watashi wa Rondon ni itta.
(I went to London.)

⟨ Purpose ⟩ *ni*⁵
僕は魚を買いに行った。
Boku wa sakana o kai ni itta.
(I went to buy fish.)

⟨ Indirect Object ⟩ *ni*²
太郎は花子に本を貸した。
Tarō wa Hanako ni hon o kashita.
(Taro lent a book to Hanako.)

⟨ Source / Agent ⟩ *ni*³
ボブはメアリーに切符をもらった。
Bobu wa Meari ni kippu o moratta.
(Bob received a ticket from Mary.)

⟨ Point of time ⟩ *ni*¹
二時に友達が来た。
Niji ni tomodachi ga kita.
(A friend of mine came at 2 o'clock.)

N

ni chigainai にちがいない　　*phr.*

The speaker is convinced that there is no mistake on his part in guessing something.

there is no doubt that ~; must be ~; no doubt

【REL. *darō*; *hazu*; *kamoshirenai*】

♦**Key Sentences**

(A)

Topic (subject)			Vinf	
下田さん　は *Shimoda-san : wa*	今日 の こと　を *kyō no koto : o*		忘れた ***wasureta***	に ちがいない / *ni　chigainai* / ちがいありません。 *chigaiarimasen.*

(Mr. Shimoda must have forgotten today's plans (lit. about things of today).)

(B)

Topic (subject)		Adj (*i*) inf	
あの 先生 の 試験　は *Ano sensei no shiken : wa*		難しい ***muzukashii***	に ちがいない / ちがいありません。 *ni　chigainai / chigaiarimasen.*

(That teacher's exams must be hard.)

(C)

Topic (experiencer)				Adj (*na*) stem	
ベイリーさん　は *Beiri-san : wa*	テニス　が *tenisu : ga*			上手 ***jōzu***	に ちがいない / ちがいありません。 *ni　chigainai / chigaiarimasen.*

(Mr. Bailey must be good at tennis.)

(D)

Topic (subject)		Noun	
あの 人　は *Ano hito : wa*		日本人 ***nihonjin***	に ちがいない / ちがいありません。 *ni　chigainai / chigaiarimasen.*

(That person must be Japanese.)

Formation

KSs (A) and (B):

{Vinf / Adj(*i*)} inf に ちがいない
              ni chigainai

{話す / 話した} に ちがいない   (s.o. will no doubt talk / s.o. no
{*hanasu* / *hanashita*} *ni chigainai*   doubt talked)

{食べる / 食べた} に ちがいない   (s.o. will no doubt eat / s.o. no doubt
{*taberu* / *tabeta*} *ni chigainai*   ate)

{高い / 高かった} に ちがいない   (s.t. is / was no doubt expensive)
{*takai* / *takakatta*} *ni chigainai*

KSs (C) and (D):

{Adj (*na*) stem / N} {ø / だった} に ちがいない
                   {ø / *datta*} *ni chigainai*

{静か / 静かだった} に ちがいない   (s.t. is / was no doubt quiet)
{*shizuka* / *shizuka*datta} *ni chigainai*

{先生 / 先生 だった} に ちがいない   (s.o. is / was no doubt a teacher)
{*sensei* / *sensei datta*} *ni chigainai*

Examples

(a) 二人は今頃ハワイで楽しく泳いでいるにちがいない。
    Futari wa imagoro Hawai de tanoshiku oyoide iru ni chigainai.
    (The two must now be enjoying swimming in Hawaii.)

(b) 一人で外国へ行くのは大変にちがいない。
    Hitori de gaikoku e iku no wa taihen ni chigainai.
    (It must be hard to go to a foreign country alone.)

(c) 山口さんは頭がいいにちがいない。
    Yamaguchi-san wa atama ga ii ni chigainai.
    (Mr. Yamaguchi must be bright.)

(d) あれはトンプソンさんにちがいない。
    Are wa Tonpuson-san ni chigainai.
    (That must be Mr. Thompson.)

Note

The sentence-equivalent that precedes *ni chigainai* can be nominalized by *no* in written Japanese, yielding more credibility to the speaker's assertion. Examples: (⇨ ***no***[3])

(1) a. 日本の経済はよくなった**の**にちがいない。

*Nihon no keizai wa yoku natta **no** ni chigainai.*

(The Japanese economy must have really improved.)

b. 家を買うのはあまり難しくない**の**にちがいない。

*Ie o kau no wa amari muzukashikunai **no** ni chigainai.*

(Buying a house is no doubt not so difficult.)

[Related Expressions]

I. There are cases where *ni chigainai* can sometimes be replaced by *hazu da*. In such cases, however, the former is always a conjecture and the latter is the speaker's expectation based on objective facts. (⇨ ***hazu***)

II. The degree of probability implied by *darō*, *kamoshirenai*, and *ni chigainai* is as follows:

Least probable		Most probable
←		→
kamoshirenai	*darō*	*ni chigainai*

N

-nikui にくい   *aux. adj. (i)*

> S.t. or s.o. is hard to ~.

hard to ~ ; difficult to ~ ; don't
do s.t. easily; not readily; not
prone to ~
(ANT. *-yasui*)

♦ **Key Sentence**

Topic (subject)			V*masu*	
この　本	は	大変	読み にくい / にくいです。	
Kono hon	*wa*	*taihen*	*yomi nikui / nikuidesu.*	
(This book is very hard to read.)				

Formation

V*masu* にくい
     nikui

話しにくい   (s.o. is hard to talk to)
hanashinikui

食べにくい   (s.t. is hard to eat)
tabenikui

Examples

(a) このドアは開きにくいですね。
   Kono doa wa akinikuidesu ne.
   (This door doesn't open easily, does it?)

(b) あの人の名前は覚えにくい。
   Ano hito no namae wa oboenikui.
   (His name is hard to remember.)

(c) あの先生は話しにくいです。
   Ano sensei wa hanashinikuidesu.
   (That teacher is hard to talk to.)

(d) この靴は走りにくいです。
   Kono kutsu wa hashirinikuidesu.
   (These shoes are hard to run in.)

Notes

1. V*masu*+*nikui* conjugates exactly like an Adj (*i*).

		Informal	Formal
Aff.	Nonpast	話しにくい *hanashinikui*	話しにくいです *hanashinikuidesu*
	Past	話しにくかった *hanashinikukatta*	話しにくかったです *hanashinikukattadesu*
Neg.	Nonpast	話しにくくない *hanashinikukunai*	話しにくくありません *hanashinikukuarimasen*
	Past	話しにくくなかった *hanashinikukunakatta*	話しにくくありませんでした *hanashinikukuarimasendeshita*

2. In both English and Japanese the subject of the *nikui*-construction can be the subject of an intransitive verb, as in Ex. (a) where *kono doa* 'this door' is the subject of *aku* 'open'. It can also be the direct object of a transitive verb, as in Ex. (b) where *ano hito no namae* 'his name' is the direct object of *oboeru* 'remember'. It can be the indirect object of a transitive verb, as in Ex. (c) where *ano sensei* 'that teacher' is the indirect object of *hanasu* 'talk'. Finally, the subject can be N+ Particle such as *kono kutsu de* 'with these shoes' corresponding in English to Preposition+N. In this construction, as in Exs. (c) and (d), note that the preposition in the English sentence is retained but the corresponding particle in the Japanese sentence is deleted.

3. *-yasui* 'easy to do ~' is an antonym of *-nikui*. The basic formation of the *yasui*-construction is identical to the *nikui*-construction.   (⇨ ***-yasui***)

~ni shite wa ~にしては   *prt.*

a phrase that indicates a generally agreed upon standard (The entire sentence that includes this phrase expresses some deviation from that standard.)

for ~ ; considering that ~
【REL. **~to shite wa**】

♦ **Key Sentences**

(A)

Topic (subject)		Noun		
高山さん *Takayama-san*	は *wa*	**日本人** **nihonjin**	に し て は *ni shite wa*	大きい / 大きいです。 *ōkii / ōkiidesu.*

(Mr. Takayama is big for a Japanese person.)

(B)

Topic (subject)			Vinf		
ボブ *Bobu*	は *wa*	日本語 を よく *nihongo o yoku*	**勉強して いる** **benkyōshite iru**	に し て は *ni shite wa*	下手だ / *hetada /* 下手です。 *hetadesu.*

(Considering that Bob is studying Japanese hard, he is poor at it.)

Formation

KS(A):

N (だった) に して は
   (*datta*) *ni shite wa*

先生 (だった) に して は   (considering that s.o. is / was a teacher)
sensei (*datta*) *ni shite wa*

KS(B):

Vinf に して は
    ni shite wa

{話す / 話した}　に して は　　(considering that s.o. talks / talked)
{*hanasu* / *hanashita*}　*ni shite wa*

Examples

(a) 八月にしては涼しいですね。
　　Hachigatsu ni shite wa suzushiidesu ne.
　　(For August it is cool, isn't it?)

(b) これは日本の車にしては大きいですね。
　　Kore wa Nihon no kuruma ni shite wa ōkiidesu ne.
　　(For a Japanese car this is big, isn't it?)

(c) 彼はレスラーだったにしては体が小さい。
　　Kare wa resurā datta ni shite wa karada ga chīsai.
　　(Considering that he was a wrestler, he is small.)

(d) 青木さんはアメリカに十年いたにしては英語があまり上手じゃない。
　　Aoki-san wa Amerika ni jūnen ita ni shite wa eigo ga amari jōzujanai.
　　(Considering that Mr. Aoki spent ten years in America, his English is
　　not very good.)

Note

~*ni shite wa* is the *te*-form of *ni suru* 'make it ~, decide on ~' plus *wa*
'if'. The literal meaning is 'if one makes it ~'.

N

~**ni suru** ~にする　　*phr.*

S.o. has decided on s.t.　　　　　　　decide on ~; make it ~
　　　　　　　　　　　　　　　　　　　【REL. *ni kimeru*】

◆**Key Sentence**

Topic (subject)		Noun		
私 *Watashi*	は *wa*	**この　アパート** **kono　apāto**	に *ni*	する / します。 *suru* / *shimasu.*
(I've decided on this apartment.)				

Examples

(a) A: あなたは何にしますか。

     Anata wa nan ni shimasu ka.

     (Lit. What have you decided on? (＝What will you have?))

  B: 私はステーキにします。

     Watashi wa sutēki ni shimasu.

     (Lit. I've decided on steak. (＝I'll have steak.))

(b) 岡田さんはアメリカの車にしました。

     Okada-san wa Amerika no kuruma ni shimashita.

     (Mr. Okada (has) decided on an American car.)

Notes

1. *Ni suru* is usually preceded by a noun or a noun equivalent. (⇨ **koto ni suru**) However, a noun with a particle is also possible. Example:

   (1) 今度の旅行はニューヨークまでにします。

      Kondo no ryokō wa Nyūyōku made ni shimasu.

      (Next trip, I'll make it as far as New York.)

2. If the tense is nonpast, *ni suru* implies that a decision has just been made, as in KS and Ex. (a). If the past tense is used, the sentence is ambiguous; it means either that a decision has been made but no action has been taken or that a decision was made and an action was also taken. (Ex. (b))

[Related Expression]

Ni kimeru also means 'decide on' and *ni suru* and *ni kimeru* can be used interchangeably, although *ni kimeru* is usually used in situations where a decision is considered significant or important. Thus, in situations like Ex. (a), *ni kimeru* is not used.

no¹ の *prt.*

> a particle which, with a preceding noun phrase, forms a phrase to modify a following noun phrase

's; of; in; at; for; by; from
【REL. *no²*】

◆ **Key Sentences**

(A)

	Noun		Noun	
これ は *Kore wa*	先生 ***sensei***	の *no*	本 *hon*	だ / です。 *da / desu.*
(This is my teacher's book.)

(B)

	Noun	Particle		Noun	
これ は *Kore wa*	友達 ***tomodachi***	から ***kara***	の *no*	手紙 *tegami*	だ / です。 *da / desu.*
(This is a letter from my friend.)

Formation

(i) N の N
　　　no

　　田中さん の 家　　(Mr. Tanaka's house)
　　Tanaka-san no ie

　　アメリカ の 大学　　(a university in America)
　　Amerika no daigaku

(ii) N Prt の N
　　　　　no

　　日本 で の 仕事　　(a job in Japan)
　　Nihon de no shigoto

　　メアリー へ の プレゼント　　(a present for Mary)
　　Meari　e no purezento

Examples

(a) 私の本　　　　　　学校の名前　　　　　　今日の新聞
    watashi no hon　*gakkō no namae*　*kyō no shinbun*
    (my book)　　　　(the name of the school)　(today's paper)

(b) 日本の寺　　　　　駅の電話
    Nihon no tera　*eki no denwa*
    (a temple in Japan)　(a telephone at the station)

(c) 美術の本　　　　　日本語の試験
    bijutsu no hon　*nihongo no shiken*
    (a book on fine arts)　(an exam on Japanese)

(d) 桜の花　　　　　　桃の木　　　　　　　バスの切符
    sakura no hana　*momo no ki*　　*basu no kippu*
    (a cherry blossom)　(a peach tree)　(a bus ticket)
    かぜの薬
    kaze no kusuri
    (cold medicine)

(e) 日本語の先生　　　音楽の学生
    nihongo no sensei　*ongaku no gakusei*
    (a teacher of Japanese)　(a student of music)

(f) ピカソの絵　　　　ベートーベンの音楽　　フォードの車
    Pikaso no e　　*Bētōben no ongaku*　*Fōdo no kuruma*
    (a picture by Picasso)　(music by Beethoven)　(a car made by Ford)

(g) 友達の大木さん　　医者の森田さん　　　カラーの写真
    tomodachi no Ōki-san　*isha no Morita-san*　*karā no shashin*
    (my friend Mr. Oki)　(a medical doctor, Dr.　(a photo in color)
    　　　　　　　　　Morita)
    十歳の子供
    jussai no kodomo
    (a ten-year-old child)

(h) 絹のドレス　　　　れんがの家
    kinu no doresu　*renga no ie*
    (a silk dress)　　(a brick house)

(i) 八時からのパーティー　先生との話し合い
    hachiji kara no pātī　*sensei to no hanashiai*
    (a party which starts　(a discussion with the
    at eight o'clock)　　teacher)

Notes

1. Generally, *no* combines two noun phrases into a larger noun phrase. In A *no* B, A *no* modifies B and indicates a specific member(s) of B among all the members of B. A and B in A *no* B relate to each other in various ways, and these relationships are determined by context. Some common relationships follow.

(A) A is the possessor of B. (Ex. (a))
  B of A; A's B

(B) A is the location where B exists. (Ex. (b))
  B in / at A

(C) B is about / on A. (Ex. (c))
  B on A; B about A

(D) A is a specific kind of B. (Ex. (d))
  AB; B of A; B for A

(E) A is the object and B is the subject. (Ex. (e))
  AB; B of A

(F) A created B. (Ex. (f))
  A's B; B by A; B created by A

(G) A is an attribute of B. (Ex. (g))
  A, B; B, who / which is A

(H) B is made of / from A. (Ex. (h))
  AB

2. In A *no* B, A is sometimes a noun phrase with a particle, as in KS(B) and Ex. (i). Note that *no* cannot be omitted in this case, because it indicates that the preceding noun phrase with a particle modifies the following noun phrase. Without *no*, the noun phrase with the particle is interpreted as an adverbial phrase which modifies the predicate in the clause. For example, in (1a) *hachiji kara* ' from eight o'clock ' modifies *ikimashita* ' went ', while in (1b) *hachiji kara no* modifies *pātī* ' party '.

(1) a. <u>八時から</u>　　パーティーに　<u>行きました</u>。
　　　<u>***Hachiji kara***</u> *pātī ni*　　<u>***ikimashita***</u>.

　　(I went to the party at (lit. from) eight o'clock.)

b. 八時からの　　　　パーティーに　行きました。

Hachiji kara no pāti ni　ikimashita.

(I went to the party which had started at (lit. from) eight o'clock.)

3. The "A *no* B" construction can be extended as in "A *no* B *no* C *no* . . ." Examples:

(2) a. 私の先生の本

   watashi no sensei no hon

   (my teacher's book)

   b. 日本語の先生の田中先生

   nihongo no sensei no Tanaka-sensei

   (the Japanese teacher, Prof. Tanaka)

4. In A *no* B, B can be omitted if it is apparent from context. Examples:

(3) これは私の(本)です。

   Kore wa watashi no (hon) desu.

   (This is mine (=my book).)

(4) このレストランの(ステーキ)はよくありません。

   Kono resutoran no (sutēki) wa yokuarimasen.

   (This restaurant's (steak) is not good.)

N

---

no² の　　*pro.*

a dependent indefinite pronoun

one

【REL. *no¹*; *no³*】

♦ Key Sentences

(A)

	Adj		
私　は	大きい	の	を　買った / 買いました。
Watashi wa	**ōkii**	*no*	*o　katta / kaimashita.*
(I bought a big one.)			

(B)

	Relative Clause		
私　は *Watashi wa*	去年　買った ***kyonen katta***	の *no*	を　使った／使いました。 *o tsukatta / tsukaimashita.*
(I used the one I bought last year.)			

Formation

KS(A):

(i) Adj (*i*) inf·nonpast　の
　　　　　　　　　　　　no

高い　の　　(expensive one)
takai no

(ii) Adj (*na*) stem　な　の
　　　　　　　　　　na no

じょうぶな　の　　(durable one)
jōbuna　　*no*

KS(B):

Same formation rules as those for relative clauses.　(⇨ Relative Clause)

Examples

(a)　A：どんな車がほしいですか。
　　　　Donna kuruma ga hoshiidesu ka.
　　　　(What kind of car do you want?)

　　　B：小さいのが欲しいです。
　　　　Chisai no ga hoshiidesu.
　　　　(I want a small one.)

(b)　友達がワインを飲みたがったのできのう買ったのを出した。
　　　Tomodachi ga wain o nomitagatta node kinō katta no o dashita.
　　　(My friend wanted to drink wine, so I served the one I bought yesterday.)

Notes

1. The indefinite pronoun *no* is a dependent pronoun; it cannot be used by itself. It must be modified by an adjective or a relative clause.

2. *No* is used in place of a noun when what it refers to is clear from the context or the situation. Things referred to by *no* are not necessarily tangible. Example:

(1) 今まで聞いたアイデアの中では田村君が言った**の**が一番よさそうだ。

*Ima made kiita aidea no naka de wa Tamura-kun ga itta **no** ga ichiban yosa sōda.*

(Among the ideas we've heard so far, the one Mr. Tamura told us seems the best.)

[Related Expressions]

The indefinite pronoun *no* (i.e., *no²*) is different from the particle *no* (i.e., *no¹*) and the nominalizer *no* (i.e., *no³*). First, [1] shows the difference between *no¹* and *no²*. Namely, in [1a] *Tomu no* is the omitted form of *Tomu no pen*. On the other hand, [1b] is not an omitted form; that is, if a noun is inserted after *kuroi no* in [1b], the sentence becomes ungrammatical as seen in [1c]. In fact, what [1b] means is [1d], if *no* 'one' refers to a pen.

[1] a. *no¹* (particle)

私はトムの（ペン）がほしい。

*Watashi wa Tomu **no** (pen) ga hoshii.*

(I want Tom's pen.)

b. *no²* (indefinite pronoun)

私は黒いのがほしい。

*Watashi wa kuroi **no** ga hoshii.*

(I want a black one.)

c. *私は黒いのペンがほしい。

Watashi wa kuroi **no pen ga hoshii.*

(I want a black pen.)

d. 私は黒いペンがほしい。

*Watashi wa kuroi **pen** ga hoshii.*

(I want a black pen.)

Next, [2] shows the difference between *no²* and *no³*. That is, the meaning of the sentence depends on whether the *no* in [2] is interpreted as *no²* or *no³*, as shown in the two English translations.

[2] 高田さんが使っていた**の**をおぼえていますか。

*Takada-san ga tsukatte ita **no** o oboete imasu ka.*

((A) [Indefinite pronoun] Do you remember *the one* Mr. Takada was using?)

((B) [Nominalizer] Do you remember *that* Mr. Takada was using (something)?)

no³ の   *nom.*

a nominalizer which is used when the nominalized sentence expresses a directly perceptible event

that ~; to do s.t.; doing s.t. 【REL. *koto²*; *no²*】

♦**Key Sentences**

(A)

Sentence (informal)†			
日本語 を **教える** *Nihongo o **oshieru***	の *no*	は *wa*	難しい / 難しいです。 *muzukashii / muzukashiidesu.*
(Teaching Japanese is difficult.)			

(B)

Topic (subject)		Sentence (informal)†				
私 *Watashi*	は *wa*	雪子さん が ビール を **飲む** *Yukiko-san ga biiru o **nomu***	の *no*	を *o*	見た / 見ました。 *mita / mimashita.*
(I saw Yukiko drink beer.)						

†*Da* after Adj (*na*) stem and N changes to *na*.

Formation

(i) {V / Adj (*i*)} inf の
　　　　　　　　　　no

　　{話す　/ 話した} の　　(that s.o. talks / talked)
　　{*hanasu* / *hanashita*} *no*

　　{高い / 高かった} の　　(that s.t. is / was expensive)
　　{*takai* / *takakatta*} *no*

(ii) {Adj (*na*) stem / N}　{な / だった} の
　　　　　　　　　　　　　{*na* / *datta*} *no*

　　{静かな　/ 静かだった}　の　　(that s.t. is / was quiet)
　　{*shizukana* / *shizukadatta*}　*no*

　　{先生　な / 先生　だった} の　　(that s.o. is / was a teacher)
　　{*sensei na* / *sensei datta*}　*no*

Examples

(a) 日本へ行くのは簡単です。

Nihon e iku no wa kantandesu.

(Going to Japan is easy.)

(b) 私は小林さんがピアノを弾いているのを聞いた。

Watashi wa Kobayashi-san ga piano o hiite iru no o kiita.

(I heard Ms. Kobayashi playing the piano.)

(c) クラークさんがフランスへ行くのを知っていますか。

Kurāku-san ga Furansu e iku no o shitte imasu ka.

(Do you know that Mr. Clark is going to France?)

Notes

1. *No* makes a noun equivalent from a sentence. KS(A) and Ex. (a) are examples of sentences where nominalized sentences are used in subject position, and KS(B) and Exs. (b) and (c) are examples where nominalized sentences are used as direct objects. A nominalized sentence can occur in any position where a noun phrase can appear, except in the position of B in "A *wa* B *da*". In that situation, the nominalizer *koto* (i.e., *koto*²) is used as in (1).

  (1) こまったの / ことは彼が来られないこと / *のだ。

   Komatta no | koto wa kare ga korarenai koto | *no da.

   (The trouble is that he can't come.)

2. Nominalized sentences are subordinate clauses, and, therefore, the topic marker *wa* cannot occur, as seen in (2). (⇨ **ga**¹)

  (2) 僕はひろ子さんが / *はピアノを弾いているのを聞いた。

   *Boku wa Hiroko-san **ga** | ****wa*** piano o hiite iru no o kiita.*

   (I heard Hiroko playing the piano.)

3. There is another nominalizer, *koto*. *No* and *koto* are sometimes mutually interchangeable. (⇨ **koto**²) For example, Exs. (a) and (c) can be restated as:

  (3) 日本へ行くことは簡単です。

   *Nihon e iku **koto** wa kantandesu.*

   (Going to Japan is easy.)

  (4) クラークさんがフランスへ行くことを知っていますか。

   *Kurāku-san ga Furansu e iku **koto** o shitte imasu ka.*

   (Do you know that Mr. Clark is going to France?)

N

However, in general, *no* is used when the preceding clause expresses something rather concrete or perceptible, while *koto* is used when the preceding clause expresses something rather abstract or imperceptible. In KS(B), Ex. (b) and (5), for example, *koto* cannot be used because the nominalized clauses in these examples all express concrete, perceptible events.

(5) 私は自分の体がふるえているの / *ことを感じた。

    Watashi wa jibun no karada ga furuete iru **no** / ***koto** *o kanjita.*

    (I felt my body trembling.)

Also, there are a number of idiomatic phrases with *koto* where *koto* cannot be replaced by *no*. (⇨ **koto ga aru**; **koto ga dekiru**; **koto ni naru**; **koto ni suru**) (6) lists verbs and adjectives and their appropriate nominalizers.

(6)

			no	*koto*
見る	*miru*	'see'	v	*
見える	*mieru*	'be visible'	v	*
聞く	*kiku*	'hear'	v	*
聞こえる	*kikoeru*	'be audible'	v	*
感じる	*kanjiru*	'feel'	v	*
止める	*tomeru*	'stop (v.t.)'	v	*
待つ	*matsu*	'wait'	v	*
見つける	*mitsukeru*	'discover'	v	?
ふせぐ	*fusegu*	'protect'	v	?
知る	*shiru*	'get to know'	v	v
忘れる	*wasureru*	'forget'	v	v
(に) 気 が つく	*(ni) ki ga tsuku*	'notice'	v	v
思い出す	*omoidasu*	'recall'	v	v

		no	*koto*
覚える *oboeru*	'learn'	v	v
認める *mitomeru*	'admit'	v	v
避ける *sakeru*	'avoid'	v	v
止める *yameru*	'quit'	v	v
後悔する *kōkaisuru*	'regret'	v	v
(が) 分かる (*ga*) *wakaru*	'understand'	v	v
(が) 好きだ (*ga*) *sukida*	'like'	v	v
(が) きらいだ (*ga*) *kiraida*	'dislike'	v	v
(が) 怖い (*ga*) *kowai*	'afraid'	v	v
(が) うれしい (*ga*) *ureshii*	'happy'	v	v
(が) 悲しい (*ga*) *kanashii*	'sad'	v	v
やさしい *yasashii*	'easy'	v	v
難しい *muzukashii*	'difficult'	v	v
期待する *kitaisuru*	'expect'	?	v
信じる *shinjiru*	'believe'	??	v
すすめる *susumeru*	'advise'	??	v
考える *kangaeru*	'think'	*	v
頼む *tanomu*	'ask'	*	v
命じる *meijiru*	'order'	*	v

N

		no	koto
（が）出来る *(ga) dekiru*	'can do'	*	v
（が）ある *(ga) aru*	'there are / were times when'	*	v
（に）する *(ni) suru*	'decide'	*	v
（に）なる *(ni) naru*	'be decided'	*	v
（に）よる *(ni) yoru*	'be due to'	*	v

no⁴ の   *prt.*

a sentence-final particle used by a female speaker or a child to indicate an explanation or emotive emphasis

it is that ~
【REL. *no da*】

N

♦ **Key Sentences**

(A)

A:		Vinf		B:		Vinf	
どうして *Dōshite*		泣いて いる **naite iru**	の? *no?*	お母さん が *O-kā-san ga*		いない **inai**	の。 *no.*
(How come you are crying?)				('Cause mommy's gone.)			

(B)

Topic (subject)			Adj (*i*) inf	
あの 人 *Ano hito*	は *wa*	とても *totemo*	やさしい **yasashii**	の。 *no.*
(He is so gentle, you know.)				

(C)

Topic (subject)				Adj (*na*) stem		
母 *Haha*	は *wa*	まだ *mada*	とても *totemo*	**元気** **genki**	な **na**	の。 *no.*
(My mother is still quite fine.)						

(D)

Topic (subject)		Noun		
主人 *Shujin*	は *wa*	**エンジニア** **enjinia**	な **na**	の。 *no.*
(My husband is an engineer.)				

Formation

(i) {V / Adj (*i*)} inf の
　　　　　　　　　　no

　　{話す　/ 話した}　の　　(s.o. talks / talked)
　　{*hanasu* / *hanashita*} *no*

　　{食べる / 食べた}　の　　(s.o. eats / ate)
　　{*taberu* / *tabeta*} *no*

　　{大きい / 大きかった}　の　　(s.t. is / was big)
　　{*ōkii* / *ōkikatta*} *no*

(ii) {Adj (*na*) stem / N} {な / だった} の
　　　　　　　　　　　　　{*na* / *datta*} *no*

　　{静かな　/ 静かだった}　の　　(s.t. is / was quiet)
　　{*shizuka na* / *shizuka datta*} *no*

　　{先生　な / 先生　だった}　の　　(s.o. is / was a teacher)
　　{*sensei na* / *sensei datta*} *no*

Examples

(a) A : どうして食べないの?
　　　Dōshite tabenai no?
　　　(How come you don't eat it?)

B : おなか (が) 空いて (い) ないの。
   Onaka (ga) suite (i)nai no.
   ('Cause I'm not hungry.)

(b) A : どうしたの?
   Dōshita no?
   (What's the matter with you?)

B : 頭が痛いの。
   Atama ga itai no.
   (I have a headache.)

(c) うちの子はまだ小学生なの。
   Uchi no ko wa mada shōgakusei na no.)
   (My child is still in grade school.)

(d) 大学はプリンストンだったの。
   Daigaku wa Purinsuton datta no.
   (My university was Princeton.)

Notes

1. The sentence-final *no* is derived from *no da / no desu* through deletion of *da / desu*.

2. This *no* is used by females or children only in an informal situation. There are times when adult male speakers use *no* in questions, as in Exs. (a) and (b), but they do not use it in declarative sentences, as in Exs. (c) and (d).

[Related Expression]

The sentence-final particle *no*[4] is the same in its meaning as *no* of *no da*.
(⇨ ***no da***)

no da のだ *phr.*

a sentence ending which indicates that the speaker is explaining or asking for an explanation about some information shared with the hearer, or is talking about something emotively, as if it were of common interest to the speaker and the hearer

The explanation is that ~ ; The reason is that ~ ; The fact is that ~ ; It is that ~

◆**Key Sentences**

A:		
Sentence (informal)†		
何　を　して　いる *Nani o shite iru*	ん / の　です *n / no desu*	か‡。 *ka.*
(What are you doing?)		

B:	
Sentence (informal)†	
日本語　を　勉強して　いる *Nihongo o benkyōshite iru*	ん / の　です*。 *n / no desu.*
(I'm studying Japanese.)	

†*Da* after Adj (*na*) stem and N changes to *na.*

‡Informal form:　何　を　して　いる　ん　だい。　　(male)
　　　　　　　　　Nani o shite iru　n dai.　　　　　　　　　(⇨ **dai**)
　　　　　　　　　何　を　して　いる　の?　　(female)
　　　　　　　　　Nani o shite iru　no?　　　　　　　　　(⇨ **no⁴**)

*Informal form:　…勉強して　いる　ん　だ。　　(male)
　　　　　　　　　…*benkyōshite iru　n da.*
　　　　　　　　　…勉強して　　いる　の。　　(female)
　　　　　　　　　…*benkyōshite iru　no.*

Formation

(i) {V / Adj (*i*)} inf　の　だ
　　　　　　　　　　　　no da

{話す / 話した}　の　だ　　(s.o. (will) talk / talked)
{*hanasu* / *hanashita*} *no da*

{高い / 高かった}　の　だ　　(s.t. is / was expensive)
{*takai* / *takakatta*} *no da*

(ii) {Adj (*na*) stem / N} {な / だった}　の　だ
　　　　　　　　　　　　{*na* / *datta*} *no da*

{静かな　 / 静かだった　　の　だ　　(s.t. is / was quiet)
{*shizukana* / *shizukadatta*} *no da*

{先生　な / 先生　だった}　の　だ　　(s.o. is / was a teacher)
{*sensei na* / *sensei datta*}　*no da*

Examples

(a) A : どうしてお酒を飲まないんですか。
　　　Dōshite o-sake o nomanai n desu ka.
　　　(Why don't you drink *sake*?)

　　B : 私はまだ十七なんです。
　　　Watashi wa mada jūshichi na n desu.
　　　((The reason is that) I'm still seventeen.)

(b) 僕は今日のパーティーに行けません。宿題がたくさんあるんです。
　　Boku wa kyō no pātī ni ikemasen. Shukudai ga takusan aru n desu.
　　(I can't go to today's party. I have a lot of homework.)

(c) あなたと結婚したいんです。
　　Anata to kekkonshitai n desu.
　　(I want to marry you.)

Notes

1. In conversation, *no da* / *desu* often becomes *n da* / *desu*. In informal speech, male speakers use *n da* and female speakers use *no*. (For the informal forms of *no da* in interrogative sentences, see *kai* and *dai*.)

2. Basically, S *no da* is used when the speaker is explaining or asking for an explanation about information shared with the hearer. The information is often what the speaker and the hearer have observed or heard. For example, in KSs, A uses *no desu* because he is asking for an explanation about what he sees B doing. B also uses *no desu* because he is explaining his actions. In this situation, (1) is odd.

⑴ A : 何をしていますか。
　　　Nani o shite imasu ka.
　　　(What are you doing?)

　　 B : 日本語を勉強しています。
　　　Nihongo o benkyōshite imasu.
　　　(I'm studying Japanese.)

If, however, A is only assuming that B is doing something, A can ask the question in (2), and B can answer as B does in (1).

⑵ あなたは今何をしていますか。
　　Anata wa ima nani o shite imasu ka.
　　(What are you doing now?)

In Ex. (a), as in KS, A uses *n desu* because A observes that B isn't drinking *sake* and wants an explanation for that. And, B also uses *n desu* because he is explaining about what A observed. In Ex. (b), the speaker uses *n desu* in the second sentence because it is an explanation about the information which has been given in the first sentence.

3. S *no da* is also used when no information is shared by the speaker and the hearer and the speaker is not explaining or asking for an explanation about anything. In this case, the speaker is talking as if some information were shared with the hearer and the effects of this are, for example,

　⒜　to involve the hearer in the affairs he is talking about (See (3) and (4) below.),

and / or

　⒝　to impose his idea upon the hearer or, at least, to emphasize his idea emotively. (See (5) below.)

Examples :

⑶ 今日フットボールがある**ん**ですが一緒に行きませんか。
　　*Kyō futtobōru ga aru **n desu** ga isshoni ikimasen ka.*
　　(There is a football game today. Wouldn't you like to go (together) with me?)

⑷ 先生，困っている**ん**です。助けてください。
　　*Sensei, komatte iru **n desu**. Tasukete kudasai.*
　　(Teacher, I'm in trouble. Please help me.)

(5)　日本語の文法は難しいですがおもしろい**ん**です**よ。
　　　*Nihongo no bunpō wa muzukashiidesu ga omoshiroi **n desu** yo.*
　　　(Japanese grammar is difficult, but it is interesting, you know.)

node　ので　*conj.*

a subordinate conjunction which expresses a reason or a cause	so; since; because 【REL. *de³*; *kara³*】

♦ **Key Sentence**

Subordinate Clause (cause / reason)		Main Clause
Sentence (informal)†		
お酒　を　たくさん　**飲んだ** *O-sake o takusan **nonda***	ので *node*	眠く　なった / なりました。 *nemuku natta	narimashita.*
(Because I drank a lot of *sake*, I got sleepy.)		

†*Da* after Adj (*na*) stem and N changes to *na*.

Formation

(i)　{V / Adj (*i*)} inf　ので
　　　　　　　　　　　node

　　　{話す　 / 話した}　　ので　　　(because s.o. (will) talk / talked)
　　　{*hanasu | hanashita*} *node*

　　　{高い / 高かった}　ので　　(because s.t. is / was expensive)
　　　{*takai | takakatta*} *node*

(ii)　{Adj (*na*) stem / N}　{な / だった} ので
　　　　　　　　　　　　　　　{*na | datta*}　*node*

　　　{静かな　 / 静かだった}　ので　　(because s.t. is / was quiet)
　　　{*shizukana | shizukadatta*} *node*

　　　{先生　な / 先生　だった} ので　　(because s.o. is / was a teacher)
　　　{*sensei na | sensei datta*}　*node*

Examples

(a) 宿題がたくさんあるのでパーティーに行けません。
Shukudai ga takusan aru node pāti ni ikemasen.
(Since I have a lot of homework, I can't go to the party.)

(b) その本は高かったので買わなかった。
Sono hon wa takakatta node kawanakatta.
(Because that book was expensive, I didn't buy one.)

(c) 私の部屋は静かなのでよく勉強出来ます。
Watashi no heya wa shizukana node yoku benkyō dekimasu.
(My room is quiet, so I can study (there) well.)

(d) ジェーンはまだ中学生なので車を運転出来ない。
Jēn wa mada chūgakusei na node kuruma o unten dekinai.
(Because Jane is still a junior high student, she can't drive a car.)

Note

Etymologically, *node* is the *te*-form of *no da*. (⇨ **no da**) However, in modern Japanese it is used as a conjunction to indicate reason or cause.

【Related Expressions】

I. The conjunction *kara* also expresses reason or cause. However, *kara* and *node* differ in the following way. *Node* is used when the speaker believes that the information he provides in S₁ *node* as cause or reason for S₂ is valid and is also evident and acceptable to the hearer. (Exs. (a)-(d)) S₁ *kara* S₂, however, does not involve that assumption. Therefore, *node* cannot be used and *kara* must be used in the following situations:

(A) S₁ (i.e., reason / cause clause) expresses the speaker's conjecture about something.

[1] 人がたくさん来るだろうから / *ので食べものを たくさん買っておいた。
*Hito ga takusan kuru darō **kara** / ***node** tabemono o takusan katte oita.*
(Because many people will probably come, I've bought a lot of food.)

(B) S₂ (i.e., the main clause) is a command, request, suggestion or invitation.

[2] *Command*

この映画はためになるから / *ので行きなさい。

*Kono eiga wa tame ni naru **kara** / ***node** ikinasai.*

(Because this movie is good for you, go (see it).)

[3] *Request*

あしたのショーはおもしろいから / *のでぜひ見に来てください。

*Ashita no shō wa omoshiroi **kara** / ***node** zehi mi ni kite kudasai.*

(Tomorrow's show is interesting, so please come to see it.)

[4] *Suggestion*

この本は とてもおもしろいから / *のでみんなも 読んだほうがい いよ。

*Kono hon wa totemo omoshiroi **kara** / ***node** minna mo yonda hō ga ii yo.*

(This book is very interesting, so you'd better read it, too.)

[5] *Invitation*

いい酒をもらったから / *ので一緒に飲みましょうか。

*Ii sake o moratta **kara** / ***node** isshoni nomimashō ka.*

(I got some good *sake*, so shall we drink it together?)

(C) S₂ expresses the speaker's volition or personal opinion.

[6] *Volition*

田中さんが行くから / *ので僕も行こう。

*Tanaka-san ga iku **kara** / ***node** boku mo ikō.*

(Since Mr. Tanaka is going (there), I'll go, too.)

[7] *Personal Opinion*

僕がよく知っているから / *ので大じょうぶです。

*Boku ga yoku shitte iru **kara** / ***node** daijōbudesu.*

(I know it well, so there will be no problem.)

II. The particle *de* is also used to express a reason or cause. (⇨ *de*³; Semantic Derivations of *De*) *De*, however, can be used only with nouns, while *node* and *kara* are used only with sentences. Compare [8] and [9].

[8] 台風で / *から / *ので家がたくさんたおれた。

*Taifū **de** / *kara / *node ie ga takusan taoreta.*

(Many houses fell down due to the typhoon.)

[9] 強い風が吹いたから / ので / *で家がたくさんたおれた。
*Tsuyoi kaze ga fuita **kara** | **node** | *de ie ga takusan taoreta.*
(Lit. Many houses fell down because a strong wind blew.)

noni[1] のに *conj.*

Contrary to everybody's expectation based on the sentence preceding *noni*, the proposition in the sentence following *noni* is the case.	even though; despite the fact that ~ ; although; but; in spite of the fact that ~ 【REL. *ga*; *keredo(mo)*】

♦Key Sentences

(A)

Subordinate Clause			Main Clause
	Vinf		
毎日　漢字 を *Mainichi kanji o*	勉強して　いる **benkyōshite iru**	のに *noni*	よく 覚えられない / *yoku oboerarenai /* 覚えられません。 *oboeraremasen.*

(Although I'm studying *kanji* every day, I cannot memorize them well.)

(B)

Topic (subject)		Adj (*i*) inf		
この ステーキ *Kono sutēki*	は *wa*	高い **takai**	のに *noni*	おいしくない / おいしくありません。 *oishikunai / oishikuarimasen.*

(In spite of the fact that this steak is expensive, it isn't delicious.)

(C)

Topic (subject)			Adj (*na*) stem			
清水さん *Shimizu-san*	は *wa*	ゴルフ が *gorufu ga*	下手 ***heta***	な ***na***	のに *noni*	大好きだ / *dai-sukida* / 大好きです。 *dai-sukidesu.*

(Although Mr. Shimizu is not good at golf, he loves it.)

(D)

Topic (subject)		Noun			
ホールさん *Hōru-san*	は *wa*	アメリカ人 ***amerikajin***	な ***na***	のに *noni*	肉 が 嫌いだ / 嫌いです。 *niku ga kiraida* / *kiraidesu.*

(In spite of the fact that Mr. Hall is an American, he doesn't like meat.)

Formation

KSs(A) and (B):

{V / Adj (*i*)} inf のに
            noni

{話す / 話した} のに   (although s.o. talks / talked)
{*hanasu* / *hanashita*} *noni*

{高い / 高かった} のに   (although s.t. is / was expensive)
{*takai* / *takakatta*} *noni*

KSs(C) and (D):

{Adj (*na*) stem/ N} {な / だった} のに
                     {*na* / *datta*}   *noni*

{静かな / 静かだった} のに   (although s.t. is / was quiet)
{*shizukana* / *shizukadatta*} *noni*

{先生 な / 先生 だった} のに   (although s.o. is / was a teacher)
{*sensei na* / *sensei datta*} *noni*

Examples

(a) 中学と高校で六年間も英語を勉強したのにまだ英語が話せません。
    Chūgaku to kōkō de rokunenkan mo eigo o benkyōshita noni mada eigo ga hanasemasen.

(I studied English for as many as six years at junior high and senior high, but I still cannot speak it.)

(b) 寒いのにオーバーを着ないで出かけた。

Samui noni ōbā o kinaide dekaketa.

(Although it was cold, he went out without wearing an overcoat.)

(c) あの人はピアノが上手なのにめったに弾きません。

Ano hito wa piano ga jōzuna noni metta ni hikimasen.

(He is good at piano, but seldom plays.)

(d) 父は九十歳なのにまだ働いています。

Chichi wa kyūjussai na noni mada hataraite imasu.

(My father is still working in spite of the fact that he is ninety years old.)

Notes

1. *Noni* is the nominalizer *no* plus the particle *ni* 'to', meaning 'in contrast to the fact that ~'. The *noni* clause expresses a highly presupposed, speaker-oriented action or state. (⇨ ***no***³) In other words, the speaker of S₁ *noni* S₂ is personally involved with the proposition of S₁. This personal involvement tends to create some emotive overtone.

2. In colloquial speech, if the content of the main clause is predictable, the clause often drops. In this case, the sentence expresses a feeling of discontent on the part of the speaker.

   (1) A：そんなもの要らないよ。

   Sonna mono iranai yo.

   (I don't need that kind of stuff.)

   B：せっかくあげると言うのに。

   *Sekkaku ageru to iu **noni**.*

   (Lit. Although I'm kindly saying that I'll give it to you. (=I'm saying I'll give it to you, you know.))

[Related Expressions]

I. Because of the speaker-oriented character of the *noni* clause, certain types of constructions involving the hearer cannot be used in the main clause in this construction. If the main clause is a request, suggestion, question, command or request for permission, only *keredo(mo)* can be used. Examples of the above categories can be seen in [1] through [5] below:

[1] 難しいけれど / *のにしてみてください。
Muzukashii **keredo** / **noni* shite mite kudasai.
(It is difficult, but try it, please.)

[2] あまりおいしくないけれど / *のに食べてみませんか。
Amari oishiku nai **keredo** / **noni* tabete mimasen ka.
(It's not so good, but do you want to try it?)

[3] a. 寒いけれど / *のに外に出ますか。
Samui **keredo** / **noni* soto ni demasu ka.
(It's cold, but are you going outside?)

  b. 寒いけれど / のに外に出るんですか。
Samui **keredo** / *noni* soto ni deru n desu ka.
(It's cold, but (lit. is it that you are going outside?) are you going outside?)

[4] つまらないけれど / *のに読みなさい。
Tsumaranai **keredo** / **noni* yominasai.
(It's boring, but read it.)

[5] 下手だけれど / *下手なのにしてもいいですか。
Hetada **keredo** / **Hetana* **noni** shite mo iidesu ka.
(I'm not good at it, but can I do it?)

N

[3b] is acceptable, because the scope of the question is not the main verb *deru* 'go outside' but the whole sentence nominalized by *n*.

II. The main clause cannot be an expression of intention as in [6], because the expression is directed not towards the speaker but towards the hearer.

[6] 分からないけれど / *のによく考えてみるつもりです / 考えて み よう と思います。
Wakaranai **keredo** / **noni* yoku kangaete miru tsumori desu / kangaete miyō to omoimasu.
(Although I don't understand it, I intend to really think about it / I think I will really think about it.)

III. Due to the nominalizer *no*, the *noni* clause tends to express something with which the speaker is emotively involved. But *keredo(mo)* is relatively free from the speaker's emotive involvement; in short, it is more objective than *noni*. (⇨ **no**[3])

IV. *Noni* in Exs. (a) through (d) can also be replaced by the disjunctive conjunction *ga* 'but'. For example, Ex. (d) can be rewritten as [7].

[7] 父は九十歳だが，まだ働いている。

Chichi wa kyūjussai da ga, mada hataraite iru.

(My father is ninety years old, but he is still working.)

The disjunctive meaning of *ga* is much weaker than that of *noni*, and *ga* is free from the restrictions imposed on *noni*. The style of the *noni* clause is always informal, but depending on the style of the second sentence, the style of the sentence preceding *ga* can be either informal or formal, as shown below:

> Sinf *ga* Sinf / fml vs. Sinf *noni* Sinf / fml
> Sfml *ga* Sfml

---

noni² のに   *conj.*

in the process or for the purpose of doing s.t. expressed in the *no*-nominalized clause	in the process of doing ~ ; (in order) to do ~ ; for the purpose of ~

【REL. *ni⁵*; *tame (ni)*】

◆ Key Sentence

Topic (subject)		Subordinate Clause			Main Clause
			Vinf·nonpast		
私	は	日本語 の 新聞 を	読む	のに	辞書 を 使う /
Watashi	*wa*	*nihongo no shinbun o*	*yomu*	*noni*	*jisho o tsukau /*
					使います。
					tsukaimasu,
(I use a dictionary to read Japanese newspapers.)					

Formation

Vinf·nonpast のに
　　　　　　　noni

話す のに　(in order to talk)
hanasu noni

食べる のに　　(in order to eat)
taberu noni

Examples

(a) すきやきを作るのには何が要りますか。
Sukiyaki o tsukuru noni wa nani ga irimasu ka.
(What do you need to make *sukiyaki*?)

(b) このレポートを書くのに一か月かかりました。
Kono repōto o kaku noni ikkagetsu kakarimashita.
(It took me a month to write this paper.)

(c) 会社に行くのにバスと電車を使っている。
Kaisha ni iku noni basu to densha o tsukatte iru.
(I am using the bus and the train to get to (lit. my company) work.)

Notes

1. In the *noni*² construction, only informal, nonpast, volitional verbs can precede *noni*.　　　　　　　　　　　　　　　　(Cp. **noni**¹)

2. When the *noni* clause is used as the topic (i.e., S *noni wa*), *no* is often deleted in conversation, as in (1).

   (1) すきやきを作るには何が要りますか。
   *Sukiyaki o tsukuru **ni wa** nani ga irimasu ka.*
   (What do you need to make *sukiyaki*?)

[Related Expressions]

I. When the main verb is a verb of motion, the *noni*² construction contrasts with that of V*masu ni* V(motion).　(⇨ **ni**⁵)　Examples:

   [1] 映画を見に銀座へ行った。
   *Eiga o mi **ni** Ginza e itta.*
   (I went to Ginza to see a movie.)

   [2] 映画を見るのに銀座へ行った。
   *Eiga o miru **noni** Ginza e itta.*
   (I went to Ginza for the purpose of seeing a movie.)

   [3] 映画を見に / *見るのに行った。
   *Eiga o mi **ni** /*miru **noni** itta.*
   (I went to see / *for the purpose of seeing a movie.)

If a destination is specified, as in [1] and [2], both constructions can be used. However, the *noni* version implies that the subject of the sentence made a lot out of the entire process. [2] can imply that the speaker shouldn't have used time and money going to Ginza to see a movie. If a location is not specified, only the V*masu ni* V (motion) construction can be used, as shown in [3].

II. *Noni²* is similar in its meaning to Vinf·nonpast *tame ni* 'in order to'. The latter purely means 'purpose' but the former retains the meaning of 'in the process of', even when it means 'purpose'. Thus, in a sentence such as [4] below in which the verb in the *noni*-clause is incongruous with the meaning of 'process', *noni* cannot be used.

[4] 生きるために / *のに食べる。
   *Ikiru **tame ni** / *noni taberu.*
   (We eat in order to live.)

Cp. この町で生きていくために / のに月二十万円は必要だ。
   *Kono machi de ikite iku **tame ni** / **noni** tsuki nijūman'en wa hitsuyōda.*
   (We need 200,000 yen a month in order to keep living in this town.)

~no wa ~da ~のは ~だ　　*str.*

a structure that indicates new, important information by placing it between *no wa* and the copula *da* (*No* is an indefinite pronoun (*no²*) that replaces 'time', 'person', 'thing', 'place' or 'reason'.)	it is ~ that ~; the one who ~ is ~; the place where ~ is ~; the reason why ~ is ~; the time when ~ is ~; what ~ is ~ **[REL.** *no³*]

N

◆Key Sentences

(A)

	Vinf		Important Information	
私　が　中国　に *Watashi ga Chūgoku ni*	行った ***itta***	の　は *no wa*	三年　前 *sannen mae*	だ / です。 *da / desu.*

(It was three years ago that I went to China. / The time when I went to China was three years ago.)

(B)

	Adj (i) inf		Important Information	
この クラスで 一番 頭 が *Kono kurasu de ichiban atama ga*	いい ***ii***	の は *no wa*	吉田さん *Yoshida-san*	だ / です。 *da / desu.*
(The brightest one in this class is Mr. Yoshida.)				

(C)

	Adj (na) stem			Important Information	
ここ で 一番 *Koko de ichiban*	きれい ***kirei***	な ***na***	の は *no wa*	山 *yama*	だ / です。 *da / desu.*
(The most beautiful things here are mountains.)					

Formation

(i) {V / Adj (i)} inf の は ～ だ
　　　　　　　　　　no wa ～ da

　　{話す　/ 話した} の は ～ だ　(it is ～ who talks / talked)
　　{hanasu / hanashita} no wa ～ da

　　{食べる / 食べた} の は ～ だ　(it is ～ who eats / ate)
　　{taberu / tabeta} no wa ～ da

　　{高い / 高かった} の は ～ だ　(it is ～ that is / was expensive)
　　{takai / takakatta} no wa ～ da

(ii) {Adj (na) stem / N} {な / だった} の は ～ だ
　　　　　　　　　　　　　　{na / datta} no wa ～ da

　　{静かな　/静かだった} の は ～ だ　(it is ～ that is / was quiet)
　　{shizukana / shizukadatta} no wa ～ da

　　{先生　な / 先生　だった} の は ～ だ　(it is ～ who is / was a teacher)
　　{sensei na / sensei datta} no wa ～ da

Examples

(a) 山田さん，あなたがシカゴに行ったのはいつですか。
　　Yamada-san, anata ga Shikago ni itta no wa itsu desu ka.
　　(Mr. Yamada, when was it that you went to Chicago?)

(b) おととい遊びに来たのは秋子さんです。

Ototoi asobi ni kita no wa Akiko-san desu.

(It was Akiko who came to see me the day before yesterday.)

(c) モーツアルトが大好きになったのは大学一年の時です。

Mōtsuaruto ga dai-sukini natta no wa daigaku ichinen no toki desu.

(It was during my freshman year that I became very fond of Mozart.)

(d) 父がきらいなのはテレビだ。

Chichi ga kiraina no wa terebi da.

(It is television that my father hates.)

(e) 日本でおいしいのは果物だ。

Nihon de oishii no wa kudamono da.

(What is delicious in Japan is fruit.)

Notes

1. The particle used with the noun or noun phrase between *no wa* and *da* usually drops if the particle does not have any concrete meaning (as in the cases of *ga* and *o*), or if the meaning of the entire sentence is somehow predictable. Examples follow.

   (1) 八時にうちに来たのは森田さん (***が**) だ。

   Hachiji ni uchi ni kita no wa Morita-san (*ga) da.

   (It was Mr. Morita who came to my house at eight o'clock.)

   (2) 森田さんが持って来たのはケーキ (***を**) だ。

   Morita-san ga motte kita no wa kēki (*o) da.

   (It was cake that Mr. Morita brought here.)

   (3) 森田さんがケーキをくれたのは弟 (に) だ。

   *Morita-san ga kēki o kureta no wa otōto (**ni**) da.*

   (It was to my brother that Mr. Morita gave cake.)

   (4) 森田さんがうちに来たのは車でだ。

   *Morita-san ga uchi ni kita no wa kuruma **de** da.*

   (It was by his car that Mr. Morita came to my house.)

   (5) a. 森田さんが来たのは東京からだ。

   *Morita-san ga kita no wa Tōkyō **kara** da.*

   (It was from Tokyo that Mr. Morita came.)

   b. 森田さんが出発したのは東京 (から) だ。

   *Morita-san ga shuppatsushita no wa Tōkyō (**kara**) da.*

   (It was from Tokyo that Mr. Morita departed.)

⑹　a.　森田さんが飲んだのは田山さんとだ。

　　　　*Morita-san ga nonda no wa Tayama-san **to** da.*

　　　　(It was with Mr. Tayama that Mr. Morita drank.)

　　b.　森田さんが一緒に飲んだのは田山さん（と）だ。

　　　　*Morita-san ga isshoni nonda no wa Tayama-san (**to**) da.*

　　　　(It was with Mr. Tayama that Mr. Morita (lit. together) drank.)

In (5b) and (6b) the particles *kara* and *to* normally drop, because *shuppatsushita* ' departed ' and *isshoni* ' together ' generally co-occur with *kara* and *to*, respectively.

3. The element between *no wa* and *da* cannot be a manner adverb. The following sentences are all unacceptable.

⑺　*花子が歩いたのは**ゆっくり**だ。

　　*Hanako ga aruita no wa **yukkuri** da.*

　　(*It was slowly that Hanako walked.)

⑻　*太郎が字を書いたのは**きれいに**だ。

　　*Tarō ga ji o kaita no wa **kireini** da.*

　　(*It was beautifully that Taro wrote characters.)

4. Unlike English, the copula *da* in this construction is normally in the present tense.

⑼　きのう買ったのはステレオです / ???でした。

　　*Kinō katta no wa sutereo **desu** / ???**deshita**.*

　　(It was a stereo set that I bought yesterday.)

5. The number of *no wa ~da* sentences which can be produced from one sentence is limited only by the number of elements which can be placed between *no wa* and *da*. For example, four such sentences can be derived from (10).

⑽　ジョンがジェーンに東京で八月に会った。

　　***Jon** ga **Jēn** ni **Tōkyō** de **hachigatsu** ni atta.*

　　(John met Jane in August in Tokyo.)

⑾　a.　ジェーンに東京で八月に会ったのは**ジョン**だ。

　　　　*Jēn ni Tōkyō de hachigatsu ni atta no wa **Jon** da.*

　　　　(It was John who met Jane in August in Tokyo.)

　　b.　ジョンが東京で八月に会ったのは**ジェーン**だ。

　　　　*Jon ga Tōkyō de hachigatsu ni atta no wa **Jēn** da.*

　　　　(It was Jane whom John met in August in Tokyo.)

   c. ジョンがジェーンに八月に会ったのは**東京(で)**だ。

     Jon ga Jēn ni hachigatsu ni atta no wa Tōkyō (de) da.

     (It was in Tokyo that John met Jane in August.)

   d. ジョンがジェーンに東京で会ったのは**八月**だ。

     Jon ga Jēn ni Tōkyō de atta no wa hachigatsu da.

     (It was in August that John met Jane in Tokyo.)

6. Normally the *no* clause takes *wa*, marking the entire clause as presupposed, old, unimportant information, and the element between *no wa* and *da* represents a new, important piece of information. But sometimes the *no* clause takes *ga*, marking the clause as new, important information. In this case the element between *no ga* and *da* indicates unimportant information.

   ⑿ 私が作っている**のが**ロボットです。

     Watashi ga tsukutte iru no ga robotto desu.

     (The one I'm making is a robot.)

   Cp. ロボット**は**私が作っています。

     Robotto wa watashi ga tsukutte imasu.

     (Speaking of robots, I'm making one.)

【**Related Expression**】

No in the present construction should not be confused with the *no* used as a nominalizer. Sentence [1] is the *no wa* ~*da* construction and [2], the nominalized sentence.   (⇨ ***no***[3])

  [1] 本を読む**の**はたいてい夜だ。

     Hon o yomu no wa taitei yoru da.

     (It is usually at night that I read books.)

  [2] 本を読む**の**はいいことだ。

     Hon o yomu no wa ii koto da.

     (It is a good thing to read books.)

One way to differentiate between the two constructions is to see if the sentence can be restated by deleting *no wa* and *da* and placing the element before *no wa* in an appropriate position. For example, [1] can be restated as [3], but [2] cannot be restated, as seen in [4].

  [3] たいてい夜本を読む。

     Taitei yoru hon o yomu.

     (I read books usually at night.)

[4] a. *いいこと本を読む。
　　　　*Ii koto hon o yomu.

　　b. *本をいいこと読む。
　　　　*Hon o ii koto yomu.

　　c. *本を読むいいこと。
　　　　*Hon o yomu ii koto.

o- お *pref.*

a prefix that expresses politeness 【REL. *go-*】

♦ **Key Sentences**

(A)

	V*masu*	
石田先生　は　英語で *Ishida-sensei wa eigo de*	お話し *o-hanashi*	に　なった／なりました。 *ni natta / narimashita.*
(Prof. Ishida talked in English.)		

(B)

	V*masu*	
私　は　きのう　山崎先生　に *Watashi wa kinō Yamazaki-sensei ni*	お会い *o-ai*	した／しました。 *shita / shimashita.*
(I met Prof. Yamazaki yesterday.)		

(C)

	Adj (*i* / *na*)
今村さん　は　ゴルフ　が *Imamura-san wa gorufu ga*	お好きだ／好きです。 *o-sukida / sukidesu.*
(Mr. Imamura likes golf.)	

(D)

Noun	
お飲み物 *O-nomimono*	は　何　が　よろしいです　か。 *wa nani ga yoroshiidesu ka.*
(Lit. As for drinks, what would be good?　(＝What would you like to drink?))	

Formation

KS(A):　お V*masu* に　なる　　　　　　　(⇨ *o ~ni naru*)
　　　　o-　　　　*ni naru*

KS(B):　お V*masu* する　　　　　　　　　　　　　(⇨ **o ~suru**)
　　　　　o-　　　*suru*

KS(C):　お Adj (*i* / *na*)
　　　　　o-

　　　　　お忙しい　　(s.o. is busy)
　　　　　o-isogashii

　　　　　お上手だ　　(s.o. is good at ~)
　　　　　o-jōzuda

KS(D):　お N
　　　　　o-

　　　　　お金　　(money)
　　　　　o-kane

Examples

(a)　田村先生は今とてもお忙しい。
　　Tamura-sensei wa ima totemo o-isogashii.
　　(Prof. Tamura is very busy now.)

(b)　毎日お暑いですね。
　　Mainichi o-atsuidesu ne.
　　(It's hot day after day, isn't it?)

(c)　上田先生はテニスがお上手です。
　　Ueda-sensei wa tenisu ga o-jōzudesu.
　　(Prof. Ueda is good at tennis.)

(d)　宮本さんの奥様はとてもおきれいだ。
　　Miyamoto-san no okusama wa totemo o-kireida.
　　(Mrs. Miyamoto is very pretty.)

(e)　野村さんからお電話がありました。
　　Nomura-san kara o-denwa ga arimashita.
　　(There was a phone call from Mr. Nomura.)

(f)　お昼ご飯はもう食べましたか。
　　O-hirugohan wa mō tabemashita ka.
　　(Have you had your lunch yet?)

Notes

1. The polite prefix *o-* is used with verbs, adjectives and nouns to express the speaker's respect, modesty or politeness. *O-Vmasu ni naru*

is an honorific polite expression and *o*-V*masu suru* is a humble polite
expression. (⇨ *o ~ni naru*; *o ~suru*)

2. *O*-Adj can be either an honorific polite expression, as in Exs. (a), (c)
and (d), or a simple polite expression, as in Ex. (b).

3. *O*-N is used in various ways:

   (1) *Honorific polite expression*:
   先生がお手紙をくださいました。
   *Sensei ga **o**-tegami o kudasaimashita.*
   (My teacher wrote me a letter.)

   (2) *Humble polite expression*:
   明日お電話をさしあげます。
   *Myōnichi **o**-denwa o sashiagemasu.*
   (I'll call you tomorrow.)

   (3) *Simple polite expression*:
   お野菜が高くなりましたねえ。
   ***O**-yasai ga takaku narimashita nē.*
   (Vegetables have become expensive, haven't they?)

4. *O*- cannot be attached to the following words:

   (A) Adjectives and nouns which begin with the [o] sound:

*おもしろい (interesting)	*おおいしい (delicious)
*o-omoshiroi	*o-oishii

*お大きい (big)	*おおじさん (uncle)	*おおび (belt, sash)
*o-ōkii	*o-oji-san	*o-obi

   (B) Long words:

*おじゃがいも (potato)	(cf. おじゃが (potato))
*o-jagaimo	o-jaga

   *おほうれん草 (spinach)
   *o-hōrensō

   (C) Foreign words:

*おエレベーター (elevator)	*おクリスマス (Christmas)
*o-erebētā	*o-kurisumasu

   *おバター (butter)
   *o-batā

There are some exceptions to this rule. For example:

おたばこ (tobacco)	おズボン (trousers)	おビール (beer)
o-tabako	*o-zubon*	*o-bīru*

おソース (sauce)
o-sōsu

These exceptions are words which have been part of the Japanese vocabulary long enough to sound like Japanese-origin words to native speakers.

5. There are a few words which are always used with the polite prefix *o-* or *go-*. (For *go-*, see Related Expression.)

   (4) おなか (stomach)   ご飯 (cooked rice, meal)
        o-naka   *go-han*

[Related Expression]

There is another polite prefix, *go-*. Basically, *go-* is used for Chinese-origin words and *o-* for Japanese-origin words. Examples follow:

[1] *Na*-type adjectives (*I*-type adjectives are all Japanese-origin words; therefore, they are all preceded by *o-*.)

   a. Chinese-origin words:

ご親切 (kind)	ごていねい (polite)	ご便利 (convenient)
go-shinsetsu	*go-teinei*	*go-benri*

   b. Japanese-origin words:

お静か (quiet)	おにぎやか (lively)	お好き (fond)
o-shizuka	*o-nigiyaka*	*o-suki*

[2] Nouns

   a. Chinese-origin words:

ご研究 (research)	ご結婚 (marriage)	ご本 (book)
go-kenkyū	*go-kekkon*	*go-hon*

   b. Japanese-origin words:

お肉 (meat)	お魚 (fish)	おはし (chopsticks)
o-niku	*o-sakana*	*o-hashi*

There are, however, some Chinese-origin words which require the use of *o-*. These exceptions are words which have become assimilated to the point that native speakers no longer consider them to be "borrowed" words. The words in [3] are examples of such exceptions.

[3] a. *Na*-type adjectives:

お上手 (skillful)   お元気 (healthy)
o-jōzu   *o-genki*

b. Nouns:

お電話 (telephone)   お料理 (dishes)   お時間 (time)
o-denwa   *o-ryōri*   *o-jikan*

お勉強 (study)   お菓子 (confectionery)
o-benkyō   *o-kashi*

There are very few examples of *go-* Japanese-origin words.

[4] ごゆっくり (slowly)   ごもっとも (reasonable)
go-yukkuri   *go-mottomo*

---

o¹ を *prt.*

a particle which marks a direct object

♦ **Key Sentence**

Topic (subject)		Direct Object		Transitive Verb
私	は	日本語	を	勉強して いる / います。
Watashi	*wa*	**nihongo**	*o*	*benkyōshite iru / imasu.*
(I'm studying Japanese.)				

Examples

(a) 前田さんはきのう車を買った。
Maeda-san wa kinō kuruma o katta.
(Mr. Maeda bought a car yesterday.)

(b) 何を飲みますか。
Nani o nomimasu ka.
(What will you drink?)

Notes

1. *O* marks the direct object. It is noted, however, that the direct object in English is not always marked by *o* in Japanese. Compare Japanese and English in the following sentences, for example.

   (1) 私は英語が分かる。
   *Watashi wa eigo **ga** wakaru.*
   (I understand English.)　　　　　　　　　(⇨ **~ wa ~ ga**; **wakaru**)

   (2) ジムはベスに電話した。
   *Jimu wa Besu **ni** denwashita.*
   (Jim called Beth.)

   (3) 僕はきのう田中さんに / とあった。
   *Boku wa kinō Tanaka-san **ni** / **to** atta.*
   (I met Mr. Tanaka yesterday.)

2. In some constructions, the direct object marker *o* can be replaced by the subject marker *ga*.

   (4) ミルクを飲む　→　ミルクを / が飲みたい　　　　　(⇨ **tai**)
   *miruku **o** nomu*　　*miruku **o** / **ga** nomitai*
   (drink milk)　　　　　(want to drink milk)

   (5) 日本語を話す　→　日本語を / が話せる　　　　　(⇨ **rareru**[2])
   *nihongo **o** hanasu*　　*nihongo **o** / **ga** hanaseru*
   (speak Japanese)　　　(can speak Japanese)

   (6) まどを開ける　→　まどを / が開けてある　　　　　(⇨ **aru**[2])
   *mado **o** akeru*　　*mado **o** / **ga** akete **aru***
   (open the window)　　(The window has been opened.)

3. *O* cannot occur more than once in a clause, whether it is the direct object marker (i.e., *o*[1]) or the space marker (i.e., *o*[2]). Thus, in the causative construction, for example, the causee can be marked only by *ni* if another element in the same clause is marked by *o*.　　(⇨ **saseru**)

   (7) 父は私に / *を酒を飲ませた。
   *Chichi wa watashi **ni** / ***o** sake **o** nomaseta.*
   (My father made me drink *sake*.)

   (8) 友達は私に / *を急な坂をのぼらせた。
   *Tomodachi wa watashi **ni** / ***o** kyūna saka **o** noboraseta.*
   (My friend made me go up a steep slope.)

4. If the direct object is presented as a topic or a contrastive element, *o* is replaced by *wa*.

(9) 日本語は知りません。

Nihongo **wa** *shirimasen.*

(I don't know Japanese.)

(10) その本はもう読みました。

Sono hon **wa** *mō yomimashita.*

(I already read that book.)

*o*² を *prt.*

a particle which indicates a space in /
on / across / through / along   which
s.o. or s.t. moves

in; on; across; through; along;
over
【REL. *de*¹】

◆Key Sentence

	Noun (space)		
私　は *Watashi wa*	**五番街** **goban-gai**	を *o*	歩いた / 歩きました。 *aruita / arukimashita.*
(I walked along Fifth Avenue.)

Examples

(a) 公園を通って帰りましょう。

Kōen o tōtte kaerimashō.

(Let's go home through the park (lit. passing through the park).)

(b) 鶴が湖の上を飛んでいます。

Tsuru ga mizuumi no ue o tonde imasu.

(Cranes are flying over the lake.)

(c) 日本では車は道の左側を走ります。

Nihon de wa kuruma wa michi no hidarigawa o hashirimasu.

(In Japan they drive (lit. cars run) on the left side of the street.)

(d) そこの交差点を右に曲がってください。

Soko no kōsaten o migi ni magatte kudasai.

(Please turn to the right at the intersection there.)

When a sentence involves the verb *noboru* 'climb', there is an important difference between the use of the particle *o* and that of *ni*, as seen in (1).

(1) a. ドンは東京タワーをのぼった。
      *Don wa Tōkyō Tawā **o** nobotta.*
      (Don scaled Tokyo Tower.)

    b. ドンは東京タワーにのぼった。
      *Don wa Tōkyō Tawā **ni** nobotta.*
      (Don went up Tokyo Tower.)

[Related Expression]

The particle *de*¹ also marks the space in which an action takes place. The difference between *de*¹ and *o* is that *de*¹ can be used with any action verb, while *o* can be used only with motion verbs such as *aruku* 'walk', *hashiru* 'run', *tobu* 'fly' and *oyogu* 'swim'. Thus, *o* is ungrammatical in [1].

[1] 私は図書館で / *を勉強した。
    *Watashi wa toshokan **de** / ***o** benkyōshita.*
    (I studied at the library.)

When either *de*¹ or *o* is possible, as in [2], there is usually a subtle difference between them.

[2] ジョンは川で / を泳いだ。
    *Jon wa kawa **de** / **o** oyoida.*
    (John swam in the river.)

First, when *de*¹ is used, other locations for an action are also implied, but when *o* is used, there are no such implications. For example, in [3] John has a choice between a pool and the river. Here, *de*¹ is acceptable, but *o* is not.

[3] ジョンはプールがきらいだからたいてい川で / *を泳ぐ。
    *Jon wa pūru ga kiraida kara taitei kawa **de** / ***o** oyogu.*
    (John usually swims in the river because he doesn't like pools.)

Second, when *de*¹ is used, the sentence often indicates that the purpose of the action is the action itself, whereas when *o* is used it seems that there is another purpose behind the action. For example, in [4] John swam in order to escape, and swimming was not the purpose of his action. Therefore, *o* is acceptable but *de*¹ is not.

[4] ジョンは川を / *で泳いで逃げた。
  *Jon wa kawa **o** / ***de** oyoide nigeta.*
  (John escaped by swimming in the river.)

o³ を *prt.*

a particle that marks the location from which some movement begins

[REL. *kara¹*]

◆ **Key Sentence**

Topic (subject)			Noun (space)		
私 *Watashi*	は *wa*	朝 七時半 に *asa shichijihan ni*	家 ***uchi***	を *o*	出る / 出ます。 *deru / demasu.*
(I leave home at 7:30 in the morning.)					

Examples

(a) 汽車がトンネルを出た。
  Kisha ga tonneru o deta.
  (A train came out of the tunnel.)

(b) バスを降りた時友達に会った。
  Basu o orita toki tomodachi ni atta.
  (I met a friend when I got off the bus.)

(c) 日本を離れて外国で暮らしている。
  Nihon o hanarete gaikoku de kurashite iru.
  (He left Japan and is living abroad.)

[Related Expression]

The particle *o³* in Exs. (a), (b), (c) can be replaced by *kara¹* 'from'. The basic difference between *o³* and *kara¹* is that *o³* marks the location from which some movement begins and *kara¹* marks the initial location in movement from one location to another. Thus, when focusing on both the new and old location of something or someone, *kara* should be used instead of *o*. Consider the following examples.   (⇒ ***kara¹***)

[1]   a.   私は今朝八時頃家を / *から出た。
        *Watashi wa kesa hachiji goro ie **o** / *__kara__ deta.*
        (This morning I left my house at about eight.)

      b.   きのうはうちから / *を外に出なかった。
        *Kinō wa uchi **kara** /*__o__ soto ni denakatta.*
        (Yesterday I didn't go outside.)

[1a] focuses on a point of detachment, so *o* is acceptable but *kara* isn't. [1b], however, focuses on a starting point, so *kara* is acceptable but *o* isn't.

o⁴ を   *prt.*

a particle that marks the cause of some human emotion

♦ **Key Sentences**

(A)

Topic (subject)		Noun		Verb (emotive)
次郎 *Jirō*	は *wa*	父　の　死 **chichi no shi**	を *o*	悲しんだ / 悲しみました。 *kanashinda / kanashimimashita.*
(Jiro was saddened at his father's death.)				

(B)

Topic (subject)			Nominalizer		Verb (emotive)
次郎 *Jirō*	は *wa*	父　が　死んだ **chichi ga shinda**	こと / の *koto / no*	を *o*	悲しんだ / *kanashinda /* 悲しみました。 *kanashimimashita.*
(Jiro was sad that his father died.)					

Examples

(a) 私は浩の大学入学を喜んだ。
Watashi wa Hiroshi no daigakunyūgaku o yorokonda.
(I was happy about Hiroshi's entering college.)

(b) ヨーロッパ人はまた戦争が起きることを恐れている。
Yōroppajin wa mata sensō ga okiru koto o osorete iru.
(Europeans are afraid that war will break out again.)

(c) 信子は京都での一年をなつかしんだ。
Nobuko wa Kyōto de no ichinen o natsukashinda.
(Nobuko nostalgically recollected her year in Kyoto.)

(d) 林は英語が出来ないことを悩んでいる。
Hayashi wa eigo ga dekinai koto o nayande iru.
(Hayashi is worried that he cannot speak English.)

Notes

1. Because the main verbs used in the KSs and the Exs., such as *kanashimu* 'sadden', *yorokobu* 'rejoice', *osoreru* 'fear', *natsukashimu* 'nostalgically recollect' and *nayamu* 'worry' are all inwardly-oriented psychological verbs they cannot be considered transitive verbs in Japanese. Therefore, the particle o^4 preceding these verbs cannot be the ordinary direct object marker *o* which normally marks an outwardly-oriented event. Rather it indicates the cause for human emotion expressed by the main verb. Thus, it is sometimes possible to rewrite the sentence in question using *node* 'because'. (⇨ ***node***) For example, KS(A) and Ex. (a) can be paraphrased as (1a) and (1b), respectively.

(1) a. 次郎は父が死んだので悲しんだ。
*Jirō wa chichi ga shinda **node** kanashinda.*
(Jiro was sad because his father died.)

b. 私は浩が大学に入学したので喜んだ。
*Watashi wa Hiroshi ga daigaku ni nyūgakushita **node** yorokonda.*
(I was glad because Hiroshi entered college.)

The original versions are examples of written style and are seldom used in conversational Japanese, but the rewritten versions can be used in both spoken and written Japanese.

2. No matter what person (first, second, third) the subject of this con-

struction is, the main emotive verb is normally in the stative *te iru /
inai* form and / or in the past tense. In a generic statement, however,
the verb can be in the non-stative, nonpast form as in (2):

(2) だれでも親の死を悲しむ。
     *Dare demo oya no shi o **kanashimu**.*
     (Everybody is saddened by their parents' death.)

3. If the emotive verb consists of adj(*i*)stem+suffix *mu* as in *kanashi-mu*
  'sadden', *natsukashi-mu* 'nostalgically recollect', *oshi-mu* 'regret', *ta-
  noshi-mu* 'enjoy', it can take the suffix *-garu* 'show signs of ~' as
  in *kanashi-garu*, *natsukashi-garu*, *oshi-garu* and *tanoshi-garu*. Thus,
  along with KS(A) we have a sentence type (3).   (⇨ **garu**)

(3) 次郎は父の死を悲しがった。
     *Jirō wa chichi no shi o **kanashigatta**.*
     (Jiro showed signs of being sad about his father's death.)

(3) is a more objective expression than KS(A), because the verb *-garu*
'show signs of ~' has an outwardly-oriented meaning.

0

ōi 多い   *adj. (i)*

> (of quantity or number) a lot

many; a lot of; much
【REL. *ōzei*; *takusan*】
(ANT. *sukunai*)

◆**Key Sentence**

Topic (location)		Subject		
日本 (に)	は	大学	が	多い / 多いです。
Nihon (ni)	*wa*	*daigaku*	*ga*	*ōi / ōidesu.*
(Lit. In Japan universities are many. (=There are a lot of universities in Japan.))				

Examples

(a) 京都(に)はお寺が多いです。

    Kyōto (ni) wa o-tera ga ōidesu.

    (There are many temples in Kyoto.)

(b) ロスさんの作文(に)は間違いが多いです。

    Rosu-san no sakubun (ni) wa machigai ga ōidesu.

    (There are many mistakes in Mr. Ross's compositions.)

(c) 一月(に)は雪が多い。

    Ichigatsu (ni) wa yuki ga ōi.

    (There is a lot of snow in January.)

Notes

1. Unlike the English 'many', the Japanese *ōi* cannot be used before a noun, except in a relative clause where *ōi* is the predicate of the clause, not the modifier of the head noun.

   (1) *京都には**多い**お寺があります。

      Kyōto ni wa **ōi o-tera ga arimasu.*

      (There are many temples in Kyoto.)

   (2) お寺が**多い**町は京都です。

      *O-tera ga **ōi** machi wa Kyōto desu.*

      (The town in which there are many temples is Kyoto.)

2. *Ōi* cannot be used in front of a noun, but *ōku no* can be used that way in written Japanese. Thus,

   (3) 多くの学生が毎年アジアから日本の大学に来る。

      Ōku no gakusei ga maitoshi Ajia kara Nihon no daigaku ni kuru.*

      (Every year many students come to Japanese universities from Asia.)

3. *Sukunai*, an antonym of *ōi*, is very similar to *ōi* in its use. Neither *sukunai* nor *ōi* can be used before nouns, except in relative clauses. *Sukunai* differs from *ōi* in that there is no counterpart of *ōku* 'the majority' and of *ōku no* 'many'.   (⇨ **sukunai**)

   (4) a. この町は車が**少ない**です。

        *Kono machi wa kuruma ga **sukunai**desu.*

        (There aren't many cars in this town.)

    b. 日本語の新聞が読める学生は少ない。

        *Nihongo no shinbun ga yomeru gakusei wa **sukunai**.*

        (Few students can read Japanese newspapers.)

[Related Expressions]

I. *Ōi* and *ōku no* can be replaced by *ōzei iru* and *ōzei no*, respectively, if *ōi* and *ōku no* refer to human beings. *Ōzei* is used only for people.

[1] この部屋(に)は学生が多い / 大勢いる。
*Kono heya (ni) wa gakusei ga **ōi** / **ōzei iru**.*
(There are a lot of students in this room.)

[2] この部屋(に)は多くの / 大勢の学生がいる。
*Kono heya (ni) wa **ōku no** / **ōzei no** gakusei ga iru.*
(There are a lot of students in this room.)

Ōzei can be used by itself as an adverb, but the adverbial form of *ōi* cannot be used as an adverb in colloquial speech.

[3] 学生が大勢 / *多く来た。
*Gakusei ga **ōzei** / ***ōku** kita.*
(Many students came.)

II. *Ōi* and *ōku no* can be replaced by *takusan aru / iru* and *takusan no*, respectively. *Takusan* can also be used by itself as an adverb.

[4] この部屋(に)は机が多い / たくさんある。
*Kono heya (ni) wa tsukue ga **ōi** / **takusan aru**.*
(There are a lot of tables in this room.)

[5] この部屋(に)は学生が多い / たくさんいる。
*Kono heya (ni) wa gakusei ga **ōi** / **takusan iru**.*
(There are a lot of students in this room.)

[6] 今年はたくさん / *多く / *大勢雪が降った。
*Kotoshi wa **takusan** / ***ōku** / ***ōzei** yuki ga futta.*
(It snowed a lot this year.)

III. *Ōku* can be used as a noun but *ōzei* and *takusan* cannot.

[7] 学生の多く / *大勢 / *たくさんは男だ。
*Gakusei no **ōku** / ***ōzei** / ***takusan** wa otoko da.*
(The majority of the students are male.)

oku おく   *aux. v. (Gr. 1)*

~~~
do s.t. in advance for future convenience
~~~

do s.t. in advance; go ahead
and do s.t.; let s.o./s.t. remain
as he/it is

[REL. *aru*[2]]

♦ **Key Sentence**

		V*te*	
あした　パーティー　を　する　ので　ビール　を		買って	おいた / おきました。
Ashita pāti o suru node biru o		***katte***	*oita / okimashita.*

(Since we are having a party tomorrow, I bought some beer for it.)

Formation

V*te* おく
　　oku

話して　おく　　(talk in advance)
hanashite oku

食べて　おく　　(eat s.t. in advance)
tabete oku

Examples

(a) 今日は昼に客が来るので昼ご飯を早目に食べておいた。
　　Kyō wa hiru ni kyaku ga kuru node hirugohan o hayame ni tabete oita.
　　(Since I'm having a guest at noon today, I had my lunch earlier.)

(b) 来年日本へ行くから少し日本語を勉強しておきます。
　　Rainen Nihon e iku kara sukoshi nihongo o benkyōshite okimasu.
　　(Since I'm going to Japan next year, I will study a little Japanese ahead
　　of time.)

Notes

1. *Oku* as a main verb means 'put' or 'place'. However, when it is
   used with V*te*, it is an auxiliary verb meaning 'do something in advance
   and leave the resultant state as it is for future convenience'.

2. With a causative verb, V*te oku* can express the idea that someone *lets*
   someone or something remain in his / its present state. Examples:

(1) a. 信子は疲れているからしばらく寝させておこう。

Nobuko wa tsukarete iru kara shibaraku nesasete okō.

(Since Nobuko is tired, let's let her sleep for a while.)

b. 飲みたいと言うのなら好きなだけ飲ませておきなさい。

Nomitai to iu no nara sukina dake nomasete okinasai.

(If he says he wants to drink, let him drink as much as he likes.)

However, if the context is not clear, causative V*te oku* can be ambiguous. For example, the following sentence can be interpreted two ways.

(2) 私はボブにビールを飲ませておいた。

*Watashi wa Bobu ni biru o **nomasete oita**.*

((A) I let (or make) Bob drink beer (for future convenience). (B) I let Bob drink beer.)

3. V*te oku* may be contracted into *toku* or *doku* in informal conversation.

(3) a. 見て おく → 見 とく (see ~ in advance)

    mite oku   *mi **toku***

b. 読んで おく → 読ん どく (read ~ in advance)

    yonde oku   *yon **doku***

---

o ~ni naru お ~ になる   *phr.*

> a phrase which expresses the speaker's respect for someone when describing that person's action or state

【REL. *o ~suru*; *rareru*[1]】

♦**Key Sentence**

Topic (subject)			V*masu*	
田中先生 *Tanaka-sensei*	は *wa*	もう *mō*	お帰り *o-**kaeri***	に なった / なりました。 *ni natta / narimashita.*
(Prof. Tanaka already went home.)				

Formation

お V*masu* に なる
o-   ni naru

お話し   に なる   (s.o. (will) talk)
o-hanashi ni naru

お教え   に なる   (s.o. (will) teach)
o-oshie ni naru

Examples

(a) この本をもうお読みになりましたか。
Kono hon o mō o-yomi ni narimashita ka.
(Have you read this book yet?)

(b) グッドマン先生は私の名前をお忘れになった。
Guddoman-sensei wa watashi no namae o o-wasure ni natta.
(Prof. Goodman has forgotten my name.)

Notes

1. In ordinary circumstances, *o-V masu ni naru* is used when the speaker describes someone's action or state with respect. However, if a social norm requires the speaker to talk in honorific speech, the honorific form is used, even if the speaker does not respect the person he talks about. (For more detail, see Characteristics of Japanese Grammar, 6. Politeness and Formality.) Politeness is expressed in this form by two elements: first by the polite prefix *o-*, and second by the verb *naru*, which describes someone's action or state indirectly. This indirectness is a common strategy in polite expressions.   (⇨ **naru**)

2. There are some verbs whose honorific forms are expressed by special honorific verbs.
(See Characteristics of Japanese Grammar, 6. Politeness and Formality.)

3. When a verb has the form "N *suru*" like *kekkonsuru* 'marry' and *denwasuru* 'call' its honorific form is "*go-* / *o*-N *nasaru*". *Nasaru* is the honorific form of *suru* 'do' and a Gr. 1 verb. (Note that V*masu* is *nasai* (*masu*), not *nasari* (*masu*).) Except for a handful of exceptions which require *o-* (i.e., *denwasuru* 'call', *benkyōsuru* 'study', *ryōrisuru* 'cook', *sentakusuru* 'wash', *sōjisuru* 'clean', *sanposuru* 'take a walk'), *go-* precedes N. (⇨ *o-*, REL.) Examples:

(1) 小山先生は四月にご結婚なさいます。

*Koyama-sensei wa shigatsu ni **go**-kekkon **nasaimasu**.*

(Prof. Koyama will get married in April.)

(2) 森本さんにお電話なさいましたか。

*Morimoto-san ni **o**-denwa **nasaimashita** ka.*

(Did you call Mr. Morimoto?)

[Related Expression]

Rareru[1] can also be used to describe respectfully someone's action or state, as seen in [1], although the degree of politeness is not as high.

(⇒ ***rareru***[1], Note 9)

[1] a. 田中先生はもう帰られましたか。

Tanaka-sensei wa mō kaeraremashita ka.

(Did Prof. Tanaka go home already?)

b. この本をもう読まれましたか。

Kono hon o mō yomaremashita ka.

(Have you read this book yet?)

o ~suru お ~ する　　*phr.*

a phrase which humbly expresses the speaker's politeness to someone when describing the speaker's action or state that involves or affects that person

【REL. *o ~ni naru*】

♦Key Sentence

Topic (subject)					V*masu*	
私	は	先生 の スーツケース を			お持ち	した / しました。
Watashi	*wa*	*sensei no sūtsukēsu o*			*o-**mochi***	*shita / shimashita.*
(I carried my teacher's suitcase.)						

お V*masu* する
o   *suru*

お話し   する   (s.o. (will) talk)
o-hanashi suru

お教え   する   (s.o. (will) teach)
o-oshie suru

(a) そのことは私がお話ししましょう。
    Sono koto wa watashi ga o-hanashi shimashō.
    (I will tell you about that matter.)

(b) 山村君は先生に本をお借りした。
    Yamamura-kun wa sensei ni hon o o-kari shita.
    (Mr. Yamamura borrowed a book from his teacher.)

1. *O-*V*masu suru* is used when the speaker wants to be polite when talking about something he or his in-group member did or will do. (For more detail, see Characteristics of Japanese Grammar, 6. Politeness and Formality.) For example, when a sales manager is talking to a customer, the manager uses this pattern to describe what his salesmen will do for the customer, as in (1).

    (1) サンプルは明日うちのセールスマンがお届けします。
       Sanpuru wa myōnichi uchi no sērusuman ga o-todoke shimasu.
       ((One of) Our salesmen will bring the sample to you tomorrow.)

2. *O-*V*masu suru* is used only when the speaker's (or his in-group member's) action involves or affects the person the speaker wants to be polite to. Thus, (2) is unacceptable under ordinary circumstances.

    (2) *私がお歩きします。
       *Watashi ga o-aruki shimasu.
       (I will walk.)

3. There are some verbs whose humble forms are expressed by special verbs. (See Characteristics of Japanese Grammar, 6. Politeness and formality.) The rule in Note 2 does not apply to these verbs. That is, these special verbs are also used as simple polite expressions and can be used even if the speaker's (or his in-group member's) action does not involve or affect the person the speaker wants to be polite to.

4. When a verb has the form "N *suru*", like *shōkaisuru* 'introduce' and *denwasuru* 'call', its humble form is "*go-* / *o*-N *suru*" or, more politely, "*go-* / *o*-N *itasu*". (*Itasu* is the humble form of the verb *suru*, do'.) Except for a handful of exceptions which require *ō*- (i.e., *denwasuru* 'call', *benkyōsuru* 'study', *ryōrisuru* 'cook', *sentakusuru* 'wash', *sōjisuru* 'clean', *sanposuru* 'take a walk'), *go-* precedes N. (⇨ *o-*, REL.) Examples:

(3) 上村さんをご紹介します / いたします。
Uemura-san o **go**-*shōkai* **shimasu** / **itashimasu**.
(Let me (lit. I will) introduce Mr. Uemura.)

(4) あしたお電話します / いたします。
Ashita **o**-*denwa* **shimasu** / **itashimasu**.
(I will call you tomorrow).

[Related Expression]

O-Vmasu ni naru is also used to express politeness. However, *o-Vmasu ni naru* and *o-Vmasu suru* are different in that the former is used when the speaker talks about someone's action or state with respect, while the latter is used when the speaker talks about his own action or state.

(⇨ Characteristics of Japanese Grammar, 6. Politeness and Formality)

0

~owaru ～終わる   *aux. v. (Gr. 1)*

~~~~~~~~~~~~~~~~~~~~~~~~~~
finish doing ~
~~~~~~~~~~~~~~~~~~~~~~~~~~

finish; end
[REL. *shimau*]
(ANT. *~hajimeru*)

♦**Key Sentence**

	V*masu*	
源氏物語　を　やっと *Genjimonogatari o yatto*	読み *yomi*	終わった / 終わりました。 *owatta* / *owarimashita*.
(I finally finished reading *The Tale of Genji*.)		

Formation

V*masu* 終わる
    owaru

話し終わる　　(finish talking)
hanashiowaru

食べ終わる　　(finish eating)
tabeowaru

Examples

(a) やっと論文を書き終わった。
    Yatto ronbun o kakiowatta.
    (I finally finished writing a paper.)

(b) ちょうどご飯を食べ終わったところです。
    Chōdo gohan o tabeowatta tokoro desu.
    (I've just finished eating my meal.)

Notes

1. ~*owaru* is an auxiliary verb derived from the intransitive verb *owaru* meaning 'end; comes to a close'.

2. ~*owaru* can be replaced by ~*oeru* in written Japanese. ~*oeru*, however, conjugates as a Gr. 2 verb.

O

rareru¹ られる　　*aux. v. (Gr. 2)*

> A state or an action cannot be con-
> trolled by s.o. or s.t.

be -ed; get -ed

【REL. *o ~ni naru*; *rareru²*】

◆ **Key Sentences**

(A)

Topic (subject)		Agent		Transitive Verb (passive)
一郎	は	花子	に	だまされた / だまされました。
Ichirō	*wa*	*Hanako*	*ni*	***damasa*reta / *damasa*remashita.**

(Ichiro was deceived by Hanako.)

(B)

Topic (subject)		Agent						Intransitive Verb (passive)
ジェーン	は	フレッド	に	夜	おそく	アパート	に	来られた /
Jēn	*wa*	*Fureddo*	*ni*	*yoru*	*osoku*	*apāto*	*ni*	***ko*rareta /**
								来られました。
								***ko*raremashita.**

(Fred came to Jane's apartment late at night (and Jane was unhappy).)

(C)

Topic (subject)		Agent		Direct Object		Transitive Verb (passive)
私	は	弟	に	ケーキ	を	食べられた / 食べられました。
Watashi	*wa*	*otōto*	*ni*	*kēki*	*o*	***tabe*rareta / *tabe*raremashita.**

(Lit. I got my cake eaten by my younger brother. (=My younger brother ate my cake (and I was unhappy).))

(D)

Topic (subject)				Verb (passive)
田中先生	は	日本 へ		帰られた / 帰られました。
Tanaka-sensei	*wa*	*Nihon e*		***kaera*reta / *kaera*remashita.**

(Prof. Tanaka went back to Japan. (Honorific))

Formation

(i) Gr. 1 Verbs:　Vneg　れる
　　　　　　　　　　　　　　reru

　　　　　　　話される　　(be told)
　　　　　　　hanasareru

(ii) Gr. 2 Verbs:　Vstem　られる
　　　　　　　　　　　　　　rareru

　　　　　　　食べられる　　(be eaten)
　　　　　　　taberareru

(iii) Irr. Verbs:　来る → 来られる　　(s.o. (X) comes to s.o. (Y) and Y is
　　　　　　　　kuru　*korareru*　　unhappy)

　　　　　　　　する → される　　(be done)
　　　　　　　　suru　*sareru*

Examples

(a)　このビルは二年前に建てられた。
　　　Kono biru wa ninen mae ni taterareta.
　　　(This building was built two years ago.)

(b)　この本は1965年にアメリカで出版された。
　　　Kono hon wa 1965 nen ni Amerika de shuppansareta.
　　　(This book was published in America in 1965.)

(c)　私は二年前妻に死なれた。
　　　Watashi wa ninen mae tsuma ni shinareta.
　　　(My wife died two years ago (and gave me sorrow).)

(d)　原田さんは奥さんに高いコートを買われた。
　　　Harada-san wa okusan ni takai kōto o kawareta.
　　　(Mr. Harada's wife bought an expensive coat (and he is unhappy).)

(e)　林先生は日本の大学のことを話された。
　　　Hayashi-sensei wa Nihon no daigaku no koto o hanasareta.
　　　(Prof. Hayashi talked about Japanese universities.　(Honorific))

Notes

1. There are two types of passive sentences in Japanese. One can be
   called " direct passive " and the other, " indirect passive ". The direct
   passive is similar to the English passive.　(KS(A), Exs. (a) and (b))
   That is, for every passive sentence, there is a corresponding active sentence. For example, the active version of KS(A) is (1).

(1) 花子は一郎をだました。
Hanako wa Ichirō o damashita.
(Hanako deceived Ichiro.)

As seen in KS(A), in direct passive sentences, the direct object in active sentences is presented as the subject; the subject in active sentences is presented as the agent and marked by *ni*. (⇨ ***ni***[3]) Note that verbs in direct passive sentences are always transitive.

2. When the speaker uses a direct passive sentence, he is making a statement from the viewpoint of the receiver of the action. The agent is frequently omitted when he / it is not important and / or unknown, as in Exs. (a) and (b).

3. The indirect object in active sentences can also be the subject in direct passive sentences. Examples:

(2) a. *Active sentence*
   ジョンは先生に質問をした。
   Jon wa sensei ni shitsumon o shita.
   (John asked his teacher a question.)

   b. *Direct passive sentence*
   先生はジョンに質問をされた。
   Sensei wa Jon ni shitsumon o sareta.
   (The teacher was asked a question by John.)

4. The agent in direct passive sentences can also be marked by other particles, such as *ni yotte* and *kara*.

(3) *Ni yotte*

   a. この絵はピカソによってかかれた。
   *Kono e wa Pikaso **ni yotte** kakareta.*
   (This picture was painted by Picasso.)

   b. 電話はベルによって発明された。
   *Denwa wa Beru **ni yotte** hatsumeisareta.*
   (The telephone was invented by Bell.)

Ni yotte, meaning 'depending on; owing to; by means of', is usually used in written form or formal speech when X in X *ni yotte* is a sort of medium through which or whom something is done. When *ni yotte* is used, X *ni yotte* is usually under strong focus. Therefore, the following sentences are unacceptable under normal circumstances.

(4) a. *私は花子によってぶたれた。

Watashi wa Hanako **ni yotte butareta.*

(I was hit by Hanako.)

b. *川本さんはいつも仕事によって追われている。

Kawamoto-san wa itsumo shigoto **ni yotte owarete iru.*

(Mr. Kawamoto's work always keeps him busy.)

Kara 'from' can be used in place of *ni* when the agent is a sort of source, that is, when there is something coming from the agent.

(5) *Kara*

a. 私は学生から日本の大学のことを聞かれた。

*Watashi wa gakusei **kara** Nihon no daigaku no koto o kikareta.*

(I was asked by the students about Japanese universities.)

b. 木田さんはみんなから尊敬されている。

*Kida-san wa minna **kara** sonkeisarete iru.*

(Mr. Kida is respected by everybody.)

The following sentences are unacceptable because the agents cannot be considered sources.

(6) a. *その時計はどろぼうから盗まれました。

Sono tokei wa dorobō **kara nusumaremashita.*

(That watch was stolen by a thief.)

b. *この写真は私の父からとられたものです。

Kono shashin wa watashi no chichi **kara torareta mono desu.*

(This picture is the one taken by my father.)

5. The other type of passive, the indirect passive, does not exist in English. The indirect passive is different from the direct passive and the English passive in the following ways:

(A) The verb can be intransitive. (KS(B), Ex. (c))

(B) The direct object can remain as the direct object. (KS(C), Ex. (d))

The indirect passive describes an event (X) involving an action by someone or something (Y) which affects another person (Z). As in direct passive sentences, the subject (Z) has no control over the event. (⇒ Characteristics of Japanese Grammar, 5. Passive) Consider the following pair of sentences. (7a), a non-passive sentence, states simply that Taro drank Jiro's beer. (7b), an indirect passive sentence, however, expresses the idea that Jiro was affected by Taro's drinking beer.

It implies that Jiro was annoyed in some way by Taro's action, perhaps because the beer Taro drank belonged to Jiro.

(7) a. 太郎は次郎のビールを飲んだ。

Tarō wa Jirō no biru o nonda.

(Taro drank Jiro's beer.)

b. 次郎は太郎にビールを飲まれた。

Jirō wa Tarō ni biru o nomareta.

(Jiro was annoyed by Taro's drinking beer.)

6. In the indirect passive construction, Z is usually presented as the topic, marked by *wa*, and Y as the agent, marked by *ni*, as seen in KS(B) and KS(C).

7. Since in many situations X negatively affects Z, this construction is also referred to as "adversity passive" or "suffering passive". (KS(B), KS(C), Exs. (c) and (d)) However, whether X affects Z negatively or positively depends on the situation. Z is not always a "victim", as seen in (8) where Z is affected positively.

(8) 高山さんは美人に横に座られてニコニコしている。

Takayama-san wa bijin ni yoko ni suwararete nikoniko shite iru.

(Lit. Mr. Takayama, having a pretty woman sit beside him, is smiling happily. (=A pretty woman sat beside Mr. Takayama and he is happy.))

8. In indirect passive sentences, the agent must be marked by *ni*. If a passive sentence contains an NP *ni*, as well as an agent marked by *ni*, the agent must precede the NP *ni*. Example:

(9) a. 私はトムにメアリーに電話された。

*Watashi wa Tomu **ni** Meari **ni** denwasareta.*

(Tom called Mary (and I was unhappy).)

b. *私はメアリーにトムに電話された。

Watashi wa Meari **ni Tomu **ni** denwasareta.*

(Tom called Mary (and I was unhappy).)

9. Passive verbs are also used as honorific expressions, as in KS(D) and Ex. (e), though the degree of politeness is lower than that of the "*o-Vmasu ni naru*" form and special honorific verbs. (⇨ *o ~ ni naru*; Characteristics of Japanese Grammar, 6. Politeness and Formality) Politeness, in this case, is conveyed through the indirectness of the passive construction.

10. Passive verbs are all Gr. 2 verbs. The basic conjugations are as follows:

   (10) 話される   (nonpast·inf·affirmative)
       *hanasare**ru***

       話されない   (nonpast·inf·negative)
       *hanasare**nai***

       話されて   (*te*-form)
       *hanasare**te***

       話された   (past·inf·affirmative)
       *hanasare**ta***

〔Related Expression〕

The potential form of Gr. 2 verbs is the same form as the passive form. (⇨ ***rareru***²) Potential, passive or honorific structures are identified through syntax and context. Examples:

   [1] 先生は刺身が食べられる。(Potential)
      *Sensei wa sashimi **ga** taberareru.*
      (My teacher can eat *sashimi*.)

   [2] 先生は刺身を食べられた。((A) Honorific, (B) Potential or (C) Indirect passive)
      *Sensei wa sashimi **o** taberareta.*
      ((A) My teacher ate *sashimi*. (B) My teacher could eat *sashimi*. (C) Someone ate *sashimi* and my teacher was unhappy.)

   [3] 先生は学生に刺身を食べられた。(Indirect passive)
      *Sensei wa **gakusei ni** sashimi o taberareta.*
      (The teacher had (his) *sashimi* eaten by his students.)

As seen in [1], if the direct object is marked by *ga*, *taberareru* can only be interpreted as potential; if there is an agent marked by *ni*, however, *taberareru* expresses indirect passive, as seen in [3]. If there is no agent marked by *ni* and the direct object is marked by *o*, *taberareru* is ambiguous; it can be either honorific, potential or indirect passive, as seen in [2].

R

rareru[2] られる   *aux. v. (Gr. 2)*

| an auxiliary verb which indicates potential | be able to do s.t.; can do s.t.; be -able; ~ can be done 【REL. *kikoeru*; *koto ga dekiru*; *mieru*】 |

♦ Key Sentences

(A)

Topic (experiencer)		Object of Action		Verb (potential)
私 *Watashi*	は *wa*	日本語 *nihongo*	が *ga*	読める / 読めます。 *yomeru* / *yomemasu*.
(I can read Japanese.)				

(B)

Topic (subject)		Verb (potential)
この 水 *Kono mizu*	は *wa*	飲めない / 飲めません。 *nomenai* / *nomemasen*.
(This water is not drinkable.)		

Formation

(i) Gr. 1 Verbs: Vcond る
                   ru

        話せる   (can talk)
        hanaseru

(ii) Gr. 2 Verbs: Vstem られる
                    rareru

        食べられる   (can eat)
        taberareru

(iii) Irr. Verbs: 来る → 来られる   (can come)
              kuru   *korareru*

              する → 出来る   (can do)
              suru   *dekiru*

Ikareru is often used as the potential form of *iku* 'go' (Gr. 1).

Examples

(a) ブラウンさんは刺身が食べられる。

    Buraun-san wa sashimi ga taberareru.

    (Mr. Brown can eat *sashimi* (=sliced raw fish)).)

(b) 寺田さんはテニスが出来る。

    Terada-san wa tenisu ga dekiru.

    (Mr. Terada can play tennis.)

(c) この字は読めない。

    Kono ji wa yomenai.

    (This letter is not readable.)

Notes

1. In potential expressions, if there is an experiencer, that noun phrase is usually marked by *wa* and the object of the action by either *ga* or *o*. (⇨ **~ wa ~ ga**) Compare (1a) and (1b).

    (1) a. *Non-potential*

          私は英語を話します。

          *Watashi wa eigo **o** hanashimasu.*

          (I speak English.)

      b. *Potential*

          私は英語が / を話せます。

          *Watashi wa eigo **ga** / **o** hanasemasu.*

          (I can speak English.)

2. In general, the choice between *ga* and *o* seems to depend on the degree of volition expressed in the action the experiencer takes. That is, if his volition is high, *o* is preferable. Thus, in the following sentences, *ga* is unnatural.

    (2) a. 私はやめようと思えばいつでも今の仕事を / *がやめられる。

          Watashi wa yameyō to omoeba itsu demo ima no shigoto **o** / ***ga** *yamerareru.*

          (I can quit my current job whenever I want to quit (lit. whenever I think I will quit it).)

      b. 僕はやっとの思いで自分を / *がおさえられた。

          Boku wa yatto no omoi de jibun **o** / ***ga** *osaerareta.*

          (I could barely control my emotions (lit. hold myself).)

3. *Dekiru* 'can do', however, always requires the object of an action to be marked by *ga*, as in Ex. (b). Another example follows:

(3) 私はチェスが / *を出来る。

*Watashi wa chesu **ga** / ***o** dekiru.*

(I can play chess.)

4. The spatial *o* (i.e., *o*²) and the detachment *o* (i.e., *o*³) do not change into *ga* in potential expressions.

(4) *Space*

a. 私はあの公園を / *が夜一人で歩けない。

*Watashi wa ano kōen **o** / *ga yoru hitori de arukenai.*

(I can't walk through that park by myself at night.)

b. この道を / *がくつをはかずに歩けますか。

*Kono michi **o** / *ga kutsu o hakazu ni arukemasu ka.*

(Can you walk along this road without shoes on?)

(5) *Detachment*

今日はうちを / *が出られません。

*Kyō wa uchi **o** / *ga deraremasen.*

(I can't leave home today.)

5. If the experiencer is clear from the context and / or the situation, or if the experiencer is a person in general, he is usually omitted and the object of the action is presented as a topic marked by *wa*, as in KS(B) and Ex. (c).

6. Non-volitional verbs like *wakaru* 'understand, be understandable'; *iru* 'need, be necessary'; *aru* 'exist'; *aku* 'open (v.i.)' and *kusaru* 'rot (v.i.)' do not have potential forms.

7. The potential forms of *miru* 'see' (*mirareru*) and *kiku* 'hear' (*kikeru*) are similar to the verbs *mieru* 'be visible' and *kikoeru* 'be audible', respectively, but their uses are different. (⇨ ***kikoeru*; *mieru***)

8. The idea of potentiality can also be expressed by Vinf·nonpast *koto ga dekiru*. (⇨ ***koto ga dekiru***)

9. Potential verbs are all Gr. 2 verbs. The basic conjugations are as follows:

(6) 話せる (can talk)

*hanase**ru***

話せない (cannot talk)

*hanase**nai***

話せて (can talk and, (*te*-form))

*hanase**te***

話せた　　(could talk)
hanaseta

10. There is another potential form for Group 2 verbs.

  (7) Gr. 2 verbs: Vstem れる
                    reru

      食べる → 食べれる
      taberu   *tabereru*

This form, however, is used only in informal conversation.

---

rashii らしい   *aux. adj.* (*i*)

an auxiliary adjective which indicates that the preceding sentence is the speaker's conjecture based on what he has heard, read or seen	seem; look like; apparently; I heard 【REL. *yōda* (*darō*; *sōda²*)】

♦**Key Sentence**

Sentence (informal)†	
松田さん　は アメリカ へ 行く *Matsuda-san wa Amerika e **iku***	らしい / らしいです。 *rashii / rashiidesu.*
(It seems that Mr. Matsuda is going to America.)	

†*Da* after Adj (*na*) stem and N drops.

Formation

(i) {V / Adj (*i*)} inf らしい
                 rashii

    {話す　 / 話した}　らしい   (It seems that s.o. (will) talk / talked.)
    {*hanasu* / *hanashita*} *rashii*

    {高い / 高かった} らしい   (It seems that s.t. is / was expensive.)
    {*takai* / *takakatta*} *rashii*

(ii) {Adj (*na*) stem / N} {ø / だった} らしい
       {ø / *datta*}   *rashii*

{静か   / 静かだった}   らしい   (It seems that s.t. is / was quiet.)
{*shizuka* / *shizuka*datta}   *rashii*

{先生   / 先生   だった}   らしい   (It seems that s.o. is / was a teacher.)
{*sensei* / *sensei* datta}   *rashii*

Examples

(a) 杉本さんはもう帰ったらしいです。
    Sugimoto-san wa mō kaetta rashii desu.
    (Mr. Sugimoto seems to have gone home already.)

(b) あの学校の入学試験は難しいらしい。
    Ano gakkō no nyūgakushiken wa muzukashii rashii.
    (That school's entrance exam seems difficult.)

(c) このあたりはとても静からしいです。
    Kono atari wa totemo shizuka rashiidesu.
    (This neighborhood seems very quiet.)

(d) その話は本当らしい。
    Sono hanashi wa hontō rashii.
    (That story seems true (lit. the truth).)

(e) ここは学校らしい。
    Koko wa gakkō rashii.
    (This place seems to be a school.)

Notes

1. *Rashii* is generally used when the speaker makes a conjecture based on some information which he has heard, read or seen. What he has heard is especially important. Unlike *sōda*[2], which expresses a simple guess based on what the speaker sees, *rashii* is used when the conjecture is based on more reliable information. (⇨ **sōda**[2]) (For a comprehensive comparison of conjecture expressions, see *yōda*, Related Expressions.)

2. If there has been relatively little conjecture in the speaker's mind, *rashii* is almost the same as the hearsay expression *sōda*[1].   (⇨ **sōda**[1])

3. Negative conjecture is expressed by a negative predicate and *rashii*, as in (1).

(1) a. 田口さんはパーティーに行かないらしい。

*Taguchi-san wa pāti ni **ikanai** rashii.*

(It seems that Mr. Taguchi won't go to the party.)

b. メアリーはビルが好きじゃないらしい。

*Meari wa Biru ga **sukijanai** rashii.*

(It seems that Mary doesn't like Bill.)

4. Another use of *rashii* is as follows:

(2) 大木さんは男らしい。

Ōki-san wa otoko rashii.

(Mr. Oki is manly.)

Here, *rashii* means likeness. That is, "X *wa* Y *rashii*" means that X is like the ideal model of Y. (Of course, (2) can also mean "It seems that Oki is a man.")

5. Since *rashii* is an *i*-type adjective, it can also precede nouns, as in (3).

(3) 私は男らしい人が好きだ。

*Watashi wa **otoko rashii** hito ga sukida.*

(I like a manly man.)

The negative version of (2) is (4).

(4) 大木さんは男らしくない。

*Ōki-san wa otoko **rashikunai**.*

(Mr. Oki is not manly.)

If *Ōki-san wa otoko* (*da*) is negated, the meaning changes.

(5) 大木さんは男じゃないらしい。

*Ōki-san wa otoko **janai** rashii.*

(It seems that Oki is not a man.)

R

Relative Clause

◆Key Sentences

(A)

Topic (subject)			Predicate
Relative Clause	Noun		
田中さん が 食べた *Tanaka-san ga tabeta*	ステーキ *sutēki*	は *wa*	高かった / 高かったです。 *takakatta / takakattadesu.*
(The steak that Mr. Tanaka ate was expensive.)			

(B)

Direct Object			Transitive Verb
Relative Clause	Noun		
ステーキ が おいしい *Sutēki ga oishii*	レストラン *resutoran*	を *o*	知らない / 知りません か。 *shiranai / shirimasen ka.*
(Do you know a restaurant which has good steak (lit. in which steak is good)?)			

Formation

(i) {V / Adj (*i*)} inf+N

　　{話す　/ 話した}　　人　　(a person who (will) talks / talked)
　　{*hanasu* / *hanashita*} *hito*

　　{高い / 高かった}　本　　(a book which is / was expensive)
　　{*takai* / *takakatta*} *hon*

(ii) Adj (*na*) stem {な / だった}　N
　　　　　　　　　　{*na* / *datta*}

　　{静かな　/ 静かだった}　家　　(a house which is / was quiet)
　　{*shizukana* / *shizukadatta*} *ie*

(iii) N {の / だった / である / であった} N
　　　{*no* / *datta* / *de aru* / *de atta*}

　　先生　{の / である}　田中さん　　(Mr. Tanaka (,) who is a teacher)
　　sensei {*no* / *de aru*} *Tanaka-san*

　　先生　{だった / であった}　田中さん　　(Mr. Tanaka (,) who was a
　　sensei {*datta* / *de atta*}　*Tanaka-san*　teacher)

Examples

(a) 日本語を教えている先生は小林先生です。

Nihongo o oshiete iru sensei wa Kobayashi-sensei desu.

(The teacher who is teaching Japanese is Prof. Kobayashi.)

(b) テニスが上手な人を教えてください。

Tenisu ga jōzuna hito o oshiete kudasai.

(Please tell me of a person who is good at tennis.)

(c) お父さんが医者の学生は三人います。

O-tō-san ga isha no gakusei wa sannin imasu.

(There are three students whose fathers are doctors.)

(d) 私がいた町は病院がなかった。

Watashi ga ita machi wa byōin ga nakatta.

(There was no hospital in the town where I lived.)

(e) 道子が行く学校は東京にあります。

Michiko ga iku gakkō wa Tōkyō ni arimasu.

(The school where Michiko is going is in Tokyo.)

(f) スティーブがあなたの写真をとったカメラはこれですか。

Sutibu ga anata no shashin o totta kamera wa kore desu ka.

(Is this the camera with which Steve took pictures of you?)

Notes

1. The procedure for making relative clauses consists of several steps. The following steps show how to relativize *sutēki* 'steak' in (1a) in order to obtain the clause modifying *sutēki* in (1b).

(1) a. ジョンは**ステーキ**を食べました。

    *Jon wa **sutēki** o tabemashita.*

    (John ate a steak.)

    b. その**ステーキ**はおいしかったです。

    *Sono **sutēki** wa oishikattadesu.*

    (The steak was delicious.)

Step 1: Delete the common noun phrase in the relative clause. ([ ] indicates the relative clause boundary.)

(2) [ジョンは ø を食べました]**ステーキ**はおいしかったです。

    [*Jon wa ø o tabemashita*] **sutēki** *wa oishikattadesu.*

Step 2: Delete the particle which remains.

⑶ ［ジョンは ø 食べました］ステーキはおいしかったです。

　　[Jon wa ø tabemashita] sutēki wa oishikattadesu.

Step 3:   Change the predicate into an appropriate form. (See Formation.)

⑷ ［ジョンは**食べた**］ステーキはおいしかったです。

　　*[Jon wa **tabeta**] sutēki wa oishikattadesu.*

Step 4:   If the topic marker *wa* appears in the clause, replace it with the appropriate particle.   (If *wa* follows another particle, delete *wa*.)   In this example, *Jon* is the subject; therefore, the particle which replaces *wa* is the subject marker *ga*.   (⇨ **ga**; **wa** (は))

⑸ ［ジョン**が**食べた］ステーキはおいしかったです。

　　*[Jon **ga** tabeta] sutēki wa oishikattadesu.*

　　(The steak that John ate was delicious.)

The clause in brackets in (5) is the final form of the relative clause when *sutēki* is relativized in (1a).

2. As seen in the procedure for relativization in Note 1, the relative clause construction in Japanese has several characteristics:

(A)   Relative clauses precede their corresponding relativized nouns.

(B)   There are no relative pronouns like *which*, *that* and *who* in English.

(C)   Particles which were affixed to relativized nouns are deleted.

(D)   The topic marker *wa* does not appear in relative clauses.

3. *No* can also be used to mark the subject in relative clauses, as in (6).

⑹ ジョン**が**／**の**食べたステーキ

　　*Jon **ga** / **no** tabeta sutēki*

　　(the steak that John ate)

No cannot be used in place of *ga*, however, if the subject of the sentence is followed by a noun, as in (7a).   If *no* is used in this construction, the meaning of the sentence changes, as seen in (7b).

⑺ a.　トムがフットボールの切符をあげた女の子

　　　　*Tomu **ga** futtobōru no kippu o ageta onna no ko*

　　　　(the girl to whom Tom gave a football ticket)

　　 b.　トム**の**フットボールの切符をあげた女の子

　　　　*Tomu **no** futtobōru no kippu o ageta onna no ko*

　　　　(the girl to whom (someone) gave Tom's football ticket)

4. Besides the relative clause construction explained above, Japanese has a construction which looks similar to the one above. As seen in Note 1, in a genuine relative clause construction, the relativized noun (the head noun) is part of the original sentence from which the relative clause was derived. In this construction, however, the "head noun" is not part of the original sentence. For example, in (8), *nioi* 'smell' is not part of the sentence *Sakana ga kogeru.* 'Fish is burning.'

(8) 魚がこげるにおい。
   sakana ga kogeru nioi
   (the smell of burning fish (lit. the smell which fish burns))

The relationship between the "relative clause" and the "head noun", as seen in (8), is as follows: Suppose that X is the "head noun". Then, X is something which was brought about by the event expressed in the "relative clause", but is not something which was explicitly stated. For example, in (8) the "head noun" *nioi* 'smell' is something brought about when fish burns, but is not an explicit part of the original sentence. Here are some more examples of this type of construction:

(9) だれかがろうかを走る音
   dareka ga rōka o hashiru oto
   (the sound of someone's running in the hall)

(10) 紙をもやしたけむり
   kami o moyashita kemuri
   (the smoke which came out when someone burned papers (lit. the smoke which someone burned papers))

(11) 山に登った疲れ
   yama ni nobotta tsukare
   (fatigue which was caused from climbing a mountain (lit. fatigue that (someone) climbed a mountain))

5. The following examples are usually considered to be appositive clause constructions rather than relative clause constructions, because in these examples what is expressed by the preceding clause is the following noun itself.

(12) 日本へ行く計画 / 考え / 予定 / 夢
   Nihon e iku keikaku / kangae / yotei / yume
   (the plan / idea / schedule / dream that (I am) going to Japan)

(13) 日本へ行った事実 / 経験 / 話 / 思い出

Nihon e itta jijitsu / keiken / hanashi / omoide

(the fact / experience / story / memory that (I) went to Japan)

6. In relative clauses in Japanese, the restrictive use and the non-restrictive use cannot be distinguished from the structure. It is usually determined from the context and / or the situation. The following examples are ambiguous.

(14) 私が日本語を教えてあげたブラウンさんはよく勉強する。

Watashi ga nihongo o oshiete ageta Buraun-san wa yoku ben-kyōsuru.

((A) Mr. Brown, to whom I taught Japanese, studies well.

(B) (Among those Browns we know the) Mr. Brown to whom I taught Japanese studies well.)

(15) よく働く日本人はきらわれる。

Yoku hataraku nihonjin wa kirawareru.

((A) Japanese people, who work hard, are hated.

(B) Japanese people who work hard are hated.)

7. The ease of relativization of a noun phrase differs depending on the particle marking the phrase. (16) shows the particle hierarchy. Here, noun phrases marked by the particles in the upper position are easy to relativize and noun phrases marked by the particles in the lower position are hard to relativize.

(16) $ga > o^1 > ni^2 > ni^6 > o^2 > e > de^1 > de^2$ (means) $> kara^1$ (source) $> no^1 > kara^1$ (starting point) $> to^2 > de^2$ (cause / reason) $> yori^1$

Concerning the relativization of noun phrases in simple sentences, noun phrases marked by de^2 (cause / reason) and $yori^1$ cannot be relativized, but those marked by the rest of the particles in (16) can.

-sa さ   *suf.*

> a suffix that makes a noun out of an
> adjective by attaching it to the stem
> of an Adj (*i*) or much less frequently
> to the stem of an Adj (*na*)

-ness; -ty
【REL. *-mi*】

♦ Key Sentence

	Adj (*i*) stem	
この うち の *Kono uchi no*	広さ *hiro*sa	は ちょうど いい / いいです。 *wa chōdo ii / iidesu.*
(The size of this house is just right.)		

Formation

Adj (*i* / *na*) stem さ
         sa

高さ　　(height)
*taka*sa

静かさ　(quietness)
*shizuka*sa

Examples

(a) 富士山の高さはどのぐらいですか。
   Fujisan no takasa wa dono gurai desu ka.
   (What is the approximate height of Mt. Fuji?)

(b) 日本語の難しさがよく分かりました。
   Nihongo no muzukashisa ga yoku wakarimashita.
   (I'm now well aware of the difficulty of Japanese.)

(c) アメリカのよさはパイオニア・スピリットでしょう。
   Amerika no yosa wa paionia supiritto deshō.
   (One of America's good qualities is perhaps its pioneering spirit.)

Notes

1. The suffix *-sa* is a very productive suffix that makes a noun out of an
   adjective. Some typical examples are given below:

S

新しさ (newness / freshness) atarashisa	大きさ (size) ōkisa
速さ (speed) hayasa	強さ (strength) tsuyosa
長さ (length) nagasa	よさ (goodness / merit) yosa
白さ (whiteness) shirosa	黒さ (blackness) kurosa

2. Adj (na) stem + sa is not commonly used. It is suggested that the learner avoid using it. Some of the most commonly used Adjs (na) stem + sa are the following:

便利さ (convenience) benrisa	正確さ (accuracy) seikakusa
忠実さ (loyality) chūjitsusa	完ぺきさ (perfection) kanpekisa
のどかさ (calmness) nodokasa	にぎやかさ (liveliness) nigiyakasa

3. When an adjective can be paired with another adjectival antonym as in ōkii 'big' vs. chīsai 'small', the positive counterpart, (i.e., ōkii) tends to acquire a meaning of absolute degree when -sa is attached, as in ōkisa 'size'. Examples follow:

Positive	Negative
厚さ (breadth) atsusa	薄さ (thinness) ususa
重さ (weight) omosa	軽さ (lightness) karusa
難しさ (difficulty) muzukashisa	やさしさ (easiness) yasashisa
うれしさ (joy) ureshisa	悲しさ (sadness) kanashisa
深さ (depth) fukasa	浅さ (shallowness) asasa

S

Positive	Negative
高さ (height) taka**sa**	低さ (lowness) hiku**sa**
暑さ (heat) atsu**sa**	寒さ (coldness) samu**sa**
濃さ (density) ko**sa**	薄さ (thinness) usu**sa**
大きさ (size) ōki**sa**	小ささ (smallness) chisa**sa**
広さ (size of space) hiro**sa**	狭さ (smallness of space) sema**sa**
強さ (strength) tsuyo**sa**	弱さ (weakness) yowa**sa**

[Related Expression]

-sa describes, in an analytical manner, the degree of the state represented by an adjective, but -mi, another noun-forming suffix, is a more emotive and concrete characterization of some state (based primarily on direct perception). Only a limited number of Adj (i) can be used with -mi. Examples:

赤み (reddishness) aka**mi**	悲しみ (sorrow) kanashi**mi**
暖かみ (warmness) atataka**mi**	深み (depth) fuka**mi**
厚み (thickness) atsu**mi**	弱み (weakness) yowa**mi**
甘み (sweetness) ama**mi**	苦み (bitterness) niga**mi**
苦しみ (painfulness) kurushi**mi**	強み (strength) tsuyo**mi**

Consider the following sentences in which -sa is unacceptable.

[1] あの人はおもしろみ / *おもしろさがないね。
Ano hito wa omoshiromi / *omoshirosa ga nai ne.
(He just lacks something that attracts people.)

S

[2] 楽しみ / *楽しさにしています。

*Tanoshimi | *tanoshisa ni shite imasu.*

(I'm looking forward to it.)

In both [1] and [2] the *-sa* version is unacceptable because both sentences express something concrete that can be expressed only by *-mi*. The fact that nouns with the suffix *-mi* indicate something concrete seems to be related to a general tendency of nasal sounds.

(⇨ Characteristics of Japanese Grammar, 8. Sound Symbolisms)

-sama 様　　*suf.*

a suffix (originally meaning 'appearance') that indicates the speaker's / writer's politeness towards s.o.	Mr.; Miss; Ms.; Mrs. 【REL. *-chan*; *-kun*; *-san*】

Examples

(a) 王様の耳はろばの耳だ。

Ō-sama no mimi wa roba no mimi da.

(The King's ears are donkey's ears.)

(b) 神様を信じますか。

Kami-sama o shinjimasu ka.

(Do you believe in God?)

(c) 花子ちゃん、今夜はお月様もお星様もきれいねえ。

Hanako-chan, kon'ya wa o-tsuki-sama mo o-hoshi-sama mo kirei nē.

(Hanako, aren't the moon and the stars beautiful tonight!)

(d) お母様、どこにいらっしゃるの？

O-kā-sama, doko ni irassharu no?

(Mother, where are you going?)

(e) お客様が見えたよ。

O-kyaku-sama ga mieta yo.

(Our guests have come.)

Notes

1. The reason why -sama 'appearance' is used to show one's respect is that -sama allows one to refer indirectly to one's superior. For instance, *Yamada-sama* is a more indirect way to refer to a person called *Yamada* than to call him simply *Yamada*, because *Yamada-sama* literary means 'appearance of *Yamada*'. Note, however, that a personal name+*sama* is not used in conversational Japanese, except in highly polite speech used to clientele by clerks / attendants of hotels, restaurants, travel agencies, department stores, etc.

2. -sama attached to a personified object shows more endearment than respect, as in Ex. (c).

3. -sama can also be attached to some action or state related to the hearer, as in (1) through (5) below:

    (1) ご馳走様(でした)。
        *Go-chisō-**sama** (deshita).*
        (It was such a treat.)

    (2) お世話様になりました。
        *O-sewa-**sama** ni narimashita.*
        (Thank you for all that you've done for me.)

    (3) お気の毒様(でした)。
        *O-ki no doku-**sama** (deshita).*
        (Lit. It was a pitiful matter. (That's too bad.))

    (4) お疲れ様(でした)。
        *O-tsukare-**sama** (deshita).*
        (You must be very tired.)

    (5) おかげ様で元気です。
        *O-kage-**sama** de genkidesu.*
        (Lit. Thanks to you I'm fine. (I'm fine, thank you.))

4. In written Japanese, esp. after the addressee's name in a letter, etc., -sama is used as in:

    (6) 山田一郎様
        *Yamada Ichirō-**sama***
        (Mr. Ichiro Yamada)

[Related Expressions]

I. Two related forms, -san and -chan are derived from -sama through phonetic modifications. *-san* is the informal version of *-sama* and there-fore less honorific and more intimate than *-sama*. Except for Exs. (a) and (b), in which the highest superiors appear, *-sama* can be replaced by *-san*. *-san* can also be attached to names of occupations and titles as in:

[1] Name of occupation + *san*

魚屋さん　　(fishmonger)
sakana-ya-san

お菓子屋さん　　(confectioner)
o-kashi-ya-san

酒屋さん　　(wine dealer)
saka-ya-san

[2] Title + *san*

校長さん　　(principal)
kōchō-san

市長さん　　(mayor)
shichō-san

課長さん　　(section chief)
kachō-san

-chan is used with children's names or in child-like language. Normally this suffix is attached only to kinship terms or first names as in:

[3] Kinship terms + *chan*

お母ちゃん　　(mom)
o-kā-chan

お父ちゃん　　(pop)
o-tō-chan

おじいちゃん　　(grandpa)
o-ji-chan

おばあちゃん　　(grandma)
o-bā-chan

おじちゃん　　(uncle)
oji-chan

おばちゃん　　(auntie)
oba-chan

[4] First name + *chan*

花子ちゃん　　(Hanako)
*Hanako-**chan***

太郎ちゃん　　(Taro)
*Tarō-**chan***

II. *-kun* is a similar Sino-Japanese suffix which can be attached to a male equal or male inferior's first name and / or last name. It is sometimes used to refer to a female or a male in an institution such as a school or a company. Etymologically *-kun* has nothing to do with *-sama* and its variants.　　　　　　　　　　　　　　　　　　(⇨ ***-kun***)

---

saseru させる　　*aux. v. (Gr. 2)*

cause s.o. / s.t. to do s.t. or cause s.t. to change its state

make s.o. / s.t. do s.t.; cause s.o. / s.t. to do s.t.; let s.o. / s.t. do s.t.; allow s.o. / s.t. to do s.t.; have s.o. / s.t. do s.t.; get s.o. / s.t. to do s.t.

♦ **Key Sentences**

(A)

Topic (causer)		Causee			Intransitive Verb (causative)
鈴木さん *Suzuki-san*	は *wa*	むすめ *musume*	を / に *o / ni*	大学　へ *daigaku e*	行かせた / 行かせました。 ***ika**seta* / ***ika**semashita.*
(Mr. Suzuki made / let his daughter go to college.)					

(B)

Topic (causer)		Causee		Direct Object		Transitive Verb (causative)
父 *Chichi*	は *wa*	妹 *imōto*	に *ni*	ピアノ *piano*	を *o*	習わせた / 習わせました。 ***narawa**seta* / ***narawa**semashita.*
(My father made (or let) my younger sister learn to play the piano.)						

S

Formation

(i) Gr. 1 Verbs:　Vneg　せる
　　　　　　　　　　　　　seru

　　　　　　　　話させる　　(cause to talk)
　　　　　　　　hanasaseru

(ii) Gr. 2 Verbs:　Vstem　させる
　　　　　　　　　　　　　saseru

　　　　　　　　食べさせる　　(cause to eat)
　　　　　　　　tabesaseru

(iii) Irr. Verbs:　来る → 来させる　　(cause to come)
　　　　　　　　kuru　　*kosaseru*

　　　　　　　　する → させる　　(cause to do)
　　　　　　　　suru　　*saseru*

Examples

(a) ひさ子は私を困らせた。
　　Hisako wa watashi o komaraseta.
　　(Lit. Hisako made me have trouble. (=Hisako caused me trouble.))

(b) このゲームはジムに勝たせようと思う。
　　Kono gēmu wa Jimu ni kataseyō to omou.
　　(I think I'll let Jim win this game.)

(c) 友達は私にチップを払わせた。
　　Tomodachi wa watashi ni chippu o harawaseta.
　　(My friend made me leave (lit. pay) a tip.)

(d) アンダーソンさんは子供達に好きなだけアイスクリームを食べさせた。
　　Andāson-san wa kodomotachi ni sukina dake aisukurimu o tabesaseta.
　　(Mr. Anderson let his children eat as much ice cream as they liked.)

(e) 私は冷蔵庫でミルクをこおらせた。
　　Watashi wa reizōko de miruku o kōraseta.
　　(Lit. I made milk freeze (=I froze milk) in the refrigerator.)

(f) それは私にさせてください。
　　Sore wa watashi ni sasete kudasai.
　　(As for that, let me do it.)

Notes

1. The idea that someone / something (=the causer) causes or allows some-

one / something (=the causee) to do something is expressed by the causative construction. In the causative construction, the causer is usually marked by *wa* in main clauses and by *ga* in subordinate clauses. When the main verb is an intransitive verb, the causee is marked by either *o* or *ni*. The choice between the two particles depends on the following general rule. When *ni* is used, the causee has taken an action *intentionally*. For example, *ni* is ungrammatical in (1) because the causee didn't intend to go to the party in this situation.

(1)　父は私を / *にむりやりパーティーへ行かせた。

　　　*Chichi wa watashi o / *ni muriyari pāti e ikaseta.*

　　　(My father forced (lit. forcefully made) me to go to the party.)

Also, *ni* is ungrammatical in (2) because the causee is a non-volitional entity and, therefore, has no intent (cannot take a volitional action).

(2)　私はハンカチを / *にしめらせた。

　　　*Watashi wa hankachi o / *ni shimeraseta.*

　　　(Lit. I made my handkerchief get damp. (=I dampened my handkerchief.))

O, on the other hand, can be used regardless of the causee's volition, as seen in (3) and (4). Whether a sentence expresses " permissive " causative or " coercive " causative depends on the context and / or the situation.

(3)　a.　私はいやがるむすこを / *にむりやり泳がせた。

　　　　　*Watashi wa iyagaru musuko o / *ni muriyari oyogaseta.*

　　　　　(Lit. I forced my son, who resisted swimming, to swim.)

　　　b.　私はむすこを / に好きなだけ泳がせた。

　　　　　Watashi wa musuko o / ni sukina dake oyogaseta.

　　　　　(I let my son swim as much as he wanted.)

(4)　a.　秋子は勉強は もうしたくないと言ったが私は彼女を / *に大学に行かせることにした。

　　　　　*Akiko wa benkyō wa mō shitakunai to itta ga watashi wa kanojo o / *ni daigaku ni ikaseru koto ni shita.*

　　　　　(Akiko said she didn't want to study any more, but I've decided to send her to college. (lit. make her go to college.))

　　　b.　秋子はもっと勉強したいと言ったので，私は彼女を / に大学に行かせることにした。

　　　　　Akiko wa motto benkyōshitai to itta node, watashi wa kanojo o / ni daigaku ni ikaseru koto ni shita.

S

(Akiko said she wanted to study more, so I've decided to let her go to college.)

2. If the main verb is a transitive verb, the causee can be marked only by *ni*, as in (5), because *o* cannot appear more than once in a clause and, in this case, there is already a direct object marked by *o* in the clause.   (⇨ ***o***[1])

(5) 一郎は雪子に / *をビールを飲ませた。
   *Ichirō wa Yukiko **ni** / ***o** bīru o nomaseta.*
   (Ichiro made (or let) Yukiko drink beer.)

Thus, when the verb is transitive, *ni* is acceptable even if the causee is not willing to take the action.

(6) 一郎は雪子にむりやりビールを飲ませた。
   *Ichirō wa Yukiko **ni** muriyari bīru o nomaseta.*
   (Ichiro forced Yukiko to drink beer.)

When the main verb is transitive, it is often difficult to tell from the sentence alone whether or not the causee takes the action willingly. This must be determined by the context and / or the situation in which the sentence is uttered.

3. Whether or not the causee is willing to do something is clear if one of the set of giving and receiving verbs is used.   (⇨ ***ageru***[2]; ***kureru***[2]; ***morau***[2])   Examples:

(7) 私は春子をパーティーに行かせてやった。
   *Watashi wa Haruko o pātī ni ikasete **yatta**.*
   (I let Haruko go to the party.)

(8) 父は私に酒を飲ませてくれた。
   *Chichi wa watashi ni sake o nomasete ｉ**kureta**.*
   (My father let me drink *sake*.)

The causee's unwillingness to do something, on the other hand, can be more explicitly expressed by the causative-passive construction explained in Note 7.

4. In causative sentences, the causer must be equal to or higher than the causee in terms of status.   Thus, the following is unacceptable:

(9) *私は先生に / をパーティーに来させるつもりだ。
   **Watashi wa sensei ni / o pātī ni kosaseru tsumori da.*
   (I'm going to let (or make) my teacher come to the party.)

5. Causative verbs are all Gr. 2 verbs.   The basic conjugations are as follows:

⑽ 話させる　(nonpast·inf·affirmative)
*hanasase**ru***

話させ**ない**　(nonpast·inf·negative)
*hanasase**nai***

話させ**て**　(*te*-form)
*nanasase**te***

話させ**た**　(past·inf·affirmative)
*hanasase**ta***

6. There is another set of formation rules for causative verbs. (Causative verbs of this version are all Gr. 1 verbs.)

⑾　a.　Gr. 1 Verbs:　Vneg　す
　　　　　　　　　　　　　　　su

　　　　　　　　　　話さす　(cause to talk)
　　　　　　　　　　***hanasa**su*

　　b.　Gr. 2 Verbs:　Vstem　さす
　　　　　　　　　　　　　　　sasu

　　　　　　　　　　食べさす　(cause to eat)
　　　　　　　　　　***tabe**sasu*

　　c.　Irr. Verbs:　来る → 来さす　(cause to come)
　　　　　　　　　　kuru　kosasu

　　　　　　　　　　する → さす　(cause to do)
　　　　　　　　　　suru　sasu

In general, this set of conjugations seems to express more direct causation. For example, in (12a) *tabesasu* means 'feed (with a spoon or something)' rather than 'make / let eat', while in (12b) *tabesaseru* is more general and means 'make / let eat (either by saying something like "Eat your meal" or "You may eat your meal" or actually by feeding with a spoon or something)'.

⑿　a.　私はジムにくだものを**食べさす**つもりだ。
　　　*Watashi wa Jimu ni kudamono o **tabesasu** tsumori da.*
　　　(I intend to feed Jim fruit.)

　　b.　私はジムにくだものを**食べさせる**つもりだ。
　　　*Watashi wa Jimu ni kudamono o **tabesaseru** tsumori da.*
　　　(I intend to make / let Jim eat fruit.)

7. Causative-passive verbs, which are used in causative-passive sentences, are constructed by affixing the passive verb ending *rareru* to causative verb stems. (⇨ ***rareru***[1]) Examples:

(13) 話させられる   (be made to talk)
    *hanasase**rareru***

    食べさせられる   (be made to eat)
    *tabe**saserareru***

Causative-passive sentences express the idea " be made to do something ". Note that they do not express the idea " be allowed to do something ". (14) and (15) show causative sentences and their corresponding causative-passive sentences.

(14) a. 父は私を歩いて帰らせた。
      Chichi wa watashi o aruite kaeraseta.
      (My father had me walk home.)

    b. 私は父に歩いて帰らせられた。
      Watashi wa chichi ni aruite kaeraserareta.
      (Lit. I was made to walk home by my father. (=My father made me walk home.))

(15) a. 和夫は夏子に酒を飲ませた。
      Kazuo wa Natsuko ni sake o nomaseta.
      (Kazuo made / let Natsuko drink *sake*.)

    b. 夏子は和夫に酒を飲ませられた。
      Natsuko wa Kazuo ni sake o nomaserareta.
      (Natsuko was made to drink *sake* by Kazuo.)

S

sekkaku せっかく   *adv.*

Some situation which seldom occurs has now occurred and one can either make use of it or, to one's regret, cannot make use of it.

with effort; at great pain; take the trouble to do ~
【REL. *wazawaza*】

♦**Key Sentences**

(A)

Subordinate Clause			Main Clause
せっかく *Sekkaku*	会い に 行った *ai ni itta*	のに *noni*	友達 は いなかった / いませんでした。 *tomodachi wa inakatta / imasendeshita.*
(I took the trouble to go to see my friend, but he wasn't at home.)			

(B)

Subordinate Clause				Main Clause
せっかく *Sekkaku*	いい 大学 に 入った *ii daigaku ni haitta*	の だ *no da*	から *kara*	よく 勉強する つもり *yoku benkyōsuru tsumori* だ / です。 *da / desu.*
(I entered a good college with great effort, so I intend to study hard.)				

(C)

Subordinate Clause					Main Clause
		Noun			
せっかく *Sekkaku*	の *no*	**日曜日** **nichiyōbi**	な *na*	のに *noni*	働いた / 働きました。 *hataraita / hatarakimashita.*
(Although Sunday is precious (to me), I worked (all day long).)					

Examples

(a) せっかくアメリカまで行ったのにニューヨークに行けなくて残念だった。
Sekkaku Amerika made itta noni Nyūyōku ni ikenakute zannendatta.
(I went as far as America at great expense, but, to my regret, I couldn't make it to New York.)

(b) せっかく日本語を三年間も勉強したのだから，是非一度日本へ行ってみたいと思います。
Sekkaku nihongo o sannenkan mo benkyōshita no da kara, zehi ichido Nihon e itte mitai to omoimasu.
(Because I studied Japanese for (as many as) three years, I would love to go to Japan once.)

S

(c) せっかくの旅行が病気でだめになりました。

Sekkaku no ryokō ga byōki de dame ni narimashita.

(My long awaited trip had to be canceled because of my illness.)

(d) せっかくですが今日は忙しくて行けません。

Sekkaku desu ga kyō wa isogashikute ikemasen.

(I appreciate your most kind offer, but I'm too busy to go there today.)

(e) せっかくのチャンスだからデートしたらどうですか。

Sekkaku no chansu da kara dētoshitara dō desu ka.

(It's a good chance, so why don't you date her?)

(f) せっかくですから遠慮なくいただきます。

Sekkaku desu kara, enryo naku itadakimasu.

(Since you took the trouble to bring it to me, I'll take it without hesitation.)

Note

Sekkaku tends to co-occur with *noni* 'although' or *no da kara* 'because (it is that) ~ ', as in KSs(A) and (B), respectively. *Sekkaku no+N*, however, can be used as a noun phrase, free from any co-occurrence restrictions, as shown in KS(C) and Exs. (c) and (e). *Sekkaku desu ga* (in Ex. (d)) is used to politely decline s.o.'s kind offer, and *sekkaku desu kara* (in Ex. (f)) is used to accept s.o.'s offer.

[Related Expression]

Sekkaku is related to *wazawaza*, an adverb whose basic meaning is 'intentionally take the trouble to do s.t., although it is not necessary to do so'.

[1] a. せっかく / *わざわざ近くまで来たのだから寄りました。

　　　Sekkaku / **Wazawaza* chikaku made kita no da kara yorimashita.

　　　(Because I came all the way to your neighborhood, I dropped by.)

　　b. わざわざ / *せっかく新しい車を買った。

　　　Wazawaza / **Sekkaku* atarashii kuruma o katta.

　　　(He went to the trouble of buying a new car.)

　　c. わざわざ / *せっかく持って来てくれてありがとう。

　　　Wazawaza / **Sekkaku* motte kite kurete arigatō.

　　　(Thanks for your trouble in bringing it to me.)

shi し *conj.*

> a conjunction to indicate 'and' in an emphatic way

and what's more; not only ~ but also ~; so

[REL. *sore kara*]

♦**Key Sentences**

(A)

	Verb		
今日 は テニス も *Kyō wa tenisu mo*	した *shita*	し、 *shi,*	映画 も 見た / 見ました。 *eiga mo mita / mimashita.*
(I not only played tennis but also saw a movie today.)			

(B)

	Adj (*i*)		
ここ は 夏 は *Koko wa natsu wa*	暑い *atsui*	し、 *shi,*	冬 は 寒い / 寒いです。 *fuyu wa samui / samuidesu.*
(Here it's hot in the summer, and what's more, it's cold in the winter.)			

(C)

	Adj (*na*)		
この アパート は *Kono apāto wa*	きれいだ *kireida*	し、 *shi,*	安い / 安いです。 *yasui / yasuidesu.*
(This apartment is clean, and what's more, it's inexpensive.)			

(D)

	Noun	Copula		
遊びたい ん です / だ が あした は *Asobitai n desu / da ga ashita wa*	試験 *shiken*	だ *da*	し *shi*	遊べない / *asobenai /* 遊べません。 *asobemasen.*
(I would like to play, but there is an exam tomorrow, and I can't fool around.)				

S

Formation

(i) {V / Adj (*i*)} し
　　　　　　　　　　shi

{話す　／話した}　　し　　(s.o. talks / talked and what's more)
{*hanasu* / *hanashita*} *shi*

{食べる／食べた}　し　　(s.o. eats / ate and what's more)
{*taberu* / *tabeta*} *shi*

{高い　／高かった}　し　　(s.t. is / was expensive and what's more)
{*takai* / *takakatta*} *shi*

(ii) {Adj (*na*) stem / N} {だ／だった} し
　　　　　　　　　　　　　　{*da* / *datta*} *shi*

{静かだ　　／静かだった}　　し　　(s.t. is / was quiet and what's more)
{*shizukada* / *shizukadatta*} *shi*

{先生　だ／先生　だった}　し　　(s.o. is / was a teacher and what's more)
{*sensei da* / *sensei datta*} *shi*

Examples

(a) 仕事もあったし，結婚も出来たし，とてもうれしいです。
Shigoto mo atta shi, kekkon mo dekita shi, totemo ureshiidesu.
(Not only did I find a job, but I was also able to get married, so I'm very happy.)

(b) 今日は天気もいいし，どこかへ行きましょうか。
Kyō wa tenki mo ii shi, doko ka e ikimashō ka.
(It's a nice day, so shall we go out somewhere?)

(c) あの人は美人だし，頭もいい。
Ano hito wa bijin da shi, atama mo ii.
(She's beautiful and what's more she's bright.)

(d) 切符は買ってあるし，是非見に行きましょう。
Kippu wa katte aru shi, zehi mi ni ikimashō.
(I've bought a ticket for you, so let's go see it, by all means.)

Notes

1. As in Ex. (a), *shi* can be repeated more than once in a clause, just like V*te* '~ and ' can be repeated.

2. There are times when a sentence ends with *shi* in order to weaken the sentence and obscure the cause / reason:

(1) A : あした映画に行きませんか。

　　　　Ashita eiga ni ikimasen ka.

　　　　(Wouldn't you like to go see a movie tomorrow?)

　　　B : えっ、あしたですか。あしたは試験があるし、...

　　　　E, ashita desu ka. Ashita wa shiken ga aru shi,...

　　　　(Tomorrow? I have an exam tomorrow, and...)

3. When the speaker wishes to be very polite, the clause before *shi* can be in the formal form if the main clause is in the formal form, as in (2).

(2) 今日は天気もいいですし、どこかへ行きましょうか。

　　　*Kyō wa tenki mo ii**desu** shi, doko ka e ikimashō ka.*

　　　(It's a nice day, so shall we go out somewhere?)   (Cf. Ex. (b))

-shi- し　*infix*

> an infix attached to the stem of an Adj (*i*) to indicate s.t. that one cannot objectively measure on any scale (e.g. human emotion)

Examples

悲し い　(sad) kana**shi**i	くやし い (regrettable) kuya**shi**i	恐ろし い (scary) osoro**shi**i
楽し い　(enjoyable) tano**shi**i	きびし い (strict) kibi**shi**i	難し い　(difficult) muzuka**shi**i
らし い　(seem) ra**shi**i	うらやまし い (envious) urayama**shi**i	恋し い　(dear) koi**shi**i
おいし い (delicious) oi**shi**i	さびし い (lonely) sabi**shi**i	うれし い (happy) ure**shi**i
苦し い　(painful) kuru**shi**i	惜し い　(regrettable) o**shi**i	親し い　(intimate) shita**shi**i
頼もし い (dependable) tanomo**shi**i	ねたまし い (enviable) natama**shi**i	涼し い　(cool) suzu**shi**i

S

Note

Adjs (*i*) that do not contain *-shi-* are, for the most part, descriptive adjectives that are dependent on the speaker's objective judgment. In other words, they are adjectives which indicate something that one can objectively measure on some scale. Typical descriptive adjectives are:

赤い (red) *akai*	低い (low) *hikui*	青い (blue) *aoi*	堅い (hard) *katai*
大きい (big) *ōkii*	浅い (shallow) *asai*	軽い (light) *karui*	白い (white) *shiroi*
小さい (small) *chisai*	黒い (black) *kuroi*	高い (high) *takai*	近い (near) *chikai*
短い (short) *mijikai*	薄い (thin) *usui*	深い (deep) *fukai*	長い (long) *nagai*
安い (cheap) *yasui*	柔らかい (soft) *yawarakai*	若い (young) *wakai*	濃い (thick) *koi*

shika しか   *prt.*

a particle which marks an element X when nothing but X makes the expressed proposition true

nothing / nobody / no ~ but; only

【REL. *bakari*; *dake*】

◆**Key Sentences**

(A)

Subject			Predicate (negative)
戸田さん ***Toda-san***	しか *shika*	たばこ を *tabako o*	吸わない / 吸いません。 *suwanai* / *suimasen.*
(No one but Mr. Toda smokes.)			

(B)

		Direct Object		Predicate (negative)
私　は *Watashi wa*	**日本語** **nihongo**	しか *shika*		知らない / 知りません。 *shiranai / shirimasen.*
(I know nothing but Japanese.)				

(C)

	Noun	Prt		Predicate (negative)
それ　は *Sore wa*	江口さん **Eguchi-san**	に **ni**	しか *shika*	話して　いない / いません。 *hanashite inai / imasen.*
(I haven't told it to anybody but Mr. Eguchi.)				

(D)

	Quantifier		Predicate (negative)
私　は　ご飯　を *Watashi wa gohan o*	**一ぱい** **ippai**	しか *shika*	食べなかった / 食べませんでした。 *tabenakatta / tabemasendeshita.*
(I had only one bowl of rice.)			

Formation

(i) N　しか
　　　　shika

　先生　が　(Subject) → 先生　しか　　(no one but the teacher)
　sensei ga　　　　　　　*sensei shika*

　先生　を　(Direct Object) → 先生　しか　　(no one but the teacher)
　sensei o　　　　　　　　　*sensei shika*

(ii) N+(Prt)　しか
　　　　　　shika

　東京　へ / に　(Direction) → 東京　(へ / に) しか　　(to nowhere but
　Tōkyō e / ni　　　　　　　*Tōkyō (e / ni) shika*　　Tokyo)

　先生　に　(Indirect Object, Agent) → 先生　(に)† しか　　(no one but
　sensei ni　　　　　　　　　　　*sensei (ni) shika*　　the teacher)
　(†*Ni* cannot drop if X *shika* can be interpreted as the subject.)

　日曜日　に　(Time) → 日曜日　(に) しか　　(only on Sunday)
　nichiyōbi ni　　　　　*nichiyōbi (ni) shika*

S

東京 に (Location) → 東京 (に) しか (only in Tokyo)
Tōkyō ni   *Tōkyō (ni) shika*

(iii) N+Prt しか
           shika

東京 で (Location) → 東京 で しか (only in Tokyo)
Tōkyō de   *Tōkyō de shika*

車 で (Means) → 車 で しか (only by car)
kuruma de   *kuruma de shika*

山田さん と (Reciprocal) → 山田さん と しか (only with Mr.
Yamada-san to   *Yamada-san to shika*   Yamada)

東京 から (Starting point / source) → 東京 から しか (only from
Tōkyō kara   *Tōkyō kara shika*   Tokyo)

五時 まで (Ending point) → 五時 まで しか (only till five o'clock)
goji made   *goji made shika*

(iv) Quantifier しか
           shika

少し しか (only a little)
sukoshi shika

Examples

(a) パーティーには学生しか来なかった。
Pāti ni wa gakusei shika konakatta.
(Only students came to the party.)

(b) 田村さんはサラダしか食べなかった。
Tamura-san wa sarada shika tabenakatta.
(Mr. Tamura ate only salad.)

(c) 私は日曜日(に)しか来られません。
Watashi wa nichiyōbi (ni) shika koraremasen.
(I can come only on Sunday.)

(d) この本はこの図書館(に)しかありません。
Kono hon wa kono toshokan (ni) shika arimasen.
(Only this library has this book.)

(e) そこは車でしか行けない。
Soko wa kuruma de shika ikenai.
(Lit. You can go there only by car. (=The only way you can go there is by car.))

(f) 私は山田さんとしか話をしない。

  Watashi wa Yamada-san to shika hanashi o shinai.

  (I talk only with Mr. Yamada.)

(g) この学校は学生が百人しかいない。

  Kono gakkō wa gakusei ga hyakunin shika inai.

  (This school has only a hundred students.)

Note

Shika always occurs with negative predicates.

[Related Expressions]

 I. *Dake* expresses a similar idea. (⇨ **dake**) However, *dake* and *shika* differ in the following ways:

  (A) X *shika* emphasizes the negative proposition of "non-X", while X *dake* merely describes the situation in neutral fashion.

  (B) *Shika* occurs only with negative predicates; *dake*, however, can occur with affirmative predicates. Compare the following sentences:

   [1] a. ボブだけ来た。

      *Bobu **dake** kita.*

      (Only Bob came.)

     b. ボブしか来なかった。

      *Bobu **shika** konakatta.*

      (Nobody but Bob came.)

   [2] a. ボブだけ来なかった。

      *Bob **dake** konakatta.*

      (Only Bob didn't come.)

     b. *ボブしか来た / 来なくなかった。

      Bobu **shika kita / konakunakatta.*

      (Everybody but Bob came.)

  (C) The verb *kakaru* 'it takes (time)' can be used with *shika*, but not with *dake*, as in [3].

   [3] a. 私の家から学校までは車で五分しかかからない。

      *Watashi no ie kara gakkō made wa kuruma de gofun **shika** kakaranai.*

      (From my house to school it takes only five minutes by car.)

S

b. *私の家から学校までは車で五分だけかかる。

*Watashi no ie kara gakkō made wa kuruma de gofun **dake kakaru**.

(From my house to school it takes only five minutes by car.)

II. *Bakari* is also used to mean 'only' in some situations. (⇨ ***bakari***) Unlike X *shika* or X *dake*, however, X *bakari* emphasizes the positive proposition of X, often with the implication that s.o. / s.t. does s.t. to X / with X / . . . a lot or more than one expects. For example, [4a] emphasizes the fact that Jim drank beer, whereas [4b] emphasizes the fact that Jim didn't drink anything but beer. [4c] is a neutral statement.

[4] a. ジムはビールばかり飲んだ。

Jimu wa bīru **bakari** nonda.

(Jim drank only beer (and a lot).)

b. ジムはビールしか飲まなかった。

Jimu wa bīru **shika** nomanakatta.

(Jim drank nothing but beer.)

c. ジムはビールだけ飲んだ。

Jimu wa bīru **dake** nonda.

(Jim drank only beer.)

Note that X *bakari* cannot be used if X is a single entity. Thus, [5a] is grammatical, but [5b] is not.

[5] a. 女の子ばかり来た。

Onna no ko bakari kita.

(Only girls came (and it was more than I expected).)

b. *メアリーばかり来た。

*Meari bakari kita.

(Only Mary came.)

Note also that ***bakari*** cannot be used with negative predicates, as in [6].

[6] 子供達だけ / *ばかり来なかった。

Kodomotachi **dake** / ***bakari konakatta***.

(Only the children didn't come.)

shimau しまう *aux. v. (Gr. 1)*

| an auxiliary verb which indicates the completion of an action | have done s.t.; finish doing s.t.; finish s.t. up
【REL. ~*owaru*】 |

◆**Key Sentences**

(A)

Topic (subject)			V*te*	
池田君 *Ikeda-kun*	は *wa*	三日 で その 本 を *mikka de sono hon o*	読んで ***yonde***	しまった / しまいました。 *shimatta / shimaimashita.*
(Mr. Ikeda finished reading the book in three days.)				

(B)

Topic (subject)			V*te*	
私 *Watashi*	は *wa*	ルームメート の ミルク を *rūmumēto no miruku o*	飲んで ***nonde***	しまった / しまいました。 *shimatta / shimaimashita.*
(I (mistakenly) drank my roommate's milk.)				

Formation

V*te* しまう
   shimau

話して しまう (have talked)
hanashite shimau

食べて しまう (have eaten)
tabete shimau

S

Examples

(a) もう宿題をしてしまいましたか。
   Mō shukudai o shite shimaimashita ka.
   (Have you done your homework yet?)

(b) 私は今日中にそのレポートを書いてしまおうと思っている。
   Watashi wa kyōjū ni sono repōto o kaite shimaō to omotte iru.
   (I think that I will finish (writing) the report today.)

(c) 早くご飯を食べてしまいなさい。
　　Hayaku gohan o tabete shimainasai.
　　(Finish (eating) your meal quickly.)

(d) シチューを作りすぎてしまいました。
　　Shichū o tsukuri sugite shimaimashita.
　　(I made too much stew (to my regret).)

Notes

1. *Shimau* is used as an auxiliary verb with Vte and expresses the idea
   of completion in terms of an action. Vte *shimau* often appears with
   such adverbs as *sukkari* 'completely', *zenbu* 'all' and *kanzenni* 'completely'. Examples:

   ⑴　a.　マイクは**すっかり**日本語を忘れてしまった。
   　　　　*Maiku wa **sukkari** nihongo o wasurete shimatta.*
   　　　　(Mike has completely forgotten Japanese.)

   　　b.　私は持っていた切手を**全部**友達にあげてしまった。
   　　　　*Watashi wa motte ita kitte o **zenbu** tomodachi ni agete
   　　　　shimatta.*
   　　　　(I gave all the stamps I had kept to my friends.)

2. Vte *shimatta* also expresses the idea that someone did something which
   he shouldn't have done or something happened which shouldn't have
   happened. (KS(B) and Ex. (d)) Thus, it often implies the agent's regret about what he has done or the speaker's regret or criticism about
   someone's action or about something that has happened. Examples:

   ⑵　a.　ジェリーはペギーのケーキを食べてしまった。
   　　　　Jeri wa Pegi no kēki o tabete shimatta.
   　　　　(Jerry (mistakenly) ate Peggy's cake.)

   　　b.　私はちがうバスに乗ってしまった。
   　　　　Watashi wa chigau basu ni notte shimatta.
   　　　　(I got on the wrong bus.)

   　　c.　雨が降ってしまったのでピクニックに行けなかった。
   　　　　Ame ga futte shimatta node pikunikku ni ikenakatta.
   　　　　(It rained, so we couldn't go on a picnic.)

3. Whether a sentence with Vte *shimatta* is interpreted as simple completion
   or regret (or criticism) depends on the context and / or the situation.
   For example, (3) can be interpreted in two ways.

(3) 僕はお酒を飲んでしまった。

Boku wa o-sake o nonde shimatta.

((A) I finished drinking *sake*. (B) I drank *sake* (which I shouldn't have done).)

4. *Te shimau* and *de shimau* are contracted as *chau* and *jau*, respectively, in informal speech, as in (4), and can be used by male and by female speakers.

(4) a. 話して　しまう → 話し　**ちゃう**　(have talked)

*hanashite shimau　hanashi **chau***

b. 飲んで　しまう → 飲ん　**じゃう**　(have drunk)

*nonde shimau　non **jau***

Chimau and *jimau*, another set of contracted forms of *te shimau*, are used only by male speakers.

【Related Expressions】

I. Vpast can also express the completion of an action. However, it is different from V*te shimau* in that Vpast expresses the completion of an action in the past, while V*te shimau* expresses completion regardless of the time of completion. Thus, [1a] is grammatical, but [1b] is not.

[1] a. ここにおいておくとジムが**食べてしまう**よ。

*Koko ni oite oku to Jimu ga **tabete shimau** yo.*

(If you leave it here, Jim will eat it (up).)

b. *ここにおいておくとジムが**食べた**よ。

Koko ni oite oku to Jimu ga **tabeta yo.*

(If you leave it here, Jim will eat it up.)

II. V*masu owaru* also means 'finish doing ~'. The difference between V*masu owaru* and V*te shimau* is that V*masu owaru* indicates the action of finishing something, while V*te shimau* indicates the completed state of the action. Thus, these two expressions correspond to the English expressions *finish doing* and *have done* in that V*masu owaru* can occur with a specific time phrase, but V*te shimau* cannot.

[2] a. きのうその本を読み終わった / *読んでしまった。

*Kinō sono hon o **yomiowatta** / ***yonde shimatta**.*

(I finished reading / *have read the book yesterday.)

b. けさ九時にやっとレポートを書き終わった / *書いてしまった。

*Kesa kuji ni yatto repōto o **kakiowatta** / ***kaite shimatta**.*

S

(I finally finished writing / *have finally written the report at nine o'clock this morning.)

It is also noted that *shimau* can be used with noncontrollable verbs like *wasureru* 'forget', while *owaru* cannot, as in [3].

[3] a. 僕はナンシーの住所を忘れてしまった。
Boku wa Nanshī no jūsho o wasurete shimatta.
(I've forgotten Nancy's address.)

b. *僕はナンシーの住所を忘れ終わった。
**Boku wa Nanshī no jūsho o wasureowatta.*
(*I finished forgetting Nancy's address.)

shiru 知る　　*v. (Gr. 1)*

S.o. gets information from some outside source.

get to know
【REL. *wakaru*】

◆ **Key Sentences**

A:		
Direct Object		
日本 の こと *Nihon no koto*	を *o*	知って います か。 *shitte imasu ka.*
(Do you know about Japan?)		

B:
はい，知って います。／ いいえ，知りません。 *Hai, shitte imasu. / Īe, shirimasen.*
(Yes, I do. / No, I don't.)

Examples

(a) 木下さんを知っていますか。

   Kinoshita-san o shitte imasu ka.

   (Do you know Mr. Kinoshita?)

(b) 山口さんの電話番号を知っていますか。

   Yamaguchi-san no denwabangō o shitte imasu ka.

   (Do you know Mr. Yamaguchi's telephone number?)

(c) A : 中国語を知っていますか。

   　　Chūgokugo o shitte imasu ka.

   　　(Do you know Chinese?)

   B : いいえ，知りません。

   　　Īe, shirimasen.

   　　(No, I don't.)

(d) 私は上田さんがアメリカへ行ったことを知らなかった。

   Watashi wa Ueda-san ga Amerika e itta koto o shiranakatta.

   (I didn't know that Mr. Ueda had gone to America.)

Notes

1. *Shiru*, a nonstative verb, takes the V*te iru* form when it means the stative 'know'. (⇨ ***iru***[2])

2. When answering in the negative to the question X *o shitte imasu ka* 'Do you know X?', the negative nonstative form *shiranai | shirimasen* is used instead of *shitte inai | shitte imasen*, as in KS(B) and Ex. (c).

S

sōda[1] そうだ　　*aux.*

an auxiliary which indicates that the information expressed by the preceding sentence is what the speaker heard	I hear that ~ ; I heard that ~ ; People say that ~ 【REL. *sōda*[2]; ***yōda*** (*darō*; *rashii*)】

♦**Key Sentence**

Sentence (informal)	
山川さん　は フランス語 を　勉強して　いる *Yamakawa-san wa furansugo o **benkyōshite iru***	そうだ / そうです。 *sōda / sōdesu.*
(I heard that Mr. Yamakawa is studying French.)	

Formation

(i) {V / Adj (*i*)} inf　そうだ
　　　　　　　　　sōda

　{話す　 / 話した}　そうだ　　(I heard that s.o. (will) talk / talked.)
　{*hanasu* / *hanashita*} *sōda*

　{高い / 高かった} そうだ　　(I heard that s.t. is / was expensive.)
　{*takai* / *takakatta*} *sōda*

(ii) {Adj (*na*) stem / N}　{だ / だった} そうだ
　　　　　　　　　　　{*da* / *datta*}　*sōda*

　{静かだ　 /静かだった}　そうだ　(I heard that s.t. is / was quiet.)
　{*shizuka*da / *shizuka*datta} *sōda*

　{先生　 だ / 先生　 だった} そうだ　(I heard that s.o. is / was a teacher.)
　{*sensei da* / *sensei datta*}　*sōda*

Examples

(a) 清水さんはお酒を飲まないそうです。
　Shimizu-san wa o-sake o nomanai sōdesu.
　(I heard Mr. Shimizu doesn't drink any alcohol.)

(b) 日本の肉はとても高いそうだ。
　Nihon no niku wa totemo takai sōda.
　(I hear that meat in Japan is very expensive.)

(c) 利子さんは英語がとても上手だそうです。
　Toshiko-san wa eigo ga totemo jōzuda sōdesu.
　(I heard that Toshiko speaks very good English.)

(d) キングさんは英語の先生だそうだ。
　Kingu-san wa eigo no sensei da sōda.
　(I heard that Mr. King is a teacher of English.)

Notes

1. Sinf *sōda* expresses hearsay. That is, this pattern is used when the speaker conveys information obtained from some information source without altering it. (⇨ *rashii*)

2. Information sources are expressed by N *ni yoru to* 'according to N'.

   ⑴ 新聞によるとフロリダに雪が降ったそうだ。
      Shinbun ni yoru to Furorida ni yuki ga futta sōda.
      (According to the newspaper, it snowed in Florida.)

[Related Expression]

The hearsay *sōda* (i.e., *sōda*¹) and the conjecture *sōda* (i.e., *sōda*²) are two different expressions. Compare their different connection patterns in [1].

(⇨ *sōda*²)

[1]

	*sōda*¹ (hearsay)	*sōda*² (conjecture)
V before *sōda*	Vinf *sōda* (Ex. 話す / 話した そうだ *hanasu / hanashita sōda*)	V*masu sōda* (Ex. 話し そうだ *hanashi sōda*)
Adj (*i*) before *sōda*	Adj (*i*) inf *sōda* (Ex. 高い / 高かった そうだ *takai / takakatta sōda*)	Adj (*i*) stem *sōda* (Ex. 高 そうだ *taka sōda*)
Adj (*na*) before *sōda*	Adj (*na*) stem {*da* / *datta*} *sōda* (Ex. 静かだ / 静かだった そうだ *shizukada / shizukadatta sōda*)	Adj (*na*) stem *sōda* (Ex. 静か そうだ *shizuka sōda*)
N before *sōda*	N {*da* / *datta*} *sōda* (Ex. 先生だ / 先生だった そうだ *sensei da / sensei datta sōda*)	✕
sōda before N	✕	{V*masu* / Adj (*i*) stem / Adj (*na*) stem} *sōna* N (Ex. 高そうな 本 *taka sōna hon*)

S

~sōda² ~そうだ　　*aux. adj. (na)*

an auxiliary adjective which indicates that what is expressed by the preceding sentence is the speaker's conjecture concerning an event in the future or the present state of someone or something, based on what the speaker sees or feels

look; look like; appear; seem; feel like

【REL. *sōda*¹; *yōda* (*darō*; *rashii*)】

♦ **Key Sentences**

(A)

Subject		Vmasu	
雨 *Ame*	が *ga*	降り ***furi***	そうだ／そうです。 *sōda / sōdesu.*
(It looks like it will rain.)			

(B)

Topic (subject)		Adj (*i* / *na*) stem	
あの　車 *Ano kuruma*	は *wa*	高 ***taka***	そうだ／そうです。 *sōda / sōdesu.*
(That car looks expensive.)			

Formation

(i) Vmasu そうだ
　　　　　sōda

　話し　そうだ　　(It looks like s.o. will talk.)
　hanashi sōda

　食べ そうだ　　(It looks like s.o. will eat.)
　tabe sōda

(ii) Adj (*i* / *na*) stem そうだ
　　　　　　　　　sōda

　高 そうだ　　(S.t. looks expensive.)
　taka sōda

静か　そうだ　　(S.t. looks quiet.)
shizuka sōda

(a) この家は強い風が吹いたらたおれそうだ。
Kono ie wa tsuyoi kaze ga fuitara taore sōda.
(It looks like this house will fall down when there's a strong wind (lit. a strong wind blows).)

(b) あのステーキはおいしそうだった。
Ano sutēki wa oishisōdatta.
(That steak looked delicious.)

(c) このあたりは静かそうだ。
Kono atari wa shizuka sōda.
(This neighborhood looks quiet.)

1. {V*masu* / Adj (*i* / *na*) stem} *sōda* expresses the speaker's conjecture based on visual information. Thus, this expression can be used only when the speaker directly observes something. The speaker's conjecture concerns an event which might take place in the future or the present state of someone or something. In other words, *sōda*² cannot be used to express the speaker's conjecture concerning a past event or state.

(⇒ *rashii*; *yōda*)

2. The adjective *ii* 'good' and the negative *nai* 'not exist / not' change to *yosa* and *nasa*, respectively, before *sōda*². Examples:

   (1) このアパートは**よさ**そうだ。
   *Kono apāto wa **yosa** sōda.*
   (This apartment looks good.)

   (2) 問題は**なさ**そうだ。
   *Mondai wa **nasa** sōda.*
   (It looks like there is no problem.)

   (3) 村山さんの家はあまり新しく**なさ**そうだ。
   *Murayama-san no ie wa amari atarashiku**nasa** sōda.*
   (Mr. Murayama's house doesn't look so new.)

3. N or N + Copula cannot precede *sōda*², as seen in (4a) and (4b), but N + Copula neg·nonpast can, as seen in (4c).

S

⑷　a.　*加藤さんは学生 ∅ そうだ。

　　　　*Katō-san wa gakusei ∅ sōda.

　　　　(Mr. Kato looks like a student.)

　　b.　*加藤さんは学生だそうだ。

　　　　*Katō-san wa gakusei **da** sōda.

　　　　(Mr. Kato looks like a student.)

　　c.　加藤さんは学生じゃなさそうだ。

　　　　Katō-san wa gakusei **janasa** sōda.

　　　　(Mr. Kato doesn't look like a student.)

To express the intended meaning in (4a) and (4b) *rashii* is used.　(⇨ **rashii**)　(4b) is grammatical if *sōda* means hearsay.　　　(⇨ **sōda**¹)

4. In this construction, the negative forms of verbs usually don't precede *sōda*². Instead, V*masu sō ni / mo nai* is used.　Examples :

⑸　クリスは車を売りそう に / も ない。

　　Kurisu wa kuruma o uri **sō** **ni** / **mo** **nai**.

　　(Chris doesn't seem to sell his car.)

⑹　この問題は学生には出来そう に / も ない。

　　Kono mondai wa gakusei ni wa deki **sō** **ni** / **mo** **nai**.

　　(It doesn't seem that the students can solve this problem.)

5. *Sōda* is also used to express the speaker's conjecture concerning his own non-volitional future actions based on what he feels.

⑺　僕はこのケーキを残しそうだ。

　　Boku wa kono kēki o nokoshi **sōda**.

　　(I'm afraid I can't eat all this cake.)

⑻　私はとても疲れていてたおれそうだ。

　　Watashi wa totemo tsukarete ite taore **sōda**.

　　(I'm so tired that I feel weak (lit. like I'm falling down).)

6. *Sōda* is a *na*-type adjective; the prenominal form is *sōna*. Examples :

⑼　高そうな車

　　taka **sōna** kuruma

　　(a car which looks expensive (=an expensive-looking car))

⑽　雨が降りそうな空

　　ame ga furi **sōna** sora

　　(lit. the sky which looks like it will bring rain)

sore de それで   *conj.*

> a conjunction to indicate that what is stated in the preceding sentence is the reason or cause for what is stated in the following sentence

and; because of that; that is why; therefore; so

【REL. *da kara*; *node*】

♦**Key Sentence**

Sentence₁	Sentence₂	
きのう は かぜ を ひきました。 *Kinō wa kaze o hikimashita.*	それ で *Sore de*	学校 を 休んだ ん です。 *gakkō o yasunda n desu.*
(I had a cold yesterday. That's why I took a day off from school.)		

Examples

(a) ちょっと大阪で用事がありました。それできのういなかったんです。
Chotto Ōsaka de yōji ga arimashita. Sore de kinō inakatta n desu.
(I had some business in Osaka. That's why I wasn't here yesterday.)

(b) A : きのうはちょっと大阪で用事がありました。
Kinō wa chotto Ōsaka de yōji ga arimashita.
(Yesterday I had to run an errand in Osaka.)

　　B : ああ，それでいらっしゃらなかったんですね。
Ā, sore de irassharanakatta n desu ne.
(Oh, that's why you weren't here.)

(c) A : きのう小川君とピンポンの試合をしたんだ。
Kinō Ogawa-kun to pinpon no shiai o shita n da.
(Yesterday I played pingpong with Mr. Ogawa.)

　　B : それで，先週新しいラケットを買ったんですね。
Sore de, senshū atarashii raketto o katta n desu ne.
(That's why he bought a new paddle last week.)

[Related Expressions]

I. "S₁. *Sore de* S₂" can be rephrased using *node* if *sore de* means cause or reason. Note, however, that the *node* construction is a single sentence. (⇨ ***node***) Example:

S

[1] ちょっと大阪で用事があった**ので**きのういなかったんです。

Chotto Ōsaka de yōji ga atta **node** kinō inakatta n desu.

(Because I had an errand to run in Osaka, I wasn't here yesterday.)

The difference is that *sore de* combines two sentences much more loosely than *node*.

II. "S₁. *Sore de* S₂" can be rephrased using *da* / *desu kara*, if S₁ indicates a reason or a cause for S₂.

[2] ちょっと大阪で用事がありました。だからきのういなかったんです。

Chotto Ōsaka de yōji ga arimashita. **Da kara** kinō inakatta n desu.

(I had an errand to run in Osaka.   So, I wasn't here yesterday.)

The difference between *sore de* and *da kara* is similar to the difference between *node* and *kara*.   (⇨ **kara**[3]; **node**)   Observe the following sentence.

[3] 今日は忙しいです。だから / *それであした来てください。

Kyō wa isogashii desu.   **Da kara** / ***Sore de** ashita kite kudasai.

(I'm busy today.   So, please come tomorrow.)

---

sore de wa それでは   *conj.*

If that is the case,	if so; then; well then
	[REL. **sore nara**]

◆**Key Sentences**

A:
この オレンジ は 甘くない です。 *Kono orenji   wa amakunai desu.*
(This orange is not sweet.)

B:	
それ で は *Sore de wa*	これ は どう (です か)。 *kore wa dō (desu ka).*
(How about this one, then?)	

Examples

(a) A : 僕は魚も肉も嫌いです。
   Boku wa sakana mo niku mo kiraidesu.
   (I hate both fish and meat.)

   B : それでは何を食べるんですか。
   Sore de wa nani o taberu n desu ka.
   (Then, what do you eat?)

(b) A : 今日の午後テニスをしませんか。
   Kyō no gogo tenisu o shimasen ka.
   (Wouldn't you like to play tennis this afternoon?)

   B : 今日の午後はちょっと都合が悪いんですが。
   Kyō no gogo wa chotto tsugō ga warui n desu ga.
   (This afternoon is not convenient for me, but . . .)

   A : それではあしたの午後はどうですか。
   Sore de wa ashita no gogo wa dō desu ka.
   (Then, how about tomorrow afternoon?)

(c) それでは二十分ぐらい休みましょう。
   Sore de wa nijuppun gurai yasumimashō.
   (Well then, let's take a break for about twenty minutes.)

(d) それではまた来週の金曜日に来ます。
   Sore de wa mata raishū no kin'yōbi ni kimasu.
   (Well then, I'll come again next Friday.)

Notes

1. *Sore de wa* is contracted into *sore ja* or *sore jā* in informal speech.

2. *Sore de wa* is often shortened to *de wa*, which is further contracted to *jā* or *ja*.

3. *Sore de wa* is used in sentence-initial position, and *sore* 'that' refers to that which is stated in the preceding sentence, as in Exs. (a) and (b), or to the preceding context, as in Exs. (c) and (d). In Exs. (c) and (d) the speaker uses *sore de wa* based on some nonverbal shared knowledge. The shared knowledge for (c) and (d) could be 'the fact of having worked long enough' and 'the fact of having finished today's discussion and an agreement for meeting every Friday', respectively.

S

sore kara それから　　*conj.*

a conjunction that indicates (1) tem-
porally contiguous actions or states,
or (2) a cumulative listing of objects,
actions or states

after that; and then; in addition
to that

【REL. *kara*[2]; *shi*; *soshite*】

◆Key Sentences

(A)

		V*te*		
きのう は 二時間 ぐらい　友達　と *Kinō wa nijikan gurai tomodachi to*		**飲んで** ***nonde***	それ から *sore kara*	うち に 帰った / *uchi ni kaetta /* 帰りました。 *kaerimashita.*

(Yesterday I drank with my friend for about two hours and then went home.)

(B)

Sentence₁	Sentence₂	
きのう は 二時間 ぐらい　友達　と 飲んだ。 *Kinō wa nijikan gurai tomodachi to nonda.*	それ から *Sore kara*	本屋 に 寄って *hon-ya ni yotte* うち に 帰った。 *uchi ni kaetta.*

(Yesterday I drank with my friend for about two hours.　Then I dropped
by a bookstore and went home.)

S

Formation

(i) {V*te* / V*masu*} それ から
　　　　　　　　sore kara

　　{話して　／ 話し}，それ から　　(s.o. talks, and then ~)
　　{*hanashite* / *hanashi*}, *sore kara*

　　{食べて / 食べ}，それ から　　(s.o. eats, and then ~)
　　{*tabete* / *tabe*}, *sore kara*

(ii) Adj (*i*) stem　く(て)，それ から
　　　　　　　　ku(te), sore kara

高く(て), それ から　　(s.t. is not only expensive but ~)
taka ku(te), sore kara

(iii) Adj (*na*) stem　で, それ から
　　　　　　　　　　de, sore kara

静かで, それ から　　(s.t. is not only quiet but ~)
shizuka de, sore kara

(iv) N_1 (と) N_2 (と) それ から N_3
　　　(*to*)　　(*to*)　*sore kara*

英語 (と) 日本語 (と), それ から　中国語　　(English, Japanese and
eigo (to) nihongo (to), sore kara chūgokugo　Chinese)

Examples

(a) 十時まで宿題をしました。それから映画に行きました。
　　Jūji made shukudai o shimashita. Sore kara eiga ni ikimashita.
　　(I did my home work until 10 o'clock. And then, I went to the movie.)

(b) きのうは朝銀座に行って, それから映画を見に行った。
　　Kinō wa asa Ginza ni itte, sore kara eiga o mi ni itta.
　　(Yesterday morning I went to Ginza and then went to see a movie.)

(c) レストランではステーキとサラダとそれからチーズケーキを食べました。
　　Resutoran de wa sutēki to sarada to sore kara chīzukēki o tabemashita.
　　(At the restaurant I ate steak, salad, and cheesecake.)

(d) 湖の色は初めは青く, それから緑になりました。
　　Mizuumi no iro wa hajime wa aoku, sore kara midori ni narimashita.
　　(The color of the lake was blue in the beginning and then turned green.)

(e) 月曜, 火曜, それから木曜もとても忙しいです。
　　Getsuyō, kayō, sore kara mokuyō mo totemo isogashiidesu.
　　(I am very busy on Monday, Tuesday, and Thursday, too.)

Notes

1. *Sore kara* can be used to indicate something which the speaker almost forgot to mention, as in (1) below:

   (1) ジョンとメリーと, ああそうだ, それからボブが来たよ。
   　　Jon to Meri to, ā sō da, sore kara Bobu ga kita yo.
   　　(John and Mary and, oh yeah, Bob came too.)

2. *Sore kara* 'and then' is often used by the hearer to elicit more information from the speaker. Example:

S

(2)　A：今日はどこへ行きましたか。

　　　　Kyō wa doko e ikimashita ka.

　　　　(Where did you go today?)

　　B：まず東京タワーに上りました。

　　　　Mazu Tōkyō tawā ni noborimashita.

　　　　(First we went up Tokyo Tower.)

　　A：それから？

　　　　Sore kara?

　　　　(And then?)

　　B：美術館に行きました。

　　　　Bijutsukan ni ikimashita.

　　　　(I went to the art museum.)

　　A：それから？

　　　　Sore kara?

　　　　(And then?)

　　B：デパートに行って，食堂で昼ご飯を食べました。

　　　　Depāto ni itte, shokudō de hirugohan o tabemashita.

　　　　(I went to a department store and ate my lunch at the cafeteria.)

3. V*te*, V*masu*, Adj (*i*) stem *ku* (*te*) and Adj (*na*) stem *de* do not have their own tense.　The tense is identical with that of the main verb.

【Related Expressions】

I.　V*te kara* and V*te, sore kara* are similar but not identical in meaning. V*te kara* expresses chronological sequence; V*te, sore kara* expresses chronological sequence and / or enumeration.　For example, [1a] expresses purely chronological order and [1b], chronological order and enumeration.

(⇨ ***kara***[2])

[1]　a.　山中さんは三時間ゴルフをしてから一時間泳いだ。

　　　　*Yamanaka-san wa sanjikan gorufu o shi**te kara** ichijikan oyoida.*

　　　　(Mr. Yamanaka swam for one hour after having played golf for three hours.)

　　　b.　山中さんは三時間ゴルフをして，それから一時間泳いだ。

　　　　*Yamanaka-san wa sanjikan gorufu o shi**te, sore kara** ichijikan oyoida.*

　　　　(Mr. Yamanaka played golf for three hours, and, on top of that, he swam for an hour.)

II. "V*te* / V*masu, sore kara*", "Adj (*i*) stem *kute, sore kara*" and "Adj (*na*) stem *de, sore kara*" are very similar to *shi* when they express enumeration.

[2] a. 今日はテニスをして，**それから**映画も見た。
   *Kyō wa tenisu o shite, **sore kara** eiga mo mita.*
   (Today I played tennis, and I saw a movie, too.)

 b. 今日はテニスもしたし，映画も見た。
   *Kyō wa tenisu mo shita **shi**, eiga mo mita.*
   (Today I played tennis, and what's more, saw a movie.)

III. *Sō shite* / *soshite* and *sore kara* are interchangeable when two events do not occurs simultaneously. Compare the following:

[3] a. 音楽を聞いて，**そうして**勉強するのが好きだ。
   *Ongaku o kiite, **sō shite** benkyōsuru no ga sukida.*
   (I like to listen to music while studying. / I like to listen to music first and then study.)

 b. 音楽を聞いて，**それから**勉強するのが好きだ。
   *Ongaku o kiite, **sore kara** benkyōsuru no ga sukida.*
   (I like to listen to music first and then study.)

sore nara それなら   *conj.*

If that is the case,	then; in that case 【REL. *sore de wa*】

♦**Key Sentence**

A:	B:	
頭　が　痛いん　です。 *Atama ga itai n desu.*	それ なら *Sore nara*	すぐ　寝なさい。 *sugu nenasai.*
(I have a headache.)	(In that case, go to sleep right away.)	

Examples

(a) A : 映画を見に行きませんか。
   Eiga o mi ni ikimasen ka.
   (Wouldn't you like to go see a movie?)

B : あした試験があるんです。
　　Ashita shiken ga aru n desu.
　　(I have an exam tomorrow.)

A : それなら，あさってはどうですか。
　　Sore nara, asatte wa dō desu ka.
　　(Then, how about the day after tomorrow?)

(b)　A : 日本にはどのぐらいいましたか。
　　Nihon ni wa dono gurai imashita ka.
　　(How long did you stay in Japan?)

B : 三年です。
　　Sannen desu.
　　(Three years.)

A : それなら，日本のことはよく知っているでしょうね。
　　Sore nara, Nihon no koto wa yoku shitte iru deshō ne.
　　(Then, you must know a lot about Japan.)

Notes

1. *Sore* 'that' refers to a previously-spoken sentence.　In KS, for example, *sore* refers to A's entire sentence.　B's sentence can be rephrased as (1):

    (1) 頭が痛いん**なら**すぐ寝なさい。
    　　*Atama ga itai n **nara** sugu nenasai.*
    　　(If you have a headache, go to sleep right away.)

    Nara in (1) expresses the speaker's supposition concerning the truth of A's statement.　　　　　　　　　　　　　　　　　　　　(⇨ ***nara***)

2. *Sore nara* has a more formal form, *sore naraba*, and a more informal one, *sonnara*.

3. For restrictions imposed on the sentence that follows *sore nara*, see the notes in *nara*.

[Related Expression]

Although *sore nara* and *sore de wa* are very similar, they differ in that the former is dependent on verbal context while the latter is not.　Thus, towards the end of one's visit with his superior or on an occasion when something is offered, *sore de wa* is used, as in [1a, b].

[1]　a.　**それでは / *それなら失礼します。**
　　　　Sore de wa* / *Sore nara* shitsureishimasu.**
　　　　(Lit. Then I must be going now.)

b. それでは / *それなら遠慮なくいただきます。

Sore de wa / ****Sore nara*** *enryo naku itadakimasu.*

(Lit. Then, I'll take it (without hesitation).)

soretomo それとも   *conj.*

| a coordinate conjunction which connects two alternatives expressed by sentences | or; either ~ or ~ 【REL. *ka*[1]】 |

♦ **Key Sentences**

(A)

Sentence₁ (informal)		
この 本 が まちがって いる *Kono hon ga machigatte iru*	か *ka*	(それとも) *(soretomo)*

Sentence₂ (informal)		
私 が まちがって いる *watashi ga machigatte iru*	か *ka*	どちらか だ / です。 *dochiraka da / desu.*

| (It's either that this book is wrong or that I am wrong.) |

(B)

Question₁		Question₂
刺身 を 食べます か。 *Sashimi o tabemasu ka.*	それとも *Soretomo*	すきやき に します か。 *sukiyaki ni shimasu ka.*

| (Will you have *sashimi*, or will you have *sukiyaki*?) |

Examples

(a) 僕が来るか(それとも)村井さんが来るかどちらかです。

Boku ga kuru ka (soretomo) Murai-san ga kuru ka dochiraka desu.

(Either I will come or Mr. Murai will come.)

(b) あの人は先生ですか。それとも医者ですか。
    Ano hito wa sensei desu ka. Soretomo isha desu ka.
    (Is he a teacher or a doctor?)

Notes

1. *Soretomo* combines statements (KS(A)) or questions (KS(B)). In KS(A), *soretomo* can be omitted.

2. In KS(B), if the context is clear, abbreviated questions may occur in informal speech. For example, (1) may be used for KS(B).

   (1) 刺身？ それとも, すきやき？
       *Sashimi? **Soretomo**, sukiyaki?*
       (*Sashimi* or *sukiyaki*?)

---

soshite そして　　*conj.*

| a coordinate conjunction that connects two sentences | and; and then 【REL. ***sore kara***】 |

♦**Key Sentence**

Sentence₁
今日 は　東京　に　行った / 行きました。 *Kyō wa Tōkyō ni　itta / ikimashita.*
(I went to Tokyo today.

Sentence₂	
そして *Soshite*	友達　　に　会った / 会いました。 *tomodachi ni　　atta / aimashita.*
And I met my friend there.)	

Examples

(a) きのうは朝ゴルフをしました。そして午後はテニスをしました。
Kinō wa asa gorufu o shimashita. Soshite gogo wa tenisu o shimashita.
(Yesterday I played golf in the morning. And I played tennis in the afternoon.)

(b) この映画はつまらない。そして長すぎる。
Kono eiga wa tsumaranai. Soshite nagasugiru.
(This movie is uninteresting. And it's too long.)

(c) この花はきれいです。そして安いです。
Kono hana wa kireidesu. Soshite yasuidesu.
(This flower is pretty. And it is inexpensive.)

Notes

1. *Soshite* and *sō shite* are normally interchangeable, but if *sō shite* is used in the original sense of 'by doing so', it cannot be replaced by *soshite*.

   (1) そうして / *そして直すんですか。
   Sō shite / *Soshite* *naosu n desu ka.*
   (Lit. Do you fix it by doing so? (= Oh, that's how you fix it?))

2. The two sentences in this construction can be combined using the *te*-form of verbs or adjectives, as in (2). This version is encountered less frequently than the above version and sounds a little redundant, because the *te*-form alone can mean ' ~ and '.

   (2) 今日は東京に行って，そうして / そして友達に会いました。
   Kyō wa Tōkyō ni itte, sō shite / soshite tomodachi ni aimashita.
   (I went to Tokyo today, and I met my friend there.)

S

sugiru すぎる   *aux. v. (Gr. 2)*

S.o. / s.t. does s.t. excessively or is in a state excessively.	too; do s.t. too much / often; over-

♦**Key Sentences**

(A)

Topic (subject)			Vmasu	
ウィルソンさん *Uiruson-san*	は *wa*	肉を *niku o*	食べ ***tabe***	すぎる / すぎます。 *sugiru / sugimasu.*
(Mr. Wilson eats too much meat.)				

(B)

Topic (subject)		Noun		Adj (*i* / *na*) stem	
この アパート *Kono apāto*	は *wa*	私達 *watashitachi*	には *ni wa*	高 ***taka***	すぎる / すぎます。 *sugiru / sugimasu.*
(This apartment is too expensive for us.)					

Formation

(i) Vmasu すぎる
　　　　 sugiru

　話し　すぎる　(talk too much)
　hanashi sugiru

　食べ　すぎる　(eat too much)
　tabe sugiru

(ii) Adj (*i* / *na*) stem すぎる
　　　　　　　　 sugiru

　高　すぎる　(too expensive)
　taka sugiru

　静か　すぎる　(too quiet)
　shizuka sugiru

Examples

(a) 私は今朝寝すぎて学校におくれた。
　　Watashi wa kesa ne sugite gakkō ni okureta.
　　(I overslept this morning and was late for school.)

(b) この机は私の部屋には大きすぎる。

Kono tsukue wa watashi no heya ni wa ōki sugiru.

(This desk is too big for my room.)

(c) 田中先生の授業は大変すぎるのでやめました。

Tanaka-sensei no jugyō wa taihen sugiru node yamemashita.

(I dropped Prof. Tanaka's class because it was too demanding.)

(d) 森さんは太りすぎている。

Mori-san wa futori sugite iru.

(Mr. Mori is too fat.)

Notes

1. *Sugiru*, which as a main verb means 'pass; go beyond some limit', is used as an auxiliary verb with V*masu* or Adj (*i* / *na*) stem and means 'do s.t. excessively' or 'be ~ excessively'.

2. The stem of *ii* 'good' changes to *yo* before *sugiru*, as in (1).

   (1) このアパートはトムにはよすぎる。

   *Kono apāto wa Tomu ni wa **yo** sugiru.*

   (This apartment is too good for Tom.)

3. The negative *nai* 'not exist / not' changes to *nasa* before *sugiru*.

   (2) ベンは力がなさすぎる。

   *Ben wa chikara ga **nasa** sugiru.*

   (Lit. Ben has too little power. (=Ben is too weak.))

   (3) 友子は野菜を食べなさすぎる。

   *Tomoko wa yasai o tabe**nasa** sugiru.*

   (Tomoko eats too few vegetables.)

4. *For* in "be too ~ for someone / something" is expressed by *ni wa*, as in KS(B) and Ex. (b).

5. *Sugiru* is a Gr. 2 verb; the negative form is *suginai*, the polite form is *sugimasu* and the *te*-form is *sugite*.

S

sukida すきだ   *adj. (na)*

~~~~~~
S.t. or s.o. is what s.o. likes.
~~~~~~

like; be fond of
(ANT. *kiraida*)

◆**Key Sentence**

Topic (experiencer)		Liked Object		
私	は	ステーキ	が	好きだ / 好きです。
Watashi	*wa*	*sutēki*	*ga*	*sukida / sukidesu.*
(I like steak.)				

Examples

(a) 僕は野球が好きだ。
Boku wa yakyū ga sukida.
(I like baseball.)

(b) ジョンソンさんはジャズが大好きです。
Jonson-san wa jazu ga dai-sukidesu.
(Mr. Johnson loves jazz.)

Notes

1. *Sukida* is a *na*-type adjective which requires the "*wa ~ ga* construction". That is, the experiencer (i.e., the person who likes someone or something) is marked by *wa* and the liked object by *ga*. (⇨ *~ wa ~ ga*) Note that the liked object is marked by *ga* not by *o*.

2. In subordinate clauses, the experiencer is also marked by *ga*, as in (1) and (2).

    (1) 私がステーキが好きなことはみんな知っている。
    *Watashi **ga** sutēki ga skina koto wa minna shitte iru.*
    (Everybody knows that I like steak.)

    (2) ジョンが好きなスポーツは野球です。
    *Jon **ga** sukina supōtsu wa yakyū desu.*
    (Lit. The sport John likes is baseball. (＝John's favorite sport is baseball.))

3. "Like a lot" is expressed by *dai-sukida*, as in Ex. (b).

sukunai 少ない   *adj.* (*i*)

> small in number or quantity

few; a small number of; little; a small quantity of ~
【REL. *wazuka*】
(ANT. *ōi*)

♦**Key Sentence**

Topic (location)		Subject		
この　　町 *Kono machi*	は *wa*	いい　レストラン *ii resutoran*	が *ga*	少ない / 少ないです。 *sukunai / sukunaidesu.*

(Lit. In this town good restaurants are few. (=There aren't many good restaurants in this town.))

Examples

(a) この大学は女子学生が少ないです。
Kono daigaku wa joshigakusei ga sukunaidesu.
(The number of female students at this college is small.)

(b) 日本は犯罪が少ない。
Nihon wa hanzai ga sukunai.
(There are few crimes in Japan.)

(c) 日本語が書ける外国人は大変少ない。
Nihongo ga kakeru gaikokujin wa taihen sukunai.
(Lit. Foreigners who can write Japanese are very few. (=Very few foreigners can write Japanese.))

Notes

1. *Sukunai* cannot be used before a noun, except in a relative clause where *sukunai* is the predicate of the subject of the relative clause.

   (1) *この大学は**少ない**女子学生がいます。
       Kono daigaku wa **sukunai joshigakusei ga imasu.*
       (Cp. Ex. (a))

   (2) 木が**少ない**町に住みたくありません。
       *Ki ga **sukunai** machi ni sumitaku arimasen.*
       (I don't want to live in a town where there are few trees.)

2. The distinction between English 'few' vs. 'a few' can be expressed by *sukunai* and *sukoshi wa* as in (3) below.

S

(3) a. 日本語が分かるアメリカ人は**少ない**。

Nihongo ga wakaru Amerikajin wa **sukunai**.

(Lit. Americans who can understand Japanese are few. (=Few Americans can understand Japanese.))

b. 日本語が分かるアメリカ人は**少しはいる**。

Nihongo ga wakaru Amerikajin wa **sukoshi wa** iru.

(There are a few Americans who can understand Japanese.)

【Related Expression】

Sukunai differs from a similar word *wazuka(da)* in both meaning and use. The latter means 'insignificant number or amount of ~' and is used before a noun or in a predicate position or as an adverb. Only in [1a] below can *wazukada* be replaced by *sukunai*.

[1] a. 私が持っているお金は**わずかだ**。

Watashi ga motte iru o-kane wa **wazukada**.

(The money I possess is very little.)

b. **わずかな**お金で暮らしている。

Wazukana o-kane de kurashite iru.

(He is living with a paltry sum of money.)

c. あの人は**わずか**のことですぐおこる。

Ano hito wa **wazuka** no koto de sugu okoru.

(He gets angry easily over a trifling matter.)

d. その時僕は**わずか(に)**六つでした。

Sono toki boku wa **wazuka(ni)** muttsu deshita.

(At that time I was merely six years old.)

S

suru[1] する   *v. (Irr.)*

S.o. / s.t. causes a state or action to take place.

do; make; play; play the role of ~ ; wear

【REL. *naru* ; *yaru***】**

♦**Key Sentences**

(A)

Topic (subject)		Direct Object		
中山さん *Nakayama-san*	は *wa*	テニス *tenisu*	を *o*	する / します。 *suru / shimasu.*
(Mr. Nakayama plays tennis.)				

(B)

Topic (subject)		Direct Object		
リーズさん *Rizu-san*	は *wa*	英語 の 先生 *eigo no sensei*	を *o*	して いる / います。 *shite iru / imasu.*
(Mr. Leeds is (lit. doing) an English teacher.)				

(C)

Topic (subject)		Direct Object		Adj (*i*) stem		
先生 *Sensei*	は *wa*	テスト *tesuto*	を *o*	やさし *yasashi*	く *ku*	した / しました。 *shita / shimashita.*
(The teacher made his test easy.)						

(D)

Topic (subject)		Direct Object		Noun		
木口 *Kiguchi*	は *wa*	息子 *musuko*	を *o*	医者 *isha*	に *ni*	した / しました。 *shita / shimashita.*
(Kiguchi caused his son to become a physician.)						

S

(E)

Topic (subject)		Direct Object		Sino-Japanese Compound	
私 *Watashi*	は *wa*	中国語 *chūgokugo*	を *o*	勉強 *benkyō*	して いる / います。 *shite iru / imasu.*
(I am studying Chinese.)					

(F)

Topic (subject)		Direct Object		
京子	は	きれいな　スカーフ	を	して　いる／います。
Kyōko	*wa*	*kireina　sukāfu*	*o*	*shite　iru／imasu.*
(Kyoko is wearing a beautiful scarf.)				

Examples

(a) 日本人はたいてい土曜日も仕事をする。
　　Nihonjin wa taitei doyōbi mo shigoto o suru.
　　(The Japanese usually work on Saturdays, too.)

(b) ビルはハムレットをするつもりだ。
　　Biru wa Hamuretto o suru tsumori da.
　　(Bill is going to play Hamlet.)

(c) 陽子は部屋をきれいにした。
　　Yōko wa heya o kireini shita.
　　(Lit. Yoko made her room clean.　(＝Yoko cleaned her room.))

(d) 僕はよく車を運転します。
　　Boku wa yoku kuruma o untenshimasu.
　　(I often drive a car.)

(e) 一男はアメリカ人を妻にした。
　　Kazuo wa amerikajin o tsuma ni shita.
　　(Lit. Kazuo made a wife of an American.　(＝Kazuo took an American wife.))

(f) いいネクタイをしているね。
　　Ii nekutai o shite iru ne.
　　(You're wearing a nice tie, aren't you?)

Notes

1. *Suru*[1] means 'to cause some state or action', and corresponds to English 'do' or 'make'.

2. KS(A) and Ex. (a) are cases in which the subject is *doing / playing s.t.* KS(B) as well as Ex. (b) are cases where the subject is *playing a social or dramatic role*. KSs(C) and (D) and Ex. (c) have causative meanings.

3. KS(C) and Ex. (c) require that either Adj (*i*) stem＋*ku* or Adj (*na*) stem＋*ni* (i.e., adverbial form of Adj (*i / na*)) be used before *suru*. KS(D) and

Ex. (e) use a Noun+*ni* in front of *suru*.

4. The Direct Objects of KS(F) and Ex. (f) are items that cover a small part of the human body such as *nekutai* '(neck)tie', *tebukuro* 'gloves' and *udedokei* 'wristwatch'. When used with such direct objects, *suru* means 'wear'.

5. The construction in KS(D) (i.e., N+*ni suru*) also has an idiomatic use, meaning 'decide on ~'.   (⇨ **ni suru**)

6. Sino-Japanese compounds+*suru* such as *benkyōsuru* 'study' and *unten-suru* 'drive' can be used as transitive verbs, as in KS(E) and Ex. (d). The Sino-Japanese compound itself can also be used as the direct object of *suru*. For example, compare KS(E) and Ex. (d) with (1) and (2), respectively.

> (1) 私は中国語の勉強をしている。
> *Watashi wa chūgokugo no benkyō o shite iru.*
> (Lit. I am doing the study of Chinese. (=I am studying Chinese.))

> (2) 僕はよく車の運転をします。
> *Boku wa yoku kuruma no unten o shimasu.*
> (Lit. I often do the driving of a car. (=I often drive a car.))

Note in Sentences (1) and (2) that the direct object in KS(E) and Ex. (d) is connected to the Sino-Japanese compound by the particle *no*, creating a noun phrase which is the direct object of *suru*.

7. In contemporary Japanese it is very common to use *suru* with loanwords. The majority of loanwords are from English verbs. Some typical examples follow:

ヒットする *hitto-suru*	(make a hit)	ノックする *nokku-suru*	(knock on the door)
ドライブする *doraibu-suru*	(drive a car)	キスする *kisu-suru*	(kiss)
タイプする *taipu-suru*	(type)	パスする *pasu-suru*	(pass an exam)

It is also common to use *suru* with sound symbolisms, especially pheno-mimes and psychomimes.

(⇨ Characteristics of Japanese Grammar, 8. Sound Symbolisms)

S

びくびくする (be in fear)	かっとする (flare up)
bikubiku-suru	*katto-suru*
ぼんやりする (be absent-minded)	はっとする (be taken aback)
bonyari-suru	*hatto-suru*
ぞっとする (shiver)	いらいらする (become irritated)
zotto-suru	*iraira-suru*

8. *Suru* basically means some causative change that is under human control, whereas *naru* 'become' basically means spontaneous change that is almost beyond human control. Since injury normally occurs due to human carelessness, *suru* is acceptable, but *naru* is unacceptable, as shown in (3) below. In contrast to injury, illness is assumed to occur regardless of human carefulness or carelessness, so it should not take *suru*. But in actuality it does. Illness can take *suru* when it is talked about as if it were something under human control, for example, cases of past illness (as in (4a)), apologies implying that one has caused illness due to carelessness on one's part (as in (4b)), and statements of one's medical history (as in (4c)). Otherwise, illness cannot take *suru*, as shown in (4d).

(3)　a.　病気 / けがをする。
　　　　Byōki / kega o suru.
　　　　(One becomes ill / sustains injury.)

　　　b.　病気 / *けがになる。
　　　　*Byōki / *kega ni naru*.
　　　　(One becomes ill.)

(4)　a.　若い頃はよく病気をした / ?になった。
　　　　Wakai koro wa yoku byōki o shita / ?ni natta.
　　　　(When I was young, I often became ill.)

　　　b.　いつも病気をして / ?になってすみません。
　　　　Itsumo byōki o shite / ?ni natte sumimasen.
　　　　(I'm sorry that I always become ill.)

　　　c.　一年に何回ぐらい病気をしますか / ?になりますか。
　　　　Ichinen ni nankai gurai byōki o shimasu ka / ?ni narimasu ka.
　　　　(About how many times do you become ill per year?)

　　　d.　きのう急に病気になりました / *をしました。
　　　　*Kinō kyūni byōki ni narimashita / *o shimashita*.
　　　　(I suddenly became ill yesterday.)

9. *Suru* can be used in the construction *o*+V*masu*+*suru*, a humble, polite form of verb. The subject of this humble verb must be the speaker or his in-group member.

   (5) 私がお読み / 書き / 持ちします。

        *Watashi ga **o** yomi / kaki / mochi **shimasu**.*

        (I will read / write / carry it (for you).)

A further degree of humbleness can be expressed by replacing *suru* with its humble version *itasu* / *itashimasu*.   (⇨ *o* ~ *suru*)

〔Related Expressions〕

I. *Naru* 'become' forms an intransitive-transitive pair with *suru*, although they are not phonetically related. (⇨ Appendix 3) Semantically, *naru* seems more passive, while *suru* seems more causative. Compare the following pairs of sentences:

  [1] a. 山田は停学になった。

         *Yamada wa teigaku ni **natta**.*

         (Lit. Yamada became suspension from school. (=Yamada got suspended from school.)

     b. 学校は山田を停学にした。

         *Gakkō wa Yamada o teigaku ni **shita**.*

         (Lit. The school made Yamada suspended from school. (=The school suspended Yamada.))

  [2] a. 山田は本を書くことになった。

         *Yamada wa hon o kaku koto ni **natta**.*

         (It's been decided that Yamada will write a book.)

     b. 山田は本を書くことにした。

         *Yamada wa hon o kaku koto ni **shita**.*

         (Yamada has decided to write a book.)

                  (⇨ ***koto ni naru***; ***koto ni suru***)

II. *Suru* can be replaced by its informal version *yaru* (Gr. 1 Verb) when it means 'do / play s.t.' as in KS(A) or 'play a dramatic / social role' as in KS(B). Also, if *suru* takes a Sino-Japanese compound as its direct object (as in *benkyō o suru* 'Lit. do a study of'), it can be replaced by *yaru*.

suru² する   *v. (Irr.)*

| S.o. or s.t. has some (semi-)perma- | have |
| nent attribute. | 【REL. ~ *wa* ~ *ga*】 |

♦ **Key Sentence**

Topic (subject, possessor)		Adjective	N (bodily part)		
洋子 *Yōko*	は *wa*	長い *nagai*	足 *ashi*	を *o*	して いる / います。 *shite iru / imasu.*
(Yoko has long legs.)					

Examples

(a) 一男は丈夫な体をしています。
    Kazuo wa jōbuna karada o shite imasu.
    (Kazuo has a strong body.)

(b) この机は丸い形をしている。
    Kono tsukue wa marui katachi o shite iru.
    (This table has a round shape.)

Notes

1. The sentence pattern is:

    Topic (subject)+Adj(*i* / *na*)+{Noun of Bodily Part / Noun of At-
    tribute}+*shite iru* / *imasu*.

   A bodily part or an attribute must be inalienably possessed by the subject. In other words, it must be such an essential part of the possessor
   (=subject) that he / it cannot exist without the part or the attribute.

2. In the main clause the verb *suru* always takes the *te iru* form, but in
   a relative clause *te iru* may be replaced by *ta* as in:

   (1) 長い足をしている / した洋子
       *Nagai ashi o **shite iru** / **shita** Yōko*
       (Yoko, who has long legs)

[Related Expression]

Sentences of this construction can be restated using the *wa-ga* construction
as follows:

N₁ *wa* Adj N₂ *o shite iru* → N₁ *wa* N₂ *ga* Adj.

Thus, the KS example can be rephrased as:

[1] 洋子は足が長い / 長いです。
   *Yōko **wa** ashi **ga** nagai / nagaidesu.*
   (Yoko has long legs.)

The only perceptible difference between KS and [1] is that the latter sentence is more analytical than the former. In other words, in KS *nagai ashi* ' long legs ' is one unit, but in [1] *ashi* ' legs ' is first presented as a single unit and is then further characterized as *nagai* ' long '.

---

suru³ する   *v. (Irr.)*

| S.t. is perceived by s.o.'s non-visual senses. | feel; smell; hear |

◆**Key Sentence**

Subject		
子供達　の　声 *Kodomotachi no koe*	が *ga*	した / しました。 *shita / shimashita.*
(I heard children's voices.)		

Examples

(a) この魚は変な味がしますね。
   Kono sakana wa henna aji ga shimasu ne.
   (This fish tastes funny, doesn't it?)

(b) このきれはざらざらしている。
   Kono kire wa zarazara shite iru.
   (This cloth feels rough.)

(c) この花はいいにおいがする。
   Kono hana wa ii nioi ga suru.
   (This flower smells good.)

S

(d) 私は寒気がします。
Watashi wa samuke ga shimasu.
(I feel a chill.)

Note

If s.t. is perceived visually, either the ~ *o shite iru* structure or the ~ *wa* ~ *ga* structure is used.   (⇨ *suru²*; ~ *wa* ~ *ga*)

(1) このりんごはきれいな色をしている。
Kono ringo wa kireina iro o shite iru.
(This apple has a pretty color.)

(2) このリンゴは色がきれいだ。
Kono ringo wa iro ga kireida.
(This apple has a pretty color.)

suru⁴ する   *v. (Irr.)*

| a verb that indicates how much s.t. costs or a duration of time | cost; lapse |

♦**Key Sentences**

(A)

Topic (subject)		Quantity	
この 時計 *Kono tokei*	は *wa*	十万円 *jūman'en*	する / します。 *suru / shimasu.*
(This watch costs 100,000 yen.)			

(B)

Subordinate Clause			Main Clause
あと *Ato*	一年 *ichinen*	したら *shitara*	大学 を 出る / 出ます。 *daigaku o deru / demasu.*
(In another year I'll graduate from college.)			

Examples

(a) A : それはどのぐらいしましたか。
    Sore wa dono gurai shimashita ka.
    (About how much did it cost?)

   B : 二十五万円ぐらいしました。
    Nijūgoman'en gurai shimashita.
    (It cost about 250,000 yen.)

(b) もう少しすれば主人が帰ってまいります。
    Mō sukoshi sureba shujin ga kaette mairimasu.
    (In a short time my husband will be here.)

Note

When *suru*[4] is used to mean 'lapse of time', it can only be used in a subordinate clause, as in KS(B) and Ex. (b). Therefore, the following sentence in which *suru*[4] is used in the main clause is ungrammatical.

(1) *三年しました。
    **Sannen shimashita.*
    Cp. 三年たちました。
    Sannen tachimashita.
    (Three years passed.)

S

suru to すると   *conj.*

a coordinate conjunction which connects two sentences (The second sentence either describes an event which takes place right after the event described in the first sentence or it expresses a logical guess related to the event in the first sentence.)

thereupon ~ ; then ~ ; and ~
【REL. *sore de wa*; *sō suru to*】

♦**Key Sentences**

(A)

Sentence₁		Sentence₂
ジョギング を 始めました。 *Jogingu o hajimemashita.*	する と *Suru to*	ご飯 が おいしく なりました。 *gohan ga oishiku narimashita.*
(I began jogging. Then, I began to have a good appetite.)		

(B)

A:
今日 は 月曜日 です よ。 *Kyō wa getsuyōbi desu yo.*
(Today is Monday, you know.)

B:
する と *Suru to* あの デパート は 休み です ね。 *ano depāto wa yasumi desu ne.*
(Then, that department store is closed, isn't it?)

Examples

(a) 私は自転車を買いました。すると弟も欲しがりました。
   Watashi wa jitensha o kaimashita.   Suru to otōto mo hoshigarimashita.
   (I bought a bike.   Then, my younger brother wanted one, too.)

(b) 頭が痛かったのでアスピリンを飲みました。すると痛みがすぐ止まりました。
   Atama ga itakatta node asupirin o nomimashita.   Suru to itami ga sugu tomarimashita.
   (I took an aspirin because I had a headache.   Then, the headache disappeared right away.)

(c) A：息子は今高校三年です。
     Musuko wa ima kōkō sannen desu.
     (My son is now a junior at high school.)

   B：すると，来年は大学受験ですね。
     Suru to, rainen wa daigakujuken desu ne.
     (Then, he is going to take a college entrance examination next year, isn't he?)

To of *suru to* is the conjunction *to*[4]. (⇨ ***to***[4]) Therefore, in KS(A), Sentence₂ normally expresses an event that is beyond the control of the speaker; that is why Sentence₂ cannot be a command, a request, or a suggestion.

[Related Expressions]

I. *Suru to* is the shortened form of *sō suru to*. These two constructions have identical meanings and can be used interchangeably. They are related to another expression *sore de wa* 'then', but unlike *sore de wa*, the second sentence in the *(sō) suru to* construction cannot be a command, request, suggestion, or something which can be controlled by the subject of the sentence. (⇨ ***sore de wa***) Thus,

    [1] A：今日は忙しいです。
          Kyō wa isogashiidesu.
          (I'm busy today.)

        B：それでは / *(そう)するとあした行きましょう。
          Sore de wa / *(***Sō***) ***suru to*** *ashita ikimashō.*
          (Then, let's go there tomorrow.)

    [2] A：(=same as [1] A)

        B：それでは / *(そう)するとあした来てください。
          Sore de wa / *(***Sō***) ***suru to*** *ashita kite kudasai.*
          (Then, please come tomorrow.)

    [3] A：あなたが来ないと困るんです。
          Anata ga konai to komaru n desu.
          (It will be difficult if you don't come.)

        B：それでは / *(そう)すると行きます。
          Sore de wa / *(***Sō***) ***suru to*** *ikimasu.*
          (Lit. Then, I'll go.)

S

II. *Sore de wa* 'then' can replace the *suru to* in KS(B) but not the *suru to* in KS(A), because *sore de wa* requires that the speakers of Sentence₁ and Sentence₂ be different.

-tachi 達　*suf.*

> a plural marker attached to personal pronouns or to human (proper) nouns

【REL. *-domo*; *-gata*; *-ra*】

Formation

(i) Personal Pronoun＋達
　　　　　　　　　　tachi

　　私達　　　　（we）
　　watashitachi

　　あなた達　　（you [pl.]）
　　anatatachi

　　*彼達　　　　（they [male]）　　Cp.　彼等　　　（they [male]）
　　karetachi　　　　　　　　　　　　　*karera*

　　彼女達　　　（they [female]）　　Cp.　彼女等　（they [female]）
　　kanojotachi　　　　　　　　　　　　*kanojora*

(ii) Human Proper Noun＋達
　　　　　　　　　　　tachi

　　山田さん達　　（Mr. Yamada and others）
　　Yamada-san- tachi

(iii) Human Noun＋達
　　　　　　　　tachi

　　子供達　（children）
　　kodomotachi

　　男達　　（men）
　　otokotachi

Note

Kanojo 'she' can take *-tachi*, but *kare* 'he' cannot.

[Related Expressions]

In addition to *-tachi* there are three other pluralizing suffixes: *-domo*, *-gata* and *-ra*. *-domo* is attached primarily to formal first person pronouns, yielding a humble 'we', as in:

　[1]　私共は何も存じません。
　　　　Watashidomo wa nani mo zonjimasen.
　　　　(We don't know anything about it.)

-domo can also be attached to a very limited number of human nouns such as *otoko* 'man' and *onna* 'woman', yielding the rather downgrading plurals *otokodomo* 'men' and *onnadomo* 'women', respectively. Although *kodomo* 'child' is *ko+domo*, it is no longer used as a plural. Instead *-tachi* is attached to it to generate the plural form, as in Formation (iii).

-gata is an honorific plural marker attached to the second person pronoun *anata* 'you' and a very limited number of nouns such as *o-kā-san* 'mother', *o-tō-san* 'father' and *sensei* 'teacher'.

[2] a. あなた方はいついらっしゃいますか。
      Anatagata wa itsu irasshaimasu ka.
      (When are you going there?)

   b. 先生方はいらっしゃらないそうです。
      Senseigata wa irassharanai sōdesu.
      (I was told that the teachers aren't coming.)

The honorific plural form for *hito* 'person' is *katagata* (as in *kono katagata* 'these people') which is the plural form of *kata*.

-ra is the least formal plural marker and is normally attached to personal pronouns and names.

| (1st Person) | 僕等 | わたし等 | わし等 | *わたくし等 |
| | *bokura* | *watashira* | *washira* | **watakushira* |

| (2nd Person) | 君等 | お前等 | あんた等 | *あなた等 |
| | *kimira* | *omaera* | *antara* | **anatara* |

| (3rd Person) | 彼等 (male) | 彼女等 (female) | それ等 (inanimate) |
| | *karera* | *kanojora* | *sorera* |

田中等 (Tanaka and his company)
Tanaka-ra

T

tai たい   *aux. adj.* (*i*)

| an auxiliary adjective which expresses a desire to do s.t. | want (to do s.t.); would like (to do s.t.) [REL. *hoshii*[1]; *hoshii*[2]] |

♦ **Key Sentences**

(A)

Topic (subject)			V*masu*	
私	は	日本 へ	行き	たい / たいです。
Watashi	*wa*	*Nihon e*	***iki***	*tai* / *taidesu*.
(I want to go to Japan.)				

(B)

Topic (subject)			Direct Object		V*masu*	
僕	は	今	ピザ	を / が	食べ	たい / たいです。
Boku	*wa*	*ima*	*piza*	*o* / *ga*	***tabe***	*tai* / *taidesu*.
(I want to eat pizza now.)						

(C)

Topic (subject)			V*masu*		
鈴木さん	は	アメリカ へ	行き	た	がって いる / います。
Suzuki-san	*wa*	*Amerika e*	***iki***	*ta*	*gatte iru* / *imasu*.
(Lit. Mr. Suzuki is showing signs of wanting to go to America. (=Mr. Suzuki wants to go to America.))					

Formation

V*masu* たい
       tai

話し たい   (want to talk)
hanashi tai

食べ たい   (want to eat)
tabe tai

Examples

(a) 僕は冷たいビールを / が飲みたい。
   Boku wa tsumetai biru o / ga nomitai.
   (I want to drink cold beer.)

(b) 今日は何を / が食べたいですか。
Kyō wa nani o / ga tabetaidesu ka.
(What do you want to eat today?)

(c) 三木さんは車を買いたがっている。
Miki-san wa kuruma o kaita gatte iru.
(Mr. Miki wants to buy a car.)

Notes

1. *Tai* is an *i*-type auxiliary adjective which expresses a person's desire to do something. Since V*masu tai* expresses a very personal feeling, it is usually used only for the first person in declarative sentences and for the second person in interrogative sentences. For the third person, V*masu ta gatte iru* 'lit. is showing signs of wanting to do s.t.' is usually used, as in KS(C) and Ex. (c). (⇨ **garu**) V*masu tai* with the third person subject is acceptable, however, in the following situations:

(1) *In the past tense*
和男はとても行きたかった。
Kazuo wa totemo ikitakatta.
(Kazuo wanted to go very badly.)

(2) *In indirect / semi-direct speech*
a. 一郎も行きたいと言っている。
Ichirō mo ikitai to itte iru.
(Ichiro says he wants to go, too.)

b. 利子は日本へ帰りたいそうだ。
Toshiko wa Nihon e kaeritai sōda.
(I heard that Toshiko wants to go back to Japan.)

(3) *In explanatory situations*
野村さんはあなたと話したいんですよ。
Nomura-san wa anata to hanashi tai n desu yo.
((The explanation is that) Miss Nomura wants to talk with you.)
(⇨ **no da**)

(4) *In conjecture expressions*
a. 村山さんはのり子と踊りたいらしい。
Murayama-san wa Noriko to odoritai rashii.
(It seems that Mr. Murayama wants to dance with Noriko.)

b. 早田さんは早く家族に会いたそうだ。
Hayata-san wa hayaku kazoku ni aita sōda.
(It looks like Mr. Hayata wants to see his family soon.)

2. In some situations, if the verb in V*masu tai* is a transitive verb, the direct object can be marked either by *ga* or by *o*, as seen in KS(B), Ex. (a) and Ex. (b). In general, the choice between *ga* and *o* seems to depend on the degree of desire. That is, when the desire to do something is high, *ga* is preferred; when it is low, *o* is used. Compare (4) and (5):

(4) [Situation: The speaker has just run five miles.]

私は水が / ?を飲みたい。

*Watashi wa mizu **ga** / ?**o** nomitai.*

(I want to drink some water.)

(5) [Situation: The speaker has been told by a doctor to drink as much water as possible. That is, he feels he has to drink water.]

私は水を / ?が飲みたいが...

*Watashi wa mizu **o** / ?**ga** nomitai ga ...*

(I want to drink water but (my stomach doesn't accept it anymore)...)

Under the following conditions, *ga* cannot be used even if the degree of desire is high.

(A) When a long element intervenes between the direct object and the verb:

(6) 私は水を / *が出かける前に飲みたい。

*Watashi wa mizu **o** / ***ga** dekakeru mae ni nomitai.*

(I want to drink water before I leave home.)

(B) When the main verb is in the passive form:

(7) 私は先生にこの絵を / *がほめられたい。

*Watashi wa sensei ni kono e **o** / ***ga** homeraretai.*

(Lit. I want to have this picture praised by my teacher.)

(C) When the preceding noun is not the direct object:

(8) a. 私は早くこの電車を / *が降りたい。

*Watashi wa hayaku kono densha **o** / ***ga** oritai.*

(I want to get off this train soon.)

b. 私は公園を / *が歩きたい。

*Watashi wa kōen **o** / ***ga** arukitai.*

(I want to walk through the park.)　　　　　(⇨ ***o***^{2}; ***o***^{3})

3. In the construction V*masu ta gatte iru*, *ga* can never be used to mark the direct object.

(9) 三木さんは車を / *が買いたがっている。
   *Miki-san wa kuruma **o** / ***ga** kaita gatte iru.*
   (Mr. Miki wants to buy a car.)

4. V*masu tai* cannot be used to express an invitation. The following sentences are inappropriate in invitation situations.

(10) a. 私と一緒に行きたいですか。
      Watashi to isshoni iki tai desu ka.
      (Do you want to go with me?)

   b. あした食事に来たいですか。
      Ashita shokuji ni kitai desu ka.
      (Would you like to come to dinner tomorrow?)

In these situations negative questions are used, as seen in (11).

(⇨ *mashō*)

(11) 私と一緒に行きませんか。
    *Watashi to isshoni **ikimasen ka**.*
    (Wouldn't you like to go with me?)

[Related Expressions]

The idea of 'want' in English is expressed by either *tai*, *hoshii*[1] or *hoshii*[2]. *Tai* is used when the experiencer wants to do something. *Hoshii*[1] is used when the experiencer wants something. *Hoshii*[2] is used when the experiencer wants someone to do something.   (⇨ *hoshii*[1]; *hoshii*[2])

T

---

tamaranai たまらない   *phr.*

The speaker or whomever he empathizes with cannot cope with a situation expressed by the -*te* phrase.	unbearably ~; extremely; be dying to do ~ 【REL. *shikata ga nai*】

♦Key Sentences

(A)

	Adj (*i*) stem		
今日 は *Kyō wa*	暑 **atsu**	くて *kute*	たまらない / たまりません。 *tamaranai / tamarimasen.*
(It is unbearably hot today.)			

(B)

	Adj (*na*) stem		
数学　が *Sūgaku ga*	嫌い **kirai**	で *de*	たまらない / たまりません。 *tamaranai / tamarimasen.*
(I really hate math.)			

Formation

KS(A):

Adj (*i*) stem　くて　たまらない
　　　　　　　kute　tamaranai

寒くて　　たまらない　　(s.t. is unbearably cold)
samukute tamaranai

KS(B):

Adj (*na*) stem　で　たまらない
　　　　　　　　de　tamaranai

不便で　たまらない　　(s.t. is unbearably inconvenient)
fuben de tamaranai

Examples

(a) この本はおもしろくてたまりません。
　　Kono hon wa omoshirokute tamarimasen.
　　(This book is extremely interesting.)

(b) 父が死んで，悲しくてたまりません。
　　Chichi ga shinde, kanashikute tamarimasen.
　　(My father died and I'm awfully sad.)

(c) おいしい魚が食べたくてたまりません。
　　Oishii sakana ga tabetakute tamarimasen.
　　(I'm dying to eat some good fish.)

(d) 僕はあの子が好きでたまらない。

Boku wa ano ko ga sukide tamaranai.

(I just love that girl.)

(e) 兄は田中先生の授業が嫌でたまらなかった。

Ani wa Tanaka-sensei no jugyō ga iyade tamaranakatta.

(My older brother really hated Mr. Tanaka's class.)

Notes

1. ~*te* / *de tamaranai* is an idiomatic phrase used to express the fact that some situation is unbearable in the extreme for the speaker or someone with whom he empathizes.

2. The adjectives used before *te* / *de* refer to human feelings.

3. There is no affirmative counterpart of this construction, *~*te* / *de tamaru*.

[Related Expression]

~*te tamaranai* (lit. ~ and I can't stand it) can be replaced by *te shikata ga nai* (lit. ~ and I don't know what to do about it). The only difference is that the former is more emotive than the latter. But when *shikata ga nai* is directly preceded by V*te mo*, it cannot be replaced by *tamara nai*, as shown in [1].

[1] そんな本は読んでも仕方がない / *読んでたまらない。

*Sonna hon wa **yonde mo shikata ga nai** / *yonde tamaranai.*

(There is no use reading that sort of book.)

tame (ni) ため（に）　　*n.*

a noun that indicates a benefit, a purpose, a reason or a cause	on account of ~ ; for the benefit of ~ ; for the good of ~ ; for the sake of ~ ; on behalf of ~ ; for the purpose of ~ ; in order to ~ ; because of ~ ; owing to ~ **[REL.** *kara*³; *ni*⁵; *node*; *noni*²**]**

♦ **Key Sentences**

(A)

Topic (subject)		Noun			
学生 *Gakusei*	は *wa*	**試験** ***shiken***	の *no*	ため に *tame ni*	勉強する / 勉強します。 *benkyōsuru / benkyōshimasu.*

(Students study in preparation for exams. / Students study because there are exams.)

(B)

Subordinate Clause (purpose)	Vinf· nonpast		Main Clause
私 は 日本 の ことを *Watashi wa Nihon no koto o*	知る ***shiru***	ため (に) *tame (ni)*	日本 へ 行く / 行きます。 *Nihon e iku / ikimasu.*

(I'll go to Japan (in order) to learn about Japan.)

(C)

Subordinate Clause (reason / cause)	Vinf		Main Clause
今年 は 雪 が あまり *Kotoshi wa yuki ga amari*	降らない ***furanai***	ため (に) *tame (ni)*	スキー が 出来ない / *suki ga dekinai /* 出来ません。 *dekimasen.*

(Because it hasn't snowed (lit. doesn't snow) very much this year, we can't ski.)

(D)

Noun			Noun Phrase	
外国人 ***Gaikokujin***	の *no*	ため の *tame no*	いい 辞書 *ii jisho*	が ない / ありません。 *ga nai / arimasen.*

(There aren't (any) good dictionaries for foreigners.)

Formation

(i) {V / Adj (*i*)} inf ため に
                   tame ni

    {話す / 話した} ため に   (in order to talk / because s.o. talks /
    {*hanasu / hanashita*} *tame ni*   talked)

    {食べる / 食べた} ため に   (in order to eat / because s.o. eats / ate)
    {*taberu / tabeta*} *tame ni*

    {高い / 高かった} ため に   (because s.t. is / was high)
    {*takai / takakatta*} *tame ni*

(ii) Adj (*na*) stem {な / だった} ため に
                  {*na / datta*} *tame ni*

    {静かな / 静かだった} ため に   (because s.t. is / was quiet)
    {*shizukana / shizukadatta*} *tame ni*

(iii) N {の / だった} ため に
      {*no / datta*} *tame ni*

    {先生 の / 先生 だった} ため に   (for the sake of the teacher / because
    {*sensei no / sensei datta*} *tame ni*   of the teacher / because s.o. is / was
                               a teacher)

(iv) Demonstrative Adj ため に
                     tame ni

    {この / その} ため に   (for the sake of this / that, because of this /
    {*kono / sono*} *tame ni*   that)

Examples

(a) 日本人は会社のためによく働きます。
    Nihonjin wa kaisha no tame ni yoku hatarakimasu.
    (The Japanese work hard for the sake of their company.)

(b) 雪のため(に)学校が休みになった。
    Yuki no tame (ni) gakkō ga yasumi ni natta.
    (The school was closed because of the snow.)

(c) ジャクソンさんは研究のため(に)ドイツに行った。
    Jakuson-san wa kenkyū no tame (ni) Doitsu ni itta.
    (Mr. Jackson went to Germany for the purpose of research.)

(d) 私は父が死んだため(に)大学に行けなかった。
    Watashi wa chichi ga shinda tame (ni) daigaku ni ikenakatta.
    (I couldn't go to college because my father died.)

T

(e) 体を強くするため (に) 毎日プールで泳いでいる。

Karada o tsuyoku suru tame (ni) mainichi pūru de oyoide iru.

(I'm swimming every day in the pool in order to strengthen my body.)

(f) 親が甘かったため (に) 子供がだめになった。

Oya ga amakatta tame (ni) kodomo ga dameni natta.

(Because the parents were soft, the children got spoiled.)

(g) 字が下手なため (に) 人に笑われた。

Ji ga hetana tame (ni) hito ni warawareta.

(I was laughed at because my handwriting is so poor.)

(h) フランスに行ったのは香水を買うためだ。

Furansu ni itta no wa kōsui o kau tame da.

(Lit. It was for the purpose of buying perfume that I went to France. (= I went to France to buy perfume.))

Notes

1. *Tame ni* expresses cause or reason when it is preceded by an Adj(*i*) or an Adj(*na*), as in Exs. (f) and (g), or when the main clause describes a noncontrollable situation and / or when the *tame ni* clause is in the past tense, as in Ex. (d). In these cases, it never expresses purpose. Consider the additional examples in (1).

(1) a. 仕事のために何もほかの事が出来ない。

   *Shigoto **no tame ni** nani mo hoka no koto ga dekinai.*

   (Because of the job I can't do anything else.)

   b. 会社のために朝から晩まで働いている。

   *Kaisha **no tame ni** asa kara ban made hataraite iru.*

   (He's working from morning till night for the sake of his company.)

(1a) gets the *reason / cause* interpretation, because the main clause describes a noncontrollable situation, whereas (1b) gets the *purpose* interpretation, because the main clause describes a controllable situation.

2. The *ni* of *tame ni* can be dropped, as in Exs. (b), (c), (d), (e), (f) and (g), if a phrase(s) intervenes between the main verb and *tame ni*.

[Related Expressions]

I. When *tame* is used to mean reason or cause, it can be replaced by *kara* or *node*. Thus, KS(C) and Ex. (d) can be rephrased as [1a] and [1b], respectively.

[1] a. 今年は雪があまり降らないから / のでスキーが出来ない。

   *Kotoshi wa yuki ga amari furanai **kara** / **node** sukī ga dekinai.*

   (We cannot ski because it hasn't snowed very much this year.)

b. 私は父が死んだから / ので大学に行けなかった。

   *Watashi wa chichi ga shinda **kara** / **node** daigaku ni ikenakatta.*

   (I couldn't go to college because my father died.)

The difference between *tame* and other markers of reason / cause is that
tame is more formal than the others and is seldom used in informal
conversation. (⇨ *kara*[3]; *node*)

II. When *tame* is used to mean purpose, it can be replaced by either Vinf·
nonpast *noni* or V*masu ni* Vmotion. However, *tame ni* can be replaced
by *noni* only when one does something *in the process of* achieving some
goal. Thus, [3a] can be paraphrased as [3b] but [4a] cannot be paraphrased as [4b].

[3] a. 漢字を調べるために辞書を使う。

   *Kanji o shiraberu **tame ni** jisho o tsukau.*

   (In order to find out about *kanji* I use a dictionary.)

b. 漢字を調べるのに辞書を使う。

   *Kanji o shiraberu **noni** jisho o tsukau.*

   (In order to find out about *kanji* I use a dictionary.)

[4] a. 体を強くするために毎日プールで泳いでいる。

   *Karada o tsuyoku suru **tame ni** mainichi pūru de oyoide iru.*

   (I'm swimming every day in the pool in order to strengthen
   my body.)

b. ??体を強くするのに毎日プールで泳いでいる。

   ??*Karada o tsuyoku suru **noni** mainichi pūru de oyoide iru.*

   (I'm swimming every day in the pool in order to strengthen
   my body.)

Note also that *tame* can be replaced by V*masu ni* Vmotion only when
tame is used with a Vmotion. The difference between *tame* and other
markers of purpose is that *tame* is the most formal and least colloquial
of the three.

~tara ~たら　*conj.*

> a subordinate conjunction which in-
> dicates that the action / state ex-
> pressed by the main clause in a
> sentence takes place after the ac-
> tion / state expressed by the subordi-
> nate clause

if; when; after
【REL. *ba*; *nara*; *to*[4]; ***toki***】

♦**Key Sentence**

Subordinate Clause (antecedent)		Main Clause (subsequence)
Sentence (informal past)		
山田さん　が **来た** *Yamada-san ga **kita***	ら *ra*	私　は　帰る / 帰ります。 *watashi wa kaeru / kaerimasu.*
(When / If Mr. Yamada comes, I'll go home.)		

Formation

{V / Adj (*i* / *na*) / N+Copula} inf·past　ら
　　　　　　　　　　　　　　　　　　　ra

話したら　　(if / when s.o. talks / talked)
hanashitara

高かったら　　(if s.t. is / were expensive)
takakattara

静かだったら　　(if s.t. is / were quiet)
shizukadattara

先生　だったら　　(if s.o. is / were a teacher)
sensei dattara

Examples

(a) 先生に聞いたらすぐ分かった。
　　Sensei ni kiitara sugu wakatta.
　　(When I asked my teacher, I understood it right away.)

(b) 私は大学を出たら小学校の先生になります。
　　Watashi wa daigaku o detara shōgakkō no sensei ni narimasu.
　　(I'll be an elementary school teacher after graduating from college.)

(c) 私は忙しいですから，おもしろかったら読みますが，おもしろくなかったら読みませんよ。

Watashi wa isogashiidesu kara, omoshirokattara yomimasu ga, omoshirokunakattara yomimasen yo.

(I'm busy, so I'll read it if it's interesting, but I won't if it's not interesting.)

(d) きらいだったら残してください。

Kiraidattara nokoshite kudasai.

(If you don't like it, please leave it.)

(e) 英語だったら分かると思います。

Eigo dattara wakaru to omoimasu.

(I think I'll understand it if it's English.)

Notes

1. The meaning of S_1 *tara* S_2 varies depending on the contents of S_1 and S_2 and also on the situation in which this construction is used. However, S_1 always represents an antecedent and S_2 a subsequence. For example, in KS, Mr. Yamada's coming precedes the speaker's returning home. Likewise, in Ex. (a), the speaker's asking his teacher precedes his understanding something. If this relation does not hold, this construction cannot be used. For example, (1) cannot be expressed by the *tara* construction because the event of S_1, the speaker's going to Chicago, does not precede the event of S_2, his going there by car.

(1) When I go to Chicago, I usually go by car.

*私はシカゴへ行ったらたいてい車で行きます。

Watashi wa Shikago e ittara** taitei kuruma de ikimasu.*

(In this situation, *toki* is used. (⇨ **toki**)) For the same reason, *tara* is ungrammatical in the situation in (2).

(2) If you go to Chicago, go by bus.

*シカゴへ行ったらバスで行きなさい。

Shikago e ittara** basu de ikinasai.*

(In this case, *nara* is used. (⇨ **nara**))

2. In S_1 *tara* S_2, it is often the case that S_1 represents a condition and S_2 an event which occurs under that condition. Therefore, the whole sentence basically means 'when S_1 is satisfied, S_2 takes place' or 'S_1 brings about S_2', as in Exs. (c), (d) and (e).

3. As seen in KS, *tara* may mean 'when' in one case and 'if' in another. *Tara* means 'when' if S₁ is a certainty; if not, *tara* means 'if'. Thus, in (3), *tara* means 'when'.

 (3) 十二時になったら帰ります。
   Jūniji ni nattara kaerimasu.
   (When / *If it is twelve o'clock, I'll go home.)

Moshi before S₁ *tara* makes sentences unambiguous; it always means 'if S₁'. Example:

 (4) もし山田さんが来たら私は帰ります。
   Moshi *Yamada-san ga kitara watashi wa kaerimasu.*
   (If / *When Mr. Yamada comes, I'll go home.)

4. In S₁ *tara* S₂, S₂ can be a command, a request, a suggestion, an invitation or a volitional sentence.

 (5) 仕事が早く終わったら僕のうちに
   Shigoto ga hayaku owattara boku no uchi ni

   a. 来なさい。
     kinasai.

   b. 来てください。
     kite kudasai.

   c. 来たらどうですか。
     kitara dō desu ka.

   d. 来ませんか。
     kimasen ka.

   (If you finish your work early,

   a. come to my place.
   b. please come to my place.
   c. why don't you come to my place?
   d. wouldn't you like to come to my place?)

 (6) 仕事が早く終わったらおうちにおうかがいします。
   Shigoto ga hayaku owattara o-uchi ni o-ukagai shimasu.
   (If I finish my work early, I'll visit your place.)

5. S₁ *tara* S₂ can also be used in counterfactual situations, as in (7).

(7) a. お金があったらこんなうちにはいない。

   *O-kane ga at**tara** konna uchi ni wa inai.*

   (If I had money, I wouldn't be in such a house.)

   b. あの時お金があったら日本へ行っていたでしょう。

   *Ano toki o-kane ga at**tara** Nihon e itte ita deshō.*

   (If I had had money at that time, I would probably have gone to Japan.)

6. When S_2 in "S_1 *tara* S_2" represents a past action, the action cannot be one intentionally taken by the agent after the action or event represented by S_1. Thus, the (a) sentences in (8) and (9) are acceptable, but the (b) sentences are not.

(8) a. 学校へ行ったら，ぐうぜん上田さんに会った。

   *Gakkō e it**tara**, gūzen Ueda-san ni atta.*

   (When I went to school, I happened to see Mr. Ueda.)

   b. *学校へ行ったら，上田さんと話をした。

   Gakkō e ittara**, Ueda-san to hanashi o shita.*

   (When I went to school, I talked with Mr. Ueda.)

(9) a. お酒を飲んだら寝てしまった。

   *O-sake o non**dara** nete shimatta.*

   (After I drank *sake*, I fell asleep.)

   b. *お酒を飲んだら寝た。

   O-sake o nondara** neta.*

   (After I drank *sake*, I went to bed.)

[Related Expressions]

Ba, *nara* and *to*[4] have similar functions but they are different from *tara* in the following ways:

I. In S_1 *tara* S_2, if the event in S_1 precedes the event in S_2, those events can be past events. This is also the case with S_1 *to*[4] S_2, but not with S_1 *ba* S_2 and S_1 *nara* S_2, as in [1].

[1] a. 先生に聞いたら / 聞くと / *聞けば / *聞いた (の) ならすぐ分かった。

   *Sensei ni kii**tara** | kiku **to** | *kike**ba** | *kiita **(no) nara** sugu wakatta.*

   (When I asked my teacher, I understood it immediately.)

b. キャシーのアパートに行ったら / 行くと / *行けば / *行った
   (の)ならアンディーがいた。
   Kyashi no apāto ni ittara / *iku to* / **ikeba* / **itta* (*no*) *nara*
   Andi ga ita.
   (When I went to Cathy's apartment, Andy was there.)

II. As stated in Note 4, S_2 in S_1 *tara* S_2 can be a command, a request, a suggestion, an invitation or a volitional sentence. This is also the case with S_2 in S_1 *ba* S_2 and S_1 *nara* S_2 but not with S_2 in S_1 *to* S_2. Example:

[2] 安かったら / 安ければ / 安い(の)なら / *安いと買いなさい。
    Yasukattara / *Yasukereba* / *Yasui* (*no*) *nara* / **Yasui to kainasai.*
    (Buy it, if it's cheap.)

III. Although S_2 in S_1 *tara* S_2, S_1 *ba* S_2 and S_1 *nara* S_2 can be a command, a request, a suggestion, an invitation or a volitional sentence, the meanings are not exactly the same. The following examples show the differences clearly.

[3] a. ベンが来たら，私は帰ります。
       Ben ga kitara, watashi wa kaerimasu.
       (When / If Ben comes, I'll go home.)

    b. ベンがくれば，私は帰ります。
       Ben ga kureba, watashi wa kaerimasu.
       (If Ben comes, I'll go home. (If not, I'll stay here.))

    c. ベンが来る(の)なら，私は帰ります。
       Ben ga kuru (*no*) *nara, watashi wa kaerimasu.*
       (If it is true that Ben is coming, I'll go home.)

As seen above, [3a] is ambiguous; it is not clear that Ben is coming. If Ben's coming is certain, [3a] indicates the time the speaker will leave. If Ben's coming is uncertain, [3a] indicates the condition under which the speaker will leave. In both cases, however, Ben's coming precedes the speaker's leaving. [3b] is similar to the second case of [3a] (i.e., the case in which Ben's coming is uncertain). However, [3b] focuses more on the condition. That is, [3b] implies something like ' the condition under which I go home is Ben's coming here '. In [3b] also, Ben's coming precedes the speaker's leaving. S_1 in [3c] also indicates the condition under which the speaker returns home. In this case, however, Ben's coming does not necessarily precede the speaker's leaving because the condition under which the speaker goes home is that Ben's coming is true, not that Ben comes (to a certain place).

IV. As stated in Note 5, S₁ *tara* S₂ can be used in counterfactual situations, and so can S₁ *ba* S₂ and S₁ *nara* S₂. However, S₁ *to* S₂ cannot be used in such situations except for the idiomatic expression S *to ii* / *yokatta* ' It would be good / It would have been good if S '. Example:

[4] あの時お金があったら / あれば / あったなら / *あると日本に行っていただろう。

*Ano toki o-kane ga at**tara** / are**ba** / atta **nara** / *aru **to** Nihon ni itte ita darō.*

(If I had had money at that time, I would have gone to Japan.)

~tara dō desu ka ~たらどうですか   *phr.*

> a phrase which expresses a suggestion (Lit. How would you feel if you do s.t.?)

Why don't you do ~?; What about doing ~?
【REL. *hō ga ii*】

◆**Key Sentence**

	Vinf·past		
もっと 日本 の 本 を *Motto Nihon no hon o*	読んだ **yonda**	ら *ra*	どう です か。 *dō desu ka.*
(Why don't you read more Japanese books?)			

Formation

Vinf·past ら どう です か。
　　　　ra dō desu ka.

話した ら どう です か。　　　(Why don't you talk ~?)
hanashita ra dō desu ka.

食べたら どう です か。 (Why don't you eat ~?)
tabeta ra dō desu ka.

Examples

(a) サラダも食べたらどうですか。
Sarada mo tabetara dō desu ka.
(Why don't you eat salad, too?)

(b) 山村先生に聞いたらどうですか。
Yamamura-sensei ni kiitara dō desu ka.
(Why don't you ask Prof. Yamamura?)

Notes

1. Vinf·past *ra dō desu ka* is an idiomatic phrase derived from the "S_1 *tara* S_2" construction and expressing a suggestion. (⇨ ~*tara*)

2. The informal version is Vinf·past *ra dō?* More polite versions are Vinf·past *ra dō deshō (ka)*, Vinf·past *ra ikaga desu ka* and Vinf·past *ra ikaga deshō (ka)*. (⇨ *darō*)

[Related Expression]

Hō ga ii also expresses suggestion, but this phrase is close to a command (especially when it is preceded by Vinf·past), and, therefore, is stronger than *tara dō desu ka*.

~tari ~tari suru ～たり～たりする *phr.*

| a phrase which expresses an inexhaustive listing of actions or states | do things like ~ and ~; sometimes ~ and sometimes ~ |

♦Key Sentences

(A)

Topic (subject)		Vinf·past		Vinf·past		
私達 *Watashitachi*	は *wa*	歌った **utatta**	り *ri*	踊った **odotta**	り *ri*	した / しました。 *shita / shimashita.*

(We did things like singing and dancing.)

(B)

Topic (subject)		{Adj (*i* / *na*) / N + Copula} inf·past		{Adj (*i* / *na*) / N + Copula} inf·past
この レストラン の ステーキ *Kono resutoran no sutēki*	は *wa*	**大きかった** ***ōkikatta***	り *ri*	**小さかった** ***chīsakatta***

り *ri*	する / します。 *suru / shimasu.*

(Steaks at this restaurant are sometimes big and sometimes small.)

(C)

A:
毎日 テープ を 聞いて います か。 *Mainichi tēpu o kiite imasu ka.*
(Are you listening to tapes every day?)

B:	{V / Adj (*i* / *na*) / N + Copula} inf·past		{V / Adj (*i* / *na*) / N + Copula} inf·past		
いいえ、 *Īe,*	聞いた ***kiita***	り *ri*	聞かなかった ***kikanakatta***	り *ri*	です。 *desu.*

(Lit. No, I listen at one time and don't listen at another (= only off and on).)

Formation

{V / Adj (*i* / *na*) / N + Copula} inf·past り（する）
                      ri (*suru*)

話したり （する）   (s.o. (does) things like talking)
hanashitari (*suru*)

高かったり（する）   (s.t. is sometimes expensive)
takakattari (*suru*)

静かだったり（する）   (s.t. is sometimes quiet)
shizukadattari (*suru*)

先生 だったり （する）   (s.o. is sometimes a teacher)
sensei dattari (*suru*)

T

Examples

(a) 私はニューヨークでミュージカルを見たりコンサートを聞いたりした。
Watashi wa Nyūyōku de myūjikaru o mitari konsāto o kiitari shita.
(In New York I did things like seeing musicals and listening to concerts.)

(b) トムは来たり来なかったりする。
Tomu wa kitari konakattari suru.
(Lit. Tom comes at one time and doesn't at another time. (=Tom doesn't always come.))

(c) あしたは雨が降ったりやんだりするでしょう。
Ashita wa ame ga futtari yandari suru deshō.
(It will probably rain off and on tomorrow.)

(d) この店の魚は新しかったり古かったりする。
Kono mise no sakana wa atarashikattari furukattari suru.
(This shop's fish is sometimes fresh and sometimes old.)

(e) 日本語の先生は日本人だったりアメリカ人だったりします。
Nihongo no sensei wa nihonjin dattari amerikajin dattari shimasu.
(Teachers of Japanese are sometimes Japanese and sometimes American.)

(f) 石川さんは来たり来なかったりであてにならない。
Ishikawa-san wa kitari konakattari de ate ni naranai.
(Mr. Ishikawa doesn't come regularly and we can't count on him.)

Notes

1. The "X *tari* Y *tari suru*" construction generally expresses an inexhaustive listing of actions or states. "Inexhaustive" means that in a given situation there may be additional, unstated actions or states. (The exhaustive listing of actions or states is expressed by the *te*-form. (⇨ *-te*))
   (Cp. *to*[1]; *ya*)

2. *Suru* usually follows "X *tari* Y *tari*" regardless of the part of speech of X and Y, and expresses the tense, the aspect (e.g., progressive, perfect) and the formality level of the sentence.

3. This construction usually lists two actions or two states, but it can list more than two actions or two states, as in (1).

(1) 本を読んだり，映画を見たり，テープを聞いたりして日本語を勉強している。

Hon o yondari, eiga o mitari, tēpu o kiitari shite nihongo o benkyōshite iru.

(I'm studying Japanese by doing things like reading books, seeing movies and listening to tapes.)

Sometimes only one action or state is listed in this construction, as in (2).

(2) 新聞を読んだりして友達が来るのを待っていた。

Shinbun o yondari shite tomodachi ga kuru no o matte ita.

(I was waiting for my friend to come, doing things like reading a newspaper.)

4. If "X *tari* Y *tari suru*" is not the final segment of a sentence and the predicate is an adjective, *suru* may be omitted, as in (3).

(3) 歌ったり踊ったり(して)とても楽しかった。

Utattari odottari (shite) totemo tanoshikatta.

(We did things like singing and dancing, and it was a lot of fun.)

If the predicate is a verb, however, *suru* cannot be omitted as in (4).

(4) *私達はテニスをしたり泳いだりして / *ø 遊んだ。

**Watashitachi wa tenisu o shitari oyoidari shite / *ø asonda.*

(Lit. We played doing things like playing tennis and swimming.)

5. As seen in KS(C) and Ex. (f), a slightly different pattern, X *tari* Y *tari da*, is also used in some situations. This pattern is used when a speaker describes someone's or something's inconstant state.

T

-tatte たって   *conj.*

even if s.o. did s.t. or s.t. were in some state (the desired result would not come about) or even if s.o. or s.t. is in some state	even if ~ 【REL. *te mo*】

♦ **Key Sentences**

(A)

Topic (indirect object)		Vinf·past		
あの 人 *Ano hito*	に は *ni wa*	話し たって ***hanashi**tatte*		分からない / 分かりません。 *wakaranai / wakarimasen.*
(Even if I tell him that, he won't understand it.)				

(B)

Topic (subject)			Adj (*i*) stem		
僕 *Boku*	は *wa*	その 切符 を *sono kippu o*	高 くたって ***taka**kutatte*		買う / 買います。 *kau / kaimasu.*
(I will buy the ticket even if it is expensive.)					

Formation

(i) Vinf·past って
　　　　　　　　tte

　　話したって　　(even if s.o. talks / talked)
　　hanashitatte

　　食べたって　　(even if s.o. eats / ate)
　　tabetatte

(ii) Adj (*i*) stem くたって
　　　　　　　　　kutatte

　　高くたって　　(even if s.t. is / were expensive)
　　takakutatte

(iii) {Adj (*na*) stem / N} だっ(たっ)て
　　　　　　　　　　　　dat(tat)te

　　静かだっ(たっ)て　　(even if s.t. is / were quiet)
　　shizukadat(tat)te

　　先生 だっ(たっ)て　　(even if s.o. is / were a teacher)
　　sensei dat(tat)te

Examples

(a) お金があったって車は買いたくない。
　　O-kane ga attatte kuruma wa kaitakunai.
　　(Even if I had money, I wouldn't want to buy a car.)

(b) 本を買ったって，忙しくて読めない。

Hon o kattatte, isogashikute yomenai.

(Even if I buy books, I'm too busy to read them.)

(c) きたなくたってかまいません。

Kitanakutatte kamaimasen.

(I don't care even if it is dirty.)

(d) 遠くて不便だってマイ・ホームならかまいません。

Tōkute fubendatte mai hōmu nara kamaimasen.

(Even if it is far away and inconvenient, it doesn't matter if it is 'my home'.)

(e) どんなにいい先生だって時々間違います。

Donna ni ii sensei datte tokidoki machigaimasu.

(No matter how good a teacher may be, he sometimes makes mistakes.)

Notes

1. *-tatte* is used strictly in informal spoken Japanese, and is used to indicate something counter to fact. However, the counterfactual (or subjunctive) nature of this construction is not very strong. See Ex. (a).

2. *-tatte* can take *donna ni* (as in Ex. (e)) meaning 'no matter how'. More examples follow.

    (1) a. どんなに考えたって分からないよ。

        Donna ni kangae**tatte** wakaranai yo.

        (No matter how hard you think, you won't understand it.)

      b. どんなに寒くたって大丈夫です。

        Donna ni samuku**tatte** daijōbudesu.

        (No matter how cold it is, it's all right.)

[Related Expression]

-tatte can be replaced by *te mo*. The difference is that *te mo* can be used in spoken and written language and that it is less emotive than *-tatte*. Thus, if Ex. (a) is replaced by the following sentence, the counterfactuality of having money is nullified, and the entire sentence sounds much less emotive.

    [1] お金があっても車は買いたくない。

        *O-kane ga at**te mo** kuruma wa kaitakunai.*

        (Even if I have money, I don't want to buy a car.)

T

-te て *te-form*

> the *te*-form ending of verbs and *i*-type adjectives (The *te*-form ending of *na*-type adjectives and the *te*-form of the copula is *de*.)
>
> and; -ing

♦ **Key Sentences**

(1)

	{V / Adj (*i* / *na*) / N +Copula} *te*	
ジム は 日本 へ *Jimu wa Nihon e*	行って ***it**te*	勉強した / 勉強しました。 *benkyōshita / benkyōshimashita.*

(Jim went to Japan and studied (there).)

(2)

ここの ステーキ は *Kokono sutēki wa*	安くて ***yasuku**te*	おいしい / おいしいです。 *oishii / oishiidesu.*

(Steaks here are inexpensive and delicious.)

(3)

この アパート は *Kono apāto wa*	静かで ***shizuka**de*	いい / いいです。 *ii / iidesu.*

(This apartment is quiet and good.)

(4)

私 の 父 は *Watashi no chichi wa*	先生 で ***sensei** de*	高校 で 英語 を 教えて いる / います。 *kōkō de eigo o oshiete iru / imasu.*

(My father is a teacher and teaches English at senior high school.)

Formation

(i) Gr. 1 verbs:

    (a) *su*-verbs: 話す → 話して (s.o. talks and)
                   *hana*su   *hana*shite

    (b) *ku*-verbs: 歩く → 歩いて (s.o. walks and)
                   *aru*ku   *aru*ite

        Exception: 行く → 行って (s.o. goes and)
                   *i*ku   *i*tte

    (c) *gu*-verbs: 泳ぐ → 泳いで (s.o. swims and)
                   *oyo*gu   *oyo*ide

(d) *mu* / *bu* / *nu*-verbs: 飲む → 飲んで (s.o. drinks s.t. and)
 nomu *nonde*

 遊ぶ → 遊んで (s.o. plays and)
 asobu *asonde*

 死ぬ → 死んで (s.o. dies and)
 shinu *shinde*

(e) *tsu* / *u* / *ru*-verbs: 待つ → 待って (s.o. waits and)
 matsu *matte*

 買う → 買って (s.o. buys s.t. and)
 kau *katte*

 取る → 取って (s.o. takes s.t. and)
 toru *totte*

(ii) Gr. 2 Verbs: Vstem て
  te

 食べて (s.o. eats s.t. and)
 tabete

(iii) Irr. Verbs: 来る → 来て (s.o. comes and)
 kuru *kite*

 する → して (s.o. does s.t. and)
 suru *shite*

(iv) Adj (*i*): Adj (*i*) stem くて
  kute

 高くて (s.t. is expensive and)
 takakute

(v) Adj (*na*): Adj (*na*) stem で
  de

 静かで (s.t. is quiet and)
 shizukade

(vi) N+Copula: N で
  de

 先生 で (s.o. is a teacher and)
 sensei de

Examples

(a) 私はコートを脱いでハンガーにかけた。
Watashi wa kōto o nuide hangā ni kaketa.
(Taking off my coat, I hung it on a hanger.)

(b) ワインを飲みすぎて頭が痛い。
Wain o nomisugite atama ga itai.
(I've drunk too much wine and have a headache.)

(c) 私の部屋はせまくて暗い。
Watashi no heya wa semakute kurai.
(My room is small and dark.)

(d) このスープはからくて飲めない。
Kono sūpu wa karakute nomenai.
(This soup is salty (or (spicy) hot) and I can't eat (lit. drink) it.)

(e) 私はテニスが大好きでよく友達とする。
Watashi wa tenisu ga dai-sukide yoku tomodachi to suru.
(I love tennis and often play with my friends.)

(f) ゆみ子は今大学三年で専攻は日本文学です。
Yumiko wa ima daigaku sannen de senkō wa nihonbungaku desu.
(Yumiko is a junior at college now and her major is Japanese literature.)

(g) 伊藤先生は今週病気で，かわりに村田先生が教えた。
Itō-sensei wa konshū byōki de, kawari ni Murata-sensei ga oshieta.
(Prof. Ito was ill this week and Prof. Murata taught for him.)

Notes

1. The *te*-form functions, in part, to link sentences. That is, if the last element of the predicate of a clause is the *te*-form, it means that that clause is not the end of the sentence and that another predicate or clause follows it. For example, in Ex. (b) the last element of the predicate of the first clause is *sugite*, the *te*-form of *sugiru* ' do s.t. too much ', and *sugite* is followed by another clause *atama ga itai* ' lit. (my) head aches '.

2. The meaning of the *te*-form varies according to context, but generally, it corresponds to *and* or *-ing* in participial constructions.

3. When the *te*-form links two predicates, the relationship between the two is often one of the following:

   (A₁: the action or state expressed by the first predicate; A₂: the action or state expressed by the second predicate)

(A) A_1 and A_2 occur sequentially, as in KS(1) and Ex. (a).

(B) A_1 and A_2 are two states of someone or something, as in KS(2), KS(4), Exs. (c) and (f).

(C) A_1 is the reason for or the cause of A_2, as in KS(3), Exs.(b), (d), (e) and (g). (This usage of the *te*-form is very common.)

(D) A_1 is the means by which someone does A_2 or the manner in which someone does A_2. Examples:

(1) 僕は歩いて帰った。
   *Boku wa **aruite** kaetta.*
   (Lit. I walked and went home. (=I went home on foot.))

(2) 健二は急いでご飯を食べた。
   *Kenji wa **isoide** gohan o tabeta.*
   (Lit. Kenji hurried and ate his meal. (=Kenji ate his meal in a hurry.))

(E) A_1 is contrasted with A_2. Example:

(3) 男は外で働いて，女はうちで働く。
   *Otoko wa **soto de hataraite**, onna wa **uchi de hataraku**.*
   (Lit. Men work outside and women work inside.)

(F) A_2 is unexpected in terms of A_1. Example:

(4) トムはいつも遊んでいてテストが出来る。
   *Tomu wa itsumo **asonde ite** tesuto ga dekiru.*
   (Tom plays around, yet he always does well on tests.)

4. The *te*-form can be repeated more than once in a clause. Just like the particle *to*[1] makes an exhaustive listing of nouns, the *te*-form can list verbs and adjectives exhaustively. (Cp. **~ tari ~ tari suru**; *ya*) Example:

(5) エミーは美しくて明るくて人に親切だ。
   Emi wa utsukushikute akarukute hito ni shinsetsuda.
   (Amy is pretty, cheerful and kind to people.)

T

5. *Te*-form verbs are also used with such expressions as *iru*[2] 'be doing ~', *kara* 'after' and *wa ikenai* 'must not do ~'. (⇨ Appendix 4, Connection forms of important expressions, F. V*te*+____)

te mo ても　　*conj.*

Te mo is used when that which is expressed in the main clause is not what is expected from the content of the dependent (*te mo*) clause.

even if; although
【REL. *keredo*; *noni*[1]; *-tatte*】

♦ **Key Sentences**

(A)

Topic (subject)			V*te*		
私	は	雨　が	降って	も	行く / 行きます。
Watashi	*wa*	*ame ga*	***futte***	*mo*	*iku / ikimasu.*
(I'll go there even if it rains.)					

(B)

Topic (subject)		Adj (*i* / *na*)*te*		
私	は	寒くて	も	出かける / 出かけます。
Watashi	*wa*	***samukute***	*mo*	*dekakeru / dekakemasu.*
(I'll go out even if it is cold.)				

(C)

	Noun		
僕　が	トム	で　も	同じ こと を した だろう / でしょう。
Boku ga	***Tomu***	*de mo*	*onaji koto o shita　darō / deshō.*
(Even if I were Tom, I would probably have done the same thing.)			

Formation

(i) {V / Adj (*i* / *na*)} *te* も

　　　　　　　　　　mo

　話して　　も　　(even if s.o. talks)
　hanashite mo

　食べて　も　　(even if s.o. eats)
　tabete mo

　高くて　　も　　(even if s.t. is expensive)
　takakute mo

静かで　も　　(even if s.t. is quiet)
shizukade mo

(ii) N で も
　　　de mo

先生　で　も　　(even if s.o. is a teacher)
sensei de mo

Examples

(a) 中山さんは本を買っても読みません。
Nakayama-san wa hon o katte mo yomimasen.
(Mr. Nakayama doesn't read books even if he buys them.)

(b) 私は四時間歩いても疲れなかった。
Watashi wa yojikan aruite mo tsukarenakatta.
(I didn't get tired although I walked for four hours.)

(c) 何を食べてもおいしいです。
Nani o tabete mo oishiidesu.
(No matter what I eat, it tastes good.)

(d) だれに聞いても分からなかった。
Dare ni kiite mo wakaranakatta.
(No matter who I asked, I couldn't get the answer.)

(e) A：たばこをすってもいいですか。
　　　Tabako o sutte mo iidesu ka.
　　　(Lit. Is it all right even if I smoke? (＝May I smoke?))

　　B：はい，いいです。
　　　Hai, iidesu.
　　　(Yes, you may.)

(f) どんなに日本語が難しくてもやってみます。
Donna ni nihongo ga muzukashikute mo yatte mimasu.
(No matter how difficult Japanese may be, I will try it.)

(g) どんなに丈夫でも体には気をつけた方がいい。
Donna ni jōbude mo karada ni wa ki o tsuketa hō ga ii.
(No matter how healthy you are, you'd better take good care of yourself.)

(h) 井上さんが先輩でも僕ははっきり言うつもりだ。
Inoue-san ga senpai de mo boku wa hakkiri iu tsumori da.
(I intend to speak straightforwardly, even if Mr. Inoue is my senior.)

Notes

1. The basic meaning of *te mo* is the same as the English phrase 'even if ~'.

2. ~*te mo iidesu ka* as in Ex. (e) is an idiomatic expression used to request permission to do s.t. If the answer is in the affirmative, it is "*Hai, iidesu.*" (Yes, you may.) If it is in the negative, it is "*Ie, ikemasen.*" (No, you may not.)

3. WH-word ~ *te mo* means 'no matter WH-', as in Exs. (c), (d), (f), and (g). Typical usages are listed below:

> だれ に 話して も　　(no matter who s.o. talks to)
> ***dare** ni hanashi**te mo***
>
> 何 を 話して も　　(no matter what s.o. talks about)
> ***nani** o hanashi**te mo***
>
> どこ で 話して も　　(no matter where s.o. talks)
> ***doko** de hanashi**te mo***
>
> いつ 話して も　　(no matter when s.o. talks)
> ***itsu** hanashi**te mo***
>
> どう 話して も　　(no matter how s.o. talks)
> ***dō** hanashi**te mo***
>
> どんな に 話して も　　(no matter how much s.o. talks)
> ***donna ni** hanashi**te mo***

[Related Expressions]

Te mo is comparable but not identical to *keredo* 'although' and *noni* 'in spite of the fact that'. The semantic difference is exactly that of English 'even if' vs. 'although'. (⇨ *keredo*; *noni*[1]) Thus,

[1] 中山さんは本を買っても / 買うけれど / 買うのに読みません。
*Nakayama-san wa hon o **katte mo** / **kau keredo** / **kau noni** yomi-masen.*
(Mr. Nakayama doesn't read books even if / although he buys them.)

However, if *te mo* is used with a WH-word, it cannot be replaced by *keredo* or *noni*.

[2] 何を食べても / *食べるけれど / *食べるのにおいしいです。
***Nani** o tabete mo* / **taberu keredo* / **taberu noni* oishiidesu.*
(No matter what I eat, it tastes good.)

~te mo ii ～てもいい　*phr.*

| a phrase which expresses permission or concession | may; It is all right if (ANT. ~ *wa ikenai*) |

♦ **Key Sentences**

(A)

A:	V*te*			B:
ここ で たばこ を *Koko de tabako o*	吸って ***sutte***	も *mo*	いいです か。 *iidesu ka.*	はい、　いいです。 *Hai,　iidesu.*
(May I smoke here?)				(Yes, you may.)

(B)

{Adj (*i* / *na*) /N+Copula} *te*		
高くて ***Takakute***	も *mo*	いい / いいです。 *ii / iidesu.*
(It is all right if it's expensive.)		
学生　　で ***Gakusei de***	も *mo*	いい / いいです。 *ii / iidesu.*
(It is all right if you are a student.)		

Formation

{V / Adj (*i* / *na*) / N+Copula} *te*　も　いい
　　　　　　　　　　　　　　　　mo　ii

話して　　も　いい　　(may talk; It is all right if s.o. talks.)
hanashite mo　ii

高くて　　も　いい　　(It is all right if s.t. is expensive.)
takakute mo　ii

静かで　　も　いい　　(It is all right if s.t. is quiet.)
shizukade mo　ii

先生　　で　も　いい　　(It is all right if s.o. is a teacher.)
sensei de mo　ii

T

Examples

(a) このいすを使ってもいいですか。

   Kono isu o tsukatte mo iidesu ka.

   (May I use this chair?)

(b) 今日の宿題は作文です。短くてもいいですがおもしろいのを書いてください。

   *Kyō no shukudai wa sakubun desu.　Mijikakute mo iidesu ga omoshiroi
   no o kaite kudasai.*

   (Today's homework assignment is a composition.　It is all right if it's
   short, but please write an interesting one.)

(c) A : テニスをしませんか。

   　　Tenisu o shimasen ka.

   　　(Wouldn't you like to play tennis?)

   B : 下手でもいいですか。

   　　Hetade mo iidesu ka.

   　　(Is it all right if I'm poor at it?)

(d) A : 何か冷たいものを飲みたいんですが。

   　　Nanika tsumetai mono o nomitai n desu ga.

   　　(I want to drink something cold.)

   B : ビールでもいいですか。

   　　Biru de mo iidesu ka.

   　　(Will beer do?)

Notes

1. When *te mo ii* is preceded by a verb, it means permission.

2. *~nakute mo ii*, the negative *te*-form with *mo ii*, means ' It is all right
   if ~ not ~' or ' do not have to do ~'.　(Cp. ***~nakereba naranai***)
   Examples:

   ⑴ 私はその試験を受けなくてもいい。

   　　*Watashi wa sono shiken o uke**nakute mo ii**.*

   　　(I don't have to take the exam.)

   ⑵ 新しくなくてもいいです。

   　　*Atarashiku**nakute mo iidesu**.*

   　　(It is all right if it's not new (or fresh).)

   ⑶ 学生じゃなくてもいいです。

   　　*Gakusei ja**nakute mo iidesu**.*

   　　(It is all right if you're not a student.)

3. Other expressions like *yoroshii(desu)*, the polite form of *ii* 'good, all right', and *kamaimasen* 'don't mind' can be used in place of *ii(desu)*. The degrees of politeness in these expressions are as follows:

(4)   *ii(desu) > kamaimasen > yoroshii(desu)*

less polite   more polite

Examples:

(5) あした休んでもよろしいですか。
Ashita yasunde mo yoroshiidesu ka.
(Would it be all right if I take a day off tomorrow?)

(6) たばこを吸ってもかまいませんか。
Tabako o sutte mo kamaimasen ka.
(Do you mind (lit. Don't you mind) if I smoke?)

Note that *kamau* 'mind' must be negated in this expression.

4. *Te mo ii* sometimes appears with WH-words like *nani* 'what' and *ikura* 'how much'. In this case, the expression means 'It is all right no matter what / who / how much / etc. ~' or 'It doesn't matter what / who / how much ~.' (See *te mo*, Note 3.) Examples:

(7) それは**だれが**してもいいです。
*Sore wa **dare ga** shite mo iidesu.*
(It doesn't matter who does it.)

(8) **いくら**食べてもいいです。
***Ikura** tabete mo iidesu.*
(It is all right no matter how much you eat.)

---

to¹ と   *prt.*

a particle which lists things exhaustively

and
【REL. *ni* (and); *to²*; *ya*】

◆**Key Sentence**

Noun		Noun		
マイク ***Maiku***	と *to*	ディック ***Dikku***	（と） *(to)*	は　学生　だ / です。 *wa gakusei da / desu.*
(Mike and Dick are students.)				

Examples

(a) 私は英語と日本語を話す。
   Watashi wa eigo to nihongo o hanasu.
   (I speak English and Japanese.)

(b) ミルズさんは来年ドイツとフランスとスペインへ行くつもりだ。
   Miruzu-san wa rainen Doitsu to Furansu to Supein e iku tsumori da.
   (Mr. Mills is planning to go to Germany, France and Spain next year.)

(c) ステーキはナイフとフォークで食べる。
   Sutēki wa naifu to fōku de taberu.
   (We eat steak with a knife and a fork.)

(d) 山本さんとスミスさんがテニスをしている。
   Yamamoto-san to Sumisu-san ga tenisu o shite iru.
   (Mr. Yamamoto and Mr. Smith are playing tennis.)

(e) 日本語とトルコ語は似ている。
   Nihongo to torukogo wa nite iru.
   (Japanese and Turkish are alike.)

Notes

1. *To* is used to list things exhaustively. The final *to* is usually omitted,
   but the others are not. Thus, "A, B, C and D" is usually expressed
   as "A *to* B *to* C *to* D."

2. *To* connects noun phrases only. Thus, it cannot be used for *and* in
   sentences, as seen in (1) – (3).　　　　　　　　　　　　　　(⇨ *-te*)

   (1) *ここのハンバーガーは安いといい。
       Koko no hanbāgā wa yasui **to ii.*
       (Hamburgers here are cheap *and* good.)

   (2) *ウイルソンさんは日本へ行ったと木村さんに会った。
       Uiruson-san wa Nihon e itta **to Kimura-san ni atta.*
       (Mr. Wilson went to Japan *and* met Mr. Kimura.)

(3) *春男はコンサートに行った**と**ゆり子は映画に行った。

　　　*Haruo wa konsāto ni itta **to** Yuriko wa eiga ni itta.

　　　(Haruo went to a concert *and* Yuriko went to a movie.)

3. "N$_1$ *to* N$_2$ (*to* N$_3$...)" is a noun phrase; it can occur anywhere nouns can occur.

4. When N$_1$ *to* N$_2$ is used as the subject of a sentence, the sentence may be ambiguous. In Ex. (d), for example, without adequate context we cannot tell if Mr. Yamamoto and Mr. Smith are playing tennis *together*. If the predicate contains reciprocal words such as *niru* 'resemble', *onaji-da* 'be the same' and *kekkonsuru* 'marry', however, sentences with "N$_1$ *to* N$_2$" in subject position are not ambiguous, as seen in Ex. (e).

[Related Expressions]

I. When Ex. (d) means 'Mr. Yamamoto and Mr. Smith are playing tennis *together*', it can be restated using *to*[2] 'with', as in [1].

　　[1] a. 山本さんはスミスさん**と**テニスをしている。

　　　　　*Yamamoto-san wa Sumisu-san **to** tenisu o shite iru.*

　　　　　(Mr. Yamamoto is playing tennis with Mr. Smith.)

　　　　b. スミスさんは山本さん**と**テニスをしている。

　　　　　*Sumisu-san wa Yamamoto-san **to** tenisu o shite iru.*

　　　　　(Mr. Smith is playing tennis with Mr. Yamamoto.)

Note that if the speaker states [1a] or [1b] instead of Ex. (d), he is speaking from Mr. Yamamoto's or Mr. Smith's viewpoint, respectively.

II. *Ya* is also used to list things, but that listing is inexhaustive. Examples:

　　[2] a. ミルズさん**や**ハリスさんが来た。

　　　　　*Miruzu-san **ya** Harisu-san ga kita.*

　　　　　(Mr. Mills, Mr. Harris, and others came.)

　　　　b. これはスプーン**や**フォークで食べる。

　　　　　*Kore wa supūn **ya** fōku de taberu.*

　　　　　(We eat this with utensils like spoons and forks.)

III. The particle *ni* can be used to combine two or more objects that usually come as a set.

　　[3] a. 毎朝みそ汁**に** / **と**ご飯を食べる。

　　　　　*Maiasa misoshiru **ni** / **to** gohan o taberu.*

　　　　　(I eat *miso* soup and rice every morning.)

b. あの人はいつも白いシャツに / と赤いチョッキを着ている。

*Ano hito wa itsumo shiroi shatsu **ni** / **to** akai chokki o kite iru.*

(He is always wearing a white shirt and a red vest.)

The difference between *ni* and *to* is that *ni* always implies that one or more than one object has been added to the first object as an indispensable member of the entire set. *To*, however, does not necessarily carry that implication.

*to*² と *prt.*

a particle marking the NP which maintains a reciprocal relationship with the subject of a clause

with; as; from
【REL. *ni*⁴ ; *to*¹】

♦**Key Sentence**

	Noun		
私 は *Watashi wa*	**アンディー** ***Andi***	と *to*	一緒に パーティー に 行った / 行きました。 *isshoni pāti ni itta / ikimashita.*
(I went to a party (together) with Andy.)			

Examples

(a) トムはジョンとよくテニスをする。
Tomu wa Jon to yoku tenisu o suru.
(Tom often plays tennis with John.)

(b) 一郎はみどりと結婚した。
Ichirō wa Midori to kekkonshita.
(Ichiro married Midori.)

(c) この車は僕の車と同じです。
Kono kuruma wa boku no kuruma to onajidesu.
(This car is the same as my car.)

(d) 日本のきゅうりはアメリカのきゅうりと少しちがいます。
Nihon no kyūri wa Amerika no kyūri to sukoshi chigaimasu.
(Japanese cucumbers are a little different from American ones.)

Notes

1. When Y is the subject of a clause, X *to* indicates that X and Y have a reciprocal relationship. For example, in Ex. (a), the fact that Tom often plays tennis with John necessarily means that John often plays tennis with Tom; in other words, it means that they have a reciprocal relationship. Thus, *to* often corresponds to the English 'with', as in 'in the company of'. *To* also appears with such reciprocal verbs and adjectives as *kekkonsuru* 'marry', *kenkasuru* 'quarrel', *hanashiau* 'discuss with', *niru* 'resemble', *chigau* 'differ' and *onajida* 'be the same'. (See Exs. (b), (c) and (d).)

2. In reciprocal sentences, the subject and X in X *to* are interchangeable. For example, Ex. (b) can be restated as in (1).

   (1) みどりは一郎と結婚した。
   Midori wa Ichirō to kekkonshita.
   (Midori married Ichiro.)

   Ex. (b) is described from Ichiro's point of view, while (1) is described from Midori's point of view. (⇨ *to¹*, REL. I)

[Related Expression]

Some reciprocal expressions take X *ni* or X *to* depending on the meaning, as in [1] and [2].

[1] a. 正男は先生と話した。
   *Masao wa sensei **to** hanashita.*
   (Masao talked *with* his teacher.)

   b. 正男は先生に話した。
   *Masao wa sensei **ni** hanashita.*
   (Masao talked *to* his teacher.)

[2] a. 明は君子とぶつかった。
   *Akira wa Kimiko **to** butsukatta.*
   (Akira bumped into Kimiko.)

   b. 明は君子にぶつかった。
   *Akira wa Kimiko **ni** butsukatta.*
   (Akira bumped into Kimiko.)

T

The difference is that *to* implies a "bidirectional" action while *ni* implies a "unidirectional" one. For example, [2a] implies that both Akira and Kimiko were moving, whereas in [2b] only Akira was moving. Thus, *to* is unacceptable in [3] because *hashira* 'post' is immobile.

[3] 明は柱に / *とぶつかった。
  Akira wa hashira ni / **to butsukatta.*
  (Akira bumped into a post.)

---

to³ と　*prt.*

~~~
a particle which marks a quotation,
sound or the manner in which s.o. /
s.t. does s.t.
~~~

that; with the sound of; in the manner of

♦ **Key Sentence**

	Quotation, sound or manner adverb		
ヒルさん は 私 に 日本語 で *Hiru-san wa watashi ni nihongo de*	「こんにち は。」 " *Konnichi wa.*"	と *to*	言った / *itta* / 言いました。 *iimashita.*
(Mr. Hill said to me in Japanese, "Hello!")			

Formation

(i) Quotation　と
　　　　　　　　　to

　「私　は　学生　です。」と　("I am a student.")
　" *Watashi wa gakusei desu.*" *to*

　私　は　学生　だと　(that I am a student)
　watashi wa gakusei da to

(ii) Phonomime と
       to

バタバタ と   (with a clattering noise)
batabata to

(iii) Phenomime と
        to

ゆっくり と   (slowly)
yukkuri to

(iv) Psychomime と
         to

うきうき と   (cheerfully)
ukiuki to

Examples

(a) トムは日本へ行きたいと言っている。
Tomu wa Nihon e ikitai to itte iru.
(Tom says that he wants to go to Japan.)

(b) これは十六世紀に建てられたと書いてあります。
Kore wa jūrokuseiki ni taterareta to kaite arimasu.
(It is written that this was built in the sixteenth century.)

(c) 私はバスで行こうと思う。
Watashi wa basu de ikō to omou.
(I think I will go by bus.)

(d) 子供達はバタバタと走り回った。
Kodomotachi wa batabata to hashirimawatta.
(Lit. The children ran around with a clattering noise.)

(e) 真知子はしっかりと私の手をにぎった。
Machiko wa shikkari to watashi no te o nigitta.
(Machiko grabbed my hand firmly.)

(f) ベンはむっつりと座っている。
Ben wa muttsuri to suwatte iru.
(Ben is sitting sullenly.)

Notes

1. *To* is basically used to mark a quotation; the literal meaning of ~ *to iu* is 'say with (the sound) ~'. This use of *to*, however, has been ex-

tended further to cover indirect quotations, as in Exs. (a) and (b), and even thoughts (i.e., internal voice), as in Ex. (c). Note that in Japanese *to* is necessary for both direct and indirect quotations, as seen in KS and Ex. (a).

2. *To* is used to mark the content of such actions as *omou* 'think; feel', *kangaeru* 'think (with the intellect)', *kaku* 'write', *kiku* 'hear' and *setsumeisuru* 'explain'.

3. *To* is also used with phonomimes, as in Ex. (d). Again, the idea is that someone / something makes the sound marked by *to* when doing something. Note that sound symbolisms in Japanese are not children's words. Rather, they are an important part of the Japanese vocabulary.

4. When a sound is repeated twice like *batabata* in Ex. (d), *to* can be omitted. When a sound is not repeated, however, *to* does not drop. Examples:

　(1) a. 子供達はバタバタと / ø 走り回った。
　　　　*Kodomotachi wa batabata **to** / ø hashirimawatta.*
　　　　(Lit. The children ran around with a clattering noise.)

　　　b. 正男はバタンと / *ø ドアを閉めた。
　　　　*Masao wa batan **to** / *ø doa o shimeta.*
　　　　(Masao slammed the door (lit. closed the door with a bang).)

5. The use of *to* with phonomimes is extended to phenomimes and psychomimes, as in Exs. (e) and (f), though these are not representations of actual sounds.

　　　　　　(⇒ Characteristics of Japanese Grammar, 8. Sound Symbolisms)

T

---

to⁴ と　*conj.*

a subordinate conjunction which marks a condition that brings about an noncontrollable event or state	if; when 【REL. **tara** (*ba*, *nara*); **toki**】

♦ **Key Sentence**

Sentence₁ (informal, nonpast)		Sentence₂
ニューヨーク に 行く *Nyūyōku ni iku*	と *to*	おもしろい 店 が たくさん ある / あります。 *omoshiroi mise ga takusan aru / arimasu.*
(If you go to New York, there are many interesting shops.)		

Formation

{V / Adj (*i* / *na*) / N+Copula} inf·nonpast と
                                          to

話す   と   (if s.o. talks)
hanasu to

高い と   (if s.t. is expensive)
takai to

静かだ   と   (if s.t. is quiet)
shizukada to

先生   だ と   (if s.o. is a teacher)
sensei da to

Examples

(a) それは先生に聞くとすぐ分かった。
   Sore wa sensei ni kiku to sugu wakatta.
   (I understood it immediately when I asked my teacher.)

(b) タイヤは古いとあぶないですよ。
   Taiya wa furui to abunaidesu yo.
   (Tires are dangerous if they are old.)

(c) 魚がきらいだと日本へ行った時困りますか？
   Sakana ga kiraida to Nihon e itta toki komarimasu ka?
   (If you don't like fish, will you have trouble when you go to Japan?)

(d) 学生だと割引があります。
   Gakusei da to waribiki ga arimasu.
   (If you are a student, there is a discount.)

Notes

1. In S₁ *to* S₂, S₁ must be nonpast even if it expresses a past event or action, as in Ex. (a). Tense is expressed in S₂.

2. In S₁ *to* S₂, S₂ cannot be a command, a request, a suggestion, an invitation or a volitional sentence. The following sentences are all ungrammatical.

(1) 仕事が早く終わると私のうちに
Shigoto ga hayaku owaru to watashi no uchi ni

　　a. *来なさい。
　　　 *kinasai.

　　b. *来てください。
　　　 *kite kudasai.

　　c. *来たらどうですか。
　　　 *kitara dō desu ka.

　　d. *来ませんか。
　　　 *kimasen ka.

(If you finish your work early,
　　a. come to my place.
　　b. please come to my place.
　　c. why don't you come to my place?
　　d. wouldn't you like to come to my place?)

(2) *仕事が早く終わるとおうちにおうかがいします。
*Shigoto ga hayaku owaru to o-uchi ni o-ukagai shimasu.
(If I finish my work early, I'll visit your place.)

(For the correct structures, see *tara*, Note 4.)

★ **Semantic Derivations of *To***

〈Accompaniment〉 *to*²:
太郎は花子と踊った。
Tarō wa Hanako to odotta.
(Taro danced with Hanako.)

to 'with'

〈Reciprocal relationship〉 *to*²:
これはあれと同じだ。
Kore wa are to onajida.
(This is the same as that.)

⟨ Exhaustive listing ⟩ ***to*¹:**

僕は刺身とてんぷらを食べた。

*Boku wa sashimi **to** tenpura o tabeta.*

(I ate *sashimi* and *tempura*.)

⟨ Direct quotation ⟩ ***to*³:**

トムは「こんにちは。」と言った。

*Tomu wa " Konnichi wa." **to** itta.*

(Tom said, " *Konnichi wa*.")

⟨ Indirect quotation ⟩ ***to*³:**

トムは学生だと言った。

*Tomu wa gakusei da **to** itta.*

(Tom said that he was a student.)

⟨ Thought ⟩ ***to*³:**

一郎は大丈夫だと思った。

*Ichirō wa daijōbuda **to** omotta.*

(Ichiro thought that there would be no problem.)

⟨ Sound symbolism ⟩ ***to*³:**

太郎はバタバタと走った。

*Tarō wa batabata **to** hashitta.*

(Taro ran with a clattering sound.)

⟨ Manner of action ⟩ ***to*³:**

花子はじっと待っていた。

*Hanako wa jit**to** matte ita.*

(Hanako was waiting quietly.)

⟨ Condition of noncontrollable occurrence ⟩ ***to*⁴:**

ニューヨークへ行くといいレストランがある。

*Nyūyōku e iku **to** ii resutoran ga aru.*

(If you go to New York, there are good restaurants.)

T

~to ieba ~と言えば　*phr.*

an expression which presents as the topic of a following discourse a phrase which has just been uttered	Speaking of ~ 【REL. *ttara*; *tte*】

◆**Key Sentence**

A:		
この　本　は　田中さん　に　借りた　ん　です。 *Kono hon wa Tanaka-san ni karita n desu.*		
(I borrowed this book from Mr. Tanaka.)		

B:		
田中さん *Tanaka-san*	と 言えば *to ieba*	もう　病気　は　治った　の　かしら。 *mō byōki wa naotta no kashira.*
(Speaking of Mr. Tanaka, I wonder if he's gotten over his illness yet.)		

Examples

(a) A：次の日曜日は京都へ行くつもりだ。
　　Tsugi no nichiyōbi wa Kyōto e iku tsumori da.
　　(I'm going to Kyoto next Sunday.)

　　B：京都と言えば，春子が京都大学の入学試験に通ったそうだ。
　　Kyōto to ieba, Haruko ga Kyōtodaigaku no nyūgakushiken ni tōtta sōda.
　　(Speaking of Kyoto, I heard that Haruko passed Kyoto University's entrance exam.)

(b) A：小西君はよく休むねえ。
　　Konishi-kun wa yoku yasumu nē.
　　(Mr. Konishi is absent frequently, isn't he?)

　　B：よく休むと言えば，山本君も最近見ませんね。
　　Yoku yasumu to ieba, Yamamoto-kun mo saikin mimasen ne.
　　(Talking about (someone's) frequent absences, we don't see Mr. Yamamoto these days either, do we?)

Notes

1. *To ieba* literally means 'if you say that ~', but it is used as a topic

presentation expression meaning 'speaking of'.

2. Usually a noun phrase is presented by *to ieba*, but any sentence element is possible. For example, in Ex. (b), a verb phrase is presented.

3. The informal form of *to ieba* is *tte ieba*.

〔Related Expressions〕

There are several other expressions used to present topics.

I. *Ttara* is the abbreviation for *to kitara* or *to ittara* and is used to present noun phrase topics in informal conversation. It is more emphatic than the topic marker *wa* and sometimes means something like 'when it comes to ~' or 'in the case of ~'. Example:

[1] よし江ったら私には何も言わないのよ。
Yoshie **ttara** watashi ni wa nani mo iwanai no yo.
(Yoshie didn't tell me anything, you know.)

II. *Tte*, the abbreviation for *to iu to* 'when you say ~', or *to iu no wa* 'what you say (or call) ~', is also used to present topics in informal conversation. Like *to ieba* any sentence element can precede *tte*, and that element is usually a part of the conversation partner's previous utterance. Examples:

[2] A: シービーを買いましたよ。
Shibi o kaimashita yo.
(I bought a CB.)

B: シービーって?
Shibi **tte**?
((What do you mean by what you call) a CB?)

[3] A: 来週から英語を教えるんです。
Raishū kara eigo o oshieru n desu.
(I'm teaching English from next week.)

B: 英語を教えるって, だれに?
Eigo o oshieru**tte**, dare ni?
(Teaching English? To whom?)

~to iu ～という　*phr.*

> a phrase marking information which identifies or explains the noun following the phrase

called; that says ~; that

◆**Key Sentences**

(A)

		Noun	
「雪国」 *"Yukiguni"*	と　いう *to　iu*	小説 *shōsetsu*	を　読んだ / 読みました。 *o　yonda / yomimashita.*
(I read a novel called *Snow Country*.)			

(B)

Message		Noun	
山田さん　が　入院した *Yamada-san ga nyūinshita*	と　いう *to　iu*	知らせ *shirase*	を　聞いた / 聞きました。 *o　kiita / kikimashita.*
(I heard the news that Mr. Yamada has been hospitalized.)			

(C)

		Noun	
もっと　がんばらなくて　は (ならない) *Motto ganbaranakute wa (naranai)*	と　いう *to　iu*	気持ち *kimochi*	が　ある / あります。 *ga aru / arimasu.*
(I have the feeling that I have to keep hanging in there.)			

Examples

(a) 「七人の侍」という映画を見たことがありますか。
   "Shichinin no samurai" to iu eiga o mita koto ga arimasu ka.
   (Have you ever seen the film called *Seven Samurai*?)

(b) ジューンが日本へ行くという話は本当ですか。
   Jūn ga Nihon e iku to iu hanashi wa hontō desu ka.
   (Lit. Is the story that June is going to Japan true? (= Is it true that June is going to Japan?))

(c) その人に会いたくないという気持ちはよく分かります。

Sono hito ni aitakunai to iu kimochi wa yoku wakarimasu.

(I am well aware of your feeling that you don't want to see him.)

(d) 友達が今日来るということをすっかり忘れていた。

Tomodachi ga kyō kuru to iu koto o sukkari wasurete ita.

(I completely forgot the fact that my friend is coming today.)

Notes

1. *To iu* is a combination of the quote marker *to* and *iu* 'call, say'.

(⇨ **to**[3])

2. The head noun in KS(B) is a noun of communication, such as *hanashi* 'story', *nyūsu* 'news', *shirase* 'information', *tegami* 'letter' and *uwasa* 'rumor'. The head noun in KS(C) is a noun of human emotion, such as *kanashimi* 'sadness', *kanji* 'feeling', *ki* 'feeling', *kimochi* 'feeling', *osore* 'fear' and *yorokobi* 'joy'.

3. *To iu* is optional if the preceding element is not a noun or a clause which represents a quotation, as in KS(C) and Exs. (c) and (d).

4. When *to iu* is used at the end of a sentence, it means *hearsay* (" I heard that ~, They say ~, It is said that ~ "). The sentence-final *to iu* is used only in written Japanese, as in (1). (⇨ **soda**[1])

(1) 学生の話によると吉田先生は教え方が非常に上手だという。

*Gakusei no hanashi ni yoru to Yoshida-sensei wa oshiekata ga hijōni jōzuda **to iu**.*

(According to the students, Prof. Yoshida's teaching method is very skillful.)

T

toka とか *conj.*

a conjunction that lists two or more
items, actions or states as inexhaustive examples

and; or
【REL. *tari*; *ya*】

♦**Key Sentences**

(A)

Topic (subject)		Noun		Noun		Noun
私 *Watashi*	は *wa*	バッハ *Bahha*	とか *toka*	モーツアルト *Mōtsuaruto*	とか *toka*	ベートーベン *Bētōben*
が 好きだ / 好きです。 *ga sukida / sukidesu.*						
(I like Bach, Mozart and Beethoven, among others.)						

(B)

	Sentence		Sentence		
疲れた 時 は *Tsukareta toki wa*	お風呂 に 入る *o-furo ni hairu*	とか *toka*	早く 寝る *hayaku neru*	とか *toka*	しなさい。 *shinasai.*
(When you are tired, do things like taking a bath or going to sleep early.)					

Formation

KS(A):

N とか N とか...
   toka   *toka*...

学生 とか 先生 とか... (students and teachers...(among others))
gakusei toka sensei toka...

KS(B):

Sinf とか Sinf とか する
    toka   *toka suru*

テレビ を 見る とか 本 を 読む とか する (do such things as watching
terebi o miru toka hon o yomu toka suru TV or reading books)

(a) 日本の茶道とか生け花とかいうものをよく知らない。

Nihon no sadō toka ikebana toka iu mono o yoku shiranai.

(I don't know much about things like the Japanese tea ceremony and flower arranging.)

(b) A : どんな日本の映画を見ましたか。

　　Donna Nihon no eiga o mimashita ka.

　　(What kind of Japanese movie did you see?)

　　B : 黒沢の「七人の侍」とか「生きる」とか「影武者」を見ました。

　　Kurosawa no " Shichinin no Samurai" toka "Ikiiu" toka "Kage-musha" o mimashita.

　　(I saw Kurosawa's *Seven Samurai*, *Ikiru* and *Kagemusha*.)

(c) A : 日曜日にはどんなことをしていますか。

　　Nichiyōbi ni wa donna koto o shite imasu ka.

　　(What sorts of things do you do on Sundays?)

　　B : 音楽を聞くとか，本を読むとかしています。

　　Ongaku o kiku toka, hon o yomu toka shite imasu.

　　(I do things like listening to music or reading books.)

1. The conjunction *toka* is a combination of the quote marker *to*[3] and *ka*[1]. That is why *toka* is often followed by the verb *iu* 'say', as in Ex. (a). When *toka* is followed by *iu*, as in (1), it is not a conjunction; it is a quote marker. The *ka* indicates the speaker's uncertainty about the quoted report.

   (1) 佐藤さんは忙しくて行けないとか言っていた。

   　　*Satō-san wa isogashikute ikenai **to ka** itte ita.*

   　　(Mr. Sato was saying he can't go there because he's busy or something.)

2. N_1 *to ka iu* N_2 meaning 'N_2 that is called N_1 or something like that' is another example of *toka* used in the above sense.

   (2) 野口とかいう人が来た。

   　　*Noguchi **to ka iu** hito ga kita.*

   　　(A person named Noguchi or something like that showed up.)

3. S *toka* S *toka suru* is used when a statement refers to something in general rather than to something specific. Thus, this structure is inappropriate in (3). (See Related Expression.)

⑶ A : ニューヨークではどんなことをしましたか。
   Nyūyōku de wa donna koto o shimashita ka.
   (What sort of things did you do in New York?)

   B : *ミュージカルを見るとか美術館に行くとかしました。
   Myūjikaru o miru **toka bijutsukan ni iku **toka** shimashita.*
   (I did things like watching musicals and visiting art museums.)

[Related Expression]

~*tari* ~*tari suru*, like S *toka* S *toka suru*, indicates an inexhaustive listing of examples. It differs from S *toka* S *toka suru*, however, in that it can be used in both general and specific statements. As noted in Note 3, the *toka* construction can only be used in general statements. Thus, the grammatical version of (3B) is [1].

[1] ミュージカルを見たり美術館に行ったりしました。
   *Myūjikaru o mi**tari** bijutsukan ni it**tari** shimashita.*

When ~*tari* ~*tari suru* indicates alternative actions or states, it cannot be replaced by *toka*.

[2] 子供が部屋を出たり / *出るとか　入ったり / *入るとかしている。
   *Kodomo ga heya o **detari** / ***deru toka haittari** / ***hairu toka shite iru**.*
   (A child is going in and out of the room.)

T

toki 時　*n.*

> a dependent noun which indicates the time when s.o. / s.t. will do / does / did s.t. or the time when s.o. / s.t. will be / is / was in some state

at the time when; when
[REL. ~*tara*; *to*[4]**]**

♦ **Key Sentences**

(A)

Topic (subject)		Subordinate Clause (informal)†			Predicate
私	は	**日本 に いた**	時	(に)	お茶 を 習った / 習いました。
Watashi	*wa*	***Nihon ni ita***	*toki*	*(ni)*	*o-cha o naratta / naraimashita.*
(I learned the tea ceremony when I was in Japan.)					

†*Da* after Adj (*na*) stem and N changes to *na* and *no*, respectively.

(B)

Topic (subject)		Noun				Predicate
ひろし	は	**試験**	の	時	(に)	かぜ を ひいた / ひきました。
Hiroshi	*wa*	***shiken***	*no*	*toki*	*(ni)*	*kaze o hiita / hikimashita.*
(Hiroshi caught cold at exam time.)						

Formation

(i) {V / Adj (*i*)} inf 時
　　　　　　　　　　 toki

　　{話す　／話した}　　時　　(when s.o. talks / talked)
　　{*hanasu* / *hanashita*} *toki*

　　{高い／高かった}　時　　(when s.t. is / was expensive)
　　{*takai* / *takakatta*} *toki*

(ii) Adj (*na*) stem {な／だった} 時
　　　　　　　　　　 {*na* / *datta*} *toki*

　　{静かな　／静かだった　　時　　(when s.t. is / was quiet)
　　{*shizukana* / *shizukadatta*} *toki*

(iii) N {の／だった} 時
　　　　 {*no* / *datta*} *toki*

　　{先生　の／先生 だった}　時　　(when s.o. is / was a teacher)
　　{*sensei no* / *sensei datta*} *toki*

Examples

(a) 松本さんは朝ご飯を食べる時いつもテレビを見る。
Matsumoto-san wa asagohan o taberu toki itsumo terebi o miru.
(Mr. Matsumoto always watches TV when he eats his breakfast.)

(b) テリーはジュースが安い時にたくさん買っておいた。
Terī wa jūsu ga yasui toki ni takusan katte oita.
(Terry bought a lot of juice when it was cheap.)

(c) 僕は静かな時しか本を読まない。
Boku wa shizukana toki shika hon o yomanai.
(I read only when it's quiet.)

(d) 私が大学生だった時妹はまだ三つだった。
Watashi ga daigakusei datta toki imōto wa mada mittsu datta.
(When I was a college student, my sister was only three.)

(e) これは出発の時にわたします。
Kore wa shuppatsu no toki ni watashimasu.
(I'll give this to you when you leave (lit. at the time of your departure).)

Notes

1. *Toki*, by itself, means 'time', but when it is used as a dependent noun with a modifying phrase or clause, it means 'at the time when' or 'when'.

2. The clause preceding *toki* is a type of relative clause; therefore, the basic rules for relative clauses apply to this construction. (⇨ Relative Clause) The following two rules are particularly important:

   (A) If the subject of the *toki* clause is different from that of the main clause, it is marked by *ga*. Compare (1) with KS(A):

      (1) メアリーは私が日本にいた時フランスにいた。
      *Meari wa watashi **ga** Nihon ni ita toki Furansu ni ita.*
      (Mary was in France while I was in Japan.)

   (B) The predicate form is usually informal except that *da* after Adj (*na*) stem and N changes to *na* and *no*, respectively.

3. The particle *ni* after *toki* is optional. With *ni*, time is emphasized and sometimes comes under focus. Compare the two sentences in (2).

   (2) a. 私は学生の時よく勉強した。
      Watashi wa gakusei no toki yoku benkyōshita.
      (I studied hard when I was a student.)

   b. 私は学生の時によく勉強した。
      *Watashi wa gakusei no toki **ni** yoku benkyōshita.*
      (It was when I was a student that I studied hard.)

4. If S_2 in S_1 *toki* S_2 is in the past tense and S_1 expresses a state, the tense of S_1 can be either past or nonpast, as in (3).

(3) a. 私は日本にいる / いた時田中先生に会った。

    *Watashi wa Nihon ni **iru** / **ita** toki Tanaka-sensei ni **atta**.*

    (I met Prof. Tanaka when I was in Japan.)

b. 肉が高い / 高かった時は魚も高かった。

    *Niku ga **takai** / **takakatta** toki wa sakana mo takakatta.*

    (When meat was expensive, fish was expensive, too.)

5. When S_1 in S_1 *toki* S_2 expresses an action, the meaning of the sentence changes depending on the tenses of S_1 and S_2.

(A) When the verb in S_1 is not a movement verb:

(4) a. 私はご飯を食べる時手を洗う。

    *Watashi wa gohan o **taberu** toki te o **arau**.*

    (I (will) wash my hands (*right*) *before* I eat my meal.)

b. 私はご飯を食べた時手を洗う。

    *Watashi wa gohan o **tabeta** toki te o **arau**.*

    (I (will) wash my hands (*right*) *after* I've eaten my meal.)

c. 私はご飯を食べる時手を洗った。

    *Watashi wa gohan o **taberu** toki te o **aratta**.*

    (I washed my hands (*right*) *before* I ate my meal.)

d. 私はご飯を食べた時手を洗った。

    *Watashi wa gohan o **tabeta** toki te o **aratta**.*

    (I washed my hands (*right*) *after* I ate my meal.)

(B) When the verb in S_1 is a movement verb:

(5) a. 私はシカゴへ行く時すしを食べるつもりだ。

    *Watashi wa Shikago e **iku** toki sushi o **taberu tsu-mori da**.*

    (I'm going to eat *sushi* (A) (*right*) *before* I leave for Chicago. / (B) *on the way* to Chicago.)

b. 私はシカゴへ行った時すしを食べるつもりだ。

    *Watashi wa Shikago e **itta** toki sushi o **taberu tsu-mori da**.*

    (I'm going to eat *sushi* after I've arrived in Chicago.)

c. 私はシカゴへ行く時すしを食べた。

    *Watashi wa Shikago e **iku** toki sushi o **tabeta**.*

494 *toki*

((A) I ate *sushi* (*right*) *before* I left for Chicago. (B) I ate *sushi on the way* to Chicago.)

   d. 私はシカゴへ行った時すしを食べた。

    *Watashi wa Shikago e **itta** toki sushi o **tabeta**.*

    (I ate *sushi* after I arrived in Chicago.)

(C) When the action in S₁ and the action in S₂ take place simultaneously or concurrently:

  (6) a. 私はシカゴへ行く時車で行く。

     *Watashi wa Shikago e **iku** toki kuruma de **iku**.*

     (When I go to Chicago, I go by car.)

    b. *私はシカゴへ行った時車で行く。

     Watashi wa Shikago e **itta toki kuruma de **iku**.*

    c. 私はシカゴへ行く時車で行った。

     *Watashi wa Shikago e **iku** toki kuruma de **itta**.*

     (When I went to Chicago, I went by car.)

    d. 私はシカゴへ行った時車で行った。

     *Watashi wa Shikago e **itta** toki kuruma de **itta**.*

     (When I went to Chicago, I went by car.)

[Related Expressions]

Unlike when-clauses in English, *toki*-clauses do not indicate condition. In other words, *toki*-clauses are genuine time clauses. In order to indicate condition as expressed in when-clauses, conjunctions like ~*tara* and *to* are used. (⇨ ~*tara*; *to*⁴) Thus, if [1] expresses a condition which causes the hearer surprise, *toki* cannot be used.

[1] You will be surprised when you see it.

In this case, *tara* or *to* must be used, as in [2].

[2] それを{見たら / 見ると / *見る時 / *見た時}おどろきますよ。

   *Sore o {**mitara** / **miru to** / *miru **toki** / *mita **toki**} odorokimasu yo.*

   (You'll be surprised when you see it.)

tokoro da[1] ところだ   *phr.*

> A place is in a location which takes a certain amount of time to get to.

~ is (in) a place where it takes ~ to get to

♦ **Key Sentence**

Topic (subject)		Noun (location)		Means	Noun (duration)	
私　の　うち *Watashi no uchi*	は *wa*	駅 *eki*	から *kara*	歩いて *aruite*	十分 *juppun*	の *no*
ところ　だ / です。 *tokoro da / desu.*						

(Lit. My house is in a place where it takes ten minutes to get to from the station on foot. (=On foot my house is ten minutes from the station.))

Examples

(a) 学校はうちからバスで三十分のところです。

Gakkō wa uchi kara basu de sanjuppun no tokoro desu.

(Lit. My school is in a place where it takes thirty minutes to get to from home by bus. (=By bus it takes thirty minutes to get from home to school.))

(b) その病院はここから車で十五分のところだ。

Sono byōin wa koko kara kuruma de jūgofun no tokoro da.

(Lit. The hospital is in a place where it takes fifteen minutes to get to from here by car. (=By car the hospital is fifteen minutes from here.))

Notes

Tokoro da is a simplified form of *tokoro ni aru* 'be located in a place (where).' This expression can be simplified even more, as seen in (1).

(1) 学校はうちからバスで三十分(のところ)だ。

Gakkō wa uchi kara basu de sanjuppun (no tokoro) da.

(By bus my school is thirty minutes from home.)

T

tokoro da² ところだ   *phr.*

S.o. / s.t. is in the state where he / it is just about to do s.t., is doing s.t., has done s.t., or has been doing s.t.

be just about to do s.t.; be in the midst of doing s.t.; have just done s.t.; have been doing s.t.; almost did s.t.

【REL. *bakari*; *toki*】

♦ **Key Sentences**

(A)

Topic (subject)			Vinf·nonpast		
春江 *Harue*	は *wa*	晩ご飯　を *bangohan o*	**食べる** ***taberu***	ところ *tokoro*	だ / です。 *da / desu.*
(Harue is just about to eat her supper.)					

(B)

Topic (subject)			V*te*			
春江 *Harue*	は *wa*	晩ご飯　を *bangohan o*	**食べて** ***tabete***	いる *iru*	ところ *tokoro*	だ / です。 *da / desu.*
(Harue is in the midst of eating her supper.)						

(C)

Topic (subject)			Vinf·past		
春江 *Harue*	は *wa*	晩ご飯　を *bangohan o*	**食べた** ***tabeta***	ところ *tokoro*	だ / です。 *da / desu.*
(Harue has just eaten her supper.)					

(D)

Topic (subject)			V*te*			
春江 *Harue*	は *wa*	晩ご飯　を *bangohan o*	**食べて** ***tabete***	いた *ita*	ところ *tokoro*	だ / です。 *da / desu.*
(Harue has been eating her supper.)						

(E)

Topic (subject)					Vinf·nonpast		
私	は	もう 少し で 宿題 を			忘れる	ところ	だった / datta / でした。 deshita.
Watashi	wa	mō sukoshi de shukudai o			**wasureru**	tokoro	

(I almost forgot (lit. was about to forget) my homework.)

(F)

Topic (subject)		Adj (*i* / *na*)			Prt	
私	は	あぶない	ところ		を	ジーン に 助けて もらった / Jīn ni tasukete moratta / もらいました。 moraimashita.
Watashi	wa	**abunai**	tokoro		o	

(I was saved by Gene when I was in a crisis (lit. dangerous state).)

(G)

Noun				Prt	
お仕事中	の	ところ		を	すみません。
O-shigotochū	no	tokoro		o	sumimasen.

(I'm sorry to bother you in the midst of your work.)

Formation

(i) Vinf ところ だ
　　　　 tokoro da

　　{話す / 話した} ところ だ　(be just about to talk / have just talked)
　　{hanasu / hanashita} tokoro da

　　{食べる / 食べた} ところ だ　(be about to eat / have just eaten)
　　{taberu / tabeta} tokoro da

(ii) V*te* {いる / いた} ところ だ
　　　　　 {iru / ita} tokoro da

　　{話して いる / 話して いた} ところ だ　(be in the midst of talk-
　　{hanashite iru / hanashite ita} tokoro da　ing / have been talking)

T

{食べて いる / 食べて いた} ところ だ   (be in the midst of eating /
{*tabete iru* / *tabete ita*} *tokoro da*   have been eating)

(iii) Adj (*i*) inf·nonpast ところ
                            tokoro

忙しい ところ   (the state in which s.o. is busy)
isogashii tokoro

(iv) Adj (*na*) stem な ところ
                     na tokoro

大事な ところ   (the state in which s.t. is important)
daiji na tokoro

(v) N の ところ
      no tokoro

休み の ところ   (the state in which s.o. is off duty / on vacation)
yasumi no tokoro

Examples

(a) 僕は今出かけるところです。
   Boku wa ima dekakeru tokoro desu.
   (I'm just about to go out now.)

(b) テリーと踊っているところをマーサに見られてしまった。
   Teri to odotte iru tokoro o Māsa ni mirarete shimatta.
   (Lit. The state in which I was dancing with Terry was seen by Martha.
   (=Martha saw me when I was dancing with Terry.))

(c) ご飯を食べ終わったところにまり子がたずねて来た。
   Gohan o tabeowatta tokoro ni Mariko ga tazunete kita.
   (Lit. Mariko came (to see me) at the state in which I had just finished
   my meal. (=Mariko came to see me when I'd just finished my meal.))

(d) 三章まで読んだところで寝てしまった。
   Sanshō made yonda tokoro de nete shimatta.
   (I fell asleep when I had read up to the third chapter (lit. in the state
   in which I had read it up to the third chapter).)

(e) 私はあぶなくおぼれるところだった。
   Watashi wa abunaku oboreru tokoro datta.
   (I was almost drowned.)

(f) お忙しいところをどうもありがとうございました。

O-isogashii tokoro o dōmo arigatō gozaimashita.

(Lit. Thank you very much (for helping me) in the state when you are busy. (= Thank you very much for sparing your precious time with me.))

(g) 利男は一番大事なところでよく勉強しなかったから何も分からなくなってしまった。

Toshio wa ichiban daijina tokoro de yoku benkyōshinakatta kara nani mo wakaranaku natte shimatta.

(Lit. Toshio has come to the point of not understanding anything because he didn't study well in the state where (the class) was the most important. (= Toshio has gotten totally lost because he didn't study hard when it was most important.))

(h) お休みのところをすみません。

O-yasumi no tokoro o sumimasen.

(Lit. I'm sorry (to disturb) the state in which you are off duty. (= I'm sorry to bother you when you are off duty / on vacation.))

Notes

1. *Tokoro* itself means 'place', but it can also mean 'state' or 'time' when it is used with a modifying verb, adjective or noun.

2. As seen in KS(A) – KS(D), verbs which precede *tokoro* are either past or nonpast and either progressive or non-progressive, and each one of the four verb forms expresses a different aspect of the action.

3. As seen in KS(E), when the preceding verb is nonpast and non-progressive and the following copula is in the past tense, the sentence may mean 'someone or something almost did something.' (The literal meaning is 'someone or something was about to do something.') When *tokoro datta* means 'almost did something', such adverbs as *mō sukoshi de* 'just by a little' and *abunaku* 'nearly' are often used also, as in KS(E) and Ex. (e).

4. *Tokoro* can be followed by either the copula, as in KS(A) – KS(E), Exs. (a) and (e), or such particles as *o*, *ni*, *e* and *de*, as in KS(F) and KS(G), Exs. (b) – (d) and (f) – (h).

5. When adjectives or nouns with *no* precede *tokoro*, *tokoro* is usually followed by a particle rather than the copula, as in Exs. (f) and (h). The following sentences are ungrammatical:

(1) a. *私は今忙しいところです。

　　　 *Watashi wa ima isogashii tokoro desu.

　 b. *私は今休みのところです。

　　　 *Watashi wa ima yasumi no tokoro desu.

【Related Expressions】

I. When *tokoro* is used as a dependent noun, its function appears to be similar to that of *toki*. However, these two expressions are different in that *tokoro* basically indicates a state, while *toki* indicates a time. Thus, [1] makes sense by itself, but [2] does not.

[1] 僕は電話をかけるところだ。

　　 *Boku wa denwa o kakeru **tokoro da**.

　　 (Lit. I'm in the state where I'm going to place a call. (= I'm just about to call someone.))

[2] *僕は電話をかける時だ。

　　 *Boku wa denwa o kakeru **toki da**.

　　 (*I am when I'm going to place a call.)

II. V*te iru* / *ita tokoro da* is similar to V*te iru* / *ita*. The difference is that the former focuses more on the state or the scene while the latter concentrates on the action. Compare the usages of the two expressions in [3] and [4].

[3] あ，ジョンが走っている / *走っているところだ。

　　 *A, Jon ga hashi**te iru** / *hashi**tte iru tokoro da**.

　　 (Look! John is running.)

[4] この写真は学生がフリスビーをしているところです / *しています。

　　 *Kono shashin wa gakusei ga furisubi o shi**te iru tokoro desu** / *shi**te imasu**.

　　 (This picture shows students playing frisbee (lit. is a scene of students playing frisbee).)

III. Vinf·past *tokoro da* is similar to Vinf·past *bakari da*. However, their implications are different. That is, the former indicates that someone / something is in the state of having just done something, while the latter implies that someone / something did something and not much time has passed since then. Thus, *tokoro da* is strange in [5] because *isshūkan mae* 'a week ago' is too far in the past to be used to express "have just done something".

[5] 私は山本先生には一週間前にあったばかりだ / *ところだ。

*Watashi wa Yamamoto-sensei ni wa isshūkan mae ni atta **bakari da** / ***tokoro da**.*

(I met Prof. Yamamoto only a week ago.)

~to shite ~として   *prt.*

> a compound particle which indicates   as ; in the capacity of
> the capacity, role or function of s.o.
> or s.t.

♦ **Key Sentence**

	Noun		
田中さん　は *Tanaka-san wa*	セールスマン ***sērusuman***	と　して *to shite*	採用された / されました。 *saiyōsareta / saremashita.*

(Mr. Tanaka was hired as a salesman.)

Formation

N　として
　　to shite

先生　　として　　(as a teacher)
sensei to shite

Examples

(a) 私は医者としてあなたに言います。

Watashi wa isha to shite anata ni iimasu.

(I'll tell you (this) as a doctor.)

(b) 木村さんとは友達としてつき合っているだけです。

Kimura-san to wa tomodachi to shite tsukiatte iru dake desu.

(I'm just keeping company with Mr. Kimura as a friend.)

(c) この部屋は物置として使っている。

Kono heya wa monooki to shite tsukatte iru.

(I'm using this room as a storeroom.)

～to shite wa ～としては   *prt.*

| a compound particle which indicates a standard for comparisons | for 【REL. ～*ni shite wa*】 |

◆ **Key Sentence**

	Noun		
この ステーキ は *Kono sutēki wa*	**日本 の ステーキ** **Nihon no sutēki**	と し て は *to shite wa*	安い / 安いです。 *yasui / yasuidesu.*

(This steak is inexpensive for Japanese steak.)

Formation

N と し て は
   to shite wa

先生 と し て は   (for a teacher)
sensei to shite wa

Examples

(a) ジョンソンさんは日本語の一年生としては日本語が上手だ。
   Jonson-san wa nihongo no ichinensei to shite wa nihongo ga jōzuda.
   (Mr. Johnson is good at Japanese for a first-year student (of Japanese).)

(b) これは日本のアパートとしては大きい方です。
   Kore wa Nihon no apāto to shite wa ōkii hō desu.
   (For a Japanese apartment, this is one of the bigger ones.)

[Related Expression]

Ni shite wa is also used to present a standard for comparisons. However, it is different from *to shite wa* in terms of the speaker's presupposition. That is, sentences with X *ni shite wa* presuppose that the person or the thing referred to by the subject is X, whereas those with X *to shite wa* have no such presupposition. In Ex. (a), for example, Mr. Johnson may or may not be a first-year Japanese student. However, if *ni shite wa* is used, it is presupposed that he is actually a first-year Japanese student. The two expressions are also different in that *ni shite wa* can be used when the speaker doesn't know exactly what he is comparing with the standard he presents, but *to shite wa* cannot be used in such situations. For example, suppose that someone receives a package and doesn't know its contents. In this situation, he can say *hon ni shite wa*, assuming that the package contains books, but he cannot say *hon to shite wa*, as in [1].

[1]　これは本にしては / *としては軽すぎるね。
　　　*Kore wa hon **ni shite wa** / *to shite wa karusugiru ne.*
　　　(This is too light for books, isn't it?)

tsumori つもり　　*n.*

an intention or conviction of a speaker (or a person with whom the speaker can empathize) about his future or past actions or current state	intend to ~ ; be convinced that ~ ; believe ; feel sure that ~ ; be going to ; mean 【REL. *hazu*; ~*yō to omou*】

♦**Key Sentences**

(A)

Topic (subject)			Vinf·nonpast		
私 *Watashi*	は *wa*	来年 *rainen*	結婚する **kekkonsuru**	つもり *tsumori*	だ / です。 *da / desu.*
(I intend to get married next year.)					

(B)

Topic (subject)			Adj (*i*) inf·nonpast		
父 *Chichi*	は *wa*	まだ *mada*	若い **wakai**	つもり *tsumori*	だ / です。 *da / desu.*
(My father is convinced that he is still young.)					

(C)

Topic (subject)			Vinf·past		
私	は	よく	読んだ	つもり	だ / です。
Watashi	*wa*	*yoku*	***yonda***	*tsumori*	*da / desu.*
(I'm convinced that I read it carefully.)					

(D)

Topic (subject)		Noun			
これ	は	お礼	の	つもり	だ / です。
Kore	*wa*	***o-rei***	*no*	*tsumori*	*da / desu.*
(Lit. This is my intention of appreciation. (=This is a token of my appreciation.))					

Formation

(i) Vinf つもり だ
　　　　tsumori da

　{話す　/話した}　つもり　だ　(intend to talk / s.o. is convinced he
　{*hanasu* / *hanashita*} *tsumori da*　talked)

(ii) Adj (*i*) inf·nonpast つもり だ
　　　　　　　　　tsumori da

　強い　つもり　だ　(s.o. is convinced that he is strong)
　tsuyoi tsumori da

(iii) Adj (*na*) stem な つもり だ
　　　　　　　　na tsumori da

　元気な　つもり　だ　(s.o. is convinced that he is healthy)
　genkina tsumori da

(iv) N の つもり だ
　　　　no tsumori da

　先生　の　つもり　だ　(s.o. is convinced that he is a teacher)
　sensei no tsumori da

Examples

(a) 休みには何をするつもりですか。
　　Yasumi ni wa nani o suru tsumori desu ka.
　　(What do you intend to do during the vacation?)

(b) 僕は大学に行くつもりはない。
Boku wa daigaku ni iku tsumori wa nai.
(I have no intention of going to college.)

(c) あんな人にはもう会わないつもりです。
Anna hito ni wa mō awanai tsumori desu.
(I do not intend to see that kind of person.)

(d) 私はまだ元気なつもりだ。
Watashi wa mada genkina tsumori da.
(I'm convinced that I'm still healthy.)

(e) 話したつもりでしたが，話さなかったんですね。
Hanashita tsumori deshita ga, hanasanakatta n desu ne.
(I thought I talked to you, but I didn't, did I?)

(f) この仕事は遊びのつもりです。
Kono shigoto wa asobi no tsumori desu.
(This work is intended to be a pastime.)

(g) それで勉強しているつもりですか。
Sore de benkyōshite iru tsumori desu ka.
(Are you sure you can study like that?)

Notes

1. *Tsumori* is a dependent noun and must be preceded by a modifier. The minimal modifier is *sono* 'that'.

   (1) A: 行くつもりですか。
   Iku tsumori desu ka.
   (Do you intend to go there?)

   B: ええ，その**つもり**です / *ええ，**つもり**です。
   *Ē, sono **tsumori** desu / *Ē, **tsumori** desu.*
   (Yes, I do.)

2. The subject of a statement containing *tsumori da* must be the first person or someone with whom the speaker empathizes. In a question, however, the subject must be the second person or someone with whom the hearer empathizes.

   (2) a. 僕 / 母 / 友達 / *あのサラリーマン / *あなたは食べるつもりだ。
   ***Boku** / **Haha** / **Tomodachi** / *Ano sarariman* / *Anata** wa taberu tsumori da.*
   (I / My mother / My friend / That salaried man / You intend(s) to eat it.)

b. **僕 / *母 / *友達 / 山田さん / あなたは食べるつもりですか。*

*Boku / *Haha / *Tomodachi / Yamada-san / Anata wa
taberu tsumori desu ka.

(Do / Does I / my mother / my friend / Mr. Yamada / you
intend to eat it?)

3. *Tsumori da* can be negated in two ways. The verb / adjective in front
of *tsumori* can be negated, as in Ex. (c), or *tsumori* can be negated as
tsumori wa nai (not **tsumori de wa nai*), as in Ex. (b). The difference
between these two negative versions is that the second version implies
stronger negation than the first one, as shown by (3) below:

(3) A：今晩の音楽会に行くつもりですか。

　　Konban no ongakukai ni iku tsumori desu ka.

　　(Do you intend to go to tonight's concert?)

B：まだよく分かりませんが，多分，行かないつもりです / ??行くつ
　　もりはありません。

　　Mada yoku wakarimasen ga, tabun, **ikanai tsumori desu** /
　　*??**iku tsumori wa arimasen**.*

　　(I can't tell for sure now, but probably I'm not going there.)

[Related Expressions]

I. *Tsumori* should not be confused with *hazu* which means 'expectation'
rather than 'conviction'. (⇨ **hazu**)

II. *Tsumori da* is comparable but not identical to *yō to omou*. Firstly, *yō
to omou* can replace *tsumori da* only in KS(A), that is, only when a
verb precedes *tsumori da*. Secondly, *yō to omou* indicates a spur-of-
the moment decision while *tsumori da* indicates a more stable conviction / intention. Thus, if you are shown a car by a car salesman, you
can say:

[1] a. この車はよさそうなので買おうと思いますがいくらですか。

　　Kono kuruma wa yosasōna node **kaō to omoimasu** *ga
　　ikura desu ka.*

　　(This car looks nice, so I think I will buy it, but how much
　　is it?)

But it is strange to say:

b. ??この車はよさそうなので買うつもりですがいくらですか。

　　??Kono kuruma wa yosasōna node **kau tsumori desu** *ga
　　ikura desu ka.*

(Lit. ??This car looks nice, so I intend to buy it, but how much is it?)

Or, if you see an interesting ad for a stereo set in the newspaper, you can say [2a] but not [2b].

[2] a. ステレオの広告を見て買おうと思ったら家内に反対された。

Sutereo no kōkoku o mite **kaō to omottara** kanai ni han-taisareta.

(Lit. Upon looking at an ad for stereos, I thought I would buy one, but my wife objected to it.)

b. ??ステレオの広告を見て買うつもりだったら，家内に反対された。

??Sutereo no kōkoku o mite **kau tsumori dattara**, kanai ni hantaisareta.

(Lit. ??Upon looking at an ad for stereos, I intended to buy one, but my wife objected to it.)

-tte[1] って *prt.*

a colloquial topic-introducer	Speaking of ~

【REL. *(no) wa*; **~to ieba** *(ttara)*】

◆ **Key Sentences**

(A)

Noun		
アメリカ人 ***Amerikajin***	って *tte*	フットボール が 好きだ / 好きです ね。 *futtobōru ga sukida / sukidesu ne.*
(Speaking of Americans, they love football, don't they?)		

(B)

Sentence		
漢字 を 覚える *Kanji o oboeru*	って *tte*	大変だ / 大変です　ね。 *taihenda / taihendesu ne.*
(Lit. To memorize *kanji*, it's terribly hard, isn't it?　(= It's really hard to memorize *kanji*, isn't it?))		

Formation

KS(A)

N　って
　　tte

先生　って　　(speaking of the teacher)
sensei tte

KS(B)

{V / Adj (*i*)} inf·nonpast　って
　　　　　　　　　　　　　　　tte

話す　って　　(to talk (topic))
hanasu tte

高い　って　　(to be expensive (topic))
takai tte

Examples

(a)　漢字っておもしろいですよ。
　　　Kanji tte omoshiroidesu yo.
　　　(Speaking of *kanji*, they are interesting, I tell you.)

(b)　日本人ってよく写真を撮りますね。
　　　Nihonjin tte yoku shashin o torimasu ne.
　　　(Speaking of Japanese people, they love taking pictures, don't they?)

(c)　外国で暮らすって難しいね。
　　　Gaikoku de kurasu tte muzukashii ne.
　　　(Living in a foreign country is hard, isn't it?)

(d)　木が多いっていいものだね。
　　　Ki ga ōi tte ii mono da ne.
　　　(It's good to have many trees, isn't it?)

(e) 家が広いっていいですね。

Ie ga hiroi tte iidesu ne.

(It's good to have a spacious house, isn't it?)

Notes

1. You should not use Adj (*na*) stem *tte*, unless it is an Adj (*na*) that can be used also as a noun as in: *kenkō* 'healthy / health', *kodoku* 'lonely / loneliness', *shinsetsu* 'kind / kindness', etc.

   (1) a. 健康ってありがたいですね。

   *Kenkō **tte** arigatai desu ne.*

   (Health is a precious thing, you know.)

   b. *元気ってありがたいですね。

   Genki **tte arigatai desu ne.*

   (Health is a precious thing, you know.)

2. You should not confuse -*tte*¹ with -*tte*² of hearsay. (⇨ ***tte***²) Consider the following sentences:

   (2) a. 山崎が医者になったって本当ですか。

   *Yamazaki ga isha ni natta **tte** hontō desu ka.*

   (I heard that Yamazaki has become a medical doctor, but is it true?)

   b. 日本の肉が高いって，どのぐらい高いんですか。

   *Nihon no niku ga takai **tte** dono gurai takai n desu ka.*

   (I heard that Japanese meat is expensive, but how expensive is it?)

3. -*tte*¹ tends to co-occur with the sentence-final particles *ne* or *yo*.

[Related Expression]

When -*tte* is attached to a noun as in KS(A) and Exs. (a) and (b), it is close in meaning to the topic marker *wa*. When -*tte* is attached to a sentence as in KS(B) and Exs. (c), (d) and (e), it is close in meaning to ~ (*to iu*) *no wa*. -*tte*, however, is more colloquial and emotive than *wa* or (*to iu*) *no wa*. In fact, if the predicate does not express the speaker's emotive judgment / evaluation -*tte* cannot be used. Thus,

[1] a. 山口さんは / *って先生です。

*Yamaguchi-san **wa** / ****tte** sensei desu.*

(Mr. Yamaguchi is a teacher.)

b. 山口さんは / って変な人ですね。

   *Yamaguchi-san **wa** / **tte** henna hito desu ne.*

   (Mr. Yamaguchi is a strange person, isn't he?)

-tte² って   *prt.*

a colloquial quotation marker	that
	【REL. *sōda*¹; *to*³】

◆ **Key Sentence**

Topic (subject)			
ジェーン *Jēn*	は *wa*	踊らない *odoranai*	って。 *tte*.
(Jane said that she wouldn't dance / They say that Jane won't dance.)			

Examples

(a) 今晩は雪が降るって。

   Konban wa yuki ga furutte.

   (They say it's going to snow tonight.)

(b) 僕も行こうかって思いました。

   Boku mo ikō ka tte omoimashita.

   (I wondered if I should go there, too.)

Notes

1. Quote + *tte*² is a colloquial version of Quote + *to*³. (⇨ **to**³) Any quotation which can precede *to*³ can precede *-tte*.

2. When there is a human topic in the *-tte* construction as in KS, the sentence is ambiguous as to whose quotation it is. The person who is quoting can be either the topic person or 'they'. But if a reporting verb *iu* 'say' is used after *-tte*, then the sentence means 'The person (topic) says that ~ '.

(1) ジェーンは踊らないって言っているよ。

　　*Jēn wa odoranai **tte itte iru** yo.*

　　(Jane is saying that she won't dance.)

3. When *-tte* is not followed by a verb, the understood verb is *iu* 'say'. Other verbs (i.e., *omou* 'feel, think') cannot be deleted after *-tte*, as shown in Ex. (b).

[**Related Expressions**]

I. *Itta / iimashita* 'said', *itte iru / imasu* 'is saying' or *itte ita / imashita* 'was saying' can be deleted after *-tte²*, as seen in KS and [1] below, but not after *to³*, as seen in [2].

　　[1] a. ジェーンは踊らないって言った。

　　　　　*Jēn wa odoranai **tte** itta.*

　　　　　(Jane said that she wouldn't dance.)

　　　　b. ジェーンは踊らないって。

　　　　　*Jēn wa odoranai **tte**.*

　　　　　(=KS)

　　[2] a. ジェーンは踊らないと言った。

　　　　　*Jēn wa odoranai **to** itta.*

　　　　　(Jane said that she wouldn't dance.)

　　　　b. *ジェーンは踊らないと。

　　　　　to.*

The difference between *-tte²* and *to³* is that the former is more emphatic and emotive owing to its glottal stop.

　　　　　(⇨ Characteristics of Japanese Grammar, 8. Sound Symbolisms)

II. When the subject of the understood *iu* is an unspecified person(s), as in the second interpretation of KS, *-tte²* is similar to the hearsay *sōda¹* 'they say ~ '. *-tte²*, however, is more colloquial and informal than *sōda¹*. (⇨ **sōda¹**) X *ga itte ita kedo* 'X was saying but' or its variants are used when specifying an informational source in the *-tte* construction, not the usual X *ni yoru to*, as shown in [3].

　　[3] a. ジョンが言っていたけど，ジェーンは踊らないって。

　　　　　***Jon ga itte ita kedo**, Jēn wa odoranai **tte**.*

　　　　　(According to John, Jane is not going to dance.)

　　　　b. ジョンによると，ジェーンは踊らないそうだ / *って。

　　　　　***Jon ni yoru to**, Jēn wa odoranai **sōda** / *tte.*

　　　　　(According to John, Jane is not going to dance.)

uchi ni うちに　　*conj.*

| during a period when a certain situation remains in effect | while; before; during 【REL. *aida* (*ni*); **mae ni**; *chū* (*ni*)】 |

♦**Key Sentences**

(A)

Topic (subject)		Subordinate Clause			Main Clause
			Verb (stative)		
前田さん *Maeda-san*	は *wa*	アメリカ に *Amerika ni*	いる ***iru***	うち に *uchi ni*	英語 が 上手に *eigo ga jōzuni* なった / なりました。 *natta / narimashita.*
(Mr. Maeda's English improved while he was in America.)					

(B)

	Subordinate Clause			Main Clause
	Vinf·neg·nonpast			
何　も *Nani mo*	しない ***shinai***	うち に *uchi ni*		今年　も　終わった / 終わりました。 *kotoshi mo　owatta / owarimashita.*
(Lit. Before I've achieved anything, this year is over.)				

(C)

Subordinate Clause			Main Clause
V*te*			
走って ***Hashitte***	いる *iru*	うち に *uchi ni*	おなか が 痛くなった / なりました。 *onaka ga　itakunatta / narimashita.*
(My stomach started to ache while I was running.)			

(D)

Subordinate Clause		Main Clause
Adj (*i*) inf·nonpast		
若い ***Wakai***	うち に *uchi ni*	本 を たくさん 読みなさい。 *hon o takusan yominasai.*
(Read many books while you're young.)		

Formation

(i) Vinf·nonpast うち に　(V: stative)
　　　　　　　uchi ni

　いる うち に　(while s.o. is there)
　iru uchi ni

　話せる うち に　(while s.o. can talk)
　hanaseru uchi ni

(ii) Vinf·neg·nonpast うち に
　　　　　　　　　uchi ni

　話さない うち に　(before s.o. talks)
　hanasanai uchi ni

　食べない うち に　(before s.o. eats)
　tabenai uchi ni

(iii) V*te* いる うち に
　　　　iru uchi ni

　話して いる うち に　(while s.o. is talking)
　hanashite iru uchi ni

　食べて いる うち に　(while s.o. is eating)
　tabete iru uchi ni

(iv) Adj (*i*) inf·nonpast うち に
　　　　　　　　　　uchi ni

　高い うち に　(while s.t. is expensive)
　takai uchi ni

(v) Adj (*na*) stem な うち に
　　　　　　　　na uchi ni

　静かな うち に　(while s.t. is quiet)
　shizukana uchi ni

U

(vi) N の うち に
    no uchi ni

休み の うち に   (during the vacation)
yasumi no uchi ni

Examples

(a) 雨が降らないうちにテニスをして来ます。
    Ame ga furanai uchi ni tenisu o shite kimasu.
    (I'll go and play tennis (and come back) before it rains.)

(b) 忘れないうちに言っておきたいことがある。
    Wasurenai uchi ni itte okitai koto ga aru.
    (There is something I want to tell you before I forget.)

(c) 考えているうちに分からなくなった。
    Kangaete iru uchi ni wakaranaku natta.
    (While thinking about it, I got lost.)

(d) 働けるうちに出来るだけ働きたい。
    Hatarakeru uchi ni dekiru dake hatarakitai.
    (I'd like to work as much as possible while I can work.)

(e) 温かいうちに飲んでください。
    Atatakai uchi ni nonde kudasai.
    (Please drink it while it is warm.)

(f) 休みのうちによく寝ておきます。
    Yasumi no uchi ni yoku nete okimasu.
    (I'll sleep a lot during the vacation.)

Notes

1. The *uchi ni* clause expresses the general time during which a given action or state occurs. *Uchi ni* is preceded by verbs describing states or progressive actions, or by adjectives, or by nouns expressing duration such as *haru* 'spring', *hiruma* 'day time' and *shūkan* 'week'. (For examples, see KSs(A), (C), (D) and Ex. (f), respectively.)

2. The tense before *uchi ni* is always nonpast, regardless of the tense of the main clause.

3. The verb before *uchi ni* is frequently negated, as in KS (B), Exs. (a) and (b).

〖Related Expressions〗

I. When it indicates an interval of time, *aida* refers to the 'time space' between two points, i.e., the beginning and the end. In other words, the time space indicated by *aida* can be measured in clocktime. *Uchi*, however, does not refer to such measurable time space; it simply means 'time space within'. Thus, in a situation where a mother wants to read books while her child is away at school, either *uchi* or *aida* can be used, as in [1a]. However, in a situation where we want to play tennis before it rains, we cannot substitute *aida* for *uchi*, as in [1b], because it is impossible to specify a time boundary.

[1] a. 子供が学校に行っている**うちに** / 間に本を読みます。

   *Kodomo ga gakkō ni itte iru **uchi ni** / **aida ni** hon o yomi-masu.*

   (I read books while my child is away at school.)

   b. 雨が降らない**うちに** / *間にテニスをします。

   *Ame ga furanai **uchi ni** / ***aida ni** tenisu o shimasu.*

   (I'll go and play tennis before it rains.)

   c. 冷たい**うちに** / *間にビールを飲んでください。

   *Tsumetai **uchi ni** / ***aida ni** bīru o nonde kudasai.*

   (Please drink the beer while it is cold.)

II. The *uchi ni* construction cannot be used for situations where a noun is an event noun such as *jugyō* 'class', *kaigi* 'conference' and *shiai* 'game'.

[2] a. 授業の間に / 中(に) / *のうちによく質問をした。

   *Jugyō **no aida ni** / **chū** (**ni**) / ***no uchi ni** yoku shitsumon o shita.*

   (He frequently asked questions during the class.)

   b. 試合の間に / 中(に) / *のうちに雨が降って来た。

   *Shiai **no aida ni** / **chū** (**ni**) / ***no uchi ni** ame ga futte kita.*

   (It started to rain while the game was going on.)

U

wa¹ は　*prt.*

> a particle which marks a topic or a contrastive element

talking about ～ ; as for ～ ; the 【REL. *ga¹*】

◆**Key Sentences**

(A)

Topic (subject)		
私 ***Watashi***	は *wa*	学生　だ / です。 *gakusei da / desu.*
(I am a student.)		

(B)

Contrastive Element₁			Contrastive Element₂		
杉田さん ***Sugita-san***	は *wa*	行きます が *ikimasu ga*	私 ***watashi***	は *wa*	行きません。 *ikimasen.*
(Mr. Sugita will go (there) but I won't go.)					

Examples

(a) ジョーンズさんは今日本語を勉強している。
　　Jōnzu-san wa ima nihongo o benkyōshite iru.
　　(Mr. Jones is studying Japanese now.)

(b) この町には大学が二つある。
　　Kono machi ni wa daigaku ga futatsu aru.
　　(There are two universities in this town.)

(c) 私はビールは飲みますが酒は飲みません。
　　Watashi wa bīru wa nomimasu ga sake wa nomimasen.
　　(I drink beer but don't drink *sake*.)

(d) 春子には人形を，秋子には絵本をあげた。
　　Haruko ni wa ningyō o, Akiko ni wa ehon o ageta.
　　(I gave Haruko a doll and Akiko a picture book.)

Notes

1. The origin of *wa* can be traced to the conditional marker *ba*. (Compare the spellings of *wa* (は) and *ba* (ば).) (⇒ *ba*) However, in con-

temporary Japanese, *wa* is used, in general, to mark information which the speaker assumes to be part of the hearer's register. In other words, when *wa* marks X, the speaker usually assumes that the hearer knows what X refers to. Thus, noun phrases which can be marked by *wa* in ordinary circumstances are as follows:

(A) Common nouns whose referents have already been introduced into the discourse linguistically or extra-linguistically. Example:

(1) 昔々，一人のおじいさんが住んでいました。
Mukashimukashi, hitori no o-jī-san ga sunde imashita.
(Once upon a time, there lived *an old man.*)
おじいさんはとてもやさしい人でした。
O-jī-san wa totemo yasashii hito deshita.
(*The old man* was a very gentle man.)

(B) Proper nouns. Examples:

(2) アメリカ 'America';   スミスさん 'Mr. Smith'
Amerika   *Sumisu-san*

(C) Nouns whose referents can be uniquely identified (that is, they are one of a kind). Examples:

(3) 太陽 'sun';   空 'sky'
taiyō   *sora*

(D) Generic names. Examples:

(4) 人 'man';   車 'car'
hito   *kuruma*

It is noted that *wa* never marks WH-words such as *nani* 'what' and *dare* 'who'. Thus, (5) is ungrammatical.

(5) *だれはパーティーに来ましたか。
Dare wa *pāti ni kimashita ka.*
(Who came to the party?)

This is because WH-words do not refer to a known thing and, therefore, their referents can never be in the hearer's register.

2. More specifically, *wa* marks a topic and / or a contrastive element. When *wa* is used as a topic marker, as in X *wa* Y, X is something the rest of the sentence (i.e., Y) is about, and the focus of the sentence falls on Y or part of Y. (Cp. *ga*[1]) The topic X *wa* normally appears at the beginning of a sentence.

3. *Wa* is also used to mark a contrastive element, as in KS (B), Exs. (c) and (d). However, whether *wa* is being used as a topic marker or as a contrastive marker is not always clear. This is not clear particularly when there is one element X marked by *wa* but there is no other element Y explicitly contrasted with X. Here are some general rules for determining whether a given *wa* is topical or contrastive.

(A) When more than one *wa* appears in a sentence, as in " X *wa* Y *wa* Z *wa* . . . ", the first *wa* is usually understood to be the topic marker, the second *wa* is more contrastive than the first one, the third one is more contrastive than the second, and so on. Examples:

(6) 太郎はテニスは出来ます。
*Tarō **wa** tenisu **wa** dekimasu.*
(Taro can play tennis.)

(7) 僕は今日はテニスはしない。
*Boku **wa** kyō **wa** tenisu **wa** shinai.*
(I won't play tennis today.)

(B) When X *wa* is pronounced with stress, it marks a contrastive element. Examples:

(8) 私は一年です。
*Watáshi **wa** ichinen desu.*
((I don't know about other people but, at least) Í am a freshman.)

(9) ビールは飲みます。
*Bíru **wa** nomimasu.*
((I don't drink other drinks but) I drink béer.)

4. When *wa* is used in negative sentences, it marks the negated element. This is a special use of *wa* as a contrastive marker. Compare the following sentences:

(10) a. 私はきのうボストンへ行かなかった。
Watashi wa kinō Bosuton e ikanakatta.
(I didn't go to Boston yesterday.)

b. 私はきのうはボストンへ行かなかった。
*Watashi wa kinō **wa** Bosuton e ikanakatta.*
(I didn't go to Boston yésterday.)

   c. 私はきのうボストンへは行かなかった。

    *Watashi wa kinō Bosuton e **wa** ikanakatta.*

    (I didn't go to Bóston yesterday.)

(10a) simply states that the speaker didn't go to Boston yesterday. (10b) negates *yesterday*, implying that the speaker went to Boston on other days or that he usually goes to Boston on that day but didn't yesterday. Likewise, (10c) negates *to Boston*, implying that the speaker went somewhere but it was not to Boston.

5. There are rules for particle ellipsis when *wa* marks noun phrases with case markers (i.e., particles such as the subject marker *ga* (=*ga*¹) and the direct object marker *o* (=*o*¹)).

  (A) When *wa* marks X *ga* or X *o*, *ga* or *o* must drop. (Exs. (a) and (c))

  (B) When *wa* marks X *e* or X *ni*⁶ (location), *e* or *ni* optionally drop. (Ex. (b))

  (C) When *wa* marks X *ni*¹ / *ni*² / *ni*³ / *ni*⁴ (time, indirect object, agent, contact), X *de*, X *to*, X *kara*, X *made* or X *yori*, the case marker usually remains and *wa* follows it, forming a double particle. (Ex. (d)) More examples follow:

    ⑾ ここではたばこを吸わないでください。

     *Koko **de wa** tabako o suwanaide kudasai.*

     (Please don't smoke here.)

    ⑿ 田中さんとはよく会います。

     *Tanaka-san **to wa** yoku aimasu.*

     (I see Mr. Tanaka often.)

6. The topical *wa* does not appear in subordinate clauses, as in (13).

    ⒀ a. 花子は私が / *はきのう酒を飲んだことを知っている。

      *Hanako wa watashi **ga** / ***wa** kinō sake o nonda koto o shitte iru.*

      (Hanako knows that I drank *sake* yesterday.)

     b. 私が / *は読んだ本は「雪国」です。

      *Watashi **ga** / ***wa** yonda hon wa " Yukiguni" desu.*

      (The book I read was *Snow Country*.)

wa² わ   *prt.*

> a sentence particle used in weak assertive or volitional sentences by a female speaker

♦**Key Sentence**

Sentence	
私　　も　あした　の　パーティー　に　行く *Watashi mo ashita no　pāti　　ni iku*	わ。 *wa.*
(I'll go to tomorrow's party, too.)	

Examples

(a) 大木さんはもう帰りましたわ。
　　Ōki-san wa mō kaerimashita wa.
　　(Mr. Oki has already gone home.)

(b) 久子はまだ学生ですわ。
　　Hisako wa mada gakusei desu wa.
　　(Hisako is still a student.)

(c) この部屋は小さいわ。
　　Kono heya wa chīsai wa.
　　(This room is small.)

Notes

1. The sentence particle *wa* is used only in female speech and expresses the speaker's weak assertion or volition. In addition, *wa* sometimes expresses the speaker's intimacy or friendliness.

2. *Wa* can follow any declarative sentence, but cannot follow the volitional forms of verbs. Thus, the following sentence is ungrammatical.

　　(1) *私が**行きましょう** / **行こう**わ。
　　　　Watashi ga **ikimashō / **ikō** wa.*
　　　　(I will go.)

　　Note that *wa* cannot be used in questions.

　　(2) a. *ジャクソンさんは学生ですかわ。
　　　　　 *Jakuson-san wa gakusei desu ka wa.
　　　　　 (Is Mr. Jackson a student?)

    b. *ジャクソンさんは学生ですわか。
       Jakuson-san wa gakusei desu wa ka.
       (Is Mr. Jackson a student?)

    c. *ジャクソンさんは学生ですわ?
       Jakuson-san wa gakusei desu wa?
       (Is Mr. Jackson a student?)

3. Other sentence particles such as *ne* and *yo* can occur with *wa*. In this case, *wa* must precede these particles.

    (3) 私も行く**わね**。
        *Watashi mo iku **wa ne**.*
        (I'll go there, too. All right?)

    (4) 私も行く**わよ**。
        *Watashi mo iku **wa yo**.*
        (I'll go there, too. (Emphatic))

~**wa** ~**da** ~は ~だ   *str.*

> S.o. or s.t. is / was s.o. or s.t. or is / was in some state, or will do / does / did s.t.

♦ Key Sentences

(A)

Topic (subject)		Noun	
これ *Kore*	は *wa*	**本** **hon**	だ / です。 *da / desu.*
(This is a book.)			

(B)

Topic (subject)		Noun	Prt	
コンサート Konsāto	は wa	八時 **hachiji**	から **kara**	だ / です。 da / desu.
(Lit. The concert is from eight o'clock. (＝The concert starts at eight o'clock.))				

Examples

(a) あの人は先生だ。
   Ano hito wa sensei da.
   (That person is a teacher.)

(b) 私はジョーンズです。
   Watashi wa Jōnzu desu.
   (I am Jones.)

(c) 授業は四時までです。
   Jugyō wa yoji made desu.
   (Lit. My classes are till four o'clock. (＝I have classes till four o'clock.))

(d) 今度の試合はワシントン大学とだ。
   Kondo no shiai wa Washinton Daigaku to da.
   (The next game is against the University of Washington.)

Notes

1. "A *wa* B *da* " is probably the most basic sentence structure in Japanese. The very basic meaning of this construction is "A is B". However, this pattern can convey more than that meaning. For example, the second sentence in (1) literally means 'My wife is tea', but actually means 'My wife drinks tea.' Here, the copula *da* is used in place of *nomu* 'drink '.

   (1) 私は毎朝コーヒーを飲む。家内は紅茶だ。
      *Watashi wa maiasa kōhi o nomu. Kanai **wa** kōcha **da**.*
      (I drink coffee every morning. Lit. My wife is tea. (＝My wife drinks tea.))

In fact, this structure is used frequently in conversation, as in (2), where the copula *desu* in B's sentence means *ikimasu* 'am going'.

(2)　A：私はハワイへ行きます。

　　　　Watashi wa Hawai e ikimasu.

　　　　(I'm going to Hawaii.)

　　B：私はフロリダです。

　　　　*Watashi **wa** Furorida **desu**.*

　　　　(Lit. I am Florida. (＝I'm going to Florida.))

In general, the copula can be used in place of a predicate if the meaning can be understood from context. Note the following examples:

(3)　このレストランはすしがおいしい。あのレストランはてんぷらだ。

　　　*Kono resutoran wa sushi ga oishii.　Ano resutoran **wa** tenpura **da**.*

　　　(*Sushi* is good at this restaurant.　At that restaurant *tempura* is good.)

(4)　ディックはスケートが上手だ。ポールはスキーだ。

　　　*Dikku wa sukēto ga jōzuda.　Pōru **wa** ski **da**.*

　　　(Dick is good at (ice) skating.　Paul is good at skiing.)

(5)　みつ子はお母さんが病気だ。つとむはお父さんだ。

　　　*Mitsuko wa o-kā-san ga byōki da.　Tsutomu **wa** o-tō-san **da**.*

　　　(In Mitsuko's family, her mother is ill.　In Tsutomu's family, his father is ill.)

What the copula *da* means may be understood from the linguistic context, as in (1) – (5), or from the extra-linguistic context, as in (6).

(6)　[In an order situation at a restaurant]

　　　僕はうなぎだ。

　　　*Boku **wa** unagi **da**.*

　　　(Lit. I am an eel.　(＝I'll have eel / I'd like eel.))

2.　In "A *wa* B *da*", B may be a noun phrase, as in KS(A) or a noun phrase with a particle, as in KS(B). General rules about particle ellipsis and retention in this construction follow:

(A)　*Ga, o, e* and *ni* (time (＝*ni*[1]), location (＝*ni*[6])) must drop. (See (1) – (6).)

(B)　*Ni* (indirect object (＝*ni*[2]), agent (＝*ni*[3]), direct contact (＝*ni*[4])) and *de* (location (＝*de*[1]), means (＝*de*[2])) may drop. Examples:

(7)　A：僕はケンにたのんだ。

　　　　　*Boku wa Ken **ni** tanonda.*

　　　　　(I asked Ken.)

B : 僕はアンディー(に)だ。

*Boku **wa** Andi (**ni**) da.*

(I asked Andy.)

(8) A : 僕はアパートで勉強する。

*Boku wa apāto **de** benkyōsuru.*

(I study in my apartment.)

B : 僕は図書館(で)だ。

*Boku **wa** toshokan (**de**) da.*

(I study at the library.)

(C) *De* (reason), *to*, *kara* and *made* usually do not drop. Examples:

(9) A : 僕は病気で休んだ。

*Boku wa byōki **de** yasunda.*

(I was absent because of illness.)

B : 僕はけがで / ??ø だ。

*Boku **wa** kega **de** / ??ø da.*

(I was absent because I got injured (lit. because of an injury).)

(10) A : 私は一郎と踊りました。

*Watashi wa Ichirō **to** odorimashita.*

(I danced with Ichiro.)

B : 私は信男と / ??ø です。

*Watashi **wa** Nobuo **to** / ??ø desu.*

(I danced with Nobuo.)

3. When the copula is used for a predicate, it usually appears in the non-past tense regardless of the tense of the predicate, as in (7) and (9).

4. In "A *wa* B *da*", A *wa* may drop if it can be understood from context, as seen in (11).

(11) A : それは何ですか。

Sore wa nan desu ka.

(What is that?)

B : (これは)辞書です。

(Kore wa) Jisho desu.

(This is a dictionary.)

~wa ~ga ～は ～が　　*str.*

a construction which relates a non-controllable state of s.t. or s.o. to a topic

◆Key Sentences

Topic (subject₁)		Predicate₁	
		Subject₂	Predicate₂
(1) 私 *Watashi*	は *wa*	英語 *eigo*	が *ga*	分かる / 分かります。 *wakaru / wakarimasu.*

(I understand English. (Lit. To me, English is understandable.))

| (2) 花子 *Hanako* | は *wa* | 目 *me* | が *ga* | きれいだ / きれいです。 *kireida / kireidesu.* |

(Hanako has pretty eyes. (Lit. Speaking of Hanako, her eyes are pretty.))

| (3) 辞書 *Jisho* | は *wa* | ウェブスター *Webusutā* | が *ga* | いい / いいです。 *ii / iidesu.* |

(Talking about dictionaries, Webster's is good.)

Examples

(a) たかしはテニスが上手だ。
Takashi wa tenisu ga jōzuda.
(Takashi is good at tennis.)

(b) 私はボーイフレンドがほしい。
Watashi wa bōifurendo ga hoshii.
(I want a boyfriend.)

(c) 僕はフットボールが好きだ。
Boku wa futtobōru ga sukida.
(I like football.)

(d) 象は鼻が長い。
Zō wa hana ga nagai.
(Elephants have long trunks.)

(e) 私はおなかがすいた。
Watashi wa onaka ga suita.
(I am hungry.)

(f) ミラーさんは背が高い。
Mirā-san wa se ga takai.
(Mr. Miller is tall.)

(g) 日本はステーキが高い。
Nihon wa sutēki ga takai.
(Steak is expensive in Japan.)

(h) 海は日本海がきれいだ。
Umi wa Nihonkai ga kireida.
(Talking about the sea, the Japan Sea is clean.)

(i) 日本の野球はどこが強いですか。
Nihon no yakyū wa doko ga tsuyoidesu ka.
(Talking about baseball in Japan, who is strong?)

Notes

1. "A *wa* B *ga* C" is one of the basic constructions in Japanese. In this construction, C usually expresses something about B and "B *ga* C" expresses something about A, as illustrated in (1).

   (1)
   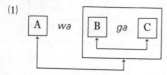

2. Sentences utilizing this construction may be categorized into three classes:

   (A) A is human, and "B *ga* C" expresses A's physical and / or mental state, for example, ability or desire, as in KS (1), Exs. (a), (b) and (c).

   (B) B is part of A, and C expresses something about B, which, in turn, expresses something about A, as in KS (2), Exs. (d), (e), (f) and (g).

   (C) B is a member of A, and C expresses something about B, as in KS (3), Exs. (h) and (i).

3. Listed below are the verbs and adjectives which usually require the "A *wa* B *ga* C" construction. (Sentences with these verbs and adjectives belong to Class (A) in Note 2.)

(2) *Ability*:

分かる (be understandable; understand)
wakaru

出来る (can be done; can do)
dekiru

られる (can)　　　見える (be visible)　　　聞こえる (be audible)
rareru²　　　　　mieru　　　　　　　　kikoeru

上手だ (good at)　　　　　　下手だ (poor at)
jōzuda　　　　　　　　　　hetada

得意だ (proudly good at)　　苦手だ (ashamedly poor at)
tokuida　　　　　　　　　　nigateda

　　　　　　　　　　　　(⇨ *kikoeru*; *mieru*; *rareru²*)

(3) *Desire / Need*:

ほしい (desirable; want)　　たい (want to)
hoshii　　　　　　　　　　tai

いる (be necessary; need)　必要だ (necessary)
iru³　　　　　　　　　　　hitsuyōda

　　　　　　　　　　　　(⇨ *hoshii¹*; *iru³*; *tai*)

(4) *Fondness*:

好きだ (be liked; like)　　　きらいだ (be disliked; dislike)
sukida　　　　　　　　　　kiraida

　　　　　　　　　　　　(⇨ *kiraida*; *sukida*)

(5) *Emotion*:

はずかしい (embarrassing)　　なつかしい (nostalgic)
hazukashii　　　　　　　　natsukashii

にくらしい (hateful)　　　　おそろしい (dreadful)
nikurashii　　　　　　　　osoroshii

こわい (fearful)　　　　　　うらやましい (enviable)
kowai　　　　　　　　　　urayamashii

くやしい (vexing)
kuyashii

~wa ikenai ~はいけない   *phr.*

<table>
<tr><td>a phrase which indicates prohibition</td><td>cannot do s.t.; must not do s.t.; Don't do s.t.; should not do s.t.
【REL. ~wa naranai】</td></tr>
</table>

◆**Key Sentence**

	V*te*	
この 部屋 に *Kono heya ni*	入って **haitte**	は いけない / いけません。 *wa ikenai / ikemasen*.
(You must not enter this room.)		

Formation

V*te* は いけない
　　wa ikenai

話して　　は いけない　　(must not talk)
hanashite wa ikenai

食べて は いけない　　(must not eat)
tabete wa ikenai

Examples

(a) 教室でものを食べてはいけません。
　　Kyōshitsu de mono o tabete wa ikemasen.
　　(You must not eat (food) in the classroom.)

(b) 花子はまだ酒を飲んではいけない。
　　Hanako wa mada sake o nonde wa ikenai.
　　(Hanako must / can not drink alcohol yet.)

Notes

1. In V*te wa ikenai*, the second person subject is usually omitted, as in KS and Ex. (a).

2. V*te wa ikenai* is often used as a negative answer to "V*te mo iidesu ka.* (May I ~?)."
　　　　　　　　　　　　　　　　　　　　　　　　　(⇨ **~te mo ii**)

[Related Expression]

V*te wa naranai* also expresses prohibition.   V*te wa naranai*, however, sounds a little stronger than V*te wa ikenai*.

wakaru 分かる　　*v. (Gr. 1)*

┌─────────────────────────────────────┐
can figure out (spontaneously) various facts——such as content, nature, value, meaning, cause, reason, result ——about s.t. whose existence is presupposed

be comprehensible; understand; can tell; figure out
【REL. *shiru*】
└─────────────────────────────────────┘

♦Key Sentence

Topic (experiencer)			Object of Comprehension		
私 *Watashi*	(に) *(ni)*	は *wa*	この　言葉 *kono kotoba*	が *ga*	分からない / 分かりません。 *wakaranai / wakarimasen.*
(Lit. To me this word is not comprehensible. (=I don't understand this word.))					

Examples

(a) 私にはこの映画の意味が分からない。
　　Watashi ni wa kono eiga no imi ga wakaranai.
　　(I don't understand the meaning of this movie.)

(b) この問題は難しくて分からない。
　　Kono mondai wa muzukashikute wakaranai.
　　(This problem is too difficult to understand.)

(c) あしたまでにこの仕事が出来るかどうか分かりません。
　　Ashita made ni kono shigoto ga dekiru ka dō ka wakarimasen.
　　(I can't tell if I can finish this work by tomorrow.)

(d) A：田中さんを知っていますか。
　　　Tanaka-san o shitte imasu ka.
　　　(Do you know Mr. Tanaka?)

　　B：ええ，知っていますが，あの人はどうもよく分かりません。
　　　Ē, shitte imasu ga, ano hito wa dōmo yoku wakarimasen.
　　　(Yes, I know him, but he is somehow incomprehensible to me.)

Notes

1. The basic pattern for this verb is the ~ *wa* ~ *ga* pattern. (⇨ ~ ***wa*** ~ ***ga***) The experiencer of *wakaru* takes *ni* optionally, as in KS.

W

2. Because *wakaru* is already a potential verb, it cannot take the potential form **wakareru* 'can understand'.

3. *Wakaru* normally takes *ga* to indicate the object of comprehension, but must take *o* when 'non-spontaneous comprehension' is involved, as in causative sentences ((1a)) or sentences in which the experiencer makes a conscious effort to understand something ((1b)).

  (1) a. 親の死を / *が小さい子供に分からせるのは難しい。

         *Oya no shi **o** / ****ga** chiisai kodomo ni wakaraseru no wa muzukashii.*

         (It is hard to make a small child comprehend the death of a parent.)

      b. ジャックはリンダの気持ちを / *が分かろうとしない。

         *Jakku wa Rinda no kimochi **o** / ****ga** wakarō to shinai.*

         (Jack does not try to understand Linda's feeling.)

[Related Expression]

Wakaru indicates 'the process of figuring something out' and is different from *shiru* which basically means 'to get some raw information from some outside source'. The primary difference between the two verbs is illustrated in the following sentences:

[1] 友達に聞いて大野の結婚のことを知っていた / *が分かっていた。

    *Tomodachi ni kiite Ōno no kekkon no koto **o shitte ita** / ****ga wakatte ita**.*

    (I knew about Ono's marriage by hearing it from a friend.)

[2] よく考えれば分かります / *知りますよ。

    *Yoku kangaereba **wakarimasu** / ****shirimasu** yo.*

    (If you think hard, you'll understand / *know it.)

[3] A : いくらか分かりますか。

       Ikura ka wakarimasu ka.

       (Can you tell how much it is?)

    B : はい，調べれば分かります / *知ります。

       *Hai, shirabereba **wakarimasu** / ****shirimasu**.*

       (Yes, I can tell / *know it, if I check into it.)

[4] A : 今晩何をするつもりですか。

       Konban nani o suru tsumori desu ka.

       (What do you intend to do tonight?)

B：まだ**分かりません** / *知りません。
*Mada **wakarimasen** / *shirimasen.*
(I don't know yet.)

wake da わけだ *phr.*

> the speaker's conclusion obtained through deductive, logical judgment or calculation on the basis of what he has heard or read

no wonder; so it means that ～; that's why; should ～; I take it that ～; naturally
【REL. *hazu da*】

♦ **Key Sentences**

(A)

Sentence₁
毎日　三時間　も　日本語　を　勉強して　いる　ん　です　か。 *Mainichi sanjikan mo nihongo o benkyōshite iru　n desu ka.*

Sentence₂		
	Vinf	
よく *Yoku*	**出来る** ***dekiru***	わけ　です　ね。 *wake desu ne.*

(Are you studying Japanese (as long as) three hours every day?　No wonder your Japanese is good.)

(B)

Sentence₁	Sentence₂	Adj (*i*) inf	
あした　試験　です　か。 *Ashita shiken desu ka.*	じゃあ　今晩 *Jā konban*	**忙しい** ***isogashii***	わけ　です　ね。 *wake desu ne.*

(Do you have an exam tomorrow?　Then, you must be busy tonight.)

Formation

(i) {V / Adj} (*i*) inf わけ だ
wake da

{話す　／話した}　　わけ　だ　　(I take it that s.o. talks / talked)
{*hanasu* / *hanashita*} *wake da*

{食べる / 食べた} わけ だ　　(I take it that s.o. eats / ate)
{*taberu* / *tabeta*} *wake da*

{高い / 高かった} わけ だ　　(I take it that s.t. is / was expensive)
{*takai* / *takakatta*} *wake da*

(ii) Adj (*na*) stem {な / だった} わけ だ
{*na* / *datta*} *wake da*

{静かな　／静かだった}　　わけ　だ　　(I take it that s.t. is / was quiet)
{*shizukana* / *shizukadatta*} *wake da*

(iii) N {という / だった} わけ だ
{*to iu* / *datta*} *wake da*

{先生　と　いう / 先生　だった} わけ　だ　　(I take it that s.o. is / was
{*sensei to iu* / *sensei datta*} *wake da*　a teacher)

Examples

(a) スミスさんは十年間もテニスをしたのだから上手なわけだ。
Sumisu-san wa jūnenkan mo tenisu o shita no da kara jōzuna wake da.
(Mr. Smith has played tennis for ten years, so he should be good at it.)

(b) A：来月から四か月フランスに行きます。
Raigetsu kara yonkagetsu Furansu ni ikimasu.
(I'll go to France next month and stay there for four months.)

B：すると、六月に帰ってくるわけですね。
Suru to, rokugatsu ni kaette kuru wake desu ne.
(Then, I take it that you're returning here in June.)

(c) 毎日プールで泳いでいるんですか。丈夫なわけですね。
Mainichi pūru de oyoide iru n desu ka. Jōbuna wake desu ne.
(Are you swimming in the pool everyday? No wonder you're healthy.)

(d) きのうは三時間しか寝ていない。道理で眠いわけだ。
Kinō wa sanjikan shika nete inai. Dōri de nemui wake da.
(Yesterday I slept only three hours. No wonder I am sleepy.)

(e) えっ？　足立さんが入院したんですか。パーティーに来なかったわけだ。

   E? Adachi-san ga nyūinshita n desu ka. Pāti ni konakatta wake da.

   (What?　Was Mr. Adachi hospitalized?　No wonder he didn't come to the party.)

(f) A：山田さんは英語のことは何でも知っています。

   Yamada-san wa eigo no koto wa nan demo shitte imasu.

   (Mr. Yamada knows everything about English.)

   B：生き字引というわけですか。

   Iki jibiki to iu wake desu ka.

   (You mean he is a living dictionary?)

(g) 父の言うことが分からないわけではないが，どうしても医者になりたくない。

   Chichi no iu koto ga wakaranai wake de wa nai ga, dōshitemo isha ni naritakunai.

   (It is not that I don't understand what my father is saying; I simply don't want to become a medical doctor.)

Notes

1. *Wake* can be used as a full noun, meaning 'reason' as in (1) and (2) below:

   (1) 会社をやめたそうですが，そのわけを聞かせてください。

   *Kaisha o yameta sōdesu ga, sono **wake** o kikasete kudasai.*

   (I heard that you quit the company.　Let me hear the reason for that.)

   (2) ここに来たわけは言えません。

   *Koko ni kita **wake** wa iemasen.*

   (I can't tell you the reason why I came here.)

2. *Wake de* is the *te*-form of *wake da*.

   (3) お母さんと二人だけですか。そういうわけで結婚出来ないんですか。

   *O-kā-san to futari dake desu ka.　Sō iu **wake de** kekkon dekinai n desu ka.*

   (It's only you and your mother?　For that reason you can't get married, eh?)

[Related Expression]

Hazu da 'expect' is similar but not identical to *wake da*.　*Hazu da* can express a speaker's expectation when there is no preceding context; *wake da* cannot.　In other words, *wake da* is highly dependent on verbal context.

(⇨ ***hazu da***)

[1] a. あしたは授業がないはず / *わけですよ。
        *Ashita wa jugyō ga nai **hazu** / ***wake** desu yo.*
        (I expect that there is no class tomorrow.)

    b. あの人は若いはず / *わけですよ。
        *Ano hito wa wakai **hazu** / ***wake** desu yo.*
        (I expect him to be young.)

-ya 屋   *suf.*

> a suffix attached to names of stores, inns and Japanese-style restaurants or to persons engaged in certain occupations

store

Examples

(a) 花屋　　　　(florist)
　　hana-ya

　　本屋　　　　(bookstore)
　　hon-ya

　　薬屋　　　　(drug store)
　　kusuri-ya

　　肉屋　　　　(butcher)
　　niku-ya

　　パチンコ屋　(pinball parlor)
　　pachinko-ya

　　パン屋　　　(bakery)
　　pan-ya

　　魚屋　　　　(fish monger)
　　sakana-ya

　　酒屋　　　　(liquor store)
　　saka-ya

(b) 酒屋さんに電話してビールを三ダース持って来てもらった。
　　Saka-ya-san ni denwashite bīru o sandāsu motte kite moratta.
　　(I called the man at the liquor store and had him bring me three dozen beers.)

(c) あの人は政治家ではなくて政治屋だ。
　　Ano hito wa seijika de wa nakute seiji-ya da.
　　(He is not a statesman but a mere politician.)

Note

The suffix *-ya* is sometimes used to downgrade a person. This use, however, is very restricted. Examples follow:

(1) はずかしがり屋   (a shy person)
     hazukashigari-ya

     いばり屋   (a haughty person)
     ibari-ya

     気取り屋   (an affected person)
     kidori-ya

Note that these examples are all derived from V*masu*+*ya*, as in *hazukashigari* +*ya*, *ibari*+*ya* and *kidori*+*ya*.

ya や   *conj.*

a coordinate conjunction that is used   and
to list two or more items (nouns or   【REL. *to*[1]; *toka*】
noun phrases) in an inexhaustive
fashion

♦**Key Sentence**

Subject				
Noun		Noun		
山田さん **Yamada-san**	や *ya*	小川さん **Ogawa-san**	が *ga*	来た / 来ました。 *kita / kimashita*.
(Mr. Yamada and Mr. Ogawa (and others) came.)				

Examples

(a) 山本さんやスミスさんがテニスをしている。
     Yamamoto-san ya Sumisu-san ga tenisu o shite iru.
     (Mr. Yamamoto, Mr. Smith and others are playing tennis.)

(b) 僕はビールやワインを飲んだ。
     Boku wa bīru ya wain o nonda.
     (I drank beer, wine and things like that.)

(c) 土田さんは大川さんや鈴木さんに手紙を書いた。
     Tsuchida-san wa Ōkawa-san ya Suzuki-san ni tegami o kaita.

(Mr. Tsuchida wrote a letter to Mr. Okawa and Mr. Suzuki (and others).)

Notes

1. *Ya* is used to combine two or more nouns or noun phrases. It cannot be used to combine predicates. Thus, (1) is unacceptable.

   (1) *きのうはデパートに行きましたや映画を見ました。
   *Kinō wa depāto ni ikimashita **ya** eiga o mimashita.*
   (Yesterday I did things like going to a department store and seeing a movie.)

   Instead of (1) we have to use ~ *tari* ~ *tari suru* to express an inexhaustive listing of predicates, as in (2).　　(⇨ **~ *tari* ~ *tari suru***)

   (2) きのうはデパートに行ったり映画を見たりしました。
   *Kinō wa depāto ni it**tari** eiga o mi**tari** shimashita.*

2. N *ya* N can be used as a noun phrase in any position where a single noun can be used. It can be used as the subject, as in KS and Ex. (a), or as the direct object as in Ex. (b), or as the indirect object as in Ex. (c).

3. N *ya* N cannot appear in the position of X in the X *ga* Y *da* construction, because *ga* in X *ga* Y *da* is a highly exhaustive listing marker.
   (⇨ ***ga*¹**)

   (3) *ジェーンやミッシェルが学生です。
   *Jēn **ya** Missheru **ga** gakusei desu.*
   (*Jane and Michelle and only they (and others) are students.)

   This idea can be conveyed using the construction in (4):

   (4) 学生はジェーンやミッシェルです。
   *Gakusei wa Jēn **ya** Missheru desu.*
   (The students are Jane or Michelle (and others).)

[Related Expression]

Toka is used to make a rather *general*, inexhaustive listing of items as examples, whereas *ya* is used to make an inexhaustive listing of items *related to a specific time and place*. Consider the following examples:

   [1] a. A: スミスさんは例えばどんな日本食が好きですか。
   Sumisu-san wa tatoeba donna nihonshoku ga sukidesu ka.
   (Mr. Smith, what kind of Japanese cuisine do you like? Give me some examples.)

B：そうですね。てんぷらとか / ?やすきやきとか / ?や刺身ですね。
*Sō desu ne.   Tenpura **toka** / ?**ya** sukiyaki **toka** / ?**ya** sashimi desu ne.*
(Well, I'd say *tempura*, *sukiyaki* and *sashimi* (and others).)

b. A：きのう料理屋で何を食べましたか。
Kinō ryōri-ya de nani o tabemashita ka.
(What did you eat at the Japanese restaurant?)

B：てんぷらや / ???とかすきやきや / ???とか刺身を食べました。
*Tenpura **ya** / ???**toka** sukiyaki **ya** / ???**toka** sashimi o tabe-mashita.*
(I ate *tempura*, *sukiyaki* and *sashimi* (and others).)

---

yahari やはり   *adv.*

| an adverb indicating that an actual situation expectedly / anticipatively conforms to a standard based on past experience, comparison with other people, or common sense | still; also; after all; as expected; you know 【REL. *kekkyoku*; *sasuga (ni)*】 (ANT. *masaka*) |

◆**Key Sentence**

Topic (subject)			
ベイリーさん *Beiri-san*	は *wa*	やはり *yahari*	来なかった / 来ませんでした　ね。 *konakatta / kimasendeshita ne.*
(As expected, Mr. Bailey hasn't come, has he?)			

Examples

(a) 雪子さんは今でもやはりきれいです。
Yukiko-san wa ima demo yahari kireidesu.
(Yukiko is still pretty.)

(b) お兄さんはテニスが上手ですが，弟さんもやっぱり上手ですよ。
O-ni-san wa tenisu ga jōzudesu ga, otōto-san mo yappari jōzudesu yo.

(The older brother is good at tennis, and the younger brother is also good at it.)

(c) やはり日本のビールはおいしいですね。

Yahari Nihon no biru wa oishiidesu ne.

(As expected, Japanese beer is good.)

(d) 僕はやはり結婚することにしました。

Boku wa yahari kekkonsuru koto ni shimashita.

(I've decided to get married, after all.)

Notes

1. *Yahari* is a speaker-oriented adverb because its use is based on the speaker's subjective and presuppositional standards. Its overuse in conversation makes a discourse overly subjective, but its proper use in conversation makes a discourse sound like real Japanese.

2. *Yahari* can be positioned sentence-initially or sentence-medially, just like other adverbs. Thus, in KS *yahari* can be positioned in two ways.

   (1) a. **やはり**ベイリーさんは来なかったね。

   　　Yahari *Beiri-san wa konakatta ne.*

   　　b. ベイリーさんは**やはり**来なかったね。

   　　Beiri-san wa **yahari** *konakatta ne.*

   　　c. ?ベイリーさんは来なかったね，**やはり**。

   　　?*Beiri-san wa konakatta ne,* **yahari**.

   The sentence-initial *yahari* is more emphatic than the sentence-medial *yahari*. The sentence-final *yahari* as in (1c) sounds like an after-thought, and its usage is slightly marginal.

3. *Yappari* is a more emphatic and emotive version of *yahari*, owing to its glottal stop -*pp*-.

   　　(⇨ Characteristics of Japanese Grammar, 8. Sound Symbolisms)

[Related Expressions]

I. *Sasuga* is an adverb / adj (*na*) whose meaning is similar to *yahari*. *Sasuga*, however, has only one meaning 'as expected' and indicates that the speaker is very much impressed or surprised by the given situation.

   [1] a. さすが(に)日本人はよく働く。

   　　Sasuga(**ni**) *nihonjin wa yoku hataraku.*

   　　(Truly Japanese people work hard!)

Y

b. さすが(に)アメリカは広い。

Sasuga(ni) *Amerika wa hiroi.*

(Exactly as I expected, America is huge.)

Sasuga(ni) can replace *yahari* only when *yahari* means 'as expected', as in KS and Ex. (c).

II. The adverb *kekkyoku* 'after all, in short' can replace *yahari* only when the latter means 'after all', as in Ex. (d). More examples follow:

[2] a. 色々薬を飲んだがやはり / 結局治らなかった。

Iroiro kusuri o nonda ga **yahari** / **kekkyoku** *naoranakatta.*

(I took all kinds of medicine, but I wasn't cured.)

b. やはり / 結局行かないことにした。

Yahari / **Kekkyoku** *ikanai koto ni shita.*

(After all, I decided not to go there.)

In [2] *kekkyoku* sounds more formal than *yahari*, because the former is a Sino-Japanese word, while the latter is a Japanese word. Yet both can be used in conversational Japanese.

III. The adverb *masaka* 'by no means, on no account, surely not' is used when a given situation is far from the speaker's expectation. In that sense, it is an antonym of *yahari*. *Masaka* is used with a negative predicate or is used all by itself, meaning 'Unbelievable!, You don't say!'.

[3] a. まさか小川さんが先生になるとは思わなかった。

Masaka *Ogawa-san ga sensei ni naru to wa omowanakatta.*

(I never expected Mr. Ogawa to become a teacher.)

b. A : トムが入院したそうだ。

Tomu ga nyūinshita sōda.

(I heard that Tom was hospitalized.)

B : まさか！ きのうテニスをしていたよ。

Masaka! *Kinō tenisu o shite ita yo.*

(You don't say! He was playing tennis yesterday.)

-yasui やすい   *aux. adj.* (*i*)

> S.t. or s.o. is easy to ~.

easy to; ready to; be apt to; prone to; do s.t. easily
(ANT. *-nikui*)

♦**Key Sentence**

Topic (subject)		V*masu*
この　漢字 *Kono kanji*	は *wa*	覚え やすい / やすいです。 ***oboe** yasui / yasuidesu.*
(This *kanji* is easy to memorize.)		

Formation

V*masu* やすい
　　　yasui

話しやすい　　(easy to speak)
hanashiyasui

食べやすい　　(easy to eat)
tabeyasui

Examples

(a) あの人のうちは見つけやすい。
　　Ano hito no uchi wa mitsukeyasui.
　　(His house is easy to find.)

(b) 佐藤先生は話しやすいです。
　　Satō-sensei wa hanashiyasuidesu.
　　(Prof. Sato is easy to talk to.)

(c) このペンは書きやすい。
　　Kono pen wa kakiyasui.
　　(This pen is easy to write with.)

(d) 上野さんは一緒に仕事がしやすかった。
　　Ueno-san wa isshoni shigoto ga shiyasukatta.
　　(Mr. Ueno was easy to work with.)

(e) 豆腐は腐りやすい。
　　Tōfu wa kusariyasui.
　　(*Tofu* rots easily.)

Y

Notes

1. V*masu yasui* is an *i*-type compound adjective and conjugates as an Adj (*i*), as seen in the following:

		Informal	Formal
Aff.	Nonpast	話しやすい *hanashiyasui*	話しやすいです *hanashiyasuidesu*
	Past	話しやすかった *hanashiyasukatta*	話しやすかったです *hanashiyasukattadesu*
Neg.	Nonpast	話しやすくない *hanashiyasukunai*	話しやすくないです *hanashiyasukunaidesu* 話しやすくありません *hanashiyasukuarimasen*
	Past	話しやすくなかった *hanashiyasukunakatta*	話しやすくなかったです *hanashiyasukunakattadesu* 話しやすくありませんでした *hanashiyasukuarimasendeshita*

2. The following sentences (1) – (4) are closely related to Exs. (a) – (d).

(1) あの人のうちを見つける。 (Cp. Ex. (a))
*Ano hito no uchi **o** mitsukeru.*
(One locates his house.)

(2) 佐藤先生に話す。 (Cp. Ex. (b))
*Satō-sensei **ni** hanasu.*
(One talks to Prof. Sato.)

(3) このペンで書く。 (Cp. Ex. (c))
*Kono pen **de** kaku.*
(One writes with this pen.)

(4) 上野さんと一緒に仕事をした。 (Cp. Ex. (d))
*Ueno-san **to** isshoni shigoto o shita.*
(One worked together with Mr. Ueno.)

The noun phrases in (1) through (4) above, such as the direct object ~ *o*, the indirect object ~ *ni*, the instrumental phrase ~ *de*, and the comitative phrase ~ *to* are the sources for the topic (subject) of Exs. (a), (b), (c) and (d), respectively.   It is important to note that all these particles drop in the *yasui*-construction, and that the topic is the new subject of the *yasui*-construction.

3. If the subject of the *yasui*-construction is under focus, it is marked by *ga*, as in (5).   (⇨ **ga**[1])

    (5) A : どの先生が話しやすいですか。

            *Dono sensei **ga** hanashiyasuidesu ka.*

            (Which professor is easy to talk to?)

      B : 佐藤先生が話しやすいです。

            *Satō-sensei **ga** hanashiyasuidesu.*

            (Prof. Sato is easy to talk to.)

4. The antonym of -*yasui* is -*nikui* 'hard to ~ ', and is used in exactly the same way as -*yasui*.   (⇨ **nikui**)

yo よ   *prt.*

a sentence-final particle that indicates the speaker's (fairly) strong conviction or assertion about s.t. that is assumed to be known only to him	I tell you; I'm telling you; you know; contrary to what you think

◆**Key Sentence**

Sentence	
坂本さん　は　たばこ　を　吸わない / 吸いません *Sakamoto-san wa tabako o suwanai / suimasen*	よ。 *yo.*
(Mr. Sakamoto doesn't smoke, you know.)	

Examples

(a) A : 日本語はおもしろいですか。

      Nihongo wa omoshiroidesu ka.

      (Is Japanese interesting?)

Y

B : ええ，とてもおもしろいですよ。
　　Ē, totemo omoshiroidesu yo.
　　(Yes, it's very interesting, I tell you.)

(b)　A : あの人はそんな本を買わないでしょう。
　　Ano hito wa sonna hon o kawanai deshō.
　　(He probably won't buy that sort of book.)

B : いいえ，買いますよ。
　　Ie, kaimasu yo.
　　(Yes, he'll buy it (contrary to what you think).)

Notes

1. In this construction, the sentence preceding *yo* can be any informal or formal sentence except a question.

(1)　a.　*読むかよ。
　　　　*Yomu **ka** yo.

　　b.　*読みますかよ。
　　　　*Yomimasu **ka** yo.

The sentences in (1) are unacceptable because the speaker's strong conviction and his act of questioning contradict each other. If (1a) is interpreted as a rhetorical question meaning 'I bet he isn't going to read it', however, the sentence becomes acceptable. But (1b), the formal version of (1a), cannot be a rhetorical question.

2. A sentence preceding *yo* can be an informal or a formal request. Examples :

(2)　a.　読めよ。
　　　　*Yome **yo**.*
　　　　(Read it.)

　　b.　読みなさいよ。
　　　　*Yominasai **yo**.*
　　　　((From a superior to his inferior) Read it.)

　　c.　読んでくださいよ。
　　　　*Yonde kudasai **yo**.*
　　　　(Please read it.)

When *yo* is used in this way, the sentence becomes more forceful.

3. Another sentence-final particle *ne* may be attached to S *yo*, yielding the meaning ' I assert S and don't you agree? '. S *yo ne* is used when the speaker wishes to mitigate the force of his assertion by talking as if the content of S were also known to the hearer. (⇨ **ne**, Note 5) Examples :

(3) a. この本はおもしろいですよね。
   *Kono hon wa omoshiroi desu **yo ne**.*
   (This book is interesting, right?)

   b. アメリカまで十時間はかかりますよね。
   *Amerika made jūjikan wa kakarimasu **yo ne**.*
   (It takes at least 10 hours to get to America, right?)

S *yo ne* can also be used when the speaker is addressing someone who doesn't know about an asserted fact and there is another person nearby who is aware of it. In such circumstances, the speaker asks the person who shares the asserted fact for his agreement at the end of the sentence.

(4) [The speaker is talking with someone about Mr. Kato, who is standing nearby.]
   加藤さんはロシア語が出来ますよ, ね?
   *Katō-san wa roshiago ga dekimasu **yo**, **ne**?*
   (Mr. Kato can speak Russian... Can't you, Mr. Kato?)

4. In nonpolite, informal speech (i.e., intimate speech) sex differences are expressed by a combination of *yo* and the female speech markers *wa* and *no*. (⇨ **wa**[2]; **no**[4]; Characteristics of Japanese Grammar, 7. Sentence-final Particles) The following chart illustrates the use of *yo* in informal male and female speech.

Male Speech		Female Speech
Vinf+*yo*		Vinf+*wa*+*yo*
Exs. 話す　よ。(I'll talk, you know.) *Hanasu **yo**.*		話す　わ　よ。 *Hanasu wa **yo**.*
話した　よ。(I talked, you know.) *Hanashita **yo**.*		話した　わ　よ。 *Hanashita wa **yo**.*
Adj (*i*)+*yo*		Adj (*i*)+*wa*+*yo*
Exs. 高い　よ。(It's expensive, you know.) *Takai **yo**.*		高い　わ　よ。 *Takai wa **yo**.*
高かった　よ。(It was expensive, you know.) *Takakatta **yo**.*		高かった　わ　よ。 *Takakatta wa **yo**.*

Male Speech		Female Speech
{Adj stem (*na*) / N} {*da* / *datta*} *yo*		{Adj (*na*) stem / N} {*da* / *datta*} *wa yo*
Exs. 静かだ よ。(It's quiet, you know.) *Shizukada* **yo**.		静か (だ わ) よ。 *Shizuka (da wa)* **yo**.
静かだった よ。(It was quiet, you know.) *Shizukadatta* **yo**.		静かだった わ よ。 *Shizukadatta wa* **yo**.
先生 だ よ。(He's a teacher, you know.) *Sensei da* **yo**.		先生 (だ わ) よ。 *Sensei (da wa)* **yo**.
先生 だった よ。(He was a teacher, you *Sensei datta* **yo**. know.)		先生 だった わ よ。 *Sensei datta wa* **yo**.
n da (*yo*)		*no* (*yo*)
Exs. 話す ん だ (よ)。(I'll talk, you know.) *Hanasu n da* (**yo**).		話す の (よ)。 *Hanasu no* (**yo**).
話した ん だ (よ)。(I talked, you know.) *Hanashita n da* (**yo**).		話した の (よ)。 *Hanashita no* (**yo**).
高い ん だ (よ)。(It's expensive, you know.) *Takai n da* (**yo**).		高い の (よ)。 *Takai no* (**yo**).
高かった ん だ (よ)。(It was expensive, *Takakatta n da* (**yo**). you know.)		高かった の (よ)。 *Takakatta no* (**yo**).
静かな ん だ (よ)。(It's quiet, you know.) *Shizukana n da* (**yo**).		静かな の (よ)。 *Shizukana no* (**yo**).
静かだった ん だ (よ)。(It was quiet, you *Shizukadatta n da* (**yo**). know.)		静かだった の (よ)。 *Shizukadatta no* (**yo**).
先生 なん だ (よ)。(He's a teacher, you *Sensei na n da* (**yo**). know.)		先生 な の (よ)。 *Sensei na no* (**yo**).
先生 だった ん だ (よ)。(He was a teacher, *Sensei datta n da* (**yo**). you know.)		先生 だった の (よ)。 *Sensei datta no* (**yo**).

5. *Ne*, the Japanese tag question marker, is another frequently used sentence-final particle. (⇨ *ne*) *Yo* should not be confused with *ne*. In contrast to *yo*, *ne* is used when the speaker and the hearer share some specific information. For example, if the speaker is looking at a delicious-looking piece of cake with his friend, he would say (5b) instead of (5a).

(5) a. *おいしそうですよ。
*Oishisōdesu **yo**.
(Looks delicious, I tell you.)

b. おいしそうですね。
Oishisōdesu **ne**.
(Looks delicious, doesn't it?)

On the other hand, if he is eating some delicious cake which his friend has not tasted, he would say (6a) rather than (6b).

(6) a. おいしいですよ。
Oishiidesu **yo**.
(It's good, I tell you.)

b. *おいしいですね。
*Oishiidesu **ne**.
(It's good, isn't it?)

---

yōda ようだ　　*aux. adj. (na)*

> an auxiliary *na*-type adjective which expresses the likelihood of s.t. / s.o. or the likeness of s.t. / s.o. to s.t. / s.o.

look like; look as if; be like; appear; seem
[REL. *darō*; *rashii*; *sōda¹*; *~sōda²*]

♦ **Key Sentences**

(A)

Topic (subject)			{V / Adj (i)} inf	
杉山さん Sugiyama-san	は wa	アメリカ へ Amerika e	行く **iku**	ようだ / ようです。 yōda / yōdesu.
(It appears that Mr. Sugiyama is going to America.)				

(B)

Topic (subject)			Adj (*na*) stem		
上田さん *Ueda-san*	は *wa*	ボクシング が *bokushingu ga*	**好き** ***suki***	な *na*	ようだ / ようです。 *yōda / yōdesu.*
(Mr. Ueda appears to like boxing.)					

(C)

Topic (subject)		Noun		
あの 人 *Ano hito*	は *wa*	**田中先生** ***Tanaka-sensei***	の *no*	ようだ / ようです。 *yōda / yōdesu.*
(That person looks like Prof. Tanaka.)				

(D)

A:		B:	Demonstrative	
石井さん は もう 帰りました か。 *Ishii-san wa mō kaerimashita ka.*		はい、 *Hai,*	その *sono*	ようです。 *yōdesu.*
(Has Mr. Ishii gone home already?)		(Yes, it looks like it.)		

Formation

(i) {V / Adj (*i*)} inf ようだ
　　　　　　　　　 yōda

　　{話す　/ 話した}　ようだ　　(It seems that s.o. (will) talk / talked.)
　　{*hanasu / hanashita*} *yōda*

　　{高い / 高かった} ようだ　　(It seems that s.t. is / was expensive.)
　　{*takai / takakatta*} *yōda*

(ii) Adj (*na*) stem {な / だった} ようだ
　　　　　　　　　　 {*na / datta*}　 *yōda*

　　{静かな　 / 静かだった}　ようだ　　(It seems that s.t. is / was quiet.)
　　{*shizukana / shizukadatta*} *yōda*

(iii) N {の / だった} ようだ
　　　 {*no / datta*}　 *yōda*

{先生　の / 先生　だった} ようだ　(It seems that s.o. is / was a teacher.)
{*sensei no* / *sensei datta*}　*yōda*

(iv) Demonstrative　ようだ
　　　　　　　　　　　yōda

その　ようだ　　(It seems so.)
sono yōda

Examples

(a) 木村さんはきのうお酒を飲んだようだ。
　　Kimura-san wa kinō o-sake o nonda yōda.
　　(It seems that Mr. Kimura drank *sake* yesterday.)

(b) この問題は学生にはちょっと難しいようだ。
　　Kono mondai wa gakusei ni wa chotto muzukashii yōda.
　　(This problem seems to be a little difficult for the students.)

(c) ここは昔学校だったようだ。
　　Koko wa mukashi gakkō datta yōda.
　　(It seems that this place used to be a school.)

(d) この酒は水のようだ。
　　Kono sake wa mizu no yōda.
　　(This *sake* is like water.)

Notes

1. *Yōda* expresses the likelihood of s.t. / s.o., or the likeness of s.t. / s.o. to s.t. / s.o. In either case, when the speaker uses *yōda*, his statement is based on firsthand, reliable information (usually visual information).

2. *Yōda* can be used in counter-factual situations, as in Ex. (d). In this case, the adverb *marude* 'just' can be used for emphasis.

　　(1) 木村さんは**まるで**酒を飲んだようだ。
　　　　*Kimura-san wa **marude** sake o nonda yōda.*
　　　　(Mr. Kimura looks as if he had just drunk *sake*.)

　　(2) あの人は**まるで**日本人のようです。
　　　　*Ano hito wa **marude** nihonjin no yōdesu.*
　　　　(That person is just like a Japanese person.)

3. *Yōda* is a *na*-type adjective and has the prenominal form *yōna* and the adverbial form *yōni*. (⇨ **yōni²**) Examples:

(3) 今日田中さんの**ような**人を見ました。
　　*Kyō Tanaka-san no **yōna** hito o mimashita.*
　　(I saw a man who looked like Mr. Tanaka.)

(4) スミスさんは日本人の**ように**日本語を話します。
　　*Sumisu-san wa nihonjin no **yōni** nihongo o hanashimasu.*
　　(Mr. Smith speaks Japanese like a Japanese.)

4. The colloquial version of *yōda* is *mitaida*, which is also a *na*-type adjective. The uses of *mitaida* are exactly the same as those for *yōda*. The formation rules are as follows:

(5) {V / Adj (*i*)} inf みたいだ
　　　　　　　　mitaida

(6) {Adj (*na*) stem / N} {ø / だった} みたいだ
　　　　　　　　　　ø   *datta*   *mitaida*

[Related Expressions]

The conjecture expressions S *darō*, S *rashii* and S *sōda*[2] convey ideas similar to S *yōda*. The differences are as follows:

(A) S *darō* expresses the speaker's conjecture, but it is not necessarily based on any information. In other words, S *darō* can be used when the speaker is merely guessing.

(B) S *rashii* usually expresses the speaker's conjecture based on what the speaker has heard or read. That is, the information his conjecture is based on is not firsthand.

(C) S *sōda*[2] expresses the speaker's conjecture about what is going to happen or the current state of someone or something. Although this expression is based on what the speaker sees or feels, it is merely his guess and the degree of certainty in his statement is fairly low. Only V*masu* or Adj (*i* / *na*) stem can precede *sōda*[2].

(D) S *yōda* is also an expression which is usually based on what the speaker sees or saw. However, unlike S *sōda*[2], this expression involves the speaker's reasoning process based on firsthand, reliable information and his knowledge. Thus, the degree of certainty in *yōda* is the highest of the four expressions compared here.

The following examples demonstrate the differences among these four expressions. The sentences in [1] present examples with the adjective *takai* 'expensive' before the conjecture auxiliaries.

[1] a. この本は高いだろう。
   *Kono hon wa takai **darō**.*
   (This book is probably expensive.)

   b. この本は高いらしい。
   *Kono hon wa takai **rashii**.*
   ((From what I heard and / or read,) this book seems expensive.)

   c. この本は高そうだ。
   *Kono hon wa taka **sōda**.*
   (This book looks expensive.)

   d. この本は高いようだ。
   *Kono hon wa takai **yōda**.*
   ((Considering the prices of similar books,) this book seems expensive.)

Here, [1a] is mere conjecture. [1b] expresses the speaker's conjecture based on what he has heard and / or read. (If the sentence involves little conjecture, it is almost like hearsay. (⇨ *sōda¹*)) [1c] is also the speaker's guess, but in this case it is based on what he sees. [1d] expresses the speaker's judgment about the price of the book. Note that in [1d] the speaker knows the book's price; therefore, this is not a guess. [2] provides examples with the noun *sensei* 'teacher' preceding the conjecture words. The differences in meaning among the sentences here are the same as those explained in [1], except that [2c] is ungrammatical.

[2] a. あの人は先生だろう。
   *Ano hito wa sensei **darō**.*
   (I guess he is a teacher.)

   b. あの人は先生らしい。
   *Ano hito wa sensei **rashii**.*
   ((From what I heard,) he seems to be a teacher.)

   c. *あの人は先生そうだ。
   Ano hito wa sensei **sōda.*

   d. あの人は先生のようだ。
   *Ano hito wa sensei no **yōda**.*
   ((Judging from how he looks,) he seems to be a teacher. / He looks as if he were a teacher.)

In [3], the verb *furu* 'fall' precedes the conjecture auxiliaries.

Y

[3] a. 今日は雨が降るだろう。

    *Kyō wa ame ga furu **darō**.*

    (I guess it will rain today.)

  b. 今日は雨が降るらしい。

    *Kyō wa ame ga furu **rashii**.*

    ((From what I heard,) it seems that it will rain today.)

  c. 今にも雨が降りそうだ。

    *Imanimo ame ga furi **sōda**.*

    (It looks like it's going to rain at any moment.)

  d. この辺はよく雨が降るようだ。

    *Kono hen wa yoku ame ga furu **yōda**.*

    ((Judging from the abundance of trees and moss,) it appears that it rains a lot around here.)

Here, [3a] is the speaker's guess. [3b] is the speaker's conjecture based on what he heard or it is almost like hearsay. [3c] is also the speaker's guess, but, in this case, he is probably looking at the sky. Like [3c], [3d] is based on what the speaker sees, but in this case the information is reliable, and involves the speaker's reasoning process.

The diagram in [4] summarizes the characteristics of the four conjecture expressions and *sōda*[1] (hearsay).

[4]

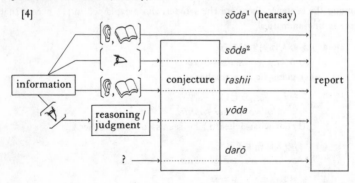

yōni[1] ように   *conj.*

> Do s.t. in such a way that ~.   so that

◆ **Key Sentences**

(A)

Vinf·nonpast(potential)		
読める ***Yomeru***	ように *yōni*	字 を きれいに 書いて ください。 *ji o kireini kaite kudasai.*
(Please write neatly so that I can read it.)		

(B)

	Vinf·neg·nonpast		
かぜ を *Kaze o*	ひかない ***hikanai***	ように *yōni*	気 を つけて いる / います。 *ki o tsukete iru / imasu.*
(I'm taking care of myself so that I don't catch cold.)			

Formation

Vinf·nonpast{pot / neg} ように
                          yōni

{話せる   / 話さない} ように   (so that s.o. can talk / does not talk)
{*hanaseru* / *hanasanai*} *yōni*

{食べられる / 食べない} ように   (so that s.o. can eat / does not eat)
{*taberareru* / *tabenai*} *yōni*

Examples

(a) 僕が分かるようにスミスさんはゆっくり英語を話してくれた。
Boku ga wakaru yōni Sumisu-san wa yukkuri eigo o hanashite kureta.
(Mr. Smith spoke English slowly so that I could understand him.)

(b) 遅れないようにタクシーで行きました。
Okurenai yōni takushī de ikimashita.
(I went there by taxi so that I wouldn't be late.)

(c) 病気が治るように薬を飲んだ。
Byōki ga naoru yōni kusuri o nonda.
(I took medicine so that I would (lit. recover from illness) get well.)

(d) 子供が本を読むようにおもしろそうな本を買って来た。

Kodomo ga hon o yomu yōni omoshirosōna hon o katte kita.

(I bought some interesting-looking books so that my child would read books.)

Notes

1. Although *yōni*[1] can be used with almost any informal, nonpast verb, it is most commonly used with potential verb forms (as in KS(A) and Ex. (a)) and negative verb forms (as in KS(B) and Ex. (b)).

2. ~*yōni iu* 'tell s.o. to do s.t.', ~*yōni naru* 'reach the point where ~' and ~*yōni suru* 'try to ~' are idiomatic uses of *yōni*.

$$(\Rightarrow \textbf{~yōni iu} ; \textbf{~yōni naru} ; \textbf{~yōni suru})$$

yōni[2] ように   *aux. adj. (na)*

an adverbial form of *yōda*   as ; like

♦ **Key Sentences**

(A)

	Vinf		
私　が *Watashi ga*	言う ***iu***	ように *yōni*	書いて ください。 *kaite kudasai.*
(Please write it down as I tell you.)			

(B)

Topic (subject)			Vinf・past		
今日 *Kyō*	は *wa*	春 に *haru ni*	なった ***natta***	ように *yōni*	暖かい / 暖かい です。 *atatakai / atatakai desu.*
(Lit. Today is as warm as if it had become spring.)					

(C)

Topic (subject)		Noun			
ドロシー *Doroshī*	は *wa*	**日本人** **nihonjin**	の *no*	ように *yōni*	日本語 を　話す / 話します。 *nihongo o hanasu / hanashimasu.*
(Dorothy speaks Japanese like a Japanese.)					

Formation

(i) {V / Adj (*i*)} inf　ように
　　　　　　　　　　 yōni

　　{話す　 / 話した}　ように　　(as s.o. talks / talked; as if s.o. (had) talked)
　　{*hanasu / hanashita*}　*yōni*

　　{高い / 高かった}　ように　　(as s.t. is / was expensive; as if s.t. were /
　　{*takai / takakatta*}　*yōni*　　had been expensive)

(ii) Adj (*na*) stem　{な / だった}　ように
　　　　　　　　　　　　 {*na* / *datta*}　 *yōni*

　　{静かな　 / 静かだった}　ように　　(as s.t. is / was quiet; as if s.t. were /
　　{*shizuka na* / *shizuka datta*}　*yōni*　　had been quiet)

(iii) N　{の / だった}　ように
　　　　 {*no* / *datta*}　 *yōni*

　　{先生　の / 先生　だった}　ように　　(like a teacher / as s.o. was a teacher;
　　{*sensei no* / *sensei datta*}　*yōni*　　as if s.o. were / had been a teacher)

Examples

(a) 前に話したように私は来月会社をやめます。
　　Mae ni hanashita yōni watashi wa raigetsu kaisha o yamemasu.
　　(As I told you before, I'm going to quit the company next month.)

(b) 上田さんのように走れますか。
　　Ueda-san no yōni hashiremasu ka.
　　(Can you run like Mr. Ueda?)

(c) 若い時のようには元気がなくなった。
　　Wakai toki no yōni wa genki ga nakunatta.
　　(I don't feel as strong as I used to when I was young.)

(d) 土井さんはいつものように朝六時に起きた。

Doi-san wa itsumo no yōni asa rokuji ni okita.

(As usual Mr. Doi got up at six in the morning.)

(e) 兄がスポーツが上手なように弟も上手だ。

Ani ga supōtsu ga jōzuna yōni otōto mo jōzuda.

(Just like the older brother, the younger brother is also good at sports.)

(f) 猫がかわいいように犬もかわいい。

Neko ga kawaii yōni inu mo kawaii.

(Lit. Just like cats are cute, so are dogs. (=Dogs are cute, just like cats.))

Notes

1. *Yōni¹* expresses purpose but *yōni²* doesn't; it expresses similarity, especially in appearance. (⇨ *yōni¹*)

2. *Yōni²* can express a counterfactual situation as in KS(B). The adverb *marude* 'just' is often used to emphasize counterfactuality. Examples follow:

　(1) a. まるで生き返ったように元気になった。

　　　Marude *ikikaetta* **yōni** *genkini natta.*

　　　(Lit. He recovered as if he had risen from the dead.)

　　b. あの子はまるで大人のように話す。

　　　Ano ko wa **marude** *otona no* **yōni** *hanasu.*

　　　(That child speaks as if he were an adult.)

~yōni iu ~ように言う　*phr.*

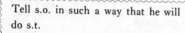

Tell s.o. in such a way that he will do s.t.	tell ~ to ~ ; say ~ in such a way

Y

◆**Key Sentence**

Topic (subject)		Indirect Object		Direct Object		Vinf·nonpast
先生 *Sensei*	は *wa*	学生 *gakusei*	に *ni*	宿題 *shukudai*	を *o*	**する** ***suru***

ように *yōni*	言った / 言いました。 *itta / iimashita.*

(The teacher told his students to do homework.)

Formation

Vinf·nonpast ように 言う
　　　　　　yōni　*iu*

話す ように 言う　　(tell s.o. to talk)
hanasu yōni iu

食べる ように 言う　　(tell s.o. to eat)
taberu yōni iu

Examples

(a) 坂本さんは雪江に図書館の前で待っているように言った。
　　Sakamoto-san wa Yukie ni toshokan no mae de matte iru yōni itta.
　　(Mr. Sakamoto told Yukie to be waiting in front of the library.)

(b) すみませんが，小林さんにあした朝九時にここへ来るように言ってください
　　ませんか。
　　Sumimasen ga, Kobayashi-san ni ashita asa kuji ni koko e kuru yōni itte kudasaimasen ka.
　　(I'm sorry, but could you please tell Mr. Kobayashi to come here at 9 o'clock tomorrow morning?)

(c) 私は聞こえるようにはっきり言ったんですが...
　　Watashi wa kikoeru yōni hakkiri itta n desu ga...
　　(I said it in such a way that it was clearly audible, but...)

Notes

1. *Yōni iu* can be used either as an indirect imperative as in KS and Exs. (a) and (b), or to mean 'say in such a way that ~,' i.e., the use of *yōni*.[1]

Y

($\Rightarrow$ **yōni**[1]) In the former case, the verb must be a controllable verb——a verb that represents something controllable by human volition, such as *suru* 'do', *matsu* 'wait', *kuru* 'come', *yomu* 'read' and *kau* 'buy'. In the latter case the verb must be a noncontrollable verb, such as *wakaru* 'understand', *kikoeru* 'be audible' (Ex. (c)), or a potential form of verbs.

2. When *yōni iu* is used as an indirect imperative, the verb *iu* can be replaced by other verbs such as *tanomu* 'ask', *meijiru* 'order' and *motomeru* 'request'.

(1) 田中さんは山本さんにすぐ来るように言った / 頼んだ / 命じた。

*Tanaka-san wa Yamamoto-san ni sugu kuru **yōni itta** / **tanon-da** / **meijita**.*

(Mr. Tanaka told / asked / ordered Mr. Yamamoto to come (to his place) immediately.)

The direct imperative versions of (1) are something like (2). Notice that there is more than one direct imperative form if the directive verb is *iu*.

(2) a. 田中さんは山本さんに「すぐ来てください（来なさい / 来い）。」と言った。

*Tanaka-san wa Yamamoto-san ni " **Sugu kite kudasai** (**kinasai** / **koi**)." to itta.*

(Mr. Tanaka said to Mr. Yamamoto, " Please come (Come) here right away.")

b. 田中さんは山本さんに「すぐ来い。」と命じた。

*Tanaka-san wa Yamamoto-san ni " **Sugu koi**." to meijita.*

(Mr. Tanaka ordered Mr. Yamamoto, " Come here right away!")

c. 田中さんは山本さんに「すぐ来てください。」と頼んだ。

*Tanaka-san wa Yamamoto-san ni " **Sugu kite kudasai**." to tanonda.*

(Mr. Tanaka asked Mr. Yamamoto, " Please come here right away.")

Y

~yōni naru ~ようになる *phr.*

> Some change takes place gradually.

reach the point where ~ ; come to ~ ; it has come to be that ~ ; have finally become

【REL. *koto ni naru*; *~naku naru*; **~yōni suru**】

♦ **Key Sentences**

(A)

Topic (subject)			Vinf·nonpast	
ジャクソンさん *Jakuson-san*	は *wa*	日本語 が *nihongo ga*	**話せる** ***hanaseru***	ように なった/ *yōni natta/* なりました。 *narimashita.*

(Mr. Jackson has reached the point where he can speak Japanese.)

(B)

Topic (subject)			Vinf·nonpast·neg	
林さん *Hayashi-san*	は *wa*	酒 を *sake o*	**飲まない** ***nomanai***	ように なった/ なりました。 *yōni natta / narimashita.*

(Lit. Mr. Hayashi has reached the point where he does not drink *sake*. (=Mr. Hayashi doesn't drink *sake* any more.))

Formation

Vinf·nonpast ように なる
　　　　　　　yōni　naru

{話す ／ 話さない} ように なる　(s.o. reaches the point where he talks /
{*hanasu / hanasanai*} *yōni naru*　doesn't talk)

{食べる ／ 食べない} ように なる　(s.o. reaches the point where he eats /
{*taberu / tabenai*}　 *yōni naru*　doesn't eat)

Examples

(a) 難しい日本語が読めるようになりました。
　　Muzukashii nihongo ga yomeru yōni narimashita.
　　(I am finally able to read difficult Japanese.)

(b) パットは私と話さないようになった。

　　Patto wa watashi to hanasanai yōni natta.

　　(Pat doesn't talk with me any more.)

(c) もうすぐおもしろさが分かるようになりますよ。

　　Mō sugu omoshirosa ga wakaru yōni narimasu yo.

　　(You'll soon come to understand the fun of it, I tell you.)

(d) この道は今通れないようになっている。

　　Kono michi wa ima tōrenai yōni natte iru.

　　(Lit. This street has reached the point where people cannot pass. (=At present we cannot use this street.))

Notes

1. Although ~*yōni naru* usually indicates a gradual change, when it is preceded by an affirmative verb the change may not take place gradually. Thus, an adverb such as *kyūni* 'suddenly' can co-occur with an affirmative verb and ~*yōni naru*, as seen in (1).

　(1) うちの子は最近急に勉強するようになったんですよ。

　　　*Uchi no ko wa saikin **kyūni** benkyōsuru **yōni natta** n desu yo.*

　　　(Lit. Recently our child has suddenly reached the point where he studies. (=Recently our child suddenly started to study.))

　When ~*yōni naru* is preceded by a negative verb (as in KS(B)), however, the change must take place gradually. If the change is not gradual, ~*naku naru* is used in place of ~*nai yōni naru*.

　　　　　　　　　　　　　　　　　　(See Related Expression II.)

2. *Yōni natte iru* emphasizes a current state that has come about after a long process, as in Ex. (d).

3. There are two ways to negate this construction, but the meanings are completely different. The verb before *yōni* can be negated, as in (2a), or the verb *naru* can be negated, as in (2b).

　(2) a. 漢字が覚えられないようになった。

　　　　　*Kanji ga oboerare**nai** yōni natta.*

　　　　　(I've reached the point where I can't memorize *kanji*.)

　　　b. 漢字が覚えられるようにならなかった。

　　　　　*Kanji ga oboerareru yōni nara**nakatta**.*

　　　　　(I haven't reached the point where I can memorize *kanji*.)

(2a) means that the speaker can't memorize *kanji* any more, and (2b) means that he is not yet able to memorize *kanji*.

4. *Yōni* by itself can be used as an adverbial phrase, along with main verbs other than *naru*. (⇨ **yōni**[1]; **yōni**[2])

[Related Expressions]

I. *Koto ni naru* 'it has been decided that ~ ' and ~*yōni naru* are related expressions in that both of them indicate some change, but they differ in that the former implies a passive decision, while the latter suggests a change brought about by a long process. Compare the following sentences:

[1] a. 私は大阪に転勤することに / *ようになりました。
   *Watashi wa Ōsaka ni tenkinsuru **koto ni** / *yōni narimashita.*
   (It has been decided that I will transfer to Osaka.)

   b. 私は英語が話せるように / *ことになりました。
   *Watashi wa eigo ga hanaseru **yōni** / *koto ni narimashita.*
   (I've reached the point where I can speak English.)

II. When the verb before ~*yōni naru* is negated, as in KS(B), this construction can be compared to the ~*naku naru* construction.

[2] a. 林さんは酒を飲まないようになった。
   *Hayashi-san wa sake o noma**nai yōni natta**.* (=KS(B))
   (Mr. Hayashi doesn't drink *sake* any more.)

   b. 林さんは酒を飲まなくなった。
   *Hayashi-san wa sake o noma**naku natta**.*
   (Mr. Hayashi doesn't drink *sake* any more.)

The *nai yōni natta* version in [2a] implies a more gradual change than the *naku natta* version in [2b]. Thus, adverbs such as *kyūni* 'suddenly' or *totsuzen* 'suddenly' can co-occur with [2b] but not with [2a].

Y

~yōni suru ~ようにする　*phr.*

S.o. causes some circumstantial or behavioral change to take place.	do ~ in such a way that ~ ; see to it that ~ ; make sure that ~ ; bring it about that ~ 【REL. ~yōni naru】

♦ **Key Sentence**

		Vinf·nonpast	
私　は *Watashi wa*	毎日 *mainichi*	**運動する** ***undōsuru***	ように　する／します。 *yōni suru／shimasu.*

(I'll make sure that I do exercises everyday.)

Formation

Vinf·nonpast　ように　する
　　　　　　　yōni　suru

{話す　／話さない} ように　する　　(s.o. makes sure that he / s.o. else talks /
{*hanasu / hanasanai*} *yōni suru*　doesn't talk)

{食べる／食べない} ように　する　　(s.o. makes sure that he / s.o. else eats /
{*taberu / tabenai*}　*yōni suru*　doesn't eat)

Examples

(a) 出来るだけ日本語で話すようにしています。
　　Dekiru dake nihongo de hanasu yōni shite imasu.
　　(I'm making sure I speak in Japanese as much as possible.)

(b) 山川には会わないようにした。
　　Yamakawa ni wa awanai yōni shita.
　　(I've made sure that I won't see Yamakawa.)

(c) 分からないことは先生に聞くようにしている。
　　Wakaranai koto wa sensei ni kiku yōni shite iru.
　　(I make a point of asking my teacher about things I don't understand.)

(d) 毎朝八時に来るようにしてください。
　　Maiasa hachiji ni kuru yōni shite kudasai.
　　(Please make sure that you come at eight every morning.)

(e) うしろからもよく見えるようにしました。
　　Ushiro kara mo yoku mieru yōni shimashita.

(I've seen to it that people can see from the rear seats, too.)

(f) 成績がよくなるようにした。

Seiseki ga yoku naru yōni shita.

(I've made sure that my grades will improve.)

1. ~*yōni shite iru* expresses s.o.'s habitual act of making sure that he or s.o. else will do (or will not do) s.t., as shown in Exs. (a) and (c).

2. The subjects in the *yōni* clause and in the main clause may or may not be identical. In (1a), the subjects are different, but in (1b), they are identical.

   (1) a. ジョンはメアリーが行けるようにした。

   *Jon wa Meari ga ikeru **yōni shita**.*

   (John has seen to it that Mary can go there.)

   b. ジョンは行けるようにした。

   *Jon wa ikeru **yōni shita**.*

   (John has seen to it that he (=John) can go there.)

3. There are two ways to negate this construction, but the meaning changes according to the pattern. The verb before *yōni* can be negated as in (2a), or the verb *suru* can be negated as in (2b).

   (2) a. 小川は山本が勉強出来ないようにした。

   *Ogawa wa Yamamoto ga benkyō deki **nai** yōni shita.*

   (Ogawa made sure that Yamamoto couldn't study.)

   b. 小川は山本が勉強出来るように(は)しなかった。

   *Ogawa wa Yamamoto ga benkyō dekiru yōni (wa) shi**nakatta**.*

   (Ogawa didn't make sure that Yamamoto could study.)

   In (2a) *Ogawa* is directly involved in preventing *Yamamoto* from studying, but in (2b) *Ogawa* just didn't bother to assist *Yamamoto*'s studying.

4. When an Adj (*i* / *na*) or N is used before *yōni suru*, the verb *naru* is used as follows:

   (i) Adj (*i*) stem く なる ように する
            ku naru yōni suru

   {高く なる / 高くなく なる} ようにする   (make sure s.t. be-
   {*takaku naru* / *takakunaku naru*} *yōni suru*   comes / won't be-
                                                      come expensive)

(ii) {Adj (*na*) stem / N} に なる ように する
　　　　　ni naru yōni suru

静か {に / で は なく / じゃなく} なる ように する
shizuka {*ni* / *de wa naku* / *janaku*} *naru yōni suru*
(make sure s.t. is / won't be quiet)

先生 {に / で は なく / じゃなく} なる ように する
sensei {*ni* / *de wa naku* / *janaku*} *naru yōni suru*
(make sure s.o. is / won't be a teacher)

【Related Expression】

~*yōni naru* 'reach the point where' is the intransitive counterpart of *yōni suru*. The former only indirectly implies human efforts behind some change that will occur or has occurred, but the latter straightforwardly indicates human efforts. For example, in [1a] the speaker can get up early in the morning almost effortlessly, but in [1b] he has to make sure that he can get up early in the morning.

[1] a. 朝早く起きられるようになりました。
　　　Asa hayaku okirareru **yōni narimashita**.
　　　(I am finally able to get up early in the morning.)

　　 b. 朝早く起きられるようにしています。
　　　Asa hayaku okirareru **yōni shite imasu**.
　　　(I am making sure that I can get up early in the morning.)

---

yori[1] より　*prt.*

a particle which indicates that s.t. / s.o. is being compared with s.t. / s.o.

than; rather ~ than ~; more ~ than ~

【REL. ~ *hō ga* ~ *yori*】

◆**Key Sentences**

(A)

Topic (subject)		Noun		Predicate
日本語 *Nihongo*	は *wa*	スペイン語 **supeingo**	より (も) *yori (mo)*	おもしろい / おもしろいです。 *omoshiroi / omoshiroidesu.*
(Japanese is more interesting than Spanish.)				

(B)

Subject			Sentence₂		Predicate
Sentence₁					
車 で 行く ***Kuruma de iku***	ほう *hō*	が *ga*	バス で 行く ***basu de iku***	より (も) *yori (mo)*	安い / 安いです。 *yasui / yasuidesu.*
(Going by car is cheaper than going by bus.)					

(C)

Topic (subject)		Predicate₁		Predicate₂
私 *Watashi*	は *wa*	旅行する ***ryokōsuru***	より (も) *yori (mo)*	うち に いたい / いたいです。 *uchi ni itai / itaidesu.*
(I'd rather stay at home than go on a trip.)				

(D)

Noun / Sentence			
これ ***Kore***	より *yori*	(ほか (に)) *(hoka (ni))*	方法 は ない / ありません。 *hōhō wa nai / arimasen.*
(There is no other way than this.)			
バス で 行く ***Basu de iku***	より *yori*	(ほか (に)) *(hoka (ni))*	仕方 が ない / ありません。 *shikata ga nai / arimasen.*
(There is no other way than to go by bus.)			

Formation

(A) KS(A) / KS(D):

    N より
      yori

    これ より   (than this)
    kore yori

(B) KS(B) / KS(C) / KS(D):

    (i) {V / Adj (*i*)} inf·nonpast より
                            yori

Y

話す より　　(than talking)
hanasu yori

高い より　　(than being expensive)
takai yori

(ii) Adj (*na*) stem な より
　　　　　　　　na yori

静かな　より　　(than being quiet)
shizukana yori

(iii) N で ある より
　　　　de aru yori

先生　で ある より　　(than being a teacher)
sensei de aru yori

Examples

(a) 漢字はひらがなより難しい。
　　Kanji wa hiragana yori muzukashii.
　　(*Kanji* is more difficult than *hiragana*.)

(b) 林さんは私より速く走れる。
　　Hayashi-san wa watashi yori hayaku hashireru.
　　(Mr. Hayashi can run faster than I can.)

(c) 僕はステーキより魚の方が好きだ。
　　Boku wa sutēki yori sakana no hō ga sukida.
　　(I prefer fish to steak.)

(d) 図書館で勉強する方がうちで勉強するよりよく出来る。
　　Toshokan de benkyōsuru hō ga uchi de benkyōsuru yori yoku dekiru.
　　(Studying at the library is more productive than studying at home.)

(e) それは赤と言うより茶色に近かった。
　　Sore wa aka to iu yori chairo ni chikakatta.
　　(That was closer to brown than to red (lit. rather than saying it was red).)

(f) 日本語を勉強したかったら，アメリカの学校で勉強するより日本へ行きなさい。
　　Nihongo o benkyōshitakattara, Amerika no gakkō de benkyōsuru yori Nihon e ikinasai.
　　(If you want to study Japanese, go to Japan rather than studying at a school in America.)

1. Either a noun phrase or a sentence precedes *yori*. When verbs precede *yori*, they are usually nonpast. However, there are a few cases where past tense verbs are used, as in (1).

   (1) その試験は思ったよりやさしかった。
   Sono shiken wa omotta yori yasashikatta.
   (The exam was easier than I thought.)

2. In KS(A), KS(B) and KS(C), *mo* is optional after *yori* and does not change the meaning of the sentence.

yori² より *prt.*

a particle which indicates a set point in terms of space or time	in ~ of; inside; outside; before; after 【REL. *kara*¹】

♦ **Key Sentence**

Topic (subject)		Noun (location / time)		Noun (location / time)
メキシコ *Mekishiko*	は *wa*	赤道 *sekidō*	より *yori*	北 *kita*

	Predicate
に *ni*	ある / あります。 *aru / arimasu.*

(Mexico is located north of the equator.)

Examples

(a) この線より内側に入ってはいけません。
Kono sen yori uchigawa ni haitte wa ikemasen.
(You must not get inside this line.)

(b) 三時より前に来てください。
Sanji yori mae ni kite kudasai.
(Please come before three o'clock.)

Y

(c) これより先はバスがありません。

　　Kore yori saki wa basu ga arimasen.

　　(There's no bus service from here (lit. beyond this point).)

Note

The use of *yori* as a marker indicating a set point in terms of location can be extended to more abstract locations, as in (1).

　⑴ 八十点より上は合格です。

　　　*Hachijutten **yori** ue wa gōkaku desu.*

　　　(Lit. Eighty point up is a pass. (=The passing mark is eighty.))

[Related Expression]

Kara can be used in place of *yori*² when *kara* indicates a set point in space, as in [1].　　　　　　　　　　　　　　　　　　　　　(⇨ **kara**¹)

　[1] この線から / より内側に入ってはいけません。

　　　*Kono sen **kara** / **yori** uchigawa ni haitte wa ikemasen.*

　　　(You must not get inside this line.)

When *yori* indicates a point in time, however, *kara* can replace it only if it indicates a starting time. Thus, *kara* in [2a] is grammatical, but *kara* in [2b] is not.

　[2]　a. 三時より / から後に来てください。

　　　　　*Sanji **yori** / **kara** ato ni kite kudasai.*

　　　　　(Please come after three o'clock.)

　　　　b. 三時より / *から前に来てください。

　　　　　*Sanji **yori** / ***kara** mae ni kite kudasai.*

　　　　　(Please come before three o'clock.)

It is also noted that *yori*² implies a comparison of two things, while *kara* has no such implication.

Y

~yō to omou ~ようと思う   *phr.*

> The speaker desires or decides to do s.t.

~ think ~ will
【REL. *tsumori*】

♦ **Key Sentences**

(A)

Topic (subject)			Vinf·vol	
私 *Watashi*	は *wa*	日本歴史 を *Nihonrekishi o*	**読もう** ***yomō***	と 思う / 思います。 *to omou / omoimasu.*
(I think I will read Japanese history (books).)				

(B)

Topic (subject)			Vinf·nonpast		
私 *Watashi*	は *wa*	もう 酒 を *mō sake o*	**飲む** ***nomu***	まい *mai*	と 思う / 思います。 *to omou / omoimasu.*
(I think I will not drink alcohol any longer.)					

Formation

KS(A):

Vinf·vol と 思う
   to omou

話そう と 思う　(I think I will talk.)
hanasō to omou

食べよう と 思う　(I think I will eat.)
tabeyō to omou

KS(B):

Vinf·nonpast まい と 思う
     mai to omou

話すまい と 思う　(I think I will not talk.)
hanasumai to omou

食べるまい と 思う　(I think I will not eat.)
taberumai to omou

Y

Examples

(a) 夏休みに日本アルプスに登ろうと思います。

   Natsuyasumi ni Nihon Arupusu ni noborō to omoimasu.

   (I think I will climb the Japan Alps during summer vacation.)

(b) 森さんはワープロ（＝ワードプロセッサー）を買おうと思っています。

   Mori-san wa wāpuro (＝wādo purosessā) o kaō to omotte imasu.

   (Mr. Mori is thinking of buying a word processor.)

(c) 僕はあの人とはもう話すまいと思う。

   Boku wa ano hito to wa mō hanasumai to omou.

   (I think I won't talk to that person any more.)

Notes

1. When the subject is not the first person, as in Ex. (b), the nonpast form of *omou* cannot be used. Thus, the following sentence is unacceptable.

   ⑴ *森さんはワープロを買おうと思う／思います。

      Mori-san wa wāpuro o kaō to **omou / **omoimasu**.*

   The reason why (1) is unacceptable is that *omou* represents an internal feeling of the speaker alone. Therefore, when the subject is the third person, *omou* has to be replaced by the stative *omotte iru* which means 'he (＝the third person subject) has indicated that he feels ～, in such a way that the speaker can see and / or hear what he feels'. Observe the following sentence.

   ⑵ 私／*父／*山下さんはその映画を見ようと思います。

      Watashi / ***Chichi** / ***Yamashita-san** *wa sono eiga o miyō to omoimasu.*

      (I / My father / Mr. Yamashita think(s) I / he will see that movie.)

   It is also to be noted that ～*yō to omou* cannot be used as a question.

   ⑶ ??あの本を読もうと思いますか。

      ??Ano hon o yomō to omoimasu ka.

      (Do you think you will read that book?)

2. The negative version of ～*yō to omou* is Vinf·nonpast ～*mai to omou*, as seen in KS(B) and Ex. (c).

3. The verb that precedes *yō* must be a verb that represents something controllable by human volition. Thus, the following sentences are all ungrammatical, because the verbs are noncontrollable.

(4) a. *車を買えようと思う。

    *Kuruma o **kaeyō** to omou.*

    (I think I can buy a car.)

  Cp. 車を買えると思う。

    *Kuruma o **kaeru** to omou.*

    (I think I can buy a car.)

  b. *お金をもらったら喜ぼうと思う。

    O-kane o morattara **yorokobō to omou.*

    (I think I'll be happy if I get money.)

  Cp. お金をもらったら喜ぶだろうと思う。

    O-kane o morattara yorokobu darō to omou.

    (I think I will probably rejoice if I receive money.)

  c. *雨に降られようと思う。

    Ame ni **furareyō to omou.*

    (I think I will be caught in the rain.)

  Cp. 雨に降られると思う。

    Ame ni furareru to omou.

    (I think I will be caught in the rain.)

A passive verb can be used with ~*yō to omou*, however, if the speaker perceives the passive situation as somehow controllable, as in (5).

(5) たまには先生にほめられようと思う。

    *Tama ni wa sensei ni **homerareyō** to omou.*

    (Lit. I think I will do my best to be praised by my teacher once in a while.)

zutsu ずつ *prt.*

a particle that indicates equal distribution of quantity

by; at a time

♦ **Key Sentence**

Topic (subject)		Direct Object		Quantifier		
私 *Watashi*	は *wa*	漢字 を *kanji o*	毎日 *mainichi*	五つ ***itsutsu***	ずつ *zutsu*	覚える / 覚えます。 *oboeru / oboemasu.*
(I memorize five *kanji* every day.)						

Examples

(a) 毎月三冊ずつ本を買っています。
   Maitsuki sansatsu zutsu hon o katte imasu.
   (I'm buying three books per month.)

(b) ゴルフが少しずつ上手になって来た。
   Gorufu ga sukoshi zutsu jōzuni natte kita.
   (I have become a better golfer bit by bit.)

(c) 私は子供達に本を二冊ずつやった。
   Watashi wa kodomotachi ni hon o nisatsu zutsu yatta.
   (I gave two books to each of the children.)

(d) どのクラスにも女子学生が六人ずついた。
   Dono kurasu ni mo joshigakusei ga rokunin zutsu ita.
   (There were six girl students in each class.)

Notes

1. The particle *zutsu* is used only after a quantifier (=an expression of quantity).

2. A sentence without *zutsu* can express virtually the same fact. Compare KS and Ex. (a) with (1a) and (1b), respectively.

   (1) a. 私は漢字を毎日五つ覚える。
          *Watashi wa kanji o mainichi **itsutsu** oboeru.*
          (I memorize five *kanji* every day.)

b. 毎月三冊本を買っています。

   *Maitsuki **sansatsu** hon o katte imasu.*

   (I'm buying three books every month.)

A sentence with *zutsu* focuses on equal distribution of quantity, but a sentence without *zutsu* doesn't.

Z

Appendixes

Appendixes

Appendix 1 Basic Conjugations

	inf., neg., nonpast	formal, nonpast (*masu*-form)[2]	inf., nonpast (dictionary form)	conditional	volitional	te-form
Group 1 verbs[1]						
書く (write) *kaku*	書かない *kakanai*	書きます *kakimasu*	書く *kaku*	書けば *kakeba*	書こう *kakō*	書いて *kaite*
行く (go) *iku*	行かない *ikanai*	行きます *ikimasu*	行く *iku*	行けば *ikeba*	行こう *ikō*	行って[3] *itte*
話す (talk) *hanasu*	話さない *hanasanai*	話します *hanashimasu*	話す *hanasu*	話せば *hanaseba*	話そう *hanasō*	話して *hanashite*
待つ (wait) *matsu*	待たない *matanai*	待ちます *machimasu*	待つ *matsu*	待てば *mateba*	待とう *matō*	待って *matte*
死ぬ (die) *shinu*	死なない *shinanai*	死にます *shinimasu*	死ぬ *shinu*	死ねば *shineba*	死のう *shinō*	死んで *shinde*
読む (read) *yomu*	読まない *yomanai*	読みます *yomimasu*	読む *yomu*	読めば *yomeba*	読もう *yomō*	読んで *yonde*
乗る (ride) *noru*	乗らない *noranai*	乗ります *norimasu*	乗る *noru*	乗れば *noreba*	乗ろう *norō*	乗って *notte*
ある (exist) *aru*	ない[3] *nai*	あります *arimasu*	ある *aru*	あれば *areba*	(あろう)[4] (*arō*)	あって *atte*
買う (buy) *kau*	買わない *kawanai*	買います *kaimasu*	買う *kau*	買えば *kaeba*	買おう *kaō*	買って *katte*
泳ぐ (swim) *oyogu*	泳がない *oyoganai*	泳ぎます *oyogimasu*	泳ぐ *oyogu*	泳げば *oyogeba*	泳ごう *oyogō*	泳いで *oyoide*
呼ぶ (call) *yobu*	呼ばない *yobanai*	呼びます *yobimasu*	呼ぶ *yobu*	呼べば *yobeba*	呼ぼう *yobō*	呼んで *yonde*
おっしゃる(say (Honorific)) *ossharu*	おっしゃらない *ossharanai*	おっしゃいます[5] *osshaimasu*	おっしゃる *ossharu*	おっしゃれば *osshareba*	(おっしゃろう)[4] (*ossharō*)	おっしゃって *osshatte*

inf., past	inf., neg., past	passive[6]	causative[6]	potential[6]	impera-tive
書いた kaita	書かなかった kakanakatta	書かれる kakareru	書かせる kakaseru	書ける kakeru	書け kake
行った[3] itta	行かなかった ikanakatta	行かれる ikareru	行かせる ikaseru	行ける ikeru	行け ike
話した hanashita	話さなかった hanasana-katta	話される hanasareru	話させる hanasaseru	話せる hanaseru	話せ hanase
待った matta	待たなかった matana-katta	待たれる matareru	待たせる mataseru	待てる materu	待て mate
死んだ shinda	死ななかった shinana-katta	死なれる shinareru	死なせる shinaseru	死ねる shineru	死ね shine
読んだ yonda	読まなかった yomana-katta	読まれる yomareru	読ませる yomaseru	読める yomeru	読め yome
乗った notta	乗らなかった norana-katta	乗られる norareru	乗らせる noraseru	乗れる noreru	乗れ nore
あった atta	なかった[3] nakatta				(あれ)[4] (are)
買った katta	買わなかった kawana-katta	買われる kawareru	買わせる kawaseru	買える kaeru	買え kae
泳いだ oyoida	泳がなかった oyogana-katta	泳がれる oyogareru	泳がせる oyogaseru	泳げる oyogeru	泳げ oyoge
呼んだ yonda	呼ばなかった yobana-katta	呼ばれる yobareru	呼ばせる yobaseru	呼べる yoberu	呼べ yobe
おっしゃった osshatta	おっしゃらなかった ossharana-katta	(おっしゃられる)[4] (osshara-reru)	(おっしゃらせる)[4] (osshara-seru)	おっしゃれる osshareru	おっしゃい[4] osshai

	inf., neg., nonpast	formal, nonpast (*masu*-form)	inf., nonpast (dictionary form)	condi-tional	volitional	*te*-form
Group 2 verbs[1]						
見る(see) *miru*	見ない *minai*	見ます *mimasu*	見る *miru*	見れば *mireba*	見よう *miyō*	見て *mite*
寝る(go to *neru* bed)	寝ない *nenai*	寝ます *nemasu*	寝る *neru*	寝れば *nereba*	寝よう *neyō*	寝て *nete*
Irregular verbs						
する(do) *suru*	しない *shinai*	します *shimasu*	する *suru*	すれば *sureba*	しよう *shiyō*	して *shite*
来る(come) *kuru*	こない *konai*	きます *kimasu*	くる *kuru*	くれば *kureba*	こよう *koyō*	きて *kite*

[1] Group 1 verbs are those whose negative, informal stems end with the [a] sound. Group 2 verbs are those whose negative, informal stems end with [i] or [e].

[2] The complete conjugations of formal forms are as follow:

nonpast	(書き)ます (*kaki*)**masu**
neg., nonpast	(書き)ません (*kaki*)**masen**
past	(書き)ました (*kaki*)**mashita**
neg., past	(書き)ませんでした (*kaki*)**masendeshita**
volitional	(書き)ましょう (*kaki*)**mashō**

[3] Irregular conjugation.

[4] This form is usually not used.

[5] Some honorific verbs (*irassharu* 'go; come; be', *nasaru* 'do', *gozaru* 'be') are irregular in the *masu*-form and the imperative form.

[6] Passive verbs, causative verbs and potential verbs are all Group 2 verbs.

[7] There are also imperative forms like *Miyo* 'See' and *Seyo* 'Do.' These are used only in written Japanese.

inf., past	inf., neg., past	passive[6]	causative[6]	potential[6]	imperative
見た *mita*	見なかった *minakatta*	見られる *mirareru*	見させる *misaseru*	見られる *mirareru*	見ろ[7] *miro*
寝た *neta*	寝なかった *nenakatta*	寝られる *nerareru*	寝させる *nesaseru*	寝られる *nerareru*	寝ろ *nero*
した *shita*	しなかった *shinakatta*	される *sareru*	させる *saseru*	できる *dekiru*	しろ[7] *shiro*
きた *kita*	こなかった *konakatta*	こられる *korareru*	こさせる *kosaseru*	こられる *korareru*	こい *koi*

	inf., nonpast	inf., neg., nonpast	inf., past	inf., neg., past	condition
i-Adjectives[8]					
大きい[9] (big)	大きい	大きくない	大きかった	大きくなかった	大きければ
ōkii	*ōkii*	*ōkikunai*	*ōkikatta*	*ōkikunakatta*	*ōkikereba*
いい[10] (good)	いい	よくない	よかった	よくなかった	よければ
ii	*ii*	*yokunai*	*yokatta*	*yokunakatta*	*yokereba*

[8] Auxiliary adjectives *-tai* (want to), *-rashii* (seem), *-yasui* (easy to), *-nikui* (hard to), *-nai* (not) are *i*-adjectives.

[9] *Ōkii* (big) and *chīsai* (small) can be either *i*-adjectives or *na*-adjectives. When they are used as *na*-adjectives, they are rather emotive.

[10] *Ii* is an irregular *i*-adjective. *Ii* is usually used as the inf., nonpast form.

	inf., nonpast	inf., neg., nonpast	inf., past	inf., neg., past	condition
na-Adjectives[11]					
静かだ (quiet)	静かだ	静かではない	静かだった	静かではなかった	静かなら(ば)
shizukada	*shizukada*	*shizuka-dewanai*	*shizuka-datta*	*shizuka-dewanakatta*	*shizuka-nara(ba)*
		静かじゃない[12]		静かじゃなかった[12]	静かであれば
		shizukajanai		*shizukaja-nakatta*	*shizukade-areba*
Copula					
だ (be)	だ	ではない	だった	ではなかった	なら(ば)
da	*da*	*dewanai*	*datta*	*dewanakatta*	*nara(ba)*
		じゃない[12]		じゃなかった[12]	であれば
		janai		*janakatta*	*deareba*

[11] Borrowed adjectives (including Chinese-origin adjectives) and such auxiliary adjectives as *-yōda* (look like), *-mitaida* (look like), *-sōda* (look) are all *na*-adjectives.

te-form	adverbial	prenominal	formal, nonpast	formal, neg., nonpast	formal, past	formal, neg., past
大きくて *ōkikute*	大きく *ōkiku*	大きい *ōkii*	大きいです *ōkiidesu*	大きくありません[13] *ōkikuari-masen*	大きかったです *ōkikatta desu*	大きくありませんでした[13] *ōkikuari-masen-deshita*
				大きくないです[13] *ōkikunai-desu*		大きくなかったです[13] *ōkikuna-kattadesu*
よくて *yokute*	よく *yoku*	いい *ii*	いいです *iidesu*	よくありません[13] *yokuari-masen*	よかったです *yokatta-desu*	よくありませんでした[13] *yokuari-masende-shita*
				よくないです[13] *yokunai-desu*		よくなかったです[13] *yoku-nakatta-desu*
静かで *shizuka-de*	静かに *shizukani*	静かな *shizukana*	静かです *shizuka-desu*	静かではありません *shizuka-dewaari-masen*	静かでした *shizuka-deshita*	静かではありませんでした *shizuka-dewaari-masen-deshita*
				静かじゃありません[12] *shizukaja-arimasen*		静かじゃありませんでした[12] *shizukaja-arimasen-deshita*
で *de*	— —	の / である *no / dearu*	です *desu*	ではありません *dewaari-masen*	でした *deshita*	ではありませんでした *dewaari-masen-deshita*
				じゃありません[12] *jaarima-sen*		じゃありませんでした[12] *jaarima-sendeshita*

[12] *Ja* is the colloquial form of *dewa*.

[13] ~*naidesu* / ~*nakattadesu* expresses a stronger feeling of negation than ~*arimasen* / ~*arimasendeshita*.

Appendix 2 **Semantic Classification of Verbs and Adjectives**

A. Stative verbs:

A stative verb usually does not appear with the auxiliary verb *iru*.

ある ((of an inanimate thing) exist);	いる ((of an animate thing) exist);
aru	*iru*
できる (can do);	いる (need)
dekiru	*iru*

(All the potential verbs are stative. (e.g., 飲める (can drink))
                                              nomeru

B. Continual verbs:

A continual verb with the auxiliary verb *iru* expresses the progressive aspect.

食べる (eat);	飲む (drink);	歩く (walk);	走る (run);	踊る (dance);
taberu	*nomu*	*aruku*	*hashiru*	*odoru*
歌う (sing);	泳ぐ (swim);	待つ (wait);	話す (talk);	聞く (hear);
utau	*oyogu*	*matsu*	*hanasu*	*kiku*
読む (read);	書く (write);	見る (see);	泣く (cry);	教える (teach);
yomu	*kaku*	*miru*	*naku*	*oshieru*
見せる (show);	使う (use);	作る (make);	笑う (laugh);	休む (rest);
miseru	*tsukau*	*tsukuru*	*warau*	*yasumu*
勉強する (study);	飛ぶ (fly);	考える (think);	会う (meet);	住む (live);
benkyōsuru	*tobu*	*kangaeru*	*au*	*sumu*

C. Stative-continual verbs:

A stative-continual verb can be either a stative verb or a continual verb.

見える (be visible);	聞こえる (be audible);	分かる (understand);	違う
mieru	*kikoeru*	*wakaru*	*chigau*

(differ); 似合う (become; be suitable)
            niau

D. Punctual verbs:

A punctual verb with the auxiliary verb *iru* expresses a repeated action or a state after an action was taken or something took place.

知る (get to know);	死ぬ (die);	忘れる (forget);	貸す (lend);	借りる
shiru	*shinu*	*wasureru*	*kasu*	*kariru*

(borrow); 跳ぶ (jump); 打つ (hit); 出る (get out); 入る (enter);
            tobu   *utsu*   *deru*   *hairu*

立つ (stand);　座る (sit down);　起きる (get up);　結婚する (marry);
tatsu　　　　*suwaru*　　　　*okiru*　　　　*kekkonsuru*

行く (go);　来る (come);　帰る (return);　言う (say);　あげる (give);
iku　　　*kuru*　　　*kaeru*　　　*iu*　　　*ageru*

もらう (get);　疲れる (get tired);　困る (get into trouble);　乗る (get on);
morau　　*tsukareru*　　*komaru*　　　　*noru*

始まる (begin (v.i.));　終わる (end (v.i.));　開く (open (v.i.));　閉まる (close
hajimaru　　　*owaru*　　　　*aku*　　　　*shimaru*

(v.i.));　なる (become);　着く (arrive);　晴れる (clear up);　覚える
　　　　naru　　　*tsuku*　　　*hareru*　　　*oboeru*

(remember);　寝る (go to bed);　止まる (stop (v.i.))　ける (kick);　付く
　　　　neru　　　　*tomaru*　　　　*keru*　　　*tsuku*

(be attached);　合う (match);　止める (stop (v.t.))
　　　　　　au　　　*yameru*

E.　Continual-punctual verbs:

A continual-punctual verb can be either a continual verb or a punctual verb.

着る (wear);　取る (take);　変わる (change (v.i.));　注文する (order)
kiru　　　*toru*　　*kawaru*　　　　*chūmonsuru*

F.　Non-volitional verbs:

A non-volitional verb usually does not take the volitional form, the imperative form and the potential form.　Non-volitional verbs are classified into emotive verbs and non-emotive verbs.

F-1.　Non-volitional-emotive verbs:

Most of the non-volitional-emotive verbs can take an NP-*o*.　($\Rightarrow$***o***^{4})

よろこぶ (be pleased);　悲しむ (be sad);　怒る (be angry);　きらう
yorokobu　　　　*kanashimu*　　*okoru*　　　*kirau*

(hate);　好む (like);　困る (get into trouble);　苦しむ (suffer)
　　konomu　*komaru*　　　　*kurushimu*

(*Komaru* and *kurushimu* do not take an NP-*o*.　They take either an NP-*de* or an NP-*ni*.)

F-2.　Non-volitional-non-emotive verbs:

できる (can do);　いる (need);　知る (get to know);　見える (be visible);
dekiru　　*iru*　　*shiru*　　　*mieru*

聞こえる (be audible);　分かる (understand);　違う (differ);　似合う
kikoeru　　　*wakaru*　　　*chigau*　　*niau*

(become, be suitable); 疲れる (get tired)
                          tsukareru

G. Reciprocal verbs:

A reciprocal verb takes the particle *to* for the direct object.

結婚する (marry);	けんかする (fight);	会う (meet);	合う (match);
kekkonsuru	*kenkasuru*	*au*	*au*

ぶつかる (bump into); 相談する (consult)
butsukaru   *sōdansuru*

H. Movement verbs:

A movement verb can take V*masu ni* to express a purpose.

行く (go);	来る (come);	帰る (return);	入る (enter);	出る (get out);
iku	*kuru*	*kaeru*	*hairu*	*deru*

(立ち)寄る (stop by)
(*tachi*)*yoru*

Appendix 3 **Pairs of Intransitive and Transitive Verbs**

Intransitive Verb		Transitive Verb	
A 1. —*eru* → —*asu*			
出る *deru*	(get out)	出す *dasu*	(take out)
逃げる *nigeru*	(run away)	逃がす *nigasu*	(let run away)
溶ける *tokeru*	(dissolve)	溶かす *tokasu*	(dissolve)
枯れる *kareru*	(wither)	枯らす *karasu*	(let wither)
A 2. —*eru* → —*yasu*			
冷える *hieru*	(get cold)	冷やす *hiyasu*	(make cold)
生える *haeru*	(grow)	生やす *hayasu*	(grow)
B. —*iru* → —*osu*			
起きる *okiru*	(get / wake up)	起こす *okosu*	(get / wake up)
降りる *oriru*	(get off)	降ろす *orosu*	(take / bring down)
落ちる *ochiru*	(drop)	落とす *otosu*	(drop)
過ぎる *sugiru*	(elapse)	過ごす *sugosu*	(spend)
C. —*u* → —*eru*			
開く *aku*	(open)	開ける *akeru*	(open)
届く *todoku*	(reach)	届ける *todokeru*	(deliver)
縮む *chijimu*	(shrink)	縮める *chijimeru*	(shrink)
育つ *sodatsu*	(grow)	育てる *sodateru*	(raise)
立つ *tatsu*	(stand)	立てる *tateru*	(stand)

D.	—*ru* → —*seru*			
乗る *noru*	(get on)		乗せる *noseru*	(put on)
寄る *yoru*	(approach)		寄せる *yoseru*	(let come near)

E.	—*ru* → —*su*			
帰(返)る *kaeru*	(return)		帰(返)す *kaesu*	(return)
通る *tōru*	(pass)		通す *tōsu*	(pass)
回る *mawaru*	(turn)		回す *mawasu*	(turn)
直る *naoru*	(be fixed)		直す *naosu*	(fix)

F.	—*reru* → —*su*			
離れる *hanareru*	(be detached)		離す *hanasu*	(detach)
倒れる *taoreru*	(fall down)		倒す *taosu*	(push / knock down)
つぶれる *tsubureru*	(crush)		つぶす *tsubusu*	(crush)
よごれる *yogoreru*	(get dirty)		よごす *yogosu*	(make dirty)
現(表)れる *arawareru*	(appear)		現(表)す *arawasu*	(represent)
こわれる *kowareru*	(break)		こわす *kowasu*	(break)

G 1.	—*aru* → —*eru*			
上がる *agaru*	(rise)		上げる *ageru*	(raise)
決まる *kimaru*	(be decided)		決める *kimeru*	(decide)
閉まる *shimaru*	(close)		閉める *shimeru*	(close)
集まる *atsumaru*	(gather)		集める *atsumeru*	(gather)
始まる *hajimaru*	(begin)		始める *hajimeru*	(begin)

高まる *takamaru*	(heighten)	高める *takameru*	(heighten)
固まる *katamaru*	(harden)	固める *katameru*	(harden)
見つかる *mitsukaru*	(be found)	見つける *mitsukeru*	(find)
かかる *kakaru*	(hang)	かける *kakeru*	(hang)
助かる *tasukaru*	(be saved)	助ける *tasukeru*	(save)

G 2.　—*waru* → —*eru*

変(代)わる *kawaru*	(change)	変(代)える *kaeru*	(change)
伝わる *tsutawaru*	(convey)	伝える *tsutaeru*	(convey)
加わる *kuwawaru*	(join)	加える *kuwaeru*	(add)

H.　--*eru* → —*u*

焼ける *yakeru*	(burn)	焼く *yaku*	(burn)
売れる *ureru*	(sell)	売る *uru*	(sell)
取れる *toreru*	(come off)	取る *toru*	(take)
切れる *kireru*	(cut)	切る *kiru*	(cut)
破れる *yabureru*	(tear)	破る *yaburu*	(tear)
折れる *oreru*	(break)	折る *oru*	(break)
割れる *wareru*	(break)	割る *waru*	(break)
抜ける *nukeru*	(come out)	抜く *nuku*	(pull out)
ほどける *hodokeru*	(be untied)	ほどく *hodoku*	(untie)
脱げる *nugeru*	(come off)	脱ぐ *nugu*	(take off)

I. Others			
見える *mieru*	(be visible)	見る *miru*	(see)
聞こえる *kikoeru*	(be audible)	聞く *kiku*	(hear)
消える *kieru*	(be extinguished)	消す *kesu*	(extinguish)
入る *hairu*	(enter)	入れる *ireru*	(put in)
分かれる *wakareru*	(get separated)	分ける *wakeru*	(separate)
終わる *owaru*	(end)	終える / 終わる *oeru* / *owaru*	(end)

Notes

(1) The "*—u → —asu*" pattern is not included in this list because this pattern applies to all intransitive Gr. 1 verbs, changing them into the causative form (i.e., the transitive form).

(2) *Suru* 'do' vs. *naru* 'become' and *korosu* 'kill' vs. *shinu* 'die' make pairs of transitive and intransitive verbs, though the two in each pair have no phonological element in common.

Appendix 4 Connection Forms of Important Expressions

A. Vneg + _____   (Gr. 2: Vstem + _____)

〜ないで 〜 nai de	(without doing 〜)
〜{なければ / なくては / ねば}ならない 〜 {nakereba / naku te wa / neba} naranai	
〜{なくては / なければ / ないと}いけない (must do 〜 (Obligation)) 〜 {nakute wa / nakereba / naito} ikenai	
〜なくてもいい 〜 nakutemo ii	(do not have to do 〜)
〜なくなる 〜 naku naru	(do not do 〜 anymore)
〜ずに 〜 zu ni	(without doing 〜)

B. Vmasu + _____

〜出す 〜 dasu	(begin to do 〜)
〜始める 〜 hajimeru	(begin to do 〜)
〜方 〜 kata	(how to do 〜; way of doing 〜)
〜ましょう 〜 mashō	(Let's do 〜; I (We) will do 〜)
〜ながら 〜 nagara	(while doing 〜)
〜なさい 〜 nasai	(Do 〜 (Polite imperative))
〜に(行く) 〜 ni (iku)	((go) to do 〜)
〜にくい 〜 nikui	(hard to do 〜)
お〜になる o 〜 ni naru	(do 〜 (Honorific))
お〜する o 〜 suru	(do 〜 (Humble))
〜終わる 〜 owaru	(finish doing 〜)

～そうだ ～ sōda	(It looks like ～ will do ～)
～すぎる ～ sugiru	(do ～ excessively)
～たい ～ tai	(want to do ～)
～やすい ～ yasui	(easy to do ～)

C. Vinf+_____

～間(に)† ～ aida (ni)	(while)
～だけ ～ dake	(just)
～だろう ～ darō	(probably)
～はず ～ hazu	(It is expected that ～)
～ほうがいい ～ hō ga ii	(had better do ～; I suggest ～ do ～)
～かもしれない ～ kamoshirenai	(might)
～かしら / かなあ ～ kashira / ～ kanā	(～, I wonder)
～けれども‡ ～ keredomo	(although)
～ことは‡ ～ koto wa	(indeed ～ (but))
～みたいだ ～ mitaida	(It appears that ～)
～(の)なら† ～ (no) nara	(if)
～にちがいない ～ ni chigainai	(must (Certainty))
～{の / ん}だ ～ {no / n} da	(It is that ～; The fact is that ～; The explanation is that ～)
～ので‡ ～ node	(since; because)
～のに† ～ noni	(in spite of the fact that ～)
～のは～だ ～ no wa ～ da	(It is ～ that ～)

～らしい ～ rashii	(It seems that ～)
～し‡ ～ shi	(～ and)
～そうだ ～ sōda	(I heard that ～)
～時† ～ toki	(when)
～わけだ ～ wake da	(No wonder ～; It means that ～: That's why ～)
～ようだ ～ yōda	(It appears that ～)
～ように† ～ yōni	(in such a way that ～; as ～ do ～)

† The formal form can also be used in very polite speech.
‡ The formal form can also be used in rather polite speech.

D. Vinf · nonpast + _____

～ことがある ～ koto ga aru	(There are times when)
～ことができる ～ koto ga dekiru	(can do ～)
～ことになる ～ koto ni naru	(It's been decided that ～)
～ことになっている ～ koto ni natte iru	(It is a rule that ～; be supposed to do ～)
～ことにする ～ koto ni suru	(decide that ～)
～ことにしている ～ koto ni shite iru	(make it a rule to do ～)
～まで† ～ made	(till)
～までに† ～ made ni	(by the time when)
～前に† ～ mae ni	(before)
～ものだ ～ mono da	(should do ～)
～な ～ na	(Don't do ～)
～のに† ～ no ni	(in order to do ～)

~ため ~ tame	(in order to do ~; because)
~と† ~ to	(if; when)
~ところだ ~ tokoro da	(be about to do ~)
~つもりだ ~ tsumori da	(intend to do ~)
~うちに† ~ uchi ni	(while)
~ようになる ~ yōni naru	(come to do ~)
~ようにする ~ yōni suru	(try to do ~)

† The formal, nonpast form can also be used in very polite speech.

E. Vinf · past + _____

~あとで ~ ato de	(after)
~ことがある ~ koto ga aru	(have done ~ (Experience))
~ものだ ~ mono da	(used to do ~)
~ら‡ ~ ra	(if; when)
~らどうですか ~ ra dōdesu ka	(Why don't you do ~?; How about doing ~?)
~り~りする ~ ri ~ ri suru	(do things like doing ~ and doing ~)
~ため‡ ~ tame	(because)
~って ~ tte	(even if)
~ところだ ~ tokoro da	(have just done ~; just did ~)
~つもりだ ~ tsumori da	(mean; believe)

‡ The formal, past form can also be used in rather polite speech.

F. V*te*+_____

～あげる ～ *ageru*	(do ～ for s.o.)
～ある ～ *aru*	(have been done)
～ほしい ～ *hoshii*	(want s.o. to do ～)
～いく ～ *iku*	(do ～ and go; keep doing ～ from now on)
～いる ～ *iru*	(be doing ～; have done ～)
～から ～ *kara*	(after)
～ください ～ *kudasai*	(Please do ～)
～くれる ～ *kureru*	(s.o. does ～ for me)
～くる ～ *kuru*	(do ～ and come; come to do ～)
～みる ～ *miru*	(do ～ and see; try to do ～)
～も ～ *mo*	(even if; even though)
～もいい ～ *mo ii*	(may (Permission))
～もらう ～ *morau*	(have s.o. do ～ for me)
～おく ～ *oku*	(do ～ in advance)
～しまう ～ *shimau*	(have done ～; finish ～)
～はいけない ～ *wa ikenai*	(must not do ～)

G. Vcond+_____   (Gr. 2: Vstem+*re*+_____)

～ばよかった ～ *ba yokatta*	(I wish ～ had done ～)

H. Vvol+_____

～ようと思う ～ *yō to omou*	(～ think ～ will do ～)
～ようとする ～ *yō to suru*	(try to do ～)

I. Adj(*i*)inf + _____	
~間(に) ~ *aida* (*ni*)	(while)
~だけ ~ *dake*	(just)
~だろう ~ *darō*	(probably)
~はず ~ *hazu*	(It is expected that ~)
~かもしれない ~ *kamo shirenai*	(might)
~かしら／~かなあ ~ *kashira* / ~ *kanā*	(~, I wonder)
~けれども‡ ~ *keredomo*	(although)
~ことは~ ~ *koto wa* ~	(indeed (but))
~(の)なら ~ (*no*) *nara*	(if)
~にちがいない ~ *ni chigainai*	(must (Certainty))
~｛の／んだ｝ ~ ｛*no* / *n*｝*da*	(It is that ~; The fact is that ~; The explanation is that ~)
~ので† ~ *node*	(since; because)
~のに† ~ *noni*	(in spite of the fact that ~)
~のは~だ ~ *no wa* ~ *da*	(It is ~ that ~)
~らしい ~ *rashii*	(It seems that ~)
~し† ~ *shi*	(and)
~そうだ ~ *sōda*	(I heard that ~)
~ため ~ *tame*	(because)
~時 ~ *toki*	(when)
~つもり ~ *tsumori*	(believe)

~わけだ	(No wonder ~; That's why ~)
~ wake da	
~ようだ	(It appears that ~)
~ yōda	

† The formal form can also be used in very polite speech.
‡ The formal form can also be used in rather polite speech.

J.   Adj(i)inf · nonpast+_____

~ことがある	(There are times when)
~ koto ga aru	
~と	(when, if)
~ to	
~うちに	(while)
~ uchi ni	

K.   Adj(i)inf · past+_____

~ことがある	(There were times when)
~ koto ga aru	
~ら	(if; when)
~ ra	
~り~りする	(~ is sometimes ~ and sometimes ~)
~ ri ~ ri suru	
~って	(even if)
~ tte	

L.   Adj(i)te+_____

~も	(even if; even though)
~ mo	
~もいい	(It is all right if ~)
~ mo ii	
~たまらない	(unbearably)
~ tamaranai	

M.   Adj(i)stem+_____

~がる	(show the sign of)
~ garu	
~み	[Noun form of Adj(i)]
~ mi	

~さ ~ sa	[Noun form of Adj(i)]
~そうだ ~ sōda	(look)
~すぎる ~ sugiru	(excessively)

N. Adj(na)stem + $\begin{Bmatrix} na \\ datta \end{Bmatrix}$ + _____

~間(に) ~ aida (ni)	(while)
~だけ ~ dake	(only)
~はず ~ hazu	(It is expected that ~)
~ことは~ ~ koto wa ~	(indeed ~ (but))
~{の/ん}だ ~ {no / n}da	(It is that ~; The fact is that ~; The explanation is that ~)
~ので ~ node	(since; because)
~のに ~ noni	(in spite of the fact that ~)
~のは~だ ~ no wa ~ da	(It is ~ that ~)
~ため ~ tame	(because)
~時 ~ toki	(when)
~つもり ~ tsumori	(mean; believe)
~わけだ ~ wake da	(No wonder ~; That's why ~)
~ようだ ~ yōda	(It appears that ~)

O. $\begin{Bmatrix} \text{Adj(na)stem} \\ \text{N} \end{Bmatrix}$ + $\begin{Bmatrix} da \\ datta \end{Bmatrix}$ + _____

| ~けれども‡
~ keredomo | (although) |
| ~し‡
~ shi | (and) |

~そうだ	(I heard that ~)
~ sōda	

‡ The formal form of *da | datta* (i.e., *desu | deshita*) can also be used in rather polite speech.

P. $\left\{ \begin{matrix} \text{Adj}(na)\text{stem} \\ \text{N} \end{matrix} \right\} + \left\{ \begin{matrix} \text{ø} \\ datta \end{matrix} \right\} + $ _____

~だろう	(probably)
~ darō	
~かもしれない	(might)
~ kamoshirenai	
~かしら / ~かなあ	(~, I wonder)
~ kashira / ~ kanā	
~なら	(if)
~ nara	
~にちがいない	(must (Certainty))
~ ni chigainai	
~らしい	(It seems ~)
~ rashii	

Q. $\left\{ \begin{matrix} \text{Adj}(na)\text{stem} \\ \text{N} \end{matrix} \right\} + da + $ _____

~と†	(when; if)
~ to	

† The formal form of *da* (i.e., *desu*) can also be used in very polite speech.

R. Adj(*na*)stem + *na* + _____

~ことがある	(There are times when ~)
~ koto ga aru	
~うちに	(while)
~ uchi ni	

S. $\left\{ \begin{matrix} \text{Adj}(na)\text{stem} \\ \text{N} \end{matrix} \right\} + datta + $ _____

~ことがある	(There were times when ~)
~ koto ga aru	
~ら‡	(if; when)
~ ra	
~り~りする	(~ is sometimes ~ and sometimes ~)
~ ri ~ ri suru	

~って	(even if)
~ *tte*	

‡ The formal form of *datta* (i.e., *deshita*) can also be used in rather polite speech.

T. $\left\{\begin{array}{l}\text{Adj(}na\text{)stem}\\\text{N}\end{array}\right\}+de+$_____

~も	(even if; even though)
~ *mo*	
~もいい	(It is all right if ~)
~ *mo ii*	

U. Adj(*na*)stem+_____

~さ	[Noun form of Adj(*na*)]
~ *sa*	
~そうだ	(look)
~ *sōda*	
~すぎる	(excessively)
~ *sugiru*	

V. N $+\left\{\begin{array}{l}no\\datta\end{array}\right\}+$_____

~間(に)	(during; while)
~ *aida* (*ni*)	
~はず	(It is expected that ~)
~ *hazu*	
~ため	(for; because of; because)
~ *tame*	
~時	(at the time of; when)
~ *toki*	
~つもり	(mean; believe)
~ *tsumori*	
~ようだ	(It appears that ~; look)
~ *yōda*	

W. N $+\left\{\begin{array}{l}na\\datta\end{array}\right\}+$_____

~{の / ん}だ	(It is that ~; The fact is that ~; The explanation is that ~)
~ {*no* / *n*}*da*	
~ので	(since; because)
~ *node*	

~のに   (in spite of the fact that ~)
~ *noni*

~のは~だ   (It is ~ that ~)
~ *no wa ~ da*

X. N+*no*+_____

~うちに   (while)
~ *uchi ni*

Appendix 5 *Ko-so-a-do*

| What is being talked about is | Non-Modifier | | Direction |
	Demonstrative Pronoun	Location	nonpolite
close to the speaker	これ **ko**re (this)	ここ **ko**ko (here)	こっち **ko**tchi (this way)
close to the hearer	それ **so**re (that)	そこ **so**ko (there)	そっち **so**tchi (that way)
removed from both the speaker and the hearer	あれ **a**re (that over there)	あそこ **a**soko (over there)	あっち **a**tchi (that way over there)
being questioned	どれ **do**re (Which?)	どこ **do**ko (Where?)	どっち **do**tchi (Which way?)

Notes

1. *Ko-so-a-do* of direction can be used to refer to persons as well as things, places and directions, as in:

   (1) a. こちらは山田さんです。
      Kochira *wa Yamada-san desu.*
      (This is Mr. Yamada.)

   b. こっちの方が安いよ。
      Kotchi *no hō ga yasui yo.*
      (This one is cheaper, you know.)

   c. お手洗いはこちらです。
      *O-tearai wa **kochira** desu.*
      (The toilet is this way.)

   d. こっちが僕の車だ。
      Kotchi *ga boku no kuruma da.*
      (This one is my car.)

| | Modifier | | |
polite	Demonstrative Adjective	Kinds	Manner
こちら **ko**chira (this way)	この **ko**no (this ~)	こんな **ko**nna (this kind of)	こう **kō** (like this)
そちら **so**chira (that way)	その **so**no (that ~)	そんな **so**nna (that kind of)	そう **sō** (like that)
あちら **a**chira (that way over there)	あの **a**no (that ~ over there)	あんな **a**nna (that kind of)	ああ **ā** (like that)
どちら **do**chira (Which way?)	どの **do**no (Which ~?)	どんな **do**nna (What kind of?)	どう **dō** (How?)

2. The *so*-series can be used to direct attention to a referent removed from both the speaker and the hearer if information about the referent has been given to the hearer, as in:

(2) A : きのう車で湖に行って来たよ。
   Kinō kuruma de **mizuumi** *ni itte kita yo.*
   (Yesterday I went to a lake by car.)

   B : その湖には魚がいたかい?
   Sono *mizuumi ni wa sakana ga ita kai?*
   (Were there fish in the lake?)

3. The speaker feels most empathetic with an item referred to by the *ko*-series, because the item is closest to him. On the other hand, the speaker feels least empathetic with an item referred to by the *a*-series, because the item is removed from him and his hearer.

Appendix 6 Numerals and Counters

A. Numerals

	Native Japanese Numerals		Sino-Japanese				
1	一 (つ) hito(-tsu)	1	一 ichi	11	十一 jū-ichi	21	二十一 ni-jū-ichi
2	二 (つ) futa(-tsu)	2	二 ni	12	十二 jū-ni	22	二十二 ni-jū-ni
3	三 (つ) mit(-tsu)	3	三 san	13	十三 jū-san	30	三十 san-jū
4	四 (つ) yot(-tsu)	4	四 {yon / shi}	14	十四 jū-{yon / shi}	40	四十 {yon / shi}-jū
5	五 (つ) itsu(-tsu)	5	五 go	15	十五 jū-go	50	五十 go-jū
6	六 (つ) mut(-tsu)	6	六 roku	16	十六 jū-roku	60	六十 roku-jū
7	七 (つ) nana(-tsu)	7	七 shichi	17	十七 jū-{shichi / nana}	70	七十 {shichi / nana}-jū
8	八 (つ) yat(-tsu)	8	八 hachi	18	十八 jū-hachi	80	八十 hachi-jū
9	九 (つ) kokono(-tsu)	9	九 {kyū / ku}	19	十九 jū-{kyū / ku}	90	九十 kyū-jū
10	十 tō	10	十 jū	20	二十 ni-jū	100	百 hyaku

Notes

1. The native Japanese numeral system is used from 1 to 10 only. For numbers greater than 10 the Sino-Japanese numeral system is used. The parenthesized *-tsu* is a counter for things.
2. 1,000 is usually read as *sen*, not as *is-sen*.
3. Telephone numbers are given in Sino-Japanese numerals. For example,

Numerals

126	百二十六 *hyaku-ni-* *jū-roku*	1,352	千三百五十二 *sen-san-* *byaku-go-* *jū-ni*	100,000	十 万 *jū-man*
200	二 百 *ni-hyaku*	2,000	二 千 *ni-sen*	1,000,000	百 万 *hyaku-* *man*
300	三 百 *san-byaku*	3,000	三 千 *san-zen*	10,000,000	一千万 *is-sen-* *man*
400	四 百 *yon-hyaku*	4,000	四 千 *yon-sen*	100,000,000	一 億 *ichi-oku*
500	五 百 *go-hyaku*	5,000	五 千 *go-sen*	1,000,000,000	十 億 *jū-oku*
600	六 百 *rop-pyaku*	6,000	六 千 *roku-sen*	10,000,000,000	百 億 *hyaku-* *oku*
700	七 百 *nana-* *hyaku*	7,000	七 千 *shichi*⎱*-sen* *nana* ⎰	100,000,000,000	(一)千億 *(is-)sen-* *oku*
800	八 百 *hap-pyaku*	8,000	八 千 *has-sen*	1,000,000,000,000	一 兆 *it-chō*
900	九 百 *kyū-hyaku*	9,000	九 千 *kyū-sen*		
1,000	千 *sen*	10,000	一 万 *ichi-man*		

389-2681 is read as " *san-hachi-kyū-no*, *ni-roku-hachi-ichi* ". However, 4 and 7 are often read as *yon* and *nana*, respectively.

4. The year according to the Western calendar is given in Sino-Japanese numerals followed by *nen*, the counter for year. Thus, 1984 is read as " *sen-kyūhyaku-hachijū-yo(n)nen* ".

B. **Counters** (The following chart lists some commonly-used counters.)

	Type A	Type B	Type C	Type D	Type E
	枚 -mai (thin object: *paper, ticket* etc.)	本 -hon (long object: *pencil, stick,* etc.)	課 -ka (lesson)	冊 -satsu (volume)	頁 -pēji (page)
1	一 枚 ichi-mai	一 本 ip-pon	一 課 ik-ka	一 冊 is-satsu	一 頁 ip } ichi }-pēji
2	二 枚 ni-mai	二 本 ni-hon	二 課 ni-ka	二 冊 ni-satsu	二 頁 ni-pēji
3	三 枚 san-mai	三 本 san-bon	三 課 san-ka	三 冊 san-satsu	三 頁 san-pēji
4	四 枚 yo(n)-mai	四 本 yon-hon	四 課 yon-ka	四 冊 yon-satsu	四 頁 yon-pēji
5	五 枚 go-mai	五 本 go-hon	五 課 go-ka	五 冊 go-satsu	五 頁 go-pēji
6	六 枚 roku-mai	六 本 rop-pon	六 課 rok-ka	六 冊 roku-satsu	六 頁 roku } rop }-pēji
7	七 枚 nana } shichi }-mai	七 本 nana } shichi }-hon	七 課 nana } shichi }-ka	七 冊 nana } shichi }-satsu	七 頁 nana } shichi }-pēji
8	八 枚 hachi-mai	八 本 hachi-hon hap-pon	八 課 hachi } hak }-ka	八 冊 has-satsu	八 頁 hachi } hap }-pēji
9	九 枚 kyū-mai	九 本 kyū-hon	九 課 kyū-ka	九 冊 kyū-satsu	九 頁 kyū-pēji
10	十 枚 jū-mai	十 本 jup-pon	十 課 juk-ka	十 冊 jus-satsu	十 頁 jup-pēji

Type F	Irregular Types			
頭 -tō (head of cattle)	人 -nin (people)	日 -ka (day of the month)	日 -nichi (day)	晩 -ban (night)
一 頭 it-tō	一 人 hitori	一 日 tsuitachi	一 日 ichi-nichi	一 晩 hito-ban
二 頭 ni-tō	二 人 futari	二 日 futsu-ka	二 日 futsu-ka	二 晩 futa-ban
三 頭 san-tō	三 人 san-nin	三 日 mik-ka	三 日 mik-ka	三 晩 mi-ban
四 頭 yon-tō	四 人 yo-nin	四 日 yok-ka	四 日 yok-ka	四 晩 yo-ban
五 頭 go-tō	五 人 go-nin	五 日 itsu-ka	五 日 itsu-ka go-nichi	五 晩 go-ban
六 頭 roku-tō	六 人 roku-nin	六 日 mui-ka	六 日 mui-ka roku-nichi	六 晩 roku-ban
七 頭 nana shichi }-tō	七 人 nana shichi }-nin	七 日 nano-ka	七 日 nano-ka shichi-nichi	七 晩 nana-ban
八 頭 hat-tō	八 人 hachi-nin	八 日 yō-ka	八 日 yō-ka hachi-nichi	八 晩 hachi-ban
九 頭 kyū-tō	九 人 kyū ku }-nin	九 日 kokono-ka	九 日 kokono-ka ku-nichi	九 晩 kyū-ban
十 頭 jut-tō	十 人 jū-nin	十 日 tō-ka	十 日 tō-ka	十 晩 jū-ban

Notes

1. Depending on the initial sound of a counter, the pronunciation of the number and / or the counter changes. Counters are classified according to the phonetic modifications they undergo. Type A counters are straight-foward cases of *Sino-Japanese Number + Counter*, with no phonetic modifications. The following is a chart of phonetic modifications for Type B through Type F. If there is no entry for a given number it indicates that there is no phonetic modification for that particular number. As for the remaining irregular types, you have to memorize them piecemeal.

Counters Numbers	Type B h-	Type C k-	Type D s-	Type E p-	Type F t-
1	[*ipp-*]	[*ikk-*]	[*iss-*]	[*ipp-*]	[*itt-*]
3	[*sanb-*]				
6	[*ropp-*]	[*rokk-*]		([*ropp-*])	
8	([*happ-*])	([*hakk-*])	[*hass-*]	([*happ-*])	[*hatt-*]
10	[*jupp-*]	[*jukk-*]	[*juss-*]	[*jupp*]	[*jutt-*]

([ ]) indicates that [ ] is optional.

2. The 20th day of the month and 20 days are not *nijūnichi* but *hatsuka*. 'Twenty years old' is referred to as *hatachi*.

3. The following is a list of other examples of each type:

   Type A:　倍 *-bai* 'time'　　　　番 *-ban* 'ordinal number'
   　　　　　度 *-do* 'frequency'　　畳 *-jō* 'tatami mat'
   　　　　　部 *-bu* 'part'　　　　　面 *-men* 'newspaper page'

   Type A':　(Exactly the same as Type A except that number 4 is pronounced *yo* not *yon*.)
   　　　　　時 *-ji* 'o'clock'　　時間 *-jikan* 'hour'　　年 *-nen* 'year'

   Type A'':　(Exactly the same as Type A except that numbers 4, 7 and 9 are pronounced *shi*, *shichi* and *ku*, respectively.)
   　　　　　月 *-gatsu* 'name of the month'

   Type A''':　(Exactly the same as Type A except that the initial sound of the counter with number 3 changes from *wa* to *ba*.)
   　　　　　羽 *-wa* 'bird'

   Type B:　杯 *-hai* 'cup of'　　匹 *-hiki* 'animal'

   Type B':　(Exactly the same as Type B except that the initial sound of the counter with number 3 is not *b-* but *p-*.)

泊 *-haku* 'stay (overnight)'   分 *-hun* 'minute'

Type C:　か月 *-ka getsu* 'month'   回 *-kai* 'frequency'

巻 *-kan* 'volume'   個 *-ko* 'piece'

Type C':　(Exactly the same as Type C except that the initial sound of the counter with number 3 can be either *k-* or *g-*.)

階 *-kai* 'floor'

Type D:　歳 *-sai* '-year old'   隻 *-sō* 'boat'

Type D':　(Exactly the same as Type D except that the initial sound of the counter with number 3 is *z-* not *s-*.)

足 *-soku* 'footgear'

Type E:　ポンド *-pondo* 'pound'

Type F:　等 *-tō* 'class, grade'   トン *-ton* 'ton'

通 *-tsū* 'letter'

Appendix 7 Compound Words

A compound is a word that consists of two or more independent words with a meaning which cannot be predicted from the combination of the constituent elements. For example, *hana o miru* means 'to see flowers', but the compound version *hana-mi* means specifically 'the viewing of cherry blossoms'.

The following is a list of basic nominal, verbal and adjectival compounds and their formation.

Formation	Examples
(A) *Nominal Compounds*	
(a) Noun + V*masu* (intransitive)	水遊び (dabbling in water) *mizu-asobi* (Lit. water-play) 昼寝 (siesta) *hiru-ne* (Lit. noon-sleep) 山登り (mountain climbing) *yama-nobori* (Lit. mountain-climb)
(b) Noun + V*masu* (transitive)	花見 (the viewing of cherry blossoms) *hana-mi* (Lit. flower-view) 人殺し (manslaughter) *hito-goroshi* (Lit. man-kill) 靴みがき (shoe polishing; shoeblack) *kutsu-migaki* (Lit. shoe-polish)
(c) V*masu* (intransitive) + Noun	乗り物 (vehicle) *nori-mono* (Lit. ride-thing) 出口 (exit) *de-guchi* (Lit. leave-mouth) 寝酒 (nightcap) *ne-zake* (Lit. sleep-*sake*)
(d) V*masu* (transitive) + Noun	飲み水 (drinking water) *nomi-mizu* (Lit. drink-water)

	食べ物　(food) *tabe-mono* (Lit. eat-thing) 借り物　(borrowed thing) *kari-mono* (Lit. borrow-thing)
(e)　V*masu* (intransitive)+ 　　V*masu* (intransitive)	上り下り　(ascending and descending) *nobori-ori* (Lit. go up-go down) 出入り　(going in and out) *de-hairi* (Lit. leave-enter) 行き帰り　(going and coming back) *iki-kaeri* (Lit. go-return)
(f)　Adj(*i*)stem+Noun	古本　(secondhand book) *furu-hon* (Lit. old-book) 黒船　　　　(black ship that came to *kuro-fune*　Japan from America and 　　　　　　Europe during the Edo 　　　　　　period) (Lit. black-boat) 青ひげ　(a blue beard) *ao-hige* (Lit. blue-beard)
(g)　Adj(*na*)stem+Noun	安全地帯　(safety zone) *anzen-chitai* (Lit. safe-zone) 健康食品　(health food) *kenkō-shokuhin* (Lit. healthy-food) 柔軟体操　(calisthenics) *jūnan-taisō* (Lit. flexible-exercise)
(h)　Noun+Noun	川魚　(freshwater fish) *kawa-zakana* (Lit. river-fish) 女子学生　(co-ed) *joshi-gakusei* (Lit. female-student)

	東京大学　(the University of Tokyo) *Tōkyō-Daigaku* (Lit. Tokyo-University)
(i)　Adj(*i*)stem + V*masu*	早分かり　(quick understanding) *haya-wakari* (Lit. quick-understand)
	早起き　(early rising; early riser) *haya-oki* (Lit. early-get up)
	長話　(long talk) *naga-banashi* (Lit. long-talk)
(B)　*Verbal Compounds*	
V*masu* + Vinf · nonpast	歩きまわる　(walk around) *aruki-mawaru* (Lit. walk-go round)
	話しかける　(speak to) *hanashi-kakeru* (Lit. talk-hang)
	話し合う　(discuss with) *hanashi-au* (Lit. talk-fit)
	読み続ける　(continue to read) *yomi-tsuzukeru* (Lit. read-continue)
	食べ始める　(begin to eat) *tabe-hajimeru* (Lit. eat-begin)
	書き終わる　(finish writing) *kaki-owaru* (Lit. write-finish)
(C)　*Adjectival Compounds*	
(a)　Adj(*i*)stem + Adj(*i*)	薄暗い　(dim) *usu-gurai* (Lit. thin-dark)
	青白い　(pale) *ao-jiroi* (Lit. blue-white)
	堅苦しい　(formal) *kata-kurushii* (Lit. hard-painful)

(b) Noun + Adj(i)	心強い (feel secure) *kokoro-zuyoi* (Lit. heart-strong) 気難しい (hard to please) *ki-muzukashii* (Lit. spirit-difficult) 義理堅い (grateful) *giri-gatai* (Lit. obligation-hard)

Notes

In compound words, the initial voiceless consonant (i.e., plosives such as *k*-, *t*-; fricatives such as *s*-, *h*-, *f*-; affricates such as *ts*-, *ch*-) of the second element of the compound tends to become voiced as shown below:

e.g. *hito* 'man' + *koroshi* 'kill' → *hitogoroshi* 'manslaughter'

ami 'net' + *to* 'door' → *amido* 'screen door'

ne 'sleep' + *sake* 'rice wine' → *nezake* 'nightcap'

naga 'long' + *hanashi* 'talk' → *nagabanashi* 'long talk'

ki 'tree' + *fune* 'boat' → *kibune* 'wooden vessel'

kokoro 'heart' + *tsuyoi* 'strong' → *kokorozuyoi* 'feel secure'

hana 'nose' + *chi* 'blood' → *hanaji* 'nosebleed'

Voicing, however, does not normally take place if one of the following conditions is met.

1. The second element is a borrowed word whose 'foreignness' is still strongly felt.

e.g. *kyōiku* 'education' + *terebi* 'television'

→ *kyōiku* $\begin{cases} terebi \\ *derebi \end{cases}$ 'educational television'

kateiyō 'home use' + *konpyūtā* 'computer'

→ *kateiyō* $\begin{cases} konpyūtā \\ *gonpyūtā \end{cases}$ 'home computer'

But if a borrowed word is free from 'foreignness', then voicing tends to take place.

e.g. *ame* 'rain' + *kappa* 'Portuguese *capa*' → *amagappa* 'raincoat'

iroha 'Japanese alphabet' + *karuta* 'Portuguese carta' → *irohagaruta* 'Japanese alphabet cards'

2. The consonant of the second syllable of the second element is voiced.

e.g. *hi* 'sun' + *kage* 'shade' → $\begin{cases} hikage \\ *higage \end{cases}$ 'shade'

ushiro 'back' + *sugata* 'appearance' → $\begin{cases} ushirosugata \\ *ushirozugata \end{cases}$ 'appearance from the back'

Appendix 8 Improving Reading Skill by Identifying an 'Extended Sentential Unit'

In Japanese, the most important principle of word order is that *the modifier precedes what is being modified*. (⇨ Characteristics of Japanese Grammar, 1. Word Order) The typical modifier modified word order in Japanese can be summarized as follows:

MODIFIER +	MODIFIED	MEANING
Adjective +	Noun	
おもしろい *omoshiroi* (interesting)	人 *hito* (person)	'an interesting person'
Adverb +	Adjective	
とても *totemo* (very)	大きい *ōkii* (big)	'very big'
Adverb +	Verb	
速く *hayaku* (quickly)	歩く *aruku* (walk)	'walk fast'
Noun +	Particle	
子供 *kodomo* (child)	が *ga* (subject)	'a child (subject)'
先生 *sensei* (teacher)	に *ni* (to)	'to a teacher'
Sentence +	Conjunction	
本を買う *hon o kau* ((I) buy books)	から *kara* (because)	'because I buy books'
雨が降った *ame ga futta* (it rained)	けれども *keredomo* (although)	'although it rained'

Sentence	+	Nominalizer	
映画を見る *eiga o miru* (see a movie)	⋮	の / こと *no / koto* (to ; -ing)	'to see a movie'
Sentence	+	Modal	
あしたは晴れる *Ashita wa hareru* (It will clear up tomorrow)	⋮	ようだ *yōda* (it appears)	'It looks like it will clear up tomorrow'
ぼくは若い *Boku wa wakai* (I am young)	⋮	んだ *n da* (It is that)	'It is that I am young'

Let's call the cohesive unit of *modifier + modified* an *Extended Sentential Unit* (= *ESU*). If all *ESU*s started at the beginning of the sentence, students would have no trouble identifying them. But in reality an *ESU* often comes somewhere between the beginning and the end of a sentence. Moreover, in written Japanese an *ESU* is quite frequently embedded within another *ESU*. The ability to identify each *ESU* in a complex sentence is a must for reading comprehension.

The following examples will serve to illustrate this point.

(1) a. 私は 辞書 をまだ使っている。
   Watashi wa 　jisho 　*o mada tsukatte iru.*
   (I'm still using the dictionary.)

   b. 私は小さな 辞書 をまだ使っている。
   *Watashi wa **chisana*** 　jisho 　*o mada tsukatte iru.*
   (I'm still using the small dictionary.)

   c. 私は父が買ってくれた小さな 辞書 をまだ使っている。
   *Watashi wa **chichi ga katte kureta chisana*** 　jisho 　*o mada tsukatte iru.*
   (I'm still using the small dictionary which my father bought for me.)

   d. 私は中学に入った時に父が買ってくれた小さな 辞書 をまだ使っている。
   *Watashi wa **chūgaku ni haitta toki ni chichi ga katte kureta chisana*** 　jisho 　*o mada tsukatte iru.*
   (I'm still using the dictionary which my father bought for me when I entered junior high school.)

If we choose *jisho* 'dictionary' as the modified word, where does its modifier start in each sentence of example (1)? In other words, exactly what part of each sentence is the *ESU*? Since (1a) obviously doesn't have any modifier, there is no *ESU*. How about in (1b)? The modifier is a simple adjective *chisana* 'small'. In (1c) the modifier is the entire relative clause which starts with *chichi ga* 'father (subject)'. Notice that the sentence-initial noun phrase *watashi wa* 'I (subject / topic)' is not a part of the *ESU* in question, because *watashi wa* is the subject of the main verb *tsukatte iru* 'am using'. Sentence (1d) is the most complex sentence of the four. Where does the *ESU* for *jisho* start in (1d)? It starts from *chūgaku* 'junior high school', because the clause *chūgaku ni haitta toki ni* 'when (I) entered junior high school' modifies the verb *katte kureta* '(he) bought for me'.

A quick and accurate identification of an *ESU* is a prerequisite for reading comprehension. The following is a list of guidelines which will help students to identify *ESU*s in written Japanese.

Guideline I

A modified element (= *m.e.*) is typically a noun, a head noun of a relative clause, a nominalizer *no* or *koto*, a coordinate or a subordinate conjunction (such as *ga* 'but', *kara* 'because', *keredomo* 'although'), a modal (such as *hazu da* 'it is expected that ~', *no da* 'it is that ~', *yōda* 'it appears that ~', *sōda* 'I hear that ~'), an adjective, a verb or a particle, as shown in the *MODIFIER + MODIFIED* chart.

Guideline II

If an element preceding an *m.e.* modifies some element that comes after the *m.e.*, that element is outside the *ESU*.

Thus, if *kyō* 'today' in (2) is judged to modify *itta* 'said', an element that comes after the *m.e. to* 'quote marker', *kyō* is outside the *ESU*. But, if the same adverb is judged to modify *nai* 'there isn't', then the adverb is a part of the *ESU*.

(2) ジョンは**今日授業がない** と 言った。

Jon wa **kyō jugyō ga nai** to itta.

(Today John said that there wasn't any class. / John said that there isn't class today.)

Guideline III

A sentence-initial topic phrase *Noun Phrase + wa*(,) is very often considered outside an *ESU*, especially when the topic phrase is the main subject of the sentence. The same is true of a *Noun Phrase + mo*(,).

Some more examples follow:

(3) a. 私は / も子供が病気だった から 行けなかった。
   *Watashi wa / mo **kodomo ga byōki datta** kara ikenakatta.*
   (I couldn't go there (either), because my child was ill.)

   b. 私は / も鈴木さんが行かなけれ ば 行かない。
   *Watashi wa / mo **Suzuki-san ga ikanakere**ba ikanai.*
   (I won't go there (either) if Mr. Suzuki won't go there.)

   c. 山本は / も雪子が結婚した こと を知らない。
   *Yamamoto wa / mo **Yukiko ga kekkonshita** koto o shiranai.*
   (Yamamoto doesn't know (either) that Yukiko got married.)

   d. きのうはここにあった 本 が今日はない。
   ***Kinō wa koko ni atta** hon ga kyō wa nai.*
   (The book which was here yesterday is not here today.)

In (3a) through (3c), *wa* and *mo* phrases are outside the *ESU* of the boxed *m.e.*'s, but in (3d) *wa* is inside the *ESU* of the *m.e.* *hon* 'book', because *wa* is used in this sentence as a contrast marker, not as a topic marker.

Guideline IV
When two sentences are combined by the conjunction *ga*(.) 'but', the first sentence is very often outside the *ESU* of the *m.e.* contained in the second sentence.

For example, in (4) the first sentence is outside the *ESU* of the respective *m.e.*'s.

(4) a. 宿題がたくさんあったが，疲れていた ので すぐ寝てしまった。
   *Shukudai ga takusan atta ga, **tsukarete ita** node sugu nete shi-matta.*
   (I had a lot of homework to do but I went to sleep right away because I was tired.)

   b. 「将軍」を読むつもりだったが，テレビで見た から 読むのをやめた。
   *"Shōgun" o yomu tsumori datta ga, **terebi de mita** kara yomu no o yameta.*
   (I intended to read *Shogun*, but I quit because I had seen it on TV.)

When two sentences are combined by the *te*-form of a verb / adjective, the first sentence is either inside or outside the *ESU* depending on the context, as illustrated by (5).

(5) a. 洋子は頭が痛くて仕方がない と 言った。
   *Yōko wa **atama ga itakute shikata ga nai** to itta.*
   (Yoko said that she had a terrible headache.)

b. 洋子は京都に行って，前から買おうと思っていた 着物 を買った。

*Yōko wa Kyōto ni itte, **mae kara kaō to omotte ita** kimono o katta.*

(Yoko went to Kyoto, and bought the *kimono* which she had been thinking of buying for some time.)

In (5a) the *ESU* includes the first sentence, whereas in (5b) it doesn't.

Guideline V

When an *m.e.* is a modal, its *ESU* normally extends to the beginning of the sentence, including *wa / mo* phrase.

(6) a. リサは来年日本へ行く らしい 。

Risa wa rainen Nihon e iku rashii.

(It seems that Lisa is going to Japan next year.)

b. ボブには日本語は難しすぎる ようだ 。

Bobu ni wa nihongo wa muzukashisugiru yōda.

(It appears that Japanese is too difficult for Bob.)

c. あんな所には行きたくない んだ 。

Anna tokoro ni wa ikitakunai n da.

(Lit. It is that I don't want to go to such a place.)

d. ナンシーは大学をやめる そうだ 。

Nanshī wa daigaku o yameru sōda.

(I heard that Nancy is going to quit college.)

Guideline VI

When an *m.e.* is the quote marker *to*, Guideline III is overridden, because a quote is supposed to follow the original source as closely as possible; if *wa* is in the original sentence, that *wa* has to be quoted. Examples follow:

(7) a. 人間は考えるあしだ と パスカルが言った。

Ningen wa kangaeru ashi da to *Pasukaru ga itta.*

(Pascal said that a human is a thinking reed.)

b. 本にペットは老人にいい と 書いてあった。

Hon ni **petto wa rōjin ni ii** to *kaite atta.*

(It was written in a book that pets are good for elderly people.)

Guideline VII

Some *m.e.*'s allow their *ESU* to extend beyond the sentence boundary. This is especially true with sentence-initial conjunctions such as *shikashi* 'but', *shitagatte* 'therefore', *sunawachi* 'namely', *tadashi* 'but', *tokoro ga* 'but' and *da kara* 'so' and the modal *no da* 'it is that ~'.

(8) a. 幸子は大学を出た。 しかし 仕事はなかった。

Sachiko wa daigaku o deta. Shikashi *shigoto wa nakatta.*
(Sachiko graduated from college. But she didn't get a job.)

b. 急に胸が苦しくなったんです。 だから 病院に行きました。

Kyūni mune ga kurushiku natta n desu. Da kara *byōin ni*
ikimashita.
(Suddenly I had a pain in my chest, so I went to the hospital.)

c. あしたは朝五時に起きます。五時半の汽車に乗る んです 。

Ashita wa asa goji ni okimasu. Gojihan no kisha ni noru
n desu .
(I'll get up at five o'clock tomorrow morning. It's because I'm going
to catch the 5:30 train.)

So far, seven basic guidelines which can be used to identify *ESU* have been
presented. The student should read Japanese carefully, searching for *ESU*s,
especially for the following four *ESU*s that create enormous difficulties.

  (i) Sentence + Conjunction
  (ii) Relative Clause + Noun
  (iii) Sentence + Nominalizer (*no / koto*)
  (iv) Sentence + Modal

For your practice, a short, simple passage containing 10 boxed *m.e.*'s is provided below. Underline the *ESU*s for each *m.e.* The answers are given
below the passage.

Practice Passage

友達に借りた 車 ¹で花子さんと一緒に先週京都まで行って来ました。ぼくはハイウェーを
走る の ²は初めてだった ので ³少し緊張しました。けれども一時間ぐらい運転している と ⁴
スピードにもなれてしまい、時々眠り そう ⁵になりました。京都までに五度ぐらいサービス
エリアに入ってコーヒーを飲みました。ぼくは隣に座っていた 花子さん ⁶といろいろ話し
ながら ⁷行った から ⁸京都もそんなに遠く感じませんでした。こんな楽しい旅行 なら ⁹もう
一度してみたい と ¹⁰思います。

Tomodachi ni karita kuruma *¹ de Hanako-san to isshoni senshū Kyōto made
itte kimashita. Boku wa haiwē o hashiru* no *² wa hajimete datta* node *³ sukoshi
kinchōshimashita. Keredomo ichijikan gurai untenshite iru* to *⁴ supido ni mo
nareteshimai, tokidoki nemuri* sō *⁵ ni narimashita. Kyōto made ni godo gurai
sābisueria ni haitte kōhi o nomimashita. Boku wa tonari ni suwatte ita* Hanako-
san *⁶ to iroiro hanashi* nagara *⁷ itta* kara *⁸ Kyōto mo sonna ni tōku kanjimasen-
deshita. Konna tanoshii ryokō* nara *⁹ mō ichido shite mitai* to *¹⁰omoimasu.*

(Last week I went to Kyoto with Hanako in a car I borrowed from my friend.
I was a little nervous because it was the first time that I had driven on the

highway. But after having driven about an hour I became used to the speed, and every now and then I almost fell asleep. Before we reached Kyoto, I stopped at service areas about five times and drank coffee. Because I drove while talking a lot with Hanako sitting next to me, I didn't feel that Kyoto was that far. If the trip is this pleasant, I would like to make it again.)

Answers: The words given below indicate the first words of the ESUs.

1. 友達 *tomodachi*　2. ハイウェー *haiwe*　3. ハイウェー *haiwe*　4. 一時間 *ichijikan*　5. 眠り *nemuri*

6. 隣 *tonari*　7. 隣 *tonari*　8. 隣 *tonari*　9. こんな *konna*　10. こんな *konna*

GRAMMAR INDEX

Note: X ⟨Y⟩ indicates that X is found under Y.

ENGLISH INDEX

Note: X ⟨Y⟩ indicates that X is found under Y.

nai⟩, nakereba ikenai ⟨nakereba nara-
nai⟩, nakereba naranai, nakute wa ikenai ⟨nakereba naranai⟩, nakute wa naranai ⟨nakereba naranai⟩, neba naranai
⟨nakereba naranai⟩

hear   suru³
how   dō
How could ~!   mono da
how to   hōhō, -kata

I

I expect that ~   hazu
if   ba, ka², nara, tara, to⁴
if it is the case that ~   nara
if it is true that ~   nara
if (or not)   ka (dō ka)
I hear / heard that ~   sōda¹
I tell you   yo
in   de¹,⁴, ni¹,⁶, o²
indeed ~ (but ~)   ~ koto wa (~
    ga)
indeed s.o. does s.t. alright (but ~)
    ~ koto wa (~ ga)
in front of   mae ni
-ing   koto², no³, te
in order to do s.t.   noni², tame ni
in place of   kawari ni
in spite of the fact that ~   noni¹
in such a way that   yōni¹
instead of   kawari ni
intend to   tsumori da, yō to omou
in that case   sore nara
in the process of doing s.t.   noni²
isn't it? / is it? / etc.   ne
it is all right if ~   te mo ii
it is expected that ~   hazu
it is natural that ~   hazu
it is that ~   ~ no da

it is ~ that ~   ~ no wa ~ da
it will be decided that ~   koto ni
    naru
I wonder   kashira

J

just   bakari, dake

L

leave   oku
leave as it is   mama
Let's do s.t.   mashō
let s.o. / s.t. do s.t.   saseru
like   sukida, yōni²
little   sukunai, wazuka ⟨sukunai⟩
look   sōda²
look as if   yōda
look like   rashii, sōda², yōda

M

make it   ni suru
make s.o. / s.t. do s.t.   saseru
manner of   -kata
many   ōi, ōzei ⟨ōi⟩, takusan ⟨ōi⟩
may   te mo ii
might   kamoshirenai
more ~ than ~   hō ga ~ yori
most   ichiban
Mr. / Mrs. / Miss / Ms.   -sama, -san
    ⟨-sama⟩
much   ōi, takusan ⟨ōi⟩
must be   ni chigainai
must do s.t.   nakereba naranai (⇨
    have to)
must not do s.t.   wa ikenai

N

need   iru³

there are times when ~ *koto ga aru²*

there was a time when ~ *koto ga aru¹*

therefore *sore de*

thing *koto¹, mono ⟨koto⟩*

things like *nado*

think ~ will *yō to omou*

though *keredomo*

through *o², made*

till *made*

to (infinitive) *koto², no³*

to *e, ni²,⁷*

to do s.t. *ni⁵, tame ni, noni²*

to make up for *kawari ni*

to the extent that *hodo*

too *mo¹, sugiru*

towards *e, ni⁷*

try to do s.t. *miru, yō to suru ⟨miru⟩*

U

unbearably *tamaranai*

unchanged *mama*

understand *wakaru*

until *made*

up to *made, made de*

used to *mono da*

using *de²*

V

visible *mieru*

W

want s.o. to do s.t. *hoshii²*

want s.t. *hoshii¹*

want to do s.t. *-tai*

way of *-kata*

what *koto¹*

What about doing s.t.? *~ tara dō desu ka*

when *tara, to⁴, toki*

whether *ka²*

whether or not *ka dō ka*

while *aida (ni), nagara, uchi (ni)*

Why don't you do s.t.? *~ tara dō desu ka*

(I / We) will do s.t. *mashō*

(I) wish ~ had done s.t. *-ba yokatta*

with *de², to²*

with effort *sekkaku, wazawaza ⟨sek-kaku⟩*

without doing s.t. *nai de, zu ni ⟨nai de⟩*

would *nara*

would like to do s.t. *-tai*

Y

yet *mada, mō*

you know *ne, yo*

JAPANESE INDEX

Note: X ⟨Y⟩ indicates that X is found under Y.

M

N

REFERENCES

Alfonso, Anthony (1966) *Japanese Language Patterns——a structural approach*, Volume I & II, Sophia University L.L. Center of Applied Linguistics, Tokyo.

Asano, Tsuruko, et al. (eds.) (1971) *Gaikokujin no Tame no Kihongo Yōrei Jiten* (Dictionary of Basic Japanese Usage for Foreigners), Bunkachō, Tokyo.

Butler, Kenneth D., et al. (eds.) (1975) *Basic Japanese——A Review Text*, Inter-University Center for Japanese Language Studies, Tokyo.

Endō, Mutsuko Simon (1984) *A Practical Guide for Teachers of Elementary Japanese*, Center for Japanese Studies, University of Michigan, Ann Arbor, Michigan.

Hinds, John and Irwin Howard (eds.) (1978) *Problems in Japanese Syntax and Semantics*, Kaitakusha, Tokyo.

Inoue, Kazuko (1976) *Henkei Bunpō to Nihongo* (Transformational Grammar and the Japanese Language), Taishūkan, Tokyo.

Inoue, Kazuko (1978) *Nihongo no Bunpō Kisoku* (Japanese Grammatical Rules), Taishūkan, Tokyo.

Jorden, Eleanor Harz (1963) *Beginning Japanese*, Part 1 & 2, Yale University Press, New Haven, Connecticut.

Kitagawa, Chisato (1983) " On the Two Forms of Negative Gerund in Japanese," A paper read on March 27, 1983 at the Annual Convention of the Association of Asian Studies, San Francisco.

Kubota, Tomio and Ikeo, Sumi (1971) *Taigūhyōgen* (Polite Expressions), Bunkachō, Tokyo.

Kuno, Susumu (1973) *The Structure of the Japanese Language*, MIT Press, Cambridge, Massachusetts.

Kuno, Susumu (1973) *Nihonbunpō Kenkyū* (A Study of Japanese Grammar), Taishūkan, Tokyo.

Kuno, Susumu (1978) *Danwa no Bunpō* (Discourse Grammar), Taishūkan, Tokyo.

Kuno, Susumu (1983) *Shin Nihonbunpō Kenkyū* (New Study of Japanese Grammar), Taishūkan, Tokyo.

Makino, Seiichi (1978) *Kotoba to Kūkan* (Language and Space), Tōkai University Press, Tokyo.

Makino, Seiichi (ed.) (1981) *Papers from the Middlebury Symposium on Japanese Discourse Analysis*, University of Illinois, Urbana, Illinois.

Makino, Seiichi (1983) " Speaker / Listener-Orientation and Formality Marking in Japanese," *Gengo Kenkyū——the Journal of the Linguistic Society of Japan*, 84, 126–145, Taishūkan, Tokyo.

Martin, Samuel (1975) *A Reference Grammar of Japanese*, Yale University Press, New Haven, Connecticut.

McClain, Yōko Matsuoka (1981) *Handbook of Modern Japanese Grammar*, Hokuseidō, Tokyo.

McGloin, Naomi Hanaoka (1980) " Some Observations Concerning No Desu," *Journal of the Association of Teachers of Japanese*, 15: 2, 117-149.

Mikami, Akira (1960) *Zō wa hana ga nagai* (An elephant has a long trunk), Kuroshio Shuppan, Tokyo.

Mikami, Akira (1970) *Bunpō Shōron Shū* (Papers on Grammar), Kuroshio Shuppan, Tokyo.

Mikami, Akira (1972) *Gendai Gohō Josetsu* (Introduction to Modern Japanese Usage), Kuroshio Shuppan, Tokyo.

Miura, Akira (1983) *Japanese Words and Their Uses*, Tuttle, Rutland, Vermont.

Monane, Tazuko Ajiro (1981) Review of McClain (1981), *Journal of Association of Teachers of Japanese*, 16: 2, 200-207.

Morita, Yoshiyuki (1977, 1980, 1984) *Kiso Nihongo* (Basic Japanese Words), 1, 2 & 3, Kadokawa Shoten, Tokyo.

Morita, Yoshiyuki (1981) *Nihongo no Hassō* (Meanings of Japanese Words), Tōjusha, Tokyo.

Nagara, Susumu (1975), " Teaching Basic Sentence Constructions in Japanese : the transition from fundamental grammatical drills to intermediate reading," *Journal of the Association of Teachers of Japanese*, 10: 2-3, 131-143.

Ogawa, Yoshio, et al. (eds.) (1982) *Nihongo Kyōiku Jiten* (Dictionary of Pedagogy of Japanese), Taishūkan, Tokyo.

Okutsu, Keiichirō (1978) ' *Boku wa unagi da* ' *no Bunpō* (Grammar of ' Boku wa unagi da '), Kuroshio Shuppan, Tokyo.

Ōno, Susumu, et al. (eds.) (1974) *Iwanami Kogo Jiten* (Iwanami's Dictionary of Old Japanese), Iwanami Shoten, Tokyo.

Ōno, Susumu, et al. (eds.) (1981) *Kadokawa Ruigo Shin Jiten* (Kadokawa's New Dictionary of Synonyms), Kadokawa Shoten, Tokyo.

Sakuma, Katsuhiko and Motofuji, Frank T. (1980) *Advanced Spoken Japanese : Tonari no Shibafu*, Institute of East Asian Studies, University of California, Berkeley, California.

Shibatani, Masayoshi (ed.) (1976) *Syntax and Semantics 5 : Japanese Generative Grammar*, Academic Press, New York and San Francisco.

Shibatani, Masayoshi (1978) *Nihongo no Bunseki* (Analyses of Japanese), Taishūkan, Tokyo.

Soga, Matsuo and Matsumoto, Noriko (1978) *Foundations of Japanese Language*, Taishūkan, Tokyo.

Soga, Matsuo (1983) *Tense and Aspect in Modern Colloquial Japanese*, University of British Columbia Press, Vancouver, Canada.

Suleski, Ronald and Masada, Hiroko (1982) *Affective Expressions in Japanese*, Hokuseidō, Tokyo.

Suzuki, Shinobu (1978) *Kyōshiyō Nihongo Kyōiku Handobukku 3, Bunpō 1, Joshi no Sho-mondai* (A Handbook for Japanese Language Teachers 3, Grammar 1, Problems of Particles), The Japan Foundation, Tokyo.

Tsutsui, Michio (1981) " Ellipsis of *wa* in Japanese," in Makino (1981), 295–319.

Tsutsui, Michio (1984) " Particle Ellipses in Japanese," unpublished Ph.D. dissertation, University of Illinois, Urbana-Champaign.

Yoshikawa, Taketoki, et al. (1983) *Kyōkasho Kaidai* (Bibliography of Japanese Textbooks), *Kyōshiyō Nihongo Kyōiku Handobukku Bessatsu* (Special Issue for a series of Handbooks for Japanese Language Teachers), The Japan Foundation, Tokyo.